THE PSYCHOLOGY OF THINKING

McGRAW-HILL SERIES IN PSYCHOLOGY

Consulting Editors
Norman Garmezy
Richard L. Solomon
Lyle V. Jones
Harold W. Stevenson

SECOND EDITION

THE PSYCHOLOGY OF THINKING

W. EDGAR VINACKE

State University of New York at Buffalo

McGRAW-HILL BOOK COMPANY

New York   St. Louis   San Francisco   Düsseldorf   Johannesburg
Kuala Lumpur   London   Mexico   Montreal   New Delhi   Panama
Paris   São Paulo   Singapore   Sydney   Tokyo   Toronto

THE PSYCHOLOGY OF THINKING

Copyright © 1974 by McGraw-Hill, Inc.
All rights reserved.
Copyright 1952 by McGraw-Hill, Inc.
All rights reserved.
Printed in the United States of America.
No part of this publication may be reproduced,
stored in a retrieval system, or transmitted,
in any form or by any means, electronic,
mechanical, photocopying, recording, or otherwise,
without the prior written permission of the publisher.

1234567890 KPKP 79876543

This book was set in Univers.
The editors were James R. Belser and Robert P. Rainier;
the designer was Nicholas Krenitsky;
the production supervisor was Leroy A. Young.
The drawings were done by John Cordes, J & R Technical Services, Inc.
Kingsport Press, Inc., was printer and binder.

Library of Congress Cataloging in Publication Data

Vinacke, William Edgar, date
    The psychology of thinking.

    (McGraw-Hill series in psychology)
    Bibliography: p.
    1. Thought and thinking. I. Title.
[DNLM: 1. Thinking. BF455 V766p 1974]
BF455.V47 1974   153   73-15756
ISBN 0-07-067486-8

TO MY PARENTS,
HAROLD M. AND EDNA L. VINACKE

CONTENTS

PREFACE

Every psychologist is acutely aware of the enormous growth of cognitive psychology during the past twenty years. Indeed, some professionals may have felt inundated by the masses of research and the multidirectional thrust of theories (both great and small). And an author must be discomforted by realizing that even as his book goes to press new materials will appear and have to be ignored. However, I feel that the main task is to identify the major developments and place them within a meaningful framework. I have tried to accomplish these aims. In doing so, I have maintained the same basic arrangement as in the first edition. The book is, perhaps, broader than will please every expert. As in the case of other psychological realms of inquiry, cognition is being subdivided ever more finely into self-contained specialties. No doubt this process is understandable, if not wholly desirable. Be this as it may, there is virtue, also, in looking across the spectrum of cognitive processes so that a person may glimpse how one group of problems relates to another. How delightful it would be if we could thereby perceive some simple theory that would at once elucidate and order them all! At our present historical position, however, no such outcome is apparent—despite some promising candidates for future theoretical unification.

No matter how difficult it is to encompass the diverse aspects of thinking, it certainly is an interesting venture. If I had to state just one reward from undertaking this revision, it would be the excitement of witnessing the brilliance of psychologists in actually coming to grips with problems that were largely ignored when I was a graduate student. We have come a long way—far enough not only to see where we came from, but also to see that we still have a long way to go.

This edition, then, attempts to bring theory and research up to date on the same topics as occupied the first edition. Although progress has been rapid in all areas of cognitive psychology, some, such as concept attainment, verbal learning, and opinion change, have virtually exploded, whereas others, such as fantasy and values, have only begun to open up. Traditional methods continue to be elaborated, with an emphasis on highly controlled laboratory experiments. At the same time, I think that there are clear signs of a turning toward subjective experience and an increasing willingness to explore new techniques for treating it. I hope that clues to this development will be evident. Unfortunately, even a comprehensive view of an area must be selective. I have tried to do justice to the investigators and theorists who are rapidly expanding the study of thinking and apologize for any errors of omission or misplaced emphasis.

I should like to express my appreciation to colleagues who have read and commented on various chapters—Richard Bugelski, Norman Slamecka, Willis Overton, and Dean Pruitt—and to Kenneth Kurtz, whose verbal comments have been very constructive. As on many previous occasions, I am deeply indebted for continuous help to Linda Hereth, whose generosity in time and effort is matched only by her skill and efficiency. I thank also the various typists who worked on the manuscript, but especially Mary Ellen Friedman.

W. Edgar Vinacke

THE
PSYCHOLOGY
OF
THINKING

1

INTRODUCTION

Thinking is distinctively human—a marvelous property that distinguishes man from other animals. Although research shows that
animals also display behavior from which we can infer the basic
processes of "thinking," this behavior is much more simple than it is
in man. Indeed, the difference is so great that whatever rudimentary
forms may be discerned in rats, monkeys, chimpanzees, and other
species investigated by psychologists, thinking is especially characteristic of man.

Man is also differentiated from lower animals by the development of the brain. The tremendously increased relative size and
complexity of the brain permit the storage and processing of information on a vast scale. Not the least of the brain's resources is
its capacity—still poorly understood—to integrate motivational and
emotional states with information in its memorial sense and information fed in from extrinsic sources.

The activity of the higher brain centers is related to thinking in
several ways.

1. *Processes That Intervene Between Stimulus and Response*
The nervous system is constructed so that at least two neurons

are involved in every response of the organism—a sensory nerve pathway leading from a sensory ending to a nerve center, and a motor nerve leading from a nerve center to a muscle or gland. The very simplest neuron arc, whereby a simple reflex occurs, may involve just two neurons—for instance, a spinal reflex such as the knee jerk. But even so simple a response does not occur independently of the total activity of the organism. It may be influenced by, and may influence, other behavioral processes by means of other neurons. Clenching one's fist facilitates the knee jerk. Most instances of human behavior are far more complex. The sensory impulse travels to a nerve center, where it may be transmitted along many other neurons, or initiate a complicated pattern of neural activity, before it ultimately reaches the motor nerve along which it travels to the muscle. The cognitive process is the activity of these nerve pathways between sensory and motor events.

2. *Context*   The notion of association pathways is really too simple, for a cognitive process occurs in the midst of complex patterns of neural activity. Sensory impulses continuously enter the brain from many different receptors; processes of muscular coordination are going on; input from the regulation of organic and emotional states proceeds; other parts of the brain not directly concerned with any of these operations are also active (e.g., memory functions). This continually shifting pattern constitutes the cognitive or mental context. Mediation theory, a central theme in this book, seeks for principles pertaining to it.

3. *Determining Tendencies*   Behavior does not occur in a random or chance fashion. Internal dynamic regulative systems, established in the brain centers, influence the course of thinking. When recurring events enable us to identify consistencies in behavior, we may draw inferences about these systems, employing terms like *set* and *attitude* to describe them.

4. *Matrix of Experience*   The brain centers contain the traces of past experience which influence the content of cognition. First, there is what we ordinarily call "memory," the conscious recall of past experiences, and the application of habits and skills when the latent traces of experience are reactivated. Second, we can

recognize the vast background of nonactive, nonconscious experience, against which a current mental process occurs, and by which it is determined in ways not easy to specify. Finally, the matrix contains repressed, but still active, components of past experience, which indirectly influence thinking. The role of unconscious forces has especially been emphasized by psychoanalysis, to which we shall refer in appropriate places.

LANGUAGE

Another especially human characteristic is language, bearing in many ways on thinking. Not only does language provide an economical vehicle for transmitting and guiding learning, but it also facilitates memorial and conceptual processes through its symbolic aspects. Kellogg (1968) suggests that language is virtually absent in other animals—even in the chimpanzee. Evidence, however, indicates that communication by systematic gestures may be attained at a fairly high level of complexity, so that one crucial factor is verbal behavior itself. It is not so much language, or communication, that distinguishes man as his ability to "reconstitute language" (Bronowski and Bellugi, 1970). This function rests on analytical and conceptual abilities that permit the combining of words into sentences.

Regardless of what may eventually be decided on these issues, we wish here merely to stress two points. One, verbal—symbolic behavior is so highly developed in man that it can scarcely be investigated in other species, and becomes critical for understanding human behavior. Two, as intimated above, we must try to determine the role of verbal acts (the use of words) in cognitive processes. For example, a word as a verbal response is not necessarily identical with the intrinsic event of which it is an expression. In this fashion we will confront problems of meaning and information processing to be considered later.

DEFINITION OF THINKING

In everyday usage, thinking refers to reflection or meditation, to belief, opinion, judgment, or fancy; it signifies "something that goes on in the mind." Thus the term has no definite meaning, perhaps because the processes involved are elusive and apparently incapable of being directly observed.

Psychological Definition

More technically, thinking is "the organization and reorganization of past learning in present situations" (Vinacke, 1968, p. 822). One implication is that thinking refers to *intrinsic* activities rather than to overt responses themselves. Such responses may express or reflect thinking and may have intrinsic effects that influence thinking, but they are not identical with thinking. Rather, we can, and do, use responses as evidence from which to make inferences about thinking. This point is especially important with reference to the role of language. Words themselves are not thinking but rather a vehicle for or an expression of thinking. The definition also implies that the content of thinking results from stored information—originating in learning prior to the time at which thinking occurs. As previously intimated, however, such information involves not only specific items but also patterns and systems of information. In this way, thinking calls on memorial processes and on conceptual and attitudinal processes. Next, the definition emphasizes the dynamic organizing and reorganizing of information. In this respect we must consider activities over time, and allow for motivational and emotional influences. Finally, "the present situation," as an integral part of the definition, points both to the continuing contribution of new information and to important relationships, to goals. Here perceptual and extrinsic conditions must be encompassed.

Cognitive Processes

Since thinking clearly bears an intimate relation to other aspects of intrinsic activity, especially memory, intelligence, and perception, many psychologists prefer not to make sharp distinctions among these psychological categories, but prefer to speak more generally about "cognition."

We may distinguish, however, between *perception*—which focuses on immediate relations to the environment (responses to stimuli at a particular time), and *thinking*—which is primarily concerned with the utilization of past experience. Evidently, thinking and perception are not separate from each other, since past experience influences the character of perceptual processes, and responses to the immediate environment influence the character of thinking. Thus the distinction is really made for convenience and, indeed, in many types of research may virtually disappear. For example, in studies of judgment and of discrimination between stimulus objects, a researcher may be concerned with complex perception or with simple forms of thinking.

Again, we may distinguish between learning which stresses the process of acquiring experience, adding responses to the individual's behavioral repertory, or altering responses, and thinking as the utilization of past experience. But the reorganization of past learning—as in problem solving—may result in the production of new responses. Changes in behavior of this sort might just as well be called "learning" as "thinking." Once a large body of information is available to a person, performance in many tasks is not so much a matter of acquiring new responses as in utilizing those already present. In the human adult, for instance, this overlapping of learning and thinking could be recognized by speaking of "complex learning." It depends on whether we wish to attend especially to changes in responses or to the properties of past learning and their role in the present task. Such emphases are often a matter of how an investigator chooses to define and measure his variables.

"KINDS OF THINKING"

Traditionally, thinking has been subdivided into *reasoning* and *imagination.* Reasoning refers to logical, problem-solving activities that occur when the environment presents a task that requires a solution. However, solutions require organization and reorganization of past experience, rather than mere production of habitual responses. Reasoning is therefore tied to an extrinsically presented task or goal. Imagination refers to the combining and recombining of past experience and is relatively free from the demands of extrinsic conditions. Reasoning is *directed* but imagination is *expressive.* It is more profitable to distinguish between the kinds of forces that influence the character of thinking. *Intrinsic* forces that arise from motivational and emotional sources determine thought processes, but so also do forces from *extrinsic* sources in the environment (stimuli associated with tasks, goals, and incentives). When extrinsic forces are dominant, thinking has a *realistic* character; when intrinsic forces are strongest, thinking has an *autistic* character. Under the former heading we can place logical analysis, decision making, problem solving, and concept attainment. Under the latter heading we can place imagery, fantasy, dreaming, and free association. It should be emphasized that thinking is never wholly determined by forces of either kind, but only relatively more by one than the other. In some instances both kinds of force intermingle complexly, as in creative thinking.

THINKING AND BEHAVIOR

The term *behavior* signifies observable responses. Since we shall regard the processes of thinking as intrinsic activities, which intervene—or mediate—between the occurrence of stimuli and the production of responses, then we must employ observed behavior as evidence from which to infer the characteristics of thinking. Such evidence includes verbal reports, and what the person says constitutes behavioral data, just as do other acts. The task of the investigator is to describe and interpret responses, and on this basis to decide what inferences are justified.

It must be stressed that the foregoing remarks do not mean that cognitive activities may not go on at a purely intrinsic level—that is, without observable responses—[1] nor that a person cannot dependably understand and describe his own thinking. Rather, we mean that the psychologist does not attempt to deal with cognitive processes in the absence of evidence in the form of behavioral records.

Our program is essentially that of the experimental psychologist. We shall be concerned with three classes of variables: independent, intervening, and dependent. By an *independent* variable we mean some stated condition that is controlled so that its effects can be observed. Such conditions include stimuli or patterns of stimuli, tasks and their properties, incentives, and the like. By an *intervening* variable we mean some condition from which intrinsic states can be inferred, such as personality traits, motives, attitudes, conceptualizing ability, and so on. The variable itself is a behavioral measure, like a test score or a physiological index, and, as with independent variables, techniques of control are used to objectify its operation. In addition, as with independent variables, we seek to determine the effects of variations in intervening variables. Finally, *dependent* variables are responses or patterns of responses recorded in an experiment, and expected to be associated with variables in either or both of the other two categories.

This plan is not always wholly clear in some of the research cited. Historically, investigators have often sought to reveal the

---

[1]We should say observable by ordinary methods because electroencephalographic and other techniques of recording intrinsic states provide evidence on which to base inferences. (See, especially, research on rapid eye movements [REMS] in dreaming in Chapter 14.)

phenomena of thinking, rather than systematically to relate variables to each other, as, for example, the kinds of activities manifested in problem-solving tasks. In the modern period, however, interest in the phenomena themselves has increasingly given way to the manipulation of variables under controlled conditions.

It is our aim in this book to survey in a broad fashion the theory and research that form a basis for understanding thinking, as a focus within the general area of cognition. This discussion sets the stage for the presentation of the general theories that have guided investigators.

SUMMARY

Thinking is distinctively human, resting on special properties of the brain and on language and symbolic processes. We can define thinking as "the organization and reorganization of past learning in present situations." Reasoning (directed thinking) and imagination (expressive thinking) are two broad aspects of thinking, with creative thinking a blend of them. We shall conceptualize conditions that affect thinking as autistic (intrinsic) and realistic (extrinsic).

2

HISTORICAL PROBLEMS IN THE STUDY OF THINKING

Man has always been interested in explaining his relation to the external world. Prior to recorded philosophy, the conception of mind existed as *animism*, a belief that all things possess souls. Gradually, Greek philosophers, beginning in the fifth century B. C., began to deal systematically with problems of knowing.

Theories were advanced about sensation and perception, feelings and emotions, creative processes, memory, reasoning, and imagination. This development culminated in the monumental works of Plato and Aristotle (the *De Anima* by the latter, indeed, is a treatise on psychology).

The Greek psychologists were engrossed with the problem of "how the outer world produces the inner perception of that world" (Brett, 1928, p. 18) and, one might add, the converse of this question, which has been equally prominent, for example, in studies of how intrinsic factors like values and motives shape perceptual response. Perhaps the chief reason why their interpretations sound naive to us is that the ancient philosophers lacked the knowledge of physiology and the nervous system which we now take for granted. Nevertheless, Alcmaeon of Crotona (550–500 B. C.) is alleged to have performed dissections leading him to posit a connection

9

between the brain and conscious life. At any rate, the Greek thinkers drew a distinction between the mind and the body that has persisted to this day.

They attempted to explain the influence of the outer world by means of *sensation*, or the power to discriminate among parts of the environment. Aristotle attributed sensation to movements of the *pneuma*, which transmits an impression of an object to the mind. The pneuma was conceived to be a medium permeating every part of the body (akin to the notion of "animal spirits"). The senses have a meeting place, or "common sense," which Aristotle located in the heart. The movements of the pneuma are unified in the common sense. Imagination is an aftereffect, fainter and less active, of the sense impression. Memory is the storage of sensory motions, and recollection, as an active process, is the stirring up of a train of imagination, which thus becomes basic to all thinking.

The Greek psychologists formulated elaborate theories of mental processes, but derived from logical systematization based on introspection, rather than from empirical evidence as we now conceive it. Plato describes memory as the preservation of sense impressions, thus making memory practically equivalent to consciousness. He adds to the usual memorial functions one of reminiscence, which is a property of the soul in knowing (or recalling) experiences not actually derived from the senses. Experiences of goodness and beauty (i.e., abstract ideas) are thus accounted for. Imagination is mental activity in sensuous form, accompanying sensation, memory, and other mental processes. In general, the mind has many functions arranged in logical fashion from low to high. The mind differs from sensation because it deals with objects not sensibly present. Plato also seems to have recognized phenomena we would call "unconscious," although he does not clearly formulate them.[1]

Plato stated laws of association to account for the effects of memory, and Aristotle carried these principles forward. The principles of similarity, dissimilarity, and contiguity, beginning in ancient Greek theory, were developed in full force by the British associationists more than 1,500 years later, and still hold an important place in psychology. The highest form of mental life is reasoning, which utilizes material from the senses and imagination, but goes far beyond them into the realm of pure ideas. Finally, Aristotle clearly recognized the interdependence of sensory, cognitive, and affective factors in behavior, just as we increasingly do today.

[1] Reeves (1965) has recently shown how the principle of the unconscious has had a long history, beginning with Plato.

This ancient psychology also separated the mind or soul from the body, ascribing to the mind an independent existence. The mind was divided into distinct parts, each with definite functions, or faculties. In the case of the highest, or rational, soul, these faculties were thinking, understanding, belief, conjecture, and so on. Here, again, the same conception persists, for example, in the formulation of distinctive intellectual abilities, bolstered by factor-analytic investigations.

Between the period of Greek scholarship and the Renaissance, little advance occurred in the study of psychology. It was a period of gradually evolving religious doctrines in the Western world (such as speculations about the soul), and of mathematics in the Arabic countries, the latter hardly known until the Crusades opened the doors of the East. Indeed, much of the classical writings of the Greek and Latin scholars were not known either until after that time. Then, in increasing tempo, there developed the stupendous trends in philosophy and science leading to modern times.

THE MIND-BODY PROBLEM

A first historical issue centers on the relationship between the mind and the body. The question arises because there appear to be differences between mental and physical events. For example, an apple hanging on a branch is clearly a material object, but an apple in the mind, no less an apple, nevertheless cannot, apparently, be a material apple. To the normal person, at least in the waking state, behavioral acts such as reaching for, biting into, and chewing the apple are quite different from imagining these acts. Going farther, the body itself, represented by the brain tissues in which the mental apple occurs, seems to be different from the idea of the apple. Under such common sense considerations, it is easy to suppose that the physical, neural counterpart of the apple and the mental apple belong to different modes of reality. One solution is to postulate the separate existence of physical and mental events, each with its own properties.

Should this position be taken, then it is logical next to inquire whether one influences the other, and, if so, how. Various possible answers to this question has each had its adherents. Descartes, in the first half of the seventeenth century, formulated a dualistic theory, completely separating the mind from the body, but supposed that they interacted in the pineal gland. Spinoza stated in 1665 that mind and body are but different facets of a single universal principle, God ("double aspect" theory). Leibnitz, in 1695, formulated another dualistic theory, a form of parallelism, according to which mind and body are not causally related but function simultaneously, in a harmonious manner. Locke developed an empiricist theory in 1690, in which he accounted for ideas by saying that they are produced from experience, rather than being innate. This position was developed more extremely by Berkeley, in 1710, who regarded mind as the ultimate reality, which generates matter. In the early nineteenth century, when psychology was emerging as a distinct discipline, Fechner tried to solve the mind-body problem by translating the identity position into mathematical form. Assuming that mind and body are merely different manifestations of the same phenomenon, he pointed to the correspondence between the physical stimulus and the internal sensations. He formulated an equation, called Weber's law (see Chapter 4), as a fundamental step toward measuring the mind-body relationship.

This problem has been taken up repeatedly down to the present day. It has often been solved through the statement of "psychophysiological parallelism." This explanation, in various forms, assumes that mental and bodily (i.e., brain) events constitute two coexisting series, either of which can be studied. This position ranges from a convenient ignoring of the problem through more thoughtful formulations that aim either to arrive at acceptable methodological solutions or to point toward more inclusive (or simple) statements, or both.

In line with the first version, many psychologists are impatient with what appears to be an abstract, philosophical problem. They simply define a realm of facts, called "psychological" or "behavioral," and base their conceptions on observations of those facts. Accompanying this strategy is an assumption, implicit rather than explicit, that these facts have a basis in, or are functions of, physiological processes. However, they leave it to the physiologist to unravel such processes, by his own methods, without worrying about their relationships to behavior. In this way the psychologist is free to investigate perception, learning, thinking, or any other aspect of behavior. In effect, then, a division of labor is implied, with different persons using different methods to penetrate separate bodies of facts. Beyond this general position, there may also be an assumption, often not stated, that in the long run the whole issue of relationships will take care of itself. When we acquire enough knowledge in both realms of facts, we shall begin to see correspondences and differences, and thus eventually reach a more inclusive view.

The second version offers greater complications. The argument here is essentially that physiology and psychology are concerned with the same facts, but that each discipline approaches them in different ways. When this argument is carried far enough, it cannot be called "parallelism," but rather becomes an "identity" position. This view probably predominates today. It signifies that there is really only one event, which can be described either in its physiological or in its psychological manifestation. Partly, the distinction rests on the use of language to describe events, so that some common denominator must be found to encompass both ways of talking about the event, or if this solution cannot be found, then we must continue to use different words for its two sides. The implication, however, is quite clear that *neither physiological nor psychological language can be preferred to the other.*

Contrasting with this position is a pervasive reductionism, which sees the physiological description as more fundamental than the psychological. The idea here is that psychological description is to be tolerated simply because we are not yet certain about the proper way to state the physiological process itself. Once investigation (e.g., of the brain) has proceeded far enough, we shall be able to account for, and to state fully, what now appears to require psychological formulation. Thus psychology will persist only as long as our ignorance of physiology continues.

My own view lies somewhere between these two versions. Although, in agreement with the second version, I see only a single event, with both physiological and psychological aspects, in accordance with the first version, I believe that neither can be wholly understood—or adequately described—solely in terms of the other. That is, whatever the correspondence between the two aspects, we shall continue to require different methods, different language, and different theoretical conceptualizations.

Research Strategies
Based on an identity solution, one procedure focuses directly on physiological processes in their behavioral significance. It searches for biological structures involved in particular behavioral acts, and seeks to identify how they work or change when those acts occur. Thus we can speak psychologically about "motivational arousal." However, we might examine physiological states and changes during variations in arousal. If we find measurable and predictable states and changes in, for example, the heart rate, skin resistance, and neural activities, we might say that motivational arousal is those states and changes. But our interest is not strictly biological, in the traditional

sense (i.e., to investigate tissues and their properties) but to describe internal states when stated behavioral acts occur.

This strategy is closely related to, but not necessarily identical with, a correlational approach. Here the aim is to systematically establish relations between physiological states and behavioral acts, to demonstrate the convergence of qualitatively different kinds of evidence on the same general fact. The difference from the first strategy is that a reductionist view is not necessarily involved. Indeed, it is closer to parallelism, since it allows for the possibility that there may be two different kinds of facts with possible variance between them. The degree to which physiological and psychological events are simply versions of the same facts should be revealed in the success with which correlations can be demonstrated. If measurement techniques can be improved to eliminate errors, then we may eventually discover whether body and mind are identical—but this outcome would not necessarily obtain.

Another strategy, increasingly pursued, is to harness physiological and psychological investigation, recognizing that at least for the present we cannot convert one to the other. That is, researchers in each realm can collaborate on similar problems in a dialogue whereby each calls on findings of the other. Thus studies of learning can provide clues to the character of relevant neural processes; and discoveries about the properties of neural circuits can yield hypotheses about the events of learning and memory. Such an interplay may lead to correlations, to a commonality of language, or to a convergence on issues not originally evident to either partner.

System Properties

Finally, there is a subtlety that transcends any of the formulated positions, pointing to the basic futility of a reductionist orientation. Regardless of the correlations that may be established between physiological and psychological variables, and regardless of how well we understand the biological workings of the organism, we are still concerned with different systems. Even though we recognize that physiological processes exactly parallel psychological events, nevertheless the properties of one are not identical with the properties of the other, and the principles required to account for the one are different from those that account for the other. Pribram (1962, p. 122) points out that "the properties of a system are not given simply by summing the properties of the component subsystems."

An analogy may help to clarify the matter. An automobile is composed of many parts, including an engine, an electrical system, a transmission, a steering mechanism, and so on. However, the automobile functions as an integrated system in which these parts are interrelated, and the activities of the total system obey principles not reducible to its parts. The automobile system, in turn, is extended into a larger system, including as components the driver and his characteristics, the environmental conditions in which the automobile is working, and the other objects (people and vehicles) with which the automobile has relationships. This larger system cannot be meaningfully described simply by reference to the separate elements —putting the components together creates new properties, those of the system itself.

Cognitive processes, then, not only correspond identically with biological processes, but also constitute systems with properties that arise from their organization and continuity. Although we can potentially fully account for each component (or subsystem) by identifying the accompanying neurophysiological processes, we still require special descriptions and principles to account for the system itself. And we must investigate cognitive processes themselves. Thus we can speak more directly about them than is possible—at least at present—when we refer to the accompanying neurophysiological events. A cognitive process, even a simple one, involves a great number of activities in the nervous system. To detail these events would demand an extremely long and intricate description. It is simpler—and necessary—to refer to a conceptual process or a dream or an association.

The complexities of cognition can be compared to neurophysiology since both involve organized systems, in which subsystems combine to produce the total pattern. However, the combinations of neural components may well require descriptions different from those of cognitive components. For example, we might be able to describe an image in neural terms by specifying a certain active circuit with its associated electrochemical activity. But to describe an image in cognitive terms may require specifying a memory process together with emotional states and the stimulus situation. Thus the principles governing how components are combined and altered may differ in the two cases.

Many readers of this book, who believe that the mind-body problem no longer has any importance for psychology, may wonder why I devote so much space to it. For one thing, I hope to show that old problems persist, and that they are not solved by ignoring them.

The truth is that this problem lies at the very heart of psychology. It will certainly continue to make its presence felt as long as the two disciplines of physiology and psychology exist. The relation between them is fundamental; it has not yet been solved.[1]

THE MECHANISM OF THINKING

The remarks about Aristotle's psychology indicate that attempts to explain how cognitive processes work extend far backward in time. Nearly all of these efforts have regarded cognition as intrinsic activity (in the brain) in which basic ingredients, defined in some way, recur in varied and complex forms. It is not always clear whether such recurrence is supposed to come about as a result of internal conditions (perhaps spontaneously) or is elicited by environmental stimuli. For the most part we can assume that both sources have been allowed, but that historical interest has been primarily in the properties of the intrinsic components and the way they work. One clear advance during the modern period has been to incorporate environmental determinants explicitly into the total system.

Locke in 1690 postulated that mental processes are composed of "ideas" derived from sensation and reflection (a sort of inner sense), or what Boring (1950) would call "meanings." Locke treats them as fundamental elements, with primary qualities (essentially the basic properties of objects, such as size and shape), and secondary qualities (presumably provided by sensory responses, such as colors and tastes). This distinction reflects the notion that objects themselves have characteristics that are directly reflected in ideas, in contrast to those characteristics that are supposedly produced indirectly by objects. Although both kinds of qualities are properties of objects,[2] primary qualities are said to correspond exactly with the object, whereas secondary qualities are only indirectly induced by some property of the object. The important thing is that these qualities are functions of the external object; ideas are the intrinsic elements of thought, produced by characteristics of objects. Thinking consists in the activities and combinations of ideas.

Hume elaborated this theory in 1739 by drawing a distinction between impressions and ideas, with impressions corresponding to more modern conceptions of sensation and perception, and ideas to

---

[1]Some modern discussions of the mind-body problem may be found in Pribram (1962), Feigl (1959), Boring (1950), and Turner (1965).

[2]Boring points out that Locke's usage is opposite to the modern view, which attributes qualities to the subjective response, not to the object itself.

what we would now call cognitive processes (concepts and images). Either form of mental content may be simple or complex. In accounting for memory and imagination, Hume stated two laws of *association,* resemblance (or similarity) and contiguity (in place or time). Ideas are combined into sequences and structures by these principles.

Hartley established associationism as a psychological system in 1749. Reducing the laws of association to contiguity, he explained that ideas can become linked either through simultaneous or successive association. In this way the associationist doctrine could be extended easily to learning and remembering, as well as to reasoning.

Later associationists developed the principles still further. In 1820 Thomas Brown added to the primary laws a series of secondary ones that deal explicitly with memory and recognize the influence of bodily, individual, and environmental conditions on mental processes. James Mill spoke of "mental mechanics" in 1829, with contiguity between ideas as fundamental, providing the basis for combinations, elements simply becoming associated according to the conditions of their original occurrence. His son, John Stuart Mill, formulated in 1843 and 1865 four laws of association: similarity, contiguity, frequency, and inseparability, not as independent principles but as aspects of a single general principle. Especially important was his theory that ideas may be fused into more complex structures —and, indeed, such fusion may produce new cognitive systems that cannot be derived merely from the adding together of the original elements ("mental chemistry"). He also anticipated the important principle of "imageless thought."

Although associationism culminated in the work of Bain (1855, 1859), it has persisted in one form or another. Learning and remembering certainly occur according to the special conditions, favorable or unfavorable, under which task materials are presented. Robinson (1932) listed a dozen or more laws of association, which perhaps should be regarded as *conditions* that influence the acquisition of experience and the characteristics of cognitive processes at later times (i.e., in recall and thinking). Associationist principles, especially in conditioning principles, are still widely employed throughout the field of cognition.

CONTENT AND STRUCTURE OF THOUGHT

Both Greek and associationist views clearly have much to say about the elements of thought, by postulating and describing sensations, images, and ideas, together with their properties (or qualities). It was however, left to the *structuralists* to focus special attention on the matter of the content, or the psychologically defined substance of thought. It is a distinction between the "how" compared to the "what" of thinking. The structuralists more or less accepted the associationist explanation of the "how" and set to work to analyze and describe the components themselves. Much influenced by the elementaristic approach of the other sciences during that period, as seen in concepts of the atom, chemical element, and cell, they sought for, and believed they found, the simplest elements of cognitive systems. Titchener was especially influential in extending principles encountered in Wundt's laboratory at Leipzig (established in 1879).

First, as to method, these early investigators developed the strict and exacting technique of *introspection*. The subject of an experiment (or the "observer") had, figuratively, to stand back from himself and examine what existed in his mind under specified conditions of stimulation and responding. He then reported his experience in as precise terms as possible. This procedure required that the observer have careful training in order to acquire objectivity and the ability to note those phenomena under study.[1] In practice, of course, introspection really means retrospection, since a mental process must occur before it can be reported. The structuralists attempted to reduce the process to such simple terms that a report could be given with a minimum of delay and a minimum of distortion.

Analysis of mental contents by this method seemed to reveal that all mental processes are composed of simple, irreducible elements, which were labeled *sensations*, *affections*, and *images*. Each element appeared to have characteristic dimensions, or "attributes." Sensations are the basic data arriving in the sense organs. They are classifiable as visual, auditory, gustatory, kinesthetic, etc. They vary in quality (e.g., cold, blue, salt), intensity, clearness, and duration. Sensations are compounded into perceptions, following the laws of

---

[1]This conception of the subject, as a trained and sophisticated observer of his own behavior, contrasts with the overwhelming emphasis today on the subject as an object to be observed by the experimenter. Most investigators deliberately choose untrained, naive subjects in order to preserve the effects of independent variables from biasing influences of the subject's knowledge about or reactions to the experimental situation. To be sure, the success of this strategy has recently been challenged by studies of "demand characteristics" (Orne, 1962). We now recognize that the subject is not a uniform, naively reacting specimen, but that he will treat experimental conditions according to his expectations and interpretations of them. Furthermore, we now also recognize that the experimenter is not merely a mechanical recorder of behavior just as it occurs, but may also participate in subtle ways in the situation. His own expectations and the cues he emits may influence the subject. We call this phenomenon *experimenter bias* (Rosenthal, 1966). Another challenge is posed by humanistic psychology, which sees persona experience as the prime concern of psychology.

such mixture. Similarly, affections with their attributes (lacking the dimension of clearness) are compounded into feelings or simple emotions. Images are derived from sensations, and constitute the elements of which ideas are composed and thus form the basic contents of thought. The differences between sensations and ideas grow out of their relationships, for an image has less distinctive quality, less intensity, and shorter duration than the corresponding sensation.

The structuralists explain all thinking as the occurrence of images combining and recombining in various ways. Memory thus consists of images with personal reference, representing definite incidents in past experience. Images of imagination, on the other hand, lack personal reference and definite associations with past events. Thought, as distinct from memory and imagination, takes the form of words (although words can readily be converted into the relevant images) (Titchener, 1914).

The early years of this century were marked by a vigorous attack on the structuralist methods and theories. Introspection was rejected in favor of the laboratory experiment as we now know it. Attention was shifted to relationships between situational variables and overt responses, instead of subjective experience and mental elements. And the interests of psychologists were extended to a great variety of problems that fell outside the narrow scope of structuralism, including development, personality, motivation, intelligence, and social processes, to say nothing of approaches to learning that the structuralists did not or could not encompass.

Imageless Thought

Of immediate concern to us, however, was the undermining of images as the basis for all thought. The notion that thinking is not reducible solely to images arose from several sources, including observations by Sir Francis Galton and Robert S. Woodworth, as well as by members of the Würzburg school, with whom this conception is generally linked (Humphrey, 1951).

In 1901 Marbe discovered that a subject could readily judge the heavier of two weights without being able to state how the judgment was made or being able to describe the content of his mind during the judgment process. Certainly no images seemed to be present. Marbe advanced the notion of *Bewusstseinslagen* (conscious attitudes) to account for the mental process. Orth showed that conscious attitudes are imageless states, not analyzable in Titchenerian terms. Watt and Ach elaborated the discovery, explaining the

imageless state as the operation of a "set" (*Einstellung*) and "determining tendency." These conditions correspond to a preparatory,
selective mechanism, permitting the thought to occur without the
manipulation of images. Thus in a judgment situation, if the subject
is prepared to make a response (and there is always some readiness
in this sense), the answer is there already, so to speak, and merely
requires the onset of the stimulus in order to appear.

The significance of these Wurzburg experiments does not lie in
the disproof of images, for that, of course, was not done—images
exist and constitute an important kind of cognitive process—but in
the following points:

> 1 They demonstrated, contrary to Titchener's position, that
> thought processes consist of more than images, and that
> thinking may occur without the necessary mediation of images.
> 2 They indicated the futility of the general structuralist position.
> If in one respect the narrow view of basic elements breaks
> down, then it is open to question in other ways as well. Further-
> more, since the principle of set implies the highly significant
> role of extrinsic and immediate determinants of response, then
> a strict orientation toward intrinsic and experiential factors is
> quite inadequate.
> 3 They recognized the importance of regulatory systems in be-
> havior by the advocacy of conditions such as set and determin-
> ing tendency. Such controlling and directing systems constitute
> more than, or differ from, the mere counterparts of perceptions,
> as the term "image" implies. Therefore the problem of under-
> standing cognition opened in directions hardly possible within
> the structuralist framework.

As a scientist, Titchener accepted the Würzburg findings, but not
their conclusions. He maintained (1909, 1910) that in fact the supposedly nonsensory and imageless components of thought could be
analyzed. One of his students, Clarke (1911), conducted a series of
experiments in which rigorous introspection was applied to perception, recognition, and verbal processes. The subjects were able to
analyze their attitudes as containing at least rudimentary feelings as
well as images. Clarke concluded that other studies had failed to
demand sufficiently intensive introspective analysis.

Titchener was therefore unshaken in his convictions. Ogden
(1911) remarked that at Cornell images were reported because subjects were trained to find them, resembling Titchener's (1909) own

criticism of the Würzburg experimenters on the opposite count! Woodworth (1906) pointed out that a thought may be primarily imageless, but "attaches itself secondarily to a word or other convenient symbol." In recall, an introspection is necessarily retrospective. Evidence on unintentional falsification in perception and memory demonstrates that an observer could find images whenever he wished.

Without pursuing the controversy farther, we can say that the Würzburg studies effectually helped to change the scene in cognition. Other forces also soon contributed to the demise of strict structuralism—notably the behaviorist revolution.

Current Views

The problem of mental content is still readily apparent in psychology. Interest in imagery, as a component of cognition, is reviving. But rather than treating images as irreducible and specific units, they are regarded as processes as reported—as aspects of *mediation.*

The term *idea* is rarely employed in the structuralist sense, but we do utilize terms that refer to mental content, such as *concept, meaning*, and *associative relationships*. Attention, however, is directed to responses, with these terms as labels for inferred mediating activities.

The general Würzburg principle of cognitive determinants of response has become indispensable. We rely on the notions of set, expectancy, attitude, and cognitive style in theorizing, and on experimentation on perception, learning, memory, and attitude formation and change.

CHARACTERISTICS OF EXPERIENCE

Another problem concerns what results from the individual's exposure to the environment. Partly it is a problem of *learning*—the acquisition of responses and sequences of responses, and partly it is a problem of *memory*—the storage and subsequent recurrence of or change in response. What does the individual learn? And what does he remember?

As we have seen, the matter had been handled in the past through assuming that external objects are converted internally into sensations, images, and ideas. These internal representations are the results of experience, and simply recur—or are called up—in later behavior. The laws of association were advanced to explain the characteristics of experience; for example, similar sensations tend to be combined or fused, and sensations contiguous to each other tend to form parts of the same experience. Thus experience consists in the acquisition and storage of counterparts to aspects of the outer world.

During the modern period this problem has mainly been pursued along two fronts. One front involves a controversy among learning theorists about what is actually learned. The second involves a concerted attempt to uncover the ways in which the effects of learning may differ from the literal characteristics of the original situation in which learning took place.

The controversy—still unresolved—concerns whether learning results in the acquisition of comparatively fixed habits of responding to stimuli, or whether it results in the establishment of cognitive systems such as expectations, knowledge, and concepts.

In the first view, experience is a matter of quite specific response mechanisms, evoked in particular situations by the stimuli that arise in those situations. The history of the individual is a matter of linkages between stimuli and responses, and the characteristics of the behavior we observe at any one time depend either on the direct eliciting of already established habits, or on the sorting out of competing habits none of which is immediately appropriate. There are several varieties of this point of view, ranging from a very strict emphasis on specific stimulus-response relationships (Guthrie, Estes, Restle) to broader conceptions that also allow for cognitive and motivational influences (Hull, Spence, Miller).

According to the other position, learning equips the individual with general cognitive systems that control his direction, choice, or patterning of response. Such systems correspond to the understanding and interpretation of situations—to meanings. They are not tied to specific stimuli so much as available in the experiential repertory of the person to assist in the discrimination of stimuli, the organization or patterning of intrinsic memorial processes, and the selection and direction of response. Again, there is a spectrum of views, ranging from a strong implication that cognitive systems may be comparatively independent of external stimulation to a conception of continuous interaction between situational influences and intrinsic activities. Psychologists who have advocated such conceptions include Tolman, Mowrer, and gestalt theorists (Koffka, Köhler, Wertheimer). A recent statement of this approach is contained in Miller, Galanter, and Pribram (1960).

As we shall see in Chapter 5, both sides of the controversy

remain lively. However, it is likely that the cognitive orientation is becoming dominant—at least in the study of human learning—as represented by mediation theory. But integral to mediation theory is the recognition that cognitive activity is tied to input from the environmental situation, rather than being independent from it.

The second front is represented by attempts to specify how past experience enters into behavior. The basic problem is to understand how and to what degree performance observed in the present differs from that expected solely from a specification of the immediate stimulus conditions. Although investigators may be interested in describing cognitive systems themselves, the more direct concern is with the description of response as it is influenced by those systems.

A simple instance of this line of attack is to be found in principles of *generalization*. Thus a conditioned response is not elicited only by the precise conditioned stimulus originally reinforced; rather, a range or class of stimuli may also elicit the conditioned response, in a gradient of diminishing effectiveness as the new stimulus differs from the original one. This phenomenon indicates that experience is acquired in broader and more complex ways than could be inferred directly from a knowledge of specific stimulus-response relationships.

Studies of memory reveal the effects of experience. This work ranges from a search for dynamic organizing processes that may lead to changes in recall following initial exposure, to current experiments on short-term memory that explore the contextual effects of prior learning on immediate recall.

Finally, we may mention research on associative organization and conceptual processes, to be examined in detail later. In a variety of ways, often ingenious, such studies demonstrate how the characteristics of experience help to determine behavior.

CHARACTERISTICS OF CONSCIOUSNESS

Behaviorism brought the term *conscious* into ill repute in psychology, as it did so many other words. As the sensible and nonsensible notions of the strict behaviorists have come into clearer focus, however, it can be seen that problems do not disappear by avoiding them.

In general, "conscious" means that the individual is aware of—knows about—his own activities. He can judge or describe his responses. But the phenomena reported have properties different from the extrinsic conditions that give rise to them, as mentioned before. If, for example, you hold before different persons a cigar, they may well characterize it differently. A young lady may see it as a distinctly larger object than its owner does. A man who has sworn off smoking may see it as harmful. And so on.

As pointed out in Chapter 1, however, conscious processes can only be inferred. The necessary evidence must rely on obtained verbal reports of imagery, associations, meanings, or other intrinsic activities, or on determining and interpreting relationships among two or more responses (verbal or nonverbal). The study of dreams and the use of projective techniques rely heavily on the first approach. The second is illustrated by studies of attention and discrimination. If a person presses a button when a green light goes on, but not when a red light goes on, we have at least minimal evidence that he is aware of differences in the stimulus situation.

The problem of consciousness really divides into at least three subproblems: (1) How are cognitive processes related to the environment? (We shall consider this matter below.) (2) How much of intrinsic activity is conscious? Here we encounter the phenomena of *unconscious* activities, and thus there arises the further issue of relationships between conscious and unconscious processes. (This problem will also be considered below.) (3) Finally, how shall we describe and account for conscious processes?

Apperception and Attention

Wundt developed the theory of *apperception*. He defined consciousness as the interconnection of psychical processes (Wundt, 1907, p. 228). The combination (or synthesis) of mental processes and their interrelations thus becomes the identifying feature of consciousness. Unconscious states are those in which this interconnection is interrupted.[1] The interconnection may be either simultaneous or successive. In the latter case, the time gap is bridged by relating the present to events that occurred earlier.

In the organization of consciousness, there is a central focus (or "inner fixation point") of maximum clarity, surrounded by a dimmer area. At any moment there exists a "field of consciousness" into and out of which moves a continuous train of "psychical compounds." In such a cycle, processes rise above the threshold of consciousness, then sink below the threshold (thus become unconscious). Apperception is the process of bringing mental content to

---

[1] Wundt also used the term *unconscious* in a somewhat different sense to refer to mental elements that have disappeared from consciousness (this fading out continually occurs, but these elements have the possibility of renewal). Contrast this view with that of psychoanalysis.

clear comprehension, attention the state of the ensuing awareness. Some contents may only be apprehended, or perceived without an accompanying state of attention. Each state is associated with characteristic feelings.

Wundt recognized two forms of apperception: *spontaneous* or *passive*, when new content thrusts itself suddenly on attention, and *predetermined* or *active apperception*, when new content is preceded by anticipatory affective preparation, so that attention is ready to be focused on it.

As Boring (1950) points out, Wundt's theory is actually three-fold: as *phenomenon*, apperception describes different degrees of consciousness; as *cognition*, apperception describes a relational process by which logical connections are formed; and, as *activity*, apperception refers to a continuous current in the stream of consciousness.

Titchener (1910) refused to accept the term apperception, preferring simply to speak about *attention*. But, otherwise, his views are similar to Wundt's, with a distinction between an upper level of clear focus and a lower, obscure, and marginal level. Functionally, he conceptualized three phases. At first, attention is passive or involuntary, determined by whatever stimuli are strong enough to intrude on consciousness. Next, some perception or idea occupies the forefront of consciousness, but is maintained in the face of opposition from other elements (secondary or active attention). Finally, a perception or idea may become dominant producing a state of "derived primary" attention or concentration, when only a powerful stimulus can disrupt it. Determinants of attention include intensity, quality, suddenness, and novelty of stimuli, repetition of a stimulus, and congruity between an intruding stimulus and the existing contents of consciousness.

Research on problems of attention has continued (Woodworth and Schlosberg, 1954; Smith, 1969), being especially visible today in studies of vigilance and tracking (see Chapter 4).

The Stream of Thought

A famous description of consciousness is James's (1890) formulation of the stream of thought. He begins with an apparently innocent statement, which, nevertheless, has vital significance. "The first fact for us . . ., as psychologists," he says, "is that thinking of some sort goes on" (vol. 1, p. 224). This statement might still today be taken as the credo of the cognitively oriented psychologist. Although we may not be able to explain just what thought is, or satisfactorily state how it can occur at all, we can accept the fact that thinking "goes on," and proceed to describe its characteristics as best we can.

James ascribes five characteristics to thought, as follows:

1 Every thought tends to be part of a personal consciousness.
2 Within each personal consciousness, thought is always changing.
3 Within each personal consciousness, thought is sensibly continuous.
4 Thought always appears to deal with objects independent of itself.
5 Thought is interested in some parts of these objects to the exclusion of others, continuously choosing from among them.

Note, first, that James emphasizes the personal side of thought. Every thought appears to be *owned*—no thought is impersonal nor existent by itself, but comes from, or occurs in, some person's mind. It is a little hard to see how this characteristic can cover all the facts; for instance, of certain pathological phenomena such as in multiple personality and hallucination, where the individual may not recognize his "self" at all. Yet, even there, one has some self ("secondary self," as James puts it), which, having thoughts, owns them. In this sense, dissociated cognitions also fit the principle. Beyond that, however, one may treat the rule as a potentiality rather than always as an actuality. That is, at least in normal persons, a thought that lacks this personal reference *may* be (and will be) recognized as belonging to the thinker, in the long run. Similarly, on awakening from a dream or revery, the thoughts are usually readily recognized as personal.[1] Aside from personal reference, James was basically concerned with a point that still needs occasionally to be made: thinking occurs in human minds and, in consequence, "thoughts" do not occur or exist outside them.

The second point states that thought continually changes. "No state," James says, "can recur and be identical with what it was before." The brain is constantly being modified by the nervous impulses that enter it, and the cumulative record influences what follows. James here expresses some of what we mean by the "mental context." He also anticipates important psychological

[1]Note, too, that therapy aims to restore this personal reference so that, for example, a hallucination is recognized as originating in the person himself.

theories that have been stated in elaborate and technical terms. Thus a basic tenet of psychoanalysis is that the individual's past experience has a profound effect on his present cognitive processes; the gestalt field theory similarly holds that the present cognitive event depends on the entire succession of past mental processes as they have modified the individual; and, indeed, general theories of learning also incorporate this principle. We might accept as a motto James's statement that "Every brain state is partly determined by the nature of this entire past succession."

The third principle expresses the continuity of thought, that it can be conceived as a "stream." Successive cognitive processes seem to belong together, even if there is a time gap between them, and shifts from one moment to the next are never absolutely abrupt. Again, this formulation may not fit pathological cases such as amnesia, but it does characterize the normal person (and, conversely, illuminates the nature of those abnormal cases where thinking is disturbed). For example, after a night's sleep, a person has no trouble in recognizing that his present mental processes are his own; that is, the gap of the night's interval is readily filled in.

In developing his third point, James describes the organization of consciousness, for thought seems to consist of resting places ("substantive parts") and places of flight ("transitive states"). In its continuous flow, thought appears to move more swiftly and with less definiteness between the resting places. Accompanying the main flow of thought are "feelings of tendency," "unnamed states," by which James seems to mean a kind of integration among mental processes. These qualities pertain to the fact that thoughts are tied together, as in speech, where words are not strung together at random but form connected series of ideas, each anticipated by the next and related to the ones before (at least as a general rule). This notion bears similarities to the "determining tendency" previously mentioned.

Finally, in discussing the continuity principle, James refers to the "fringe of consciousness," or the "psychic overtone." The stream of thought contains a central focus and fades off from that into vaguer, less conscious accompanying states, which nevertheless influence the course of thought. This conception is related to Wundt's theory of apperception.

The fourth principle states that thought tends to deal with objects rather than with the thought itself. We do not think about thought but of objects, or ideas, for which the thought is simply a representation.

The fifth principle implies that a selective process operates continuously in thinking, with the result that from the total store of possibilities, some are accepted and some are rejected. In this fashion James anticipates the body of research on attitudes and sets, ego mechanisms and values, cognitive styles, and so on.

A Behavioristic View

Lashley (1923) presented a forthright statement on the question of consciousness that expresses a position taken by early behaviorism on the mind-body problem. It is inappropriate to describe consciousness in introspective terms. Consciousness is behavior and nothing else, and can be reduced to the "physicochemistry of bodily activity." He proposed that "the statement 'I am conscious' does not mean anything more than the statement that 'such and such physiological processes are going on within me.'" By analyzing, one by one, the various characteristics ascribed to consciousness, he attempted to show that each can be fully understood strictly in physiological terms. He linked consciousness to the language mechanisms, so that the supposed phenomena of consciousness are simply the verbalized (or verbalizable) outcomes of neural activities. Thus verbal responses may be mistaken for the facts of consciousness.

The Psychoanalytic View

In some respects, Freud had a conventional conception of consciousness. He regarded its contents as consisting of perceptions and impulses; that is, the contents depend on the dynamics of attention as it is bombarded by environmental stimuli, on the one hand, and by internal stimuli on the other (Rapaport, 1960). What enters into attention depends on how intense or persistent it is, relative to the already existing content of attention—and the dominance of such content may wax and wane in a variable relation to external input. On the environmental side, the major determinants of consciousness are stimulus properties such as those already mentioned, for example, intensity and duration. On the internal side, however, the boundaries of consciousness are to an important degree subject to positive control by the individual (ego defense). It is at this point that we encounter one of the most distinctive features of psychoanalysis, namely, the key emphasis on *unconscious* forces.

Conscious activities, as just mentioned, are those mental processes of which the individual is aware, whereas unconscious activities are those of which he is not or cannot be aware. The conscious level has a peripheral region, which Freud designated as "preconscious," and processes in it are capable of attaining consciousness. Activities in the unconscious are held in check because they disturb or threaten in some fashion the conscious behavior of the individual. Although conscious and unconscious processes obey different laws, they nevertheless have dynamic relations with each other through the mechanism of *repression.* By this concept, Freud signifies the barriers erected against the direct or uncontrolled intrusion of unconscious impulses into consciousness. But the former may have effects in the following ways: (1) impulses originally unconscious may penetrate into consciousness if they are deprived of dangerous emotion, or if they are converted into acceptable forms of expression; (2) unconscious activities are assumed to bombard the barriers to their direct outlet and to exert modifying influences on conscious processes; (3) unconscious ideas may gradually be brought into consciousness by converting them first into the transitional forms that characterize the preconscious and thereafter admitting them into consciousness.

Whereas conscious processes are comparatively logical, orderly, rational, and realistic, unconscious processes are nonlogical, uncontrolled, and impulsive. This identification of two sides to mental life is fundamental in psychoanalytic theory, and contrasts sharply with the emphasis on primarily rational thought characteristic of other early theories.

It should be strongly stated that psychoanalytic theory from its beginnings incorporated motivational forces into its model of behavior. But it also allowed for extrinsic forces, and, indeed, we have in this theory a broad conception of the interplay of external and internal determinants of thought. Furthermore, by stressing the unconscious side of behavior, psychoanalysis has greatly broadened and deepened our understanding of cognition.

With this brief look at the psychoanalytic conception, we leave the matter of consciousness. Although today few psychologists concern themselves explicitly with it, the problem of awareness continues to receive experimental attention, as in studies of subliminal perception, vigilance, perceptual judgment and conditions that influence it, and so on. However, the measurement of performance in stated tasks is the central concern, rather than the subjective character of awareness. Our modern interest lies in processes more than in content. If we had to state a modern definition of consciousness, it would probably be safe to say that it corresponds to whatever the individual can (or could) verbalize, if he is asked to do so.

SUMMARY

In historical perspective, we can see the following basic problems: (1) the *mind-body* problem concerns the status of mental and bodily events and the relation between them, with psychophysiological parallelism as the principal position; (2) the problem of the *mechanism of thinking* has historically been treated in associationist terms; (3) the problem of the *content and structure of thought* has been approached through introspection and postulation of mental elements, principles of imageless thought and intrinsic determinants, and mediating processes; (4) in dealing with the *characteristics of experience,* views based on responses are contrasted with those that draw inferences about cognitive systems; and (5) theories that bear on the issue of *consciousness,* or the person's awareness of his own activities, include apperception and attention, the organization of consciousness, the stream of thought, stimulus-response relations (behaviorism), and psychoanalysis.

3

MEMORY, MOTIVATION, AND INTELLIGENCE

The historical perspective of the last chapter revealed several general issues that have pervaded the treatment of thinking. This background can be rounded out by looking at certain conditions usually assumed to be related to thinking—even if they have not always been sufficiently considered.

THE ROLE OF MEMORY

Whenever we speak of "experience" or the effects of learning, we imply that something retained from prior events in the individual's history now exerts some kind of influence on behavior. There are three major aspects of the problem.

1. If prior events are recorded in the nervous system, they may constitute a store of information that may be called on directly. This conception of memory may be called the *reappearance* hypothesis (Neisser, 1967). It is best exemplified by the associationist position, which maintains that ideas are composed of fainter replicas of sensations. Thought then becomes a shifting reoccurrence of bits from the memory store, combined or recombined according to the laws of association. The structuralist view of thinking similarly

31

implies the reappearance of images as traces of past events. Through-out the experimental study of memory, we can see a heavy reliance on this principle. Experiments on recall and recognition often have the aim of testing the withdrawal of information from the memory store. If there are errors or inadequacies, the implication has often been that the initial input was too weak or in some other way failed to produce a good record, or, if there was a record, it simply faded out.

2. In contrast, memory may be an active process in which the effects of experience undergo changes with time. This view of intrinsic dynamic organization was strongly advocated by the gestalt psychologists (see especially, Koffka, 1935). They postulate that memory consists of *traces* of past experience, but that these residues are subject to change as a function of their relations to each other and to those already laid down. Fundamental to this theory is the principle of closure, which states that a cognitive organization tends to become as "good" as possible. That is, it constitutes a field of active forces that tends toward a stable structure. Thus changes may take place to produce a more complete, more mean-ingful, or better organized system.

Unfortunately, it has, in general, proven to be impossible to define precisely what constitutes a "good" organization. Experi-ments certainly reveal many kinds of change in recall, so that there is evidence for the dynamic character of memory,[1] but such changes are not really predictable. For example, if subjects are presented with line drawings and asked to reproduce them, some subjects may lengthen particular lines and others may shorten them. Or, in remembering stories, people leave out different details, or "shape" the story differently. Thus we could accept a weaker statement of the principle of closure, that the properties of the initial trace field determine changes in memory.

A still stronger position on dynamic memorial processes is possible; namely, that response to stimulation is never a precise and literal trace of the stimulus input. Neisser (1967) points out that the gestalt position, like others, rests fundamentally on the postulate that the raw materials of memory correspond to the initial registration of the stimulus object. Thereafter, traces may change. He suggests that a *utilization* hypothesis is more acceptable. He says, "The only plausible possibility is that [cognition] consists of traces of *prior processes of construction*. There are no stored

---

[1] Classic studies of this kind were conducted by Bartlett (1967).

copies of finished mental events, like images or sentences, but only traces of earlier constructive activity. . . . We store traces of earlier cognitive acts, not of the products of those acts. The traces are not simply 'revived' or 'reactivated' in recall; instead, the stored fragments are used as information to support a new construction" (Neisser, 1967, pp. 285–286).

3. Finally, however we may eventually come to describe the record of experience, memory may be said to provide a general context that indirectly influences present cognitive events. Either of the first two views of memorial processes can allow for such effects. Already-existing memorial systems may influence what is recorded in the first place, as well as exerting effects on whatever traces are added to the storage. In this view there is a continuing interplay of immediate cognitive events and the total memorial system. Even if a precise replica of some previous experience were available to the subject—and this would depend on whether the mental context at the time provides an isolated niche, as it were—nevertheless it may not be producible or be only partly reproducible if other memorial processes interfere or alter its appearance.

At the present time all three of these aspects of memory are under intensive investigation. The first two are represented by attempts to clarify "decay" and "interference" factors in recall (especially in short-term recall). Controversy over these two possibilities continues to be too active to envisage its resolution in the near future. The third aspect is represented by studies of meaningfulness and other variables in associative processes, and also by studies of repression and other ego-defensive mechanisms in learning and recall.

THE ROLE OF MOTIVATION

In general, the concept of *motivation* has been used in a variety of ways in psychology, and a very large number of terms can be found under this heading. We shall take the central reference to be conditions which instigate and determine the course of sequences of behavioral acts (see Vinacke, 1960b, 1962). These conditions are intrinsic states, to be distinguished from extrinsic stimuli, although stimulus situations may often be called motivational. In this case, however, emphasis is placed on the induced intrinsic state, rather than on informational input.

We may recognize three major kinds of treatment of motivation in psychology.

Motivation as a Postulate

It is doubtful that any psychological theory ever failed to allow for some intrinsic condition, however general, that makes the organism vary in its activity. But such conditions may be treated as an assumption, signifying little more than the fact that behavior occurs in a living organism, which is therefore active. Historically, early theories, like those of the associationists and structuralists, simply ignored what we would now regard as motivational variables, except for this underlying assumption. In keeping with their major interest, the structuralists attempted to describe "feelings of volition" (regarded as complex reactions) as components of mental content, but problems of motivation were not directly examined. Early behaviorism also ruled out such variables, allowing only for fundamental biological viability[1] and variations in organic structure. A similar assumption characterizes some later theories, such as those of Guthrie and Estes and Skinner. Much current theorizing in the information-processing approach may also be characterized in this way. That is, the energizing of behavior is assumed, with little attention to the possibility that individuals differ in their intrinsic characteristics (save for specific effects of learning).

Motivation as Intrinsic Drive(s)

The individual may be inferred to possess special internal properties as a function of which behavior varies in characteristic ways. Put another way, a theorist may draw inferences about motivational variables, which are then considered to influence performance, either in their own right or in interaction with extrinsic forces. The chief point here is the distinction between intrinsic and extrinsic variables, as a consequence of which both must be taken into account.

We may further differentiate among three usages of drive.

1. Drive as General Life-Force Some basic urge may be postulated that characterizes all organisms. Lying beyond the possibility of understanding in physical or chemical terms, it is a property of living things. Although this conception has had proponents since the time of the Greeks, it has usually been replaced by views described below. However, something like this principle is

[1] Watson (1924) suggested the term *stream of activity* to express his belief that we need not speak of intrinsic motives (instincts) but only of developing systems of response.

implied in certain personality theories that postulate a general "drive for superiority" (Adler, 1964; Jung, 1956) or a drive toward "self-actualization" (Rogers, 1961).

2. Drive as an Explicit Intrinsic State In this sense drive means an inherent biological mechanism that characterizes a given species. In the case of human beings, such conceptions range from emphasis on a single major drive to formulations based on many different drives. The Freudian principle of libido as a general sexual drive is one example (in actuality, Freud's views are not readily reduced to this simple notion, especially if we accept his distinction between life and death instincts). Conceptions based on several or many drives include older doctrines of instinct and more recent drive theories. The former described a large number of specific mechanisms, each supposedly instigating well-defined patterns of response. The latter proposed an indeterminate number of generalized biological instigators (primary drives).

The demise of classical instinct theory came after a period of intensive criticism advancing four principal objections. (1) A careful review of evidence showed that the human organism does not have the biological properties apparently required to infer instincts. (2) The doctrine involves a circular argument—for example, the gregarious instinct was defined by pointing to aggregating phenomena such as crowds, but these same phenomena were attributed to the operation of an instinct. (3) The doctrine implies mysterious forces that cannot be understood by reference to known biological facts. (4) Finally, and most important, the instinct principle fails to allow sufficiently for the effects of the environment, which, through learning, may produce a large part—and perhaps all—of the behavioral tendencies attributed to innate impulses.

Instead of instincts, psychology turned to the concept of "drives," since, evidently, one cannot ignore the fact that intrinsic instigative forces *are* properties of the living system. This concept rests, first, on the simple postulation of energizing forces. But energy acts through organic structures, or systems, which have recognizable functions: supplying the tissues with nourishment, increasing the level of activity, and so on. Changes in these systems influence the behavior of the organism. The chief problem is to decide how to classify these functions, and it has usually been solved by speaking about general kinds of physiological needs, especially hunger, thirst, excretion, respiration, general activity, maternal impulses, and sex. Aside from bypassing some of the unsatisfactory features of the instinct doctrine, the concept of drive has clear advantages. Needs can be treated as strictly biological, independent of learning, experience, or specific modes of stimulation.[1] Thus we can conceive of motivational changes solely by virtue of continuing intrinsic changes, and seek to determine their effects on learning and performance. By linking drives with definite organic needs, we can devise systematic ways to vary and measure the drive. The *deprivation* technique is the major approach. If we can meaningfully recognize a need for food, and infer a hunger drive, then by withholding food, we increase the need, and thus strengthen hunger. The general implications of this usage of the term drive are twofold. (1) Only well-defined physiological needs can be linked with drives : All other tendencies either depend mainly on learning or are wholly produced through learning. (2) All motivation arises fundamentally from variations in drives.

3. Drive as Synonymous with Activity Level[2] Any factor that alters the intensity of behavior is regarded as a drive. Such factors may be physiological states (primary drives), secondary (acquired) drives, extrinsic influences (instructions, incentives, punishment), or special conditions attendant on goal attainment (such as frustration) (see especially, Brown 1961). Although several criteria for defining a drive variable may be advanced, the chief one is its ability to facilitate or interfere with learning. To the extent that different variables have similar effects on learning, they are regarded as equivalent drives. Perhaps no one is quite willing to propose that all the classes of conditions mentioned above are fully equivalent—thus obviating the necessity to distinguish one from another, save in methodological fashion—but much of the research literature carries this implication. Drive in this sense does not signify any particular kind of motivational force. It refers just as meaningfully to manifest anxiety as to hunger, to the possibility of losing money as to the threat of receiving an electric shock.

Thus in order to deal systematically with the problem of motivation, it is necessary to decide which meaning of the term drive to adopt (if we use the term at all). My preference is for the second usage, thus distinguishing drives from other components of motivation.

[1]To be sure, this notion is not strictly accurate because the organism at every instant interacts with the environment. But to adopt it provides a way to clarify the effects of learning.

[2]This view leads to a unitary conception.

Motivation as a System

Finally, there are a variety of theories that see motivation as a complex system of variables. The major features of these positions include: distinctions among several classes of motivational influences, interactions among variables, and emphasis on components established by learning.

Historically, theories of this kind have been especially influenced by the *functionalist* tradition of American psychology, of which Woodworth, Murphy, Murray, and McClelland are outstanding examples. In this line of development, dynamic influences on behavior have steadily been a central interest, accompanied by an eclectic treatment of learning, an orientation toward human behavior, and an attention to individual differences. The open-mindedness of functionalism has also made it receptive to diverse theories and research findings, so that an effort, more or less systematic, has been made to comprehend and encompass psychoanalytic, behavioristic, and cognitive principles within a broad framework. Functionalism has also had a pervasive evolutionary and biological outlook as well, so that it might better be called *biosocial* theory. These positions generally recognize both innate and physiological variables and sociocultural contexts and influences. The principle of the unconscious is typically accepted, but not strongly developed; indeed, the problem of how to fit it into motivation theory appears to be not yet solved effectively.

Two contrasting treatments of motivation in this general tradition can be designated as *drive-modification* and *activation* theories.

Drive-modification Theory

In this view, motivational influences are seen as operating at different "levels," each serving a special function within the total system.

Activation Arousal, or General Energizing Basic to the system is the level of energy expenditure, which varies quantitatively as a function of the internal need-state.

Forms of Predominance The individual expends energy in different ways, depending on the organic subsystem most activated. Variations in predominance may be labeled as "drives" and "motives." *Drives* are inherent biological properties, associated with organic need-states. During development, primitive drives may undergo modification, leading to altered biological properties (or *biogenic motives*). Such instigators are continuous with drives, and often there is no necessity to distinguish the later from the earlier form. In some instances, however, notably in the case of sex, it would be very misleading to assume that the two are the same. In addition, the distinction is essential in comparing man with lower animals, since the modification of drives is so very much greater in the former. Becoming gradually established is a third class of instigators, namely, *psychogenic motives.* If acquired tendencies become typical and regular in instigating behavior, they have an importance equivalent to biogenic motives. The chief criteria by which acquired tendencies may be recognized as motives are the permanence of the tendency, its operation independently of biogenic motives (or drives), and its ability to influence behavior (such as learning) comparably to drive states. The principle of the functional autonomy of motives is a classic statement of this viewpoint (Allport, 1961). Note how this view treats the distinction between primary and secondary instigators: All three classes are fundamental instigators, representing alternative forms of energy expenditure, but drives are earlier forms, and both biogenic and psychogenic motives are later (i.e., secondary only in this chronological sense). For example, hunger in its innate form is a drive, but may undergo such pronounced changes that it is scarcely recognizable (as in anorexia nervosa or in obese persons) (Schachter et al., 1968). The wide departures from the original drive that we see in sexual behavior hardly need to be mentioned. With respect to psychogenic motives, anxiety, achievement, affiliation, and power have been widely investigated. None of these basic instigators could be described or predicted solely from knowledge about drives. Some instigators, such as aggression and cognition, cannot clearly be assigned to biogenic or psychogenic categories. In such instances it is uncertain to what degree development is continuous with drives, or whether the instigators are established by learning.

Regulation   At another level we can identify functions of direction, orientation toward a goal, and systematic control of response, signifying that motives are channeled in certain alternative ways. Diverse terms familiar in psychology for these functions, including habit, value, ego mechanism, sentiment, and cognitive style, may all be subsumed under the general heading of *attitudes*. These intrinsic systems are learned regulators of motives, providing continuity and organization in response sequences.

As distinctly different components of the motivation system, motives and attitudes can be measured and separately manipulated in experiments. For example, we can assess latent achievement by the Thematic Apperception Test (McClelland et al., 1953; Atkinson, 1958), and compare the performance of persons low and high in this respect as a function of differences in manifest anxiety. Instigative and regulative variables interact, as has been repeatedly shown (Vinacke, 1962).

Adjustment   At a level still closer to the specific response is the function of selection or focusing. Following the contributions of the Würzburg research, and calling also on Tolman's principle of expectancy (Atkinson, 1964), we shall designate this process as *set*. It refers to the effects of the immediate state of preparation of the subject, as induced by instructions or other properties of the environment just prior to performance.

Situational Variables   The foregoing variables are all intrinsic, and it is necessary to recognize that extrinsic variables also affect the motivation system. We cannot adequately represent this system without allowing for goals, incentives, and stress. It is especially important to do so in view of the patent fact that in many investigations such conditions are manipulated to establish variations in "motivation." It therefore seems best to include them as an additional level.

Activation Theory

Some theories primarily emphasize the role of emotional arousal and utilize hedonic principles. They separate the fundamental emotional arousal as an instigative process from its expression or regulation in various forms, employing the term motive for the latter function.[1]

Behavior is viewed as depending on a fundamental activating process—an alerting and energizing system. Arousal is associated

[1] See Cofer and Appley (1965) for a review.

with feelings of tension that instigate activity. The feelings themselves are perceived as pleasant or unpleasant, and behavior is guided accordingly. Learned systems, or motives, maintain, alter, or reduce arousal by determining patterns of response.

Motives and attitudes are distinguished in two ways. (1) Stimulus factors influence the expression of motives by presenting alternative goal objects or by inducing expectancies about the outcomes of behavior. (2) Responses depend on whatever habits were acquired in the past. In both respects, the regulation and direction of response is a function of conditions present in the situation. Broadly conceived, the motive is regulative—that is, it directs and expresses affective arousal. Thus motivation has three levels: emotional arousal, regulative patterning, and extrinsic influence.

More generally formulated activation theories avoid the distinction between pleasant and unpleasant affect by postulating a general arousal process, ranging from low activity to high degrees of excitement. In this fashion, arousal becomes the major variable (corresponding to the general drive concept), without necessarily distinguishing among the levels of instigation, regulation, and adjustment.

Motivational Variables
The point of this sketchy discussion is not so much to formulate a systematic approach to motivation as to pave the way for an understanding of research that concerns the effects of motivation on thinking. I intend to show that many different variables can be chosen, but that various functions are involved. The role of motivation depends on the kind of function with which an investigator is concerned.

THE ROLE OF INTELLIGENCE
Surprising as it may appear, not much attention has been devoted to the relationship between intelligence and thinking. In general, earlier theories regarded thinking as intellectual activity and broadly equated one with the other. Since the classical views for the most part dealt primarily with logical reasoning, individual differences in its exercise were largely ignored. That is, reasoning was treated in a formal way as dependent on definite rules and as generally similar from one situation to another. There is a strong implication that training and skill are mainly responsible for variations in the effectiveness of thought. In addition, as we have seen, the problem of

describing content and its organization dominated much of the psychology of the past, and therefore the special properties of the thinker were seen as a matter of differences in experience. Within the body of laboratory research, however, intelligence has typically been treated like other intrinsic variables: by randomizing or control procedures an effort is made to rule out the effects of intelligence.

Investigators during the first half of this century operated on two general assumptions, apparently supported by research. (1) The more intelligent the subject, the better his performance in tasks that call on fairly complex functions (i.e., learning, recall, and problem solving). Performance here usually signifies quantitative rather than qualitative variation. That is, the more intelligent the subject, the faster the learning, the more problems solved, and so on.[1] It is only recently that qualitative aspects of performance have assumed much importance, as seen in research on concept formation and creativity —and even here the quantitative emphasis continues strong. (2) Intelligence increases with increasing age, and therefore developmental level is an important factor in performance. But, again until recently, this assumption has had a quantitative implication, that children perform less well (or require simpler tasks) because they are less intelligent. The overwhelming preference for college students as subjects in experiments has made age variations in intelligence a minor concern in formulating theories about performance. However, as the field of developmental psychology has become more empirical, this problem is now under intensive scrutiny, strongly influenced by the work of Piaget.

One stumbling block to an effective attack on the role of intelligence in thinking has been a reliance on the concept of general intelligence (Hunt, 1961). We need not review the history of attempts to define intelligence, which range from a conception of general adaptibility to the environment through associating intelligence with learning ability to vaguer notions of a fundamental common element in diverse tasks. Perhaps two factors contribute to the tenacious grip of the concept on psychology. In the first place, the testing movement had a very practical interest in producing a total score that could, in unitary fashion, be employed for selection and prediction purposes. The sole concern was to determine a useful correlation between this score and a criterion of success— and the criterion itself was a general unitary variable, rather than

---

[1] But correlations between measures of intelligence and performance have been low often enough to prevent sweeping generalization. The relationship varies with other conditions, such as motivation.

differentiated into different kinds of performance. It was natural for the investigator, who was searching for general variables, to seize on the test score (or IQ) and to employ it without worrying about its adequacy for his purposes. It may also be observed that the experimenter has not wished to act in a "clinical" capacity, and therefore has accepted measures of intelligence as they were made available. In the second place, the concept of general intelligence has an inherent logic. The test is composed of diverse items, on which enormously varied patterns of response are possible. An average score appears to do justice to performance, allowing for the fact that performance on some items is better, on others worse.

Stemming, however, from the work of Thurstone, the concept of general intelligence has increasingly come under criticism. It has become evident that a large variety of distinctive abilities enter into intellectual performance. Modern intelligence tests, especially those developed by Wechsler, have endeavored to incorporate the principle of diverse abilities instead of relying on the IQ as a general measure. Instrumental in our changing ideas about intelligence is the factor-analytic research of Guilford (1967) that points to a large number of different abilities. Thus it is clear that the role of intelligence in thinking must be assessed by exploring relationships between well-defined special abilities and the kinds of tasks to which they are relevant. For example, rather than using IQ measures in studies of associative processes, we might better employ scores on tests of flexibility or fluency. We are led therefore to a third assumption, which is being increasingly emphasized in research. Performance in different kinds of tasks varies with the abilities appropriate to those tasks. It must be remarked that, so far, quantitative implications continue to be more salient than qualitative ones. There are signs of movement toward a better balance in studies of conceptual functioning and verbal learning, where the possibility of variations in the characteristics of performance associated with variations in ability is coming to be better recognized.

SUMMARY

Conditions fundamental to the study of thinking are: (1) *memory,* or the storage and retrieval of experience—here we can contrast "reappearance" and "utilization" hypotheses, and can speak about the general context of experience; (2) *motivation*, which refers to processes that instigate and regulate sequences of behavioral acts—conceptions of drive, motive, attitude, set, and situational variables must be differentiated, with drive-modification theory as a general orientation; and (3) *intelligence*, which has mainly been treated by assumptions that performance is correlated with ability and that increased intelligence with age is associated with changes in the character and level of thinking—however, difficulties with the conception of general intelligence has now led to an emphasis on many abilities.

4

RELATIONS BETWEEN PERSON AND ENVIRONMENT

Broadly speaking, psychology has the mission of investigating how variations in states of the person are related to variations in the properties of the environment. For strategic reasons—or out of theoretical preference—it has usually seemed desirable or easier to deal systematically with only one set of variations at a time. Yet it is easy to see that behavior is always the resultant of conditions both of the person and of the environment.

The problem is therefore how to cope adequately with the interactions between such conditions. As sophistication increases, the question shifts from asking how a given stimulus or task variable influences response, or how differences in a personality variable are correlated with performance, to the issue of the relative contributions of both kinds of variables.

Intervening Variables

The general model of psychological research treats conditions that can be brought under experimental control as *independent variables*. From this standpoint, extrinsic influences are most readily defined as independent variables. But when the principle is introduced that performance also varies with intrinsic conditions, the question arises concerning how to conceptualize such intrinsic conditions. They might be regarded as independent variables too, if we define them as conditions antecedent to performance (or if we manipulate them systematically independently of performance). Thus we would have two classes of independent variables, personality and environmental, either or both of which may have significant effects on response. We must also allow for the fact that neither kind of variable operates in an absolute fashion, as if the person were a static mechanism. Rather, the intrinsic state changes from one moment to the next, depending on preceding events, on the alteration of the behaving system by current events, and so on. That is, a personality variable has changing degrees of influence and input from the environment, which thus modifies existing states. In part these remarks concern the problem of *feedback*, and in part the problem of *pervasive* or *spreading organization*, by which varying properties of the intrinsic system become involved in the response process. We have referred to the adjustment level in this connection. We shall differentiate in this general sense between independent, intervening, and dependent variables. An intervening variable, then, is an intrinsic state that represents the temporary condition induced by whatever variables can meaningfully be defined as operating in the situation.

MODELS OF PERSON-ENVIRONMENT RELATIONS

Several treatments of how intrinsic and extrinsic variables are related can be recognized. These models tend to emphasize certain kinds of problems in preference to others, and thus differ in the variables that might be chosen to test them.

Input-Output Models   We will begin with the formulation that has guided most psychological investigation. It is the simple conception founded on the definition of extrinsic stimulus variables and ensuing response variables. Since we have frequently referred to it in preceding sections, it needs only to be mentioned here. Research on threshold phenomena and signal detection depends heavily on it, as will be discussed in the next section.[1]

Cognitive Models   In contrast to the foregoing conception, emphasis may be placed primarily on the operation of intrinsic process-

[1] This and the next two models are developed further in Chapter 5.

es. The organism is considered to acquire properties that determine the selection of responses and to influence their characteristics (such as rate, intensity, duration, etc.). An important difference from the simple input-output model is that no one-to-one relation is attributed to stimuli and responses. That is, the intrinsic process is regarded as relatively enduring, linking series of events and generalizing across situations. The implication therefore is that information about cognitive properties is seen to be more significant than information about the particular components of a single situation.

Mediation Models Except for the analysis of quite specific behavioral events, neither of the preceding models is really typical of modern psychology. Rather, they appear mostly as heuristic devices to focus on the effects of certain kinds of variables. Indeed, many cases can be found when investigators concerned with the same problem begin with such an emphasis and then move toward a more inclusive conception. Vigilance research illustrates this trend. In the mediation model, however, the input-output and cognitive formulations are combined to allow both for stimulus and intrinsic variables, and also to take account not only of immediately effective input conditions but of past and future influences. In this way the organism is treated not as a mechanical instrument (input-output model) nor as a programmed agent for operating on the environment (cognitive model), but as a structured and dynamic participant in behavioral processes. The person is thus both a responder to stimulation and a determiner of response. The intrinsic activities that link these two aspects of behavior are mediating processes. Potential inferences about mediating processes appear whenever either of the first two models proves insufficient, for example, when response characteristics cannot be adequately predicted from known stimulus properties, or when presumably different intrinsic characteristics are nevertheless associated with similar response properties.

Information Theory This theory also considers input variables as leading to activities internal to the system (information processing), including the combining of elements, incorporating material already stored in memory, and selecting and sequencing of phases, eventuating in response processes. We shall see this version especially clearly in the development of computer-simulation approaches to thinking. It is not entirely clear whether information theory should be considered "mediational" or represents a contrasting point of view. Some investigators seem to use mediation and information processing as synonymous, others as different conceptions.

Models of the input-output and cognitive types are frequently described as "two stage," with mediation types as "three stage"; or we might say that the first two explicitly deal with two components, and the third with three.[1]

General Situational Models   Any of the first three formulations may be extended more broadly to the person *and* the environment. Here emphasis is placed on adjustment or behavioral change, rather than on specific stimulus response events. Indeed, both person and environment are recognized to be complex systems of variables, for which general definitions are provided. Especially to be noted are conditions of frustration and conflict. In such cases, the situation in effect has two poles: a person and a goal. The two poles are separated by time or space and are bridged by inferred cognitive states (expectation, intention). Each of the poles may have both extrinsic and intrinsic aspects. Thus the goal is both an actual and a perceived (positively or negatively valued) object; the person is both an observable responding system (e.g., making movements or uttering words) and a feeling, cognizing system (e.g., interpreting or valuing his relation to the goal).

Any set of variables may be described either by objective measurement or by obtaining evidence about the individual's subjective state, with no necessary agreement between them. In frustration, for example, we have four kinds of variables: the person, the barrier, the goal, and the distance (or space) between person and barrier and between barrier and goal, easily viewed as objectively definable by the use of direct observation or operations of physical measurement. Such procedures are especially easy for distances, barrier, and goal. However, there might be problems about the person, whose physical size, speed of movement, and so on are probably irrelevant to the characteristics we wish to treat as variables. Of course, we *could* content ourselves merely with simply recording his movements—a strategy that is fairly successful with rats. Or, we could adopt the opposite approach and administer procedures that yield information about the subjective counterpart of the main variables. Thus we might define them on the basis of how the person perceives the goal and the barrier, and how he judges distances between them and

[1]Actually, in a broad sense with four, if structural, content, and organizing cognitive factors are distinguished from affective and motivational factors. The latter might ultimately be treated as intrinsic input variables.

himself. As in so many areas of psychological research, general situational variables have been treated in both ways, depending on the investigator's predilections. As a result we have for the most part two apparently similar bodies of results—often appearing very similar —with no clear evidence that they can be reconciled. For example, there is strong evidence for gradients of approach and avoidance in ambivalent conflict situations (Brown, 1948; Miller, 1959) in which the strength of the tendency is found to vary with distance from the goal, with the avoidance gradient steeper. Presumably the individual's subjective state varies comparably so that his anxiety increases as he comes closer to a negatively valued goal, and his desire to attain the goal increases as he comes closer to a positively valued goal. At the same time these tendencies are influenced by personality characteristics (Ringuette, 1965; Speisman et al., 1964). Therefore the behavior elicited in a situation cannot be fully predicted without considering how the person construes its properties. In more common sense terms, the *same* object may be a negative goal for one person and a positive goal for another. Beyond that, the mere fact of its valence does not necessarily enable the observer to predict behavior in relation to it. A person for whom a goal has negative valence may nevertheless approach it vigorously, and with increasing vigor the closer its inevitability becomes. In short, we are faced again with problems of interaction, in which the effects of extrinsic variables depend on intrinsic variables, and vice versa.

Research on relations between person and environment thus calls on two levels of analysis. On the one hand, we can use models that look at specific, well-defined behavioral events (as in the first three types), paying attention primarily to stimulus, response, and mediating conditions; or we can employ general models of adjustment that attempt to cope with broad, complex sets of variables, paying attention to processes over time and to large patterns of behavioral change.

Dynamic Models   In none of the foregoing conceptions does the major interest lie in the characteristics of cognitive processes themselves.[1] But these properties may be examined to determine how they vary with changes in the environment. Freudian principles contribute here a distinction between primary and secondary processes (Rapaport, 1951, 1960).

From its inception, psychoanalysis has incorporated affective

[1]To some extent this statement does not apply to mediation theory, but even here there is less concern with intrinsic processes than with how they serve to link stimuli and responses.

and motivational influences into its view of cognition. It has also recognized that thought is determined not only by dynamic intrinsic influences, but also by extrinsic stimulus influences. On the one side, instinctual impulses seek for expression, and on the other, conditions in the environment impose constraints and demands. The ego is the agent for reconciling these potentially competing forces, subject also to supervision by the superego (which may be regarded as strong and continuing moral and ideal attitudes). Strictly speaking, all cognition is activity of the ego, which therefore consists of the images and other symbolic processes that we ordinarily call "thinking." However, they may be of two kinds, under the headings of *primary-process thinking* and *secondary-process thinking*. The former refers to "wish-fulfilling" cognitions induced by instinctual impulses, the latter to "realistic" cognitions oriented toward the environment. Primary-process thinking is determined by the pleasure principle, secondary-process thinking by the reality principle. In general the primary process corresponds to irrational thinking, reflecting the free and direct expression of emotions and impulses (as in fantasy or dreams), whereas the secondary process is rational, logical, controlled, problem solving cognitive activity.

The question of what conditions determine whether cognition will have primary or secondary properties is bound up with the ego as a mediator between instincts and the demands of reality. Psychoanalytic theory is more concerned with the former than the latter.[1] The relation between the ego and the id therefore requires explication.

The id is the great reservoir of primitive instinctual impulses that seek outlet in behavior. The ego manages these impulses by means of mechanisms that control impulses and direct them into forms of behavior that protect and enhance the person's best interests in relation to environmental demands. From a cognitive standpoint, this process is a matter of how unconscious forces influence the character of conscious events. There are at least three aspects to the relation between unconscious and conscious, which we may label as *arousal, sublimation*, and *repression* (see Madison, 1961).

1. *Arousal.*   In this relationship, instincts function like the biological drives of many other psychological theories, as discussed in the last chapter. That is, they simply represent forces at the instigative level of motivation systems. Such forces are not directly accessible to conscious awareness, but are known only by their

---

[1]Rapaport (1960), however, points out in some detail that it is a matter of emphasis rather than neglect of situational influences. In fact much psychological research appears to complement the psychoanalytic viewpoint by systematic study of realistic factors.

affective and cognitive effects (for example, feelings of hunger versus the energizing process). Rather than speaking of unconscious forces, we might simply refer to nonconscious conditions of arousal. Present in all behavior, these conditions do not imply threat to the ego, which in many areas simply responds to and expresses changing states of instigation.

2. *Sublimation.*   During the course of socialization, instinctive impulses are deprived of their original energy,[1] which the ego acquires to serve its own interests. Once the ego assumes control of energy, it can direct it into realistically determined channels—that is, in those directions that cope with the environment as presented to the individual. Thus systems of motivation develop that correspond to the psychogenic motives discussed in the last chapter, such as achievement, affiliation, nurturance, and so on. In contrast to the primitive gratification of instincts, the operation of such systems leads to forms of behavior we consider "higher human" endeavors, such as love and altruism, religion and humanitarianism, constructive accomplishment, and so on.

Here again the unconscious component is not to be considered threatening to the person's welfare. Rather, the unconscious side simply is the levels of motivation and memory that lie outside—or perhaps below—cognitive awareness but within the boundaries of the ego. Whether these levels are accessible to cognition depends on the degree to which attention is directed to them, as well as on the characteristics of storage. Be that as it may, the relation between conscious and unconscious in sublimation is frequently a direct one. That is, ego-instigative impulses feed directly into the attitudes whereby they are satisfied—and the cognitive process (imagery or symbolic representation) is conscious and verbalized.

3. *Repression.*   In this third relationship, the instinctual forces of the id remain unharnessed and continuously active. Since they are unconscious, they are conceived to impinge on or to intrude into conscious levels. To maintain control, the ego utilizes the mechanism of repression, which generally signifies the exercise of energy in opposition to the instinctual energy. Barriers to the direct expression of instinctual wishes prevent their expression, or permit the ego to disguise or divert them into forms that protect the individual from harmful consequences (such as unacceptable or threatening cognitive expression, immoral acts, etc.).

[1]Since Freud at first considered this energy to be sexual, the process is called desexualization of instincts. However, it is not necessary to limit the principle to sexual drives, it may be presumed to apply to any drive on which socialization acts. In the extended Freudian view, for example, aggressive-destructive impulses are parallel to sexual drives.

There may be several effects of repression. An impulse may be restrained in the unconscious (primal repression), requiring continuous expenditure of energy to prevent its expression. If an impulse succeeds in escaping, the ego may utilize energy to push it back again (afterexpulsion). At times the ego may control the expression of an impulse by defensive mechanisms, converting it into its opposite (reaction formation), neutralizing the threat (denial, intellectualizing, rationalizing), disguising the source (as in projection), concealing its aim (as in displacement), or in other ways. Repression may also have even more indirect effects because the impulse continues to exert an influence on the ego, for example, by partially escaping in some new direction, or by draining the resources of the ego so that activities of kinds unrelated to the repressed impulse are reduced. Finally, the ego may fail to maintain repression, so that the impulse penetrates into cognition, appearing in a primitive form, perhaps as an image or hallucination, or as an act that gratifies the wish.

Primary versus Secondary Processes

We may now distinguish between primary- and secondary-process thinking. The former occurs as the direct effect of an unconscious impulse, the latter as cognitions under the control of the ego. One extreme is therefore especially represented by escape, the other extreme by cognitions associated with sublimated motivation systems. Between lies a continuum on which fall cognitions that to some extent reflect the influence of unconscious impulses. The most striking examples of primary process are found when there is a wish fulfillment and, indeed, we might limit primary process to such instances. But the only clear examples of secondary process are those when cognition is strictly under the control of the ego in its reality-oriented functions. In any case, it is important to recognize that a continuum is really involved, and that a large share of thinking is neither wholly primary nor wholly secondary.

At this point it is necessary to reiterate that *all* cognition is a function of the ego. In the unconscious, processes obey their own rules and, by definition, it is impossible to describe them; only their effects are describable. It appears more meaningful to regard the unconscious as containing processes (impulses, wishes) different from conscious processes than to employ the same term for both. Thus we should not refer to unconscious cognitions, for it is only the consequences of unconscious forces that are cognitive.

Instead of two distinct categories, as seems to be implied in the psychoanalytic view, a conception based on two interrelated kinds of forces better describes cognition. One set is represented by affective-motivational influences, the other by ego-directive influences. The former may be called *autistic*, the latter *realistic*. Both are always to some degree present in all cognition, but in varying intensities, leading to the autistic-realistic continuum shown in Figure 4-1. At one pole autistic forces are the major component, and at the other pole environmentally determined forces are the major component. As the importance of one component increases, the other decreases (see Martin, 1968, for a discussion of the Freudian concept of stimulus barrier along somewhat similar lines). Whatever serves either to strengthen or weaken one relative to the other alters the character of cognition. When instigative forces intensify, cognition shifts toward the autistic pole, acquiring greater need-oriented or need-expressive properties; and when extrinsic forces impose stronger demands, cognition shifts toward greater realism. Of course, such changes do not correspond precisely to the forces themselves, because properties of the cognitive system partially determine response. For example, the ego may delay or otherwise exert influence on the expression of needs or on the effects of environmental input. But in general the relative contributions of autistic and realistic forces determine the character of cognitive events.

Thus we can readily cast into perspective the strategies open to the investigator in seeking to ascertain the effects of one force or another. Autistic forces can be increased by acting on instigation, as in imposing conditions of deprivation on the subject, or by the experimental inductions used to increase arousal. Conversely, we can potentially weaken autistic influences by alleviating need-states or by trying to reduce some relevant instigative condition—for example, by reassuring instructions when anxiety is the state under study or by using neutral instructions to decrease the likelihood of achievement arousal. At the opposite pole, realistic influences can be increased by providing more structured and demanding tasks, by orienting instructions, or in other familiar ways.

The aim then is to establish conditions that either free autistic forces from realistic demands or maximize the effects of environmental forces. In addition to the experimental tactics outlined above, it is evident that sleep is a state in which environmental input is greatly reduced, thereby releasing autistic forces, as in dreams. Similarly, the withdrawal of attention from extrinsic objects frees autistic

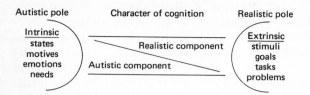

FIGURE 4–1   Autistic-realistic continuum.

forces, as in fantasy. In complementary fashion, orientation to environmentally imposed tasks promotes realistic forces, as in problem solving. Thus dreams and fantasy represent one end of the continuum, problem solving the other.

Psychoanalytic theory also incorporates values and ideals as influences on behavior, through the principle of the *superego* (See Chapter 18).

Field Models

Finally, some theories have formulated relations between person and environment as systems of forces that act at each moment to produce response.

One historical example is Lewin's (1936) theory of the *life space*, in which at any instant in time, behavior is treated as a function solely of the immediately given properties of the person and of the environment as it exists for that person (the principle of *contemporaneity*). To describe person and environment, Lewin uses various structural and dynamic concepts to specify the conditions present in each component of the life space and to indicate direction of change. Rudimentary forms of this treatment are apparent in the situational models previously mentioned.

More recently, Helson (1964) has developed a field theory with the principle of *adaptation level* as a focus. At a particular moment, all relevant forces combine to determine the response. *Focal stimuli* are the directly influential properties of the immediate situation, such as the intensity, size, variation, and nearness of objects. *Background stimuli* are contextual factors in the situation, removed from the immediate object(s), such as the color of the background against which a figure appears. *Residual stimuli* are intrinsic determinants arising from past experience, including memorial, attitudinal, and affective states.

As behavior continues, stimuli of all these kinds interplay in an averaging process, with changes occurring as a function of their relative weights, resulting at a particular moment in the *adaptation level*: a net resultant of the forces present. The adaptation level is considered to be a psychologically neutral or "zero" state, acting as a reference point for subsequent stimuli.[1]

The occurrence of a new stimulus tends to alter the adaptation level according to its properties. If it is above the existing level, the level shifts in that direction; if below the level, there is a shift downward. (However, since the several classes of stimuli mentioned above are weighted, a particular influence may be counteracted by the stronger or counterbalancing effect of another.) For example, if we present a series of geometric objects as stimuli, judgments of shape are a function of the characteristics of the series. To provide a simple demonstration of adaptation level, we would ask the subject to respond in a fashion that most directly reflects the comparison of one stimulus with another. We might require him to judge whether the stimulus is "more square" or "less square." Then as the objects become progressively less square, the adaptation level moves in that direction.

From this perspective Helson derives the following characteristics of behavior:

1 *Bipolarity.* When a new stimulus is presented, response tendencies occur in contrasting directions with respect to the existing state (e.g., "more than" or "less than"; "pleasant" or "unpleasant"; "toward" or "away from"; "hostile" or "friendly."
2. *Pooling.* In a series of responses, sensory, cognitive, and sensorimotor data are integrated to produce the adaptation level.
3. *Distinctiveness of stimuli.* Despite pooling, stimuli preserve their individuality, the more so the further they depart from the adaptation level.
4. *Nonlinearity of response.* Response does not vary in one-to-one relation to objective stimulus properties (e.g., subjects typically overestimate small quantities and underestimate large quantities).
5. *Oscillation and variability.* Since forces are continuously reactive and counterbalancing, the adaptation level oscillates about a general mean—over long sequences oscillation may display a direction, so that the mean rises or drops.

[1]Unlike in equilibrium and balance theories, however, the adaptation level is not a "goal," or a state toward which behavior aims, but simply the net resultant of forces.

6. *Optimal levels.* Performance is most efficient at intermediate points along stimulus continua—such optima depend on the averaging of converging forces (i.e., the adaptation level).

7. *Output-input matching.* The response tendencies adjust to the changing operating forces.

Helson proposes these seven principles to generalize the theory beyond specific stimulus-response relationships. However, despite limited application to problems of attitude measurement, the theory has not received widespread acceptance outside of psychophysics. Like all field theories in psychology, its major virtues as a general approach to behavior lie in its descriptive and conceptual aspects. This does not mean that it cannot be useful in an empirical sense— for example, by increased attention to the role of residual and background stimuli in their interdependent relations to focal stimuli, a development already apparent in investigations of sensory thresholds and signal detection. Rather, it means that a field theory serves as an important framework for recognizing both the complexity and the dynamics of behavior.

IMMEDIATE BEHAVIORAL EVENTS

Although psychology in general is always concerned with person-environment relations, the most explicit treatment of them lies in the psychophysical tradition. In this respect we see a concerted attempt to measure and explain the basic character of these relationships by focusing on what may be called *minimal stimulus-response events*.

The conception of the *threshold* is familiar enough : under given conditions of sensory receptivity, a stimulus must have some minimum value in order to elicit a specified response. Originating in the theories of Weber and Fechner in the middle of the last century, the fundamental strategy rests on the measurement of response in relation to stimulus variations.

The *absolute threshold* is the minimum stimulus required to elicit a response above the absence of a stimulus (i.e., the zero level of stimulation). Examples include the introduction of light under conditions of total darkness, and the presentation of sound beginning from the point of silence. The *difference threshold* is the amount by which one stimulus must be increased to elicit a judgment of difference in comparison with another stimulus. Examples include the presentation of two patches of light, one of which gradually increases or decreases in intensity, and the sounding of a standard pitch alternating with a sound that gradually changes in pitch. These principles have been extended widely to many problems of the scaling of ratings, opinions, and other psychological responses (Stevens, 1951). Beyond the fundamental stimulus-response relationship lie problems of contextual relationships, traditionally assigned to the topic of attention, and currently treated actively under the heading of signal detection and vigilance.

Weber's Law

The difference threshold leads to the notion that we could compare two stimuli at any level of intensity. In each case one stimulus must differ enough from the other to elicit a judgment of more than or less than. This amount is a *just noticeable difference*. Weber proposed that just noticeable differences are equivalent regardless of stimulus magnitude because the increment is a constant fraction of the comparison stimulus. A systematic study might use as standard stimuli squares ranging in size from small to large. The subject makes judgments of larger for comparison squares. As the size of the standard stimulus increases, it requires increasingly greater increments in the comparison stimulus for the subject to report a difference. Weber's law states that the ratio of the comparison to the standard stimulus is constant.[1]

Research has disclosed that Weber's law holds approximately for moderate degrees of stimulus dimensions but breaks down at extremes (when the fraction increases). In fact, curvilinear relations are found. Nevertheless, three fundamental points remain: (1) change in response is a function of stimulus magnitude, (2) there are limits to this relationship, and (3) the effect of a given stimulus depends on its magnitude relative to other stimuli.

SIGNAL DETECTION

In recent years the theory of signal detection has considerably clarified the threshold problem. In general we can distinguish between issues of the absolute threshold and the identification of stimuli discontinuously presented over a period of time—attention, or vigilance. The absolute threshold, as defined above in the classical sense,

---

[1]Fechner developed this principle into a psychological law to the effect that just noticeable differences are subjectively equal. If the metaphysical features of Fechner's treatment are ignored, then his law underlies much psychological scaling. That is, units can be developed on the basis of perceptual judgments. Adaptation-level theory provides a conceptualization for this strategy.

implies that under standardized conditions there is no effect on response of magnitudes smaller than this minimum quantity. Careful
investigations indicate that in fact evidence for an absolute threshold
depends on the criterion adopted. Suppose that we present a graduated series of stimuli, each time calling for a judgment of the
presence or absence of the stimulus. A definition of the threshold
requires that we decide how frequently it is necessary that a particular magnitude elicits the judgment "yes." Ordinary statistical
considerations require that "yes" be significantly more frequent than
"no." Let us say that with a sufficiently large number of observations,
a frequency of "yes" greater than 50 percent identifies a stimulus of a
magnitude greater than the threshold. Additional increments above
that point will result in an increasingly greater proportion of "yes"
judgments. If there were an absolute threshold, then magnitudes below
that point should elicit approximately chance results (i.e., 50 percent
"yes") regardless of actual magnitude. This result would occur if the
subject were merely guessing, as would be necessary if the stimulus
did not influence his judgments. Experiments, however, show that
the proportion of "yes" judgments increases regularly from some
intensity well below the 50 percent magnitude. These data become
quite reliable when the attendant conditions are highly standardized
and when a procedure is included to detect "false alarms" (i.e., trials
when no stimulus is actually presented, thus permitting the experimenter to differentiate random judgments from correct judgments).[1]
It appears that there is no sharp break between response and signal
intensity, but rather that response has some determinable probability
of occurring at any signal intensity. But response probabilities do not
begin at the absence of stimulation (at zero intensity), rather they are
displaced upward. In this sense there is an absolute threshold. The
concept of *noise*, however, introduces a qualification. A stimulus
always occurs against a background of other kinds of stimulation (or
of generalized stimulation) : therefore the stimulus must exceed not
only the possible absolute threshold for that stimulus dimension but
also whatever noise is present. (Note that the concept of noise corresponds to the background and residual stimuli of adaptation-level
theory.) One way to refine the measurement of threshold would be
to establish a standardized noise level, rather than simply to allow
random and unknown noise to interfere with the process of judgment. Since some noise is probably always present, it is impossible to

---

[1]For detailed discussion of these matters, see Tanner and Swets, 1954; Swets, 1961; Bevan,
1967; Galanter, 1962; and Corso, 1963.

establish conditions under which a truly absolute threshold could be determined. Thus we must distinguish between a *sensory threshold* and a *response threshold*. The former can only be hypothesized as some level lower than the latter. The probabilities of response are then shifted upward from the probabilities of minimal sensory effects. Both thresholds vary, so any definition of either must be based on the averages of many determinations.

The classical view of the threshold has therefore been revised in several ways.

Response is considered a continuous function of stimulus intensity rather than an all-or-none matter. In determining the effects of stimuli, the response, rather than the sensory function, is measured, yielding the notion of two or more threshold values for a given stimulus, depending on the criterion adopted (see Figure 4-2). The response or judgment obtained from a subject depends on factors other than the environmental stimulus itself. This point is especially well recognized in adaptation-level theory (Swets, 1961; Bevan, 1967). The subject's expectancies and motives, as well as contextual conditions such as incentives (the "payoff martix"), add their weights to the sheerly sensory information.

Vigilance

A situation in which a subject is instructed to respond selectively over a period of time to a stimulus display calls on *vigilance*. A common theme is an arousal principle. Vigilance is not a simple state of receptivity to stimuli, but a condition of active and focused attentiveness.

The kind of task frequently used is illustrated by the Mackworth clock test (Mackworth, 1948). Here a subject monitors a pointer that moves clockwise against a plain white background. Normal movement is short jumps, but at intervals the pointer makes a double jump, which is the signal to be detected.

In such situations the subject typically manifests a decrement over time. Considerable controversy exists over the reasons for this phenomenon (Frankmann and Adams, 1962). One theory advances principles of classical conditioning (Mackworth, 1948). That is, during initial observation, a conditioned response is established to the signal to be detected; the period of the watch serves as an extinction period, with an increase in internal inhibition and, consequently, a decline in performance. However, predictions from this theory are not always confirmed and the introduction of additional variables

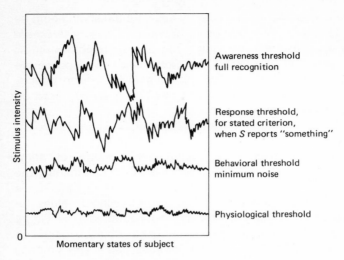

FIGURE 4–2   Definitions of the threshold.

leads to a more complex view. An information model, proposed by Broadbent (1953, 1957), is based on the assumption of a limited nervous system that can deal only with some aspects of information input. Selective processing depends on stimulus properties such as intensity, biological importance, and novelty. The decrement depends on competing stimuli. This interpretation emphasizes input variables without sufficiently allowing for other influences, such as expectancy. Deese (1955) went farther by incorporating intrinsic variables. The subject begins with some degree of interest or arousal, depending on his experience with the task. Actual stimulus events induce an expectancy for the next event, and this determines the level of vigilance (or probability of detecting a signal). The expectancy principle has been extended by Baker (1959), but with a primary emphasis on immediate situational conditions. Frankmann and Adams (1962) invoke an activation principle, linked with stimulus input, which is seen to have two aspects, the cue functions stressed in other theories, and an arousal function, by which attention is maintained. The decrement during watches stems from the lack of stimulus variation, as a consequence of which arousal declines. Mackworth (1968) has developed an habituation theory, which considers the decrement to depend on both arousal and cue functions. Habituation of the arousal response leads to decreased sensitivity, whereas habituation of the cue component reduces response both to background stimuli (false alarms) and to signals. She suggests

that the first process is greater under conditions of rapid or continuous background events, with the second process more significant
when background events are discrete and slow.

Conditions Affecting Performance in Vigilance Tasks   Efficiency varies as a function of numerous special conditions. The
effects of *stimulus and task variables* are shown by a reduced decrement when the length of the watch is shortened (Mackworth, 1948),
when rest periods are introduced (Bergum and Lehr, 1962), or when
stimuli are presented at regular intervals to facilitate pacing of response
(Baker, 1959). Detection depends both on the brightness and
the duration of the stimulus, but especially on the latter, with brief
signals being harder to detect (Adams, 1956). Highly distinctive
objects (marked by several different dimensions) are easiest to
identify (Lappin, 1967). Redundant signals (e.g., simultaneous
sound and light) are significantly better than signals presented in a
single sensory modality (Baker, Ware, and Sipowicz, 1962). Auditory
stimuli appear generally to be more efficient than other stimuli
(Baker et al., 1962; Loeb and Hawkes, 1962).

   Instructions and cognitive variables are illustrated by the fact
that feedback about "right" and "wrong" answers improves performance (Hardesty, Trumbo, and Bevan, 1963)—one reason may lie
in increased arousal (Locke, Cartledge, and Koeppel, 1968). Providing alternative responses prior to or after exposure facilitates performance (Lawrence and Coles, 1954), as do instructions to pay attention to all relevant dimensions (Lawrence and LaBerge, 1956). Such
findings have led Egeth (1967) to conclude that subjects use coding
strategies, or "adaptive mediational processes."

   Personality and motivational variables also influence response.
Thus in a tracking task, with peripheral stimuli, a high financial
incentive markedly facilitated the central task, but impaired the
peripheral one (Bahrick, Fitts, and Rankin, 1952). Easterbrook (1959)
proposes that motivational arousal reduces the range of cues used,
but the effect depends on the task. In the least demanding tasks,
little effort is required and only small amounts of information are
needed, so that the subject has a "surplus capacity" for noticing
irrelevant cues. In more demanding tasks, nonrepetitive serial operations are required and complex responses are most successful;
therefore performance is impaired as the span of cue utilization is
reduced from interference in the integration of relevant cues—and
high arousal should produce poor performance. Impairment under

stress (threat of electric shock) does not occur when the subject has some means to cope with it (if he can avoid the shock). Personality variables affect such relationships since individuals high in test anxiety perform less well under the coping conditions (Wachtel, 1968). Furthermore, extraverts adapt better to incidental stimuli than do introverts (Bakan, 1959).

It is clear from research that even minimal relations between person and environment depend on the interplay of many variables. Stimulus properties, sets, and intrinsic motivational variables all partly determine response. In general the adaptation-level conception of response averaging as a resultant of the weightings of the relevant forces accords best with the facts.

SUBLIMINAL EFFECTS

A question has been repeatedly raised in psychology about whether stimuli so weak as to fall below the threshold can influence response by adding sufficient input to tilt responses one way or another, or by triggering off events sensitively primed to occur (see reviews by Vinacke, 1942; and Goldiamond, 1958).

The definition of threshold is crucial. From the vantage point of signal detection, response probabilities are determined in relation to the level of "noise," and if we assume that there is always some noise in the system, then any signal must be sufficiently above the noise level to have any probability of detection. If there is an absolute sensory threshold, it must lie somewhere between zero stimulus intensity and the zero point of the response probability curve. Finally, if we employ different response criteria (e.g., "guess" versus "report only when you think you see something"), the curve for response probabilities will shift upward on the scale of stimulus intensity. In general we can differentiate several levels.

1 At or above the noise level—or the *behavioral threshold*— there is some probability of detecting a signal; below this threshold, stimuli may have some neural or physiological effects not evident in detection measures. The limits of the latter effect are represented by a *physiological threshold* (some intensity greater than zero).

2 According to some criterion, significant effects may occur that lie above the behavioral threshold and are used to define a *response threshold*.

3 Still other effects may be found in which the subject perceives something but cannot be certain what it is, defining an *awareness* (or psychological) *threshold*.

Thus we have points on a scale corresponding, at any moment in time, to the following order of thresholds : physiological → behavioral → response → awareness. Research and controversy center on effects at the second and third levels; that is, whether stimuli below the response threshold or below the awareness threshold can influence acts. In general, studies labeled *subliminal* are concerned with the first of these two problems, and studies of *defense* and *unconscious influences* deal with the second. Typically, subliminal effects are sought by establishing minimal, controlled, and neutral stimulus-response relationships, in which effects can be linked as simply as possible to variables of stimulus intensity. In contrast, defense effects are studied by maximizing intrinsic emotional, motivational, and selective factors in the person's relation to special classes of stimuli. The first approach assumes that threshold values occur at relatively narrow ranges of stimulus intensities; the second approach assumes that threshold values occur over a wide range. In either case the same response criterion could be used, such as the report of seeing "nothing" (and, indeed, false alarm trials can be used in both), but subliminal perception emphasizes physical stimulus variables, whereas in defense studies the emphasis lies on psychological cues or significance variables. We can devise a subliminal experiment merely by specifying a sequence of stimulus intensities; but to perform a defense experiment, we would need to specify in addition the characteristics of the stimulus and their relevance to the person.

The defense issue is evidently a special aspect of the problem of intrinsic and mediational influences on behavior. The wealth of evidence on such effects at supraliminal levels need not concern us here, for we shall invoke it in appropriate contexts later.

There now appears to be no doubt that stimuli below the response threshold have significant effects on response[1] [see, for example, Lazarus and McCleary (1951)]. Bevan (1964) points out that interest has shifted from simply confirming the phenomenon to an exploration of the influence of subliminal processes. That is,

---

[1]In this discussion, I shall simply assume the criterion in the subject's report that he could not recognize the stimulus, rather than tediously citing the precise criterion, such as degree of certainty. Since it is customary to set stimuli at intensities far enough below the response level, much stricter criteria have held in various experiments.

subliminal perception has come to be treated as an independent rather than dependent variable.

Response Theories

From the signal-detection approach comes the principle that minimal stimuli feed at least some information into the cognitive system and thus increase the probability of response (Howes, 1954; Goldiamond, 1958). Hence there is no need to postulate a subliminal discrimination process since properties of the stimulus can sufficiently well predict outcomes. For example, *partial cues*, such as images, emotional reactions, and fractions of the total stimulus may be responsible (Eriksen, 1958) for increasing response. The verbal report is only one criterion, and does not allow for cases when the subject is unable to report, refuses to do so, or makes errors, even when he may have some information. However, since serious advocates of the principle that stimuli of which the subject is not aware influence response would not deny that cognitive events of some kind are elicited, this argument merely points to the operation of some mechanism.

Two-process Theories

Psychoanalytic theory suggests that response events are not necessarily correlated with stimulus properties but may rather express intrinsic dynamic processes. The effects of minimal stimuli must thus be distinguished from those of strong and active internal stimuli. The subliminal principle is that under certain conditions very slight stimuli may elicit intrinsic changes that affect response. Beyond that, such changes may be different from those elicited by strong (supraliminal) stimuli.

Crucial evidence for two processes requires a demonstration that subliminally produced responses differ from supraliminally produced responses. If awareness has a restricting effect, so that a person is actually made less sensitive to minimal cues, then the greater the intensity of the stimulus, the *less* the likelihood that intrinsic processes will affect response.

Rather than obtaining reports about subliminally presented objects, some investigators have determined the effect of subliminal stimuli on response to stimuli at supraliminal levels (Klein, et al., 1958; Smith, Spence, and Klein, 1959; Eagle, 1959). For example, subliminal sexual or aggressive stimuli influence the perception of supraliminal, neutral stimuli. However, partial cues may account for some of these results (Guthrie and Wiener, 1966).

In clarifying the controversy between partial-cue and intrinsic-effect interpretations of subliminal stimulation, Spence and Holland (1962) point out that the partial-cue hypothesis assumes a continuum of response from minimal cues to developed stimuli, with the former being merely an attenuated copy of the latter. Furthermore, it assumes that increasing awareness simply means that more information is being fed in, and response therefore becomes better (more in line with the stimulus). Contradicting these assumptions are findings that the effect of an impoverished stimulus seems to vary *inversely* with its intensity. As an alternative, Spence and Holland offer a two-process theory, broadly derived from Freudian principles with the following assumptions: (1) registration and awareness are separate aspects of cognition; (2) the degree of awareness is not appropriate to predict the degree of effect of a stimulus; (3) weak and faint stimuli do not necessarily have less effect than strong and clear stimuli; and (4) reduction of awareness changes the character of cognition. In contrast to the intensity argument, they suggest that a different class of responses is elicited as stimuli diminish below threshold.

Awareness, they state, actually has a restricting effect. If a stimulus word is presented supraliminally, it dominates cognition. But a subliminal word may evoke wide-ranging associative processes. They hypothesize that this spread of effect is inversely correlated with stimulus intensity, and predict that subjects who recall *fewer* test words correctly will recall more meaningfully related words presented in conjunction with the critical word. This effect should be greater for subliminal words. To test this prediction, the subliminal word CHEESE was periodically flashed on a fixation screen while the experimenter read a list of words that contained cheese associates and control words (matched for length and frequency). In a control condition, subjects closed their eyes. In a third condition, CHEESE was presented supraliminally. Cheese associates were recalled significantly better than control words under the subliminal condition (see Figure 4-3). Recall of the five most frequent associates displayed a high *negative* correlation with frequency ($r_s = -.91$), indicating that the subliminal effect was greater for weak associates, and that recall was better with fewer correct discriminations of CHEESE. The role of partial cues was shown by a tendency

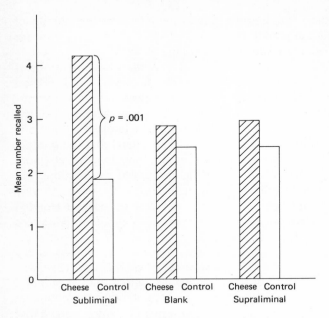

FIGURE 4–3 Mean recall of CHEESE associates and control words under three conditions. (Based on Spence and Holland, 1962.)

for control words containing fragments of CHEESE to be better recalled.[1]

Partial Cues and Intrinsic Release

It may well be a long time before investigators are agreed on how to resolve this controversy. As pointed out, the possibility of partial cues can perhaps never be fully ruled out. If the notion is extended to "registration," then surely a stimulus of *any* intensity *may* provide information of some degree.

At present, advocates of the two-process theory appear to have the better of it. They have shown how a crucial phenomenon can be explained, and their opponents have yet to demonstrate that strict reliance on stimulus intensity can do so. Furthermore, the two-process

[1] Luborsky et al. (1968) showed that eye fixations begin to concentrate on a subliminal stimulus when the first awareness is reported; however, they also obtained evidence that registration begins before that level is reached.

view actually incorporates the partial-cue hypothesis by predicting such effects at levels of partial awareness, and different effects at lower levels.

PERCEPTUAL DEFENSE

The principle of defense is derived from Freudian theory, in which the ego is considered to maintain control over stimulus input. When stimuli are threatening, barriers are erected against their untrammeled perception; in complementary fashion, stimuli that are especially acceptable may be afforded ready ingress. Thus ego mechanisms may be treated as having sensitizing and defending functions in relation to the environment. It is easily seen that the defensive aspect is comparable to repression. Strictly speaking, however, we should distinguish repression from perceptual defense, using the term *suppression* for the latter. Repression is especially applicable to the relation between cognitive processes and unconscious impulses, rather than to that between cognition and extrinsic stimuli.

The general role of noxious stimuli, values, motivational variables, and stress has often been reviewed (Jenkin, 1957; Eriksen and Pierce, 1968). In relation to perceptual responses, experimental work on this problem has come to be called the "new look", and owes much to studies by Bruner and Goodman (1947), Bruner and Postman (1947), and Postman, Bruner, and McGinnies (1948).

Of immediate interest are the questions "Is the threshold raised by a stimulus that threatens or endangers a person's ego structure?", "Is the threshold lowered by a stimulus that promotes or harmonizes with a person's ego structure?"

Blum (1954) used pictures from his Blacky test (devised to assess characteristics derived from psychoanalytic theory) in the following procedure: (1) four pictures were exposed subliminally, with instructions to report which quadrant stood out the most; (2) sensitization was induced by presenting a neutral and a threatening picture, accompanied by descriptions and a request that the subject think about his own experiences; (3) repetition of the subliminal condition; and (4) presentation under increased exposure with instructions to locate a specified picture. As predicted, each sex in the third case more often chose the threatening (sensitized) picture, and in the fourth case less often chose it (indicating defense). Such results provide evidence for complementary processes. When repression operates, the subject should be especially sensitive to relevant cues below conscious awareness, but when threatening cues are strong enough that it is risky to perceive them, defense should occur.

To meet the criticism that stimulus properties can account for defense (Postman, 1953), Blum (1955) conducted a second study. A similar procedure was followed with subjects thoroughly familiar with the pictures, but preceded by an intensive clinical process to assess actual conflict associated with them. Again the results strongly supported defense as a perceptual rather than response principle (see Figure 4-4).

Although concluding that evidence for response suppression is sufficient, Eriksen (1958) questioned whether a principle of intrinsic defense is necessary. Rather than discrimination at unconscious levels, he advocates an explanation based on anxiety. A particular response (such as a word) may acquire noxious or unpleasant associations so that its occurrence serves as a conditioned stimulus for anxiety. Such a response would become weaker relative to other responses elicited by the same stimulus. Thus the stimulus would evoke some alternative response rather than the anxiety-producing response. As a test, Eriksen and Browne (1956) compared subjects high and low on proneness to anxiety on a very difficult anagram task under stress. The recognition threshold for the anagram words was not significantly different from that for control words. However, subjects judged as nonrepressers had lower thresholds for the anagrams compared to the control words. The authors interpret these results as supporting their theory but say that the principle of defense also explains them.

Interactions appear also in other experiments. Carpenter, Wiener, and Carpenter (1956) found that sensitizers recognize stimuli relevant to conflicts sooner than do repressers (see Figure 4-5). Silverman and Silverman (1964) found that differences in ego function are significantly related to changes in Rorschach responses, after subliminal exposure of a sexual stimulus. Bootzin and Natsoulas (1965) also reported significant defensive effects associated with personality differences like those found by Eriksen and Browne (1956), but decreasing with repeated trials.

Subliminal Perception and Defense

It thus appears that subliminal stimuli probably have effects different from supraliminal stimuli, and also that their potential depends on

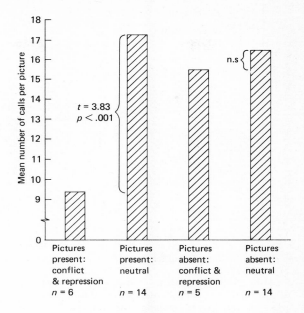

FIGURE 4-4　Mean frequencies of picture calls under four conditions of subliminal presentation. (Based on Blum, 1955.)

ego mechanisms of sensitization and defense. Spence (1967) has summarized the main points. First, stimulus conditions must be relevant to the subject: he must be primed or appropriately aroused or possess certain characteristics. Second, systems of cognitive content are maintained over time in active storage, apart from conscious awareness, so that extremely small amounts of information can touch them off. These two propositions are nicely brought together in a study by Spence and Ehrenburg (1964) employing the technique of the CHEESE-associates experiment. They manipulated relevance by using smokers and nonsmokers, on the supposition that a food stimulus would be more important for the nonsmokers. The storage aspect was introduced by contrasting food-deprived and satiated conditions, in the belief that greater relevant arousal under deprivation would maintain the intrinsic system in a more active state. The recall of associates to the subliminal CHEESE stimulus was compared with such associates elicited by a blank slide. The

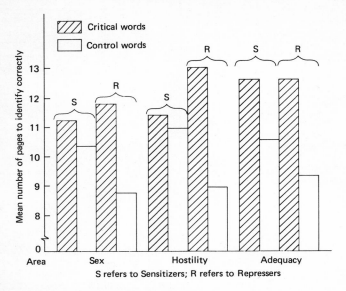

FIGURE 4–5 Perceptual sensitivity to control words and to critical words in three content areas in relation to preferred defense (N=10 in each group). (Based on Carpenter, Weiner, and Carpenter, 1956.)

combination of active storage and relevance was highly favorable to the subliminal effect (see Figure 4-6).

The conception of an autistic-realistic continuum also helps to clarify these matters. Shifts in the threshold, and the characteristics of cognition elicited by faint stimuli, depend on the relative importance of motivational-affective and stimulus-situational components. Experiments on general subliminal and signal-detection effects illustrate the dominance of realistic factors by demonstrating how perception becomes increasingly veridical as stimulus intensity increases, when neutrally treated or standardized subjects are used. (The partial-cue theory stresses realistic determinants.) Studies of perceptual defense complement this approach by showing that autistic factors become increasingly dominant when the stimulus structure becomes more relevant to intrinsic conflicts and when subjects are aroused in some appropriate way. (The defense theory rests on a principle of autistic forces.)

	——————— Relevance ———————	
	Smokers	Nonsmokers
Satiated	− 1.12	− 1.0
Deprived	.43	2.30

(left margin label: Storage)

FIGURE 4–6 Difference between subliminal and control effects on relative recall of CHEESE associates as a function of hours since last food and amount of smoking. (Adapted from Spence, 1967.)

SUMMARY

Relations between person and environment require specification of independent, intervening, and dependent variables; intrinsic states may, on occasion, be treated as independent or dependent variables. Models of behavior include: input-output, cognitive, mediation, general situational, dynamic, and field. Thresholds of responsiveness are a focus of research on immediate behavioral events, such as studies of signal detection, subliminal perception, and perceptual defense. Evidence indicates that the two-process theory better accounts for subliminal effects than does the partial-cue theory, with the former holding that response at minimal levels is inversely related to the intensity of the stimulus. Perceptual defense, shown by a rise in the threshold, occurs when a minimal stimulus is strong enough to elicit repression; but a weaker stimulus may avoid repression, with a lowering of the threshold (sensitization).

5

THEORIES OF COGNITION

Let us consider the problems faced by the investigator of human thinking. First, since cognitive processes cannot be directly observed, they must be described and interpreted by inferences drawn from behavioral events. Such inferences would be much easier to draw if we could experiment directly on the human brain, as we can on the animal brain. Since society does not tolerate this approach, knowledge of the functioning of the human brain itself must wait on studies of brain pathology and medical treatment. In the meantime there must inevitably be heavy reliance on inferences drawn from normally functioning subjects. Even when we experiment systematically on animal brains, the gap between observation and interpretation is great, particularly because animals cannot verbalize. Perhaps an understanding of verbal behavior is not absolutely essential to an understanding of human cognition, but in any case we certainly cannot be sure without allowing for the involvement of one with the other. Beyond the role of language, there is also the problem of images. Even if imagery also occurs in animals, it is extremely difficult to obtain evidence for it without overt signs such as verbalization can provide.

Second, cognitive events are not isolated from each other but occur continuously in the life of each person. An adequate theory must somehow allow for relationships among events since the problem of past experience is intimately entwined with the study of cognitive processes. Part of the theoretical enterprise is to explain how prior events act as influences on present events. In this way we see attention to memorial processes and to cognitive organization. Again, it is apparently difficult to obtain direct evidence on the role of past experience—to separate those forces that owe their character to past experience and those that arise from properties of the immediate situation.

Third, cognitive events are continuously influenced by emotional and motivational states. Theoretical treatments are incomplete without incorporating such relationships. Sometimes the problem is handled by formulating dynamic variables in simple or general ways, sometimes in more complex and differentiated ways. For the most part there is uneven attention to motivation, and many theoretical analyses of cognitive processes continue to be insufficient in this respect.

Systematic discussions of thinking elaborate in one fashion or another on the basic components that fall into the classes of input, intervening, and output variables. Under *input* fall problems of sensory response and registration. *Intervening* variables pose problems of motivational arousal, withdrawal of past experience from memory and its integration with currently active intrinsic processes, and selection of responses. *Output* variables pertain to the quality and quantity of overt acts, together with their sequence and patterning. The logic of conceptualizing these three aspects of behavior as successive in time is compelling. However, principles of feedback—for example, proprioceptive cues from overt acts—introduce loops that modify the strict succession in its simplest form. In addition, if we assume that influences may arise by virtue of changes within the organism, whether partially or wholly independent of extrinsic input, the simple succession is further complicated.

As we have emphasized, all of these characteristics are inferred from what we can observe about the organism's behavior in relation to what we can meaningfully state about conditions of stimulus input. For example, if it were possible to account fully for responses simply by specifying the properties of immediate stimuli, we would not need to allow for the role of past experience or memory. We would then require some reference to memorial functions if we conducted an experiment in which stimulus conditions are held constant, but some operations were introduced that altered response processes through a plausibly inferred variation in memory. In a broader fashion, revealing the role of past experience depends on establishing relationships between variations in subjects, known background characteristics and variations in present performance, for example, in studies of class and cultural differences and the effects of personality variables. Intrinsic aspects can be inferred from introspective data, or more generally by evidence that at least some features of mental activity are not precisely expressed in or interpretable from specific observed responses. Selective and organizing properties can be shown experimentally when a stimulus is perceived or judged differently by different subjects, when variations in instructions produce variations in response, or when rules and techniques (such as mnemonic devices) produce systematic response sequences. Delay functions require for their demonstration only a comparison among different stimulus-response situations, such as the time differences among simple, choice, and associative reactions. Another kind of evidence comes from experiments in which the length of the time interval between onset of a stimulus and the subject's required response is associated with the proportion of correct responses. When an increased interval produces improved performance, we can infer that the cognitive process delays response until the probability of correct response is maximized.

On the physiological side, thinking refers to activities in the nervous system, primarily in the cerebral cortex. Neuron circuits represent the past experience of the organism, as a consequence of the modification of the neurons themselves and of the relationships among them. Thinking consists of the activity of such circuits, on the one hand initiated and continually influenced by impulses from the receptors, and on the other hand leading to sequences of effector activity—that is, overt behavior.

But the neural activity corresponding to thinking does not have a specific locus in the brain. It is very likely that, from moment to moment, thought processes depend on the total organization of neural activities, as it shifts and changes. Rather than being a matter of definite neuron arrangements and connections, thinking probably depends on complex patterns (or circuits), or of relations between active currents in the cortical tissues.

Neural components bear active relationships to each other, and a change in one may induce changes in others, depending on the magnitude of the change and the closeness of the relationship. Because changes occur continually—for example, from input via the receptors—we may assume continual instability that results in

continual activity. Therefore not only are thought processes themselves active, but there is a continual modification of the traces of
past experience.

Finally, we must reiterate that other parts of the organic system,
in addition to the brain itself, enter into processes of cognition.
Motivational and affective states are integrated into the course of
thinking through their neural communication with the brain. In short,
in a genuine way the organism thinks with its whole body.

THEORIES OF THE THINKING PROCESS

Historically, there have been three general kinds of explanation for
how thinking may work. They differ in their treatment of how
processes in the brain are related to response processes. The basic
problem concerns how intrinsic activities can control and direct
response sequences, even though no new stimuli appear to be
involved in bringing about a partially or wholly new response. How
can there occur a train of organized manipulation of the environment,
involving the utilization of past experience, without overt activity and
without the physical presence of the prior environmental objects or
conditions?

The *central* theory merely assumes that the characteristic
features of thinking depend on activities in the brain. A weak form
emphasizes the intervening character of such activities, with a
continuing role of stimulus input—that is, direct contact with the
environment. A stronger form stresses the potential independence of
the intrinsic processes from the environment—that is, that thinking
can go on autonomously in the brain (see Figure 5-1). Both forms
of the theory correspond to the commonsense view of thinking;
neither appears to have serious status in modern psychology.
Nevertheless certain kinds of evidence point to the possibility of
autonomous central processes, and a final theory cannot ignore them.

The *stimulus-response (S-R) theory* is built on principles of
continuous participation by stimulus and response processes in
cognition, with the assumption that these processes or their direct
counterparts are the fundamental mechanism. Thinking is a matter of
sequences of greatly reduced, or "implicit," muscular responses,
initiated by an external stimulus and terminating in an overt response.
The reduced S-R units correspond to originally occurring behavioral
events.

Since its original statement, this theory has led toward a
position based on Hullian principles (especially as influenced by the

CENTRAL THEORIES

Weak

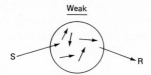

Strong

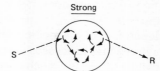

Generally described
or unspecified
activities in the brain

S may be
incidental
or absent

Generally
described
or formally
specified (e.g.,
reasoning,
imagination)

R may merely be
expression of
activity, not
necessarily related
to S; may be evoked
by mental process
independently of S

CENTRAL PERIPHERAL THEORIES

S-R

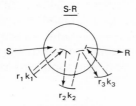

Behavioral

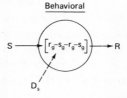

r = Implicit motor response
k = Kinesthetic impulse
r → k   Connections in chained sequence

r_g = Fractional anticipatory goal response
s_g = Fractional anticipatory goal stimulus
D = Drive stimulus
$r_g \rightarrow s_g$ Mechanism has proprioceptive basis-
some reduced form of S-R process

MEDIATION THEORIES

Mediation

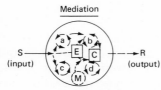

S   R
(input)   (output)

Intrinsic Organization

a, b, c, d = Associative systems
(c, d not aroused)
E = Expectancy
M = Motivational component
C = Net cognitive process
R = Always partly determined by S

a, b, c = Cognitive systems active in a sequence.
Brackets indicate system may function as a
whole (including regulative and motivational
components)
d, e = Cognitive systems not active
E = General expectancy (attitude)
E' = Specific expectancy (set)
M = Motivational component
F = Feedback
S, R = Partly or wholly incidental to cognitive
system, but input and feedback always
influence process

FIGURE 5-1   Models of thinking.

work of Tolman), which we shall call *behavioral theory*. It adds the notion of special cognitive mechanisms, fractional anticipatory goal responses ($r_g - s_g$), which are to a large degree treated as being independent of a specific stimulus input, and thus capable of acting as intervening processes. In this theory, thinking corresponds to the activities of $r_g - s_g$ mechanisms.

Mediation theory differs from S-R theory primarily by emphasizing the inferred central processes, leading to a more complex view (especially through conceptions of associative processes). There is more attention to the structure and functioning of intervening variables. It is for this reason that we distinguish it from behavioral theory, which actually has acquired a decidedly mediational character. For convenience, we recognize two forms of mediation theory. One, which we shall call *mediation*, is closely related to behavioral theory, and treats mediating processes as relatively simple linkages between stimulus input and response output. In the other, which we shall call *intrinsic organization*, mediation theory comes closer to the central theory, in allowing greater autonomy and self-contained structure to processes in the brain.

THE MOTOR THEORY

The mechanism described by James (1890) for habit presented this theory in a simple form. During learning, separate responses become linked to form automatic sequences, in which one act elicits the next with hardly any attention by the individual. Watson (1924) developed this principle to explain thinking as subvocal speech (Titchener, 1909, anticipated this view). Words, as substitutes for objects, may be "spoken" subvocally so that implicit movements of the muscles involved may take the place of overt language. In chains of implicit responses, each event provides a kinesthetic stimulus for the next. Watson saw no need to refer to "meaning" independent of specific S-R relationships—a person's action shows his meaning. Criticized for limiting the mechanism to implicit vocal habits (see, for example, Bartlett and Smith, 1921), Watson (1930) responded by extending the theory to include other implicit habits— manual, visceral, visual, and so on—any of which could serve as "conditioned substitutes." Thus thinking could still go on even without words.

To test the motor theory, early experimenters tried to correlate various behavioral and physiological measures with mental activity (Clarke, 1922; Thorson, 1925). The development of electronic recording systems offered more refined procedures to pick up minute electrical potentials in muscle fibers.

Jacobson (1932) found that action currents were elicited when subjects imagined bending the forearm, without overt movements. The currents appeared in muscles that would actually be involved, but not when the subject was told to relax or to imagine acts with other parts of the body, or when he actually slightly bent the opposing foot or arm. The records during imaging and overt movement were identical. Furthermore, the location of the potentials differed with the character of thought. If it entailed visualization, they occurred in the ocular region; if imagining a movement of the right arm, they occurred in those muscles. Thus there seemed to be good support for the Watsonian theory.

Max (1934, 1935a, b, 1937) used deaf subjects for whom fingers serve as language mechanisms; thus potentials should be found there when linguistic responses are involved. As supposed, action currents were obtained from the arms and hands of the deaf, but not the hearing, for implicit linguistic activity. Action currents decreased from waking to sleep in both groups of subjects, with a gradual increase in the reverse phase. External stimuli applied during sleep produced action currents in the peripheral musculature of the deaf. When engaged in abstract thinking, action currents from the arms of deaf subjects were much larger and more frequent than for the hearing subjects. Finally, action currents during "vocal" responses, such as nodding the head, occurred in the hand and arm muscles of the deaf, but only slightly in those muscles of the hearing. Again, the evidence supported the motor theory.

Criticisms and Counterevidence

Taken literally, the motor theory signifies that thinking consists in the reactivation of past experience by means of implicit activities of the muscles originally involved in that experience—that is, one thought (implicit response) follows another because a sensory stimulus (kinesthetic) aroused by the previous thought (implicit response) sets off the next in the series. The selective factors that determine what response will be produced depend, supposedly, on the nature of the original associations and on the conditions of organization in the nerve centers. The significance of this theory is twofold. First, it supplied a comprehensible explanation for thought without merely postulating vaguely defined or "magical" processes in the brain. In this way thinking was brought within the orbit of systematic, objective psychology. Second, the formulation of the theory identified processes and variables in relation to which specific empirical questions could be raised.

Despite the evidence that implicit motor responses accompany thinking, there are objections against accepting them as the specific mechanism of thinking. First, the implicit muscular responses may not be essential to thought, but may simply be an incidental overflow of energy. The initial activity during earlier learning phases could sensitize the sensorimotor pathways so that at later periods they provide ready outlets for surplus neural energy aroused by relevant stimulus input. If this were the case, then the motor mechanism itself would not account for thinking. Second, even if an essential role were found in some cognitive processes, if perhaps not in all, the possibility remains that additional mechanisms are also required. Beyond that, some cognitive processes might actually occur entirely in the absence of implicit motor responses. Finally, if it were proven that implicit muscular responses *are* always involved in thinking, it is nevertheless not certain that the mechanism works as it has been described. This possibility would lead to the proposition that thinking requires more than one mechanism, and that the sensorimotor components have certain functions to be distinguished from those of other components.

Phantom Limbs   One type of evidence comes from conditions where cognitive processes can be separated from the motor source of stimulation, as in persons from whom a limb has been amputated. Jacobson (1931) reported that a subject with a missing arm could imagine or recall acts involving that arm. But after repeated tests the subject said that he could not imagine movements independent of the intact arm. Combined with action-potential evidence from the stump, Jacobson interpreted the findings as evidence for "substitute reactions," and thus supportive of the motor theory. However, other studies (see, in particular, Riddoch, 1941) indicate, on the contrary, that it is typical for amputees to have images and illusions of feelings and movements of the missing parts ("phantom limbs"). From interviews with above-the-elbow amputees, Haber (1956) reported that all of them had illusions, which he interpreted as favoring a central theory of cognition. These effects are related to the distance of the missing part—phantoms are generally stronger in above-the-elbow amputees than in below-the-knee amputees (Weiss and Fishman, 1963).

However, amputation sensitizes the stump, and cues from that source may interact with central images. That experience may influence the character of phantom-limb phenomena is indicated by variations associated with stress (Weiss and Fishman, 1963), and the length of preoperative illness (phantoms are longer lasting with longer illness) (Hirschenfang and Benton, 1966). In these studies some individuals report an absence of phantom-limb sensations, so that Jacobson's case could be an exception.

Although the weight of evidence supports the conclusion that cognitive processes do not require peripheral stimulation for their occurrence, nevertheless, the phantom-limb phenomenon is not absolutely a crucial test. In addition to the possibility that stump cues provide the necessary kinesthetic input contained in the motor theory, this input could be supplied by kinesthetic impulses from a companion part (i.e., the other arm or leg), which is then simply attributed to the missing part.

Absence of Peripheral Stimulation   Long ago, Lashley (1917) reported a study of a subject with anesthesia of a leg. Since this person displayed almost normal movements of the leg, he concluded that some mechanism apart from stimuli arising from the movements themselves must be responsible. Lashley could not decide whether this control is central or located in some other body part. The most definitive evidence so far available comes from experiments with the drug curare, which produces paralysis of the muscles. If such a condition were complete, then any cognitive processes occurring during the period of paralysis must be centrally controlled. Smith, Brown, Toman, and Goodman (1947) administered the drug to an adult male subject, in a dosage $2\frac{1}{2}$ times greater than that required for complete respiratory paralysis and sufficient to induce complete skeletal muscular paralysis. Under these conditions, the subject reported that he remained "acutely conscious" and without impairment of memory. Normality of the central stage was also indicated by a lack of change in the electroencephalograph. Leuba, Birch, and Appleton (1968) administered the drug until the subject could no longer make any movements (artificial respiration, of course, was necessary). During paralysis, the subject was asked to solve five problems, similar to those previously given during the normal state (as a control), and told to remember his answers and to connect them with those of the previous problems. Not only did he comply with these instructions by producing correct answers, but

he also reported that his mental processes had been normal throughout the session. With a still stronger injection, similar results were
obtained.

In general, then, this evidence shows that a peripheral sensorimotor mechanism cannot account for cognitive activity. Lashley
(1967) in fact argued for a central theory. Analyzing phenomena of
serial order of responses, such as in speech, he pointed out that the
time required, as well as the lack of correspondence between
internal and overt speech, rule out a strictly motor regulation. For
example, a piano virtuoso may play a cadenza so rapidly that there
could not be a separate sensorimotor arc for each successive
movement.

In a detailed analysis of the serial-order problem in speech,
Wickelgren (1969) agrees that Lashley was correct in rejecting a
strictly motor theory. However, he points out alternative possibilities
that rely on associative processes that do not require a mechanism
independent of the units composing the sequence. Furthermore,
he suggests that discussion of the serial-order problem has been
confined to noncreative sequences, so that additional theoretical
attention to productive and creative cognitive sequences is required.

Rejection of the motor theory does not signify that implicit
responses and their kinesthetic feedback have *no* function in
thinking, since they may fulfill important functions. (1) In the
normally behaving person the sensorimotor arc may serve as an
overflow mechanism for surplus energy not actually demanded in
the thought process. The implicit response could represent a
reserve supply of energy, available if required (analogous to the
governor on a motor). (2) Kinesthetic input may facilitate the
maintenance of cognitive sequences or patterns. Such input may
provide information about prior events and their relationships,
which, even if delayed, may still be critical in influencing current
processes (i.e., a kind of "reassurance" concerning their properties); or, as learning progresses, the flow of kinesthetic feedback might be organized in groups, with only certain implicit
responses periodically supplying facilitating (or inhibiting) information. In a regular segment of behavior the implicit system could
thus, at intervals, "catch up" with cognition and help to keep it
"on the track." (3) Finally, kinesthetic impulses may also have a
signalling function (another kind of feedback), serving to identify
errors, irregularities, or other inappropriate elements in the sequence.
In this way the sequence may be slowed down or interrupted, with
subsequent correction or even gross change in behavior.

The efficiency of behavior does not require an immediate correction so much as prevention of inordinately extended, inappropriate, or badly controlled sequences. None of these functions means that cognitive processes *cannot* occur without them, nor that all these functions are equally important at all times. Presumably their operation and the significance of their effects would vary from definitely specified automatized sequences across ranges of more freely occurring cognitive events to wholly autonomous central processes in which implicit responses are really incidental and noninfluential. Adams (1968) presents a detailed analysis of the proprioceptive feedback problem as it is conceived in closed-loop theory, where proprioceptive stimuli are assigned a role similar to (2) and (3) above.

BEHAVIORAL THEORY

In the motor theory, central processes operate as little more than simple linkages (or associations) between separate sensorimotor units. The behavioral theory allows, in addition, for more elaborate central functions and incorporates motivational (drive) influences into the total response process. Although the basic concepts of this approach were formulated several decades ago (Hull, 1930), it has only been recently that the implications have been realized, strongly influenced by Tolman's (1932, 1948) insistence on the role of expectancy and purpose in behavior (acknowledged by Hull, 1952, p. 152).

Hull (1952; Atkinson, 1964, Ch. 6) postulated the establishment of intrinsic counterparts of overt responses, which can function in the absence of the original response. The internal response (r_g) elicits a covert stimulus s_g. The r_g, a *pure stimulus act,* has no overt effect itself, it merely produces the critical stimulus s_g whose function is to evoke some response (which may be another r_g) that advances the organism toward some overt goal response. Thus the $r_g \rightarrow s_g$ mechanism represents expectancy of subsequent goal attainment.

Suppose that an organism carries out a sequence of acts symbolized as follows: $S_1 \rightarrow R_1$, $S_2 \rightarrow R_2$, $S_3 \rightarrow R_3$, $S_4 \rightarrow R_4$ . . . $S_G \rightarrow R_G$. Here the capital letters designate extrinsic stimuli and overt responses. G refers to the goal (for example, a food box). It is assumed that motivation (drive) is high, so that stimuli associated with a need-state S_D accompany the consummatory behavior R_{Gc} that occurs in the goal region. As a consequence of R_{Gc}, the need-state is reduced (S_D becomes weaker, that is, reinforcement takes place).

The stimulating conditions continue to occur. The need-state persists (until satisfied) and other stimuli leave internal traces. Thus it is possible (from R_G) for S_D to be reinforced, and for traces of S_1, S_2, S_3, S_4, and S_G to be established throughout the sequence. However, there is likely to be conflict between the consummatory response R_G and the instrumental acts represented by other responses (R_1, R_2, etc.). But the instrumental act dominates whatever components of the intrinsic process (the antedating counterpart of R_G) conflict with it. There still remains r_g, the nonconflicting intrinsic components of R_G, and this covert response is the *fractional anticipatory goal reaction*.

The internal response r_g continuously elicits an internal stimulus s_g, called the *fractional goal stimulus*. Although S_D, a stimulus associated with a need, is specific and steers behavior in definite directions, fractional goal stimuli are highly varied and are not attached to specific responses. At any point in a sequence, the fractional goal response r_g has a strength related to all preceding events in the sequence. Through generalization, the traces of those events all elicit r_g. If r_g is elicited by the trace of S_4, it is also elicited by traces of S_3, S_2, and S_1. But if r_g is elicited by S_1, only the trace of S_1 is associated with it.

The ability of the goal response R_G to reinforce connections between stimuli and responses (primary reinforcement) is complemented by the ability of the internal response r_g to reinforce such connections (secondary reinforcement). That is, the anticipatory response itself can reinforce connections.

When during actual behavior the anticipatory event leads to the actual goal response—that is, when $r_g \rightarrow s_g \rightarrow S_G \rightarrow R_G$—an anticipation is confirmed, and the strength of the connection between stimulus traces and r_g increases. In the same way, the connection between s_g and preliminary responses leading to the goal response R_G becomes stronger. However, if the anticipation is not confirmed, the absence of the goal stimulus S_G eventually brings to an end the goal behavior originally elicited by s_g; this produces inhibition that results in extinction.

After learning has occurred, an increasing sequence of responses followed by primary reinforcement serves to reduce inhibition because the anticipatory goal response becomes attached to the traces of nonreinforced stimuli, and through secondary reinforcement strengthens these connections. Thus very long sequences of response may take place without primary reinforcement.

In sum then, the organism can acquire covert responses that substitute for the overt relation between goal stimuli and goal responses. The $r_g \rightarrow s_g$ is, in fact, a mediator between some cue and a goal. Presumably, the cue that elicits r_g could either be an internal drive stimulus (S_D), such as hunger, or an external stimulus, such as a landmark at the entrance to a maze. Hull's discussion was scrupulously specific to the particular kinds of evidence he regarded as most appropriate, namely, experimental studies of rats. For the most part he eschewed the larger steps required to fit his theory to human behavior. This extension has been developed by some of his students.

Spence (1956) modified the theory by showing that motivating factors in behavior include extrinsic incentives as well as intrinsic drive states. Although Hull came to include incentive (K) in his conception, he did not see it as having an effect independent of drive, but posited a multiplicative relation between them. Spence, however, allowed for their separate influence on behavior (that is, for an additive relation). In this fashion he proposed that r_g is the internal counterpart of the incentive, and therefore has a motivating influence. This makes the intrinsic mechanism correspond more nearly to the notion of purpose.

Applications of $r_g \rightarrow s_g$

Hull used the anticipatory goal response to explain certain phenomena stressed by Tolman. In the *double-drive situation,* an animal learns to turn in one direction—say, to the right—when hungry, but to the left when thirsty. How does he "know" which way to go? Hull follows the analysis by Spence, Bergmann, and Lippitt (1950) in showing how, in the course of learning, the anticipatory response for eating provides the stimulus to turn right, and that for drinking the stimulus to turn left. Thus when one of the two needs is aroused, associated covert cues steer the animal in the appropriate direction. *Latent learning* (Blodgett, 1929) occurs when animals satiated with food are allowed to explore a maze, but display no overt evidence of learning. During the course of their wanderings they eventually reach a goal box. If at some later time food is located in the goal box, errors abruptly decline, as if the animals "knew" where to go as a result of previous experience, but only went there directly when

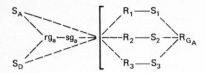

FIGURE 5-2   A habit-family hierarchy produced by a divergent and a
convergent mechanism. (From Maltzman, 1955).

sufficiently motivated—this behavior, too, can be explained by
invoking the anticipatory goal response.

Problem Solving

Hull discussed how the $r_g \rightarrow s_g$ mechanism might apply to various
complex processes, including problem solving. Maltzman (1955),
however, has presented an especially thorough treatment, invoking
the concept of *habit-family hierarchies* in conjunction with the
anticipatory goal response. Such a hierarchy is a system of interrelated stimuli and responses. It contains two mechanisms, a
divergent one by which a stimulus (either internal or external) tends
to evoke several responses, and a convergent one by which several
stimuli tend to elicit the same response (see Figure 5-2). During
learning, the status of components changes; the correct response
and the correct cue become dominant in the hierarchy. The $r_g \rightarrow s_g$,
also contained in the hierarchy, is related to all the responses, and
may be evoked by either internal or external stimuli. Thinking,
according to this view, depends on the development of compound
habit-family hierarchies (see Figure 5-3). The stimulus for a
divergent mechanism becomes an element in a convergent
mechanism. That is, a particular stimulus not only evokes its own
habit family but, at least to some degree, other habit families also.
Similarly, responses become elements in convergent mechanisms
so that they are elicited by several stimuli, and the anticipatory goal
response also may be elicited by different stimuli and to some degree
may lead to different responses. In short, there is a hierarchy of
hierarchies, within which connections ramify in complex ways
(not all indicated in Figure 5-3).

Applying principles like these in simple learning, Maltzman
proposes that in problem solving changes in order of dominance
occur within the compound hierarchy. (1) Incorrect families initially

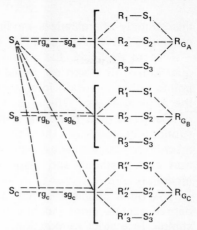

FIGURE 5-3 A compound habit-family hierarchy produced by a combination of habit-family hierarchies (other possible relations and drive, stimuli omitted to avoid cluttering). (From Maltzman, 1955.)

dominant decrease in strength as a function of extinction (from failure). (2) Correct responses initially low in the hierarchy become stronger as a function of reinforcement. (3) The anticipatory goal response of a particular habit family may be aroused in some way, for example, through verbal instructions. In this fashion the multiple possibilities within the system become sorted out and rearranged in a manner appropriate to the problem. In reproductive thinking the dominant family already contains the correct response, so that it is primarily necessary for initially incorrect dominant responses within this family to be extinguished, but in productive thinking the correct habit family rises to dominance, accompanied by extinction of the incorrect families.

Criticisms of Behavioral Theory

This view presents an extremely intricate and cumbersome model. It may be asked what is gained by reducing cognitive processes to such specific and detailed units. Instead, recognizing that such a model is possible, we might better employ a simpler approach to inferred components of cognition, and thus speak about associations, concepts, attitudes, and other processes. To a large degree, this strategy characterizes modern mediation theorists, who might otherwise fall into the category of behavioral theorists.

More explicitly, the notion of single, chained events may be questioned. Research on verbal learning and conceptual processes points rather to fusion into systems, with properties different from the original events. The r_g is not necessarily an internal duplicate of the overt goal response, but may undergo change since it is supposedly unstable. Therefore the character of the mediating mechanism cannot necessarily be accurately inferred from specification of the stimuli and responses that occur at the time of its inception.

Another criticism is that mediating mechanisms may to some degree operate independently of either external or internal (drive) stimuli. In a strict formulation, $r_g \rightarrow s_g$ is apparently aroused only when its proper stimulus occurs. And yet in thinking we can easily suppose that traces of past experience may be aroused by stimuli with which they have never had any previous connection. We must allow for greater flexibility in the operation of mediating mechanisms than behavioral theory permits. In addition, the Hullian formulation makes the mediating process a passive connection that awaits the occurrence of a suitable stimulus, and then merely evokes an internal stimulus that leads to a subsequent act (whether another r_g or an overt response), which itself is relatively predetermined. Even with Spence's principle that the anticipatory goal response possesses motivating properties, it is hard to see how sufficient allowance is made for the possible role of dynamic influences within the intrinsic cognitive system itself.[1]

In Hull's formulation the only property attributed to the anticipatory goal response is its ability to link stimuli with overt goal responses. As a pure stimulus act, it has no dynamic characteristics, but is simply some unspecified internal response that represents the overt goal response. Such factors might be handled by postulating some additional (and separate) mechanism. But, cannot the mediating process *itself* have components of an affective character? If the overt goal response can achieve internal representation, why cannot the covert emotional (and motive) activities that occur during behavior also have a comparable result? The individual may recall and anticipate his own impulses, as well as incentives or goals. More important, however, these components are not necessarily separable in their internal representation, but form interrelated systems.

[1] The unconscious also poses a special problem for behavioral theory. It might be handled via a class of drive stimuli.

In sum then, the behavioral theory advances beyond the motor theory by including a mediating mechanism. But it only offers a foundation for moving toward a fuller description of cognitive processes. We must allow for greater complexity of the mediating process than the anticipatory goal response entails, for greater flexibility in the covert mechanisms, for greater degrees of independence from specific stimuli and responses, for fusions between and among mediating processes, and for the integration of affective-motivational components with other mediating components.

MEDIATION THEORY

The need to extend the expectancy principle has led to positions that fall under the general heading of mediation theory. Developing naturally from the convergence of Tolman's expectancy principle and the fractional anticipatory goal response suggested by Hull, mediation theory modifies the older treatment in important ways.

Two Forms of Mediation Theory

Our distinction between two forms of mediation theory lies mainly in two points: (1) how closely the internal mechanism is tied to specific stimulus events and to immediate situational determinants, and (2) how complex the mechanism is considered to be. The weak form of the theory is simply an extension of the Hullian conception, but the strong or intrinsic organization form breaks with this view by assigning properties to the mediating process not directly derivable from specific stimulus-response events.

Consider the notion of *expectancy*, which has two rather different usages corresponding to the distinction we drew earlier between attitude and set. In the latter sense, an expectancy is a mechanism derived from experience with a succession of stimuli that exerts a controlling influence on later events in the sequence. In the former sense, an expectancy is a mechanism established during experience prior to the presently observed sequence of events, but aroused by the immediate situation, and determining response in it. Neither is wholly independent of the other: the set focuses the attitude, and the attitude helps to determine the set. The conception of mediating processes must incorporate both functions. The attitude principle primarily demands antecedent measurement of individual differences in expectancy. The set principle primarily calls for examination of properties of sequences of situational stimuli. The corresponding research strategies contrast subject selection (or assessment) and subject assignment or special induction procedures with planned instructions or programmed sequences of stimuli. In terms of the anticipatory goal response, an *attitude* is a general mechanism that influences selection of particular r_g's, whereas a *set* is closer to the actual r_g elicited by a stimulus. Mediation theory differs from behavioral theory in allowing for the more general mechanism.

The weak form of the theory takes only a few steps beyond the specific $r_g \rightarrow s_g$ mechanism (Osgood, 1952, 1953; see, also, Berlyne, 1954). Resting on the Hullian foundation, the essence of the theory continues to be an internal, but reduced, representation of the actual behavior toward an object, which is a partial *replica* of that behavior. "Detachable" from the stimuli that originally elicit it, some part of the representational reaction becomes the stable mediation process. Once aroused, it has the property of "self-stimulation"; that is, it can influence the selection of instrumental acts. Possessing energizing properties, the mediating process has motivational and reinforcing effects and contains emotional components that, indeed, are especially independent of the original object that elicits the reaction.[1]

Finally, this theory allows for certain kinds of change in the mediation process; chiefly, either a shift in the connection between a "sign" (the stimulus that elicits a mediator) and the mediator or a shift in the instrumental responses evoked by the mediator. Although both kinds of change concern what we ordinarily call "meaning," the first corresponds with modification of associations, and the second with decisions or response selection. For example, the stimulus word *page* normally elicits associations to which the word *book* serves as a label. But it is not difficult to make it elicit associations with the label *boy*. Even more distinctively, the word *page* normally has a somewhat neutral meaning. But if an electric shock were administered in conjunction with its presentation, it would tend to elicit mediating processes of a noxious character. A shift in an instrumental response would be illustrated by first learning that an object can be obtained from a vending machine by the insertion of a nickel, then discovering that a dime is now required.

The Osgood theory, however, does not clearly allow for fusions between or among mediators since it still rests largely on the conception of discrete and separate rather specific mechanisms. Nor does it fully recognize that affective-motivational representations

[1] Like Hull, Osgood assumes that the mediator may be aroused either by external or internal (drive) stimuli.

may become integrated into a single system. In fact it adopts one of two alternatives. One is that a stimulus elicits internal reactions that, although separate from each other, occur simultaneously, and the total mediating process is a combination of such units. This alternative seems to mark Osgood's treatment. The other is that a stimulus elicits a total system, as an interrelated whole. Thus, for example, the stimulus word *horse* could evoke an image of the animal in question *and* feelings of love (the implication of Osgood's approach), or could evoke a reaction that is both an image and a feeling. The strong form of mediation theory would introduce this second alternative.

Mowrer (1960b) accepts the principle of mediation, relying strongly on images (conditioned sensations) as its basis. In Mowrer's general theory, motivation is the basis for all learning. However, he is not clear whether conditioned emotions and conditioned sensations (images) are two different consequences of learning (with images fulfilling mainly a memorial or information function), or whether one is derived from the other. He is clear, however, in saying that images act as mediators.

By postulating simple basic units, weak mediation theory does not do justice to complex mediating systems, such as we see in abstract concepts. The complex system becomes a collection of mediators held together in some way. We suggest, however, that complex systems may develop in which originally discrete elements lose their identity and fuse into a new, directly elicitable entity.

INTRINSIC ORGANIZATION

Strong mediation theory (1) recognizes important and continuing relations between the cognitive process and operations of extrinsic stimulus and overt response; (2) endeavors to specify the intrinsic mechanisms of the cognitive process; (3) maintains close dependence on principles of learning to account for the establishment of and change in cognitive mechanisms; and (4) stresses the continuous role of emotional and motivational influences. Hebb (1949) has been especially influential, providing an explanation for autonomous central processes inferred to represent the essential characteristics of thinking. He begins with a neural assumption: "When an axon of cell A is near enough to excite a cell B and repeatedly or persistently takes part in firing it, some growth process or metabolic change takes place in one or both cells such that A's efficiency, as one of the cells firing B, is increased." On this fundamental principle, relationships gradually develop between and among neural elements, at three stages or levels of organization. The first is a *cell assembly*, formed when two or more cells converge on each other and through lowered synaptic relations activate each other. Rather than a closed chain or sequence, however, a cell assembly must be conceptualized as a network or system. Energy reverberates through the system, which thus may maintain its organization more or less indefinitely (i.e., as long as any excitation exists in it). The second stage is a *phase sequence*, or an interrelated system of cell assemblies. Again, by the reverberation principle, such an organization can maintain itself indefinitely. Finally, the third stage involves cycles of phase sequences. Whereas perceptual behavior is in large degree a process of activating cell assemblies, the more complex processes of conceptualizing and thinking call on the second two stages. These kinds of organization serve three functions: (1) to store information, (2) to maintain cognitive activity once it is aroused, and (3) to provide a basis for extended trains of thought. (Function (1) depends on reverberation within the system, function (2) on activation from outside the system, and function (3) on transmission along sequences.) None of these systems is wholly static, but is subject to internal changes, to changes in relationships between systems, and to changes induced by other neural activities (an important point in stressing the continuous responsiveness of intrinsic processes to both the effects of external stimuli and to other central states). But in complex systems, such as concepts, organization rather than the "core" of the system changes. For example, an object that we might describe as a "horse" can be large, small, of various colors, with or without a saddle, and so on; or it can be classified as a herbivore or judged as friendly or mean, and so on. Although aspects of meaning vary, depending on conditions of stimulation, the central components are fairly stable.

Interrelationships among emotional and motivational components of thinking and cortical systems are handled in two ways. First, motivation is equated with the cortical activity itself, that is, with the maintenance and direction of phase sequences. Second, emotions and needs are represented by separate cortical systems acting to arouse and influence cell assemblies,[1] rather than becoming integral components of them (i.e., participating directly in the cell assembly or phase sequence). Here is one point at which a full-fledged mediation theory might differ from the Hebbian view.

[1] In general Hebb's conception of motives corresponds to attitudes and sets, as described in Chapter 3. Learning establishes mechanisms to control and direct arousal, rather than to modify drives. His view is similar in this respect to McClelland's affective-arousal theory.

In explicating the role of motivation in Hebb's theory, Milner (1957) addresses himself cogently to the problem of the self-maintenance of cortical systems. Originally ambiguously treated, the principle of reverberation seems to point to a "snowballing" effect. Activity in the brain could conceivably ramify endlessly, in a multiplicative way, as impulses from any neuron pass to all others via synaptic connections. To solve this problem, Milner adds an *inhibition* postulate that leads to an equilibrium principle. He suggests that some neurons have long axons with excitatory connections with other parts of the cortex and that others have short axons with local inhibitory connections. The short-axon cells could receive impulses from long-axon cells; the latter could receive impulses both from other neurons and from the arousal system. The long-axon type could fire numerous other cells (the multiplicative effect), but would be checked by the inhibitory neurons, except for a small proportion of the connections ("primed" by earlier firing). Milner then shows how a balance would be produced between activity within a system of cells and surrounding inhibition, since increased firing would also increase inhibition and, conversely, decreased firing would increase total activity. A second postulate proposes that short-axon cells have fewer inhibitory connections with long-axon cells in a particular system than with other cells. In this way a system could tend to re-excite itself, and maintain itself indefinitely.

Blum (1961) presented a strong version of mediation theory, which can be considered an extension of the Hebbian view (see Figure 5-4). The cognitive subsystem acts as the "master," sending impulses to the motoric and affective subsystems. Input comes from sensory sources, both external and internal, with effects depending on the signal's intensity and on relations based on past experience. Cognitive components have complex properties of storage, reception, and transmission. They form *circuits* when contiguously and repeatedly fired, and may be linked into *networks*.

The system operates on the following principles:

1 *Facilitation*—the strengthening of connections when components are activated, up to some asymptote, but decreasing in strength when activation is absent.

2 *Integration*—combining into more complex processes.

3 *Hyperfacilitation*—an attention function by which the strongest composite is amplified from moment to moment.

4 *Reverberation*—reactivating initiating circuits by positive feedback loops, with spread of activity to other parts of the network.

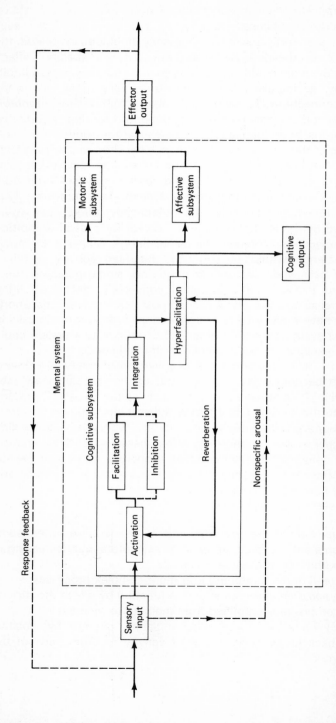

FIGURE 5-4 Overview of a conceptual model of mental functions.
Note: Arrows indicate the direction of signal passage. Signals from the external world or response feedback always pass (by way of sensory input) through the cognitive subsystem before reaching the motoric and affective subsystems. Effector output is by way of the latter subsystems, whereas cognitive output refers to the products of hyperfaciliation in the cognitive subsystem. (From Blum, 1961.)

5 *Response feedback*—additional feedback from motoric and affective subsystems, when they are activated.

6 *Inhibition*—a cognitive mechanism, linked with an anxiety network, which interferes with transmission, thus producing a balancing process, like that suggested by Milner.

Blum has used hypnosis in preliminary experiments to show how internal characteristics of the system can be manipulated. For example, by increasing the facilitation function, the effect on consequences (such as recall) can be tested.

Criticisms of Mediation Theory

Osgood himself pointed out the chief weakness of mediation theory, namely, that it attempts to describe conditions and processes that are not observable, and therefore inferences are difficult to test. The advantage of behavioral theory lies in its effort to attach variables and processes as closely as possible to what *is* observable : stimulus input and response output, attributing only what is absolutely necessary to the covert aspects of behavior. Acceptance of the mediation principle makes it easy to speak about intrinsic processes without any certain justification.

A second weakness stems from incomplete knowledge about the nervous system. Insofar as mediation theory is built on assumptions about the character of neural activity, it rests on the soundness of those assumptions. Until we know how the nervous system actually works, mediation theory is open to question.

Finally, we have speculated about the kinds of problems that arise in the analysis of cognition. Like other theories, the mediation approach adopts certain solutions to those problems, which may or may not prove correct. The issue that has frequently recurred in this discussion is a good example—how do emotions and motives influence thinking ? We have generally distinguished between conceptions that separate emotion from cognition, although allowing for the former to impinge on or influence the latter, and conceptions that see the two as integrated components of the same process. No theory will be wholly adequate until it satisfactorily resolves this issue.

INFORMATION PROCESSING

We turn next to an approach that formalizes the operations of cognition by examining the succession of events from the moment of stimulation to the production of a response outcome. But it avoids much of the S-R terminology in favor of concepts drawn from communication theory and computer technology. Both treat the sequence of events by reference to the input of information, with subsequent processes of arousing activities in the system, followed by the organization and direction of those activities, and eventuating in the output of new information.

To clarify the expression "information processing," we can distinguish three usages. (1) It has become fashionable to employ the phrase as a title for almost any treatment of thinking, particularly as a term nearly synonymous with mediation. (2) It refers to special models of cognition in which the variables are described strictly with reference to input and output characteristics, together with connecting processes that can be described by direct reference to other externally observable events. (3) Information theory often signifies a computer model, with characteristics derived from properties of computers. The first usage may be ignored. The second usage is more general, with computer models as special instances, and aims to specify and precisely test information-processing principles. One reason for making this distinction is that traffic is properly in one direction: the computer aims to simulate human information processing, rather than the reverse.

Haber (1969) states that information processing rests on three major assumptions.

1 Perceptual response is not an immediate result of stimulation, but involves a succession of stages each requiring some time for organization to take place. The total time involved can be divided into intervals, during each of which some different operation occurs.

2 The information-processing system has limited capacities. This means that activities depend on how much information is imposed, what kind it is, and what mechanisms exist for selecting and organizing information. The process by which some of the available content is retained and/or rendered more salient is called *recoding*.

3 Perception and memory are not wholly distinct but in fact have important commonalities. Both, for example, always occur following stimulation, and must be treated as interrelated processes.

Drawing on concepts of communication theory (Shannon, 1948), and signal detection, Miller (1953, 1956) formulated the fundamental principles. A source of input presents information as the alternatives open to the individual in producing a response. The greater the number of alternatives, the larger the quantity of information. The unit for measuring the quantity of information is a *bit:* the amount needed to decide between two equally possible alternatives. Each bit of information reduces the alternatives by one-half; conversely, each added bit doubles the number of alternatives. However, because the channel capacity of the transmitter (e.g., the perceiver or learner) is limited, the amount of effective information quickly reaches an asymptote, a condition that limits how well the individual can match his response to the stimulus situation. Miller estimates that an asymptote is reached at about three or four bits of information. For absolute judgments of unidimensional stimuli this means that the observer is highly accurate for as many as seven or eight items. When dimensions are added to stimuli, the channel capacity increases but at a decreasing rate, and accuracy for any particular dimension decreases. (It is as if the added dimensions reduce the number of alternatives by facilitating classification. Thus a bit of information shifts from individual items to groups—or kinds—of items.) In accordance with the principle of limited capacity, the number of dimensions is also limited (estimated to be about ten).

The individual does not treat input in simple direct ways, but rather organizes or groups stimuli and their properties—when exposed to stimuli, he does not remember details, but larger units, or *chunks*. For example, if the letters XRAY are exposed, he does not store the separate letters but rather the entire word. There is also a limit on the number of chunks that can be remembered from an exposure, just as there is a limit on the number of bits of information that can be transmitted. By chunking (or *recoding*), the individual increases the amount of information available, thereby facilitating recall and subsequent use of information. The input code (e.g., a sequence of letters) contains many separate chunks, each with a few bits of information, but the observer reorganizes (recodes) the sequence—if possible—by remembering many fewer chunks, each with several bits. Put more simply, the subject in an experiment groups letters, gives names to the groups, and remembers these names.

The merit of this approach is that an experimenter can study perceptual, memorial, and conceptual processes by systematically varying the properties of stimulus arrays. It becomes possible to examine the characteristics of information, the effects of varying the amount of information, and the manner in which requirements of the task affect performance.

In a basic paper, Newell, Shaw, and Simon (1958; see also, Simon and Newell, 1971) postulate that information-processing systems have these characteristics: (1) *memories*, consisting of symbolized information, interconnected by various ordering relations; (2) *primitive information processes*, definitely specifiable operations acting on the information in the memories; and (3) explicit *rules* for combining these processes into complete *programs*.

Viewed as an explanation or theory about behavior, a program is specific to particular observed situations, incorporating those information processes that will generate the behavior in question. Computer simulation is a method of representing—clearly and un-ambiguously—the information-processing activities of human beings. It starts with protocols of human behavior—for example, in choice situations or in problem solving—and translates them into terms such that a computer can do the same things in a similar fashion. Such a specification includes the weaknesses and irregularities of human cognition, as well as its strengths (Hovland, 1960).

In developing the computer analogy, emphasis has chiefly been placed on relatively clearcut problem situations, that is, cases in which there is a definite solution that can be assessed for its ade-quacy or accuracy in the light of stated input conditions.[1] Thus the program contains rules, that is, *algorithms* and *heuristics*, that facili-tate arrival at the correct solution (Newell, Shaw, and Simon, 1958). An algorithm is a procedure that guarantees a solution—an exhaust-ive search process that encompasses all available information, sorts it out, and follows the best possible (or only possible) path to the outcome. A heuristic is a rule of thumb or a procedure that pursues likely avenues that shortcut the detailed process, but it does not guarantee a solution. In fairly simple problems algorithms work very well—and indeed it would often be foolish to adopt some other method. But in complex problems a complete search process would be tedious, or economically impracticable. In such cases the problem solver employs devices to classify groups of alternatives, or seeks for techniques that have worked in the past. By taking a step likely to be helpful, the thinker runs some risk of failure, but is willing to do so as a means to arrive more quickly and directly at the goal. It is uncertain whether computer programs have actually duplicated human heuristic procedures (because their full range is difficult to identify

---

[1]Reitman (1965, p. 166), however, describes how a creative process—composing a fugue—might be handled as an "ill-defined problem." In such a case the "initial and terminal states and the transformational procedures are left entirely unspecified except for some property [here the production of a fugue] associated with an object of the terminal state."

explicitly), but at least they have gone a long way in this direction.

Finally, information processing requires a specification of the cognitive elements and structures on which the program can operate (Reitman, 1965). This can be accomplished by utilizing principles of *sets* and *relations*.

Set refers to an aggregate of objects, such as may be represented in the memory component of the system. In computer simulation, a code would be developed to represent each item in whatever way we wish, such as by a series of digits, with each position corresponding to a certain attribute. For example, to record data about geometrical figures, the first digit might stand for form, the second for color, the third for size, the fourth for the presence or absence of a stripe, and so on. Suppose that squares are 1, circles 2; red is 1, blue 2; large is 1, small 2; and stripe is 1, no stripe 2. A square that is red, small, and striped would be represented as 1111; a circle that is red, small, and unstriped would be 2122; and so on. These elements of the system can be drawn on or grouped, according to some rule, to form a set (e.g., all the squares, all the large red figures, etc.). If the set must be listed in a fixed order, then it is an *ordered set*; for example, if sets of colored figures must always be produced in the order red, green, blue.

A relation is some connection between elements, and specifies an ordered set of members that have this connection. That is, a rule determines a characteristic that elements have in common—for example, if a set of figures must be red, or both red and small. Or the rule may generalize across pairs (or triples, etc.), such as all the instances in which a red circle is next to a blue square.

We shall pursue these principles farther when we consider concept formation. By following them, we can quite precisely manipulate variables associated with the elements themselves or with the rules on which sets and relations are based. Note also that we could examine the effects of conditions that may lead to errors or variability of performance—for example, some elements might be partly square or partly round. Or a rule might be ambiguously stated, such as requiring that a set be figures that look alike.

Criticisms of the Information-processing Viewpoint

The question may be raised whether theories of information processing actually do justice to the characteristics of human cognition. They usually present strictly formal models in which elements and rules are explicitly stated. Although advocates of the approach argue that this very requirement is a great advantage, nevertheless the severe constraints thus imposed may not be really typical of human thinking. Perhaps a better way to state the point is to say that information processing deals only with limited and special cases.

Beyond this, we encounter again a problem apparent in the behavioral approach, namely, that information processing demands, even for fairly simple cases, an enormously complex set of specifications. It is doubtful that such intensive detail greatly adds to our understanding of cognition, which might better be described in other terms. After all, human thinking employs symbolic and language devices rather than the highly specific fractional elements of the computer. It is not certain that the human system has as yet been really duplicated by computers, or if inherent differences do not make this impossible. Critics might propose that the human system, after all, is the essential object to investigate.

Other criticisms have been advanced by Neisser (1963a, b), who suggests that human thinking is multiple, with several independent processes operating concurrently (1963b), but with consciousness as a main sequence. In contrast, information-processing models emphasize sequential operations. Although a computer can be programmed for multiple processes, the theory is clearly of limited value if it is tied to a strictly sequential conception.

Neisser (1963a) sees the following similarities between human and computer: (1) *purposiveness*: if this concept refers to "anticipation" of a goal, and persistence of related activity, then the machine is, if anything, superior to man; (2) *learning by experience*: the computer displays this effect and in fact must do so whenever continuous input is intended to improve efficiency; and (3) *creativity*: since a computer can be made to act unpredictably, to perform in ways not fully programmed, and even to find original solutions (e.g., for mathematical propositions), it can cautiously be concluded that the machine is similar to the human.

But Neisser also points to important differences. (1) The human displays growth and development; the machine is a system with fixed properties, to which can be added specific content or new rules only by external input. (2) Human thinking displays an "intimate association with emotions and feelings," but this characteristic is absent from the machine. (3) The human system is featured by a multiplicity of motives, but the machine functions as if it had only a single need, that is, to respond fully to input conditions.

Responding to these criticisms, Simon (1967) recognizes that the relation between affect and cognition has been ignored by information-processing theory, and therefore addresses himself mainly to the second and third of Neisser's points. He states two assumptions: that the central nervous system is organized to operate in serial fashion, and that the course of behavior is regulated (or motivated) by tightly organized hierarchies of goals.

With respect to serial organization, some "indivisible" time unit is required, assumed to correspond with the simplest reflex action (about 100 milliseconds), and an "elementary" symbol (or a "chunk"). Simple sequences consist of such units, more complex processes of syntheses of these units over longer intervals. With respect to "emotion," Simon points to mechanisms that control the *hierarchy* of operations and *goal completions*. The machine is provided with subroutines to execute instructions in the proper order, leading to "apparently single-minded, single-purpose behavior." But human behavior is markedly different since it is subject to interruption by threats, unexpected stimuli, changes in intrinsic states, and so on. Goal completion requires mechanisms to terminate a subroutine and restore control to the next higher level. Among the criteria for completing subgoals are: (1) aspiration attained (that is, reaching the subgoal), (2) satisficing (a term that signifies "good enough," indicating reasonable approximation), (3) impatience (a sufficient time has been spent), and (4) discouragement (indication that specified steps have been taken and failed). According to Simon, these four mechanisms have already been incorporated into information-processing systems.

The problem of multiple goals is to show how a system may respond to several goals simultaneously without altering the basic serial character of performance. As one mechanism, he proposes a *queuing of goals*, by which some goals may be postponed when the system is otherwise occupied, and time allocated to various phases of the operation concerned with particular goals. A second is incorporating *multifaceted criteria*, to which the machine can respond and thus choose among alternatives as work proceeds.

Emotion and motivation, Simon suggests, do not require representation by special mechanisms since they refer merely to whatever process influences attention at a given time. This problem might be handled by an *interrupt system*, which would, so to speak, monitor performance to "notice" when conditions exist that demand interruption, and then set aside programs in operation. Another interrupt system would operate on a cyclic principle. A "drive" or "need" built into the system would increase as a function of minutes or hours of "deprivation," with some "threshold" defined when it becomes so strong as to interrupt the operating program. In developing these ideas, Simon discusses several possible kinds of "needs" that could be programmed. He also indicates how the learning of emotional behavior might be simulated by using an interrupt system. Thus the effects of certain stimuli might be made to change, or as the situation becomes more familiar, the "emotionality" mechanism in the system might decrease.

In these ways Simon has boldly explored steps to take in coping with the problems raised by Neisser. It is a very healthy sign that advocates of information-processing models are willing to extend their treatment to encompass not only "irrational" aspects of human thinking, but also variables of emotion and motivation.

GUILFORD'S MODEL

In the *structure-of-intellect* model, Guilford (1967) has systematically ordered the general kinds of variables revealed in factor-analytic studies of ability tests. Earlier conceptions of intelligence were based on a rather limited number of general abilities with a common core of general intelligence, but Guilford's work has produced a very large number of distinctive factors, together with little evidence for a general factor (see Figure 5-5). The dimensions should be regarded as categories, within each of which a large number of factors can be identified. Furthermore, each factor is itself measured by many different tests. Finally, the three-dimensional form of the model indicates that the categories of one dimension intersect with those of the other dimensions.

The *content* dimension refers to the forms of intellectual processes, including categories designated as figural (concrete information in the form of images), symbolic (signs that code information, like numbers, letters, musical notation), semantic (meanings, whether verbalized or unverbalized), and behavioral (added as a logical necessity to allow for information involved in perceiving and thinking about other people—or what Thorndike once called "social intelligence").

The *operation* dimension orders categories from most basic to most inclusive, each more dependent on the others, namely, cognition (immediate comprehension or understanding), memory (storage), divergent production (generation of information from that already given), convergent production (dealing with logical necessities, and with constraints that demand correct answers, as in problem solving), and evaluation (comparison and decision or judgment).

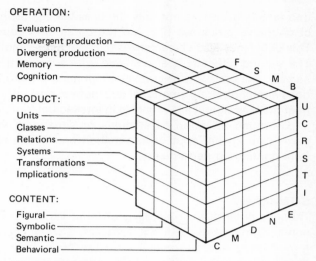

OPERATION:

Evaluation
Convergent production
Divergent production
Memory
Cognition

PRODUCT:

Units
Classes
Relations
Systems
Transformations
Implications

CONTENT:

Figural
Symbolic
Semantic
Behavioral

FIGURE 5-5   The structure-of-intellect model, with three parameters (other parameters may need to be added). (From Guilford, 1967.)

The *product* dimension concerns the outcomes of intellectual activity, such categories as units (or distinctive "things"), classes (sets of units), relations (connections between units), systems (complexes or organizations), transformations (changes or modifications by which one product moves to another state), and implications (predictions, expectations).

To do justice to Guilford's formulations, we would need to examine in detail the relations between categories and dimensions. For example, the four content and six product categories together comprise categories of information, and in combination yield twenty-four subcategories (e.g., figural units, symbolic classes, semantic relations, etc.). The five categories of operations act on the information categories. Thus cognition is a decoding of information, memory is the storage of figural units (or whatever), convergent production yields symbolic classes, and so on.

Although there can be little doubt about the importance of Guilford's systematizing of human abilities, it is impossible to discern its ultimate impact, outside of the realm of intelligence testing. Despite his versatile treatment of intersections among the categories, the model suffers from two weaknesses. The first stems from its logical formality. The use of discrete special tests and their ordering into factors overlooks not only the possible interlacing and blending of cognitive processes but also the continuing course of thinking. This deficiency also characterizes the computer-simulation approach. The second difficulty is also shared with some of the other models, namely, the omission of crucial components of cognitive activity. It does not incorporate emotional and motivational influences, nor even treat them as significant variables in intellectual functioning. Nor does it pay much attention to stimulus or situational variables, which participate in the input of information and in the feedback effects from continuing performance.

SUMMARY

Theories differ in their handling of input variables, intrinsic components, output, and feedback variables. *Central theory*, in its weak form, simply refers to activities in the brain, and in stronger form specifies kinds of thinking and their characteristics. The motor version of *S-R theory* posits sequences of implicit muscular movements with kinesthetic feedback as the mechanism of thinking. Research on phantom limbs and conditions when peripheral stimulation is absent undermine the generality of the theory, but kinesthetic feedback may be important in the latent monitoring and maintenance of cognition. *Behavioral theory* has adduced principles based on the fractional anticipatory goal response ($r_g \rightarrow s_g$), and applied them to explain double-drive situations, latent learning, and problem solving, advanced by cognitive theorists as evidence against a strictly S-R view. Criticisms include the resulting fractionated and cumbersome description, the orientation to single, chained events that merely duplicate behavioral responses, and inadequate attention to properties of the postulated mechanism (especially insufficient allowance for affective components). In a simple form, *mediation theory* extends the $r_g \rightarrow s_g$ mechanism to account for meaning or introduces images and conditioned emotions. In the stronger form of *intrinsic organization*, mediation theory incorporates principles of cognitive structure, integration of affective components, and feedback, and allows for at least some autonomy of thinking. Criticisms include speculation about unobservable processes, reliance on unconfirmed notions about neural processes, and inadequate attention to emotion and motivation. This theory, however, is the position of this book. Other approaches are *information theory* that calls on concepts from communication theory and computer technology and the *model of intellect*, each also subject to criticism.

6

CONCEPTUAL DEVELOPMENT OF CHILDREN

Research on conceptual processes has been pursued on two broad fronts, the fundamental stages of development during the early years and the behavior manifested by adults. The theories of Piaget have played a central role in the first area, and mediation theory has been a focus in the second. The two bodies of investigation are not necessarily incompatible—indeed, there are signs of movement toward putting them together into a broader perspective. Studies of children and of adults deal with rather different problems since processes of acquiring intellectual experience and skills especially characterize children, whereas adults typically exercise and manipulate already acquired intellectual components.

Recall that we drew a distinction between autistic and realistic poles of thinking. In this and the next six chapters we shall be oriented primarily toward the realistic pole—that is, toward cognitive processes as they are related to and determined by the environment. In experiments this signifies the responses observed when particular kinds of tasks are presented under specified situational conditions.

WHAT IS A CONCEPT?

"Concept" can be defined in various ways. We might emphasize behavioral aspects by citing certain defining responses, or we might

stress the inferred properties of the person who produces those responses. Behavioral aspects include activities of classifying objects, of
making decisions based on relationships between objects, and so on.
On the intrinsic side, we could cite cognitive structures that serve to
organize information about objects, linking previous experience and
current states with stimulus objects—in short, systems that act as
mediators. I shall adopt the latter definition, and define concepts as
"cognitive organizing systems which serve to bring pertinent features
of past experience to bear on a present stimulus object" (Vinacke,
1954).

I intend to distinguish concepts from other mediating processes,
notably from attitudes (see Chapters 17 to 20). Concepts have the
function of selecting and organizing the effects of extrinsic stimuli
(i.e., experience, knowledge, information), whereas attitudes have
the function of selecting and regulating responses. Thus concepts
concern the *meanings* of objects, but attitudes concern *choice* and
decision. In a broader sense, concepts and attitudes are not independent of each other, but represent components of complex
cognitive systems.

Another complication arises from the role of language in conceptualizing. Words may serve in three distinct capacities: as stimuli,
as symbolic mediating agents, and as responses. These functions
can easily be confused, as when we assume that a name for an
object defines it. But the word is merely a label for intrinsic processes, which may vary from one person to another, or even from one
time to another in the same person. The term *concept* refers to cognitive processes themselves, insofar as we can make inferences about
them, partly occurring as verbal symbols—tools, so to speak, for the
manipulation and efficient organizing of experience, so that conceptualizing to some degree makes use of words. Words here are treated
as being different from concepts, however closely parallel they may
become under suitable circumstances.

To begin with, there are certain general characteristics of concepts. They are *mediating processes* rather than direct sensory data,
and represent the elaboration, combination, and reorganization of
those data. They call on *previous experience*, as it is tied together in
relationships and classes of events. Such linkages are *symbolic* (often
with words as the agent). As intrinsic selective and organizing
systems, concepts have both *denotative and connotative* components
(or "meaning") (Hayakawa, 1964). Denotative components correspond to the "objective" properties of objects regularly provided by

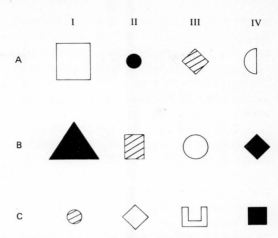

FIGURE 6-1 An array of stimuli to illustrate characteristics of concepts.

the senses (color, shape, size, etc.). Connotative components correspond to properties derived from the individual's unique experiences—"subjective" properties such as feelings or projected attributes. We would expect all or most people to have similar denotative components in the case of a given object, but to differ in connotative components. Concepts vary in *consistency,* or the "completeness" and "correctness" of their components. For instance experiments by Reed (1946a, b, c, 1950) demonstrated that subjects may classify words into consistent or logical categories, or may classify unrelated words into "incorrect" or inconsistent categories. In both cases the category has a name by which it is identified. Finally, a conceptual system may be organized *horizontally* or *vertically* (Welch, 1940; Welch and Long, 1940a, b). The same object has different points of reference to other objects, either at equivalent levels of inclusiveness, or at different levels of generality.

An array of stimuli, such as that in Figure 6-1, illustrates these points.

A person may place figures into classes on the basis of shape, producing the groups IA, IIB, IIIC,[1] and IVC; IC, IIA, IIIB, and IVA;[1] and IB, IIC, IIIA, and IVB. Such a response is based on denotative properties, as could be confirmed by the fact that quite similar results

[1] Note that these figures may offer some difficulties.

would appear for different subjects. Similarly, classes might be based on color (here represented by white, black, and cross hatching), or on whole versus half-figures, or small versus large figures. The connotative property would appear if the subject were asked to select the figures that he likes best (he might still form a logical class, such as choosing all the figures except IIIC and IVA, indicating a preference for regular objects).

Consistent concepts depend on the criterion of "correctness." Ordinarily, a relationship of "roundness" would be consistent for a classification of IC, IIA, IIIB, and possibly, IVA; then a class including IIA, IIB, and IIC would be inconsistent (note that one-third of the responses are "correct"). This characteristic bears on the matter of rules in conceptualizing (see Chapter 9).

Vertical classes might be as follows: hierarchy 1: twelve figures, as separate and equivalent objects; hierarchy 2: square, round, and triangular; hierarchy 3: roundish and angular; hierarchy 4: all the figures as a set of geometrical objects.

BASIC PROBLEMS OF CONCEPT FORMATION
Research on conceptual behavior bears on three fundamental issues.

1. Ability to Conceptualize How can we explain and describe how the child comes to form and use concepts? Is there a general intellectual function that displays itself during development? What roles do maturation and environmental influence play? Guilford's model does not allow for a separate explicitly conceptual function. But a strong implication of Piaget's theory is that conceptualizing shows a well-defined progression with increasing age. On the whole, a definite solution to this problem has not been reached.

2. Acquisition of Concepts, or Repertory What concepts—or systems of concepts—are present at various stages in development? Whether or not a general ability or several interrelated abilities are involved, there remains the issue of what is learned, so that we still need to examine the character of experience and its expression in specific behavioral acts.

Since a major thrust of research on children deals with this problem, especially in the Piagetian tradition, the answer is becoming increasingly clear.

3. Attaining a Specific Concept How does an individual learn a particular conceptual response? Typically, a subject is exposed to an array of stimulus objects and required to respond in a systematic way to instances of them, on the basis of relationships or class membership. The investigator works out the process of attainment by observing errors, inquiring into reasons for the decisions made, comparing subjects with each other, and relating his response measures to variations in the task, to inferred cognitive characteristics, to motivational conditions, and so on. Although this third problem is clearly important for understanding the child's behavior, it has dominated the investigation of the conceptual behavior of adults, who do not so much acquire new concepts as apply the ones already possessed in new variations, systems, and hierarchies.

METHODS OF INVESTIGATION

Research on conceptual behavior has displayed remarkable versatility in recent years. The aims have been to objectify procedures and to contrive techniques of control that permit the operation of stated variables to appear as unequivocally as possible. These aspirations are difficult to achieve in the case of concepts, where our interest lies in inferring mediational processes. The study of children is especially difficult, both because we cannot rely on language exclusively as a communication medium and because verbal responses, when they can be elicited, may not adequately correspond to conceptual behavior.

The Interview-Questionnaire Method

In this approach, verbal inquiry is employed to obtain information about a child's interpretation of objects, relations, or various natural, moral, causal, or social phenomena. Piaget (1929, 1930, 1952; Flavell, 1963) developed a "clinical" procedure, a rather free and informal interaction between child and experimenter, with considerable flexibility allowed in the types of questions asked and in adapting to variations among children. Piaget has also made extensive use of demonstrations as a means to test the child's comprehension and ability to carry out certain tasks.

Numerous investigators have further developed the method in an attempt to achieve greater control and objectivity. For example, the interview may utilize standardized questions in a predetermined order. At suitable ages, actual questionnaires may be used. There has also been a proliferation of carefully prepared demonstrations and of apparatus. These developments have been particularly important since they help to overcome the language obstacle in dealing with young children and yield readily quantifiable responses. Finally, there has been increasing attention to experimental design and sampling.

The Performance Method

Various laboratory techniques have been adapted to the study of children's cognitive processes. In the performance method, the investigator places the child in a situation that requires the learning or use of one or more simple responses to solve more complex problems. For example, a child is taught that if he opens a box that has a triangle on the front he will find a piece of candy. He is then presented with two boxes, one marked with a triangle, the other with a square, to see if he can discriminate between them. Other examples include operant conditioning procedures, display panels, and sequences of paired stimuli of which one member is correct according to some rule.

This method has proven to be especially valuable in testing hypotheses concerning the effects of specific variables on performance, such as the role of pretraining or cognitive style. In this respect it is a direct parallel to experimentation with adults. However, the progressive changes that occur in children's thinking make it important to maintain a time perspective by sampling different ages. Furthermore, interpretation in mediational terms is sometimes hampered by focusing too directly on motor responses or by the restrictions that stem from the control of stimulus variables. For example, errors in a conceptual task may arise from the child's failure to understand instructions. Although most investigators are surely aware of these problems, the problems demand continuous attention, accompanied by revision of procedures if necessary.

THEORETICAL PERSPECTIVES

Currently there is considerable attention to theoretical treatment of children's thinking. We shall discuss four major categories: psychoanalytic, developmental progression, mediational,[1] and cognitive

---

[1] Behavioral models based on classical or operant conditioning might be separately recognized, as might also cue sampling. However, these orientations are especially pertinent to concept attainment as an aspect of adult behavior, and therefore are deferred to Chapter 8. Mediation theory, of course, has in large degree been derived from behavioral theory.

adaptation (Piaget). At the present time Piagetian views are receiving widespread attention, and they shall be discussed in greatest detail. It is noteworthy that investigators in the behavioral-mediational tradition are increasingly seeking to relate their hypotheses to Piaget's work. All theories discussed in this section assume the principle of mediating processes.

Psychoanalytic Principles

The Freudian theory of development emphasizes a progression from narcissistic, pregenital cognitive expression to increasingly realistic, ego-controlled thinking—toward the relative dominance of second-ary-process thinking. With the advent of the latency period, follow-ing resolution of the Oedipus complex, the superego becomes a force that shapes cognition in the direction of socialized, moralistic, and idealistic judgment. In addition we can trace the changes atten-dant on the successive cathexes of the oral, anal, and phallic stages, with their implications for later projections and defensive processes. Indeed, an essential feature of psychoanalytic theory, largely ignored in other treatments of children's thinking,[1] is the reservoir of affective influences associated with experiences at very early ages. Surely the ultimate study of the great realm of connotative meaning will call on psychodynamic principles.

Psychoanalysis has been mainly a reconstructive theory rather than one directly concerned with children, but Rapaport (1951) has undertaken an explicit description of conceptual development as it appears in psychoanalytic theory.

He notes that concepts are one aspect of the total thought process. They appear to become dominant as realistic determinants become stronger. If we view thinking as a merging of three compo-nents, namely, memorial content, environmental input (perception, as shaped by the special conditions of attention at the time), and motivational forces ("drive-derivatives," emotional states), then the characteristics of concepts depend on the relative strength of these components. When motivational forces are expressed in their most direct forms, concepts have a "primitive" character, but when ego control, representing socialized and environmentally oriented con-trols, operate most strongly, then concepts assume their most logical properties. The actual content of the concept is composed of memories, and is altered as the other components vary. Memories can

[1] Except for Werner (1948).

primarily serve the requirements of motivational forces, as in fantasy, or be drawn on to meet environmental demands, as in the sense of information. (Or we might say that there are two kinds of memory organization.)

These aspects of concepts appear in the adult partly as connotative and denotative properties, partly as those variations in the organization and control of the concept system that we would otherwise call dimensions of illogical and logical, plastic and structured, and so on.

In the child, thinking moves from a dominance of autistic properties in which ideas are undifferentiated (Rapaport refers here to Piaget's principle of egocentrism) toward a relative dominance of realistic elements. The process of socialization begins with the establishment of affective cathexes, especially with the parents, on the basis of which identification is built. Through the medium of identification, the child begins to introject (take into himself) characteristics of the object of identification. This process begins the movement away from primitive autism toward self-awareness. At first, introjected thought organizations tend to remain distinct from the rest of the ego. Later they are progressively integrated into the ego.

Comment   One of the chief merits of the psychoanalytic view is its recognition of the complex interplaying character of conceptual processes, in particular the continuous influence of motivational forces. A second merit is explaining cognitive development in relation to the social and emotional context of the child's experience.

Unfortunately, psychoanalytic theory is especially vague on just those points of greatest interest to the systematic investigator. Rapaport borrows heavily from other theories in order to make psychoanalytic principles more precise from the behavioral standpoint. By the very fact of stressing dynamic, intrinsic forces, psychoanalysis underplays the role of situational demands. For this reason it often appears to have the least to offer at the moments when such demands are most salient. Since experimenters favor conditions when psychoanalytic principles are mostly irrelevant, it has been easy for critics to scoff. The lack of communication in this dialogue is obvious, and can probably be alleviated by more attention to the autistic-realistic continuum.

Developmental Progression

Some students of child conceptualizing have seen it as a continuous process in which earlier acquisitions lead gradually to more advanced and inclusive kinds of thinking. Earlier characteristics are not so much lost as built into the later forms, as if the child first learns simple intellectual skills, then learns to employ them in more complex and interrelated ways. This progression has been described traditionally as moving from global (or undifferentiated) concepts through phases of differentiation into more highly organized and integrated systems.

Diffuse to Integrated Functioning   Werner (1948) has presented the thesis that there are parallels between the thinking of primitive people, children, and psychotics.[1] *Syncretic* thinking is the fusion of sensorimotor, affective, and perceptual elements. Thus images and "concepts" are not distinguished by the very young child—objects are separate things, closely determined by immediate perceptual and affective experiences. *Diffuseness* signifies that names stand for whole situations, or sequences of ideas, rather than for differentiated objects. The concepts of childen spread out in many directions instead of having a relatively limited meaning. For example, "ball" may refer to playing a game like the one played yesterday, including many additional elements such as wanting to play, desiring the parent's attention, going out into the yard, and so on. Since a single cognitive process may have various affective and experiential elements, it appears to the adult as illogical, cryptic, or idiosyncratic. *Lability* means that the child's perceptions and cognitions (as reflected in his use of words) do not have the relatively fixed content and reference of more advanced thinking. For example, the child may seemingly emphasize different properties of the same object on different occasions. Today he may treat a toy as a plaything, tomorrow as a weapon. Or names may have shifting meanings. A "bow-wow" may be a dog, a teddy bear, or a fur hat, on various occasions.

These characteristics of early childhood pass through stages marked by increased differentiation of objects and their attributes, accompanied by increased precision in language, and culminating in the hierarchical integration of adult thinking.[2]

[1] Recognizing, however, important differences, such as that adult primitives have a more adequate language than do children, and that pathological thinking in significant ways reverses the processes.

[2] Bruner's approach is rather similar (see Bruner, Olver, and Greenfield, 1966).

Werner's orientation toward the functions of language and the symbolic properties of words is illustrated by the detailed study of word meanings he conducted with Kaplan (Werner and Kaplan, 1952, 1963). They argue that the child acquires meanings as a function of the adult's direct naming of objects or verbal definitions, and also through implicit or contextual relations among words. In these processes the young child probably learns primarily by the use of words in concrete situations, in conjunction with manipulation of objects, pointing, and so on. Subsequently, the contextual factor increases in importance.

A word-context test was devised to measure changes in the understanding and use of words. It consists of twelve series of sentences, in which a nonsense word is embedded in six successive contexts. Here is the first series:

CORPLUM   (adequate translation—stick, or piece of wood):
1 A CORPLUM may be used for support.
2 CORPLUMS may be used to close off an open place.
3 CORPLUMS may be long or short, thick or thin, strong or weak.
4 A wet CORPLUM does not burn.
5 You can make a CORPLUM smooth with sandpaper.
6 The painter used a CORPLUM to mix his paints.

After each sentence the subject was queried to see if he had grasped the meaning. Pains were taken to promote rapport between the experimenter and the subject, and the situation was kept flexible. Children in five age groups, nine, ten, eleven, twelve, and thirteen, served as subjects.

As would be expected, correct definitions markedly increased with age (from a mean of 0.8 to a mean of 5.7). Conventional or standardized definitions increased, with a corresponding decrease in unique definitions. Word-sentence fusions, as when a word signifies the whole context (sentence-core concept) or part of the context (holophrastic gradient), immature usages (like fluid meanings and syncreses), egocentric and imaginative usages, and concrete symbolism decreased. Autocriticism, the ability to evaluate the adequacy of solutions, increased.

These investigators concluded that both gradual and saltatory changes are apparent. The evidence for sudden changes, however, is based mostly on the fact that statistically significant differences were found between adjacent ages for some characteristics, with non-significant differences between other ages. There were few, if any, instances in which truly abrupt changes appeared.

Another point of some interest concerns the principle of analogous functioning. They suggest that during development similar performance may be achieved by "genetically different" processes. For example, relationships may be grasped by perceptual organization or by verbal-abstract conceptualizing. These processes are not necessarily linked to different stages in development but may represent alternative and overlapping functions. If, as appears likely, perceptual organization is the typical process in childhood, and verbal-abstract conceptualizing is more typical of the mature adult, then this difference may well not be absolute, but a matter of degree. Certainly both processes are readily observable in the adult (hence the notion of alternatives), depending for their occurrence on the nature of the task. The developmental process, from this standpoint, is not a succession of distinctly different stages so much as the differentiation of processes or abilities, together with an increasing ability to adapt them to the demands of the situation, or an increasing integration of functions into the total resources of the person.

Cumulative Learning   Gagné (1965, 1968) states that "new learning depends primarily upon the combining of previously acquired and recalled learned entities, as well as upon their potentialities for transfer of learning." "Learned entity" means a system of previously acquired functions that combine to constitute a more complex ability—not merely a variation in the number, complexity, and organization of association, but a new level, at which new processes come into play (see Figure 6-2).

First, performance at a particular level depends on the functions already learned at lower levels. Thus the attainment of concepts utilizes prior associations (S-R connections) and available chains (mediators). The person faced with a concept problem is not really learning associations, nor fitting them into chains, but is applying these functions. Clearly, concepts, according to this view, cannot be learned *without* these prerequisites. But the individual is learning *concepts*—not chains of associations. Similarly, once the individual is equipped with concepts, he uses them to arrive at the formulation of simple rules and, in turn, after these rules are acquired, to derive more complex rules.

Second, development is a progression in the kinds of performance of which the individual is capable. At a particular age the level of ability is a combination of those of lower levels. The acquisition of S-R connections is typical of very young children, who cannot yet acquire concepts. At older ages multiple discriminations become

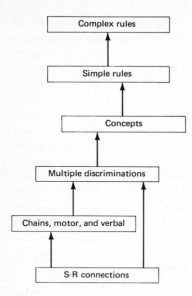

FIGURE 6-2 Gagné's general model of cumulative learning. (From Gagné, 1968).

possible because the prerequisite functions are available. By the time that concepts can be learned, this kind of performance is typical since the required abilities are now present. In this fashion, performance is a cumulative integration of antecedent skills.

Third, the principle of levels does not mean that each successive ability is fixed at a particular age. The individual at any age can learn S-R connections—and continues to do so; once that ability has been gained, it no longer dominates his behavior, but becomes a resource for more advanced levels; similarly for other functions. Furthermore, the abilities actually employed depend on the task to which the individual is exposed. If a person who has acquired an ability to perform at one level is placed in a task that calls on more advanced abilities, he must first learn the necessary capabilities. For instance, if a child has achieved adequacy at the level of multiple discriminations, and we now expose him to a task in which simple rules must be applied, he must learn the concepts that underlie the rules. We can also always establish task conditions that demand an ability at a level below that at which the individual is capable of operating. Thus we can require an adult to make multiple discriminations, to attain concepts, and so on. A person *can* use any of the abilities he has already learned, if he needs to do so. It is important to recognize, however, that he does not typically do so (save under special situational requirements). In this sense it is misleading to regard association learning as the basic process in learning concepts (or rules). In a conceptual task, the adult is learning concepts, not associations.

A study that illustrates a derivation from the theory has been reported by Lee and Gagné (1969). Tenth-grade subjects were exposed to a complex rule-learning task, after prior training on the identification of attributes and an intermediate contingent rule. Experience with these antecedent levels facilitated performance on the complex rule.

Comment The fundamental principles of developmental progression offer an attractive view of the person embarking on life, accumulating experience, and gradually (for the most part) becoming more highly organized, better able to cope with increasingly difficult and complex tasks, and moving toward more competent control over his own resources in relation to environmental demands. Thus conceptualizing is not treated as a matter of bits and pieces put together into packages, but as a process of mastering and utilizing experience. It is true that Gagné distinguishes specific kinds of learning, with particular conditions associated with each. And the investigations of Werner and Kaplan have shown some very specific changes in the use of language. Nevertheless, a theorist who favors a carefully constructed step-by-step approach to conceptual development would find both views unsatisfactory. Gagné's view may be seen as so eclectic in accepting many kinds of learning that it loses the impact that would come from closely examining the degree to which specific processes at one level might actually be similar to those at another level. These theories provide broad frameworks for treating conceptual development but await more extensive data to confirm their validity. It should be noted that the implication of continuous, cumulative progression is opposed by the conception of distinctive stages, each possibly marked by particular biological conditions.

Werner's view is limited by frequent reliance on observational and anecdotal materials, rather than empirical data, and he tends to impose his own interpretations on these supposed "facts"—especially in the parallels he finds between primitive, infantile, and pathological thinking—so that we should consider his views as more hypothetical than conclusive. Werner also appears to rely heavily on words as verbal responses, without sufficient attention to what can legitimately be inferred about meaning.

In the case of Gagné, we have more a program for managing learning situations than an explanation of learning itself. This limitation can certainly be overcome as evidence accumulates that the program works when it is translated into explicit operations.

My bias lies with the viewpoint of progressive development. In general the case for separate, abrupt, age-linked stages in development has not convincingly been established. Of course, it depends on what is meant by a "stage," a point we must face in evaluating Piaget's theories. I simply find conceptions of processes, abilities, and functions that become interrelated in the course of development more tenable.

Mediational Views

On the principle of mediation, two points have received most attention, namely, fundamental establishment of the principle itself, and the functions of words as mediators.

Research comparing rats, very young children, and older subjects is especially relevant to the mediational principle. Such studies have made use of situations in which the subject must *shift* his response from one alternative to another in order to perform correctly (see Figure 6-3). The subject is first trained to respond to one member of a pair of stimuli. After he has learned to do so, the correct member is changed. In a *reversal shift* the correct member lies on the same dimension—it is merely the other member of the pair. In a *nonreversal shift* the correct member is identified by a different property of the stimuli—that is, correct members fall into a new class. In the first instance there must be an *intradimensional* shift, in the second an *extradimensional* shift.

Rats and very young children (three to four years of age) learn the extradimensional shift more easily, whereas older subjects learn the intradimensional shift more easily (Kelleher, 1956; T.S. Kendler, Kendler, and Wells, 1960; T. S. Kendler, 1963; Guy, 1969); retarded children resemble young children in this respect (Sanders, Ross, and Heal, 1965). This difference can be interpreted in mediational terms. The reversal shift really calls for the application of a general principle: the stimuli are classified by a certain attribute, and it is only necessary to determine what the subclasses are. The

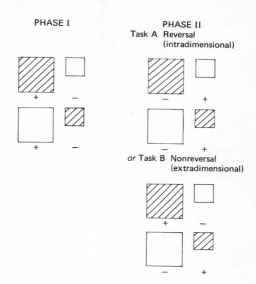

FIGURE 6-3   Arrangements for studying reversal and nonreversal shifts. (After Kendler and Kendler, 1961.) The symbols + and — indicate the member of pairs of stimuli reinforced during that phase.

subject learns this classification, then merely responds appropriately to the members of the class. But the nonreversal problem demands that a new classification be learned, so that the already acquired concept will not work. The very young child, like the rat, apparently does not learn the first discrimination conceptually but perceptually. When the nonreversal problem is presented, the task is quite similar to the first one—merely learning a new discrimination. In this sense the conceptual mediator of the adult interferes with learning the extradimensional-shift solution.

We can infer that equipping the subject with suitable mediators should facilitate learning. This result can be achieved by acting on verbal symbols. For example, the reversal-shift experiment has been conducted under conditions of verbalization versus no verbalization. No difference was found for four-year-olds (T. S. Kendler, Kendler, and Wells, 1960; H. H. Kendler and Kendler, 1961). However, when verbalization was varied, a difference appeared. Under the relevant condition the subjects spoke aloud the characteristics of the stimulus that determined correctness in the test situation. Thus, if "large" was

Table 6-1

Mean Trials to Criterion on Reversal Shift
under Verbalization Conditions (from T. S.
Kendler, 1963).

Age	Verbalization	Condition	
	Relevant	Irrelevant	None
4 years	16.1	30.4	22.2
7 years	8.3	35.6	8.8

to be correct, they were first trained to say "small"; in the irrelevant
condition, they were trained to say "black." Relevant verbalization
markedly facilitated performance of four-year-old children, but had
little effect on the seven-year-olds (see Table 6-1). (Irrelevant
verbalization was obviously detrimental for both ages.) These
findings are consistent with the supposition that older children
generate mediating processes spontaneously, but that younger
children must learn to do so.

But other variables also affect the rate of learning, as shown in
the optional-shift procedure. Here the test series is not reinforced;
the subject is simply allowed to indicate his choice between the
stimuli so that the basis for the initial response can be ascertained.
After a test to determine the preferred (dominant) dimension of color
or form of kindergarten children (sixty-two-to-seventy-three months),
Smiley and Weir (1966) found a highly significant tendency for
the dominant dimension to be learned more rapidly, indicating that
the performance is partly determined by characteristics of the child
apart from stimulus variables.

The effects of mediation are also apparent when the irrelevant
dimension varies during the shift phase. Tighe and Tighe (1967)
compared a condition when the irrelevant dimension was held
constant on each trial with a variable state in which the irrelevant
dimension varied within each trial. The nonreversal shift was learned
faster by the younger children under both stimulus conditions, with
little effect of the state of the irrelevant dimension. However, the
variable state produced a slower rate of learning on both kinds of
shift for the older subjects. Thus the variable dimension made it
more difficult for them to identify the correct dimension, in line with
a mediational interpretation.

Evidence for mediation in children also comes from experiments
on inferential behavior. Kendler and Kendler (1956) arranged for

preschool children to have different experiences which, when adequately combined, led to the solution of a problem. An apparatus was constructed to provide two subgoals $A \rightarrow B$ and $X \rightarrow Y$ and a major goal G. The experimental subjects had an opportunity to observe that one subgoal led to the major goal—that is, that $A \rightarrow B$ and that $B \rightarrow G$, therefore $A \rightarrow B \rightarrow G$, whereas the control subjects did not. The three experiences ($A \rightarrow B$, $X \rightarrow Y$, $B \rightarrow G$) were presented in four orders. All the experimental groups were superior to the control groups, showing that they could make the logical inference $A \rightarrow G$, derived from the separate experiences. The *order,* however, was significant, for when the $B \rightarrow G$ experience came first, there was little difference from the controls.

Comment   It is difficult to distinguish weak from strong mediation theory because, as mentioned, this approach either rests on a largely undifferentiated assumption or leads to the experimental testing of specific hypotheses. The evidence is quite compelling that intrinsic processes relatively separate from immediate stimulus conditions operate in children. Increase in this function (if not necessarily its abrupt appearance) with age also seems thoroughly established. However, before an adequate picture of the development of mediating processes can be formulated, many details must be worked out, including the effects of specific variables, some of which may prove powerful in explaining efficiency, and the interplay of language and conceptualizing.

The chief weakness of mediation theory resides precisely in its programmatic character. Investigators are still engrossed in trying to decide just what model (e.g., one-stage versus two-stage interpretations) should serve as a theoretical focus. For the most part then, mediation is more a principle than a theory. Little attention has been paid so far to emotional and motivational influences. While experimental conditions may include incentive or even arousal variations, dynamic principles have not really achieved an adequate treatment.

Piaget's Theory

The fourth kind of approach to children's conceptualizing is contained in the elaborate system adumbrated in numerous books over several decades by the Swiss psychologist Jean Piaget.

In its broad aspects the theory presents a systematic treatment of intellectual development from infancy to adulthood. In its specific aspects it contains a great many descriptions of age-specific behavior.

The general theory is based on an equilibrium model, in which basic processes proceed in an interrelated, balancing fashion to produce organized patterns of intellectual functions. Distinguishable within this progression are *schemes,* or holistically conceived behavior sequences characterized by consistency of response. A scheme may be a reflex, a skill (such as manipulation), a cognitive style, or any other recognizable mode of acting.

Equilibrium is featured by two general processes, *adaptation* and *organization.* Adaptation refers to any result of interaction between the person and the environment that renders behavior more efficient. It depends on *assimilation,* or using already present resources to act on the environment, with ensuing changes in the organism (this may depend on active effort, such as manipulating objects, or on intrinsic change, such as in meaning—in general, it refers to what is otherwise called "habit," "discrimination," etc.). Adaptation also depends on *accommodation,* or modifying behavior in accordance with environmental conditions (corresponding closely to what we usually call "learning"). Neither process can clearly be distinguished from the other, for they act in an interrelated fashion. Elements that have been assimilated, or incorporated into cognitive structure, determine the character of accommodation, but the latter, in turn, can lead to additional assimilation.

Organization refers essentially to cognitive structure. At any point in time some already-present system of experience and skills determines what behavior can occur. These systems change from one developmental period to another, partly as a function of biological factors—heredity and maturation—partly as a function of adaptation. Broadly speaking, organization proceeds from egocentric, perceptually determined, simple structures toward realistic, conceptually based, complex structures. The specific aspects of Piaget's theory concerns these changes.

A *period* in development is a subdivision when certain characteristics typify performance. With each period Piaget distinguishes *stages,* when the general characteristics are expressed in particular ways, representing steps, so to speak, along the way. In addition some stages are further subdivided, almost to the point of identifying highly specific responses.

I. Sensorimotor Period   (Ages birth to two years.) The origins of intellectual functioning lie in the acquisition of perceptual and manipulative skills, accompanied by an increasing control and direction of behavior. During the six successive stages, the infant progresses from simple innate reflexes through increasingly complex, coordinated, and skillful treatment of objects. By stage 5 (twelve to eighteen months), the child displays active discovery and experimentation. In stage 6 (eighteen months to two years), the child is capable of inventing new means to reach an objective—for example, he may reach through the bars of a playpen for a toy too wide to pull through, and, apparently without previous experience, turn the toy sideways so that it comes through the bars. (But we cannot assume that the child has had no relevant learning experience, since his performance could be based on inference based on past experiences with thin objects.)

II. Intuitive or Preoperational Thought[1]   (Two to seven years.) During this period the child begins to acquire truly symbolic functions, the ability to represent objects internally, anticipate consequences, and move more definitely toward controlled, planned behavior. Flavell (1963) points to the following distinguishing features. (1) *Egocentrism*: thought is personal, with an inability to view things from another person's point of view, a lack of awareness of his own thought processes, and what we have previously called a dominance of autistic components; (2) *centration:* an intensive focus on some particular aspect of an object, or an orientation to especially salient stimulus properties—this contrasts with decentration in which the older child can encompass various elements of the situation simultaneously and deploy attention in a wider, more versatile fashion; (3) *phenomenal states:* a succession of discrete, static impressions rather than integrated flowing patterns, in which one state is transformed into another; (4) *absence of stable equilibrium:* the relation between accommodative and assimilative processes has not achieved harmony—there are frequent contradictions between experience and antecedent cognitions; (5) *concreteness:* representations are closer to action than to abstract symbols, tending to be sequences of events; (6) *irreversibility:* lack of considered logical analysis, by which a thought process can change direction, return to previously tried possibilities, move back and forth—that is, it is inflexible. Thus the child uses *preconcepts,* or concrete, perceptually dominated modes of thinking (corresponding to the primitive thinking described by Werner).

The period of intuitive thought has been extensively investi-

---

[1] Flavell (1963) treats this and the next period as subperiods of a phase characterized by preparation for and organization of concrete operations.

gated, with a number of stages formulated in many areas, such as causality, space, and play. Roughly, there is a stage of rudimentary representational thought (two to four years), followed by simple representations (or intuitions) (four to five and a half years), and culminating in organized, articulated representation (five and a half to seven years).

III. Concrete Operations   (Seven to eleven years.) During this period the child has achieved complex, integrated systems of action, and has definite cognitive structures in which the equilibrating process is well established. Concrete operations, however, do not yield true classification, in which defining properties are independent of actual members, but rather *groupings*. However, the child at this period increasingly shows an ability to understand the logic of combining objects and of relationships among objects, including addition, multiplication, asymmetry, symmetry, and so on. Although Piaget deals with some nine aspects of grouping, research has concentrated on the operations of *transitivity* and *conservation*. Transitivity refers to inferences in which two objects are related by virtue of their relations to a third (e.g., if $A=B$ and $B=C$, then A? C; or if $A>B$ and $B>C$, then A ? C). Conservation means the ability to recognize that some property of an object remains invariant despite transformations in other properties (e.g., the amount of a piece of clay is the same regardless of its shape; the distance between two points is the same no matter what objects are placed between them).

IV. Formal Operations   (Eleven to fifteen years.) During adolescence, thinking becomes mature. Abstract concepts can be used, as the child becomes freed from close dependence on perception—indeed, he can now deal with objects in strictly symbolic fashion, without their actual presence. Formal operations include the formulation and logical ordering of propositions, the development of systematic arguments, the formation of true classifications and their manipulation, and the ability to cope with complex relationships (such as incongruities, opposites, and inferences).

This period is marked by a change in orientation (Piaget and Inhelder, 1956). Whereas the child at the concrete-operational stage is immersed mainly in the real, immediate situation, at the period of formal operations he begins to consider the *possible*. That is, he can mentally assemble alternatives and hypotheses by combining facts and applying logical analysis, and then decide on the most plausible or likely solution to a problem, thus transcending the data of sensory experience. He can move into the realms of scientific and mathematical thinking, philosophy, social problems, and so on.

SUMMARY

With conceptual behavior, we begin our discussion of thinking oriented to the realistic pole. Concepts are organizations of meaning, in contrast with attitudes (regulative systems that influence choice and decision making). In conceptual behavior words serve as eliciting stimuli, mediators, and responses. Concepts have denotative and connotative components, and vary in consistency and organization. Basic problems include development of conceptualizing ability, kinds of concepts acquired, and processes of attaining specific concepts. Theoretical approaches to conceptual development include: (1) *psychoanalysis,* which points to trends toward realistic, ego-controlled, secondary-process thinking, with an emphasis on early experience as the determinant of later behavior— however, situational determinants are insufficiently recognized; (2) *developmental progression,* which sees trends from diffuse to integrated cognitive systems—these theories tend to be global and sometimes rest on vague principles of learning; (3) *mediational* theories, which stress the acquisition of cognitive linking of facilitating mechanisms—however, this view continues to be more problem-oriented than truly systematic; and (4) the Piagetian theory of *cognitive development,* which employs an equilibrium model based on processes of adaptation and organization, and formulates successive periods with various stages from immature, sensory functioning through preconceptual and concrete operations to symbolic-abstract operations (criticisms appear in Chapter 7).

7

CONCEPTUAL BEHAVIOR IN CHILDREN

The several theories presented in the last chapter share at least two major characteristics. First, they unanimously posit that conceptualizing changes with age. They differ in their views of the fundamental processes themselves, as well as in the factors that determine change. Thus controversy continues on the comparative roles of maturational and environmental-experiential conditions, and on whether change is gradual, continuous, and cumulative, or sudden, discontinuous, and in stages. Second, all the theories emphasize that children's concepts differ from those of adults—especially in early properties of perception bound, concrete, global, and inaccurate (or "illogical") cognitions, which give way to perception free (symbolic), abstract, integrated, and informed (or "logical") cognitions. Disagreement is apparent in whether these differences should be viewed as primarily qualitative or mainly quantitative, and also on the most meaningful way to view the basic abilities involved. There is no final resolution in sight.

CAUSALITY

One area that has evoked considerable interest is the explanations that children give of natural phenomena. Piaget (1929) distinguished between "precausal" (five to six years of age) and more objective types of explanation (eleven to twelve years). The young child's thinking is characterized by realism, artificialism, and animism.

Realism is a confusion of the representation and the object—that is, the child does not separate his own experience from external reality. Four stages were described: (1) absolute realism, or no attempt to differentiate between thought processes and where objects seem to be; (2) immediate realism, or a distinction between thought processes and objects, although the former are located in the latter; (3) mediate realism, or continuing to treat thought processes as "a kind of thing... situated both in the body and in the surrounding air," and (4) subjectivism or relativism, or recognition that thought occurs inside oneself. Thus the child is said to pass from a confusion of self and world to a distinction between them. For example, Piaget gives protocols about the notion of thought, names, and dreams. At first the child confuses thought with the object thought about and only later understands the difference between thing or word and thought. With respect to names, the child moves from a stage of assuming that names are in the things themselves to a stage of recognizing that names are in the voice, the head, or the thought itself. Dreams are first considered to come from outside and to remain external, then to arise in the self but to be external, and finally to be internal in origin and to remain internal.

Artificialism means treating things as created by human acts. For example, the origin of the sun may at first be explained by saying that it was lighted with a match, and then, by intermediate stages, to the point where it is recognized that human activity had nothing to do with it.

Animism is treating objects as if they were alive. In the first stage (four to six years), the child believes that everything active is conscious (e.g., if a stone is moved, it feels it). At the second stage (six to seven years), consciousness is attributed to things that can move, such as the sun and moon, clouds, rivers, bicycles, and so on. At the third stage (eight to ten years), consciousness is attributed to things that can move of their own accord. A distinction is therefore drawn between movement exhibited by the object itself and that introduced by an external agent: the sun and wind are conscious, but not the bicycle. Finally, consciousness is restricted to the animal world (eleven years and older).

Some early studies found good agreement with Piaget (Grigsby, 1932; Russell and Dennis, 1939; Russell, 1940; Dennis, 1940;

Bruce, 1941). Others cast doubt on the distinctions drawn by Piaget, and on the conception of well-defined age-linked stages (Deutsche, 1937; Huang, 1943; Huang, Yang, and Yao, 1945; Huang and Lee, 1945—on examining the last of these studies, Strauss, 1951, suggested that animism was more evident than they thought; Oakes, 1947).

Efforts to clarify the issue of animism have continued. Klingensmith (1953) proposed that it is necessary to determine what the child means by "alive." He asked questions aimed at the attribution of sensory and functional properties to objects. His subjects (kindergarten, grades 1, 3, 5, 7) more frequently said that inanimate objects such as a burnt match, a broken dish, an alarm clock, and so on, were alive than attributed to them functions such as pain, ability to hear or see, thinking, and so on. After the kindergarten age there was a decrease in stating that inanimate objects that do not show activity are alive and in attributing to them sensory and functional properties. A clock and a lighted candle were said to be "alive" more often than the other four objects—and this tendency was still clearly evident at grade 7. Klingensmith concluded that children mean much less by the word "alive" than adults do, and much less than Piaget implied.

Crowell and Dole (1957) found considerable evidence of animism in college students. This phenomenon was examined by Simmons and Goss (1957) in the light of sentence context and type of instruction. Stimulus words included sea, earth, sun, pearl, wind, and match. The contexts in which they appeared were scientific statements, poetic metaphors, and mixed. Instructions were either "regular" (indicate whether living or nonliving), judge as if you were a scientist, or judge as if you were a poet. Forty percent or more in each of twelve groups of subjects (context and instructions varied) produced one or more animistic responses. And 100 percent did so under poetic instructions. The contexts had little effect. Thus, again, what the subject actually means by the word "living" depends on circumstances. This point is further demonstrated by Nass (1956), who found a greater incidence of "nonnaturalistic" (precausal) responses in children of grades 3 and 4 who were withdrawn and had less experience with the causal agent, and in response to the question "Why" versus "How." Cultural factors, such as traditional religious beliefs and language characteristics, also influence the incidence of animistic responses (Jahoda, 1958a).

Finally, we come to the most definitive study yet produced on this problem. Laurendeau and Pinard (1962) conducted a very careful and thorough study of the concept of dream (realism), the concept of life (animism), the origin of night (artificialism), the movement of clouds (explanation of natural motions), and the floating and sinking of objects (prediction and understanding of elementary physical laws). The first four areas began with general questions, leading progressively to more specific ones. The fifth area made use of concrete materials such as predicting whether a boat or a wooden bead or a marble would float. Samples consisted of fifty children (half of each sex) at each age from four to twelve. Four stages (with substages) were found for each of the five areas. (1) The very young child could not understand the problem (no comprehension, refusal). (2) At about age four or five, precausal types of explanation appeared. (3) Precausal explanations were mixed with the mention of physical or objective factors. (4) At age eight to ten, the child attained a mature understanding of causality, with the disappearance of precausal answers. Each stage, however, was spread widely over the age range, and the "age of accession" varied considerably. Although the various types of precausal explanation were associated with the problem posed (see Table 7-1), nevertheless there was internal consistency in the child's thinking. Answers among the five problems displayed high correlations (tetrachoric correlations range from .59 to .78), providing some support for the generally precausal character of the young child's concepts.

　　　Looft and Bartz (1969) have raised a number of unresolved issues. It is questionable whether the young child's explanations should really be regarded as animistic, or simply as reflecting inadequate knowledge. They also point to the difficult issue of "stages," discussed below. The role of experience and training, they suggest, has not been adequately investigated. Finally, the occurrence of animism in adults merits further attention, and at least some of what passes for adult animism may be quite different from that in the child. These authors cite the desirability of searching for additional theoretical approaches, such as might be derived from analyses of adult concept attainment, and of utilizing methods other than those so far mainly adapted from Piaget.

CONSERVATION AND TRANSITIVITY

Many studies have shown that physical concepts change with age, beginning with shape and size in the first couple of years and progressing toward more complex relations like "larger-smaller,"

Table 7-1

Frequency of Occurrence of Various Modes of Precausal Thinking in Various Problems. (Based on Laurendeau and Pinard, 1962).

| | Mode of Precausal Thinking | | | | |
Problem	Realism	Animism	Artificialism	Finalism	Dynamism
Concept of dream	143	0	184	49	0
Concept of life	0	198	0	0	0
Origin of night	0	48	257	309	0
Movement of clouds	13	205	218	74	152
Floating and sinking	6	65	0	80	127
	162	516	659	512	279

"middleness," and contradictory relations. Indeterminate numbers (such as "few," "many," "part") appear in the first few years (Pratt, Hartman, and Mead, 1954), and are vague at first, becoming increasingly differentiated during the elementary school years. Determinate numbers show a similar progression. Experiments reveal a gradual improvement in understanding concepts of number, quantity, and size, increasing discrimination, and growing versatility in the vocabulary needed (W.E. Martin, 1951).

With respect to the development of mathematical concepts, including the conservation of number (changing the arrangement, but not the number of items), and the projection of a straight line, Estes (1956) found that performance improves with age, but that no stages were evident. If the children could count, they counted correctly, even if the appearance of the array changed, and they did not confuse an apparent with an actual increase. If they could project a straight line in one direction, they could do so in another. She noted that the use of words is a possibly complicating factor. For example, a child might indicate that of two jars containing an equal number of marbles, one had more. When questioned further, the child would admit that it simply looked like more because of the difference in shape, but, in fact, he knew that he had placed the same number of marbles in the second jar.

Dodwell (1962) has pointed to Piaget's implication that the solution of number and conservation problems requires antecedent skills, including the concept of *class* and *linguistic facility* with names and logical relationships. Using children in kindergarten and the first three grades, he found that understanding of classification and of the concept of cardinal number develop rather independently of each other, although during the same age span. Thus, contrary to Piaget, the suggested sequence is variable at best.

Elkind has been especially assiduous in testing hypotheses from Piaget's numerous special theories. With respect to the ability to compose classes by adding subclasses, Piaget (1965a) stated that the child passes through stages of a general global impression of the class (five to six years), to a more differentiated conception, with recognition of subclasses (also five to six years), to an abstract conception. Piaget presented brown and white wooden beads in two boxes, with the former more numerous. At stage 1 the children knew that both kinds of beads were wooden, but could not correctly answer the question whether there were more brown or white wooden beads. At stage 2 they said that the brown beads were the same as the wooden beads, but only with difficulty learned that the brown beads were fewer than the wooden beads. At stage 3 they readily saw that the wooden beads were more numerous, because the white as well as the brown beads were wooden. Elkind (1961c) replicated Piaget's experiment with a different problem, calling for the number of boys and girls in the school class (subclasses), and the number of children (total class). There was a marked shift in frequency with age, but few fell into stage 2, explained by Elkind as a matter of the transitional character of the stage; substantial numbers of children at all four ages fell into both stages 1 and 3.

Number and Quantity

Similar stages were confirmed by Elkind (1964) for seriation (ability to arrange size variations in sequential order) and numeration (ability to count extending to the concept of number independent of counting). Discrimination was easiest, followed by seriation, and numeration was hardest. With respect to dimensionality, one dimension (sticks) was easiest, two dimensions (slats) intermediate, and three dimensions (blocks) was hardest. Three stages were also found for quantity concepts (Elkind, 1961d), associated with differences between gross quantity (e.g., "longer than"); intensive quantity (e.g., longer and wider); and extensive quantity (e.g., X is half of Y, X is twice Y).

Elkind (1961a) has also confirmed the findings of Piaget and Inhelder (1940) that the conservation of mass is achieved approximately by age seven to eight, of weight by age nine to ten, and of volume by age eleven to twelve. This performance was studied by using two clay balls, equal in quantity, with one subsequently changed in shape.

In a series of experiments, Wohlwill (1960a, b, 1963) demonstrated a progressive improvement with age in the transposition and transfer of both relational and absolute discrimination of numbers. The former is the ability to identify the larger of two numbers (e. g., 1 or 2, 2 or 3, etc.), whereas the latter refers to knowledge of a number itself (e.g., 5 versus any other number). Children of five and three-quarters years of age display good transposition and transfer of the learning of relational problems, but a full understanding of absolute numbers is not well established until the later elementary school years. Wohlwill interprets his findings as confirming the three familiar stages: (1) initial, preconceptual, and predominantly perceptual use of numbers; (2) intermediate and transitional processes; and (3) mediating, conceptual performance. This trend is especially apparent with symbolic (i.e., numbers) compared to perceptual (patterns of dots) or abstract materials (sets of geometric forms with shape, color, and orientation as irrelevant dimensions—the latter is a task that even adults find difficult in concept-attainment experiments).

Quantity

Bruner (1966) points out that ability to maintain quantity in the face of transformations depends on a distinction between the concept of identify (e.g., two samples of a liquid are the same amount) and the concept of equivalence (e.g., a liquid changed to a different container is the same liquid). Identity is presumed to be more fundamental than equivalence. Five-year-old children who recognized identity were found also to understand equivalence, but the reverse did not hold—that is, children who recognized equivalence did not necessarily manifest identity. The order of asking the questions is important since conservation was much more often demonstrated when the first query concerned identity than when it concerned equivalence. Bruner emphasizes that "sameness" is initially vague and global, then passes through a phase of differentiating the two concepts, and finally reaches an integration of the two. In another experiment a special training procedure demonstrated that children of five years or older can learn to separate their immediate perceptions from the correct interpretation. The four-year-olds, however, cannot do so because they focus on some single salient attribute (e.g., a change in shape of the vessels into which water is poured) and do not recognize contradictions in their own responses (e.g., that a judgment of the equality of two amounts conflicts with a judgment of different amounts when one of them is poured into a vessel of different shape).

Braine (1959) has shown that ability to infer length ("longer" or "shorter") improves with age (see Figure 7-1). Of special interest, however, is the fact that success appears much earlier than Piaget states (at ages five to six rather than seven to eight).[1] It is significant that Braine's use of a nonverbal method may have more objectively revealed an ability that verbal methods obscure.

In a similar vein, Mehler and Bever (1967) found that children as young as two years and six months can correctly make judgments of "more." First, two rows of four objects were presented in identical spacing, followed by a similar row of four paired with a shorter row of six. When clay pellets were used, the children were asked which row had "more"; when M & M candies were used, they were told to select the row they wished to eat and to eat them. Under both conditions the youngest children were quite accurate, with a *decrease* to age four, followed by an increase, but this change was much less apparent with the candies. The authors suggest that the very young child actually possesses the necessary cognitive capacities to achieve simple conservation, but that he later develops an explicit strategy (he learns to count). The decline in conservation stems from a temporary close dependence on perceptual processes, which may be overcome, for example, by strong enough incentives. Beilin (1968) severely disagreed with Mehler and Bever, pointing to certain methodological features of their experiment that might have confused "more of" with "more than in the face of transformation." He devised a task to separate judgments when elements are added or subtracted from those when transformations in arrangement occurred. His youngest children displayed a high level of performance on additivity, with an increase in age (that is, not a decline and rise). Even the oldest children (four years four months to four years seven months) displayed a low level of conservation under transformation. Bever, Mehler, and Epstein (1968) responded by reporting additional studies that reaffirm their contention that even very young children possess the requisite cognitive skills to conserve number, but that they are limited in their exercise by insufficient development of memory, attention, and other resources. Beilin (1968) adduces still other criticisms of this position, maintaining that the weight of

---

[1] Braine also tested the appearance of the concept of position order, with similar results. He finds, in support of Piaget, a high correlation between this concept and the inference of measurement.

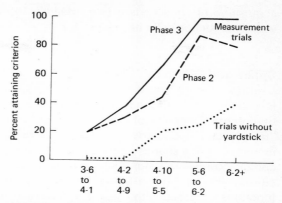

FIGURE 7-1   Percentage of subjects finding the correct upright by inference (measurement trials) and by direct comparison (trials without yardstick). (From Braine, 1959.)

evidence runs against conservation in very young children. Piaget (1968) himself criticized the Mehler and Bever experiments because of their interpretation of the results, particularly that the procedure permitted a valid test of conservation. In reply, Mehler and Bever (1968) point to some differences between the studies conducted by Piaget and their own, and to their use of controls that further support their findings. They agree, however, that their use of the term *conservation* may not be in accord with Piaget's.

Thus there remains a point of considerable interest, practical as well as theoretical. Regardless of which view ultimately wins, the implications for educational strategy are extremely important. Can we train children to think in certain ways earlier than has been accepted? Or is educational practice inevitably linked with characteristics that only appear at a relatively fixed age?

Smedslund (1961 a-e) has reported several experiments that show little effect on conservation of reinforcement and special training conditions, once it has been "normally" (i.e., not experimentally) attained. He suggests that the development of conservation is facilitated by conditions when experience with addition and subtraction conflicts with evidence of deformation of objects. Results obtained by Gruen (1965) also tend to support the principle of cognitive conflict. However, negative evidence has been reported by Winer (1968) and by Smith (1968). The possibility that Smedslund's principle is untenable does not rule out other ways to facilitate the acquisition of conservation (e.g., Beilin's 1965 demonstrations and verbal instruction) (Smith, 1968).

Space and Distance

Using a variety of tasks modeled on Piaget's, Dodwell (1963) has investigated spatial concepts in children from kindergarten through third grade. Examples of the tasks are constructing a straight line of "telephone poles" between two points designated by the experimenter, drawing shapes ranging from irregular to geometrical to more complex forms, and reproducing geometrical sections resulting from cutting an area from a figure. The general ability to perform such functions increased with age, but without a well-defined progression. He differentiated the three familiar stages, but found that most of his subjects were "mixed" in this respect, rather than clearly assignable to a particular stage.

Smock and Cox (1969) have studied the conservation of multiple space relations in a situation devised by Piaget and Inhelder (1956). Objects are located in a miniature landscape. Under "static" or "copy" conditions, the subject's landscape lies in the same orientation as the model's; under "transformed" conditions, the test landscape is rotated 180 degrees. Children of higher mental ability, at the hypothesized critical age (seven to eight and one-quarter years) displayed more progress toward conservation, as reflected in fewer errors and less use of prelogical strategies.

Prerequisite to understanding the spatial coordinate system, according to Piaget and Inhelder (1956), is attainment of the conservation of distance (about seven years, with the coordinate system at about nine years). Shantz and Smock (1966) hypothesized that every child who uses the spatial coordinate system also manifests distance conservation, and that the reverse would also hold true (inability to conserve distance is associated with inability to use the coordinate system). Distance conservation was measured by several tests. One was placing between two toy trees a board taller than the trees and asking whether the distance was the same as when the space was empty. Another was asking whether the distance was the same when the experimenter's finger was moved from left to right as when it was moved from right to left. The coordinate system was assessed by horizontality and verticality tests. For example, a bottle one-quarter full of liquid was presented, and the subject was asked to point with his finger on an identical empty bottle to the level there would be if the empty bottle were upside down. For verticality, a pyramid ("mountain") was presented, with the child asked to stick pins with objects attached in a straight line at locations designated by the experimenter. If verticality is not understood, the pins are placed perpendicular to the slope, rather than with reference to some external axis. The hypotheses were supported, although not totally.

Ford (1970) has also employed the "waterline" task to test the hypothesis that grasping distance conservation is prerequisite to correct performance (i.e., correct judgment of horizontality), with subjects judging drawings either against an actual jar (perception task) or in its absence (prediction task). Results were generally in line with the Piagetian hypothesis, but a lack of relationship between the perception and prediction tasks casts doubt on the notion of a general coordinate system since Piaget regarded both versions of the task as equivalent predictors.

College Students

Beyond the critical periods of childhood, only limited numbers of subjects at ages eleven to eighteen manifest conservation of volume (considerably more can conserve mass and weight). Testing the age range of seventeen to thirty-seven years, Elkind (1962c) reported a much higher incidence of conservation of volume (however, significantly less often for females). This better performance can be attributed partly to intelligence (since college students average higher than high school students). No systematic trend with age was apparent for the males, but there was a significant increase for the females. Elkind suggests that sex role is one factor, since girls who continue in college tend to be characterized by less feminine role characteristics. In any event it is quite evident that there is no sharp break between younger and older persons in the development of quantity concepts.

OTHER KINDS OF CONCEPTS

Varying in details, but within the same broad distinctions between preoperational and mature characteristics, investigators have dealt with many other areas of children's thinking (Russell, 1956). Strauss (1954) developed Piaget's ideas with regard to *rules* by proposing a seven-stage scale, from a "realistic" phase (rules exist by definition) through the social-interaction phase mentioned by Piaget to concepts of personal responsibility. He has also presented a nine-stage scale for the development of monetary meanings (Strauss, 1952).

Concepts of time manifest consistent changes, moving from vague, poorly informed, and inconsistent notions to the differentiated system of the adult (Oakden and Sturt, 1922; Springer, 1951).

Nagy (1948) found that concepts of death change from animism (everything is alive) through artificialism[1] (death is personified) to an understanding of death as an inevitable process. Other studies show age-related changes in social concepts (Meltzer, 1925; Ordan, 1945), kinship terms (from precategorical through categorical to relational) (Danziger, 1957; Elkind, 1962a), and religious concepts (Elkind, 1961b, 1962b, 1963). Economic concepts are learned quite slowly through the first six grades (Sutton, 1962). When adapted to the school curriculum, the learning of social concepts is facilitated (Rogers and Layton, 1966).

Conceptions of bodily functions in the early years are global and inaccurate (Nagy, 1953), but become increasingly accurate and differentiated with age (Gellert, 1962). Concepts of right and left similarly display Piaget's distinctions among global (age seven to eight), concrete differentiation (ages seven to eight and ten to eleven), and abstract differentiation (age ten to eleven) stages.

Finally, moral judgment has been discussed by Piaget (1965b). This topic will be postponed to Chapter 18.

THE CONCEPTION OF STAGES

Piaget has chosen to treat conceptual development as a matter of successive, qualitatively different stages. Opposed to this view is the principle that cognitive growth is the progressive and gradual acquisition of skills, in which quantitative changes, such as increased knowledge, vocabulary, attention span, and so on, are important. It is therefore necessary to look for a reconciliation of these positions.

First, Piaget has recognized that stages are not wholly fixed and invariant, but are influenced by conditions of the task, by the sociocultural conditions of learning, and by individual differences. Hunt (1969), especially, has reviewed the matter of experience and special circumstances.[2] Therefore it is desirable to distinguish between a "stage" as a level or step in a particular process and a "stage" as an overall state (Flavell, 1963).

Second, the criteria by which Piaget defines successive stages are not precise, specifically stated properties (Pinard and Laurendeau,

[1] Not found in Catholics by Gartley and Bernascini (1969).

[2] For example, the attainment of conservation quantity is delayed in deaf children (Nass, 1964). But Furth (1961) shows that this depends on how relevant language experience is for the task.

1969). Rather, they emphasize the holistic, patterned character of thinking, which represents one of Piaget's most important contributions. Piaget implies that all components of a stage develop in unison. The evidence runs counter to this view. Flavell and Wohlwill (1969) present a revised model that differentiates as determinants of performance: (1) the actual cognitive characteristics of the child at the time (i.e., the level and kind of skill), (2) the task properties (the rules or demands posed by the structure of the task), and (3) the weight (a coefficient) to be assigned to the task for a particular child. This treatment affords considerable flexibility in describing the child's performance, and can lead to greater freedom in linking theoretical predictions to empirical data.[1]

Third, the conception that stages are inherently qualitatively different appears to be untenable insofar as specific processes are concerned. (The holistic, interrelated patternings mentioned above, however, appear to provide a useful qualitative distinction.) At best, the question remains open whether *some* changes may be qualitative rather than quantitative (Flavell and Wohlwill, 1969).[2]

Fourth, the tight linking of stages, whether specific or general, with specific ages, implying a mainly maturational basis, requires examination. The chief problem concerns the invariant character of acquisition. Are the requisite attainments always acquired in the same order? Once attained, are they permanent? Some of the work we have reviewed clearly casts doubt on both matters. Fowler (1962) concludes that children can probably learn many things earlier than is conventionally supposed.

One direction needed to resolve continuing ambiguities in the stage theory is longitudinal studies, as recognized, for example, by Laurendeau and Pinard (1962). A major effort is a study by Almy, Chittenden, and Miller (1966), who investigated conservation of number, conservation of liquid, seriation, and concepts of floating and sinking. The subjects were drawn from a lower-class and a middle-class school, from kindergarten, first, and second grades. In addition to a cross-sectional study, the investigators continued to interview the kindergarten children who remained in the schools, at approximately half-year intervals until the beginning of the second grade. The cross-sectional data agreed quite well with the stages described by Piaget. The longitudinal data, however, strikingly revealed the significance of individual variation. Thus, of forty-one

[1] Ultimately, too, theory may well find a meaningful reconciliation between the views of Piaget and of Werner (Glick and Wapner, 1968).

[2] Witness the shift to dominantly conceptual thinking in the reversal- nonreversal-shift experiments.

children in the middle-class school, 68 percent displayed irregular progress (including deviations from age expectations and many instances of regression) ; of twenty-four children in the lower-class school, 75 percent did not follow the expected sequence. Some evidence was also found for the role of experiential factors, including differences between the schools and a generally higher level of performance for the longitudinal subjects (possibly reflecting both the effect of repeated interviews, and also the character of school instruction, which included some innovations in the mathematics program).

EVALUATING PIAGET

The enormous impact of Piaget's work is sufficient testimonial to the fecundity of his ideas, not only in generating research but also in affecting the character of the whole field of education.

The general theory requires little comment. In many respects, particularly in its description of the broad course of development, it resembles long-existing views. The principle of progressive adaptation and trends toward higher, complex forms of thinking accord with the evolutionary, biological character of much psychological theorizing at the general level. This view has the great merit of counterbalancing the atomistic, specific acquisition position contained in conditioned-response treatments of learning. Piaget stresses the holistic, interrelated course of conceptual learning, with progress from one level of organization to another.

Criticisms of Piaget's methods continue to be expressed, including his reliance on small numbers of subjects, inadequacy of sampling, and the lack of careful controls. However, these criticisms have become secondary in the wake of so many studies that rectify these defects.

The tendency of Piaget (and some of his followers) to impose a logical structure on the performance of children, as required by the theory, is certainly open to criticism. There often seem to be interpretations that fit the theory better than the actual data. This point is evident in the various specific formulations of stages. Rather than well-defined fixed qualitatively different phases, appearing at definite ages, there is much overlapping and mixture of stages. It is only in the modal findings of cross-sectional studies that the expected succession emerges. Although these general patterns cannot be ignored, the actual course of conceptual acquisition, as well as the status and change in individual children, can be considerably obscured by adhering to the demands of the logical structure.

Despite ostensibly allowing for environmental and other conditions, Piaget does not stray far from the principle of invariant sequences closely tied to inherent biological properties. It would be foolish to ignore hereditary and maturational factors, but to err on the other side is equally limiting. Much remains to be learned about special conditions (not the least of which is educational techniques) in conceptual development. There is evidence that the processes involved can be modified, both in their time of acquisition and in their properties. Part of the problem involves the study of actual process, of not so much *how* the child learns as *why* he learns. Piaget is more helpful in describing children's concepts than he is in explaining them. Gagné and Bruner clearly have an advantage in this respect.

Finally, we can point to Piaget's very heavy reliance on specific tasks (and questions) and on the child's verbalizations. Some of the studies mentioned above illustrate the risks of equating the child's words with his understanding (or his ability to behave successfully given certain conditions). We require better perspective on the relation between language development and the ability to mediate. While not denying the importance of this relation, we do point to the potential difference between understanding and experience and the particular verbal facilities of the child. Of significance here are the comparative roles of denotative and connotative meanings, to be discussed below.

CONDITIONS AFFECTING CHILDREN'S CONCEPTS

There are several explicit factors that investigators have linked with conceptual development. Most of them have already been mentioned, but the Piagetian approach has tended to treat them in a peripheral manner. *Age*, of course, is central in Piaget and requires no additional discussion.

Intelligence

In general, IQ, as customarily measured, shows little or no relation to conceptualizing (Peterson, 1932, Deutsche, 1937; Schuessler and Strauss, 1950). The problem, however, is complicated by a kind of circular reasoning, since increasing intelligence is partly a function of increasing ability to conceptualize.

Osler and her associates (Osler and Fivel, 1961; Osler and Trautman, 1961) point out that the role of intelligence depends on the task. Their high-IQ subjects frequently displayed "sudden" solutions, indicative of an hypothesis-testing strategy. When formal, abstract conditions were compared with concrete (object) conditions, children of superior intelligence were slower under the latter condition. The concrete condition, containing more irrelevant cues, permits the generation of more hypotheses, and also promotes learning by gradual S-R association [this part of the interpretation was not supported in a replication by Wolff (1967)]. Mishima and Tanaka (1966) have further reported that hypothesis-testing strategy is typical not only of superior intelligence but also of older children of lower intelligence, indicating the role of mental age rather than IQ.

Such studies illustrate the complex problems that persist in the study of conceptualizing. Not only do tests of intelligence provide inadequate predictors of performance in concept-attaining tasks, but general qualitative differences may be found at different levels of intelligence. In many tasks, strategy variations may make little difference, but if we establish conditions especially appropriate for the presumed qualitative differences to operate, performance differences may emerge more sharply. That is, abilities of "hypothesis testing" and/or "problem finding" may prove more significant than the abilities reflected in intelligence tests.

Language and Meaning

We have already discussed the problems that arise in attempting to analyze relations between language acquisition and conceptual development. Bruner (1964) reports studies that show the successive emergence in the child of action, image, and word, with an increasing importance of language as the "implement of knowing." The acquisition of language mediators helps to free the child from dependence on immediate perceptual information, and thus provides efficient mechanisms for symbolic and abstract treatment of objects. Sigel (1953, 1954) has shown that the classification performance of children is largely independent of stimulus conditions, such as whether the task uses objects or words, relative to perceptual classifications: Conceptual behavior increases regardless of whether objects or names are used. He suggests that *meaning* is the crucial variable.

The *type* of definition of words changes gradually with age, with younger children more often providing uses, descriptions, and demonstrations, and older children more often giving synonyms and explanations (Feifel and Lorge, 1950).

Connotative meaning increasingly gives way to *denotative meaning*. In a study using Osgood semantic differential scales, first-graders much more than sixth-graders reported objects as differing in dimensions other than those in which they actually differed (Ervin and Foster, 1960). Other studies also reveal changes toward more conventional, stable, and denotative meanings (Donahoe, 1961; Palermo, 1963). A very important question, mostly ignored in studies of conceptual development, is to what extent children's concepts depend on the dominance of connotative meaning. Definitions of "correct" invariably refer to adequacy from the mature point of view. And yet the child may be quite accurately reflecting his own experiences or feelings. Again, the necessity to examine what the child "means" is evident.

DiVesta (1965) investigated connotative meaning through the use of modifiers (adjectives) elicited by familiar nouns. Evaluative and potency aspects decrease, with little change in colors (a denotative property) or activity. Some words become more common in their meanings, and others become more idiosyncratic. These changes are indicated by the standard deviation of the index. It appears, according to my calculations, that abstract concepts acquire more diverse connotation, with the opposite holding for concrete concepts. Figure 7-2 presents mean ranks for the twelve words judged most abstract and the twelve considered most concrete. This interesting result merits further research since it suggests that the effects of experience differ for different kinds of concepts—and that a key element in so-called "abstract" concepts is actually their connotative meaning. Experience appears to lead to *more denotative* emphasis in concrete objects, but more *connotative* significance in abstract ideas. The widening world of the child thus seems to lead in two directions.

DiVesta (1966) has further shown that age changes in connotative meaning are most likely for concepts with an emotional character. Neutral words produce semantic differential ratings in children more like those of adults, indicating the effects of early learning. Too much overlooked, this point suggests that the highly standardized, emotionally neutral tasks almost invariably used in experiments need to be balanced by the study of more personally relevant and emotionally arousing tasks.

Social Class and Milieu

Lower- compared to middle-class children seem to display slower conceptual development (Almy et al., 1966), even at comparable IQ levels (Findlay and McGuire, 1957). The greater experience of middle-class children with intellectual "games," as well as moti-

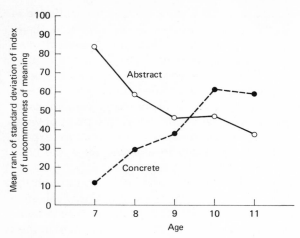

FIGURE 7-2 Changes in connotative meaning for abstract and concrete words. (Computed from data in DiVesta, 1965.) Note: The lower the mean rank, the larger the standard deviation, and hence the less common the meaning. The abstract words were freedom, life, knowledge, pleasure, peace, success, truth, progress, death, and sympathy. The concrete words were horse, cloud, cup, smoke, egg, cat, girl, book, rope, river, star, and chair.

vational factors, may be partly responsible. For example, differences appear in verbal, but not in nonverbal tasks (Siller, 1957; Salzinger et al., 1967). Lower-class children perform better when offered a tangible reward (a prize), middle-class children better with intangible rewards (verbal reinforcement) (Zigler and DeLabry, 1962, using seven-year-olds with mental age controlled). Although lower-class children are inferior on discrimination learning, pretraining on this kind of task eliminates the difference in subsequent concept attainment (Scholnick, Osler, and Katzenellenbogan, 1968). These investigators used a tangible reward, which may also have benefited the lower-class subjects.

Cultural differences in beliefs, attitudes, and concepts stem from variations in experience. Nevertheless, the broad pattern of conceptual development may well be similar in widely different milieus. For example, Goodnow (1962) found that European and Chinese children in Hong Kong, from different social-class backgrounds, manifested the same sequence in attaining conservation of space, weight, and volume, although the European children performed at a somewhat higher level.

Perhaps more crucial than cultural milieu is schooling (Green-field, 1966; Maccoby and Modiano, 1966; Greenfield, Reich, and Olver, 1966). The child who does not go to school continues to rely heavily on perceptual, concrete modes of representation and thus makes slow progress in conservation and grouping, especially when verbal contexts are involved. However, schooling forces the child to learn alternative ways of treating objects, induces comparisons, promotes verbal expression, and encourages the development of the symbolic functions on which abstraction depends.

Differences between sociocultural groups, assuming compar-able intelligence, may reflect variables of interest, verbal understand-ing, experience with test situations, and the like, rather than cognitive processes themselves. A principle to be stressed is the relevance of task, situation, and incentive to the characteristics of the subject.

It appears likely that differences between milieus are greater in older than younger children because factors such as schooling and home environment can be expected to have cumulative effects. Probably it will be necessary to make careful distinctions between conceptual *ability* and conceptual *performance*. Perhaps they cannot be completely differentiated—and perhaps both are similarly influ-enced by milieu. Nevertheless, it may turn out that lower-class children are disadvantaged more predictably in certain kinds of tasks—for example, verbal, conceptual ones. And the difference may increase more with age in level of performance than in the funda-mental abilities required.

Cognitive Style

Coming increasingly under intensive investigation are variables of *how* individuals organize and manage information. I have touched on this point in distinguishing possible differences in strategy between children high and average in intelligence. Cognitive style, in some respects, may be a general function of age. Heidbreder (1928), for example, pointed out that responsiveness to problems is strongly evident in children older than age six, but is only occasionally evident in younger children. She also noted the change from more subjective to more objective attitudes, so often mentioned above. Kagan et al. (1964) showed in detail how analytic and reflective attitudes in-crease with age. Field independence also increases with age (Witkin, Goodenough, and Karp, 1967), signifying a general movement from global perception, dominated by perceptual response, toward differ-entiation and greater freedom from stimulus properties. Saltz and Sigel (1967) suggest that young children tend to "overdiscriminate" (that is, distinguish objects as separate entities when they are actually alike), leading to narrow conceptualizations. In their study, the youngest subjects (age six) actually made *fewer* errors than adults in the most difficult discrimination, when a correct response called for comparing similar stimuli (i.e., they noticed very small details). Thus lack of conservation may stem from narrow conceptualizing.

Sex differences in cognitive style appear as early as the pre-school years (Lewis et al., 1968). Wallach and Kogan (1965) show that fifth-grade boys categorize more broadly than girls, as holds also for adults (Pettigrew, 1958).

Training and Experience

In general, special training procedures facilitate performance. One example is improvement in "learning set," or accomplishment in a series of related tasks (Reese, 1963). Another example is "over-training," or continued practice beyond the criterion. This procedure results in better performance on "shift" problems, both intradimensional and extradimensional (Eimas, 1966). Still another is verbal training, which can be interpreted as promoting the "acquired distinctiveness of cues" (Spiker, 1963).

An experiment by Lacey (1961) was explicitly designed to equip children with verbal mediators. He first trained subjects to label sets of stimuli (drawings of houses or faces) by a nonsense name (e.g., HUV). A transfer phase followed in which the subject had to learn new names for these stimuli, as follows: (1) a new name for the same set of stimuli as before (e.g., the four HUV houses or faces were now to be named CEY; or if two houses had been named NAZ and two others DIT, each pair was to be called BAW and GOS, respectively)—thus in effect the subject merely had to substitute a new label for a previously learned category; (2) new names had to be learned either for subsets within a larger category or for two subsets previously separately labeled (e.g., the four HUV houses now formed two subcategories to be named GOS and CEY, respectively, or two pairs previously called NAZ and DIT now formed a single category to be named BAW). In the first condition, the name learned initially operates as an effective mediator for the transfer task, but does not do so in the second condition. Control groups performed the same tasks, but with different stimuli introduced into the transfer phase (i.e., faces were substituted for houses, or houses for faces). No mediation should have operated in these groups. In fact, under the mediating conditions, the experimental groups were significantly superior to the control groups, with the opposite effect demonstrated for the interfering conditions.

In the reversal-nonreversal-shift situation, Tighe (1965) showed that reversal shifts in first-grade children require fewer trials to learn if preceded by training in same-different discriminations. This effect depends on the amount of training—it occurs only with "over-training" (here, fifteen or twenty-five trials beyond achieving the criterion of learning) (Youniss and Furth, 1965) and, apparently, only when training does not call for verbalizing (Mumbauer and Odom, 1967).

Finally, special training facilitates the kinds of performance studied by Piaget, such as conservation of length and area, substance, number, and weight (Beilin and Franklin, 1962; Brison, 1966; Sonstroem, 1966; Brainerd and Allen, 1971).

It would be difficult to overestimate the importance of experience and special training for an ultimate clarification of conceptual development. Not only do these variables have great significance for the resolution of theoretical issues (the age-stage linkage, the role of individual differences, and the accumulative-growth versus qualitative pattern-succession interpretations), but they also concern the practical matter of educating children. It makes a great deal of difference to know how much and in what ways training influences the child's conceptualizing.

Situational Variables

Smedslund (1969) has pointed out several sources of error that may enter into experiments, unless they are controlled, such as failure to understand instructions, failure to process other information correctly (i.e., as the experimenter expects), forgetting, guessing or acting on previously acquired irrelevant tendencies, direct perception (i.e., he makes the correct response without the cognitive processes hypothesized to operate—he already knows, as it were, or behaves in a simpler manner than the experimenter supposes), and irrelevant procedures generated in the experimental session.

Variations in the *form* of presentation appear in a study by Glick and Wapner (1968). Subjects throughout the age-range of eight to eighteen years showed a higher level of solving transitivity problems under concrete (physical comparison) than under strictly verbal modes of presentation. Conservation was found by Sigel, Saltz, and Roskind (1967) to be inversely related to irrelevant cues.

An experiment by Siegel and Andrews (1962) varied *incentives* (a button versus a small toy) in a two-choice uncertain-outcome situation that required guessing in which of two containers an object, which could be kept if found, was hidden. The incentive difference influenced the child's tendency to approximate the objective probability of occurrence. Although the choice of the more probable alternative increased for both rewards, it was consistently greater under the high reward. As the authors point out, these results indicate a considerably earlier age for the concept of probability than Piaget implies.

Research thus indicates that gross age trends can be misleading by failing to allow for the effects of other variables. Similarly, as repeatedly shown, any variable may be modified in its influence by some other condition. The principle of relevance applies to situational as well as to personality variables.

SUMMARY

We have reviewed research based on Piagetian principles. Children's concepts develop from preoperational to more differentiated, abstract stages. These changes are apparent in their explanations of natural phenomena (causality), conservation, transitivity, and other concepts. Evidence shows that the postulated stages are not fixed but overlapping, and are not tightly linked with specific ages. Individual variations are common, and progress is influenced by task properties, sociocultural factors, and personality variables. In evaluating Piagetian theory, we must recognize that it imposes logical structure on cognitive development and that it relies heavily on specific tasks, verbalizations, and performances. Conditions that affect children's concepts include intelligence, language development, class and cultural milieu, cognitive style, training and experience, and situational variables.

8

THEORY AND METHOD IN THE STUDY OF CONCEPT ATTAINMENT

Experiments with adults entail tasks in which the subject must determine how to name and classify stimulus objects with which he has already had a great deal of experience, and where he must decide whether some concept, or relationship, or rule he has previously had ample opportunity to acquire will work in this particular situation.

Concepts represent linkages between objects; a child must first learn them before he can use them. The adult knows much about these linkages, and therefore needs primarily to select those that are appropriate. The development of language increasingly equips the individual with an efficient mechanism for dealing with such linkages—that is, with convenient, readily manipulated symbols. Once sufficient experience has accumulated, symbolic processes can be used to label, compare, and classify objects. It is with these cognitive activities that experiments on concept attainment are mainly concerned.

The adult makes use of past experience in at least the following ways:

1. *Identification and classification of objects.* Concepts at the lowest level represent generalized categories of objects. For example, a concept of "cat" refers to no particular cat, but constitutes a

general cat in reference to which never-before-seen-cats can be identified or recognized. This means that the individual is not continually confronted with totally new experiences requiring new responses. In addition, possessing experience that has yielded other categories, the individual readily distinguishes cats from dogs, Siamese from alley cats, black from yellow cats, and so on. At higher levels, recognition may be more complex. Thus "animal" refers to no particular animal, for both cats and dogs may be identified as animals. At any level, it must be understood, the object is identified and classified on the basis of both denotative and connotative dimensions. The general cat has properties of size, color, composition, shape, and so on—it is a rather small, furry, black animal with a long tail, rounded paws, pointed ears, and so on, but it may also be purring, playful, soft, and agreeable to one person, while sinister, slinking, uncontrollable, and vicious to another person.

2. *Symbolic manipulation.* The organization of experience involves more than the integration of sense impressions against the background of which recognition occurs; it is represented by symbolic responses that may occur in the absence of external objects. The predominant modes of symbolic responses are words, gestures, and images, which are probably not distinct from each other, although words have come to be the most common means of symbolizing, at least in communicating concepts. Through symbolic responses, concepts can be given names, and in this way manipulated in many complex ways. Putting it another way, the concept can be detached from specific instances, by means of a word, and thus used to organize experience over and beyond the more simple recognition function. This symbolic process corresponds to mediation, and includes both the weak and intrinsic organization versions discussed in Chapter 5.

METHODS

The foregoing remarks suggest the major directions in which investigative techniques have gone. The subject must learn how to respond to stimuli in some fashion not determined by the properties of the stimuli considered as separate objects. As Gardner (1962) points out, no concept is involved when each stimulus is assigned a separate, individual response—such situations may be employed to measure reaction time, discrimination, absolute judgment, or simple learning. The basic requirements for a concept problem are that the same response is demanded for more than one stimulus, and that the stimuli vary in more than one dimension. From that point of departure, the situation can be rendered more complex by requiring different responses for different groups of stimuli, by including properties or combinations of them that distinguish positive from negative responses, and so on.

In a concept problem, two kinds of criteria are available to assess performance. First, we could record responses to determine when the subject is able to name the stimuli correctly. This criterion can be extended to measure transfer to related or new sets of stimuli, thus differentiating a learning from a performance stage. Second, we could interrogate the subject at selected points to determine what principle or rule he is following in responding to the stimuli. For the most part we would expect that the response measure and the verbal statement would correspond, and that we could infer the concept from either. However, there may be occasions when this relation does not hold true. For example, the subject may solve problems correctly without being able to formulate the principle that makes them correct (see, for example, Bugelski and Scharlock, 1952). By the same token, what the experimenter records as "incorrect" may actually be indicators of a rule the subject is using (for example, the inconsistent concepts noticed by Reed, 1946a). Thus one must be careful in drawing inferences about the cognitive process itself.

The Introspective Technique   One method calls on the subject to report about his cognitive processes. Early investigators relied on this device (English, 1922; Fisher, 1916; Moore, 1910). For instance, a series of figures may be exposed tachistoscopically until the subject believes that he has discovered something about them. The exposures are stopped while the subject reports what he has discovered.

Although this approach has mainly historical interest, it has not been abandoned. In fact, recent investigators of hypothesis sampling have found that direct questioning of the subject yields crucial information (Levine, 1962; Rogers and Haygood, 1968). Introspective procedures may in the future provide evidence bearing on connotative and unconscious aspects of conceptualizing. Perhaps other valuable uses will also be found.

The Learning Method   Here the subject is placed in a situation where he must learn to respond to varied stimuli according to a rule or principle. The response may be verbal (such as a name) or a motor act (such as pressing a certain lever or button when the appropriate stimulus is present (Bourne and Haygood, 1959). Typically, the conditions resemble a memorizing experiment. The subject may first be taught some names (perhaps nonsense syllables) for a series of stimuli, say, by the anticipation method. He is then shown a second series of stimuli, each of which has something in common with the first series, to see if he can name them correctly (Heidbreder, 1924, 1946; Hull, 1920; Kuo, 1923; Reed, 1946a; Trabasso and Bower, 1968; Johnson and White, 1969).

The Problem-solving Technique   The third approach is similar to the preceding one, except that the subject does not go through a controlled learning phase. He may be presented with a collection of stimuli, either simultaneously arrayed or successively appearing, and required to classify them or to select them in a way that satisfies the experimenter. The subject may be told, for example, that each drawing in a series is, or is not, an instance of the same concept; he is to examine them and explain, or define, the concept (Smoke, 1932; Hovland and Weiss, 1953). Or an instance may be chosen by the experimenter and the subject asked to select others that belong with it (Bruner, Goodnow, and Austin, 1956). In another variation, the subject is exposed to an array of stimuli and asked to select those that belong together (Bolles, 1937; Goldstein and Scheerer, 1941; Heidbreder, 1949); or categories may be indicated by examples, with the subject asked to sort instances accordingly (Grant and Berg, 1948).

GENERAL THEORIES OF CONCEPT ATTAINMENT

In conceptualizing problems, the individual can start with an idea, or principle, and endeavor to name or classify instances in accordance with it. Or he can begin with specific instances, examine their properties, and evolve a basis for relating one object to another, or for grouping objects together. Traditional terms for these approaches are *abstraction* and *generalization*. The process of abstracting signifies the linking of one sensory experience to another, in which some details are left out and others become dominant—in this sense the concept is a symbolic response for these dominant details. The process of generalizing signifies that a dominant detail (or group of details), is adopted as a basis for responding similarly to separate objects, and for responding to other objects similarly characterized.

In actual practice it is often difficult to distinguish abstraction from generalization. For example, the question may be asked whether concepts result only from the activity of successively abstracting "common elements" in a series of stimulus patterns, or whether concepts are formed by setting up a generalization (or hypothesis) and then confirming or disproving it by examination of stimulus patterns. Experiments reveal both types of behavior. It is safest to conclude that they are not mutually exclusive activities, and that either or both may occur, depending on conditions and individuals. We need to keep in mind the three problems of conceptual behavior. In the investigation of adults we cannot assume that the subject is really acquiring a "new" concept because he is probably learning to apply concepts (or dimensions of concepts) already in his possession. In this sense both abstracting and generalizing can be, for the adult at least, quite conscious, controlled, and motivated activities. The distinction between abstracting and generalizing breaks down.

Nevertheless, these considerations lead directly into two general theories of concept attainment.

Composite Photograph Theory   The primary emphasis in this view is on abstraction, in which the features objects have in common "summate" (Woodworth, 1938).

Smoke (1932, 1933) criticized this theory on the grounds that the phrase "common features (or elements)" is misleading. He suggested that it is not specific components common to a series of stimulus patterns that summate in the concept, but relationships between them.

Active Search Theory   By contrast, another view emphasizes generalization, in which the subject has some hypothesis that he tests on successive instances (Woodworth, 1938). This approach assigns to the individual a more active, deliberate role than the preceding one. Perhaps more significant than the condition of beginning with an hypothesis is the principle of active search, shown in many experiments (English, 1922; Heidbreder, 1924; Smoke, 1932; Reed, 1946b).

Although terminology and treatment have changed, these traditional views still permeate current formulations of concept attainment. The first kind of theory underlies approaches in which the individual is regarded as responding to a series of stimuli in order to evolve the rule by which he can correctly name or classify them. It is true that controversy continues over whether this process is a gradually increasing incrementation of information or consists of more discrete steps. Nevertheless, the principle that abstracting leads to generalization is apparent. We also find deliberate attempts to establish conditions in which active search can ensue, whether by first teaching the subject a rule and then testing him in its application, or by using instructions to influence his behavior.

Podell (1958) has examined the operation of summation (composite photograph) and active search processes in a complex concept-attainment problem. The stimuli were combinations of numerous distinctive elements, with either twelve or two instances. To promote summation, subjects were given an "unintentional set," under which they inspected the instances as preparation for making aesthetic judgments; to emphasize active search, they were given an "intentional set," under which they were asked to notice similarities among the instances (hypothesis testing). The results supported the expectations that the summation condition should yield less memory of common features and less inclusion of them in definition of classes; and, further, that this difference should depend on exposures—with many varied instances, active search produces more knowledge of common features than do few instances, with the reverse holding for summation. Thus summation leads to considerable information about separate instances (so that a small number is efficient), whereas active search leads to considerable information about specific aspects or dimensions (so that a large number is efficient).

By way of summary, we can say that the two general theories really state two aspects of the total conceptualizing performance. Depending on tasks, conditions, and personality characteristics, the individual may be essentially a passive recipient of sensory impressions that gradually summate into the concept. Under other conditions, we may see the individual proceed by establishing a hypothesis and then deliberately checking it against instances. More than likely, as suggested, they are compatible and complementary approaches to a situation.

THE CONTINUITY-DISCONTINUITY CONTROVERSY

Research on discrimination learning has led to the issue of how to account for progress toward correct performance. Is it a function of a gradual increase in the strength of a response tendency? Or is it a matter of acquiring specific acts, each complete by itself? The first position makes learning a *continuous* process, whereas the second regards learning as *discontinuous*. The continuity view has been dominant in psychology, and arises from orthodox conditioning theory, with emphasis on reinforcement as the agent for strengthening the direction in which response will go. The discontinuity position has two major versions. One also grows directly from conditioning theory, but conceives the result to be the acquisition of a specific response (all-or-none theory). The other makes a break with simple conditioning, seeing the learning process as resulting in the acquisition of hypotheses or other cognitive structures—concepts— that in turn determine responses (mediation theory). We shall examine the second of these notions in this section because of its historical connection with continuity theory, reserving the all-or- none principle for a separate section.

Research on Discrimination

Krechevsky (1932) suggested that in solving problems, rats display systematic behavior, from which one might infer the operation of a "hypothesis," thus differing from the random, chance behavior apparently postulated in S-R theory. In opposing this view, K.W. Spence (1945) tested rats in a brightness-discrimination task. Continuity should be apparent if an association were established between a cue and a reinforced response during the period when there is evidence that a different hypothesis (e.g., a dominant position habit) was operating. His rats first learned a position habit (i.e., food on one side of the apparatus) with neutral gray runways. Training followed on black and white runways, with experimental animals reinforced only when they chose one color, and control animals reinforced 50 percent on each color. Next, the animals were given reversal training on the gray runways (reinforcement on the side opposite to the original position habit). Tested again in the colored runways, the experimental group displayed significantly worse performance when rewarded for the cue opposite to that previously reinforced. Spence interpreted these results as supporting the principle of continuity since the earlier reinforcement seemingly produced conflicting associations that retarded performance. When Ehrenfreund (1948) attempted to render the position habit salient by forcing rats to jump against the stimulus window, subsequent learning was retarded, indicating that the rat *did* learn something in the preliminary training, thus supporting continuity theory. Familiarizing rats with cues that later become relevant facilitates learning (Lawrence, 1949, 1950)—leading to the principle of acquired distinctiveness of cues. However, Lawrence was unwilling to accept an extreme discontinuity interpretation, and suggested that past experience has a relative rather than all-or-none effect.

Concept Formation and Discrimination Learning

Martin (1967) has proposed that generalization, discrimination learning, and concept formation fall on a continuum, in which *inhibition* is the key factor. Once basic conditioning has occurred, variations in response strength produce a particular response as a consequence of the inhibition of alternative responses. Generalization is merely a "failure to discriminate"; responses to several stimuli are similar because competing tendencies are inhibited. Discrimination learning is the overcoming of generalization, when a response becomes particular to a stimulus by inhibition of that response to other stimuli. Concept formation is an extension of this notion and involves more complex inhibitory processes, by which already-acquired internal representations become conditioned to the common elements in stimulus situations. That is, some of the response tendencies are inhibited, others are elicited. "Concept labeling" is incidental—a conditioned response that in itself can be evoked by a stimulus. When the individual learns such labeling responses, he also learns to be aware of concepts.

Unfortunately, the major function attributed to inhibition may be incorrect. Holland (1967) points to experiments on operant conditioning that show how discrimination can be learned without evidence of any inhibitory stimulus. Furthermore, one of Martin's chief points seems to lead toward a more complex model than he may have intended. He emphasizes that attention should not be restricted to overt responses, but should also be directed toward "receptive" responses, such as orienting and perceiving. In fact, he states that it can be very misleading for the experimenter to impose his own logic on the subject. It appears that once more we are led toward individual differences and mediating processes. These properties may originate in specific conditioning, but surely require additional formulations. Levine (1963) has presented a preliminary model that leads in this direction by dealing directly with the subject's hypotheses.

Shift Behavior

The reversal and nonreversal problems mentioned in Chapter 6 also bear on the continuity-discontinuity controversy.

When subjects were required to shift from one dimension to another in card sorting, performance improved with an increasing number of reinforcements (Grant and Berg, 1948; Grant and Cost, 1954). However, Buss (1953) found that both reversal and non-reversal (more for the latter) are impaired after prior training on one dimension, in accord with the continuity principle. He invoked partial reinforcement as an explanation for the nonreversal results: during the reversal phase, the nonrelevant stimulus has been "fortuitously" reinforced 50 percent of the time.

In opposition, Kendler and D'Amato (1955) advanced a mediational interpretation, arguing for a two-stage process. First an association is formed between the overt stimulus and an implicit symbolic response, then an association is formed between an implicit symbolic stimulus and the overt card-sorting response. Even with partial reinforcement controlled, reversal should be superior because the *implicit cues are present in the reversal condition, and would not be changed by ruling out partial reinforcement in the nonreversal condition*. That is, learning "appropriate" symbolic cues should facilitate concept attainment, even though they are connected to the "wrong" responses. When partial reinforcement was removed during the shift phase, by simply eliminating the pertinent instances during an intermediate stage and then reintroducing them, reversal shift was faster than nonreversal, supporting the mediational view. In four-category problems, however, the difference disappears (Kendler and Mayzner, 1956). This task still requires the learning of a single dimension, but with four values. Reversal demands learning the opposite of pairs. Thus if arrows point up, down, left, and right, reversal means assigning "down" to "up", and so on. This increases the number of possible rules and decreases the likelihood that the same general dimensional rule will work. Responding on the basis of the initial concept increases opportunities for nonreinforcement of the correct response, and the mediating process should be weakened. In four-category problems with two dimensions, each representing a single concept, pretraining on one of them facilitates both reversal and nonreversal shifts for the compound concept and the former is easier, as in other tasks (D'Amato and Ryan, 1967).

Buss (1956) criticized Kendler and D'Amato on the ground that partial reinforcement was not really eliminated in nonreversal: both groups actually learned a reverse shape concept (see Table 8-1). If we assume that shape continues to operate in the intermediate stage, nonreversal suffered from partial reinforcement of the shape concept, and the problem did not involve a shift at all for the reversal

Table 8-1
Design for Groups Learning the Shape Concept First in the Kendler and D'Amato (1955) Study. (From Buss, 1956.)

		Second Concept	
Group	**First Concept**	Intermediate Stage	Final Stage
Reversal	Shape	Reverse shape or Reverse color	Reverse shape
Nonreversal	Shape	Reverse shape or Reverse color	Reverse color

group. He checked on which concept had been learned by asking subjects to continue responding in the final stage in the same way as in the intermediate stage. Of twenty-five subjects, seven learned the nonreversal shift, but still required significantly more trials. Since even with partial reinforcement controlled, reversal was still faster, he accepted the mediational interpretation. Harrow and Friedman (1958) further ruled out partial reinforcement by using different stimuli in the shift stage, but still found that reversal was superior. When O'Connell (1965) compared partial (60 percent) with continuous (100 percent) reinforcement, the latter yielded significantly better performance in both phases, but the difference between reversal and nonreversal was not significant. However, the very large number of reinforcements (fifty) probably established the rule so strongly that when the shift occurred without warning, the reversal task might simply have become as difficult as nonreversal. Even cross-cultural studies show that reversal is typically easier for the adult (Cole, Guy, and Glick, 1968).

In addition to mediation, perceptual and attentional factors affect performance. Kendler, Glucksberg, and Keston (1961) influenced the "perceptual orienting act" by varying the position of the relevant stimulus. If the position were unchanged, orientation should be more favorable than if changed. Reversal, was, in fact, better with favorable orientation and better than nonreversal with either orientation. Kendler and Woerner (1964) compared orientation directly with mediation, by interposing nonreinforced (blank) trials to extinguish the orienting response, or the same stimuli previously

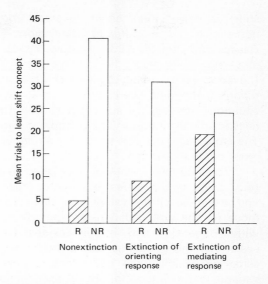

FIGURE 8-1   The comparative contributions of orienting and mediating responses on shift performance. (Based on Kendler, Glucksberg, and Keston, 1961, and Kendler and Woerner, 1964.) Note: R and NR refer to reversal and nonreversal, respectively.

categorized to extinguish the mediating response. Extinguishing the orienting response had little effect, but when the mediating response was extinguished, the reversal shift was no longer significantly easier (see Figure 8-1). Kendler, Kendler, and Marken (1970) further argued that a critical test would be to change the external stimuli, but not the mediating response, which should not affect speed of learning after the shift. Subjects first learned to discriminate between words in two different categories (e.g., clothing, fruit). In two reversal conditions, the *same* sets of words were presented, but with reversed categories, or new sets of words from the same categories were introduced (e.g., "orange" for "apple"). The two groups, as expected, did not differ significantly. A second experiment showed that memory for specific words is reduced when categories are involved.

Task Conditions   The characteristics of the stimuli have also been examined. Nonreversal to the same dimension (*within-dimension* shift) is easier than either reversal (*intradimensional* shift) or nonreversal to a different dimension (*extradimensional* shift) (Isaacs and Duncan, 1962; Harrow, 1964). An example of within-dimension shift would be to have the subject learn a shape rule (hexagon versus triangle), then another shape rule (square versus triangle). However, we cannot say that *no* mediation occurs in this situation—indeed, the subject may learn the rule that *shape* is the relevant dimension and simply apply it directly to the second task. The more necessary it is to modify a rule, or to learn a new rule, the more difficult the task.

To determine whether mediation represents the dimension (e.g., color) or the values (e.g., red or green), P. J. Johnson (1967) first presented all the values and dimensions in initial learning, but those for the within-dimension shift did not appear together. The within-dimension and intradimensional (reversal) shifts were both easier than the extradimensional (nonreversal) shift. Shifts with the same dimension were equivalent, indicating that the important variable is the dimension, not the specific values.

Reversal shifts appear to be easier, even with more difficult rules. Harrow and Buchwald (1962) compared a consistent with an inconsistent rule. In the former case, cards (for example, containing stars) were marked with one, two, three, or four lines in the corners, and could be sorted either by position or number. In the latter, the cards had to be sorted according to an imposed rule not readily apparent (e.g., for number, $n + 1$ so that a card with two stars had to be placed in the "3" location). Reversal shifts were easier, regardless of the rule, but the inconsistent rule increased the difficulty of the nonreversal shift much more than the reversal.

Verbal Associations   One kind of evidence for mediation rests on examining the properties of the inferred mediator. Lachman and Sanders (1963), for example, showed that the rate of learning shift problems differs in accordance with the semantic character of the relationship. Thus the verbal counterparts of intradimensional and reversal stimuli may be treated as "similar" and "opposite" pairs, compared to the "neutral" relation of the nonreversal pair—and they are correspondingly easier. A refinement of their procedure revealed that the meaningfulness of the first two situations yields positive transfer, whereas the lack of association in the nonreversal situation produced *negative* transfer.

Still more definitive are studies with actual verbal materials. Kendler, Kendler, and Sanders (1967) compared trigrams, arbitrarily assigned to two categories, with real words drawn from different conceptual categories (e.g., clothing and vegetables). With four items per category, a partial shift was devised by reversing some proportion of the stimuli. There was little effect with the trigrams, but for the words, 100 percent reversal was easier than partial reversal.

Overlearning The better learned the initial rule, the stronger its effect should be on subsequent shift performance. In both two-hair and four-category problems, Ludvigson and Caul (1964) found that ease of learning *both* shifts increases after overlearning. Again, the reversal shift was easier for two categories, but there was little difference for four categories. Uhl (1966) confirmed this result for two categories and also showed that reversal is superior, though less so, when the stimuli changed. This finding indicates that the mediating process is fairly specific to the set of stimuli used initially.

In fact, the efficiency of the subject depends on what concept is learned. In the studies by Grant and Berg (1948) and Grant and Cost (1954), the problems were all alike by demanding a simple shift from one dimension to another. The subject apparently learned that the solution demands a shift. In successive problems, he merely needed to ascertain which dimension was correct. This kind of improvement in a series of identical problems is a "learning set" (Harlow, 1949). In the reversal situation, no doubt, the subject would, also improve on successive problems, once he learns the reversal rule. When the stimuli are changed, as in Uhl's and similar studies, the altered cues in effect create a new problem, weakening the apparent applicability of the rule already learned. As a result the reversal shift should become more difficult to learn, but the extra-dimensional shift should become easier since the change makes the new problem more similar to the initial learning situation.

Individual Differences Although we shall look at cognitive style and motivation later, a couple of studies should be mentioned at this point. Martin (1968) has analyzed in detail the performance of subjects who were fast and slow in solving the initial discrimination problem. Overlearning had little effect on the fast learners, but produced significantly more rapid solution of the shift problem for the slow learners. The fast learners displayed significantly worse recall of the relevant attributes. These differences might be expected if the initial training serves to establish the relevant dimension as a basis for mediation.

Ohnmacht (1966) saw the possibility that certain attitudinal characteristics may influence the ease with which subjects adapt to the demands of the shift task. Rigidity, difficulty in assimilating new information, stubborn adherence to a judgment, and so on, may well interfere with a performance that requires a change in response. Using measures of field dependence (Witkin et al., 1954) and dogmatism (Rokeach, 1960) to test this hypothesis, he found the now-familiar greater difficulty of the extradimensional compared to the reversal shift. Field-dependent and dogmatic subjects, as predicted, had more difficulty with both types of shift problem, and those individuals with both characteristics were especially poor.

Thus personality variables, as well as training, task, and situational conditions affect performance in the shift problem. But such factors do not override the fundamental point that it is easier for adult subjects to solve problems that call for a dimensional rule, which has already been learned, than problems that require the identification of a new dimension. Both situations illustrate the principle that a concept (or mediating process) is operating, but in the first case it works (after correction), in the second case it does not. These findings, now thoroughly established, constitute an impressive foundation for the mediational view.

Slamecka's Analysis Not content to consider the available research completely definitive, Slamecka (1968) has carefully reviewed the methods employed in shift experiments (see Figure 8-2). He points out that the progressive elaboration of procedures has clarified a number of uncontrolled factors. The mediational interpretation has steadily been strengthened, with an accompanying likelihood that other explanations can be ruled out. The fifth design may offer the most definitive setting for further research. It is a "total change" design that potentially permits the investigator to test both shifts at least somewhat independently of the initial task. Although the intradimensional shift is still superior to the extradimensional one, the design might be pursued to explore other problems, such as generalization across dimensions.

Comment
At one level research has at least clarified distinctions between several aspects of behavior in concept attainment. Thus we can see

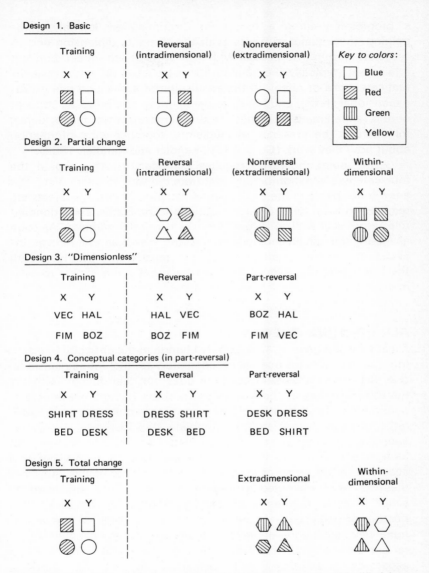

FIGURE 8-2   Various designs employed in shift experiments. (Modified from Slamecka, 1968.)

a progression along a line from discrimination learning (pre-training to acquaint subjects with the stimulus dimension and to associate distinctive names with the stimuli), to direct concept attainment (typically the training that establishes the initial conceptual categories or rules), to the acquisition of a changed rule (intra-dimensional shift[1]), and finally to the learning of a different concept or rule (extradimensional shift). In this perspective we gain evidence for inferring the presence of mediators, together with information about how they work (Goss, 1961 ; Kendler and Kendler, 1962).

One point, however, requires clarification. Why should the four-category situation be different from the two-category one ? The answer lies partly in the experimental situation in which subjects are required to learn quite explicit solutions to problems. The attendant rules work very well so long as the task is not too complex. As soon as additional dimensions are added, the response alternatives increase in number. In effect the subject must learn new rules, with the result that the reversal problem becomes more similar to non-reversal.

ALL-OR-NONE THEORY

Except for the general evolutionary change in the difficulty of learning the extradimensional shift compared to the intradimensional one, the research on shift behavior does not deal directly with the question of whether the acquisition process is continuous or discontinuous. The establishment of a mediator could still be gradual, rather than an immediate and complete step beyond random responding. Is concept attainment a matter of the slow dawning of understanding, in the trial-and-error sense, or is it sudden and accurate, in the sense of insight ? In order to answer this question, theorists have attempted to reduce the task of the subject to its simplest terms. It is as if a typical problem were composed of a number of parts, each of which is a unit by itself. In the all-or-none view, each unit—if we can identify it properly—is either solved or not solved. And, if solved, mistakes no longer occur on that aspect of the problem. We shall first examine the basic kinds of argument advanced on this matter, then see how they have fared in systematic research. More than one version of all-or-none theory can be recognized, but we shall concentrate on the general themes that characterize them.

[1] In a sense this phase is a reversion to the situation that characterizes the original direct concept attainment, with the special feature that the subject has isolated one of the possible rules.

Guessing State, Sampling, and Conditioning

The subject is assumed to exist in a state of exposure to many stimuli, each of which elicits a particular response. When such stimuli are sampled, one or another response may receive reinforcement, thus increasing the probability of its being produced subsequently. If no conditioning occurs, the subject remains in the same guessing state as before. Learning therefore consists in the increased probability that a sample of stimulus elements will consistently produce a certain response (or class of responses). As trials continue, more and more samples of stimuli become conditioned to the same response.

Prior to an error, the subject is assumed to be sampling available hypotheses about the correct response at random. On successive trials, the total population of hypotheses is available—that is, the subject samples with replacement into the population of the previous possibilities. An error alters response probabilities, since now there are two categories, potentially correct and incorrect (assumed to be equal, so that each error eliminates one-half of the hypotheses). The subject learns nothing so long as he remains in a guessing state— or, alternatively, he exhibits no systematic preference for one set of hypotheses over another. He is treated as having little or no memory for what has taken place on previous trials. Once the correct response occurs, the subject moves completely to that step, supposedly merely repeating it and learning nothing more from it. Thus there is said to be no "information processing" during correct responding.

All-or-None Principle

Experiments by Rock (1957) suggested that the elements of a task are learned in one trial, if they are learned at all. In this situation, the rate of paired-associate learning was not affected when an item missed was replaced by a new one. Despite the criticism by advocates of the incremental position that this procedure may simply produce in the long run a list of the easiest items (J. Jung, 1968), other evidence has supported the all-or-none principle (Estes, 1960, 1964). The principle rests on reducing the total learning process to its simplest components. In the typical procedure, data are pooled for groups of subjects or groups of trials. But if we link specific events to particular subjects, then one subject may acquire the correct response on trial n, another on trial $n + 1$, and so on. Pooling of data yields a continuous function of average performance, artificially indicating incremental learning and obscuring the discontinuous events. All-or-none theorists therefore search individual learning curves for evidence of abrupt change from a stage of random responding to a stage of correct responding. By constructing backward learning curves, they can identify the point when learning appears, then analyze the preceding trials. One implication is that until a response is learned, the subject samples hypotheses at random, and the number of correct responses should remain constant prior to the last error (*stationarity*) (Trabasso, 1963; Bower and Trabasso, 1963).

Hypotheses

It is a key issue whether the subject samples with replacement or whether, in fact, past experience with the components affects his current behavior. Research on dimensional shifts supports the latter view (e.g., Guy, Van Fleet, and Bourne, 1966). Beyond that, characteristics of the dimensions themselves partly determine the kinds of hypotheses employed. In a study by Schlag-Rey and Suppes (1968), the task called for classifying strings of the letters D and K into two categories. For combinations of one, two, three, or five letters, the solution consisted in identifying those ending in either DD or KK. This rule is abstract enough to permit numerous hypotheses, but the stimuli were simple enough to place little strain on memory. The subjects showed gradual, but nonlinear, improvement over trials. Inquiry disclosed that complex hypotheses (combining two properties of the stimuli) *increased* with progress, with a decrease in other types.

Erickson, Zajkowski, and Ehmann (1966) suggested that the subject's response latency is indicative of the size of the pool of hypotheses from which he is sampling. From the all-or-none standpoint: (1) the latency should be greater following errors than following correct responses (because after an error the sampled hypotheses should return to the pool, but should be retained after a correct response); (2) latency should be constant across trials that precede the last error; (3) latency should be constant across trials following the last error and should be equal to that on trials following correct responses prior to that time; (4) latency, for binary dimensions, on error trials and on correct trials should be equal (because it is assumed that trials are independent during the presolution period); and (5) latency following uninformed errors should be equal to that following correct responses (because, lacking information that an error has occurred, the subject has no reason to resample).

A procedure was adopted in which each subject worked on three problems, a control in which treatment was consistent across trials, a second in which a reversal shift was imposed after every other error, and a third with an extradimensional shift after every other error. In this way, about half of the errors were uninformed. Predictions 1, 4, and 5 were supported. However, although the latency after errors was greater than after correct responses, it decreased more after errors than after correct trials;[1] furthermore, the latency of postsolution trials decreased, as in a typical learning curve. Thus the size of the hypothesis pool is not constant, but decreases, as if the subject remembers at least the most recently incorrect hypotheses. The authors propose a principle of sampling with partial replacement.

In a later experiment, Erickson and Zajkowski (1967) increased the difficulty of the task by requiring subjects to solve three problems concurrently. Overloading of memory in this fashion made the results agree more closely with the expectations of sampling with replacement. Erickson (1968) further pursued the "no memory" implication in an experiment using a procedure of hypothesis tracking. As devised by Levine (1963), this method permits the investigator to identify the hypothesis under test by the subject. Stimuli are arranged in a sequence such that the pattern of responses can be examined for consistencies along one of the dimensions. For example, if there are four binary dimensions, a set of four stimuli can be developed that can be classified into any of the four possible categories. Call these dimensions one, two, three, and four, each having the values of either X or Y. The subject is instructed to label each stimulus A or B. Suppose the four stimuli in sequence have the values XXXX, XXYY, XYXY, and YXXX. The subject could respond, A, A, A, B, showing that the X value of dimension one is his hypothesis, or A, A, B, A, showing that the X value of dimension two is his hypothesis, and so on. For any set, the sequence can be inconsistent, from which no single hypothesis can be deduced. In the study two problems were presented, one in which the experimenter chose the solution, reinforcing accordingly, and one in which the subject chose his own solution. In the latter situation, the hypothesis apparently adopted by the subject on the first set of four stimuli was called incorrect, but thereafter that hypothesis was reinforced by the experimenter. The assumption of "no memory" should be confirmed if the two problems were solved, after the first block, in the same number of trials. With complete (or permanent) memory, the second problem might never be solved. On an assumption of short-term memory, the second

---

[1] Vincentizing of the data sustained these conclusions.

problem should be more difficult by whatever difference limited storage would produce. The second problem did, in fact, take longer to solve, clearly indicating that the subject does not sample with replacement, and that the pool of hypotheses changes as a function of information.

Other evidence counter to the replacement principle is that subjects show an increased tendency to choose the relevant cue, rather than replacing it (R. C. Anderson, 1966), and that subjects often retest previously tested hypotheses, sometimes more than once after they are told it is incorrect and may test the correct hypothesis before it has been learned (Gettys and Gettys, 1968; Kenoyer and Phillips, 1968). Rogers and Haygood (1968) queried the subject at five-trial intervals to discover what hypotheses he was using. In an attempt to slow down the solution process, they introduced conditions of misinformative feedback (at times informing the subject that he was incorrect when he was correct and vice versa) and non-contingent feedback (the subject was reinforced on a random basis). Contrary to the replacement assumptions, there were many *spontaneous* changes following a series of correct responses (when there should be none), and instances when the subject *failed to conform to his verbalized hypothesis* or *retained the same hypothesis after an error*. Falmagne (1968) found that rated confidence in the correctness of hypotheses increased for relevant (i.e., correct) hypotheses, with very low (and somewhat decreasing) confidence for irrelevant and incorrect hypotheses.

Nahinsky (1968), after a detailed analysis, adduced strong evidence that subjects follow systematic strategies. They change— or at least refine—their hypotheses on correct, as well as on incorrect trials. Furthermore, he points out that subjects can hold several alternative hypotheses at the same time, which can then be tested, at least partially, over more than one trial. Under these circumstances information obtained in early trials can be very influential, regardless of whether responses are correct or incorrect. Research by Nahinsky and Slaymaker (1969) supports this view. Dodd and Bourne (1969), through special analysis of data from Trabasso and Bower (1966) and additional experimentation, also find that hypotheses may be changed after correct responses, that subjects "misuse" information from error trials, and that failures to check the consistency between errors and immediately preceding trials occur. They suggest the need for a revised model that allows for variations in probability of resampling (and the elicitation of new hypotheses) stemming from these tendencies. Levine (1970) has also shown that several hypotheses are adopted simultaneously.

Four-Category Problems

An important point, not sufficiently investigated, concerns the proposition that complex problems are treated as subproblems and are solved independently (Bourne and Restle, 1959; Trabasso and Bower, 1964). In an experiment not explicitly directed toward this theory, Kendler and Vineberg (1954) examined the effects of learning simple concepts on the later learning of a test concept compounded from them (e.g., shape and size, then four shape-size categories). As anticipated, prior learning of both relevant components significantly facilitated acquisition of the compound concept, with prior learning of one component superior to prior learning of irrelevant components. The crucial point is that the rate of learning the compound concept was certainly not the sum of the two simple concepts.

Research on hypothesis behavior indicates that subjects are actually acting in a complicated fashion. They may examine combinations of dimensions, as well as separate dimensions, or retain a possibly correct hypothesis while testing it against others that may be compatible with it, and so on. Nahinsky and McGlynn (1968) arranged a procedure whereby it was possible to determine whether responses reflected single or combined hypotheses. Their evidence points very strongly to the latter. Subjects sampled combinations rather than single and independent dimensions.

Comment

Theories prompted by the all-or-none principle continue to exist in a state of flux, and space limitations prevent me from reviewing all the pertinent research. The all-or-none basis for learning may prove to be valid in the fundamental sense that when an appropriate unit is used, the subject moves from a state of guessing (or no understanding) to a solution state of making correct responses. However, it seems clear that the assumptions about the characteristics of the guessing state and about the subject's goals are incorrect. Before solution, the subject typically does not guess purely at random. He uses whatever cues he can, whether or not derived from correct responses or from errors, and whether his interpretation of either kind of feedback is actually valid. (He can derive the wrong information from a "correct" instance, for example.) With respect to the subject's goals, it is fallacious to suppose that he is solely concerned with achieving a correct solution. He is also interested in understanding why it is correct, whether it is the complete solution, and so on. Thus it would be surprising if all subjects invariably repeated a "correct" response uncritically. It would often be intelligent to test a hypothesis against an instance one believes to be incorrect, but would like to make sure. Certainly the assumption of no memory is unjustified, as is the total replacement assumption.

The theories under consideration have begun with simplified principles of concept attainment, based on logical analysis of the stimulus situation, regarding the subject as the mere recipient of information. Thus the subject is expected to have only minimal perceptual and cognitive properties at the time the experiment starts, and to be without response preferences or varied motives. It has taken much research to lead back again to an approach in which the actual behavior of people can serve as a point of departure for theories that can account for concept attainment. It will be necessary to develop more complex models, which not only include revisions of variables already considered but also additional variables. An example of the first modification is the recognition of varied degrees of "replacement" dependent on memory, dimension preferences, confidence, and so on. The second sort of modification is exemplified by cognitive styles and variations in strategy, as well as by interactions between intrinsic and situational variables.

We must distinguish the fundamental *outcome* of learning from the *processes* leading to that outcome. If the task is rendered sufficiently simple, or if a complex task is properly broken down into its smallest components, it is probable that the all-or-none outcome occurs. In this sense, learning is discontinuous rather than incremental. At levels beyond that, however, it is extremely difficult to see how all-or-none principles contribute much to our understanding of learning (with special reference here to concept attainment). In fact, aside from the possibility of enormously detailed and specific analysis of individual subjects, calling for masses of information difficult or impossible to obtain, an incremental principle appears more workable. That is, if each small aspect of a complex task is separately learned, at different times for different subjects, the permutations become so numerous that one might as well concentrate on more general variables to begin with. Furthermore, if we allow for the fact that the learning of separate elements by no means guarantees the learning of their combinations, then an additional complication ensues. A subject might attain the elements, which he can utilize correctly, but appear to make errors when they must be transcended. In arriving at their correct integration, he may make errors (or partial errors) at different rates for different combinations. Again, the permutations become extremely numerous. The net picture could easily be much better described in incremental rather than in all-or-none terms. Once, however, the more complex rule is achieved, we might again see a genuine discontinuity—or what has in a problem-solving context been called *insight*.

It is likely that theorists have struggled with an insoluble problem in attempting to apply all-or-none principles in complex tasks. They have assumed that a one-stage, or possibly a two-stage process, can account for attainment. They appear to have confused an intermediate stage with either an initial or final stage, or both.

I suggest that a three-stage model may be required. The first stage is all-or-none learning of specific aspects of the task (assuming that it is meaningful to reduce the task to very small parts). The second stage is the fitting together, or integration, of those elements to produce relationships, patterns, combinations, or other systems of elements. It is likely that an incremental principle can best describe this stage. Finally, the third stage is the complex rule, or solution, which, when attained, also displays all-or-none properties. The trouble arises mainly, then, in examination of the second stage, in which the intricacies of progress toward solution are probably unlimited. Of course, the three-stage sequence is not necessarily fully elaborated in all cases, since the "jump" to the integrated rule may be fast or slow, as a function of many variables, such as experience and training, the characteristics and "accessibility" of task properties, strategy, and cognitive styles.

INFORMATION PROCESSING

This approach, like the foregoing, relies heavily on analyzing the properties of stimuli and their relationships so that they can be reduced to simple units. It differs by incorporating conceptions of memory and allowing for the operation of internal rules (the program of the computer, or the intrinsic processes of mediation theory). It treats the subject as an active decision-maker, but looks for the constraints that influence outcomes. As we have seen, this approach is closely tied to principles derived from computers, but it also considers actual human conceptual behavior via simulation studies (Hunt, 1962).

In a sense, all theories of concept attainment use information-processing models in varying degrees of emphasis. The subject is regarded as receiving input from the environment, which activates internal processes of registry, discrimination, response selection, or response organization, and decisions that eventuate in naming objects, differential responding to objects, or verbalizing a rule. The information-processing approach, as such, is especially concerned with specifying the various components of these activities in precise terms.

Posner (1964) has suggested distinctions between tasks based on the characteristics of the information processing required. A basic feature of most tasks is *preserving* information, but this function is especially apparent in simple reaction time, perceptual, and memorizing situations. In other tasks, however, information *reduction* becomes important, marked by omissions, combining or condensing components, discarding irrelevancies, and so on. Tasks used in concept-attainment studies fall into this category. Finally, there are situations that call for the *creation* of new information, such as invention, discovery, and theorizing. When the prime requirement is conserving, optimal performance results in a matching of input and output ("in" = "out"). Information reduction is best when input exceeds output ("in">"out"). Creation is greatest when output is new information at least equal to and possibly more than the starting point ("in" ‡ "out"). Multiple association and divergent-thinking tasks exemplify this outcome.

Posner orients his analysis especially to conceptual learning. The key process is regarded as information reduction, whether the task is attainment of a concept (as in the first phase of a typical shift experiment), or learning to modify or change a concept already acquired (as in the transfer phases of shift situations). If we consider rote learning to require information conservation, then the minimum needed to produce a classification problem is the presentation of more than one stimulus per response. Posner describes two mechanisms of information reduction. *Gating* signifies that the subject can ignore much of the available information without affecting his performance. For example, if there are irrelevant stimulus dimensions, the subject must learn which ones to omit in finding the correct rule. *Condensation* refers to the combining of relevant dimensions into a smaller number of categories. Unlike in simple gating, the subject must incorporate all relevant dimensions of the stimuli into his definition of the response classes.

The chief point is that performance can be related systematically to task conditions by determining the amount of information reduction demanded. Concept tasks are more difficult the more it is necessary to reduce information (see Figure 8-3). When gating is the main process, information reduction and difficulty are related during the stages of learning the rule, but not after the rule is learned. That is,

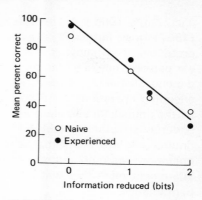

FIGURE 8-3   Percentage of correct responses in concept formation as a function of information reduction required. (From Posner, 1964, and after Shepard, Hovland, and Jenkins, 1961.)

the introduction of irrelevant information may show little effect on utilization of the rule. However, the relationship appears in condensation tasks both during periods of initial learning and at later stages of applying the rule(s) in new test situations, or in problems of reclassifying objects. We can surmise then that the intradimensional shift calls more on gating, whereas extradimensional shifts demand condensation. Since investigators have expended a great deal of effort in exploring task variations that add up to manipulations of difficulty, it may be that principles derived from information theory can assist in bringing order into this work. Such application, however, calls on more than simply formally specifying the "information properties" of the task. Thus Fitts and Biederman (1965) show the importance of "perceptual demands," since performance becomes more efficient as the compatibility between stimulus and response aspects of the task increases.

Memory
It is easy to see that the storage, organization, and retrieval of information are basic in the information-processing approach. Hunt (1967) has shown by an artificial-intelligence procedure that the quantity of available memory is related to performance. (See also, Hunt, Marin,

and Stone, 1966.) An impressive simulation experiment by Gregg (1967) goes farther in several ways. The utilization of individual protocols clearly shows the wide variety of processes whereby different persons may manage the same type of problem. Such variations depend on the characteristics of memory, not only the coding and encoding operations conducted in "short-term memory" as induced by the immediate stimulus situation, but also on the antecedent and enduring structures established during past learning. Playing a continuing role are the verbal labels by which coding and encoding operations are rendered more or less efficient. Research on concept attainment must find ways to get at such memorial influences on performance.

Denny (1969) has shown that memory loss is greater when the task involves complex rules than when it demands simple rules, generally in line with Posner's analysis. But when memory load is reduced (e.g., by "refreshing" the subject's recall by displaying previously seen instances between trials), the difference decreases. As Denny points out, errors in memory do not necessarily reflect an actual loss of information, but may also come from the application of strategies. Such cognitive processes appear to be inefficient but might be regarded as information reduction, in the sense of condensation. The subject is not forgetting information so much as endeavoring to apply a rule, but in doing so he concentrates on some aspects while ignoring others.

SUMMARY

In adults, central problems concern utilization of concepts in solving problems and organizing information in new ways. Abstraction and generalization are salient themes in composite photograph and active search theories. With respect to the continuity issue, research on discrimination tends to support the continuity position, while experiments on shift behavior and mediation support the discontinuity view. All-or-none theory formulates principles of conditioning from samples of stimuli. Although there is evidence for the basic all-or-none principle, evidence runs counter to principles of cue neutralization, no memory, and sampling with replacement. Especially significant are tendencies of subjects to formulate hypotheses and adopt strategies. A conservative position is that all-or-none learning may hold for sufficiently small S-R units. If we distinguish outcome from process, in a three-stage model, all-or-none outcomes may characterize a first stage, followed by an integrative stage of gradual incrementation, and a third stage of rule or solution attainment ("insight"). The first and third stages may be discontinuous, the second continuous. Information-processing theory distinguishes among preserving, reducing, and creating information. Concept formation involves reduction, with gating and condensation as basic mechanisms, and specification of memory as a central problem.

9

CONDITIONS RELATED TO CONCEPTUAL BEHAVIOR

Most experiments on concept attainment deal with situations in which a particular concept or group of concepts is to be derived from or applied to a particular set of formally constructed stimuli. In the typical case a rule for classifying or naming stimuli must be discovered; sometimes the rule is supplied and the subject must learn the properties that define it. Although studies are often prompted by the kinds of theoretical issues discussed in the last chapter, a large proportion of them are directed toward quite specific problems that arise independently of systematic theory—and these problems are clearly discernible in experiments conducted many decades ago. Modern investigators have added a few new and important questions, but much of their effort has been directed to the improvement of technique, the measurement of variables, and refining the conditions under which performance is facilitated or degraded.

As we previously observed, verbal responses play a highly significant role in conceptual behavior, both in implicit symbolic (mediating) ways and in explicit evoking and responding ways. Certainly, in many experiments concept attainment appears as a kind of verbal behavior, such as in the learning of names for certain sets of stimuli. In general, however, we can draw a distinction between processes of classifying objects—and of treating particular objects in some fashion dependent on their class membership—and processes of acquiring and using words, or *verbal learning*. The two interests overlap with every indication that the convergence will increase in the future, as the significance of *meaning* becomes more evident.

CONCRETE AND ABSTRACT PERFORMANCE

Contrasts between concrete and abstract behavior were drawn in treating developmental processes in children. Despite the trends described in that context, both kinds of behavior occur in adults. However, whereas the young child is predominantly concrete—and in fact can behave abstractly only with great difficulty, if at all—the adult can utilize both concrete and abstract processes.

Studies with sorting tests revealed contrasting concrete and categorical performances, with the former primarily determined by sensory impressions, the latter by class membership (Weigl, 1941; Bolles, 1937; see also, English, 1922). To assess these differences, Hanfmann and Kasanin (1937, 1942) devised the Vigotsky test. It consists of small blocks, varying in size, height, color, and shape. On the bottom of each is a nonsense syllable to serve as a name for one of the four classes formed by a double dichotomy of size and height (tall-large, tall-small, flat-large, and flat-small). Variations in color and shape constitute irrelevant dimensions. One of the names is revealed, and the subject is asked to select all those that belong with it. The experimenter turns up one of the wrongly allocated blocks, and asks the subject to try again. (For example, he might have chosen blocks of the same color.) This procedure is continued until all the blocks are correctly sorted.

By this test, Hanfmann and Kasanin distinguished three levels of performance, (1) primitive "concrete," at which the names are not related to the properties of the blocks, so that solution proceeds only by trial and error; (2) intermediate, at which the nature of classification is not fully grasped, as when the task is seen as a game with rules, or only the possibility of grouping is discovered; and (3) conceptual or abstract, at which the task is understood as a problem of classification.

Goldstein and Scheerer (1941) interpreted the concrete mode as realistic, that is, as dependent on immediate sensory impressions, and the abstract mode as detached from immediate reality, thus including more than the actual stimulus object. These investigators pointed to degrees and gradations of these approaches, and noted that the normal individual (unlike the pathological cases of their study) can combine them, or shift from one to another as the situation demands. Hanfmann (1941), in fact, formulated "personal patterns," such as predominantly "thinking" or abstract, compared to predominantly "perceptual" or concrete. When one of these tendencies is strongly marked, the pattern is "concordant," but if they conflict, it is "discordant" (leading to less efficient performance).

Efficiency depends on what the task requires. In a concrete response the specific object and its unique properties dominate, but in an abstract response it is relationships between objects or dimensions that cut across objects that dominate. There are, of course, occasions when optimum performance depends on finding and properly using specific objects, others when classification is required for good performance. Efficiency may be impaired when either approach is inappropriate. A homely example may illustrate the point. Suppose that a person wished to write a letter at a desk well equipped with various pencils, pieces of charcoal, paint brushes, pens, crayons, and so on, among numerous other objects. It would be foolish to treat all available writing implements as equivalent and thus to write the letter with a crayon—he would choose a pen. Or suppose that a man wishes to purchase a blouse for his wife. To him all blouses of the proper size are essentially equivalent (he has an abstract conception of blouses). He is likely to choose one at random from this class of objects. But his wife probably has a very concrete approach to blouses, treating members of the class as quite separate objects. Therefore concrete performance is quite as efficient as abstract performance when it is called for. It is clear that the normal person behaves both concretely and abstractly, shifting from one mode to the other as required, but with individual differences in the ease of shifting. It is likely that the predominantly abstract person, however, encounters much less difficulty with concrete tasks than the reverse, with some persons arrested at the more primitive concrete level.

Experiments show in general that performance becomes more efficient the more concrete the stimuli (such as pictures versus words, or words referring to objects—e.g., *furniture*—versus words referring to abstract ideas—e.g., as *punishment*) (Davidon, 1952; Reed and Dick, 1968).

Harvey, Hunt, and Schroder (1961) treat concreteness and abstractness as a general dimension of conceptual development, marked by the acquisition of alternatives (or schemata). The differentiation and integration of information passes through stages, with transitions. Stage 1 is featured by highly concrete, absolutist systems, with the person dependent on external control in coping with situations. At stage 2 there is resistance to external sources, accompanied by adherence to one's own opinions and the use of defensive mechanisms against cognitive change. Stage 3 brings on greater differentiation, with concern for success or failure and a premium on maintaining positive relationships to avoid negative consequences of action. By stage 4 the person has become complex, neither dependent on external rules (or people), nor opposed to them—he can assess his own actions and work out alternative ways to organize the same stimuli.

Progression through these stages may be continuous or arrested at some point, so that adults may display any of the foregoing patterns. Such variations in the general concrete-abstract dimension have a fundamental significance in how the person responds to and acts toward the world, not only in dealing with specific stimuli, but also in interpersonal relations, in perceiving and striving toward goals, in reacting to frustration, and in other ways. Their theory is especially important in recognizing differential *cognitive styles* associated with the dominance of one stage or another.

Various studies have revealed an "order of dominance," in which concepts of objects are easiest to learn, with color and form harder, and number still more difficult (Heidbreder, 1947; Wenzel and Flurry, 1948; Grant, Jones, and Tallantis, 1949; Komachiya, 1957). The distinction between concrete objects and classes based on properties like color, form, and number clearly corresponds to variation along the concrete-abstract continuum. With sorting tests of the Goldstein-Scheerer variety, which present a large assortment of diverse objects that vary in many dimensions (including number of identical objects), subjects typically produce classes based on kinds of objects or functional relationships (such as objects used in a poker game) more readily than those based on texture, color, or form.

TYPES OF CLASSIFICATION RULES

Bruner, Goodnow, and Austin (1956) pointed out distinctions among *conjunctive, disjunctive,* and *relational* concepts, each associated with a rule of classification. A conjunctive rule is defined "by the *joint presence* of the appropriate values of several attributes," a disjunctive rule by the presence of one attribute *or* of another attribute, a relational rule by a relationship between attributes. Conjunctive concepts would be represented by classifying figures on the basis of form and color, for example, red circles versus black crosses versus green squares. A disjunctive class would be exemplified by figures that are either square or red (thus all squares, all red figures). A relational rule would be a class based on more than and less than, for example, a set on which there are fewer figures than borders.

There are many variations of these rules (Neisser and Weene, 1962; Haygood and Bourne, 1965; Laughlin, 1968b). Where A designates one attribute (e.g., red) and B another attribute (e.g., square), the following rules can be noted: *affirmation* (A present); *negation* (A absent); *alternative denial* (either A absent or B absent); *joint denial* (A absent and B absent); *conjunctive presence* (A and B both present); *conjunctive absence* (A and B both absent); *exclusion* (A present and B absent); *inclusive disjunction* (A present or B present or both present); *exclusive disjunction* (A present or B present, but not both); *disjunctive absence* (A absent or B absent or both absent); *conditional* (if A present then B must be present; if A absent, then B present); *biconditional* (A present, but positive if and only if B present; or at a more complex level, *both/neither*—A and B must both be present, unless neither is present).

In addition to the foregoing there are numerous relational rules, ranging from the simple one stated above to complex ones, such as those that might be based on combinations of several attributes.

Conjunctive and relational rules are preferred by subjects (E. B. Hunt and Hovland, 1960), and are easier than disjunctive rules (S. H. Schwartz, 1966). In a situation where stimuli can be classified according to any of three types of rules, disjunctive solutions are much less frequently found than conjunctive and relational solutions. Conditional rules appear to be most difficult of all (Laughlin, 1968b).

Difficulty varies with the complexity of the rule (Shepard, Hovland, and Jenkins, 1961; Neisser and Weene, 1962; Bourne and Guy, 1968a; Laughlin, 1968a). Thus rules based on a single dimension (A present) are easier than rules based on two dimensions (A and B present), and these are, in turn, easier than rules based on three dimensions (A and B and C present). Beyond this perhaps obvious condition lie internal characteristics of the rules. Bruner, Goodnow, and Austin (1956) point out two difficulties with disjunctive rules. First, there is an asymmetry between attributes and classes. That is, if defining attributes are known, then class membership is readily ascertained; but a knowledge of class membership does not provide certain information about attributes. Second, an attempt to test the relevance of attributes directly is very inefficient since all members of the class do not have the same attributes. In contrast, under conjunctive rules attributes and classes are symmetric and the relevance of attributes is readily tested directly. Under conjunctive rules relevant attributes must be checked to find out if an instance is positive, whereas under distinctive rules, attributes must be checked to determine whether an instance is negative (Nickerson, 1967). However, rules differ in difficulty, even when relevant attributes do not need to be identified (Bourne and Guy, 1968a). This suggests that complexity is the important factor. Another reason may be familiarity, since ordinary experience is probably much greater with conjunctive than with other types of rules.

It is evident that a concept-attainment task has two aspects, learning the defining attributes and learning the rule. Procedurally, one could supply no information on either aspect or the subject could be told the rule and asked to define the attributes of positive instances, or the attributes could be stated and the subject required to discover the rule. Haygood and Bourne (1965) compared these conditions directly, under four rules: conjunction, disjunction, joint denial, and conditional. When subjects were first given preliminary training on disjunctive, conditional, and biconditional rules (with only conjunction explained), then tested on rule identification, order of difficulty was similar: conjunction, disjunction, conditional, biconditional. They found, as would be expected, that when "complete learning" is required (i.e., both to identify attributes and attain the rule), the task is hardest. But rule learning is easier than attribute identification.

It would be superficial to conclude that rule learning is actually easier or a lower order of conceptual behavior than attribute identification. At least under the conditions of these experiments, the latter is simply more tedious and requires a more extensive search or testing process, thus demanding more time and leading ordinarily to more errors.

MEANING

When a stimulus object is presented to a subject, we infer that intrinsic activities are aroused that correspond to the properties of the object, their relation to each other and to other memorial, cognitive, and affective states in some manner operative at that time. Such intrinsic processes are components of the systems that link stimuli and responses—that is, they are mediators. They also represent the "meaning" of the object. But meaning signifies more than the minimum mediating process—that is, meaning is involved when the stimulus evokes processes greater than or different from representations of the stimulus itself (Osgood, 1952). The problem of meaning is commonly treated in relation to words, and their significance—whether this significance is a matter of what a speaker *intends* that another person understand or of what the recipient of a verbal stimulus actually understands. However, it is evident that any stimulus object, not only a verbal stimulus, can elicit meaning.

Reference to various theories shows how meaning can be treated as little more than a simple, direct connection between stimulus and response, with content represented by implicit S-R linkages. From this standpoint there is scarcely any need to allow for complex structures of personal experience. The principle of mediation is a sufficient extension to allow for processes not directly accounted for by specific stimulus properties. At the opposite pole are theories that attempt to describe the mediating structures themselves—that is, that examine meaning.

If experience were closely similar in all persons and, further, if properties of overt stimuli were the sole determinants of response, meaning would be a minor problem (Adams, 1953). Both these conditions are well met in the laboratory, and, as a consequence, it is easy to ignore meaning. Actually, of course, there are all kinds and degrees of variation in learning and its memorial effects, and response is complexly influenced by intrinsic as well as extrinsic variables, including emotional and motivational states, and the structure of already-established and functioning cognitive systems.

Of course, even were concepts to have only denotative components, meaning would still pose difficulties, but connotative components very greatly complicate the problem.

Response Dominance

Research on verbal learning has led to proposals for the objective manipulation of variations in meaning. The notion is that words as stimuli differ in the degree to which they elicit other words as responses (associates). The greater the tendency to evoke a single response, the higher the dominance (or the more specific and predictable the meaning). Underwood and Richardson (1956) have prepared a list of words with stated dominance values by determining the typical percentage of associations for each of 213 nouns. There were forty response categories, such as "dark," "round," "smelly," "green," "painted," "heavy," and "rough." For example, CAVE and CLOSET have, respectively, 66 and 64 percent "dark" associations, whereas FOREST and SEWER have 14 and 10 percent "dark." Thus an investigator can choose stimuli that differ systematically in meaning in this sense.

Kendler and Karasik (1958) showed that response dominance affects the interference of irrelevant verbal stimuli. Sets of eight words were composed, in which four were related to a medium degree (elicited the concept "round" from 25 to 38 percent of the time). The other four were related by a highly dominant but different response (e.g., "white" 71 to 83 percent of the time), or had in common a low-dominant response (e.g., "white" 10 to 28 percent of the time), or were unrelated but each elicited a highly dominant but different response (67 to 96 percent of the time). Least interference occurred when the four irrelevant words shared a highly dominant response. Thus the strong relationship among the irrelevant words served to organize them effectively, facilitating their differentiation from the four critical "round" words.

The role of response dominance has been extended by Kendler and Watson (1968) to the reversal situation. In one experiment employing two categories, high dominance facilitated initial learning, but the difference from low-dominant associates was nonsignificant after reversal. In a second experiment using only a single category, but with a shift to a different category, performance was facilitated when the second concept was a high associate of the first. It appears that in the first case, experience in the task produced equivalence between high- and low-dominant associates; in the second case, a high-dominant relation served to make a critical word a salient cue to the solution.

The effect of meaning is shown in another way by Glixman (1965). When subjects classified statements characterized by the "meaning domains" of objects, war, and self, more categories were produced for objects and least for self, as if the latter had a more distinctive and consistent meaning. When examined for connotative meaning (see below), the category of self-statements was more differentiated than that for objects, again indicative of greater meaning (Glixman and Wolfe, 1967).

Finally, an experiment by Zimring (1969) exemplifies still another approach. He drew on the theory of personal constructs (Kelly, 1955) to hypothesize that "the more representative a word is of the common usage of the words in that construct system, the slower the reaction time will be in giving an associate to that word." In Kelly's theory, personal constructs represent individualized ways of viewing important persons and their relationships to oneself. By means of the Rep test, sets of three statements are presented, with the subject asked to state how two of them are alike, and how the third differs. Thus the central characteristics of personal constructs can be identified. From this test Zimring derived for each subject lists of words interrelated within construct systems, and these words could then be used for a word-association test. The results sustained the hypothesis, indicating that the more typical a word is of a personal construct system—that is, the more comprehensive its special meaning, or the more information it holds—the longer it takes to produce a different response word. Zimring suggests that components of a construct system differ in their functions within that system.

CONNOTATIVE MEANING

Building on his theoretical treatment of mediation, Osgood (1952) perceived the significance of connotative properties of concepts. Past learning in relation to objects provides associations of various kinds, not solely those arising directly from physical characteristics of stimuli. Indeed, affective and other intrinsic components are especially important in demonstrating the mediation principle since they cannot be inferred from the stimulus itself. Rather, we must search for inferences about cognitive structure.

Connotative properties, like denotative properties, are descriptions of objects. A peach is not only round, pink, and fuzzy, but also pleasant, sunny, and gentle. If adjectives denote sense impressions, they also connote feelings, judgments, and personal relevance. Although there are many available adjectives, it is easy to see that they can potentially be grouped into various categories, and that, as a consequence, connotative meanings can be treated as dimensions of objects, similar to denotative dimensions like color, form, and number. Borrowing from principles of scaling, it should be possible to express the degree to which adjectives are judged to describe objects.

Osgood proposed the semantic differential (S.D.) as a device for achieving this aim (Osgood, Suci, and Tannenbaum, 1957). First, it is assumed that verbal indicators (i.e., adjectives) can serve as indexes to connotative components of concepts. Second, connotative dimensions range between extremes that can be represented by opposing adjectives, with intermediate degrees of applicability, and a neutral midpoint. Third, there are groups of related dimensions with an underlying general characteristic.

Possible scales were selected by developing pairs of adjectives that might define the opposite poles of a scale. Items were cast as seven-point rating scales, as follows :

good——— :——— :——— :——— :——— :——— :———bad

The subject is presented with the name of an object (or concept) and

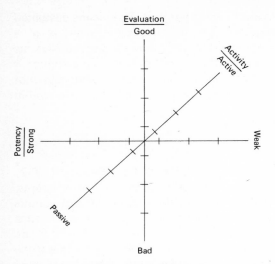

FIGURE 9-1   Three major dimensions of connotative meaning, as revealed in factor-analytic studies
by Osgood, Suci, and Tannenbaum (1957).

instructed to mark the place on the scale that most closely expresses
the meaning of the object to him. Responses can be scored either
by assigning the numbers 1 through 7 to successive subdivisions, or
by treating the middle space as zero and treating one side as positive
(+1, +2, +3) as one moves to the left, and the other as negative
(—1, —2, —3) as one moves to the right.

    Although a great number of such polar scales can be construc-
ted, factor-analytic studies have produced the familiar dimensions
widely used today, which are regarded as essentially orthogonal to
each other: evaluation (e.g., good—bad, pleasant—unpleasant,
beautiful—ugly), potency (e.g., strong—weak, large—small, heavy—
light), and activity (e.g., fast—slow, active—passive, sharp—dull)
(Figure 9-1). Note that sets of scales can be chosen on the basis of
their relevance to the object. For example, one would ordinarily not
use the scale lush-austere for the concept *psychology,* but might use
the scale rich-thin.

    The three dimensions just mentioned are not necessarily the
only dimensions of connotative meaning. They are simply those
that appear most commonly with the methods, objects, scales, and
subjects used. In fact other dimensions may also be important
(Osgood, Ware, and Morris, 1961 ; Pervin, 1967). Cross-cultural studies,

furthermore, reveal distinctive variations in dimensions (Tanaka and Osgood, 1965).

Furthermore these dimensions define the descriptive practices of people in general. Idiosyncratic connotative meaning is measured only in the following ways: (1) by variations in polarity (e.g., one person may rate Napoleon +2 on the good-bad scale, another —3; (2) by the "profile" of ratings (i.e., the pattern of scores across a set of scales); and (3) by relationships among ratings across concepts (e.g., a set of objects highly positive in evaluation for one person, compared to highly negative for another person). Otherwise, special, "personal meanings" are not taken into account.

Finally, we must note that the S. D. is a *verbal* device. There is a danger that words may be treated as equivalent to concepts—but they are indexes to them, or expressions of them. The S.D. is most obviously a method for studying words and for obtaining overt verbal descriptions. In the long run, the S. D. must be complemented by attention to other indexes, such as imagery, autonomic measures, and so on. It may, of course, prove that different indicators of connotative meaning are related. For example, McMurray (1958) has shown that symbolic drawings chosen to "fit" a word (such as *rhythm, storm,*) have S. D. ratings similar to the word.[1]

Conditioning Connotative Meaning[2]

If concepts have connotative components, we should be able to condition them. C. K. Staats and A. W. Staats (1957) employed nonsense syllables as conditioned stimuli, with words representing S. D. poles as unconditioned stimuli. For example, the syllable YOF might be reinforced by the word *beauty*, and the syllable XEH by the word *ugly*. Control syllables were followed by neutral words.

[1]Certain technical criticisms of the S. D. can also be advanced. Thus the scales are strictly bipolar assuming that the two anchoring words are truly opposite. This assumption is probably justified for the most part, but nevertheless imposes artificial constraints on judgment. It is quite possible that an object may be both good and bad (i.e., either complex or arousing ambivalent feelings); if forced to make a judgment, a person may be hard put to choose one side or the other, possibly ending with a neutral rating. Furthermore, it is assumed that the two polar words are equivalent in their information value. This assumption may work fairly well for practical purposes, but it has been shown that this is not always the case (Ross and Levy, 1960; Terwilliger, 1962). Differences between the anchoring words, in this respect, affect ratings. The more meaningful an adjective, the greater its polarity on the S.D. Green and Goldfried (1965) elucidate several ways in which the Osgood techniques impose artificial restrictions on the measurement of connotative meaning. Heise (1969) has reviewed these and other points, in general concluding that sources of error and bias do not vitiate the merits of the scales. His point that responses are markedly affected by individual differences should be emphasized.

[2]Some materials especially prepared for experimental use include lists of words for which S. D.; ratings have been determined, such as hose by Jenkins, Russell, and Suci (1958), and Heise (1965).

After an extensive conditioning series, the syllables were rated on S. D. scales, showing that they had acquired connotation corresponding with the reinforcing words, for all three dimensions. A later experiment (A. W. Staats and C. K. Staats, 1958) confirmed this result, with nationalities as conditioned stimuli. Although this experiment has been criticized on the ground that demand characteristics were responsible, since the rather transparent procedure might merely make subjects aware of the contingency (Page, 1969)[3] other studies confirm such effects (Miller, 1966; Yavuz, 1963).

Less direct effects of acquired connotation are perhaps more convincing, as revealed in studies of *generalization*. Here a set of words is first conditioned, and then associated words are tested to see whether they have acquired meaning similar to that induced by conditioning. In one experiment, neutral words were reinforced by positively or negatively evaluative words. Generalization appears in changes in S. D. ratings for synonyms of the conditioned words (Staats, Staats, and Heard, 1959). In another experiment, Brotsky (1968) conditioned subjects to the brand names of automobiles and white noise, using the galvanic skin response as a measure of conditioning. Significant generalization occurred to the word CAR and new automobile names, for both the galvanic skin response and S. D. measures (see Figure 9-2). Similar evidence appears in other studies (Dicken, 1961 ; DiVesta and Stover, 1962).

Satiation and Generation of Meaning

A commonsense phenomenon that has a long history in psychology (Basette and Warne, 1919) has recently come under intensive scrutiny. It is the observation that the intensive repetition of a word produces a loss of meaning. The word seems to become only a sound.

Smith and Raygor (1956) exposed words with very common responses from the Kent-Rosanoff list. For the experimental condition a word was exposed for three 7-second periods, during which the subjects fixated the word, with 3-second intervals, writing the word while pronouncing it subvocally. There ensued a brief exposure of the word, with the subjects writing anonymously an association to it. For the control period the words were given as a simple association test, with a brief exposure, followed by writing a response. Under satiation, significantly more subjects produced un-

---

[3]Staats (1969) points to other evidence in replying to Page, suggesting that the principle holds despite methodological problems.

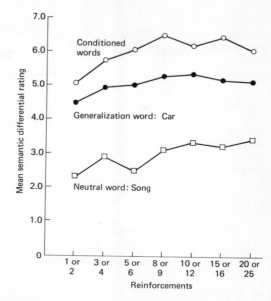

FIGURE 9-2 Generalization of conditioned connotative meaning. (Based on Brotsky, 1968.)

common than common responses, and vice versa for the control condition. In a replication with a continuous 20-second exposure, the difference was even more pronounced.

Lambert and Jakobovits (1960) found that satiation decreased the polarity of ratings on S. D. scales, indicating loss of connotative meaning (see Table 9-1). A second experiment showed that a central mediating process is responsible. Thus, although the muscular responses in saying "nuka nuka" are the same as "canoe canoe" (except for the first and last segments), the former showed no loss of meaning. In paired-associate learning, satiation not only decreased connotative meaning, but brought about slower learning and increased retroactive inhibition (Kanungo, Lambert, and Maurer, 1962).

Fillenbaum (1963, 1964a) has also reported significant satiation effects, including evidence for generalization to related words. Gampel (1966) found that satiation increases with the length of the repetition interval, stabilizing after 60 seconds. Recovery of meaning was very rapid, reaching a maximum at delay intervals between 5 and 15 seconds.

Table 9-1

Change in Polarity per Word over the Sum of Nine S. D. Scales. (From Lambert and Jakobovits, 1960.)

		Change in Polarity		
Condition	N	Mean	S.D.	t
Satiation	22	−2.85	2.93	4.45*
Silence control	19	0.03	1.41	0.09
Different-word control	19	−0.66	1.91	1.46
Retest control	22	−0.21	0.73	1.31

$*p < .01$

An interesting opposite effect appeared in experiments by Yelen and Schulz (1963). Instead of a decrease in meaning, they found an increase, or a *generation* of meaning. Further analysis disclosed the possibility that some S.D. scales are apparently susceptible to satiation, others to generation. Accordingly, they repeated the experiment, endeavoring also to approximate more exactly the Lambert and Jakobovits conditions, with "satiation scales" (good-bad, active-passive, beautiful-ugly) and "generation scales" (wide-narrow, fast-slow, large-small). The results confirmed this distinction, with ratings on satiation scales initially more extreme, but becoming less so, while the opposite effect happened for the generation scales. A related finding is that words high in associative dominance display satiation effects, while words low in dominance display generation.

Amster (1964), after reviewing the evidence, points to certain methodological differences. Regression effects can account for some of the discrepancy, but not all. Thus control groups do not display such effects. Furthermore, Amster shows that the mean difference score used by Yelen and Schulz may typically yield a positive (or generation) value, whereas the polarity difference score adopted by Lambert and Jakobovits may produce a negative (or satiation) value. There is also the matter of initial polarity to consider, which is not yet fully clarified. If ratings are low in polarity at first, then the repetition procedure may well increase meaning. Gumenik and Perlmutter (1966) have shown that some of the effect attributed to repetition may be a function of set, since they obtained similar results under both oral repetition (20 seconds) and a 2-second presentation of a word followed by a 18-second blank period.

As shown by some of the studies mentioned, connotative satiation (a neutralization of meaning) may be distinguished from associative satiation (an interference with the production of customary associations). Amster discusses theories advanced to explain these effects. A counterconditioning principle might be invoked to say that the repeated word tends to become so well learned that it facilitates the response that matches the stimulus, thus interfering with other response processes, whether connotative or associative. Generation effects would be expected under brief exposure, since associations would at first be available. Or repetition might produce reactive inhibition, with a consequent reduction in the availability of meaning responses (connotative and/or associative). Generation might occur if, at first, habit strength increases more rapidly than reactive inhibition. Finally, Amster favors an adaptation-level interpretation, based on Helson's theory. Continuous repetition of a word, with only itself as a context, brings about gradual shifting of the adaptation level in the direction of neutrality. Generation could be explained at least partly by the connotation of the situational context. There should be a shift in the connotation in that direction, if both are on the same side of the neutral point.

Following this line of argument, Amster and Glasman (1966) point out that results obtained by Johnson, Thomson, and Frinckee (1960) show consistent generation when meaningless words are repeated. Furthermore, words in satiation studies have usually been pleasant to begin with, but neutral in generation experiments, and the verbal contexts may also be important. Accordingly, they conducted two experiments in which meaningless (Turkish) words were compared with meaningful words (adjectives) matched closely in length, frequency, and neutrality of evaluative connotation, and with additional Turkish and meaningful buffer words. In general, evaluative meaning (i.e., "goodness") increased with frequency of repetition. This change was greater for the meaningless material. With respect to context, evaluation increased when buffer words were meaningless, but there was an opposite (though nonsignificant) effect for the meaningful context. It appears then that generation and satiation effects depend on the type of word repeated, together with the context in which it is placed. The degree of initial meaning (or polarity) is a basic consideration, with repetition tending to neutralize (satiate) highly meaningful words while establishing greater meaning (generation) in initially meaningless words. In general these experiments show how the mediating process can be influenced.

In their attempt to rule out regression effects, Schulz, Weaver and Radtke (1965) employed a posttest-only design, obtaining no difference between repetition and control groups. These results, however, cannot be interpreted clearly without knowing how well matched the groups were in their initial ratings. Furthermore, some difference from other studies in the interval between repetition and rating might be involved. Shima (1966) also found generation rather than satiation. His procedure was rather complex, and included a phase of producing associations to the repeated word between repetition and rating. It appears very likely that this condition at least served to restore meaning, if not to override satiation.

Similarly, the failure of Hupka and Goss (1969) to find either significant generation *or* satiation effects can possibly be explained on methodological grounds. Especially important to note are the relatively slight differences between their high- and low-polarity words (those with higher polarity ranged from 2.25 to 2.75, those with lower polarity from .66 to 1.29, with two words rated on one scale of each of three S. D. dimensions). These considerations plus other methodological variations render this study questionable as a test of connotative change.

Finally, Jakobovits (1965) has introduced satiation into a concept-attainment task. Sets of twelve words could be classified into equal subsets either on the basis of semantic class or physical similarity (e.g., rhyme or length). Under the experimental condition, one word was repeated for four 15-second periods; in the control condition, an irrelevant word was satiated. The subjects then classified the words, with their responses judged as semantic, phonetographic, or idiosyncratic. The experimental condition produced significantly more phonetographic classifications. Without further research it is not clear whether the repetition served to reduce the connotative meaning component or to emphasize the physical (more concrete or denotative?) component [Esposito and Pelton (1971) suggest that the effect is perceptual rather than semantic]. Certainly, however, the possibilities for influencing the intrinsic mediating basis of conceptual behavior are evident.

Concept Attainment

Various studies have sought to bring connotative variables into line with the denotative dimensions usually employed. Haygood (1966) directly tested the possibility that subjects can classify words on the basis of S. D. dimensions. Lists were selected containing words from each end of an evaluative (good-bad) or a potency (hard-soft) scale. The task of the subject was to assign each word to one of two categories (X or not-X). These sets were used for a "concept" condition; in a contrasting "no concept" condition, words were randomly assigned to the two categories, so that correct classfica- tion could be learned only by rote memory. In addition, subjects learned either under instructions to memorize or under instructions to discover the correct principle. As shown in Figure 9-3, there was significant evidence for attaining the connotative classification.[1] Although there was some improvement under the "no concept" condition, a somewhat greater rate occurred under the "concept" condition ($P <$ .05). The instruction conditions differed little, attributed to the fact that all the subjects had previously participated in another concept-attainment experiment.

It is important to note that the previously mentioned lack of complete equivalence of the two ends of S. D. scales emerges also in conceptual learning. Rhine (1965) found that positive evaluative concepts are more easily acquired than negative concepts. In a subsequent experiment, Rhine, Cole, and Ogilvie (1968) further demonstrate that such effects are influenced by word frequency and types of words. Thus resistance to change (introduced by reversing word assignments) is greater for positive concepts incorporating high-frequency words. Resistance is also greater when the two phases employ the same type of words rather than different types.

In summary, the introduction of connotative meaning into the study of conceptual behavior opens important avenues for research. Its significance lies in complementing denotative variables in media- tion with intrinsic components not readily accessible from specifica- tion of stimulus properties.

VARIATIONS IN COMPLEXITY

If we treat a conceptual class as defined by the dimensions of the objects that belong in the class, then it follows that we can render a category more complex by increasing the number of dimensions relevant to it. Dimensions can be *relevant,* that is, required to identify the rule of classification, or *irrelevant,* that is, not related to the rule. We can ascertain the rule by properly noticing relevant dimensions and their values, but we cannot discover the rule by attending to irrelevant dimensions. Many experiments have sought

---

[1] Despite the separation, evaluative and potency were not significantly different.

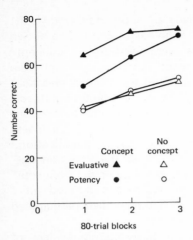

FIGURE 9-3   Attainment of concepts with connotative dimensions. (From Haygood, 1966.)

to determine the effects on performance of varying the number of either relevant or irrelevant dimensions, or both. We could, for example, make a conjunctive rule depend on color and form, on color and form and size, on color and form and size and number, and so on; irrelevant dimensions can be limited to one, as when stimuli are constructed to vary in just three dimensions, but two are relevant, or to more than one, when additional dimensions are incorporated. In general, the greater the number of relevant dimensions, the more distinctive the instances of different classes become; at the same time, the more necessary it is to test the various dimensions available and their combinations. The greater the number of irrelevant dimensions, the more chances there are of making errors. Thus, as complexity increases in either fashion, we would expect the difficulty of attaining the correct concept to increase.

Redundancy
When dimensions are redundant, instances can be classified correctly on one or more properties (e.g., all *red* stimuli are also *large*); similarly, two or more irrelevant redundant dimensions are correlated, so they must be ignored equally (e.g., although form and number correspond, neither is correct). Redundancy increases complexity without affecting the number of instances required.

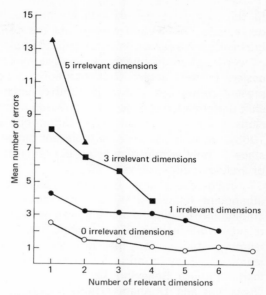

FIGURE 9-4 Mean number of errors to solution as a joint function of number of redundant relevant and nonredundant irrelevant stimulus dimensions. Each plotted point represents the data from fifteen subjects. (From Bourne and Haygood, 1961.)

As relevant redundancy increases, performance improves, and this facilitation is greater the larger the number of irrelevant dimensions, but irrelevant redundancy interferes with performance, although less than when irrelevant dimensions are nonredundant (Bourne and Haygood, 1959, 1961; Keele and Archer, 1967) (see Figure 9-4). The addition of nonredundant dimensions, whether relevant or irrelevant, makes the problem more complex, and hence more difficult (numerous studies, including Archer, Bourne, and Brown, 1955; Bulgarella and Archer, 1962; Pishkin and Shurley, 1965). Similarly, performance declines as the number of irrelevant values within dimensions increases (Battig and Bourne, 1961). However, this applies much more to attribute learning than to rule learning (Haygood and Stevenson, 1967; Bower and King, 1967).

After a concept has been learned, the introduction of irrelevant cues (Braley, 1962) interferes with the learning of concepts utilizing those cues. But a cue that was positive in a previously learned concept facilitates the attainment of concepts based on newly introduced dimensions. These two situations are versions of the shift paradigm.

In the first case the extradimensional shift produces the usual decrement. The second case is not the conventional reversal shift but in effect the same principle seems to apply : the previously learned concepts, when they become negative, make the new discrimination easier. In the regular shift situations, when irrelevant cues are present throughout both stages, both reversal- and extradimensional-shift performance decline with increased number of irrelevant dimensions, but the within-dimension shift is not affected (P. J. Johnson, 1966). However, when new irrelevant dimensions are introduced in stage 2, only within-dimension performance declines with number of irrelevant dimensions.

Richardson and Bergum (1954) proposed that concept attainment follows a three-stage sequence, beginning with discrimination of dimensions and values, followed by identifying the relevant dimensions ("dimension selection"), and ending with learning names for the defining characteristics ("associative learning"). They found that most time was spent in the associative-learning phase. Believing that these conditions maximized difficulty, Overstreet and Dunham (1969) sought to render the dimension-selection process more comparable in difficulty. The difficulty of associative learning was varied by using different numbers of values per dimension, and the difficulty of dimension selection was varied by introducing different numbers of irrelevant dimensions. After initial training on dimensions and values (the first stage above), the subjects went through a stage of learning the relevent dimensions, then acquired labels for the correct categories. The difficulty of dimension selection was a function of the number of irrelevant dimensions, but the difficulty of associative learning depended on the number of values per dimension. This distinction is worth further investigation since it points to two quite distinct aspects of complexity.

In general then, the more complex the stimuli the more difficult it is to attain concepts, whether added dimensions are relevant or irrelevant. However, redundant relevant dimensions facilitate performance and the higher the proportion of available dimensions that are relevant, the better the performance; redundant irrelevant dimensions interfere with performance.

CONDITIONS OF PRACTICE

The concept-attainment task provides a wide variety of factors that can influence the subject's efficiency. One can determine the effects of particular kinds of prior experience on the main task, leading to a distinction between *pretraining* and *training*. At either stage, numerous variables can be identified, including instruction, feedback, the sequence of instances, complexity, and so on.

Pretraining to acquaint subjects with the stimuli and/or their names (especially when the labels are meaningful) generally facilitates learning (Kendler and Vineberg, 1954; Lacey and Goss, 1959; Rasmussen and Archer, 1961; Petre, 1964). Practice in the task itself, as would be expected, improves performance (Hull, 1920; Peterson, 1968). In tasks depending on mediating processes, sufficient time must be allowed during or between instances (Bourne et al., 1965). The more *obvious* the relevant features, the better the performance (Hull, 1920; Archer, 1962), but special cues to irrelevant dimensions impair concept learning (Rasmussen and Archer, 1961; S. H. Simon and Jackson, 1968).

Presentation of Instances

Underwood (1952) has argued that contiguity of stimuli is necessary for concept attainment—and without doubt, contiguity usually facilitates performance (Dominowski, 1965). Thus when instances of a concept are presented in succession, it is more readily attained than when instances are intermixed with exemplars of other concepts (Kurtz and Hovland, 1956). And the greater the number of noncritical instances that precede a "key" instance or that intervene between such an instance and test stimuli, the more performance declines (Hunt, 1961; Jacoby and Radtke, 1969). Increasing the contiguity of positive instances facilitates the attainment of disjunctive as well as conjunctive concepts (Haygood et al., 1969).

The intermixing of successive instances has been extended to require the subject to learn more than one concept at a time (Restle and Emmerich, 1966). Errors increased slightly for two concurrent problems, but sharply increased for three at a time, with little further increase for six at a time. A person can manage a few dimensions very well, but beyond that, interference is considerable. Additional experimentation indicated that short-term memory is especially important for single-concept problems, but multiple-concept problems depend more on remembering the correct hypothesis than the stimuli themselves.

In the typical experiments, the experimenter imposes the rule on the subject. Mandler and Pearlstone (1966) allowed subjects in a *free* condition to sort cards into any categories they wished; in a *constrained* condition the experimenter imposed rules corresponding to those freely adopted by "yoked" partners. The free condition produced faster attainment with fewer errors.

Positive and Negative Instances

Kuo (1923) found that a problem becomes more difficult as the proportion of negative instances increases. Despite Smoke's (1932, 1933) failure to confirm this principle, it has generally been supported, although with some refinements. Analyzing the concept-attainment task as a communication situation, Hovland (1952) suggested that the experimenter transmits information by labeling instances as "correct" or "incorrect." Therefore the information conveyed by instances should be ascertainable by determining the number of possible hypotheses and how many are eliminated by successive positive or negative instances. The instances required could be specified by number of dimensions, the number of values of each, the proportion of correct hypotheses, and so on.

Following this approach, Hovland and Weiss (1953) constructed stimuli from which a concept could be attained by deduction either from all-positive or all-negative instances. In several experiments, all-positive sequences proved markedly superior—even with variations to equalize the information available; intermixed series were next, and all-negative series were worst. Simultaneous presentation facilitated all-negative series, but not enough to overcome the advantage of all-positive sequences. Other experiments similarly point to the increasing ease of attainment as the proportion of positive instances increases (Buss, 1950; Mayzner, 1962; Schvaneveldt, 1966). However, continued practice reduces the difference between the two kinds of instances (Fryatt and Tulving, 1963).

As noted by Smoke (1933) and Schvaneveldt (1966), in some problems negative instances are required to eliminate hypotheses—that is, nonconjunctive problems. Huttenlocher (1962), drawing on Bruner, Goodnow, and Austin (1956), points out that in disjunctive concepts informational value is reversed since one cannot as readily determine whether an instance exemplifies the concept, as whether it *does not*. Therefore negative instances should transmit more information and should be more efficient. Although two negative instances proved harder than either two positive instances or a positive followed by a negative instance, the easiest condition was a negative followed by a positive instance. Haygood and Devine (1967) pointed out that both relevant attributes are present in conjunctive problems, but only one may be available under nonconjunctive rules. When the proportion of instances in such problems containing both relevant attributes was increased, performance was facilitated. Thus the important factor is not so much positive instances as the amount of relevant information conveyed (see also, P. J. Johnson and White, 1969). In fact, for this reason negative instances are actually more efficient than positive instances in disjunctive problems (Freibergs and Tulving, 1961; Chlebek and Dominowski, 1970). For example, if the concept is "blue" *or* "circle," but not both (exclusive disjunction), then all negative instances are "blue circle," and each positive instance conveys only half the necessary information. The opposite holds for conjunctive concepts. Thus, for "blue circle," a positive instance contains all relevant information, whereas a negative instance, such as "blue square," contains only half the essential information. For disjunction, one could discover the complementary conjunctive concept, then simply reverse the classification (i.e., designate the conjunctive concept as negative). In general then, the role of positive and negative instances depends on the conceptual rule.

All-positive, all-negative, or mixed series were employed in conjunctive, disjunctive, and conditional problems by Bourne and Guy (1968b) under attribute identification and rule-learning training procedures. On subsequent test trials, the mixed series was most efficient across all rules (see Table 9-2).

For attribute identification, however, positive instances proved best in conjunctive and disjunctive problems, and worse in conditional problems. Negative instances were much more efficient in disjunctive and conditional problems than in conjunctive problems. Rule-learning performance (discovering how to combine relevant attributes according to a principle) thus seems to depend on the variety of instances during training: the mixed series was best. Attribute-identification efficiency (discovering which attributes to combine under a stated rule) depends, by contrast, on training that minimizes the variety of stimuli: positive for conjunctive rules, negative for conditional rules. In addition, positive instances being most efficient for disjunctive rules (although the negative category is more homogeneous) suggests additional factors, namely, that positive focusing strategy, as described below, is easier, or that the task is more difficult simply because negative information must be converted into positive form.

Table 9-2

Mean Number of Trials to Solution for Attribute Identification (AI) and Rule Learning (RL) Procedures in Test Trials, for Three Rules. (Modified from Bourne and Guy, 1968b.)

Instances	Conjunction		Disjunction		Conditional	
	AI	RL	AI	RL	AI	RL
Positive	3.9	6.6	12.9	4.7	28.8	20.5
Negative	46.3	3.0	19.8	15.3	16.9	23.3
Mixed	6.1	.9	16.5	2.4	17.9	17.1

Davidson (1969) has further pointed out that the character of the problem determines the role of positive and negative instances. Analyzing the type of problems described by Hovland (1952), he suggests that simple disjunctive concepts are "mirror" images of Hovland's conjunctive concepts. For example, suppose that the concept is a combination of number (one, two, or three) and form (circle, square, triangle), with a fourth value of each (four and hexagon) and with color (four values also) as irrelevant. Negative instances would be four circles, four squares, one hexagon, and two hexagons. But for the disjunctive concept—four and hexagon—these instances are positive and the formerly positive instances negative. By inverting the problem, the logical aspect can be distinguished from the negative character of the series. With this approach, disjunctive problems were solved faster than conjunctive problems, and although the all-negative series was much slower for conjunctive problems, little difference appeared for disjunctive problems. The logical difference (conjunctive positive and disjunctive negative versus disjunctive positive and conjunctive negative) accounted for two-thirds of the variance, compared to less than a tenth for the positive versus negative series.

Instructions   As might be expected, special instructions (or information) may significantly influence performance. Instructions to be analytical decrease variability and facilitate more complex tasks (Archer, Bourne, and Brown, 1955).

Laughlin (1964) found that instructions to attain a concept as fast as possible facilitated speed of solution, but that instructions to make as few choices as possible did not affect the number of choices required to reach a solution.

Performance also improves when subjects are allowed to verbalize freely (Wolfgang, 1967) or required to state a hypothesis on each trial (Byers and Davidson, 1967). Finally, the more precise the information about the probabilities of occurrence of dimensions, the better the performance (Bornstein and Grier, 1968; Laughlin, 1969).

Feedback   During the period when the subject is working on a problem, performance is influenced by the information provided. There are beneficial effects of allowing previously exposed instances to remain in view (Bourne, Goldstein, and Link, 1964). But a small number is optimal, since more than five produces a decline—at least with a limited time interval.

The effect of available information depends on the kind of feedback, with negative feedback much the worst (Pishkin and Wolfgang, 1965). When incorrect responses are corrected by feedback, performance improves (Pishkin, 1967). The greater the percentage of information feedback, whether positive or negative, the better the performance (Bourne and Pendleton, 1958), and misinformation, not surprisingly, has an adverse effect (Pishkin, 1960; Bourne, 1963). All these effects become more pronounced as the problem becomes more complex.

STRATEGY

The active search and summation theories, discussed earlier, lead to conceptions of differential strategies in concept attainment. On the one hand, the subject may pursue a course of deliberately testing instances against hypotheses or he may wait for information to build up as it occurs and thus evolve his hypothesis. Viewed in this way, strategy is a function of attitudes that characterize the subject's approach to the problem. As a potential intrinsic variable, strategy thus becomes an aspect of *cognitive style*, to be discussed in the next section. There has, however, been little research that explicitly formulates active search and summation attitudes as cognitive styles, although various studies suggest that it would be possible to do so. Instead, strategy has been treated as *patterns of responses*, without attempts to draw inferences concerning the cognitive mechanisms responsible. In fact, differences in strategy have been linked more with task properties than with attitudes.

Interest in strategy, in the sense of typical response sequences, has been stimulated by the work of Bruner, Goodnow, and Austin

(1956). In general their approach to strategy compares processes of attaining concepts when the subject chooses instances himself, after the experimenter has presented a positive instance, with those when the experimenter successively presents instances. The first condition is said to produce *selection* strategies, the second *reception* strategies.

Selection strategies may take several forms, as follows:

1 *Simultaneous scanning* is using each instance as a test for all possible hypotheses. Clearly this approach is extremely demanding since it requires complete memory both for stimulus properties and for retained or rejected hypotheses. Such demands become increasingly great as complexity increases.

2 *Successive scanning* calls on testing one hypothesis at a time, with the subject choosing instances that directly test it. This procedure is a simplifying one; however, there is a risk of choosing poorly informing instances.

3 *Conservative focusing* is a process of selecting a positive instance as a point of reference and then choosing instances that systematically alter one attribute at a time. If an instance is positive, the changed feature is not part of the concept, but if an instance is negative, then the changed feature is relevant. Clearly this process can be very efficient for it permits attention to attributes rather than hypotheses, and thus reduces the complexity of the problem. Indeed, it renders the task more concrete (and thus easier). In general this strategy appears to involve summation rather than active search.

4 *Focus gambling* carries the just-mentioned procedure a step farther by altering more than one attribute at a time. It is obviously riskier than the tedious but careful procedure of conservative focusing. However, since it is risky, it may require more choices, in opposition to the possible advantage of securing information more quickly.

Bruner, Goodnow, and Austin (1956) found in general that focusing is superior to scanning when instances are not perceptually available (e.g., when the stimulus display is removed), as might be expected from the greater demands on memory of scanning strategies. With ordered arrays, focusing is also superior, but with random arrays, scanning seems to be better. With abstract materials (those stimuli typically used), focusing is better, but scanning works very well with thematic materials (i.e., meaningful objects rather than figures or designs), perhaps because the familiarity of actual objects facilitates memory, thus making it possible to capitalize on the greater information obtained by scanning. Finally, subjects often employ modifications or combinations, as shown also in research on hypothesis testing.

Two forms of reception strategy were described:

1 *Wholist,* or a continuous focusing process, by which the subject adopts at the outset a hypothesis based on the total instance, and then retains or changes it as new instances come along.

2 *Partist,* or the application of scanning, by which the subject begins with a hypothesis based on some aspect of an instance, and uses new instances to test it; if it is incorrect, he then seeks to remember preceding instances and to use this information in developing a new hypothesis. Clearly this procedure can be very demanding.

Wholist strategy was more frequently employed by the Bruner, Goodnow, and Austin (1956) subjects, and it was more successful than partist strategy. Subjects tended consistently to use one strategy or the other, suggesting that we might infer the operation of cognitive styles.

The foregoing picture applies to conjunctive concepts. In disjunctive problems, which depend on negative instances, *negative focusing* and *multiple negative* strategies were described. The former involves systematically altering values of negative instances. The latter involves searching for two or more negative instances, comparing them, and using their opposites to define the concepts. This procedure is likely to be awkward and less efficient than negative focusing.

One implication is that appropriate strategies depend in large degree on the character of the problem. In a study by Peterson and Colavita (1964), for example, not only did the more efficient subjects employ wholist strategy, but they shifted to a partist strategy in later stages, when this procedure represented a more effective use of information. In line with Bruner, Goodnow, and Austin, Bourne (1965) found conservative focusing that begins with a broad initial hypothesis to be especially efficient in conjunctive problems. In fact, subjects shift to this strategy as soon as an especially informative positive instance becomes available (Nahinsky and Slaymaker, 1970). Focusing strategy increases in more complex problems (Laughlin, 1965, 1966), no doubt because it makes less demand on memory.

Conant and Trabasso (1964) showed that positive focusing strategy is adopted more readily in conjunctive problems than negative focusing is in disjunctive problems. Subsequently, Laughlin (1968a) extended the analysis to eight rules. The order of decreasing use of focusing was as follows: conjunction, exclusion, conjunctive absence, biconditional, exclusive disjunction, inclusive disjunction, disjunctive absence, and conditional. Efficiency followed a similar order with minor changes. In general, focusing strategy appears to be especially appropriate when memory requirements are least demanding.

Several variables were investigated by Laughlin, McGlynn et al. (1968). There were no general effects of sex or memory (paper and pencil allowed the subjects to keep a record) on the use of focusing, but females were more efficient than males when they were permitted to use paper as a memory aid. Subjects working cooperatively on the problems were more efficient than individuals, and more often adopted focusing strategy. Male pairs more often used focusing strategy than did female pairs, but there was no sex difference under the individual condition. In general more-intelligent subjects tend to adopt focusing and wholist strategies (Rao, 1971).

In disjunctive problems, instruction in negative focusing (the appropriate one) facilitates attainment, compared to the information that a disjunctive concept is required (Wells and Watson, 1965). Practice improved performance under both conditions, and the availability of a negative instance was more effective than display of a positive instance. Conjunctive concepts were investigated by Byers, Davidson, and Rohwer (1968) under conditions of displaying instances versus no display, with subjects either uninstructed or given instructions designed to promote conservative focusing. The strategy instructions significantly facilitated attainment only when no memory aid was present.

COGNITIVE STYLE

The principle that conceptual behavior varies with the cognitive structure of the person is complementary to strategy in the sense just described. A cognitive style is associated with consistent modes of responding to, organizing, and using information. It may be shown in characteristic patterns of attention and choice (Gardner et al., 1959; Klein, 1958; Wachtel, 1968), in contrasting perceptual (or concrete) and analytic (or abstract) treatment of stimuli (Grant, 1951; Harvey, Hunt, and Schroder, 1961), and in varying degrees of rigidity or flexibility (Schroder and Rotter, 1952). Cognitive styles appear to be consistent across a wide range of conceptual tasks (Gardner and Schoen, 1962).

Interference Proneness

The Stroop Color-Word Interference Test (Stroop, 1935) has been developed to measure cognitive styles that differentiate between flexible and constricted control in coping with conflicting stimuli. This test consists of three parts: part 1, serving as a "warm up," presents four color names (e.g., RED, BLUE) in random order in black ink. The subject is instructed to read the *names* as rapidly as possible. Part 2 presents strips of colored asterisks in positions corresponding to the words in part 1 and matched for length, position, and color of words in part 3. Instructions are to name the *colors* as rapidly as possible. In part 3, colors and color names are presented in competing combinations—that is, the name is in a different color (e.g., RED is in blue ink). The subject now must report the *color*, not the word, as rapidly as possible. An interference measure is the difference between the time required for part 3 and the time predicted from the regression of time on part 3 from time on part 2. Other scores can also be derived. For example, Broverman (1960) distinguished "conceptual" versus "sensorimotor" cognitive styles, with the former naming colors (part 2) relatively faster than color names (part 1), and "strong" versus "weak automatizers," with the former having greater difficulty on part 3. Each style was associated with greater efficiency in certain kinds of tasks: conceptual in a difficult addition task; perceptual in a difficult pattern-tracing task; and strong automatization in simpler, more routine versions of these tasks.

Amster (1965) devised a concept-attainment task in which complex designs alternated with pictures. Instructions to examine one set of stimuli induced an intentional set, with the other stimuli as incidental. Concept attainment was measured by verbal definitions and drawings. No effect appeared for the former, but for the representational measure, subjects low in interference proneness were better than those high in this characteristic under intentional set, and were worse under incidental set. Thus low interference proneness promotes attention to relevant features, with nonrelevant cues being less distracting. At the same time, of course, ability to produce information about incidental stimuli is reduced.

Category Width

Pettigrew (1958) has devised a test to measure the degree to which individuals set limits on a class of objects. One item, for example, starts with an estimate of the average length of whales; the subject is asked to indicate from four alternatives what he thinks is the greatest length of a whale in the Atlantic Ocean, and then the shortest length. Pettigrew found that females tend to produce narrower categories than males. Broad categorizers are less sensitive to differences among events, and therefore should tend to generalize from one set of events to future events. In fact, Phares and Davis (1966) had female subjects estimate their performance on Rorschach and word-association tests. The Rorschach was administered and fictitious scores attributed to induce failure, followed by new estimates for the word-association test. The broad categorizers lowered these estimates more than did narrow categorizers, indicating generalization from the failure experience—that is, less sensitivity to the difference between the two tests.

Cognitive Complexity

Some investigators have attempted to distinguish more concrete from more abstract styles. McGaughran (1954) took his lead from Goldstein in defining a variable of "conceptual freedom" ranging between closed and open poles, and representing the degree to which an individual can incorporate new and varied members into a class. To this he added a principle of conceptual extensionality ranging between public and private poles, and corresponding generally to the dominance of denotative or connotative components. Conceptual areas were treated as combinations of these characteristics. *Hypostatic* conceptualizers form relatively closed concepts in which denotative elements dominate; *metastatic* conceptualizers have open-end concepts with emphasis on denotative properties; and *autistatic* conceptualizers are dominated by connotative elements, with undetermined status on the other continuum.[1] The hypostatic category corresponds most closely to what is typically

[1] Actually, logic suggests that there should be two kinds of autistatic conceptualizers, perhaps distinguished by impulsivity (open end) and obsessive compulsivity (closed).

regarded as abstract, with the autistatic' more concrete, although McGaughran's systems may be more useful than such an oversimplification might suggest. These differences were assessed by performance on an object-sorting test. On a subsequent picture-interpretation task, the hypostatic subjects displayed less spontaneity, flexibility, and autonomy; they tried to be more exact and literal, and were more resistant to ambiguity in the materials.

Another approach stems from the theoretical position of Harvey, Hunt, and Schroder (1961), summarized above. Here concreteness or abstractness is measured by items indicative of variations in ability to make differentiations and integrations, tendencies toward extreme and biased versus more balanced judgments, dependence on external versus internal cues, and other characteristics. Studying the attitudes of pro-Mormons toward the Mormon religion, White and Harvey (1965) found that concrete subjects more often used extreme categories, used fewer categories, showed larger gaps in their scales, and displayed a stronger tendency to produce pro-Mormon statements when asked to write new attitude statements. It has further been found that more-complex subjects achieve better integration of information, and are better at solving problems involving complex information (Streufert, Suedfeld, and Driver, 1965; Suedfeld and Hagen, 1966).

There is also some evidence that *field-independent* persons, described (by Witkin et al., 1954) as more analytical, freer from environmental support, and better able to initiate and organize judgmental processes, compared to field-dependent persons, perform better in abstract tasks or situations that involve analyzing and differentiating complex stimuli (Elkind, Koegler, and Go, 1963; Wachtel, 1968).

Dogmatism

Rokeach (1951a, 1960) has defined an attitudinal dimension of open- and closed-mindedness, representing "the extent to which the person can receive, evaluate, and act on relevant information received from the outside on its own intrinsic merits, unencumbered by irrelevant factors arising from within the person or from the outside" (1960, p. 57). Relative to closed-minded persons, open-minded persons are hypothesized to be receptive to new information, to be able to reconcile ideas discrepant with their preexisting beliefs, and to have flexible cognitive structures.

In one study, subjects high on Rokeach's dogmatism scale and

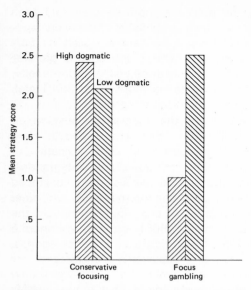

FIGURE 9-5   Use of strategy by subjects high and
low in dogmatism. (Based on Torcivia and Laughlin,
1968.) Note: A special scoring system was used to
measure strategy. Results were similar for abstract
and social displays. The figure gives results for the
abstract display, consisting of cards containing
combinations of + and — signs. The social display
consisted of drawings of social situations.

on the F-scale measure of authoritarianism were found to employ fewer
and broader categories in sorting items of a socially relevant sort, compared to items low in relevance (White, Alter, and Rardin, 1965). In
another study, closed-minded subjects displayed difficulty in adapting to the initial demands of a task (Ladd, 1967). In a third, dogmatism had little relation to use of conservative focusing (a highly
efficient strategy), but persons low in dogmatism more often adopted
focus gambling (high risk and more variable in efficiency) (Torcivia
and Laughlin, 1968) (see Figure 9-5).

Generality of Cognitive Styles
Variables like those mentioned above appear to have certain common
denominators of flexibility, broadness or inclusiveness of definition,
ability to differentiate components of stimuli, and ability to integrate

information. Baggaley (1955) correlated with card-sorting performance a variety of tests regarded as measures of important cognitive factors. Significant relations were found for inductive and deductive reasoning, speed of closure, and strength of closure. In a more recent study, Vannoy (1965) conducted a factor analysis of twenty tests proposed by investigators as measures of complexity and simplicity. All correlations were very low, and some eight factors emerged, with little indication of the hypothesized general dimension. One must conclude that we are a long way from identifying cognitive styles that can validly be given general definitions. Instead, we have numerous, quite specific tests, each of which has some predictive value in some tasks. Of crucial importance, no doubt, will be direct attention to the problem of relevance and to providing a wide spectrum of tasks along dimensions of complexity, concreteness and abstractness, and meaning. Furthermore, motivational variables must be included to reveal interactions.

MOTIVATION

So far, investigators have been concerned mainly with mapping the general characteristics of conceptual behavior and with the effects of variations in task and situational variables. Similarly, students of motivation have devoted much of their effort to the differentiation and measurement of fundamental variables. Pursuit of this interest has entailed the use of perceptual and learning tasks that are usually simpler than those employed for concept attainment. Even in those studies that might bear on conceptualizing, little attention has been paid to the principle of relevance—that is, some instigative or drive variable has been manipulated without considering clearly whether a distinctive conceptual effect might be elicited by it. Although variations in biogenic motives, or in the psychogenic motives typically studied (achievement, affiliation), are surely important for wide ranges of behavior, there is no reason to suppose that their influence is uniform for all aspects of response. Indeed, conceptual behavior might be very little affected by motivational states that produce pronounced effects in perception, memory, speed of learning, and so on. In fact there is considerable evidence that conditions that facilitate or degrade simple learning may have little effect on performance in complex tasks (Vinacke, 1960b). In distinction to other forms of instigation, cognitive motives may be especially significant for conceptual performance (Cohen, Stotland, and Wolfe, 1955).

Some situational variables can certainly be interpreted as having an arousal or instigation effect. A favorite is electric shock. Ross, Rupel, and Grant (1952) found that it impaired performance on the Wisconsin Card-sorting Test, whereas other forms of distraction did not. There was, however, rapid recovery with little effect in later stages of the experiment. False norms were invoked by Juzak (1955) to induce feelings of success or failure in solving conceptual problems. Test problems were then administered, in which either of two solutions was possible. The success induction had no effect, but failure led to a preference for the solution with which it had previously been associated, suggesting that this result may depend on aroused achievement motivation.

Manifest Anxiety

Anxiety is a somewhat ambiguous variable since it can be treated either as an instigative variable[1] or as a regulative variable. Research with anxiety has often employed the J. A. Taylor (1953) scale as a measure, in relation to various conditioning and learning tasks (J. A. Taylor, 1951; J. A. Taylor and Spence, 1952; K. W. Spence, 1958). In general, subjects high in anxiety perform better in simple tasks and under relatively nonstressful conditions (Sarason, 1956; Sarason and Palola, 1960), than do subjects low in anxiety. When the task becomes more difficult or when stress is introduced, this tendency is usually reversed. In an experiment in which a standard concept-attainment task was used, the difference between subjects high and low in manifest anxiety was not significant (Braley, 1962). As we have seen, however, concepts can vary widely in difficulty (complexity). Dunn (1968) compared the effects of high and low anxiety at three levels of complexity. Prior to the concept-attainment phase, subjects were given positive reinforcement in half of the instances, and mild negative reinforcement (shock) in the other half. First, as in other studies, performance declined with increased complexity. Second, fewer concepts involving stress-related instances were attained. Finally, the anxiety variable displayed interactions with complexity. At the simplest level, both groups performed better for previously stressed items. At the intermediate level of complexity, subjects low in anxiety performed better with the stressed items than did subjects high in anxiety. At the most complex level, subjects high in anxiety were little affected by the stress, but the subjects low in

[1]Clinical anxiety might be regarded as an instigative condition, whereas situationally related anxiety, such as test anxiety, appears to have a regulative implication. However, regardless of its intrinsic character, anxiety seems to be a state of arousal.

anxiety showed an impairment, relative to nonstress. Across all three levels of complexity, the low group reached a higher level of performance, except at level 2 for nonstress, suggesting that even the simplest version of the task is more difficult than perceptual, conditioning, or paired-associate learning.

Finally, it is important to note that intelligence partly determines the effect of anxiety (Spielberger and Weitz, 1964). At high levels of ability, even under stress (rendering the task relevant to academic proficiency), persons high in anxiety have been found to outdo subjects low in anxiety in a concept-attainment task (Denny, 1966).

SUMMARY

Research on adult conceptual behavior reveals concrete and abstract processes and order of dominance. Conjunctive classification rules are easiest, disjunctive next, and conditional hardest. High response dominance, as a measure of meaningfulness, facilitates performance. Experiments show that connotative meaning can be conditioned, and conceptual classes may be based on connotative as well as denotative properties. As the complexity of stimuli increases by added dimensions, the difficulty of attaining concepts increases. However, redundant relevant dimensions facilitate attainment, while redundant irrelevant dimensions have an interfering effect. Increasing the number of values within dimensions also makes the task more difficult. Other facilitating conditions include relevant pretraining, practice, obviousness of instances (but emphasizing a cue may interfere with later shift performance), and "free" rather than "constrained" conditions. Successive presentation of instances helps in easy tasks, while simultaneous presentation helps in difficult ones. The effect of positive and negative instances depends on the amount of information, with positive better for conjunctive rules, and negative for nonconjunctive rules. A mixed series facilitates rule learning. Special instructions, opportunity to verbalize, and positive feedback improve performance. With respect to selection strategies, focusing is better when instances are not continuously available, and with ordered arrays, and abstract materials; scanning is superior with random arrays and thematic materials. Wholist reception strategy is more effective than partist strategy. Other effects of strategy depend on the conceptual rule. Also influencing conceptual performance are cognitive style and motivational variables.

10

VERBAL LEARNING

Tasks that require practice with words (and letter combinations)—those used to study "verbal learning"—can be distinguished from other kinds of tasks, such as those used to study classical and operant conditioning and to investigate perceptual and motor skills. It is, however, difficult to define the exact boundaries of this psychological field—and perhaps that is a good thing. In one direction it merges into the study of fairly simple perceptual-discriminative learning, as when an investigator merely exposes words or parts of words for more than one trial to determine the effects of stimulus structure or to measure transient recall. In another direction verbal learning converges on concept attainment, as when the task involves verbal labels for complex classifications or rules.

The common denominators of verbal learning lie in the materials of the task—components of language, letters and their combinations—and in the effects of practice (repeated trials). The tasks utilized in studies of verbal learning, unlike those in conceptual learning, rarely incorporate rules or principles that, once discovered, permit the subject to arrive at correct performance with no further practice. A few attempts have been made to compare paired-associate rote learning with concept attainment. Metzger (1958) suggested that one difference lies in associating a single response to a single stimulus compared to linking the same response to different stimuli. That is, rote learning could be transformed into concept attainment either by increasing the number of stimuli, while holding number of responses constant, or by decreasing the number of response alternatives, while keeping the number of stimuli constant. The first procedure significantly increased the difficulty of learning, but the second did not. It is noteworthy that as the number of stimuli increased, so did the length of the list, but inspection of his data indicates that this factor was not wholly responsible for the difference. Fallon and Battig (1964), in a partial replication of Metzger's experiment, also found concept attainment to be more difficult than rote learning. The concept task became easier, however, when response difficulty was increased, apparently pushing subjects toward a more classificatory approach; in addition, when concept pairs were based on actual groupings (of the geometric stimuli) produced by the subjects, both rote and concept performance markedly improved, with the latter becoming superior to rote learning with increased response difficulty. Finally, Dick and Combs (1965) also found concepts to be harder to learn than paired associates, but generalization after learning was greater.

Assuming nearly comparable conditions,[1] several possible reasons for the greater difficulty of concept learning could be advanced. Especially important is the complexity variable discussed in the last chapter, which signifies the necessity to identify relevant and irrelevant stimulus components.

The field of verbal learning originated in the study of the formal properties of rote-learning situations. Ebbinghaus, the founder of this tradition, devised nonsense syllables to determine the rate of learning and the efficiency of recall under conditions of minimal meaningfulness. Recent years have seen a rapid shift in interest from formal variables to the role of meaningfulness and other conditions arising from the subject's past experience. Certainly, as Osgood (1961) pointed out, meaning is the central issue in verbal learning.

PHASES OF VERBAL LEARNING

Systematic research has subdivided the total learning process into acquisition, transfer, and recall stages (see Figure 10-1). It is evident that one could focus on any of the successive stages, or on relations

---

[1]That is, equivalent exposure to instances. An extremely long rote list would surely be far more difficult than an equally long list of conceptual instances for which classification rules could be discovered during early trials.

between them—and, in fact, these relationships become a crucial matter.

Tasks generally fall into classes of *serial learning* (a simple list of items is presented to the subject) and *paired-associate learning* (the list consists of two members, one serving as a stimulus, the other as a response). The latter has come to be preferred since it helps to separate cues from responses, thus making it possible to manipulate separately properties of each. Methods of presentation include a series of exposures of the entire list, often with items in different orders on successive trials to control for position; alternation of study (exposure) trials and test (recall) trials; and anticipation (on successive trials, the subject attempts to produce the correct response).

Paired-associate Paradigms

A glance at Figure 10-1 readily discloses the logic by which stimulus-response (S-R) pairs can be varied both within and between lists. Either can be varied or controlled to suit the problem under investigation. Recent practice has been to employ *mixed* lists, in which several variations are included within the same list, using subsets of pairs to exemplify pertinent conditions (e.g., pairs with similar stimuli with a defined S-R relation, containing responses that will either remain the same or differ in a second list, etc.). Twedt and Underwood (1959) reported that results for mixed lists are essentially the same as for unmixed lists. Although Slamecka (1967) generally sustained this conclusion, he found that transfer to new items (a sequence of A-B to C-D) was easier for mixed lists, suggesting that they produce negative transfer, whereas unmixed lists yield negative transfer only as the number of new pairs increases.

The major paradigms are formulated in Figure 10-2. In studies that compare one paradigm with another, the commonest procedure is to employ at least A-B, A-Br, A-C, C-B, and C-D. A-Br is an "interfering" list, with the pairs rearranged so that associations initially established must be unlearned before the correct pairing can be acquired. A-C allows the effects of response variation to be determined. C-B permits variation in stimuli to exert an influence. C-D represents a control situation, with new pairs free from associations present in A-B.

Some of the paradigms may be irrelevant if only acquisition is involved, in which case, for example, A-B, C-B, and C-D might represent systematic variation in relations between stimulus and response, such as degree of meaningfulness. For the transfer phase, the paradigms correspond to differences either in the original or

Phase	Prior Experience	Original Learning (OL)	Interpolated Learning (IL)	Recall	Relearning or Application
Explanation	Sets, concepts, knowledge, or other characteristics of subject invoked by the situation.	Task experimentally assigned to subject	Second task or tasks experimentally assigned to subject.	Subject reproduces items from either OL or IL, or both.	Subsequent relearning of either OL or IL, or both; undetermined later consequences in behavior.
Example	[Knowledge of English words.]	List 1—Paired Associates: S R BIRD RAIN COLD SEAM etc.	List 2: S R FIRST LOAD MORN TOAD etc.	List 1 or List 2	Relearn list 1 or list 2; expose S to relevant concept-attainment task; etc.
General Effects	[Not specified; contingent on instructions; or experimentally induced context or set; etc.]	Acquisition (rate, errors, etc.)	Transfer: positive, negative, or none, depending on conditions.	Retroaction or proaction: Facilitation or inhibition or none, depending on conditions.	

FIGURE 10-1   Phases of verbal learning.

Acquisition Phase (OL)	Transfer Phase (IL)	Recall Phase‡
A—B	A—B	Any set of pairs, usually with S presented and R to be reported.
A'—B	A—B$_r$†	
A"—B	C—B	
A—B'	C—D	Backward associations may be studied by presenting R, with S to be reported.
A—B"	A'—B	
A'—B'	B—A	
A'—B"	B'—A	
A"—B"	A'—B'	
Etc.	Etc.	

FIGURE 10-2 Paired-associate paradigms. Note: The first letter is the stimulus member, the second letter the response member. Primes ',' refer to variation in one of the members. Different letters signify a new member (e.g., A-B vs. A-C, A-B vs. C-D, etc). Any combination may be employed. In a mixed list, OL would contain subsets corresponding to the transfer phase, which is arranged so that the second list is identical for all subsets (e.g., if A-B is the second list, then the necessary conditions are established by using in the first list A-B, A-B$_r$, C-D, etc.).

†Repairing of A and B members.
‡This phase may occur as test trials after either OL or IL.

second-list learning. The first list can be the same for all subjects (e.g., list A-B), followed by the assignment of subgroups to the requisite paradigms (such as A-B or relearning, A-B$_r$, A-C, C-B, and C-D). As pointed out above, however, investigators currently prefer to vary lists in original learning, with all subjects presented with the same second list, thereby simplifying the problem of analyzing transfer effects. For the recall phase the appropriate list is simply administered as a test; relearning effects can then be determined by additional trials.

BASIC VARIABLES
The conditions that influence acquisition, transfer, and recall fall under several headings.

Formal Task Properties These conditions represent characteristics of stimulus and response, as specified by the experimenter and assumed to operate mainly independently of the past experience of the subject. Among such conditions are the rate of presentation, the length of the task, the amount of practice, and any pretraining. The paradigmatic variations just described and their sequences also belong here. One of the most widely investigated formal properties is degree of similarity among or between members, when this condition is defined solely by components of the items. For example, stimulus members may be based on the position and/or number of common letters.

An important consideration here is the distinction between *formal* and *functional* stimuli (Underwood, Ham, and Ekstrand, 1962), that is, between the stimulus (e.g., a word) designated by the experimenter versus the cue actually utilized by the subject. This point has become the topic of special investigation in which the stimulus is deliberately made compound in order to determine which aspect is effective. But the notion can usually be extended to any situation in which the subject may employ cues other than those intended.

Situational Variables   These conditions are manipulated to influence the subject's performance—and thus receive their sharpest emphasis when formal task properties are held constant. Special instructions, method of presenting materials, environmental context, and individual versus group administration are illustrative of these variables.

Meaningfulness   It is likely that no fully satisfactory simple definition can be produced for meaningfulness. Noble (1963) points out that this term is not identical with meaning, suggesting that the latter depends on relations or connections between words, whereas meaningfulness concerns the facility with which a word is produced by a person. The advantage of this distinction in research is that it avoids difficult epistemological issues of meaning and permits a focus on variables that can be measured with respect to the ease of producing a verbal response. In fact, investigators have adopted precisely this strategy. It turns out that a number of such variables can be identified, as we shall see. Even connotative meaning, as measured by the S.D. can be manipulated as a factor in meaningfulness.

Intrinsic Variables   Finally, verbal behavior, like other human activities, is influenced by the special characteristics of the subject— those variables we include under the heading of personality (arousal, motivational characteristics, cognitive structure, etc.).

MEANINGFULNESS

Since meaning can be regarded as implicit relationships among cognitive components (which need not be verbal-symbolic in character), mediation implies meaning. These terms have both structural and functional significance since we can infer both potentially available relationships and also activities that organize them as a function of stimulus conditions. Much of the research discussed previously emphasizes the functional side of mediation, especially by using procedures that induce cognitive relationships experimentally. Probably it is impossible—or at least very difficult—to separate structural from functional properties of mediation. Even if we can justifiably assume an already-existing cognitive system, which is merely elicited in a situation, it would be subject to modification or variation by continuing informational input and by other concomitantly active intrinsic processes. In this respect, the analogy to a computer encounters an especially severe problem of interpretation.

The phenomenon of clustering in recall illustrates the relational character of meaning. Bousfield (1953) presented subjects with lists of words randomly arranged, but falling into general categories—for example, animals, names, professions, and vegetables. During recall, subjects tended to produce words in the same category in sequence. Bousfield and Puff (1965) presented each of two groups with a different list, one of taxonomically related pairs (e.g., TABLE-CHAIR, SNOW-ICE), the other of nontaxonomically, but associatively related pairs (e.g., SKY-BLUE WINTER-SNOW). In the recall test, clustering occurred to a greater degree in the taxonomic list. This difference could not be attributed to associative strength, which was controlled, but rather to stimulus equivalence (or nondirect associations). Clustering tends to increase with repeated trials (S. Rosenberg, 1966), and is facilitated by conditions promoting intrinsic organization of items, such as providing a general name for subsets (Segal, 1969; Shuell, 1969). When members of associatively related paired associates (e.g., ACCORDION-(piano)-KEY are presented contiguously in a serial list, they tend to cluster during recall, whereas this effect is less evident after random presentation (Shapiro and Palermo, 1967). Experimental induction of relationships also produces mediated clustering (Wiley and Horton, 1968).

The associative priming technique utilized by Cramer (1965, 1966) further demonstrates the relational character of meaning. In one version of this procedure, the A and C words in A-B-C chains (e.g., LONG-(short)-TALL) are included in lists along with unrelated words; they are presented either contiguously or noncontiguously.

Recall is tested after an interval which is either unfilled or filled by having the subject circle the missing B terms (priming). Clustering appears both under the contiguous and the priming conditions.

Let us turn now to experiments on meaningfulness. As suggested previously, this term does not pretend to be synonymous with meaning; rather, it refers to the ease with which a word is produced. Although we can suppose that the more meaning a word has, the more readily it is elicited, meaningfulness variables are oriented toward objectifiable indicators of response readiness. Since no one has yet proposed a fully acceptable definition of meaning—primarily, perhaps, because idiosyncratic or connotative components merge with denotative representations, and emotional interfusions complicate the problem—the manipulation of meaningfulness has contributed notably to progress in understanding verbal learning.[1]

Frequency   One approach to the problem of meaningfulness arises simply from the idea that the more frequently words occur in a language, the more readily they can serve as agents for verbal expression. The more frequent a word, the more likely it is that a person will have encountered and learned it, and will have experienced it in varied contexts and in conjunction with other words.

Variations in frequency can be determined simply by counting how often words occur. The classic study of this kind was carried out by Thorndike and Lorge (1944), resulting in norms that have since widely been used to investigate verbal learning and recall.

Generally speaking, this method shows a positive relation between frequency of words and efficiency of learning and recall (Hall, 1954)—the spew hypothesis (Underwood and Schulz, 1960). However, such effects depend, in paired-associate learning, on the frequency of both stimulus and response members. Postman (1962) found that acquisition is more rapid for middle-frequency stimulus terms than for either high- or low-frequency words, although it is slowest for the latter; acquisition, however, is directly related to frequency of response terms. Recall shows a similar effect for stimulus terms, but is little influenced by frequency of the response terms.[2]

Frequency has also been induced by varying the number of times items are exposed in an experimental setting. In general,

[1]Pertinent surveys may be found in Underwood and Schulz (1960); Deese (1965); Goss and Nodine (1965); and Creelman (1966).
[2]Studies like this employ items with minimal associative or formal relation to each other. Interitem similarity is a different problem.

induced frequency of response rather than stimulus terms facilitates learning (Sheffield, 1946; Underwood and Schulz, 1960).

Association Values   Among the limitations of word frequency as a measure is the fact that items must be treated as discrete, essentially unitary occurrences, detached from other components of cognitive systems. Accordingly, Noble (1952a) shifted attention to measures of associative frequency. Subjects are presented with a word and asked to write down as many other words or phrases as they can think of that are called forth by the stimulus. Means can then be computed and utilized as a measure of meaningfulness.[1] Starting with low- and high-frequency nouns from the Thorndike-Lorge count and paralogs, Noble developed a list of ninety-six items, covering a wide range. Examples that define approximately equal intervals are, as follows: (1) GOJEY (0.99); (16) NOSTRAW (1.34); (32) ROMPIN (1.90); (48) TARTAN (2.63); (64) ZENITY (4.44); (80) UNCLE (6.57); (96) KITCHEN (9.61). High reliability was indicated by a mean correlation of .975 among four groups of subjects.

This measure (M)[2] was incorporated into a study of serial learning (Noble, 1952b), producing a strong relation to acquisition (see Figure 10-3). Furthermore, the superiority of high-M items was strongly apparent at all positions in the list. An extension to paired-associate learning had similar results (Noble and McNeely, 1957).

Response Dominance   A variation of the associative conception of meaningfulness was described in Chapter 9. Underwood and Richardson (1956) determined the frequency with which a stimulus elicits various responses. For example, a word like small frequently elicits village, less often bungalow, and infrequently earthworm. In concept-attainment tasks, learning is facilitated by using responses high in dominance (Coleman, 1964). Similarly, the rate of paired-associate learning is related to the dominance of the response words.

Pronounceability   In a series of experiments concerned with the characteristics of S-R terms, using single letters, two letters, and

---

[1]This approach had long been established, especially for nonsense syllables (Glaze, 1928; Hull, 1933).
[2]The abbreviation M will be used for all measures of meaningfulness based on associations. M may be defined either by the number of associations elicited by a word, or by the proportion of subjects who produce some association in a specified short interval.

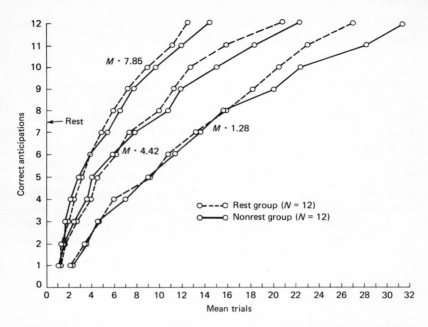

FIGURE 10-3   Mean number of trials required to anticipate correctly successive number of items with and without a 2-minute rest pause of naming colors introduced after reaching a criterion of 7/12 correct under different conditions of meaningfulness. (From Noble, 1952.)

trigrams, Underwood and Schulz (1960) found a consistent tendency for pronounceability (based on ratings) to display a strong relationship to learning. The effect was greater for response members than for stimulus members.[1]

Comparison of Measures
Investigators have naturally sought to assess the differential effects of these potential aspects of meaningfulness, all of which display significant relations to learning and recall, at least under some conditions.

Noble (1954) found a curvilinear relation between rated famil-

---

[1]It is worth mentioning that the sample of three-letter units include about 11 percent "real" words, and about 13 percent combinations of three consonants (CCC trigrams). All but one of the real words fall among the 29 percent most easily pronounced (ratings of 3.00 or less); the exception is *STY* with a rating of 3.19. Of these easiest items, 45 percent are real words; among the others are some that actually serve as words, such as *FEM, KIM,* and *KIX.*

iarity of words (and paralogs) and M; a similar relationship appeared between frequency of exposure and familiarity. Thus words of high M vary less in familiarity than do words of low M. Lindley (1960) found that words high in frequency (familiarity), assessed by the Thorndike-Lorge word count, produce results in serial learning similar to words high in association value (confirmed by Epstein, Rock, and Zuckerman, 1960, and Runquist and Freeman, 1960).

In a paired-associate study, however, Saltz (1967) varied the M and frequency of stimulus terms, with response terms all high in M. Learning was facilitated by high M, but impaired by high frequency. Thus it is possible that high M allows for numerous associations to operate, facilitating the development of mediators; by contrast, high frequency may depend partly on quite specific functions or uses of words, thus making it more difficult to attach them to new responses (in this case nouns).

An important variation of formal measures of M (i.e., obtained norms) comes from experiments with *natural language mediators* (Montague, Adams, and Kiess, 1966; Montague and Wearing, 1967). Here a procedure is used to determine whether subjects adopt a device to link members of a pair or to recall items. Montague and Kiess (1968) have derived from this source a special measure of M, which they call *associability*. After exposing pairs of trigrams (CVC's, or consonant-vowel-consonant combinations), subjects indicated whether an associative device occurred to them, providing associability values for pairs. Examples are given in Table 10-1, indicating how pairs matched for association value may differ in associability and vice versa. (Note the relation between the two: as associability increases so do the S and R association values.) Experiments demonstrate facilitation by associability, in general comparable to association value. Since the earlier experiments took into account individual differences in the use of natural language mediators, this result suggests that meaningfulness exerts its maximal effect when idiosyncratic factors are allowed to operate. For example, those subjects who can actually generate a mediator for VUP-NEJ may find it little more difficult than WAX-GEM. The norms indicate that very few persons can produce a mediator for the former.[1] But those who can would be expected to learn the pair more easily than those who cannot. Bearing on these points are findings that subjects can discriminate differences in associative strength immediately after

[1]Temporal and instructional conditions no doubt would play an important role. Allowed sufficient time, or explicity asked to develop a mediating association, a high proportion of subjects might find VUP-NEJ quite associable.

Table 10-1
Examples of CVC Pairs Varying in Association Value and
Associability. (From Montague and Kiess, 1968.)

CVC Pair		Association Value		Mean
S	R	S	R	Associability
VUP	NEJ	14	15	17
GUC	PEV	47	46	15
YIW	POJ	14	15	23
KEV	GOC	46	46	22
HUJ	XAN	14	14	35
HEG	TUD	45	47	35
QEP	XAS	13	14	43
LIG	VOX	46	46	43
JUP	WEZ	39	39	55
DAS	NAC	72	72	55
HUY	LUW	39	39	68
DUG	ZIP	100	100	68
MAZ	DUS	72	73	79
BEL	MAC	99	99	79
CIV	CER	71	71	89
PAT	RIB	99	100	89
LAZ	DEY	68	68	95
WAX	GEM	100	100	95

Associative values are from Archer (1960); separate values were obtained
for males and females (associability), and these should be considered,
especially at low levels.

presentation of items, and that those subjects who report the likelihood of recalling perform significantly better than those who do not
(Arbuckle and Cuddy, 1969).

Reinforcement Value   The significance of individual factors in
meaningfulness is nicely revealed in studies by Rychlak and his
associates (Rychlak, 1966; Abramson, Tasto, and Rychlak, 1969).
Subjects rated trigrams on a likeability scale, which was used to vary
reinforcement value. Experiments showed that this variable is positively related to learning, and is independent of association value (see
Figure 10-4). Especially interesting, however, is the finding that the

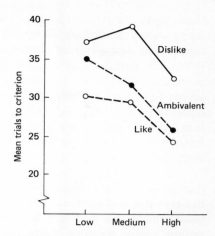

FIGURE 10-4 Effects of reinforcement value (likeability) of trigrams in relation to association value. (Based on Abramson, Tasto, and Rychlak, 1969.)

advantage of the idiosyncratic variable of reinforcement value disappears when association value is also obtained idiographically. (Subjects were asked to report when a trigram resembled a word.) If anything, association value in this case is a superior measure.[1]

Pronounceability and Other Measures   R. C. Johnson (1962b) points out that Underwood and Schulz (1960) employed a peculiar logic in determining the frequency of trigrams. They counted the occurrence in textual materials of successive three-letter groups. For example, ANGRY contains ANG NGR, and GRY. (Similar counts were made of single letters and bigrams.) Clearly this procedure could be quite an artificial way to treat functional aspects of language. From this standpoint the frequency of occurrence has little to do with letter combinations as language units, and it is not surprising that frequency was not significant.

Johnson classified trigrams as words (e.g., WAS, ART, VIZ),), syllables (ZON, STI, CHA), and nonsyllables (RCH, IFO, DFL). These three groups were judged to be levels of functional occurrence in the English language. The results of Underwood and Schulz were reanalyzed to compare

[1] It is likely that reinforcement value is related to the evaluation dimension of the semantic differential.

these three groups, and to compare more versus less pronounceable items within each group. Although learning was directly related to the degree of functional significance, pronounceability made little difference. Furthermore, syllables that did not form words (but were pronounceable) were assessed for their perceived incidence in words (e.g., MEL—melody, mellifluous, caramel, etc.). The reanalysis displayed a significant correlation with this measure, again indicating that pronounceability is less important than other aspects of meaningfulness—if, in fact, pronounceability is not actually incidental to them (supported in a study by Lindley, 1963).

DiVesta and Ingersoll (1969) investigated the effects of articulation (audibly pronouncing trigrams). Groups either articulated both the stimulus and response, the stimulus only, the response only, or were silent. The first and last of these conditions (called "congruent") were superior, especially for the items low in pronounceability (as if speaking the items made them more pronounceable).

Concreteness   Finally, both frequency and abstractness and concreteness were assessed in several experiments by Winnick and Kressel (1965). The materials were nouns classified according to Gorman's (1961) listing, and by the Thorndike-Lorge frequency count. Examples of the four categories are: (1) high-frequency abstract—OPINION, BIRTHDAY, PRINCIPLE; (2) high-frequency concrete—TEACHER, BEDROOM, HOSPITAL; (3) low-frequency abstract—APPROVAL ANECDOTE, IDLENESS; and (4) low-frequency concrete—VOLCANO, FILAMENT CALCIUM. Note that these words are all long and fairly difficult.

It was found that, in tachistoscopic recognition, thresholds did not differ for abstract versus concrete items. But frequency was significant, contributed almost entirely by lower thresholds for high-frequency concrete words. Both variables were significant in paired-associate learning (with nonsense syllables of medium associative value as stimuli). Again, the frequency variable was consistently, although not significantly, more potent for the concrete words. In immediate recall, frequency was not significant, but concrete words were better recalled. Finally, in line with other research, the concrete words were more meaningful, as determined by the number of associations produced; frequency was related to associations for concrete, but not for abstract, words. Following this procedure, recall for concrete words was superior to abstract words, as in free recall, with no effect on frequency.

Aside from showing the importance of the kinds of verbal

materials employed, an interesting point is the difference between the results for recognition and the other tasks. Evidently, frequency is especially likely to influence performance in simple tasks, less so in complex tasks. Such findings indicate that meaningfulness facilitates mediation. Although mediation is not wholly established in the Winnick and Kressel study, the greater meaningfulness of concrete words is not in doubt.

CONNOTATIVE MEANING

Imagery, to be discussed in Chapters 13 and 14, is one kind of non-verbal activity by which mediation can occur. Connotative meaning, implying feeling or emotional relationships, is another. We would have only a very limited understanding of verbal learning were such variables to be ignored, or to be regarded as incidental or transient components of meaning.

Following the work of C. K. Staats and A. W. Staats (1957), Pollio (1963) examined connotative meaning in a paired-associate situation. Items to be conditioned (corresponding to stimulus terms) were CVC (consonant-verb-consonant) trigrams of low association value (thus presumably neutral in meaning). Unconditioned stimuli (corresponding to response terms) were words of positive, neutral, or connotative meaning,[1] lower in intraset than in interset common associates. Each trigram was paired with nine words of the same category. Following this phase, the trigrams were presented for 20 seconds and subjects were asked to write down the first word that came to mind for each syllable. These responses were then rated by a separate group of subjects on the "good-bad" S.D. evaluative scale. These ratings corresponded closely to those of the original unconditioned words. More significant, however, is the character of the associations. Half of the associates were *different* words, and the S.D. ratings for these cued associates corresponded with the unconditioned stimuli. These results support the principle that facilitation can be produced by connotative processes.

Sassenrath (1967) obtained significantly better learning of pairs of words positive or negative in connotative meaning than of neutral words. An interesting feature was that for a parallel list of pairs high or low in denotative meaning, the former were easier to learn.

The role of connotative meaning in serial and paired-associate

---

[1] From S. D. norms obtained by Jenkins, Russell, and Suci (1958), with which new ratings, obtained by Pollio, closely agreed.

learning remains to be fully elucidated. Employing the evaluative S.D. dimension, Keppel (1963) found that positive (good) nonsense syllables were learned faster than negative (bad) syllables. However, Harbin and Wright (1967) point out that the syllables also differed in pronounceability (or difficulty). In a series of experiments in which the activity and potency dimensions were manipulated by means of S.D. ratings of CVC's, they found that both paired-associate and serial learning were impaired by high activity, but not by high potency. This suggests that connotative meaning functions differently from meaningfulness (as defined by the measures previously described), since M typically displays a direct relation to learning. In addition, whereas response M has a greater effect than stimulus M, in these experiments it made no difference which term was high in activity. Whether these effects stem from the greater diffuseness of connotative relations—as seems quite possible—or from other conditions not yet clear, further research is greatly needed.

ASSOCIATIVE PROCESSES

As attention to mediating processes has increased, investigators have become less satisfied with formal properties of materials as adequate explanations for verbal learning. As a consequence there is a pronounced trend toward examining cognitive structure. From one standpoint, this movement comes closer to a search for the role of meaning (in contrast to meaningfulness), conceived in general terms. From another standpoint, it may be interpreted as an attempt to consider the effects of experience and the contribution that the individual makes to a learning situation.

The Structure of Associative Meaning

Deese (1962) proposed that relations among associations are more important than logical classification of words. Associative meaning refers to the "verbal environment" of a particular word—the associations that words have in common. This conception contrasts with the approach that sees words as linked together in such a fashion that one word elicits another (corresponding to the free-association frequency). Deese (1965) has therefore examined overlapping associations of words, and applied factor analysis to clarify the categories that emerge. The result is a class with a functional character rather than a logically imposed one like subordination, coordination, and so on. For example, these words constitute a category of associative meaning: MOTH, INSECT, WING, BIRD, FLY, BUG, COCOON, BEES, BUTTERFLY. It is easy to see how they could be related to each other, but no rule of formal logical relationships can describe the class.

This approach leads Deese to emphasize cognitive structure, in opposition to the traditional "laws of association" based on contiguity and assimilation. Instead, he suggests that *contrast* and *grouping* are better conceptions of relations among ideas. These new laws may be stated as follows: (1) "Elements are associatively related when they may be contrasted in some unique and unambiguous way" and (2) "elements are associatively related when they may be grouped because they can be described by two or more characteristics in common" (Deese, 1965, p. 165). The first principle expresses the fact that experience leads to unique kinds of relationships among cognitive components; the second provides an avenue for arriving at normative data on cognitive structure. Both laws propose that we examine actual systems of associations rather than logically sequential relations. Influencing this approach is the changing conception of memory to which we referred in Chapter 3. Acts of registry and recall are not mechanical, not literal and fixed representations, but active in character. The person's intrinsic system influences them at the moment of experience and subsequently.

Also pertinent to the importance of associative structure is Cofer's (1967) search for contextual conditions, such as priming and stimulus compounding. Direct priming (Storms, 1958) is shown when responses to stimulus words in a free-association test display increased frequency after they have been previously exposed for a different task, compared to their frequency in free association without the prior experience. Indirect priming (Cramer, 1966) occurs if the prior experience involves a group of words associated with the to-be-primed response word, which itself is not previously exposed. Stimulus compounding is somewhat similar (Howes and Osgood, 1954; Podell, 1963). Here two or more related words are presented to see whether this joint occurrence influences associative responses. In one procedure the frequency of responses to one of the words is compared to their incidence without the related words. In another procedure the words in the set may separately elicit the same response to some degree; when presented together this response may be augmented. Such studies show again that cognitive events do not necessarily depend on discrete and fairly fixed components, but on associative systems. In general, it appears that relationships among words are a function of their combinations rather than of their individual, separate properties. That is, a pair of words acquires characteristics that cannot be entirely accounted for by looking at the members in isolation from each other.

Associability

In a similar vein, Kammann (1968) has devised a measure of associability. Two words are presented, and subjects are asked to rate from 1 to 10 "the degree to which it is likely that the two words would appear together" in certain contexts, a sentence, a line of poetry, in association (one calling forth the other), or in relatedness (a way to relate them to each other). The four different instructions yielded similar results, although the correlation between sentences and poetry was higher than between either of these and association.

With respect to other measures of meaningfulness, associability was significantly correlated with an index of natural language mediation (.62) and to a lesser degree with distance on the S. D., but not to Noble's M, or word frequency. (The correlation of .64 between these last two measures indicates a factor contrasting with associability.) In a paired-associate learning experiment, associability produced higher correlations with learnability in the forward direction, but M was a better predictor for the backward direction (in keeping with a response availability principle). It is important to note that for learning trials the 2 :2 rate of presentation was used, but 8 seconds were used for the backward recall trial. We can only conclude that associability is especially favorable at brief intervals in the learning phase. Whether longer intervals would show that associability fosters mediation cannot be stated.

The effects of associative structure also appear in studies by Pollio and his associates. In one study (Pollio, Kasschau, and DeNise, 1968), associates of a single word (e.g., MUSIC) were presented as a learning list, and latencies of free recall were determined. Individual records were examined to identify fast and slow sequences. Analysis disclosed that the former were connected associatively, and also were more similar semantically than the latter.

Subsequently, Pollio Dietchman, and Richards (1969), have obtained evidence to support Deese's (1965) law of contrast. This principle implies that "words can (be) and often are brought together in association despite the fact that they have never been experienced in contiguity." These investigators examined the characteristics of oppositional word pairs (like HOT-COLD), arguing that such pairs share many overlapping attributes, except for one that emphasizes the contrast. The S. D. failed to identify such an attribute. An effort was therefore made to compare opposites with non-opposites (like HOT-WARM). These words can be regarded as falling on a scale (e.g., Cold-Cool-Mild-Warm-Hot). In this case, there is potentially a serially ordered set of words, and the end terms might act like the semantically most distant members. Thus, pairs with COLD and HOT should be learned most readily. Furthermore, an analysis of errors should disclose no unusual tendency to produce each other as intrusions. Paired associates were constructed with nonsense syllables as stimulus terms with the five words above as response terms.

The results, overall, yielded the expected serial-position curve, but an interesting seasonal difference appeard. The HOT end was distinctly easier in summer and the COLD end easier in winter. (A replication confirmed this finding for summer, but not for winter.) Scrutiny of errors showed that words adjacent to Hot and Cold were confused with these words more than they were with each other.

There appear to be two contradictory kinds of findings: Oppositional word pairs elicit each other with high frequency in word-association tests; yet they differ markedly in attributes (S. D. ratings) and do not produce confusion in paired-associate learning. The law of contrast can be interpreted to signify that oppositional relationships are *conceptually convenient*. In this experiment they apparently define a scale in an economical way, and therefore do not interfere with each other. At the same time, Pollio and his associates suggest that contiguity and frequency also play an important role. These conditions are imposed, so to speak, *on* associative structure, rather than primarily determining it. They serve to strengthen particular relationships in a given task.

The seasonal results offer additional considerations. Although the investigators prefer to interpret the results as evidence for frequency (HOT for example, in summer), it is also plausible to infer the effects of contextual factors in cognitive structure. There are certainly numerous experiential factors that may converge to render HOT salient in the summer. We might, indeed, invoke a notion of *rules*, whether stated or implied in the instructions, that govern associative systems. For example, these investigators assume that HOT-COLD are opposites, whereas HOT-MILD are not. Nothing in the experimental conditions would alter this expectation. But clearly, as season (and the experimental conditions) serves as a context, so a different context could also operate. For example, HOT-MILD are actually opposites of a sort, if one speaks about mustard; and HOT-COOL are contrasting terms when one refers to jazz. In this sense it is surely probable that contextual factors are as significant as frequency. The context certainly affects the frequency with which a term is used ("mild" is used more frequently in describing summer weather than is "cold"); and if we focus on the potentialities of inferred associative structure, we might say that those properties determine processes, without any need to be concerned with frequency.

Coherence

Asch (1969) has sought to break away sharply from traditional principles of contiguity, since it is misleading to conceive of association as a linking or changing of components. Rather, the fundamental property is coherence, "a name for the general fact that we refer given experiences to each other in a manner that unifies them." The basic condition is the experience of *relations*. We should be concerned, not with separate elements of association, but with their interdependence. Simple demonstrations show how figure-ground relations, part-whole relations, and so on, enhance the unitary character of materials, and thus promote learning. Recognizing the relation is essential. Sheer contiguity of elements may lead to such recognition, but it is an inefficient condition (almost a matter of chance). Establishing the relation is a more direct and certain way to facilitate learning.

From these different directions then, we can see considerable progress toward an ultimate understanding of how the properties of cognitive systems influence learning and recall. In general there has been a pronounced shift in emphasis. Associative structure is coming to be seen as offering more significant clues to verbal learning than the specification of general stimulus and response characteristics. This conception allows far more scope for the role of individual experience and of the particular situational context in which verbal learning takes place. We can agree with Asch that in this fashion research is coming more actively to grips with the actual life of the person.

MEDIATION AND TRANSFER IN VERBAL LEARNING

The term *mediation* has a significance beyond simple, direct S-R relationships, since mediation signifies in some degree at least a state or process that can be defined independently of S and R. The experimental problem is to influence such an inferred process. The basic three-stage specification is the sequence A-B, B-C, A-C, in which A-B is established, with B-C either explicitly established or inferred, and A-C represents a test. Appropriate controls involve a variation at any of the three stages, so that mediation is weakened or absent. For example, control sequences might be A-B, X-Y, A-C; A-B, X-C, A-C; X-B, B-C, A-C; and so on.

Experimental Background

Influential in promoting the mediation principle were studies of generalization stemming from work by Russian investigators. Razran (1935–1936) used classical conditioning methods to study semantic generalization. In one extensive study (Razran, 1949), subjects were first conditioned to words by reinforcement with mints or pretzels, then the subject was tested with other words related to the original word in several ways. For example, a word derivative (such as LOCK-LATCH) yielded more than 60 percent generalization; subordinates (e.g., DOG-TERRIER), contrasts (e.g., DARK-LIGHT), and part-whole relations (e.g., DAY-WEEK) produced about 40 percent generalization. Even pseudoderivatives (e.g., BAKE-BOOK) showed some effect. Variations in the number of common phonemes and letters displayed a roughly quantitative scale—for example, FLOWER-GLOWER 35 percent, DARK-MARK 32 percent, DAY-MAY 20 percent.

Following the lead of such research, Cofer and Foley (1942) pointed to the important role of mediated generalization in verbal behavior and thinking, emphasizing how such processes provide indirect links between stimulus and response. They formulated the basic techniques, including preexperimental reinforcement of verbal responses, assessment of meaningfulness by word frequencies or associations, inferences derived from "language biographies," and procedures for differentially strengthening verbal symbols. A series of investigations demonstrated mediational effects in serial learning by means of homophones and synonyms (Foley and Cofer, 1943), antonyms (Cofer, Janis, and Rowell, 1943), language learning (Foley and Mathews, 1943), and specially acquired associations (Foley and MacMillan, 1943).

Implicit Chaining

In another early experiment, Peters (1935) obtained evidence for "mediate association" in a procedure where subjects learned two lists, linked by a common term, and then were tested 24 hours later for recall. The greatest effect of mediation was found in the sequence A-B, BC, A(c), where A=a word, B=a letter, C=a number, and (c)=instructions to say the first number that came to mind. Peters' experiments, however, were not wholly successful in demonstrating mediation.

These equivocal results led Bugelski and Scharlock (1952) to devise a new test of the mediation principle. Using nonsense syllables in paired-associate lists, they ran their subjects through the sequence A-B, B-C, A-C. Control pairs consisted in the third list of random pairings of A and C syllables (in contrast to those that had a common B associate). The experimental A-C pairs were learned in significantly fewer trials, and of sixteen pairs, twelve showed a difference in the predicted direction. Martin and Parrott (1966) extended the linked sequence to A-B, B-C, C-D, A-D, and found facilitation here too.

Noting that the Bugelski and Scharlock experiment employed direct learning of the B–C relation, Russell and Storms (1955) tested mediation as a function of inferred association (i.e., implicit relations present prior to the experiment). For this purpose empirically established associative norms for real words were used to link the A and D terms in the sequence, A-B, B-C, C-D, A-D, with the two middle relations inferred. Nonsense syllables constituted the A terms. The control sequence substituted X, or unrelated words, for the D terms Here is an example :

List 1	Inferred Associations		List 2
A B	(B C)	(C D)	A D
CEF-STEM	(STEM-FLOWER)	(FLOWER-SMELL)	CEF-SMELL
			A X
			CEF-JOY

The chained pairs were facilitated, indicating the operation of mediation (a control experiment in which subjects learned in succession two forms of the test list showed that the facilitated pairs were not easier to learn).These effects have been confirmed in subsequent studies (Norcross and Spiker, 1958; McGehee and Schulz, 1961; Crowder, 1968).

Eight different three-stage paradigms were utilized by Horton and Kjeldergaard (1961). It can be seen in Table 10-2 that the sequence takes account of the several ways in which A and C might acquire a common mediating process by chaining (I to IV), by coming to elicit the same response (V to VI), or by coming to be elicited by the same stimulus (VII to VIII). The assumed associations act in a forward direction in paradigms I, II, VI, and VII, but in a backward direction in paradigms III, IV, V, and VIII. Greater generalization was predicted for the forward direction. Furthermore, in each category the assumed association is either contiguous (I, IV, VII, and VIII) or remote (II, III, V, and VI), and more generalization was expected for the more contiguous arrangement. Difficult five-letter words were used to form the required pairs, and control words were substituted for the common member in some pairs in one of the first two stages. Highly significant facilitation was found for all paradigms except III.[1] Evidence for the greater benefit of forward than backward associations was markedly stronger than for the effect of contiguity.

J. G. Martin et al. (1963) employed the sequence A-B, C-B, A-D, C-D, with the first two stages inferred from norms, so that both A and C commonly elicited B as a response, but rarely elicited each other; D was a lever-pressing response. Learning actually began then with A-D, which was regarded as an interfering condition. In accordance with the mediation principle, the mediated (C-D) pairs were learned faster than nonmediated pairs (X-D). This effect diminished with A-D trials, showing that continued practice under this condition tends to disrupt the mediated association.

Other investigators (Weaver and Schulz, 1968) have shown that the operation of mediating processes actually strengthens them. Thus, following the usual sequence A-B, B-C, A-C, subjects recalled A-B. A control group passed through the sequence A-B, B-E, A-C, then also recalled A-B. Not only was significant mediated facilitation of A-C evident, but the recall of A-B was better under the mediated condition and was not affected by repeated trials on A-C. However, A-B recall became worse with increased A-C trials under the nonmediated condition.

An interesting complement to the preceding study has been reported by Glucksberg and King (1967). They adopted the Russell and Storms paradigm (A-B, B-C, C-D), in which C is an inferred mediator and is never actually presented to the subject. A-B was learned first, then the D words were presented, some accompanied by electric shock, and, finally, there was a recall test of A-B. Significant forgetting was found for the B words inferred to be chained with the D words, showing something like "mediated repression."

Thus these representative studies demonstrate the mediation

---

[1]The authors suggest that individual differences may have been responsible since the results are generally in the same direction as in the other paradigms.

Table 10-2
The Mediation Paradigms Investigated by Horton and Kjeldergaard (1961).

	Stage 1	Stage 2	Test	Assumed Association
Chaining				
I	A–B	B–C	A–C	$[B]{\nearrow}^{A}_{\searrow C} \to A \to [B] \to C$
II	B–C	A–B	A–C	$[B]{\nearrow}^{C}_{\nwarrow A} \to A \to [B] \to C$
III	B–A	C–B	A–C	$[B]{\nearrow}^{A}_{\nwarrow C} \to A \leftarrow [B] \leftarrow C$
IV	C–B	B–A	A–C	$[B]{\nwarrow}^{C}_{\searrow A} \to A \leftarrow [B] \leftarrow C$
Acquired Stimulus Equivalence				
V	A–B	C–B	A–C	$[B]{\nwarrow}^{A}_{\nwarrow C} \to A \to [B] \leftarrow C$
VI	C–B	A–B	A–C	$[B]{\nwarrow}^{C}_{\nwarrow A} \to A \to [B] \leftarrow C$
Acquired Response Equivalence				
VII	B–A	B–C	A–C	$[B]{\nearrow}^{A}_{\searrow C} \to A \leftarrow [B] \to C$
VIII	B–C	B–A	A–C	$[B]{\nearrow}^{C}_{\searrow A} \to A \leftarrow [B] \to C$

principle both by direct establishment of associations and by inferring their presence from free-association norms. However, J. Richardson (1968) has shown that the inferred relation between B and D, via B-C and C-D, should not always be accepted as valid. He ascertained such relations by having subjects actually match the words. Based on this congruence, learning of A-D pairs was better than for the inferred pairs. Although he suggests that this result weakens the supposition that implicit chaining is involved in this situation, it would rather appear that a more direct relation is simply more efficient. It is not surprising that this should be the case, and does not vitiate the mediation principle.

Imagery

The experiments just described treat the mediation process by reference to presumable verbal-symbolic mechanisms. But, as we have mentioned before, internal representations may be nonverbal as well. Commonsense illustrations abound, although some ingenuity is required to achieve a systematic experimental approach. The use of special mnemonic devices is familiar. They may assume various forms, verbal and nonverbal, and may indeed resemble conceptual classifications in their complexity. For example, in memorizing telephone numbers, a person may deliberately strive to associate a number with a familiar combination of dates or events. The number 835-2956, for example, could be identified as follows: 8 need not be coded since it is common to all local numbers, 35 is the year of the person's graduation from high school, 29 is the date of the stock market crash, and 56 is one year past the middle of the 1950 decade. (Of course, this seemingly cumbersome process can be short-circuited to increase its efficiency, but we need not elaborate the point.) A nonverbal device may be used by a lecturer. If he has five major topics to deal with, he can "locate" them in the four corners of the room, and proceed in an orderly fashion from right front to right rear, and so on, returning to right front for the fifth. To remember the general idea itself, he can "place" a cue in the proper corner, such as an object that suggests by a pun or homophonic relation the idea involved.

As in the case of verbal mediation, investigators have employed both inference about relations and explicit induction. Paivio and his associates have pursued the first of these tactics. The *imagery hypothesis* (Paivio, 1963, 1965, 1970) proposes that concrete nouns serving as stimulus terms facilitate paired-associate learning compared to abstract nouns, because concrete nouns evoke sensory images that act as mediators. This hypothesis is readily derived from the general mediation theory discussed in Chapter 5. A series of studies has supported the imagery hypothesis. When stimulus terms are concrete, imaginal mediators are discovered more quickly than when they are abstract, but the speed of verbal mediation is not affected by the concrete-abstract variable (Yuille and Paivio, 1967).

The question arises: Is the efficacy of concrete nouns a function of imaginal mediators, or simply of their greater availability because they are easier, more familiar, more meaningful, and so on? This possibility was tested by Paivio and Madigan (1968). The capacity of nouns to evoke sensory images (I) was determined (e.g., ACROBAT and ACCORDION are high-I nouns, ANECDOTE and AMENDMENT are low I. Matched for M and frequency, they were combined with nonsense syllables high or low in association value AV (e.g., CIR and NUF are high AV, XDL and WGP low AV, with the noun and syllable serving as stimuli in half of the lists, in the four combinations of high and low members. Significant advantages appeared for lists with syllables as the stimulus term, pairs containing high-I nouns, and pairs containing high-AV syllables (see Figure 10-5). Thus the imagery-evoking character of nouns is important, entirely aside from their meaningfulness, defined in other ways. It was found that high imagery is significantly more facilitative than high meaningfulness in the free recall of words; but under conditions of serial recall, this difference was not significant.

Mediating instructions to link pairs of nouns with a mental image or with a word or phrase are both markedly superior to repetition instructions (i.e., simply to repeat each pair aloud several times) (Yuille and Paivio, 1968), and, in addition, subjects increasingly report imagery under all three conditions as trials continue (Paivio and Yuille, 1969).

Paivio (1969) concludes that imaginal and verbal processes are alternative symbolic representations; either may be employed in mediation, whether fairly directly or evoked associatively. The more concrete the stimulus items, the more likely they are to evoke sensory images that can serve as mediators. Paivio proposes that concrete words, from association both with concrete objects and with other words, can evoke both images and verbal processes. Either can function as an effective coding system. But since abstract words depend primarily on intraverbal experiences, they especially evoke verbal associations. In general, imaginal mediators are "preferred" if at least one member of a pair is concrete. Concrete imagery operates as a parallel processing system, whereas verbal symbolism is mainly sequential (Paivio and Csapo, 1969).

Induced Imagery Bugelski has borrowed a simple mnemonic device to demonstrate the efficacy of imagery. Subjects first learn a

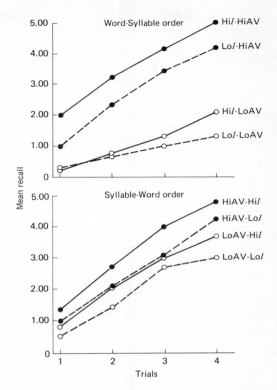

FIGURE 10-5   Recall as a function of S-R order, noun, imagery (I), and trigram association value (AV). (From Paivio and Madigan, 1968.)

set of pairs consisting of rhymes for the digits 1 through 10—for example, 1-BUN, 2-SHOE, 3-TREE, and so on. There follows a phase of learning a list of common object names, with a recall test. In learning, a person can use the number associate to picture an object —for example, if word 1 is BOOK, he could visualize a sandwich with the book in a BUN. Experimental subjects instructed in this way perform significantly better than control groups who merely learn the rhymes without instruction in their mnemonic use or who have no instruction with the rhymes, if the rate of presentation is not too fast (Bugelski, Kidd, and Segmen, 1968) (see Figure 10-6). With a self-pacing procedure, this mnemonic device proved to be highly effective with six successive lists (Bugelski, 1968). It is interesting that some subjects reported a continuous sequence to tie together successive words for the same number. For example, for 9 (WINE)

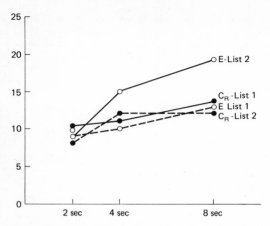

FIGURE 10-6 Effect of an imaginal mnemonic device and presentation rate on serial learning of concrete words. (Based on Bugelski, Kidd, and Segmen, 1968.)

Bugelski cites "a drunken SOLDIER, cutting a ROSE with his SWORD, while lying on a COUCH."

TEMPORAL FACTORS

Evidently, if mediation involves processes that intervene between the stimulus and response, leading to a multistage view, then the time permitted to the subject becomes a crucial consideration. A very brief exposure of materials may not suffice for mediation to operate. It does not follow, of course, that learning will not occur, but rather that mediation may not be possible. At least two different factors may be involved: the *confirmation* of response merely by virtue of opportunity to continue inspecting the relation between the stimulus and response—here an important process may be rehearsal, and there need be no mediation at all; and *mediation,* or facilitation by processes of implicit organization, enhancement of meaning, and so on. Decreasing the rate of presentation could improve learning for either of these reasons.

Many experiments have demonstrated that learning is facilitated by *decreasing* the rate of presentation of verbal materials. The standard rate for presenting paired associates is 2 seconds for the stimulus term, followed by 2 seconds for the S-R pair (2:2 rate).[1] The inter-

[1]The anticipation interval is thus 2 seconds when this method is used.

val between trials is often zero (i.e., the next stimulus term is presented immediately after S-R), or fixed at some convenient rate such as
2 or 4 seconds. In general increasing any of these intervals has a
beneficial effect. This means small increases, usually to 3 or 4
seconds, but up to 15 seconds (Bugelski, 1962). However, the length
of the S-R presentation is most important, and, compared to 1:2 or
2:2 rates, 2:3 or 3:3 or slower rates typically produce learning
in fewer trials and fewer errors (Hovland, 1938; Bugelski, 1962;
Williams, 1962; Richardson and Brown, 1966; Schulz and Weaver,
1968; Wood and Bolt, 1968; Ley, 1968). There is therefore no
doubt that slower rates of presentation are decidedly advantageous.

Total-Time Hypothesis

Before considering the effects of mediation, it is necessary to point
out that a slower rate of presenting materials also signifies a longer
time per trial. It has therefore been suggested that a given degree of
learning demands about the same total time, whether the time is
allocated to a few trials or to many trials (Murdock, 1960, 1965;
Bugelski, 1962). The hypothesis was confirmed for total rates of 6, 8,
10, 12, and 19 seconds (stimulus at 2 seconds plus S-R rate plus a
2-second intertrial interval). Subsequent investigators have generally
confirmed the total time hypothesis (Bugelski and Rickwood, 1963;
Keppel and Rehula, 1965; Cooper and Pantle, 1967; Keppel and
Mallory, 1969; Zacks, 1969; Mueller and Slaymaker, 1970[1]). However, Carroll and Burke (1965) show that the total-time hypothesis
applies only to quite slow rates and to difficult materials or those low
in meaningfulness. Zavortink and Keppel (1969) failed to support
the total-time hypothesis with paired nouns, finding in fact that the
time allowed for "study trials" has a significant effect relative to the
total time. Cooper and Pantle (1967) concluded that total time holds
only "when task requirements do not exceed simple rehearsal and
when effective time bears a positive linear relationship to nominal
time." *Effective* time refers to the period during which "representational responses" are evoked; *nominal* time signifies the potential
period for this evocation. Effective time reduces to simultaneous
presentation of stimulus and response terms. This condition also
clearly facilitates rehearsal.

The development of more refined procedures has disclosed
another limitation of the total-time hypothesis, namely, that the
relation between exposure time and learning is not constant.

[1] In this study high imagery of the R word markedly facilitated learning.

Stubin, Heimer, and Tatz (1970), for example, found that relatively more is learned with shorter exposure than with longer exposure times (see also, Bugelski, 1970). Such findings at least indicate, that in tasks of this kind there is some optimal (and fairly brief) exposure time. Clearly sufficient time must be allowed, as Bugelski points out; beyond that, increased exposure facilitates learning in regular increments to a maximum.   At increased exposure, such factors as boredom, strategy changes, or information overload may interfere with learning (Bugelski and McMahon, 1971).

Time to Mediate

The critical point concerns whether mediation, given sufficient time, facilitates learning compared to nonmediation for the same length of time. In the latter case, learning is indeed strictly by rote (sheer repetition, perhaps augmented by REHEARSAL), with emphasis on the capacity of the stimulus to elicit the response automatically. In the former case, learning depends on improving the distinctive relation between the stimulus and response so that they become part of the same "system."

Few experiments have decisively compared mediation and nonmediation during the same interval. In some studies mediation is inferred to be probably, but not directly, correlated with the rate of learning; it has seldom been ascertained whether mediation may be used spontaneously by some subjects, and, if so, whether they learn faster or slower than nonmediators. The Bugelski, Kidd, and Segmen (1968) study certainly confirms the advantages of mediation, given sufficient time. Clearly, with these meaningful object names, the total-time hypothesis is not supported.

Other studies also indicate the limitation of the total-time hypothesis to conditions when mediation is difficult, irrelevant, transient, or not used at all. King's (1971) findings that the hypothesis does not hold for connected discourse supports this conclusion. In Bugelski's (1962) study, subjects were queried about the means whereby they remembered the correct response, and several categories of devices were identified. Analysis disclosed that "the longer the interitem interval, the more likely the occurrence of a mediator." However, the data are not presented so that the rate of learning can be compared at a given interval for those who mediated and those who did not. Again, the analysis presented by Richardson and Brown (1966) does not permit a really direct test of mediation effects. If, however, the inference is warranted that a "two-step implicit chain" is involved in the paradigm A-B, A-D (with B-C-D- inferred by manipulation of association norms), then it can be compared with the "direct association" paradigm A-C, A-D. The length of the anticipation interval should benefit the A-B, A-D sequence more than it does A-C, A-D. We may also suppose that this effect should be greater for low-meaningful stimuli because of the greater difficulty in forming a mediational relationship. Examination of their tables 1 and 2 suggests that both these effects did, in fact, occur. Confirmation of the first of these effects was obtained by Richardson (1967), inferring mediation from the latency of "implicit verbal responses."

Wood and Bolt (1968) actually provided a mediator during study trials. Experimental subjects were presented paired associates composed of the first letter of a word highly associated with the response word, accompanied by the word itself [e.g., T (table)— CHAIR], and told that the mediator could aid in learning, whereas the control group was merely presented with the letter-word pair. The mediator-provided subjects performed significantly better. To determine whether the mediator itself was effective, a second experiment utilized the same procedure, but with nonassociated mediators (e.g., TOWN instead of TABLE), or a nonassociated response (such as DOCTOR instead of CHAIR). The difference significantly favored the nonmediator group for the nonrelated stimulus, with no significant difference for the nonrelated response. Finally, in a third experiment, the effect of the interval was assessed by varying both study and test times from 1 to 4 seconds. The results showed that particular combinations of these intervals were more important than either alone. In general, however, given favorable combinations, the mediator group benefited more than the non-mediator group. Furthermore, it is important to note that the nonmediator subjects reported significantly more use of mediators with increased study time, whereas no such difference appeared for the mediator group. Probably we should expect this outcome since the mediators were provided for the experimental group from the beginning. We are forced to suggest that Wood and Bolt are not really justified in concluding that mediation is independent of temporal factors for either their mediator or nonmediator groups. Other experiments also show that instructions to use verbal mediators facilitate learning, and that mediators generated by the subject himself are superior to those supplied by the experimenter (Bobrow and Bower, 1969; Schwartz, 1969a, b, 1971; Schwartz et al., 1970).

The weight of evidence therefore supports the principle that not only does mediation require some minimum time beyond sheer exposure of materials but also that, given items for which mediation is appropriate, performance is facilitated when mediation actually occurs.

In addition, the efficacy of mediation may in many cases be quite independent of temporal considerations. If it is extremely important to remember something, a person may be quite willing to devote extra time to "mediated rehearsal." In our example of the telephone number, the time spent in developing a mnemonic device may be well worth it if it guarantees future recall (e.g., if an attractive girl gives you her telephone number and you have nothing to write with!). If one is simply endeavoring to "carry" the number from the directory to the dial, it would hardly pay to search for mediators.

HOW DOES MEDIATION WORK?

We have already referred to the general conception that when mediation enters into verbal learning, three aspects are involved. The first occurs when the stimulus evokes some internal process; the second when this event calls into play memorial, organizing, and selecting cognitive processes; and the third when these events elicit the response. Only a beginning has been made toward explicating the functional significance of the central, or mediation, aspect. Although there continue to be efforts to "explain away" this process, by seeking either for relatively direct linkages between the stimulus and response, or by translating the intrinsic activites into distinguishable stimulus and response units (Jakobovits, 1966), there has finally come to be a widespread acceptance of the principle of mediation. To this extent we are led to the notion that mediating processes require an exploration of the special laws that govern them—and to the recognition that such laws cannot necessarily be derived from knowledge concerning stimulus and response properties.

Two-Phase Conception

Underwood, Runquist, and Schulz (1959; see also, Underwood and Schulz, 1960) suggested that mediation can be separated into a phase of *response acquisition* and a phase of *linkage*. On the one hand the subject must learn what responses to make, but on the other hand it is still necessary to connect the stimulus and response in an efficient manner.

McGehee and Schulz (1961) argued that the first aspect depends on rendering the response more available in the subject's response repertory (supported, for example, by Weinstock and Daly, 1971). In the chaining paradigm A-B, A-D, with B-C-D inferred, B might simply enhance the availability of D, without any necessary associative relationship. In one experiment, following the Russell and Storms procedure a special availability paradigm was contrived by employing different stimulus-terms for first and test lists. But no advantage appeared for this situation. A second experiment introduced additional comparisons (especially, the A-Br, or interfering, paradigm). The results agreed with those of Russell and Storms, confirming that it is the linkage, or associative, phase that is facilitated by mediation.

Currently, the two-phase view distinguishes between *discovery* of mediators and their *utilization* (Schulz and Lovelace, 1964). The study interval is considered critical for the former, the test interval for the latter. Manipulation of these intervals by Schulz and Weaver (1968) supported the latter of these relations but not the former. A further study (Weaver, Hopkins, and Schulz, 1968) also failed to confirm the relation of the study interval to the hypothesized discovery process. This outcome, of course, does not mean that the interval is not important—performance improves for both mediated and nonmediated pairs as the interval increases—but in this study, at least, the mediated pairs were not differentially affected. There are several weaknesses in this approach, however, especially because the actual occurrence of mediators was not assessed. Furthermore, the range of intervals reported was only 0 to 2.5 seconds.

McCormack and Hannah (1967) found by monitoring eye movements that subjects pay more sustained attention to low-M than to high-M materials. In combined lists this should result in greater viewing of the response under high-stimulus–low-response conditions, but the reverse should hold for the low-stimulus–high response situation. The two-phase interpretation leads to a different prediction. Viewing of the response should exceed viewing of the stimulus in the early stages of low and high learning and should be continued longer in the high and low stage. Although McCormack and Moore (1969) found some support for the two-phase view, they suggest that a more complex—perhaps multiple-phase explanation—may be required.

The two-phase hypothesis has not received strong support. On the whole it may be quite an artificial separation. It depends fundamentally on traditional distinctions between the stimulus (or the implicit stimulus) and the response (or the implicit response) variables. While mediation may indeed involve subcomponents, they are not necessarily separable in this fashion. Successive phases could very well occur, but "discovery" (and/or retrieval) and "utilization" (and/or operation) may be intricately interrelated.

Interference

Mandler and Earhard (1964) suggested that it is not mediation that facilitates performance in the A-B, B-C, A-C paradigm, but rather that there is relatively more interference in the control A-B, D-C, A-C paradigm. The argument runs that the learning of A-B also strengthens B-A; in the mediational sequence the presentation of B-C produces interference between B-A and B-C. In a nonmediated sequence there is no such unlearning (since D-C is presented). Therefore in the final stage, A-B remains stronger in the nonmediated sequence and produces greater interference, thus, of course, making the mediated pairs easier to learn.

Using the mediated sequence B-A, B-C, A-C and the standard control sequence B-A, D-C, A-C, and also control paradigms ("pseudomediation" B-A, B-D, A-C; mediated interference B-A, B-C$_r$,[1] A-C; and warm-up control E-F, G-H, A-C), Earhard and Earhard (1967) found that the standard and warm-up controls were superior at stage 2, showing the anticipated effects of interference and unlearning. All but the standard control displayed facilitation at stage 3. The mediated facilitation and warm-up-control conditions were superior to pseudomediation and mediated-interference conditions.

The major weaknesses of this study are similar to those previously mentioned. The presentation rate was brief (2:2) and there was no way to know whether mediation actually occurred or not. To deal with these points, Earhard and Earhard (1968) investigated the effects of overlearning, lengthening the test interval, and instructions that provided a mediating rule. Under the last of these conditions, when combined either with overlearning of the first list or a lengthened interval, the mediated pairs showed facilitation. These findings run counter to a strict interference interpretation.

THE BROADER CONTEXT

Although we have concentrated on meaning and mediation, numerous experiments have shown that verbal learning is affected

[1] Repairing of C terms so that they are not the same in A-C as they would be by reference to B-A.

by the kinds of situational, task, and motivational variables mentioned at the beginning of this chapter. For example, incentives facilitate recall (Weiner, 1966; Kahneman and Pearler, 1969), and severe stress has interfering effects (Beam, 1955). Persons high in manifest anxiety typically perform worse than those low in anxiety as the task becomes more difficult or as stress becomes greater (Sarason, 1960), but are benefited, under such conditions, under reassurance (Sarason, 1958). As it does in concept tasks, pretraining facilitates performance for verbal learning. (Hovland and Kurtz, 1952; Saltz, 1961), especially with materials initially low in meaningfulness (Saltz and Felton, 1968).

Another factor depends on the structure of the language, or the degree to which words form a regularly used context. For example, G.A. Miller and Selfridge (1950) developed sets of words that varied in their "approximation to English." Thus the same words can be rearranged with respect to the probability with which one would usually follow another. The phrase "the greedy starlings ate all the sunflower seeds" makes excellent sense. "All starlings ate the greedy seeds the sunflower" contains some structural peculiarities, but still reads fairly well. But "sunflower the greedy the all seeds starlings ate" has very little sensible structure.

Special Cues

Left to their own devices, subjects select different elements in a compound stimulus to serve as cues (Harrington, 1969). In a situation such as the appearance of a verbal element against a colored background, the transfer effect of each cue can be tested. Color is fully effective as a cue when trigrams are the other element, but words are better than color (Underwood, Ham, and Ekstrand, 1962). But if color is present in a compound, it facilitates learning by making the stimulus more distinctive (Saltz, 1963). Such effects do not appear when color is added to the response term (S.C. Brown and Read, 1968). Mediational interpretations have been offered for the facilitation of compound stimuli (Birnbaum, 1966; Steiner and Sobel, 1968; Solso, 1968).

When items are constructed according to a rule, similar to those for concepts, cues to the rule facilitate performance. For example, S-R pairs in one experiment consisted of similar-sounding syllables, and alerting subjects to a relation between the stimulus and response, or to the sound, or to what the "mouth" was doing all facilitated performance, especially the last (Jenkins, Foss, and Greenberg,

1968). In another experiment, trigrams were treated as anagrams (e.g., XAW can be converted into AWX or WAX). Alerting subjects to a systematic rule, in which numbers refer to position such as 2,1,3, promotes learning. Lists containing conceptually related words also produce faster learning than noncategorizable words (Robinson and Rabin, 1969; Henry and Voss, 1970). In all such cases, mediation is a unifying principle (Richardson, 1960).

In all these ways—and many others, which space limitations preclude citing—verbal learning depends on much more than the purely formal specification of stimulus and response terms: It varies with the situational context and characteristics of the person.

SUMMARY

The study of verbal learning originated in studies of rote memorization, but has increasingly turned to problems of meaning and mediation. Paired-associate paradigms may be adapted to sequences of acquisition, recall, transfer, and relearning phases. Variables manipulated in experiments include formal task properties, situational conditions, meaningfulness, and intrinsic states. The role of meaningfulness is demonstrated by clustering in recall, categorizing and organizing effects, and associative relationships. Measures are frequency, associative value, response dominance, pronounceability, associability, reinforcement value, and concreteness. Each shows some relation to rate of learning, but those founded on associations are generally most potent. Connotative meaning can be conditioned. Instead of relying strictly on formally defined properties of materials, theorists are developing principles based on associative structure, with contrast, grouping, coherence, and experience of relations as fundamental conditions. Mediation is investigated by using paired-associate paradigms of chaining, acquired stimulus equivalence, and acquired response equivalence. Experimental background is found in studies of semantic generalization, mediated generalization, implicit chaining, imagery, and induced imagery. Temporal effects are important. Mediation has been analyzed by formulating a two-phase process and a principle of interference, but neither view has received strong support. In a broader perspective, verbal learning is affected by motivational, situational, pretraining, language structure, special cues, and other factors beyond formal specification of stimulus and response terms.

11

PROBLEM SOLVING

Concept-attaining and verbal-learning situations fall toward the realistic end of the continuum formulated earlier, although investigators are increasingly recognizing that autistic components interplay with the realistic ones. We can turn our attention now to more complex problem solving, in which realistic processes typically predominate. Distinctions from the kinds of tasks previously discussed depend not only on the somewhat vague matter of complexity, but also on the diversity of behavior that may be elicited and on the degree to which the person must produce varied and reorganized responses.

Diversity is reflected in the shifting of behavior from one mode to another as the subject seeks to adapt his performance to the goal of the problem. Thus we may see various sequences and combinations of perceptual, cognitive, motor, and verbal acts. The varied and reorganizing feature appears in the necessity for the person to alter customary, fixed, or familiar patterns of response in order to arrive successfully at the solution because the goal usually cannot be reached in a simple, direct fashion. Since these processes call for changes in behavior and increasing integration of responses into smooth sequences, problem solving can be regarded as a form of complex learning.

Another characteristic of problem solving appears when we focus on the goal, or solution. The person's objective is to arrive at the correct outcome; furthermore, such an outcome can be specified in advance: The problem is "solved" when this outcome is produced. In a problem solving task every subject either succeeds or fails, and when they succeed all subjects display the same solution. Thus even very complex problem solving retains formal requirements.

These distinctions are drawn partly to stress differences from routine and rote situations, but also to introduce a preliminary comparison with creative tasks. Later we shall see that these latter situations not only call intimately on autistic processes, but also do not have "correct" solutions that can be identified in advance—whatever the person produces is correct and can only be judged adequately by qualitative criteria.

A great variety of problems have been used in experimentation. Among them are mazes, multiple choice, and alternation problems, which demand the development of a pattern or sequence of choices; anagrams, word building, and other verbal tasks in which the subject must manipulate letters or words to produce meaningful structures; puzzles and brainteasers, which require a disentangling of ambiguities or obstructions and a fitting together of parts to arrive at the solution; mathematical problems, which call for the application of logical principles; construction problems, in which the subject must use and combine discrete materials to produce a structure; and many games involving the utilization of strategies to win points or awards, often with the object of defeating an opponent. (We shall not deal directly with gaming.)

Three major stages can logically be distinguished.

1 *Confrontation by a Problem.* The situation involves a goal, accompanied by some difficulty or obstacle in attaining it. Problem solving behavior occurs when the person *perceives* the goal, *encounters* the difficulty, is *motivated* to achieve the goal, and exerts *effort* to overcome the obstacle.

2 *Working toward a Solution.* Assuming that the person strives to attain the goal, rather than withdrawing from it or not responding, his behavior involves *mental or symbolic processes,* such as inspection, calling on past experience, relating one part of the situation to another, and so on; *manipulation* of materials; and *verbalization,* such as interpreting the situation, asking questions, expressing feelings, labeling materials, citing rules, and so on. The chief concern of the cognitive psychologist lies

not in cataloguing responses, but in describing their sequencing and patterning, together with their effects on and relations to outcomes. Thus we arrive at principles of organization and re-organization, cognitive style and strategy, and goal-relatedness. 3 *Solution*. Finally, the person may reach the goal, or he may fail to reach it. *Results for the individual* may be understanding, relief of tension, emotional expressions of satisfaction or plea-sure, a cessation of activity, and so on. We should also recognize longer-range effects, such as subsequent modification of behavior, shift to a different goal, or an instrumental relating of the immediate goal to some more remote or more inclusive goal. Each particular problem situation thus typically serves as a subgoal. However, laboratory studies seldom consider more than the immediate task. *Results in the environment* may be an organization or reorganization of materials, the removal of the obstacle, or a change in the situation. In an important sense problem solving is a matter of the person's altering or con-structing his own environment in ways that fulfill his needs. Finally, *failure* may also be an outcome. Although often employed as an experimental induction to observe its effects on subsequent performance, conditions related to failure have for the most part been treated incidentally, or by inference from factors leading to successful solution.

More attention has been paid to the intermediate stage than to the other two.

EXPERIMENTATION ON ANIMALS
Many lines in the investigation of problem solving have originated in experiments with animal subjects.

Thorndike
At the turn of the century, trial-and-error behavior was described by Thorndike (1898). He placed cats in a puzzle box where the door could be opened by moving a button, by pulling a loop of wire, or by some other simple mechanism. An incentive, food, was placed within the sight and smell of the animal, to elicit effort to obtain the reward. It is not certain that the food served as the real incentive; Thorndike suggested that escape is more important than the food, at least at first. In the course of time, an accidental movement would result in

opening the door, and the cat would get out and obtain the reward. Upon successive repetitions, much the same process would be repeated, until the cat would quickly and efficiently perform the required act to open the door.[1] The learning that occurred in this kind of situation led Thorndike to the view that the animal was solving the problem in a blind and accidental fashion. Later investigators have repeated Thorndike's experiments (Adams, 1929; Guthrie and Horton, 1946). Much the same general results were found, although theoretical interpretations differ.

Other types of problem situations have also been devised to study animal behavior; most of them have also been extended to the observation of human subjects. In many ways the maze is ideal, since it has definite structure, an explicit starting point, a correct or successful pathway, and a goal. Furthermore, the subject cannot attain the goal without encountering choice points, at which the alternatives carry some risk—that is, limited probability of moving directly toward the goal. In the double-alternation problem, either of two pathways could lead to the goal, but the subject must learn the rule that two successive correct choices must be followed by two successive choices of the alternative pathway. Thus, if the two choices are a right (R) and a left (L) alleyway, correct performance requires learning the sequence RRLLRRLL (Gellerman, 1931). Or the subject may be presented with two boxes to choose between (W. S. Hunter and Bartlett, 1948).

When human subjects are presented with these problems, they show the same general kinds of behavior as animals. Quantitatively, the record of performance, in the form of a learning curve, is quite similar. Qualitatively, there is exploration, chance success, and gradual increase in mastery. Some important additional characteristics appear, however, that make human trial-and-error activity at least more complex than that of animals, if not actually fundamentally different. Human subjects often employ visual imagery (evidence for which can hardly be obtained in animals) and verbalization, both of which increase the efficiency of performance in comparison with a purely motor mode of attack (Warden, 1924; Husband, 1931). Facilitation is especially associated with verbal methods.

Woodworth (1940, p. 294) has clearly set forth what we may call the classic features of trial-and-error behavior as it appears in animal studies: (1) a "set" to reach a goal; (2) inability to see any clear way to the goal; (3) exploring the situation; (4) seeing or

---

[1] Today we would refer to this process as *instrumental* or *operant conditioning* (see Skinner, 1938).

somehow finding leads, or possible ways to reach the goal; (5) trying these leads; (6) backing off when blocked in one lead, and trying another; and (7) finally finding a good lead and reaching the goal.

Köhler

Some experiments with chimpanzees by the gestalt psychologist Köhler (1927) set the stage for later experimental work on insight. His research is complemented by Yerkes' (1927) investigations of a young gorilla.

Köhler devised a variety of situations that required "roundabout" methods of solution. Among them were fetching an object when it was thrown through a window, using implements like sticks and boxes to reach bits of food, making implements, building simple structures to obtain objectives dangling out of reach, and employing one implement to obtain a second one by which food could be secured.

From detailed protocols, Köhler noted that the chimps would try out various tactics, which proved ineffectual, then apparently engage in random acts or even seem to abandon attempts to solve the problem. At a later point, however, the animal would quite suddenly use the resources available to obtain the objective in a smooth sequence with a minimum of confusion.

Yerkes also noted that "insightful" solutions apparently evolved only after considerable preliminary learning—even in many cases requiring careful demonstration by the experimenter.

Utilizing similar problem situations, later investigators repeated Köhler's and Yerkes' experiments, attempting to describe more fully the characteristics of insight. Pechstein and Brown (1939) compared the performance of a gorilla, chimpanzees, and children. They found that "learning never takes place immediately when the problem is, in reality, new." Immediate solution occurred only when it was possible to transfer what had previously been learned. The subject typically explored the situation and gradually developed appropriate responses. Insight, they suggest, refers primarily to the fact of learning and not to how the learning takes place.

In experiments with preschool children, Alpert (1928) obtained valuable quantitative data on the incidence of various kinds of behavior and types of solution. Responses were classified as *primitive* (such as simple reaching with the hand), *random exploration and elimination* (characterized as the deliberate trying out of possibilities), and *immediate solution*. Primitive responses tended to become less frequent as familiarity with the situation increased. Of all responses, exploration and elimination were most frequent, followed by primitive responses and immediate solution, with random response very infrequent.

Alpert also reported the incidence of four types of solution: (1) solution after immediate insight (33 percent); (2) solution after gradual insight, either partial (5 percent) or complete (16 percent); (3) solution after sudden insight, either matured during exposure (14 percent) or matured between exposures (4 percent); and (4) failure to solve (28 percent).

Primitive behavior most often led to failure, but successes tended to be immediate; random responses were too infrequent to display a consistent relation to solution; and exploration and elimination led more often to success than failure, with gradual solutions accompanied by complete insight most frequent. The same child would attack one problem in one way, and another problem in a different way, and no one problem was solved in the same way by all children.

Thus, insightful behavior, like trial and error, is more complex than early conceptions indicated.

HUMAN PROCESSES OF PROBLEM SOLVING

Important contributions to a more inclusive view of problem solving have come from experiments in the gestalt tradition, which emphasize the characteristics of adults in complex tasks.

Functional Fixedness and Recentering

Experiments by Duncker (1926, 1945) have played an influential role in elaborating principles of insightful problem solving. Like some pioneers—for example, Piaget—he was less concerned with controlled experimentation than with exploring the activity of his subjects. His experiments were often little more than illustrations of points of departure for analytic interpretation. Furthermore, his studies must be considered in the light of his general point of view. Since he linked problem solving ("productive thinking") with certain limited kinds of problem situations, conditions were devised to evoke the kinds of performance in which he was interested. "Insightful" signified "intelligent"—or responding effectively (in a "good" manner) to relevant features of the situation, implying that one is intelligent only when acting in a specified fashion.

In presenting a problem to his subjects, he asked them to "think aloud." (See also, Claparède, 1934.) In contrast to classical intro-spection, in which the subject reported and/or analyzed his mental content, he was supposed simply to verbalize what he was doing. There are serious limitations with this procedure, since it may inhibit thought, slowing it or interfering with its free flow. Furthermore, there are differences between speech and thought, such as demands for greater coherence and orderliness in verbalization and the "private" characteristics of thought. Nevertheless, introspective data have much to recommend them in the study of cognitive processes (Natsoulas, 1970). We have, indeed, already pointed to their crucial significance in the investigation of mediation in verbal learning.

In the process of solution, Duncker distinguished as "heuristic methods" between *analysis of the situation* and *analysis of the goal*. The subject must ascertain conflicting elements of the situation, since, in Duncker's view, the solution always requires some variation of crucial relationships. Furthermore, it is necessary to analyze the materials available in order to resolve conflicting elements (to remove the difficulty). Thus the subject looks over the situation to determine where the difficulty lies and tries to find what can be used to remove it. In a "genuine" solution process, the person also analyzes the goal, that is, considers what must be done if the solution is to be achieved.

Duncker regarded solutions reached by analytic means as rational and desirable, compared to solutions reached by *resonance*, which he considered to be "banal" and less rational, "the process by which, in the perceptual field or in memory . . . an object or a situation is sought out through specific signalling. . . ." Resonance may operate whenever previous experience, or learned structures, affect the process of solution. The instructions presented to the subject arouse past experience, leading to the adoption of "models of search," or general schemes that guide behavior in the situation, based on previously learned strategies or habits.

Especially important is the *functional fixedness* of available objects, or the degree to which an object is in some manner tied into the environmental situation. For example, a specific function may be strongly attached to an object that must be used for a different function, or an object might require alteration to fulfill the required function, or an object might be required for one function and later for a new one, or an object might be poorly suited for a new function. Experiments to be cited illustrate these points.

Therefore when the person must successively reformulate the elements of a situation, conditions of functional fixedness can make it more difficult for him to reach a solution. Then it is necessary to utilize objects in new ways or to reorganize the elements of a situation. The problem is analyzed to see where the trouble lies, what needs to be done, and what is available for solving it. To be sure, the solution may occur immediately if a simple perception locates the difficulty and there is readily available the means for coping with it. For instance, if I wish to hang a picture, all I need is a hammer and a nail; I would go to my toolbox and obtain the equipment. Such a solution would exemplify a solution by resonance—and it would be a perfectly sensible and successful solution.[1] On the other hand, no hammer and nail may be available; in this case there is a real difficulty that might, for example, be solved by wedging a small strip of wood into a crack in the wall and hanging the picture on this improvised peg.

Recentering

Wertheimer (1959) has further clarified the characteristics of "sensible" solutions. A fundamental requirement is an understanding of the structural and functional relationships in the situation. In a sensible solution the person must grasp the meanings, the principles, the *inner relations* of the situation, and be oriented to the whole problem. The solution is not a matter of mechanically applying rules or principles—of simply invoking operations that have worked before, but grows out of understanding the specific requirements of the immediate problem. One can construct, reconstruct, or reorganize features of the situation to cope with the inner relations of the problem as a whole. Thus problem solving becomes a dynamic, fluid process, beginning with a *centering* of attention on the essential elements and their relation to the basic difficulty, followed by some reorganization, or modification, of previously known principles—leading to a *recentering* of attention. Without these processes, problems cannot be solved, except by accident. In short, a rule or concept has no practical use unless it is fully understood.

Method of Instruction

Clearly, the foregoing analysis of problem solving contains implications for training. Katona (1940) conducted an important series of experiments to compare *memorizing* as a technique of practice with

[1] Unless we argue that no "problem" exists—but to do so misses the ordinary, daily character of coping with the environment in a goal-oriented manner.

methods that seek to promote *understanding* of principles or rules. Ingenious card-trick and match-stick problems served as tasks. An example of the former is to lay the top card on the table, then to return the next card to the bottom, the third on the table, and so on, until all cards have been laid out in such a manner that the colors red and black alternate. The solution lies in prearranging the deck according to a principle. In a match-stick problem, matches are used to form adjacent squares or triangles, and the subject is asked to produce a smaller number of squares or triangles by moving only a specified number of matches. For example, with this arrangement he should make four squares by moving only three matches.

For the memorizing condition, Katona had his subjects merely learn the concrete steps (e.g., the specific order of cards required). Understanding was taught by explanation and demonstration (card tricks) or by stating crucial requirements (e.g., functions of match positions) or principles (e.g., make a hole). In general, Katona found a slight advantage for memorization during practice on initial tasks but, as variations or new problems were introduced, the understanding methods were markedly better.

Direction

Maier (1930, 1933) has added another principle, namely, a relevant set, or direction. Even if the subject observes and analyzes the problem and locates the difficulty in attaining the goal, nevertheless he may not be able to achieve a solution without an appropriate guiding principle, an adequate set serving to integrate the elements of the problem and to organize them in relation to the goal.

Maier has employed a variety of difficult problems to reveal the significance of direction. The pendulum problem is one example (Maier, 1930). The task is to construct two pendulums, each designed to swing over a designated point on the floor. Various materials are available to the subjects, such as coils of wire, two kinds of clamps, chalk, and lengths of wood. The solution depends on three part responses: (1) suspending the chalk at the end of a wire by tying the wire to a clamp that holds a piece of chalk; (2) making a pole long enough to reach the ceiling by clamping together two lengths of wood; and (3) supporting the two pendulums at either end of a board by wedging it against the ceiling with the long pole. The necessary direction was a statement that the problem could easily be solved if the pendulums could be hung from the ceiling. Five groups participated in the experiment: (1) problem only (control); (2) part solutions demonstrated by analogous operations, but not presented in relation to the problem; (3) part solutions demonstrated and directly related to the problem, that is, the subjects were told that the solution was constituted in separate parts; (4) direction given, after which the problem was presented; and (5) same as group 3, plus direction.

The subjects displayed six different types of solution, five of them unsuccessful, such as achieving one of the part solutions without discovering how to complete the structure, or building up from the floor (e.g., a tripod). Of sixty-two subjects in the first four groups, only one achieved the correct solution, whereas eight of the twenty-two in group 5 achieved it (1.6 versus 36.3 percent).

The beneficial effect of hints further reveals the importance of direction. Administered prior to the task, the hints suggested that it is necessary to vary one's attack on the problem and that new combinations should be sought when previous attempts have proven unsuccessful.

RESEARCH ON INSIGHTFUL PRINCIPLES

Taking their departure from these historic treatments of problem solving, later investigators have systematically examined various theoretical points. Attention has been devoted especially to explicit facilitating or interfering conditions. The general principles of centering and recentering appear to be accepted, although our understanding of problem solving would be advanced by intensive study of the processes by which these central features of problem solving actually operate. In this respect, introspective reports could be valuable.

Analysis of the Goal

Reid (1951) employed two puzzles to test Duncker's contention that problem solving is advanced by knowledge about the goal. One group of subjects was supplied with several "aids" designed to explicate progressively the requirements of the solution, another group was given the same number of "aids," but these did not explicate the goal. For example, the match problem required the subject to make four equilateral triangles with six matches. Explicative aids pointed to critical requirements such as, "What does this problem mean? What would that mean for each match involved?" and "The terms mean that twelve triangle sides must be formed by only six matches." Nonexplicative aids took the following forms: "Are you still clear what the problem is?" and "There really is a solution to this problem." Approximately one-third of the subjects who attempted each problem solved it without aid. Each successive aid helped some subjects, but the explicative aids were markedly more helpful than the nonexplicative aids. And in both problems, many more failed under the latter condition (in one problem 62 versus 20 percent, in the other 32 versus 6 percent).

An experiment by Anthony (1966) dealt both with analysis of the goal ("working backward") and analysis of the situation ("working forward"), although recognizing that neither is necessarily opposed to the other. He devised a map test that required the subject to find a route from city A to city B, so that information could be supplied by the experimenter in the vicinity of either A or B. Although subjects often changed direction during the course of the problem, in general they tended to work in the more effective direction.

Clearly the principle of analysis is related to Maier's principle of direction. In fact relevant aids or hints or the acquiring of information should influence the establishment of direction. Burke, Maier, and Hoffman (1966) have pursued this point in a study with a hatrack problem using two sticks and a clamp. The solution lies in clamping the sticks together and wedging the resulting pole between the floor and ceiling, with the clamp handle serving as a hook for a hat. The experimenter introduced hints at various times, intended to help overcome two assumptions, one that a hatrack is a vertical structure that rests on the floor, another that the hat must be hung from the end of a stick. The first hint was, "In the correct solution the ceiling is part of the construction"; and the second was, "In the correct solution the clamp is used as the hat hanger." Aids of these kinds may arrest an already adopted direction, facilitate the finding of a correct direction, or can provide a point of departure for later reference when unsuccessful attempts are abandoned.

Functional Fixedness

Birch and Rabinowitz (1951) point out that experience in a situation enters into problem solving both by providing a repertoire of pertinent information and by supplying specific cues that affect how that knowledge will be used. This second aspect bears on the role of functional fixedness as advanced by Duncker. They used Maier's (1931) two-string problem. In this situation two strings hang from the ceiling too far apart for the subject to reach one while holding the other. The goal is to tie them together. The solution is to tie a weight to one string and to make it swing so that it can be caught close enough to the other string. Available (as weights) were an electrical switch and a relay. Groups of subjects were given different prior experiences. One first used the switch to complete an electric circuit, another first used the relay for this purpose, and a control group had neither experience. In the test situation both switch and relay were available. Direction (hint) was introduced, such as the experimenter's "accidentally" causing one of the strings to swing after 9 minutes. As predicted from the principle of functional fixedness, each experimental group significantly more often used for a weight the object with which they had not had previous experience (see Figure 11-1). Similarly, Adamson (1952) showed that the preutilization of an object for a function other than that required by the solution induces functional fixedness.

As intimated by Duncker, the perceptual characteristics of objects may signal their possible use. Glucksberg (1964), for example, devised a problem in which a metal screwdriver could be used to complete an electrical circuit. When this object was conspicuous, with a bright blade and a red handle, the same hue as the binding posts, solution time was faster than when it merely looked like a small, nearby screwdriver (therefore its functional fixedness was strong). Thus differentiating objects helps to overcome their fixedness. In another experiment, labeling of available objects increased the rate of solution, compared to no labels (Glucksberg and Weisberg, 1966). Similarly, in the electrical circuit problem, the use of novel names (nonsense syllables) reduced the functional fixedness of objects (Glucksberg and Danks, 1968). In the two-string problem, several solutions are possible (besides the pendulum, extending one string, hooking one string from a distance, etc.). Objects appropriate for particular solutions are readily used when presented alone, but less often when another object is simultaneously available, as if the latter distracts the subject from perceiving the function in question (Maier and Janzen, 1968). Finally, initial satiation on the relevant word *swing* slows performance (Wakin and Braun, 1966).

In summary then, Duncker's principle of functional fixedness has received strong experimental support. Not only do the directly

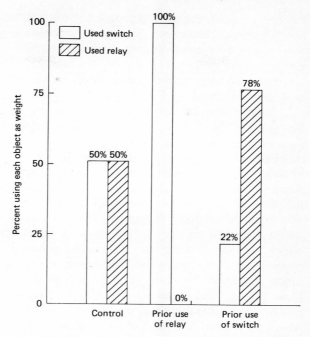

FIGURE 11–1   The effect of prior utilization in promoting functional fixedness.   (Based on Birch and Rabinowitz 1951.)

perceived and habitual functions of objects interfere with their utilization in different or new ways, but factors that help to render the required functions more salient reduce fixedness of the prior or usual function (or the reverse). To make the picture more complete we would need to also consider individual differences in tendencies toward functional fixedness. Furthermore, if functional fixedness corresponds to a set induced by situational conditions, then techniques, such as special instructions or training, ought to help subjects to overcome the set.

Availability of Functions

Weaver and Madden (1949) repeated the pendulum problem with somewhat equivocal results. When the data were classified according to Maier's specifications, only four solutions were obtained from fifty-four subjects. Including another variation of the correct solution, the groups given the part responses achieved about as many correct solutions as did the group given part responses plus direction. Further analysis revealed slightly more advantage for the direction group (more subjects attempted the correct solution). Actually, direction also appears to operate, at least implicitly, in the group given only part responses.

Such findings suggest that direction by itself is insufficient. Saugstad (1955, 1957) points to certain untested assumptions: (1) part experiences in the pendulum problem were the only ones required, (2) subjects actually perceived the demonstrations as intended, and (3) subjects understood the statement of the problem. Accordingly, it is necessary to determine whether the required functions of the objects are available to the solver.

In one experiment (Saugstad, 1955) this proposition was tested with the candle problem, which calls for constructing a device by which to blow out a lighted candle some distance away. Present are glass tubes, putty, and a rod. The solution consists in adjoining the tubes and fastening them to the rod with putty, so that one can blow through the extended mechanism. Before the problem was presented, an experimental group had an availability test during which they listed functions of the objects, whereas a control group did not have this experience. Of the fifty-seven experimental subjects, thirteen showed on the test that the necessary functions were available, and all solved the problem. Of the remaining forty-four, only 58 percent achieved a solution. Only 57 percent of the twenty-eight control subjects were able to solve the problem.

The possibility that the critical part response in the pendulum problem (i.e., wedging a T-shape against the side of a doorway) merely called attention to the ceiling, rather than inducing the essential "direction," was also tested (Saugstad, 1957). To make the ceiling more available perceptually, a miniature hallway was compared with a life-size one, but neither the supposed "direction" nor a change in the situation affected performance. Next, an attempt was made to increase the availability of the required function by presenting three tasks representative of the three part responses, and instructing subjects in the principles themselves. When the pendulum problem was administered, significantly more of the subjects were successful. Finally, 94 percent solved the problem when additional controls maximized certainty that the ceiling principle was understood; at this point none of the subjects failed to grasp the idea. Similar evidence for the importance of understanding the principle was obtained with a different problem (Saugstad and Raaheim, 1960) (see Figure 11-2).

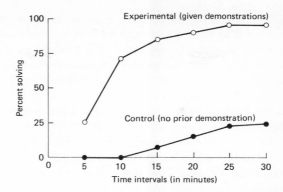

FIGURE 11–2   The effect of demonstrations to enhance the availability of functions. (Based on Saugstad and Raaheim, 1960.) Explanation: The ball problem presents the task of transferring steel balls from a glass on a movable frame to a metal cylinder, both a considerable distance away. Available are newspapers, string, pliers, rubber bands, nails. Solution is to bend the nail with the pliers and tie it to the string, then to throw the improvised hook to catch the frame and pull it within reach, then to roll the newspapers to form tubes inserted into each other and held by rubber bands, and finally to roll the balls down the tube to the cylinder. Demonstrated were hook and tube functions.

Saugstad's research does not necessarily mean that the principle of direction is incorrect, as much as it indicates that Maier's procedures were insufficient to ensure understanding. Subjects can and do solve problems when the necessary functions are available to them, whether or not the integrating guideline is explicitly provided. It appears that Maier's assumed direction added little or nothing to the subjects' self-generated application of principles, or, perhaps, Saugstad's demonstrations and instructions themselves induced an appropriate direction.

Maier and Burke (1966) argue that even when functions are available, the crucial factor is the subject's ability to select from and to organize his relevant past experience. They conducted a further test, using the hatrack problem described above. Some subjects solved the problem without hints, some solved it with hints, and some failed even with hints. As a means to avoid an influence on the problem solving process, the availability test was administered *after* the experiment in another room. The correct structure was already mounted in this room (with the sticks painted white to reduce similarity), and the subjects were asked to list as many uses or functions for it as they could think of. There were no differences among the three groups of subjects in the functions listed. Not only were they similar in almost unanimously mentioning the hatrack function, but they also gave others with comparable frequency.

Additional factors appear in a study by Maier and Burke (1967). Here the horse-trading problem was used, namely, "A man bought a horse for 60 dollars, sold it for 70 dollars, bought it back again for 80 dollars, then sold it again for 90 dollars. How much did he make in the horse-trading business?" It is usual for males to perform much better than females. The investigators undertook to track down the reasons.

First, under the standard conditions, five alternatives are available: (1) he lost 10 dollars, (2) he broke even, (3) he made 10 dollars, (4) he made 20 dollars, and (5) he made 30 dollars. As usual significantly more males gave the correct answer (48 versus 27 percent). But, interestingly enough, significantly more females chose "broke even" (28 versus 9 percent). Next, a "rationale" was provided for each alternative—for example, for alternative I, "He lost 20 dollars by paying 80 dollars for a horse which he originally bought for 60 dollars, but he made 10 dollars by selling it again for 90 dollars. The sum of his gains and losses still yields a loss of 10 dollars." These additions produced an increase in correct responses, but aided males more than females (67 versus 34 percent), thus indicating that the latter were not simply jumping to conclusions. Once again, "broke even" was more often preferred by the females (27 versus 2 percent). A third step was taken, by eliminating the broke even alternative and now no sex difference appeared (48 percent of the males and 47 percent of the females were correct). This finding suggested that this choice served to distract the females. Next, a special version intended to appeal more to females was used; it involved a secondhand car and the financial figures were eliminated. This problem went as follows: "A man bought a secondhand car for his wife. She didn't like it so he sold it. How did he make out financially? One of the following alternatives is correct. Please choose one of them. (1) He lost money. (2) He broke even. (3) He made a small profit. (4) He made a good profit." Now the females again favored broke even (28 versus 6 percent) and less often chose lost money (36 versus 75 percent). The fifth step used the secondhand car version, but with the husband-wife relationship reversed. Again the females more often chose broke even (31 versus 6 percent), but there was a significant increase in lost money, suggesting that the "protective response" of minimizing loss decreased when *she* conducted the sale. Finally, the horse-trading problem was modified to make the broke even alternative correct. It now read, "A man bought a horse for 60 dollars and sold it for 70 dollars. Then he bought it back for 90 dollars and sold it for 80 dollars." This produced a nonsignificant difference in correct responses (82 percent for males, 71 percent for females).

It is evident from these studies that "availability" of response depends on factors other than some logically defined function. In this case, the females display both a special response preference and a marked influence of their perceived sex role.

A different approach to the availability function appears in studies that induce tendencies to produce unusual responses (Maltzman, Brooks, Bogartz, and Summers, 1958). Subjects were administered a test of verbal fluency (writing in 3 minutes as many words as possible beginning with *s* and ending in *l*), and were then asked to think of as many uses as possible for a screwdriver, a block of balsa, wood, and a length of string. These instructions failed to increase rate of solving the two-string problem. However, performance was significantly improved when subjects were presented with lists of uncommon uses and asked to check which ones they were likely to use. (Exposure to the uncommon uses alone yielded significantly better performance for men than for women.) Experiments by Duncan (1961) add a cautionary note since he found that none of the following procedures significantly influenced problem solving: prior instructions to think of a relevant object, instructions to think of something new, instructions to use imagination, or practice on insight problems. Thus rather general and nonspecific experience is not sufficient to promote availability of functions.

These findings thus show that new functions of objects may under appropriate conditions be rendered more available by influencing the flexibility or attention of subjects, but that it is not easy to accomplish. It probably depends on whether functional fixedness is actually reduced.

Discovery

Taking their cue from Katona's research, several investigators have examined the efficiency of various training methods. Hilgard, Irvine, and Whipple (1953) tested three propositions, namely, that, compared to learning by rote, learning by understanding (1) does not necessarily show an advantage in original learning since it may take longer, (2) produces better retention, and (3) yields better transfer to new related tasks. A series of Katona's card tricks was used. As mentioned, these problems require that a set of cards be pre-arranged so that they would appear in a specified order (e.g., numerical) when played first face up and then returned to the bottom (or two cards could be returned, etc.). In the rote-memorization condition the experimenter simply gave the subject the correct order for placing the cards in the deck. In the understanding condition the experimenter taught a general scheme by which the proper order could be worked out.

The first and third propositions were well supported. More time was needed to instruct the understanding group, although the understanding group was slightly better on a transfer task that merely called for transposition of the same rule to a different outcome (even-odd order, rather than red-black); on the other transfer tasks that could not be solved except by developing a new formula (which could be worked out by the method taught), the understanding group was vastly superior.

The second proposition was not sustained since there was no difference between the groups in overnight retention. To be sure, this study is not a definitive test of retention since there might be a difference over a longer time. Furthermore, retention might differ for more complex problems.

The investigators noted that the understanding subjects made many errors, including a tendency to rely on rote memory once the solution was found, careless mistakes, and incomplete grasp of the method. In a further experiment utilizing five different methods for teaching "understanding," carelessness rather than lack of understanding emerged as most important (Hilgard, Edgren, and Irvine, 1954).

Forgus and Schwartz (1957) devised an alphabet-learning task with symbols for letters; successive groups of letters could be derived according to a rule, and a transfer task called for applying this rule to discover a new alphabet. Instruction took one of three forms: (1) demonstration—the alphabet was presented and the principle explained; (2) discovery—the alphabet was presented and the subject was asked to find the principle; and (3) memorization—the letters were rearranged to conceal the principle and the subject was told to memorize it. Memorization here took more time than in the Hilgard et al. study, probably because of greater length. Furthermore, retention was worse for the memorization group, probably again for the same reason. These subjects performed better on the transfer test, in line both with Katona and Hilgard et al. studies.

Gagne´ and Brown (1961) related Katona's principle of understanding to a programmed-learning situation designed to instruct boys in the ninth and tenth grades in the solving of number series. After an introductory program to provide the basic concepts, subjects worked under a special instructional program: (1) *rule and example*—statement of the correct formula, which the subject wrote down, followed by items in small steps with examples that took him through the identification of terms and determination of numerical values by applying the formula; (2) *discovery*—items in large steps, requiring the subject to answer basic questions, with hints interspersed that provided progressively greater guidance, but without supplying the answer; (3) *guided discovery*—generally similar to step 2, but in small steps that led the subject toward statement of a general rule. On the day after training, the program was repeated, and then new problems were presented, with hints introduced if a problem was not solved after 5 minutes.

All three teaching conditions displayed significant gains from the first to the second session but, in general, discovery required less time. On the problem solving tasks, the rule-and-example method was significantly worse than the other two, with guided discovery nonsignificantly better than discovery (see Figure 11-3). Thus Katona's principle is supported, but with an emphasis on "what is learned" rather than "how it is learned."

Studies like these thus point to the ultimate significance of understanding for successful problem solving. Although rote methods—which could be interpreted as promoting resonance—are easier to acquire and to use, they are much less efficacious in solving new problems. The long-range advantage of understanding thus emerges. The general tenor of research on mediating processes points in the same direction (Cofer, 1957). To the extent that understanding depends on the acquisition of concepts, rules, principles, or other information-interpreting and organizing processes, the role of mediation compared to sheer S-R linkage (or covert automatized response evocation) is evident.

Missing again, however, from these contributions to problem solving is direct attention to emotional or motivational components. Potentially significant factors in understanding are the possible arousing function of this method of instruction, the possibly greater personal involvement of the subject, and the emotional gains derived

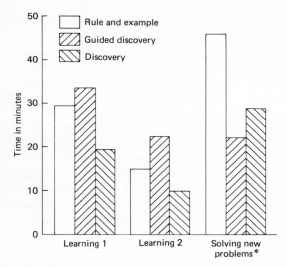

FIGURE 11–3   The effects of training method on problem solving. (Based on Gagné and Brown, 1961.) Weighted time scores for solving new problems : minutes plus a value assigned to each hint required.

from perceived intensive mastery of a problem. Beyond that we must also consider the influence of individual differences in problem solving attitudes.

MODES OF ATTACK
When the foregoing aspects of problem solving behavior appear in distinctive patterns, we can speak about *modes of attack*. They are clarified by distinguishing among the strategy of the solver, the properties of the problem situation, and the type of solution achieved.

Apart from individual differences in approaching problems, determining factors include the complexity of the task, the degree to which the goal can be understood, the kinds of resources available, the extent to which logical principles are involved, and so on. Such conditions impose requirements that determine what is possible— and necessary—for a person to do. For example, if no logical princi- ple will work, then there is no recourse but to manipulate or explore more or less at random. Here we have the classic situation in which trial-and-error behavior occurs, as in mazes and puzzles. On the other hand, when rules or formulas or the discovery of relationships can lead directly to the goal, recentering or understanding processes are required. Here we have the classic insight problem. In still other situations progress depends on attaining successive stages in mastery, with one stage contingent on the next. Then a systematic stepwise process is necessary. Such tasks are exemplified by mathematical exercises and reasoning problems of both deductive and inductive types.

Important also is the final outcome and its characteristics. The solution may be the result of a tedious process of specific decisions and acts, each of which must be perfected before performance becomes efficient. Very often in such situations, the person does not (or cannot) understand the complete pattern without considerable repetition. A jigsaw puzzle is a good example. Or the solution may be a gradual working out of successive aspects of the problem. Here it is unlikely that understanding can be attained prior to the last step, but at that point it may be complete. Finally, the solution may actually *be* the understanding itself of some principle. In such cases it is quite possible for a person to move suddenly or quickly to the goal, without the necessity to deal any more with details of the task (or with the requirement only of putting the principle into practice).

The crucial point is that general strategies (processes of coping with the task-requirements) and solutions may occur in various combinations. For example, an individual's strategy may be to acquire understanding, but the task may impose such restrictions that his search exhibits apparently random manipulation and exploration. Or a strategy of systematic analysis accompanied by step-by-step solution and partial understanding begun in a task where a principle leads to the solution may rather abruptly end with a resulting leap to the goal.

Durkin (1937) described three basic behavioral patterns: trial and error, insight (or sudden reorganization), and gradual analysis. If we add to them the sharper distinctions indicated above and separate behavioral processes from types of solution (Sargent, 1940), we arrive at a conception like that shown in Table 11-1.

Bartlett (1958) has emphasized the continuous character of problem solving, seeing it as a "gap-filling" process from one step to the next, guided by directions (in Maier's sense). How gaps will be filled depends on such conditions as the amount of information available and the contingency of one step on the next (e.g., the selection of appropriate items). In this "classic" pattern of gradual analysis, evidence is sought to fill up gaps in information through

Table 11-1
Modes of Attack, Behavior, and Solutions in Problem Solving. (Based on Durkin, 1937.)

	Trial and Error	Insight	Gradual Analysis
General SET or attitude	To match pieces	To look for wholes or interrelations	To satisfy goal needs
	Attention to goal distant, diffuse	Attention not centered on goal	Attention concentrated on specific goal needs
	Attitude not definite, but wandering, haphazard	Passive, receptive	Active, directed search
General behavior	"Blind" groping	Groping suddenly stopped	No groping but a gradually developing understanding
Intermediate characteristics	Error curve irregular, errors may not drop out after solution; transfer poor	Curve irregular, then sudden drop; transfer good	Error curve steplike; transfer good
	Manner baffled	Baffled; then well organized, efficient	Calm, well organized
Emotional characteristics	Confusion till last moment; hopeless feeling	Confusion suddenly cleared; excitement, elation, sometimes relief	Cleared away step by step; satisfaction
Character of understanding	Hindsight	Sudden foresight	Foresight

interconnected steps. This pattern is associated with essentially closed systems, when there is a limited number of components, it is known that they are to be used, and they do not change. Such situations may be distinguished from more open systems, like those commonly employed in experiments on insight, reaching an extreme in creative problems. Here the components are not fixed and successive steps open up rather than narrow the possibilities of goal attainment. "Leaps" then occur more often, in contrast to a step-by-step process.

Seeing some affinities between Duncker and Bartlett, Hayes (1965) formulated problem solving as a "sequence of linked phases or steps which form a chain or path connecting the initial conditions of the problem with its goal." Accordingly, an important consideration should be information about topological properties of the problem, such as the length of the path and its degree of branching. He devised "spy" problems involving a communication network with the subject instructed to get a message to the goal. There were eight types of problems that varied in length and in blind alleys. He found that subjects typically started in the forward direction, although often in the backward direction when they were at the goal, especially when the forward strategy failed. Time increased both with the length of the minimal chain and with the number of blind alleys, but disproportionately with the latter factor. Time increased, similarly, with the number of steps involved. Blind alleys were entered with less than chance expectancy, indicating that the subject took into account the properties of both correct and blind alleys. As the goal was approached (and the number of steps to go decreased), the entering of blind alleys decreased. Additional experiments confirmed the tendency for solution to accelerate as the goal was approached. In general, therefore, gradual analysis appeared as a rather distinctive pattern.

An attempt to differentiate antecedent phases from the solution itself has been made by Johnson (1960). The first step, marked by the occurrence of errors, he calls *preparation*, with the remainder designated as *solution*. Johnson, Lincoln, and Hall (1961) have reported a simple experiment to confirm this distinction. The problem is presented in two panels. On one side a number of "specifications," are stated, and on the other side several alternatives are given. Each alternative satisfies some of the specifications, but only one meets them all. An example of the specifications is "flat, readable, descriptive, gummed," with the alternative solutions shown as "map," "book," "label," "paper," "globe." In the basic experiment only one side is illuminated at a time. The left (specification or preparation) side is lighted;

when the subject is ready he uses a switch to expose the right (solution) side. The results for both verbal and numerical problems showed that as the number of specifications increased, preparation time increased, but solution time did not increase. Variations, such as allowing switchback or exposing both sides, did not affect this result. Thus there is good reason to maintain that preliminary aspects of problem solving should be distinguished from the solution.

There are signs of dissatisfaction with the state of knowledge about problem solving. The complexities of the behavior observed, together with the diversity of situations that have been studied, have necessitated a continuing effort to describe phenomena. I have tried to show that distinctions among strategy, situational demands, and solutions lead to a clarification of patterns of trial and error, insight, and gradual analysis. These are not different kinds of problem solving but distinctive combinations of processes that may occur in a wide variety of problems, with the relative dominance of certain processes dependent on the conditions present at the time.

In an attempt to reunite the Duncker, Wertheimer, and Maier views, Hoffman (1961) has treated problem solving as a process of developing a new organization of previously dissociated experiences. The basic conditions are: (1) coexisting but different cognitions, each with positive and negative valence, accompanied by a process of resolving these forces in an acceptable way; (2) reaching a state when at least two cognitions acquire above-threshold positive valence sufficiently equal to produce an impasse (only then can analysis and recentering occur); and (3) a situation that requires a decision that cannot be resolved by mere resonance or appeal to an external agent. When such conditions exist, solution depends on the explicit recognition of conflicting elements and the discovery of an appropriate direction to resolve them. The concept of valence leads to the principle that the intensity of behavior is a function of the net level of the forces present. At a low level, little effort may be expended, but as the level increases, involvement increases, with important consequences on performance.

Davis (1966) has advanced a view in a more traditional behavioristic tradition. For him, problem solving is primarily a form of complex learning, and the common denominator is trial-and-error behavior (see also, Duncan, 1959). But he distinguishes two types. Type C, or *covert* trial and error, occurs in such situations as anagrams, "insight" problems, and arithmetic. Here the outcomes of response alternatives are known, the pertinent sequence of acts is not observable, the task is concrete, and the solution is likely to be total and unitary. Type O, or *overt* trial and error, occurs in mazes, probability-learning tasks, classification problems, and the like. Here the outcomes of response alternatives are not known, the behavior sequence is observable, the task is unfamiliar and uses abstract materials, and the solution is a relatively continuous process of acquisition.

Davis recognizes that some cases cannot be assigned clearly to either type. The preceding discussion also indicates that the distinction may well be greatly oversimplified. Covert and overt processes may *both* occur in the same task—and it may be typical for them to do so. The conditions that Davis links with each type correspond to the constraining considerations pointed out above. It does not appear especially useful to see trial-and-error learning as the essential process, any more than to make understanding basic.

"Switch-light" problems were devised to test the distinction (Davis, 1967). In these problems, the subject is confronted with a panel of lights, and must operate switches so that only two designated lights remain on. Although a systematic principle could locate the covert switches, in practice they could be operated in any order. Thus the subject had to manipulate and explore—that is, use trial and error—to solve the problem. Performance declined with reinforcement of incorrect (distracting switches), with increased number of available switches, and with complexity (the number of switches required). But, after pretraining on basic S-R relationships, subjects shifted to "implicit" (type C) behavior, characterized by a long latency of response and nearly errorless solutions.

These studies demonstrate that different patterns of problem solving can occur in the same task, depending on the kinds of conditions involved. It can hardly be concluded that both groups of subjects are displaying the same behavior (i.e., trial and error). In fact, pretraining here can be interpreted simply as providing relevant experience that promotes understanding, which then permits a direct solution. In this way conditions of the situation produce shifts in the relative importance of one pattern compared to another.

INFORMATION PROCESSING

Principles from information theory have been invoked for problem solving tasks. Whitfield (1951), for example, distinguished between "stimulus difficulty," or the number of possible responses when all available information is taken into account, and "phenomenal difficulty," inferred from the subject's performance. Using matching problems, he found that qualitative differences in information (such as amount forgotten or perceived bases of classification) were more related to phenomenal than stimulus difficulty.

In line with principles of information theory, Brush (1956) found that performance varies with both stimulus and response uncertainty, with relative gain in information an inverse function of both factors. Solley and Snyder (1958) found that discrimination time in a jigsaw puzzle task is a linear function of the number of pieces, and that this variable seemed to be additive.

Posner (1965) applied the analysis reported earlier to information-reduction tasks like those used to study problem solving. Information handling, he suggests, can be regarded as a matter of the storage and transformation of information. In general, the subject selects information relevant to his hypothesis—and thus stores in memory not the actual information but a transformation of it. The more difficult the transformation, the less the information that can be stored. In concept-formation tasks, as we have seen, redundancy typically facilitates performance (see also, Biederman and Checkosky, 1970). That is, redundancy makes it easier to select information relevant to a hypothesis. In an experiment by Campbell (1968), however, redundant information was introduced into a word-coding problem, and here solution was impeded. It is not so much amount of information, as its character, that makes a task easy or difficult. In Campbell's problems, redundancy, although relevant, opened up false trails and thus delayed solution.

The difficulties that still await the information theorist are illustrated in a study by Bendig (1953). He endeavored to adapt the game of twenty questions (Taylor and Faust, 1952) to an information analysis. In this familiar game persons try to identify a particular object by asking questions to progressively narrow the alternatives. At first it seems a natural task to examine processes of information utilization. However, the situation offers extremely free response on the part of the subject, so Bendig modified the task both to limit the possible topics and to standardize the possible questions. Theoretically, each question should reduce the amount of uncertainty by comparable amounts. Bendig found that the actual amount transmitted was less than theoretical expectation, since the first three questions accounted for 85 percent of the reduction. One of the reasons lay in topic preferences, which prevented the subjects from using available information in an objectively efficient manner. Furthermore, theory would predict a learning effect over successive problems, but no consistent trend appeared.

This experiment, as well as one by Levine (1966), reveals that systematic problem solving is accompanied by a progressive reduction in the size of the hypothesis under consideration. To this extent subjects act generally in accordance with the information available to them. However, this behavior cannot be understood merely by reference to the objectively defined stimulus or the task situation. It is phenomenal information, as Whitfield (1951) indicated, that determines performance. The subjects themselves alter the theoretical expectations that might be deduced from properties of the task itself. Donaldson (1959), for example, devised matching problems that could be solved by obtaining either positive or negative information. Despite the fact that both kinds of information were logically equivalent, they were not psychologically equivalent. Her fourteen-year-old subjects seemed to be unable or unwilling to use negatives, even if the task favored them. They also failed to employ derived positive information, whether because they distrusted negative information or felt that positive information has an appearance of finality. In addition, they displayed a tendency to search for a rule or principle, which in this task interfered with efficient solution. By contrast, in a task that called for choosing between two alternatives, with the subject asked to predict which would come next, the problem could be solved by deducing a rule. But the subjects did not try to make inferences about the generating source nor to analyze sequences in order to discover the rule; instead they searched for order by looking at recurring events. Neimark (1967) utilized a problem situation in which the reward for "gambling" moves was varied. Information reduction depended on the alternatives chosen. In general, subjects tended consistently to follow either a safe strategy when rewards for gambling were low or a gambling strategy when such rewards were high. However, they did not shift from one to the other at the predicted point, but instead displayed a more conservative policy. Variations in situational conditions (properties of the problem, reinforcement contingencies) had little effect once the subject had formulated a rule, as ascertained from postexperimental questioning.

It appears that principles of information theory can lead to a better understanding of problem solving. However, a conception of the human problem solver as responding solely to the information display, as extrinsically defined, and as operating mechanically on this basis, is artificial. Memory, past experience, and cognitive structure (to say nothing of emotional and motivational characteristics) must be taken into account. Performance is a resultant of all these influences. As indicated in Chapter 5, models of information processing in the future may well develop increased powers of description by incorporating intrinsic variables. The human problem solver *acts on* information in distinctive ways rather than responding to it. This principle is increasingly evident in the development of information-processing theory.

SUMMARY

Problem solving is realistic, goal-oriented behavior in complex tasks having definite and correct outcomes, in which the following phases can be distinguished: confrontation by a problem, working toward a solution, and reaching a solution (or failing). Basic principles concern resonance and functional fixedness, centering and recentering, and analysis of situation and goal. Although direction seems important, availability of functions and perception of direction are probably more significant. In transfer to new problems, techniques of instruction that promote understanding and discovery are superior to rote methods. Behavior in problem situations varies with the kind of problem and strategy, falling generally into patterns of trial and error, insight, and gradual analysis. One view treats trial and error as fundamental, distinguishing between overt and covert forms. Information-processing theory involves principles of stimulus and response uncertainty, and storage, transformation, and reduction of information, but encounters difficulties in application to problem solving.

12

EFFICIENCY IN REASONING AND PROBLEM SOLVING

So far we have looked at the variety of behavior that can be observed in problem solving, and outlined a general approach to incorporate diverse principles. Although there are indications of movement toward theoretical integration, no really satisfactory system has yet emerged. Counterbalancing the descriptive research, there has been a continuing concern about conditions that influence successful performance in problem solving tasks. In keeping with earlier treatments, we can recognize here too the effects of situationally induced variables, task conditions, and intrinsic characteristics of the subjects.

FORMAL LOGIC

Traditionally, the terms *thinking* and *reasoning* have been closely linked. This treatment grows out of the tradition that thinking must be logical and that the process of thinking inevitably leads to predetermined outcomes. In reality such attitudes represent values rather than a truly informed analysis of cognitive behavior. Not only does freely expressive cognition (imagination) have its own merits but, in fact, reasoning, like other aspects of thinking, is subject to the influence of autistic forces.

Logical thinking is linked with special rules to control the problem solving process; such formal prescriptions clearly place logic toward the realistic end of our continuum. If the rules are properly followed, then presumably special characteristics of the person, whether properties of his cognitive structure or of his motivational system, would have little effect on performance. A major interest of psychologists has been to determine whether the formal character of the task actually controls the reasoning process.

In logical tasks, as in others, we must consider whether their verbal form corresponds with the intrinsic cognitive processes elicited. Not only must we distinguish between denotative and connotative properties of words, but also recognize that logical analysis may impose technical definitions on terms—often quantitative—that create conditions different from ordinary usage. In addition, relationships between words must carefully be identified in formal logic. Successive statements are related by explicit rules that cannot be violated, whereas in ordinary discussion they can be (or often are) treated independently.

Under formal conditions a logical relation is not necessarily objectively correct. A logical argument is valid when the rules are followed properly, regardless of the actual content of the statements. A valid conclusion may be drawn from false premises, or an invalid conclusion from true premises. For example, the statement "All birds fly south for the winter" is logically equivalent to the statement "All birds lay eggs." Formal logic does not guarantee the truth of premises or conclusions, but only their validity; incorrect reasoning is not the same as "false" reasoning.

It is easy to be impressed with the thesis that logical thinking can resolve our confusions, doubts, and ignorance. The application of systematic, consistent, and realistic principles can certainly work to this end when properly invoked. However, we must also evaluate the premises on which reasoning is based, a process far from easy to accomplish in a wholly logical manner, for the cultural context, personal values and needs, and the goals of thinking must also be considered. Beyond that, what might otherwise be viewed as illogical or purely expressive cognitive processes also have functions and valuable outcomes of their own.

SCIENTIFIC METHOD

Disciplined reasoning includes procedures developed to facilitate the scientist's solving of problems. They vary all the way from highly formalized steps with rigorous prescription of rules across behavior that can scarcely be distinguished from the processes described for problem solving or for creative thinking (discussed in Chapter 15).

A distinction can be drawn between formal logic and scientific method by saying that the former is *deductive* and the latter *inductive*. Deduction, crudely defined, is reasoning from the general to the particular, or more precisely from stated premises to a proper conclusion; induction signifies reasoning from the particular to the general. These distinctions frequently break down, however, in actual cases of reasoning, although deduction is often the only observable process in formal syllogistic problems. If syllogisms are extended to everyday life discussion, where a person does not feel bound by rules, then inductive processes are mingled with this form of argument. But scientific reasoning is not entirely inductive, and it is better to treat deduction and induction as mutually operating processes rather than to differentiate sharply between them.

To rid logic of such rigid distinctions, Dewey (1938, p. 419) defined deduction as "the methods by which already existing generalizations are employed" and induction as "the methods by which generalizations are arrived at." Both kinds of method are fundamental in science (except in disciplines deliberately kept on a deductive basis). One process can be distinguished from the other only at particular points in a sequence. Thus generalizations reached in one series of experiments may be used deductively to formulate a further generalization in the form of a hypothesis. Then inductive procedures may be employed to collect evidence relevant to that hypothesis. That is, specimens may be collected, or samples assayed, or particular instances examined. After appropriate analysis of these data, a generalization or conclusion may be reached that either supports or rejects the original hypothesis. But even this is too simple a picture, because at any time deduction may temporarily be introduced; and it cannot be said that—even during the inductive stages—there is no deduction, because "already existing generalizations" may be applied in collecting the data, in the acceptance and rejection of data, in the analysis and evaluation of the data, and so on.

In any case, logic has endeavored to establish and explain conditions under which reasoning can efficiently and dependably be carried out: for deduction, the proper statement of propositions, the relations between them, and the conclusions to which they lead; for induction, techniques for observing and measuring facts, determining validity and reliability of measures, formulating hypotheses, and evaluating evidence (M.R. Cohen and Nagel, 1934; Larrabee, 1964).

THE SYLLOGISM

A situation in which the reasoning of formal logic takes place is called the *syllogism.* It is a group of three assertions or propositions, of which one is said to follow when the other two are granted.

An example of three assertions arranged in syllogistic form is as follows :

All books copyrighted in the United States are in the' Library of Congress.

All of Dr. Jones's books have been copyrighted in the United States.

All of Dr. Jones's books are in the Library of Congress.

There are certain important characteristics of such a sequence of assertions. Without going into all the details, which may be found in any elementary logic textbook, the following points are relevant to the experiments presently to be reviewed.

1 The first two assertions (or *propositions*) are called the *premises*, the third proposition is the *conclusion* which is inferred from (or—logically—said to follow from) the premises.
2 Any proposition may be one of four kinds, depending on whether it is affirmative or negative and universal or particular (that is, includes all of a class or some of it). In the example above, all three propositions are affirmative and also universal (designated as A propositions). Other arrangements may be universal negative (E), particular affirmative (I), or particular negative (O). An instance of an I proposition would be to state the second proposition above as "Some of the books by Dr. Jones were copyrighted in the United States."
3 The manner in which AEIO propositions are arranged determines the validity of the conclusion. That is, only certain combinations yield valid (correct) conclusions; otherwise the conclusion is invalid. If the second premise above, for example, is stated as an I proposition, the conclusion cannot be an A proposition.
4 Each proposition contains two terms, but the syllogism itself contains only three different terms (the items connected in the assertions), which, to be valid, must be arranged according to certain rules.
5 Since only two of the terms appear in the conclusion, they must be the two that yield a valid conclusion. The one omitted

is the *middle term*, or that which brings the other two into the asserted relationship. In the example above, "Books copyrighted in the United States" is the middle term since it relates Dr. Jones's books to the Library of Congress.

The syllogism is, therefore, a framework into which propositions may be placed to assist in the formulation of conclusions, or to test the validity of conclusions.

EXPERIMENTAL STUDIES OF SYLLOGISTIC REASONING

Research on syllogisms has mostly been concerned with revealing the kinds of factors conducive to errors in logic, although some investigators have seen this situation as a convenient and well-structured problem solving task for testing hypotheses derived from mediation theory.

Characteristics of the Material

Logical problems can be cast in various forms, such as in concrete words, symbolic notation, or abstract terms. According to Thorndike (1922), propositions stated in familiar forms produce more correct solutions than propositions expressed in changed or less familiar forms. Wilkins (1928) tested this hypothesis with syllogisms stated in four different versions: *familiar, symbolic* (abstract notation), *unfamiliar* (technical or nonsense), and *suggestive* (everyday common sense). The following examples illustrate the four types:

> *Familiar*   All the people living on this farm are related to the Joneses. These old men live on this farm. Therefore (1) these old men are related to the Joneses; (2) all the people related to the Joneses are these old men; (3) some people related to the Joneses are not these old men.
>
> *Symbolic*   All *x*'s are *y*'s. All *z*'s are *x*'s. Therefore (1) all *z*'s are *y*'s; (2) all *y*'s are *z*'s; (3) some *y*'s are not *z*'s.
>
> *Unfamiliar*   All lysimachion is epilobium. All adenocaulon is lysimachion. Therefore (1) all adenocaulon is epilobium; (2) all epilobium is adenocaulon; (3) some epilobium is not adenocaulon.
>
> *Suggestive*   All Anglo-Saxons are English. All British are Anglo-Saxons. Therefore (1) all British are English; (2) all English are British; (3) some British are not English.

For some items all three alternative conclusions were invalid (even when they might factually be true), for others the alternatives were valid (but sometimes true, sometimes false).

The familiar material was easiest, with the suggestive items next, then the symbolic, and the unfamiliar hardest. (Sells [1936] also found concrete (verbal) syllogisms to be easier than abstract syllogisms.) There were, however, individual differences, varying with the type of material, which were interpreted as "bad habits" that especially affect familiar material.

Henle (1962) has reached a similar conclusion by examining deduction in everyday life. She identified as sources of errors failure to follow the rules (not distinguishing between logically valid and factually correct conclusions), restating premises or conclusions to change the intended meaning, omission of a premise, and slipping in additional premises.

"Atmosphere"

Woodworth and Sells (1935; Sells, 1936) called attention to a characteristic *atmosphere* generated by statements. An A proposition has an *all-yes* atmosphere and calls for an A, or weaker I conclusion; an E proposition has an *all-no* atmosphere and calls for an E, or weaker O conclusion; an I proposition has a *some-yes* atmosphere and calls for an I conclusion; and an O proposition has a *some-no* atmosphere and calls for an O conclusion.

Additional hypotheses are necessary when the combination introduces a contradictory element. For example, if one premise is universal and the other particular, then the latter seems to weaken the atmosphere, making it less than "all," or equivalent to "some." Therefore the presence of a negative proposition creates a *negative* atmosphere and calls for an E or weaker O conclusion, and the presence of a particular proposition creates a *particular* atmosphere and calls for an I or O conclusion.

Accordingly, Sells developed syllogism tests of two forms, abstract (symbolic) and concrete (verbal). The items included every possible combination of propositions for each of nine fallacies; about a fourth were valid, the rest invalid. The subjects rated the conclusions on a five-point scale, ranging from absolutely true through uncertain to absolutely false. The errors predicted on the basis of atmosphere effect occurred to a highly significant degree (see Table 12-1). (See Hunter [1957a] for another interesting demonstration of an atmosphere effect.) Although persons trained in logic

Table 12-1

The Effect of Atmosphere on the Acceptance of Invalid Conclusions (slightly modified from Sells, 1936). (In average percent; $N=65$.)

Premises	Types of Invalid Conclusions			
	A	E	I	O
A atmosphere	*58*	14	*63*	17
E atmosphere	13	*51*	17	*55*
I atmosphere	32	9	*72*	35
O atmosphere	12	29	30	*62*

Note: Italic figures refer to incidence predicted for atmosphere effect.

would no doubt make many fewer errors than Sells' naive subjects, there can be little doubt that atmosphere has a powerful effect.[1]

Atmosphere effects are especially pronounced in neutral items, whereas personal convictions play a greater role in controversial items (Morgan and Morton, 1944) (see Table 12-2). People tend to accept an invalid argument when they disagree with it (Janis and Frick, 1943). Although more errors occur on emotionally toned than neutral items, first presenting the emotional items induces more errors on the neutral items, whereas first presenting neutral items increases correct responses to emotional ones (Lefford, 1946). Further consideration indicates that affective factors induce errors of accepting invalid conclusions, rather than of rejecting valid ones, with the principle location of errors lying in universal positive statements (Kaufmann and Goldstein, 1967).

Related to these findings is Frase's (1968b) introduction of connotative meaning by composing syllogisms that contained words high, moderate, or low in incompatibility of rated meaning. Significantly fewer correct conclusions were drawn when highly incompatible words were used.

In further pursuing the atmosphere issue, Chapman and Chapman (1959) constructed a carefully controlled syllogism test in which all items had the same correct answer (none of these). As might be expected from this somewhat tricky device, the percentage of correct answers was very low. Departures from predictions based on the atmosphere effect mainly occurred for "mixed" items (like IE, OE, and EO premises), suggesting the operation of

[1] Henle and Michael (1956) found that instruction in syllogistic reasoning greatly improved performance.

Table 12-2
Comparative Effects of Various Influences on Choice of Conclusions (in Percent).
(From Morgan and Morton 1944.)

| | Condition | | |
| | Neutral | | Controversial |
Influence	Letter Symbols	Words	
Atmosphere	44	46	26
Logic	27	33	20
Personal conviction	—	—	36
Other (unknown or chance)	30	21	18

expectations derived from everyday experience. For example, the converse of a statement frequently holds in everyday statements. "All right angles are 90 degrees" is equivalent to "All 90 degree angles are right angles." However, in logical terms, the expression "are" signifies "included in," so that the two statements are not the same. In addition, we often employ probabilistic inference in everyday problems, correcting conclusions, as necessary, but in logic this tactic leads to invalid conclusions. Chapman and Chapman give this example. A chemist argues: "Yellow and powdery material has often been sulfur. Some of these test tubes have yellow, powdery material. Therefore some of these test tubes contain sulfur." That is a perfectly reasonable supposition, which, of course, would then be checked, but the conclusion is logically invalid. The middle term produces the difficulty since we expect that objects sharing common characteristics are very likely the same, when this is not necessarily correct. Other investigators have shown that a potential source of error lies in the character of the syllogism itself, such as difficulty in interpreting the premises, or in their complexity (Ceraso and Provitera, 1971).

Simpson and Johnson (1966) identified syllogisms for which predictions based on atmosphere and conversion effects can most unequivocally be stated. They included not only the indeterminate forms used by Chapman and Chapman, but also determinate arguments. First, as expected, the determinate syllogisms were easier. Second, items intended to produce atmosphere effects tended to do so, and a similar result occurred for intended conversion items. Third, the two effects were largely independent of each other—that is, subjects

susceptible to one kind of error did not necessarily display the other
($r = -.21$). Finally, training had a significant effect. Antiatmosphere
instructions reduced this type of error, with similar but less-
pronounced effects for anticonversion instructions.

Begg and Denny (1969) have pointed out that Sells' supplementary hypotheses are based on principles of *quality* and *quantity*.
Thus, when one premise has a negative quality, the most frequently
accepted conclusion will be negative, and when neither premise is
negative, an affirmative conclusion is indicated. And when at least
one premise is a particular quantity, a particular conclusion is preferred, whereas if neither premise is particular, a universal conclusion seems called for. On this basis, specific predictions were
developed for pairs of premises, which were generally sustained, rather
than the predictions of Chapman and Chapman, which were based
on probabilistic inference. (Further scrutiny disclosed that the
Chapman and Chapman results actually agreed with the quality and
quantity principles in twelve of fourteen instances.)

By and large, the original atmosphere hypotheses have been
well supported, with evidence that other set or attitudinal variables
also influence logical reasoning. Beyond those already cited, a significant negative correlation was found by O'Connor (1952) between
ethnocentrism and syllogistic performance ($r = -.37$ for total score).
Intolerance of ambiguity, although significantly correlated with
ethnocentrism ($r = .55$), had no relation to performance in this task.
An interesting situational variable was introduced by Rosenhan,
DeWilde, and McDougal (1963), namely, the pressure to conform
to majority opinion. They used a procedure originated by Asch
(1956), where a naive subject is located so that he must make a
judgment after several of his peers have already stated their opinions.
The other subjects are actually confederates of the experimenter and
are instructed to choose an incorrect alternative on certain critical
trials. This condition produced 49 percent errors on a syllogism test,
compared to 0.5 percent for the control subjects.

Psycho-Logic

A recent development of considerable promise is the search for
systematic principles of subjective logic (Abelson and Rosenberg,
1958), or the special properties of cognitive structure as they affect
reasoning. This research is clearly an outgrowth of that just discussed,
but represents an orientation toward the cognitive process rather
than toward the formal situation.

In one study, Gilson and Abelson (1965) devised an approach using "evidence matrixes," which varied in the number of positive and negative entries, type of verb, and character of evidence (object-specific, subject-specific, mixed). The verbs expressed "unit relations" (such as produce, buy), "sentiment relations" (such as like, get angry with), and other more ambiguous relations. The components were combined to constitute sets of items containing the two types of evidence (object-specific and subject-specific) for various subjects, verbs, and objects with the content "Tribes have magazines." Examples of the two types are as follows:

Object-specific
Altogether there are three kinds of tribes—Southern, Northern, Central.

Southern tribes have sports magazines.

Northern tribes do not have sports magazines.

Central tribes do not have sports magazines.

Do tribes have sports magazines?

Subject-specific
Altogether there are three kinds of magazines—sports, news, fashions.

Southern tribes do not have sports magazines.

Southern tribes do not have news magazines.

Southern tribes have fashion magazines.

Do Southern tribes have magazines?

Object-specific evidence showed more generalization ("yes" responses) than subject-specific evidence. Although certain peculiarities of the items might explain this difference—for example, the subject in a sentence comes first and might therefore be more salient—the authors stress the probability that types of people are psychologically more important than types of objects. As a consequence, objects may be more "interchangeable" than people. A difference was also found for the type of verb, with more generalization for *produce, buy, have,* and *steal* than for *get angry with, understand, like,* and *avoid*. Although no definite explanation was advanced, the investigators suggest that the first group are "manifest" verbs, whereas the second are "subjective." Possibly the manifest verbs simply have a more global character, or are less influenced by negative implications. Another possibility is that connotative meaning is a stronger factor in subjective verbs, thereby rendering either the subject or object more variable among individuals.

DeSoto, London, and Handel (1965) hypothesized that people have a preference for linear orderings. An experiment was conducted with syllogisms, employing sequences of "better" to "worse," or the reverse, both within and between premises. For example "A is better than B. B is better than C," or "B is worse than A. B is better than C." Each such combination was used four times, with one of these questions, "Is A better than C?" "Is C better than A?" "Is A worse than C?" or "Is C worse than A?" Clearly shown was a tendency for more correct answers to be given with the consistent within- and between-premise better-to-worse order; least with the consistent worse-to-better order; the inconsistent orders fell in between. Furthermore, ends-to-middle forms were easier than middle-to-ends.

The investigators propose two *paralogical* principles: (1) "People learn orderings better in one direction than in the other." (2) "People end-anchor orderings."

A second experiment disclosed that judgments of "better" and "worse" and of "has lighter hair than" and "has darker hair than" have a preferred spatial direction, with the first pair located, respectively, at the top and bottom, with no such allocation for the second pair. The first pair was rarely assigned to a horizontal direction, whereas "lighter" and "darker" were often treated in this fashion, but both in a left-to-right direction rather than opposite to each other. A third experiment combined conditions from the first two experiments, yielding the predicted results.

Huttenlocher (1968) took issue with Hunter's (1957b) analysis of "three-term problems"—syllogistic items employing terms like "Tom is taller than Sam. John is shorter than Sam. Who is tallest (or shortest)?" These problems, Hunter contended, are solved by changing the premises so that they are ordered transitively, either by converting the second premise or by reordering the premises, or both. Thus all problems assume the following form: "Tom is taller than Sam. Sam is taller than John." Reference to the initial example shows that it takes this form when the second premise ("John is shorter than Sam" is converted to "Sam is taller than John"). If the premises were "Sam is taller than John. Tom is taller than Sam," reordering the two premises produces the basic transitivity. Finally, in some problems both operations are required; for example, in the case "Sam is taller than John. Sam is shorter than Tom, " the second premise must be converted and placed before the second premise.

Huttenlocher points out that the order or difficulty is predicted to be (1) simple transitivity (the basic form), (2) converting or re-ordering, (3) both converting and reordering. Although step 3 is hardest, problems requiring conversion appear to be the easiest from evidence in her own research, as well in that of DeSoto, London, and Handel (1965). She further points out that subjects themselves report use of the spatial ordering described above for the first premise, making the second one contingent on the first, with an object to identify the third term, and then ascertaining its position. Her experiments confirm this imaginal ordering as the preferred operation instead of the analytic logic suggested by Hunter.

Clark (1969a, b) proposes still another explanation based on fundamental linguistic principles. First, there is a *primacy of functional relations*, of which Chomsky (1965) mentions as universal "subject of," "predicate of," "direct object of," and "main verb of." Such relations are presumed to be stored in memory immediately after comprehension and to be especially available compared to other kinds of information (e.g., the theme of a sentence). Second, *lexical marking* signifies that certain simple positive adjectives (like *good* and *long*) are stored in a less complex form than their opposites. From this principle there appears an asymmetry in relationships. Third, *congruence* refers to the likelihood that the person searches prior knowledge for information "congruent, at the level of functional relations, with the information asked for in the question."

On this basis Clark makes his own predictions. According to the primacy of functional relations, the basic information "John is bad" is more readily available than a comparison like "more than." The principle of lexical marking indicates that statements containing words like *good* or *better* should be easier than those containing words like *worse* and *bad*. Finally, from the principle of congruence, it should follow that a question like "Who is best?," which is congruent with the statement "If John is better than Pete," is easier than the question "Who is worst?" when preceded by the same statement. (The same analysis applies to three-term problems.)

Experiments supported the theory. In interpreting his results, Clark indicates certain critical differences from predictions based on paralogic (DeSoto et al., 1965) and of spatial imagery (Huttenlocher, 1968). In some types of problems these theories agree, but in others they do not. With respect to paralogic, the principles of directional preference and end anchoring lead to predictions opposite to

Clark's. For example, "A isn't as bad as B. B isn't as bad as C" is a "top-down problem," whereas "C isn't as good as B, and B isn't as good as A" is a "bottom-up problem." From paralogic the former should be easier than the latter, but the linguistic analysis predicts the reverse, and this is supported by Clark's results. In the case of spatial imagery Clark's argument does not seem to be as sound, so the alleged discrepancy is less justified. In any case, Clark himself recognizes that imagery may play a significant role.[1]

Clearly there are some difficult issues yet to be resolved before we shall have a definitive understanding of subjective logic. However, all these studies point to the fact that reasoning processes cannot be explained by reference to the traditional principles of formal logic.

Mediation in Syllogisms

Investigators are beginning to apply the principle of mediation to syllogistic tasks. Frase (1968b) points out that a syllogism corresponds to a three-stage mediational paradigm, as follows:

1 All B are C. All A are B. Hence all A are C—corresponds to BC, AB, AC, or a forward chain.
2 All C are B. All A are B. Therefore all A are C—corresponds to CB, AB, AC, or stimulus equivalence.
3 All B are C. All B are A. Therefore all A are C—corresponds to BC, BA, AC, or response equivalence.
4 All C are B. All B are A. Therefore all A are C—corresponds to CB, BA, AC, or a backward chain.

On this basis, syllogism 4 should produce the most errors, and 1 the least. These predictions were confirmed on a syllogism test.

This study utilized syllogisms in abstract form (i.e., with letters rather than words), but mediation should operate more strongly with meaningful materials. Pezzoli and Frase (1968) varied the associative strength of terms in the premises from a control condition using nonsense syllables (CCC's of low associative value) through words of low associative strength to words of high associative strength. They adopted the stimulus-equivalence and response-equivalence paradigms (2 and 3 above), predicting that the latter should display interference, and hence more errors in reasoning, increasing with associative strength between the mediating term and other terms. The opposite should hold for the stimulus-equivalence paradigm. As shown in Figure 12-1, this prediction was borne out.

[1] Although Huttenlocher implies that her subjects used imagery, it is difficult to determine how universally they did so. Clark (1969b) reports that 49 percent of his subjects employed imagery.

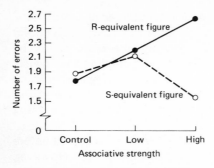

FIGURE 12–1   Number of reasoning errors as a function of meaningfulness and syllogistic paradigm. (From Pezzoli and Frase, 1968.)

Thus steps can be taken to bring reasoning problems within the scope of mediation theory. Granted that the syllogism is a comparatively simple and well structured task, compared, for example, with typical recentering problems; nevertheless, these investigators have paved the way for interesting research.

SCIENTIFIC REASONING

In scientific thinking there must be a minimum of two inductive stages: (1) sufficient observation to suggest a tentative conclusion (a question or a hypothesis), and (2) steps taken to collect enough facts, or data, or observations, and to analyse those data clearly enough that a generalization may be made. This second conclusion may be in the form of accepting the tentative conclusion, or of rejecting it, or of revising it. The situation may be more complicated at any point in this sequence. For example, instead of one tentative conclusion, there may be several alternative ones. The data may require any number of intermediate inductive analyses prior to the conclusion. The final conclusion itself may be merely tentative, leading to further inductive procedures, or to the deduction of sub-hypotheses which need to be tested, and so on.

In any case, four conditions appear to be always involved: (1) *Observation*: facts or instances of phenomena begin the inductive sequence; (2) *objectivity*: the collection of data or experience follows, under conditions related to the observer and to what is observed, and therefore the conditions of their occurrence and recording must be specified and an effort made to control them so that the facts are understandable; (3) *evidence*: once facts are objectively observed, they must be assessed for their relevance and significance, to determine their adequacy for answering the question, both for the investigator and for other people as well; and, finally, (4) *warranted conclusions*: the final stage of an inductive sequence is the statement of the conclusion, or generalization, to which the data lead, involving problems of the relation between the data and the conclusion, and the strength with which the conclusion is accepted.

Research by Rosenthal (1966) and Orne (1962) bear on these conditions. The former has shown that *experimenter bias* may unwittingly influence the results obtained (especially revealing factors that affect objectivity). The latter has demonstrated that *demand characteristics* may disguise or distort the evidence obtained in an experiment. A situation may contain conditions that influence the subject's behavior, apart from those intended by the experimenter. A good example is in studies that find sex differences, for females may perceive the purpose of the task quite differently from males (perhaps to please the experimenter, whereas males are more concerned to achieve success).

ANAGRAMS

Perhaps because of their possible significance for understanding verbal learning, anagrams have received considerable attention. In such tasks the subject is presented with scrambled letters (such as ACEHP) and asked to rearrange the letters to form words. Many experiments have focused on factors that determine the difficulty of anagrams, with particular attention to properties of the items and to set (Johnson, 1966).

Formal and Task Variables

With respect to *letter order*, the more displacement from the original word, the more difficult the problem (Mayzner and Tresselt, 1958), with some evidence that difficulty is affected by the frequency with which one letter follows another in the language (*transition probability*) (Mayzner and Tresselt, 1959; Hunter, 1961; Harris and Loess, 1968). More significant is *word perseveration* since anagrams as meaningful words are harder than nonsense forms (e.g., FROTH is harder than ROFTH for the solution FORTH) (Beilin and Horn, 1962; Ekstrand and Dominowski, 1968). A high-frequency solution word is easier than a low-frequency word (Mayzner and Tresselt,

1958; Dominowski, 1967), but words containing letters of low frequency are easier (J. L. Cohen, 1968), partly because of the *"rule-out"* factor (Ronning, 1965) or unlikely rearrangements, such as ITLGH versus REPIC. Difficulty also increases nonlinearly with *length* (at great length, fewer solutions are available and the probability of familiar suffixes increases) (Kaplan and Carvellas, 1968). As *information* increases, performance improves—for example, supplying a correctly placed letter or sequence (Dominowski, 1968), and displaying many random rearrangements rather than only one for the same period (Gavurin, 1967).

Set   Efficiency is greater with definite rather than indefinite instructions, but training with anagrams solvable in only one way establishes a set that interferes with solutions that can be achieved in other ways (Rees and Israel, 1935; Maltzman and Morrisett, 1953a). When special instructions refer to a class of words, the number of set solutions increases, and experience with fixed letter orders has a similar effect (Maltzman and Morrisett, 1953b). A set is more resistant to extinction under partial than under every-trial reinforcement (Adamson, 1959). When the set involves order rules, an attentional factor is involved since the pattern of eye movements changes when the rule changes (Kaplan and Schoenfeld, 1966).

Other Intrinsic Variables   Better solvers utilize more efficient hypotheses, looking for letter combinations, rather than whole-word solutions (Rhine, 1959). The special role of abilities is shown by significant correlations with anagram performance of spatial aptitude, general intelligence, and spelling achievement (r's from .22 to .54). Induced failure, as in other tasks, has an inhibitory effect.

Field-dependent persons tend to make more errors than field-independent persons, indicating greater impulsiveness or an over-dependence on the experimenter, who urged the subjects to try as many problems as possible (Bloomberg, 1965).

Mediational Studies   Safren (1962) has shown how a conceptual component can be introduced. In one condition, six sets of anagrams contained a common relationship (e.g., DOROCT, URNES

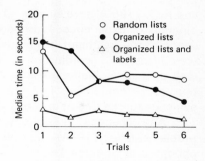

FIGURE 12–2 Median anagram solution time per trial for each of three experimental conditions. Each point is based on data of 36 subjects. (From Safren, 1962.)

EHALHT, etc.) ; in another, these sets were accompanied by identifying labels (e.g., *hospital*) ; and in a third, the sets were drawn randomly, one from each of the six lists. The mediated lists were easier than the random lists, and the labels were markedly facilitating (see Figure 12-2).

Other studies also contribute to a mediational view (Mayzner and Tresselt, 1963; Mayzner, Tresselt, and Helbock, 1964). For example, one may infer that greater word frequency induces greater frequency of implicit responses—and, in fact, subjects tend to produce first words with higher digram frequency. Furthermore, for multiple-solution anagrams (e.g., AEPHS), solution time varies with digram frequency and word frequency, indicative of mediational variables (Mayzner and Tresselt, 1966).

Priming techniques applied to anagrams also show facilitating effects (Dominowski and Ekstrand, 1967).

DEVELOPMENTAL TRENDS

As we saw, young children are able to integrate discrete experiences to solve a problem by inference (Kendler and Kendler, 1956). Kendler and Kendler (1962) have further shown that this behavior increases with age (from kindergarten to the third grade) and also that it increases with mental age.

It is, however, possible that chronological age is more important than mental age in some aspects of problem solving behavior. Smith and Roth (1960) have suggested that "sophistication" is primarily a function of experience. Preschool children were observed in their spontaneous treatment of naturally occurring problems. Responses were classified according to their effectiveness in coping with ten well-defined problems identified for each child. A significant relation to chronological, but not mental age, was interpreted as evidence for the role of experience.

Age changes in strategy appear in simple discrimination problems (Weir, 1964). In one such problem, the subject must choose one of three knobs, the correct one of which delivers a marble, with the aim of obtaining as many marbles as possible. Reinforcement is varied by having the correct knob yield marbles only 33 or 66 percent of the time—the problem is unsolvable since no strategy can lead to a 100 percent correct outcome. Over the ages of from three to ten years, the level of correct responding displays a pronounced curvilinear trend, with the middle ages reaching a lower level than either the younger or older ages. An examination of response patterns suggests that different strategies are typical of the various age groups. The youngest subjects tend to repeat previous responses, whether correct or not. Children at the middle ages (seven to ten) are likely to follow a win-stay, lose-shift strategy, reflecting a stereotyped approach. The oldest subjects appear to look for a complex solution, and develop hypotheses accordingly, but succeed in arriving at a simpler and more appropriate strategy. Since little or no understanding of a rule or principle is demanded, the simple approach of the youngest children is fairly successful, and the oldest children readily reach the conclusion that no principle is involved. The children of middle ages, on the other hand, are apparently able to search for a complex solution, but cannot easily discover its inappropriateness. Thus it appears in line with our earlier discussion of conceptualizing behavior in children, that there is little mediation in the youngest subjects, inefficient or transitional mediation in the next ages, and quite efficient mediation after the age of ten.

SEX DIFFERENCES

During the course of investigating problem solving, it has often been found that females tend to perform worse than males.

Milton (1957) hypothesized that sex-role identification, rather than biological differences themselves, may be related to problem solving success. The tasks typically employed in experiments, such as insightful (recentering), numerical, and reasoning problems, significantly favor males. However, masculinity and femininity, as assessed by three different tests, manifested significant correlation with problem solving performance. Although the relationship was not in all cases significant for the females, it was consistently so for the males.

Further evidence is provided by Carey (1958), who found that males typically have a more favorable attitude toward problem solving than do females. Scores on an attitude test were positively correlated with performance but, again, the relationship was markedly higher for males. The introduction of a discussion condition, intended to induce a more favorable attitude, produced significant improvement for the female subjects, but had little effect on the males.

These findings indicate that sex differences in problem solving stem not so much from intellectual abilities as from conditions of socialization leading to different interests and sex roles. When content is changed to make problems more appropriate to the feminine role, sex differences are reduced. In experiments with three-person games (Vinacke, 1959b, 1964; Bond and Vinacke, 1961), males typically display an exploitative pattern of behavior, featured by competitive bargaining, ruthless focus on winning, and a struggle for individual gain. Females, in contrast, manifest accommodative behavior, marked by an orientation toward the social interaction aspects of the situation, and are concerned with arriving at mutually satisfactory outcomes. By using a quiz game with items of feminine interest, — e. g., clothing and cosmetics, compared to sports — the incidence of accommodative (feminine) strategy can be increased (Uesugi and Vinacke, 1963). Feminine versions of reasoning tasks do not always benefit females, however (Hoffman and Maier, 1966).

Other experiments have similarly sought to make the problem situation more appropriate for feminine characteristics. Raaheim (1963) found that when practical construction problems were presented in written form, females performed as well as males. Burke (1965), however, obtained the usual sex differences on such problems when a brief rationale for each of the five alternative answers was provided. Furthermore, each sex performs better when the experimenter is of the same sex (Hoffman and Maier, 1966). Priest and Hunsaker (1969) tried to improve the performance of females on the horse-trading problem described in the last chapter, by allowing more time, providing more explicit instructions, or both. Only the last condition was effective.

PROBLEM-SOLVING ABILITY

It may be assumed that variations in problem solving are correlated with intelligence. However, although positive, correlations between general measures of intelligence and problem solving are typically low (Forster, Vinacke, and Digman, 1955; Burke and Maier, 1965) over the ranges of ability tested. It is more meaningful to consider whether problem solving calls on special kinds of abilities, which are obscured by the concept of general intelligence.

Guilford and his associates have pursued this issue from the standpoint of the "model of intellect" discussed in Chapter 5 (Guilford, Kettner, and Christensen, 1956; Kettner, Guilford, and Christensen, 1959; Merrifield et al., 1962). These studies show that there is no unitary problem solving or general reasoning ability. Rather, different tasks call on various combinations of abilities, very often with common factors that account for only a fraction of the variance (see also, Guilford, 1960). Thus predictions of performance based on ability require the measurement of fairly specific abilities known to be correlated with tasks of that kind. Guilford's structure of intellect clearly allows for the numerous patterns of abilities that enter into problem solving. In addition, as just pointed out, and as will be further apparent below, even were intellectual ability to be equated, problem solving varies markedly with situational and intrinsic conditions of other sorts.

CONDITIONS OF TRAINING

From the principle of *learning set* (Harlow, 1949), we might expect that repeated practice on a single problem would be superior to practice on many problems presented during the same period. Although this point was confirmed by Adams (1954), training on many problems was better when new problems were introduced, showing that intensive practice on much the same task is beneficial only so long as a specific skill can be routinely applied. Diversified training increases versatility. Furthermore, transfer is greater with multiple training (Callentine and Warren, 1955; Morrisett and Hovland, 1959), which permits greater generalization across problems. Therefore *two* requirements are evident—thorough mastery of training problems and sufficiently varied experience with the type of problem.

Generally comparable to the methods of discovery and demonstration discussed in the last chapter are *correction* and *modified correction* procedures. The former requires the subject to continue making choices until the correct one is found; the latter permits the subject one choice, after which the correct one is presented. Correction procedures are typical of maze learning, modified correction of verbal learning. Thompson (1958) compared these methods in verbal mazes,[1] finding that correction demands much more time and produces more errors (as does discovery). As the number of alternatives increases, the correction procedure becomes increasingly less efficient, but on transfer tests, the correction procedure produces increasing positive transfer (but also retroactive inhibition) as the number of choices increases (Ernst, 1967). Unfortunately, comparison with modified correction was not made, and we can only surmise that the latter would prove to be less efficient in transfer tests. Some support for this inference comes from a study by Rieber and Lockwood (1969) of preschool children on double-alternation learning. None of these subjects solved the problem under noncorrection (one guess only, leaving to inference that the other choice must be correct), but 50 percent did so under the correction procedures. The authors point out that correction leads to complete, concrete knowledge of the solution, forcing attention to the inferred event.

Finally, it must be recognized that situations involving multiple alternatives can encompass different values. In the experiments cited, the objective is to solve problems in the single best way. But an opposing goal may be to achieve varied or new solutions—that is, to promote flexibility and originality. Ray (1966), for example, has shown that training on single-solution problems inhibits the production of varied solutions in new situations, thus establishing a set. Ray further showed that the production of multiple solutions can be increased by manipulating the subject's expectancy. Originality increases if the subject is informed that many solutions are possible rather than only a few.

Complementary to the foregoing studies are those in which the information available to the subject is manipulated. For example, performance is better when subjects participate in demonstrations of principles than when they are simply exposed to them (Székely, 1950; Anderson and Johnson, 1966).

Verbalization

As pointed out above, techniques that force the subject to pay closer attention to the task tend to facilitate performance. In an early experi-

---

[1] The subject makes a succession of choices, such as between right and left (two choices) or, in addition, up and down (four choices), and so on.

ment by Ewart and Lambert (1932), it was found that subjects who were provided with a verbally stated principle of solution performed better than those given other types of instruction. At first it appears obvious that such a statement would be facilitative. Gagne' and Smith (1962), however, suggested that the same effect might be evident if the subject did his own verbalizing—in this case explaining the reasons for his moves. This result, in fact, occurred, leading to the interpretation that verbalizing by subjects has "the effect of making them think of new reasons for their moves, and thus facilitates both the discovery of general principles and their employment in solving successive problems."

STRATEGY
So far, only limited attention has been paid to the patterning of responses in complex problem situations, perhaps because primary interest has been directed toward identifying the kinds of variables that influence solutions.

Hypotheses
How do subjects develop and employ guiding hypotheses? This topic, well investigated in concept-attainment tasks, has been raised in other kinds of situations as well. Goodnow and Postman (1955) show that subjects search for principles, even when this strategy is inappropriate. In their experiment, correct choices were predetermined by the experimenter; even though the subjects continued to search for a principle, their choices actually came to approximate the externally imposed probabilities. A complementary finding in a study by Hillix, Lawson, and Marx (1956) was that the degree of reinforcement during training had no effect on the tendency to prefer one hypothesis rather than another. In fact, subjects tended to *avoid* hypotheses based on common properties of the problems. There appears to be, however, an important relation between the perceptual properties and logical demands of a problem. Benjafield (1969) has shown that as the former become less compelling, logical analysis increases. Goodnow and Pettigrew (1956) observed that in simple repetitive tasks the subject seems to develop a "response hypothesis" that interferes with his noticing consistencies in stimulus events and therefore delays solution. By providing advance training that emphasized consistent patterns, the mastery of a subsequent problem was facilitated.

The type of hypothesis adopted depends on the problem for, as

Markova (1969) has shown, simple versions tend to evoke general hypotheses based on overall evaluation of the problem, whereas complex versions induce differentiated hypotheses with subgoals based on logical analysis. In examining the game of chess, Simon and Simon (1962) have pointed out that success depends on the use of "selective heuristics," and that by applying such tactics perhaps anyone can discover difficult combinations of moves.

Measures of "defense effectiveness" and "adaptive regression," based on Rorschach responses (Blatt, Allison, and Feirstein, 1969), have yielded significant correlations with problem solving performance, suggesting that efficiency in complex logical problems depends on the integration of "drive-determined and/or unusual types of thinking into realistic and appropriate responses." Primary-process components were not related to efficiency.

These observations accord with our earlier discussion of mediation theory. People typically approach problems by formulating and testing hypotheses, tactics not readily identified from merely the objective characteristics of the task. Nor is hypothesis forming necessarily appropriate, and, if not, the subject finds the task more difficult than it really is. Success in solving problems thus depends more on experience with relevant situations, on the complexities of the problem, and on the accessibility of information, than on failure to develop and test hypotheses.

Cognitive Complexity

Strategy varies with cognitive complexity (Harvey, Hunt, and Schroder, 1961; Karlins, 1967; Karlins, Coffman, Lamm, and Schroder, 1967). Compared to cognitively simple persons, complex persons ask more questions (directed toward acquiring broader information pertinent to the goal), are willing to explore the environment directly and to act on the environment, and more readily maintain differentiated classes of information. Sieber and Lanzetta (1964), along the same lines, show that complex persons employ complex strategies.

SET

Implicit in principles such as functional fixedness, direction, and strategy is the idea that established response tendencies influence the character of problem solving. Regulative processes induced by the immediate situation can be called *sets*. Special tendencies to persist in a given fashion fall under the general heading of *rigidity*.

Interest in rigidity was prompted by some experiments by Luchins (1942). He used water-jar problems, by which a particular method of dealing with the problems—or an *Einstellung* (fixed tendency or set)—could be induced, followed by presentation of test problems that could be solved either by the set method or by an alternative (and more direct) method. (An exhaustive discussion of the problem of rigidity may be found in Luchins and Luchins [1959].)

Water-jar problems take this form. Given empty jars that hold the following amounts in quarts: jar A, 21 ; jar B, 127 ; jar C, 3, obtain the following amount: 100 quarts. The solution can be generalized by a rule: jar B minus 2 times jar C minus jar A equals 100. In a series of identical problems (save for variations in the amounts given and required), the subject is likely to learn this rule very well and to apply it with increasing efficiency. When the test problem is presented, the set operates if the subject still uses the same rule, even though a new and much simpler solution is possible (e.g., with jars holding 23, 49, and 3 quarts, obtain 20 quarts). Luchins not only demonstrated the persistence of the set but also that it could be disrupted by such devices as having subjects write on their papers, prior to the critical problems, "Don't be blind." The set operates more strongly as it becomes better established and, concomitantly, it becomes more difficult to shift to a new solution (Gardner and Runquist, 1958).

The strength of the set also varies with the amount of effort expended in acquiring it. If the initial problem is easy, subjects shift to a new procedure more readily than if it is difficult (Knight, 1963). Although some studies have reported personality correlates of *Einstellung* effects (Cowen and Thompson, 1951 ; Cowen, Wiener, and Hess, 1953), most efforts to establish a general trait of rigidity have been unsuccessful (Guetzkow, 1951 ; Forster, Vinacke, and Digman, 1955 ; Goodstein, 1953).

In general, research indicates that rigidity is a kind of behavior rather than a generalized personality trait (Levitt, 1956; Chown, 1959). A person who is rigid in one task is not necessarily so in another. This conclusion, however, should not be taken to discount the importance of sets, which clearly have two effects. They facilitate performance, once acquired, when a series of similar problems calls on the same solution (by the same token, solutions by resonance, as pointed out, can be quite appropriate). But when a better or new solution is demanded, then the persistence of a set interferes with a more efficient performance.

MOTIVATIONAL VARIABLES

A variety of studies have demonstrated how differences in intrinsic states are related to problem solving efficiency.

Deprivation

A classic study by Birch (1945) found that the performance of chimpanzees in insight problems is curvilinearly related to food deprivation. At low levels, the animals were easily diverted and displayed activities not directed toward the goal; at high levels, the animals seemed to concentrate so strongly on the goal that other relevant conditions were ignored. This relationship, the Yerkes-Dodson (1908) principle, has become well established, at least for biogenic motives and with a sufficiently wide range of intensity (Bindra, 1959; Malmo, 1959). It has been demonstrated for human subjects under sensory and social deprivation (Suedfeld, Glucksberg, and Vernon, 1967). A curvilinear relation to performance on Maier's candle problem appeared when deprivation and monetary incentive combined to produce low, moderate, and high levels of motivation (see Figure 12-3).

Stress and Arousal

In general, arousal increases with the difficulty of the task (R. C. Davis, 1938; W. A. Shaw and Kline, 1947). And the relation of arousal to performance is curvilinear (Burgess and Hokanson, 1964). Both effects, however, depend on interactions with other variables.

Ego-involving instructions increase arousal (muscle-action potentials) in easy tasks, whereas task-orienting instructions increase arousal in difficult tasks (Reuder, 1956). Under distraction, arousal is decreased in difficult tasks, as measured by the heart rate (Gibson and Hall, 1966; Harleston, Smith, and Arey, 1965). Autonomic activity, however, in general increases with the difficulty of the task (Kahneman et al., 1969). Further analysis discloses that the heart rate decelerates during information-intake phases of the task, but accelerates during cognitive processes. Skin resistance manifests a generalized arousal pattern during both phases (Tursky, Schwartz, and Crider, 1970). These findings support Lacey's (1967) view that physiological components of arousal reflect different demands of the task, with the heart rate depending on the direction of attention, decelerating with orientation to the environment and accelerating with a shift to cognitive manipulation.

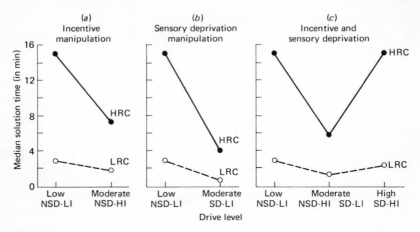

FIGURE 12–3   The effect of incentive and sensory deprivation on problem solving. (From Suedfeld, Glucksberg, and Vernon. 1967.)

Note: NSD=no sensory deprivation; LI=low incentive; SD=sensory deprivation; HI=high incentive; HRC=high response to competition; LRC=low response to competition.

With respect to performance, stress (such as verbal challenge, failure, or threat) typically impairs performance (Combs and Taylor, 1952; Cowen, 1952). But arousal increases with success (Clites, 1935), and is beneficial in easy problems, although detrimental in hard problems (Bills and Stauffacher, 1937). Similarly, better problem solvers are more aroused than poor solvers (Beckman and Stein, 1961). These findings indicate that effective problem solving is a function of adaptation to the demands of the situation.

Achievement

Of the social motives related to performance, achievement has been most extensively investigated. In early studies, persons high in latent achievement (i.e., those whose pretest scores are high under neutral conditions) were found to be more efficient problem solvers than persons low in achievement (Lowell, 1952; French and Thomas, 1958). However, it has become increasingly evident that such effects depend importantly on other variables. That is, individuals with a predisposition to achievement even under neutral conditions tend to generate their own eliciting cues. When appropriate inductions are employed, persons low in latent achievement may show improved performance matching that of persons high in achievement. For example, under neutral instructions the maze-learning time of sub-jects high in achievement was considerably faster than that of those low in achievement, but under threat of shock, there was no differ-ence (the high group actually displayed some impairment compared to a great improvement in the low group) (Johnston, 1955). A similar effect was shown under achievement-orienting instructions versus multi-incentive instructions, which added the offer of a prize and "pleasing the experimenter" (Atkinson and Reitman, 1956). A more complex interaction appeared in a study by Williams (1955). Subjects worked under nonfailure or failure conditions with goals set either by the subject himself or by the experimenter. The group high in achievement performed best under failure when they set the goals themselves, and were worst under nonfailure when they set their own goals; the low-achievement group were best when the experi-menter set the goals, especially under failure.

In addition, relevance among conditions must be taken into account. These points are nicely illustrated in a study by French and Lesser (1964). They identified women characterized by strong "intellectual" values, by strong "women's-role" values, or by both. Arousal conditions appropriate to one or the other of these orienta-tions were employed in one of two tasks (anagrams and a social-skills test), similarly designed to be especially suitable for one of the values. Achievement arousal was assessed by French's test of insight, with items containing either a male or female stimulus figure.[1] As hypothesized, achievement motivation is high when activity leads to a valued goal, but not otherwise, and achievement motivation is positively related to performance only when it leads to a valued goal. Greater achievement motivation was displayed by the women with strong intellectual values under intellectual arousal, and by the women with strong women's-role values under women's-role arousal. Similarly, level of performance sorted itself out into patterns of relevant conditions—that is, intellectual orientation under intellectual arousal in anagrams and women's-role under women's-role arousal in social skills (the relevance of motivation to group problem solving is evident in another study by French [1958]).

Anxiety
A host of studies have also examined the effects of anxiety, as mea-sured by the Taylor Manifest Anxiety Scale or by the Sarason-Mandler

[1]This test is semiprojective, calling for brief explanations of statements like "John (Jane) always lets the 'other fellow' win."

Test Anxiety Scale. In reviewing this research, Sarason (1960) concluded that individuals high in anxiety typically display impaired
performance in complex and stressful tasks, whereas those low in
anxiety are relatively better under these conditions. As might be
expected, however, situational variables influence these effects.
For example, although stress may have similar effects on all subjects
in easy problems (producing generally better performance), in
difficult problems stress impairs subjects high in anxiety, but facilitates those low in anxiety (Sarason and Palola, 1960).

Motivation and Problem Solving

From this brief look at relations between motivational variables and
performance, certain conclusions emerge. In the first place, increases
in arousal, by the employment of inductions or incentives, generally
improve performance, in line with commonsense notions. Individuals
who adapt best to the situation are more efficient at problem solving
that those in whom an inappropriate intrinsic state is elicited. Individual differences in antecedent characteristics such as latent achievement or level of anxiety depend for their effects on situational conditions such as the difficulty of the task or stress. Equally important is
the relevance of situational and goal conditions to motivational
characteristics. If the task is inappropriate or the goal unsuitable,
arousal or incentive procedures may have little or no effect.

INDIVIDUAL VERSUS GROUP PROBLEM SOLVING

Two questions arise with regard to the efficiency of group problem
solving. The first concerns differences between individuals and
groups, the second whether proficiency differs under the two conditions. It is not always possible to say that differences in the first
respect are accompanied by differences in the second. One reason is
that outcomes of group discussion (or of individual behavior, for
that matter) may pertain to opinions, values, affective states, or
interpersonal relationships, and in such cases it would be dubious to
assess performance by ordinary measures of accuracy, speed, and
so on.

Differences between Individual and Group Problem Solving

When a group faces a task, it really encounters two sorts of problems
—not only finding a way to reach the goal but also of organizing and

directing intragroup relationships. Processes of resolving issues internal to the functioning of the group therefore constitute a major difference between group and individual problem solving. Even when there is little conflict—for example, in a clearly structured group which has, at least temporarily, achieved a smoothly operating system—the necessity to coordinate the activities of the members demands effort beyond that devoted to the task itself. This difference is related to proficiency because the group requires extra time solely for this reason, regardless of whatever advantages or disadvantages it may have with respect to the problem itself.

Another difference has recently received a great deal of attention, namely, the proclivity of groups under some conditions to take more risks than individuals in arriving at decisions (but they may also be more cautious—and a more general principle of *choice shifts* is more appropriate). Stoner (1961) observed that persons are typically more willing to take risks when they become members of groups than during individual decision making [this has often been confirmed (Wallach, Kogan, and Bem, 1962; Pruitt and Teger, 1967; Dion, Baron, and Miller, 1970)]. This phenomenon is known as the *risky shift*. The principle of *diffusion of responsibility* maintains that membership in a group releases the individual from facing the consequences of his own actions, so that he can endorse positions he would otherwise hesitate to accept (Wallach, Kogan, and Bem, 1964). A second view proposes that certain individuals in the group influence others to adopt a riskier course than they would otherwise adopt (Marquis, 1962). One such effect might stem from the leader, another from members high in achievement or extraversion (Rim, 1963, 1964). In a third interpretation, the group situation provides *familiarization* with ideas, thus promoting their acceptability (Bateson, 1966; Flanders and Thistlethwaite, 1967). Research to test these explanations has failed to sustain them (Pruitt and Teger, 1967, 1969; Hoyt and Stoner, 1968). Therefore a fourth view has been advanced, that the character of group decisions depends on *cultural values* (R. Brown, 1965; Nordhφy, 1962).

When risk is condoned or valued, decisions will tend to move toward greater risk; when caution is the keynote, then risky shifts will not occur. Assessments of the three preceding interpretations point in this direction. That is, such conditions as exercise of influence and familiarization sometimes produce risky shifts, sometimes not. Risky shifts result from a situation when risk is valued, but less risky (or conservative) shifts occur when caution is valued (Stoner, 1968; Pruitt, 1969; R. D. Clark and Willems, 1969).

When the problem has an impersonal character, people seem more willing to endorse actions that lead to reward, but that violate ethical standards (Rettig, 1966). The group situation apparently permits individuals to test censure and reduces anxiety about it, with a concomitant strengthening of the force of possible gain. Discussion produces a shift toward enhancing the social value of risk (Rettig and Turoff, 1967), revealed by the fact that persons believe themselves to take more risks than their peers, so that the group situation contains a potentially pervasive value that tends to become a norm (Wallach and Wing, 1968; Levinger and Schneider, 1969; Moscovici and Zavalloni, 1969).

Finally, Vidmar (1970) has proposed that when the composition of the group is considered, the value hypothesis entails assumptions that riskiness is valued, that each member conceives himself as taking more risks than others, and that the shift toward risk depends entirely on differences in preference between less-risk-taking members and the most-risk-taking member. On this basis, Vidmar used the Choice Dilemmas Questionnaire (Kogan and Wallach, 1964) to measure variations in risk-taking proclivities, then composed five-member groups of high, moderate, low, or mixed (two high, one moderate, two low) risk takers. His predictions were sustained that all groups would manifest a risky shift, but that the degree of shift would be greater for the mixed groups, that there would be an inverse relationship between initial individual risk preference and judgments made (individually) following the group discussion (unanimity was required). However, the riskiest members themselves displayed a significant average risky shift, rather than no change. Since an individual can take more risks on some items than on others, a separate analysis was conducted to identify the riskiest person on each item—and now this part of the prediction was sustained.

Some investigators have also begun to question the value theory of risk. Thus Zajonc et al. (1970) have reported a study in which, unlike the results of Wallach and Wing subjects displayed little difference between their own and others' estimates of risk, and, further, knowledge about the risk positions of others had little effect on risk taking. They suggested that the most important factor lies in the interaction processes of the group, with decision-making rules (e.g., majority, consensus, etc.) as salient considerations. From this perspective risky shifts may well be more inevitable than conservative shifts. One might argue that the principle of cultural values can encompass such considerations (conservatism and decision-making norms or rules may operate as values). But the notion that groups are invariably more prone to take risks than individuals is clearly not established. The problem, in the future, will probably be to explicate in detail the *conditions* that promote risky (or conservative) decisions and to elaborate relationships among those conditions, together with their outcomes.

Group Proficiency

A simple experiment from the introductory laboratory nicely demonstrates the effects of group discussion. A large square of cardboard containing several hundred 1/4-inch dots is displayed before a group of subjects. They are given 30 seconds to estimate the number of dots. After this guess is written down, the subjects are formed into pairs and allowed to discuss the problem for 5 minutes or so. They then are asked to write down a new estimate of the number of dots. Four effects are revealed by comparison of the initial and final estimates :

1 The average is closer to the correct number than either of the two first guesses—that is, the judgments tend to converge on the correct answer.

2 The average of the final estimates is often closer to the correct answer than the average of the initial estimates—that is, the discussion-influenced guess may be better than the pooled individual judgments.

3 The pairs display less variability after discussion than before— that is, there is movement toward greater agreement.

4 *Both* people individually are typically closer to the correct number after discussion than before—that is, final performance is actually better in many instances than that of the better of the two judges.

We may label the first and third effects as *convergence* (or change toward agreement) ; the second effect may be called *movement toward increased efficiency;* and the fourth effect reflects the *transcendence* of a group-produced judgment. Any group, of course, may manifest an exception to any or a combination of these effects. For example, both individuals may arrive at similar estimates that are farther away from the correct judgment than either of their initial judgments. Experiments show all these effects (Shaw, 1932; Marquart, 1955 ; E. J. Hall, Mouton, and Blake, 1963).

The superiority of groups, however, is contingent on two considerations. In the first place, since two or more persons are working on the same problem, actual efficiency rests on allocation of time.

The *total time* to arrive at a comparable level is greater than for an individual working alone (except for very slow persons). Thus groups are comparatively slow (Taylor and Faust, 1952; J. H. Davis and Restle, 1963; Kelley and Thibaut, 1969). Second, the superiority of groups depends on the type of problem, such as the distribution of information among members (Kelley and Thibaut, 1969), and the degree to which efficiency increases with a division of labor. J. H. Davis (1969), for example, found that groups are actually *faster* than individuals under conditions when a division of labor and social interaction are appropriate.

The dot problem illustrates the convergence of individuals on some middle ground. Kelley and Thibaut (1969) have pointed to the transcendent feature by reviewing evidence that groups may actually perform at a level above the most proficient member. Issues of this kind are mostly irrelevant when group outcomes represent policies, values, and other intangible products, although there are instances when some objective evidence or an evaluation of subsequent events may lead to an assessment of accuracy or some other proficiency measure. But a variety of studies indicate that in appropriate types of problems, groups tend to reach better outcomes than any of the members separately (and, in some cases at least, better than a pooling of the performance of separate individuals).

This point has historical precedence in Dashiell's (1935) study. A simulated jury was found to reach a more accurate, though less complete, report on an accident than any individual. Barnlund (1959) utilized a syllogism task in which the alternatives were controversial, and here again most of the groups (four to six members) produced a larger number of correct solutions than the member identified on a pretest as the best. Similar results have been reported by Perlmutter (1933) and N. H. Anderson (1961).

The influence of the type of problem is illustrated in a study by Faust (1959). On spatial puzzles, which demand a one-step straightforward solution, group performance was no better than that of "nominal" groups (i.e., a combination of separate individuals chosen at random). On anagrams, however, the real groups were superior. An important reason lies in the probability that different members could solve different words, so that individual abilities were added.

In other types of situations, groups may be inferior to nominal groups (thus to the most competent individuals). For example, Faucheux and Moscovici (1958) found that when a coordinated strategy of following a succession of steps is involved, members may interfere with each other. There arises the necessity, as pointed out above, to solve problems of group organization; once these issues are resolved, the group may again be superior to individuals.

Brainstorming

Another interesting question is whether groups are more or less creative than individuals. Here proficiency depends not on accuracy or time or agreement, but on the number of novel ideas proposed. As advanced by Osborn (1957), the technique calls for a kind of free-associative verbal production, with participants instructed to suspend critical judgment, and merely to suggest anything that occurs to them.

Taylor, Berry, and Block (1958) conducted a systematic study of the principle that brainstorming increases creativity. Three different problems were presented under brainstorming instructions to individuals and to groups of four. The latter produced a significantly greater number of ideas, on the average. However, when individual responses were pooled into randomly constituted nominal groups, the real groups were significantly inferior, not only in number of ideas, but also in the number of unique responses (see also, Dunnette, Campbell, and Jaastad, 1963).

However, Meadow, Parnes, and Reese (1959) found that brainstorming instructions produced more qualitatively good ideas when given to individuals working alone than occurred without such instructions. Their subjects had participated in a course on creative problem solving, and therefore may have reflected this training in their performance (see also, Cohen, Whitmyre, and Funk, 1960).

In general it is unlikely that creative solutions are more frequent in group than in individual settings—at least in the kinds of situations so far studied. But this conclusion should not be taken to mean that brainstorming lacks value. Participants may very well feel that they have been changed by the experience and validly believe that their thinking has been especially stimulated. It is, unfortunately, easy to confuse the personal significance of cognitive activity with objectively evaluated merit. In any case, brainstorming procedures may have the advantage of increasing the productivity of a group, regardless of whether or not separate individuals would do as well or better.

SUMMARY

Formal logic is concerned with the promotion of successful reasoning through the proper application of rules by which valid conclusions may be reached. Scientific method utilizes hypotheses and tests them through the development of evidence. Deductive processes entail the use of generalizations, in contrast to inductive processes that involve arriving at generalizations. The syllogism is a set of three propositions, the first two (premises) leading to the third as a conclusion. Any of the propositions may be affirmative or negative, general or particular. Valid reasoning depends on the arrangement of the propositions. Experimental studies show that difficulty varies with the characteristics of the material, and that atmosphere effects and personal convictions influence performance. Studies of psycho-logic show that variables of cognitive structure partly determine reasoning. Scientific reasoning, less investigated experimentally, involves observation, objectivity, evidence, and warranted conclusions. The solving of anagrams is influenced by letter order, transition probability, word and letter frequency, rule-out factor, amount of information, and mode of presentation. Conditions that enhance mediation facilitate solution. Failure inhibits, while the appropriate set facilitates performance. Better solvers utilize more efficient hypotheses. Inferential ability increases during childhood, as does the ability to adopt an appropriate strategy. Although males are typically more efficient problem solvers than females, this difference is mainly a function of sex-role identification. There is probably no general problem solving ability. Within the same type of problem, learning sets facilitate performance, but multiple training increases efficiency when the task involves diverse problems. Efficiency is also affected by the mode of presenting information and by verbalization. With respect to strategy, the forming of hypotheses is typical, but their effectiveness depends on the type of problem, the availability of information, and other conditions. Cognitively complex and simple persons differ in strategy, as do good versus poor solvers. Although an acquired *Einstellung* may interfere with changing to a new rule, the search for general measures of rigidity has not been successful. Efficiency is also affected by motivational variables. Of the principles advanced to explain risky and cautious shifts in group problem solving, those based on values appear most convincing. Compared to individuals, group decisions may display convergence of individual judgments, movement toward increased accuracy, or transcendence of group judgment over that of individual members. Important factors include division of labor and coordination of effort. Under certain conditions, groups may outperform the best member. Brainstorming may have psychological benefits, but creativity of outcomes is probably less than for individual performance.

13

IMAGINATION

In this chapter and the next we shall deal with cognitive processes dominated by intrinsic conditions, such as imagery, fantasy, and dreams. Earlier we formulated the realistic-autistic continuum of cognition. In the past few chapters we have concentrated on the realistic pole, although recognizing that autistic components are not absent but rather much reduced in their influence when environmental stimuli dominate the course of thinking.

Traditionally, the distinction between realistic and autistic processes has been apparent in formulating two broad categories, "reasoning" and "imagination." These terms, however, are inadequate. For one thing, they imply a sharper difference in kind than accords with our conception of interrelating components. From the traditional view stem assumptions that reasoning is (or should be) logical, controlled, and free from emotional entanglements, and that imagination is incidental or trivial. In addition, by postulating two different categories of cognitive events, methodological implications appear. Since reasoning signifies the application of rules and the generation of definite and overtly produced outcomes, it would appear that it is more directly or objectively amenable to study, whereas imagination implies wholly covert and personal events that demand indirect methods. Although it is certainly true that important methodological issues arise, and that the same techniques may not be applicable to realistic and autistic components, nevertheless, to treat them as distinctly different categories fails to consider sufficiently the variables that should be defined in investigating the full spectrum of cognitive processes.

Thus, although there are special conditions when autistic influences are strongly dominant, as previously pointed out, realistic factors are very rarely, if ever, totally absent. Murphy (1947, p. 363) has stated the relationship this way for perception: "the outer world can never be so completely unstructured as to make perception depend solely upon the perceiver; but it can never be so sharply and clearly organized as to obliterate individual differences among perceivers."

IMAGERY

In the formalistic tradition, imagination has often been defined as "the manipulation of images." This view is inherited from the structural psychology of the last century, and implies both that images are the ingredients of imagination, and that something else is the element of reasoning (once said to be "ideas"). In our treatment the ingredients are the same in all thinking, although not necessarily always in the same proportions or forms (e.g., we would distinguish images and verbal responses as symbols that are not always simultaneously present). It is more meaningful to say that it is not so much the ingredients that differ, as the situational and functional determinants. This point is well illustrated by the earlier discussion of mediation, in which both words and images appeared as agents.

Images play a very prominent role in imagination, especially in the extreme forms represented by fantasy, dreams, and disordered states of drastic dissociation. An *image* may be regarded as a subjective quasi-perceptual response that occurs in the absence of an extrinsic stimulus, and to this degree it can be described analogously to corresponding stimulus-induced experiences, but with different consequences (Richardson, 1969). In fact, unusually intense images may actually be mistaken for extrinsically induced responses, as in hallucinations.

An image typically differs in several ways from a perception induced by an environmental stimulus: (1) Images are usually fainter, less detailed, and less definite than immediate perceptual responses. (2) Images are unsteady and shifting or fleeting, and cannot be maintained as dependably as can perceptual responses. (3) Images cannot supply new factual information about an object or situation, but contain only information stored in memory, whereas in perception new information may be obtained by continued examination of objects or by changes in attention.[1] (4) Images are facilitated by shutting out external stimuli, such as by closing the eyes, or stopping up the ears, thus increasing the dominance of intrinsic states. (5) Images need not correspond to actual, real objects, and, in fact, frequently display bizarre, distorted, exaggerated, incomplete, or unusual combinations of impressions.

Imagery is far more responsive to intrinsic need-states than is perception. The less thinking is influenced by direct perception for whatever reason, the more likely it is that images will predominate because, up to a point at least, images express the changing intrinsic state more easily than do the processes of direct perception. Thus, with respect to the autistic-realistic continuum, as thinking shifts toward the realistic pole, images tend to decrease and perceptual response to dominate; and, as thinking shifts toward the intrinsic need pole, environmental influence decreases, and images become more numerous and stronger. Either realistic or imaginative thinking may, at any moment, be carried out at a verbal level by translating images or perceptions into words. In either case, the translating (or coding) represents at least a minimal organizing and integrating process. There are many occasions when imaginative thinking occurs in words, with images absent or incidental. Imagination, according to this view, is mental activity relatively free from extrinsic demands, not merely the "manipulation of images."

Needless to say, images may have as many properties as would be allowed by the properties of the sense organs in which the original responses occurred and as permitted by the properties of memory and the cognitive systems that process memorial input. Because visual images are usually the strongest and most frequent, it is easy to overlook other kinds. Nevertheless, auditory, tactual, thermal, kinesthetic, olfactory, gustatory, and even organic images are readily reported (Brower, 1947).

When the actual variety of imagery is recognized, it becomes an interesting exercise to inquire into individual differences. Does different imagery predominate in different people? This question is another of the historic typology hypotheses. Betts (1909) showed that

---

[1]But imagery may involve novel combinations of memorial material, and, in this sense, represent "new" information.

persons cannot be classified according to their dominant imagery. Rather, those persons who have imagery at all tend to display comparable degrees of all kinds. Recently, Sheehan (1967) has used a technique derived from Betts' work to distinguish between persons who report vivid imagery and those who are poor "imagers." He reports that the former perceive the environment in a literal fashion, whereas the latter employ coding devices.

Especially valuable information about imagery can be supplied by individuals who lack the normal basis for sensory experience, such as the blind. A case in point comes from a lucid report by Duran (1969). Having lost all sight during early childhood, Duran learned about objects primarily through touch. Although he could experience color images, visual properties of objects were lacking, and, instead, his cognitions assumed other forms. For example, his knowledge of a female tutor was based on her voice and pleasant perfume, rather than her shape, size, etc. The interesting point is his ability to "know" and to "think" in special ways different from the sighted person.

Classes of Images
Images vary in their characteristics and the conditions under which they occur.

Afterimages These are sensory experiences that continue after the initiating stimulus is removed, and are most readily recognized in visual and vestibular modalities. For example, when a subject fixates a blue square and then shifts his gaze to a neutral field, a negative afterimage (a yellow square) is experienced. Similarly, when a person is stopped, after rotation, the experience of turning in the opposite direction occurs. These effects have a secondary interest for the study of cognition, except for the general principle that any stimulus may reverberate in the cognitive system, with effects that interact with subsequent events.

Memory Images These include virtually any recall of previously experienced objects or events that correspond closely to the original perception. They differ from afterimages because there is an interval between perception and recall. Feelings of recognition or familiarity accompany memory images.

Eidetic Images   These are unusually strong, persistent, and accurate representations of complex stimulus situations, usually more frequent in children (Jaensch, 1930), and are apparently independent of cultural background (Doob, 1966). Because an eidetic image so closely resembles an actual perception, some observers regard them as more like aftersensations than memory images. For example, Hanawalt (1954) described compelling "recurrent images" of blackberries after an extended period of picking them, suggesting that such images have an affinity to eidetic images. Others propose that eidetic images display characteristics both of afterimages and of memory images (Barber, 1959). Rather than using a stimulus to induce an image, Barber had his subjects first imagine an object, then "project" the image. Classic features of eidetic images were evident: Children were more successful than adults, and the subjects insisted that the image did not differ from an actual object and behaved as if actually "seeing" the object. In addition, physiological indices, such as alpha blocking and alteration of pupil size, resembled those obtained in actual perception. Using the standard technique of having children inspect pictures, then report what they saw after their removal, Haber and Haber (1964) found that 55 percent reported images of at least one picture and that accuracy and duration were positively related. Only a few children could be identified as "eidetic," displaying very high accuracy and long duration of the image. After the image faded, their memory was about the same as that of the "noneidetic" children. These results are more in line with an afterimage interpretation than Barber's, although a cortical basis is not ruled out. Hebb (1968) believes that eidetic images belong in the same class as memory images but, unlike them, involve both sensory and central processes.

Hypnagogic and Hypnopompic Images   These occur in the intervals between waking and sleeping (hypnagogic) or the reverse (Slight, 1924). These phenomena resemble eidetic images, with perhaps a greater role of sensory aftereffects (Hebb, 1968). A questionnaire study (McKellar and Simpson, 1954) indicated that hypnopompic imagery is not frequent, although most people have experienced it. More than 60 percent reported hypnagogic images, but only 20 percent reported hypnopompic images. The former were said to be more vivid and realistic than dreams, to be quite instantaneous, and not to involve participation by the subject, who seemed merely to "watch" them; they were described as clearer, more vivid, less subject to conscious control, and more varying than memory images. These images occur in all sensory modalities, but most frequently in the auditory mode, with visual images next (McKellar, 1957).

Images of Imagination These are continuous, plastic, free forms of memory images that may depart widely from their original perceptual origins. They may be constructive and subject to some voluntary direction, as in creative thinking, or be aimless, as in daydreams.

All these forms of imagery are quite normal, but there are also pathological forms, to be mentioned later.

STUDIES OF IMAGERY
Conditioning
In keeping with the behavioristic tradition, some investigators have sought to show that images are simply conditioned sensations. Under hypnosis, Leuba (1940) applied stimuli (e.g., a bell and a pinprick on the hand). Posthypnotic amnesia was induced, and then, after being awakened, the subject was asked to report any experiences when a series of stimuli occurred. Images ("conditioned sensations") were reported when the conditioned stimulus was presented (e.g., "smarting and itching" and scratching the previously stimulated area when the bell was sounded). Ellson (1941) devised a more conventional procedure, with control groups, using a light as the conditioned stimulus and a tone as the unconditioned stimulus. Of forty subjects, thirty-two reported on test trials hearing the tone on presentation of the light. Ellson, however, was not willing to call this phenomenon "conditioning" in the usual sense because, for example, the latency of the response was greater and more variable than in standard motor conditioning, and furthermore, neither acquisition nor extinction was gradual.

Leuba and Dunlap (1951) showed that conditioned sensations (i.e., images) can be elicited by images of the conditioned stimulus. After conditioning under hypnosis, the subject was asked in an amnesic posthypnotic session to *imagine* the conditioned stimulus. Despite having no memory of the original situation, all four subjects reported the associated images.

Information Theory
Recently, experiments have been undertaken on the role of images in memory and in information processing. Giddan (1967), for example,

tested the principle advanced by Hilgard (1962b) that unreported aspects of stimuli persist and can be incorporated into cognitive processes. Giddan argues that conditions conducive to fantasy should facilitate such effects. Subjects witnessed brief tachisto-scopic exposure of stimulus pictures and then attempted to draw what they had seen; next "fantasy" drawings were obtained; and finally another drawing of the original picture was made, with evidence for a significant amount of recovery of the original stimulus.

Antrobus, Singer, Goldstein, and Fortgang (1970) report several studies with a signal-detection technique. The subject was supplied periodically with a signal to indicate the occurrence of a "stimulus-independent thought," something for which there was no signal on the preceding trial (e.g., thinking about a boyfriend while working on the task). Subjects were trained to identify such occurrences and to press a button when one occurred during a signal-detection task. If perceptual responses and stimulus-independent thoughts (arising from events previously stored in long-term memory) have cognitive stages in common, such an "operator" should become less available as the information rate increases, assuming that the payoff for correct response to the perceptual task exceeds that for the stimulus-independent thought (the reverse could hold under certain conditions, perhaps, for example, if the intrinsic component were anxiety-laden). As predicted, the subjects tended to produce at least some stimulus-independent thoughts even under a high rate of information input, although some subjects did not under the highest rate.

To examine the question whether stimulus-independent thought is a parallel or sequential process, the amount of information and the duration of the interval were manipulated separately. If the sequential process holds, then decreasing the interval should reduce the time available and thus decrease stimulus-independent thought. Increasing the amount of information should increase the load on the central operator and reduce the amount available. Were the sequential process to hold, increasing the interval should increase stimulus-independent thought, but increasing the amount of information should have no effect; but if the parallel process were to hold, there should be no effect by increasing the interval, but stimulus-independent thought should decrease as the amount of information increases. Both parallel and sequential processes were evident since response probability increased as a function both of the amount of information and the duration of the time interval. In general, performance of the detection task interfered with stimulus-independent thought, and they concluded that a single, central cognitive operator is responsible for all processes of the detection response and of the stimulus-independent thought response. Comparison of auditory and visual coding showed that imagery was disturbed more in the same sensory modality. Thus there is a rather complex integration between imagery and immediate information processing. Events in long-term memory apparently initiate stimulus-independent thought, but influences also stem from the particular sensory modality, so that stimulus-independent thought operates partly parallel to perceptual processing and partly in the intervals between the sensory processing by the central operator. Similar results have been reported by Segal and Fusella (1970), but they propose that imagery, as an internal signal, is confused with the external one. Performance is impaired when the subject attends to mental imagery during a discrimination task.

IMAGINATION

Although images represent cognitive activity that responds freely to intrinsic states, imagination is not a simple matter of imagery, but may involve complex integrations of conceptual, motor, affective, and verbal components. The distinguishing condition is not so much imagery as the relatively lesser role of extrinsic forces in determining cognitive activity. Imagination is the reoccurrence or utilization of past experience, mainly independently of immediate realistic determinants in the expression of intrinsic states.

From this standpoint, imagination may serve the following general functions: (1) *enjoyment and play*, as in reliving pleasurable past experiences merely for their own sake, or in free manipulation of a present situation; (2) *interpretation and appreciation*, as in aesthetic responses or in observing others (children playing, people at a party); (3) *guidance of action*, as in anticipating future events, or considering alternative goals; (4) *constructive or creative thought*, as when an artist allows his feelings and memories free expression; (5) *anxiety*, as when states of tension evoke painful memories or feared outcomes, an upwelling of imaginative activity with a self-reinforcing quality that tends to become greater the longer it persists, as if the cognitive processes increasingly release and elaborate needs and fears that cannot be alleviated by imagery.

These functions are all normal and common, but when they become exaggerated, each encroaches on the pathological. For example, enjoyment of reliving the past may become a withdrawal from the present, an absorption in memories. A normal appreciation of the external world in one person may in another be a refusal to perceive reality except in accordance with personal wishes. Preparation for action through imaginative activity might become an inability to accept the actual event when it happens. Constructive imagination may become exaggerated into bizarre, impossible, or misshapen creations. Anxious imagination may become neurotic fears, agonizing conflicts, painful and debilitating worry.

PLAY

In childhood imaginative activity assumes the form of play.

Many theories of play have been proposed, but no one interpretation is entirely satisfactory. Klinger (1969), for example, could not formulate a positive definition, but instead offered specifications of what it is *not,* namely, consummatory behavior, behavior of an instrumental character that leads "detectably" to consummatory behavior or a goal extrinsic to the play, competition with a standard of excellence, socially prescribed or formalized or ritual activity (when such behavior occurs in the context of social sanction and enforcement), or behavior constrained by demands of social interaction. Although everyone might not agree even here, play is clearly an activity in which extrinsic rewards and future goals are absent, or at least secondary. We might add that play is autistic, rather than realistic, but it is a matter of degree, for play may be governed by rules and be responsive to situational conditions that limit the free expression of intrinsic states.

Piaget (1962) sought to bring play within the scope of his conception of intelligence, and to assign definite functions to it. Sutton-Smith (1966) has criticized this view because it places undue stress on formal and directed properties of play. Piaget (1966) has commented in response that "play manifests the peculiarity of a primacy of assimilation over accommodation which permits it to transform reality in its own manner without submitting that transformation to the criterion of objective fact." But Sutton-Smith's point nevertheless remains valid, that Piaget is unsuccessful in assigning a distinctive intellectual function to play, and ends by relying on affective and intrinsic conative factors to account for it.

Observers of children's play have documented a great range and variety of activities, including the exercise of motor skills and verbal expression, processes of familiarization with the environment (including the social environment), and adjustment processes such as relief of emotional tensions and the working out of conflict and problem situations.

Development of Play

The development of play may be viewed both from the standpoint of characteristic mental activity and fantasy, and from that of overt behavior. In the very young child, of course, it is difficult or impossible to obtain data of the former kind, and in older children they are closely interrelated. It should be remembered that successive stages merge gradually into each other, with the result that changes are continuous rather than sharply distinct from each other (Lehman and Witty, 1927; Marshall, 1931; Hartley and Goldenson, 1957).

The origins of play lie in *motor behavior* (Britt and Janus, 1941; Guanella, 1934; Hurlock 1934). Manipulative play is characteristic of the first two or three years, during which time a wide variety of motor skills are practiced and improved. At about the second year, *language* becomes important (Guanella, 1934; Markey, 1935; Hartley and Goldenson, 1957), although not all children verbalize in play (Hurlock, 1934). As growth proceeds, and play becomes more varied and elaborate, language, for those children who verbalize, also becomes more complex. Other important trends begin to emerge during the second and third years. In building with blocks, children gradually learn to *control more space* (Guanella, 1934). Their initial nonstructural, linear, and areal play leads into tridimensional and more extensive structures. *Construction*, in general, and *dramatic play* become more frequent and skillful (Hurlock, 1934; Markey, 1935).

Gradually, the *end becomes more important than the activity* itself, so that by four, children are definitely carrying out ideas in their play and dealing with complicated relations and themes (Amen, 1941; T. D. Jones, 1939; Markey, 1935). Imitation of adults also becomes increasingly more important up to the age of six and after (Hurlock, 1934). Although the period between the ages of two to five has been called "egocentric," *social* play of various kinds certainly has its origins in that period; nursery schools probably encourage earlier development of social play. Coincident with the usual point of entering school and the consequent broadening of experience, at age five or six, children become increasingly social in their play (Britt and Janus, 1941; Hurlock, 1934; Lehman and Witty, 1927; Hartley and Goldenson, 1957). Competitive and cooperative activities engage the child's interest, inaugurating experience with group membership and structure. At the later ages of childhood and during adolescence, *group* play is the most typical, carrying with it the codification of rules and a very wide variety of games (Britt and Janus, 1941; Lehman and Witty, 1927; Hartley and Goldenson, 1957). Although imaginative play involving physical activity persists into adulthood, more *sedentary* and often more solitary activities become dominant, such as gardening, reading, and the development of special hobbies.

At any age play serves a variety of functions, varying with the special characteristics and differing needs of the child (or adult). The expression and enjoyment of affective states and the practice of skills are evident, but many observers have also seen play as contributing in a more practical way to the child's development, by pointing to the implications of play activity for the resolution of emotional problems and for learning about the environment. A salient aspect is identification with and imitation of adult behavior. Greenacre (1959) has suggested that play, by the repetition of experience, is necessary in establishing the "sense of reality." As a reality-emulating and reality-testing process, play aids children in bringing their own feelings, concepts, and values into meaningful relation to the external world. Furthermore, by facilitating the harmonizing of fantasy (especially in its unconscious aspects) with reality, play serves as an avenue for creativity.

Factors Related to Play

Individual differences, which deserve more systematic attention, influence the character of play. Amen and Renison (1954) have examined the effects of anxiety. They classified the play patterns of preschool children into *manipulative, imaginative* or *fantasy*, and *constructive-creative* (involving goals or purposes, the expression of ideas, and solving of problems), with the third category regarded as the most mature. Anxiety and IQ were correlated positively with time spent in mature play ($r = .52$ and $.44$, respectively; in this study, IQ and anxiety displayed a correlation of $.77$). In addition, older children tended to display both greater anxiety and greater maturity of play.

In relation to *intelligence*, an early study found that bright children play more (longer) during the day than do duller children (Boynton and Ford, 1933). The difference lies more in mental forms of recreation than in physical activity. Other studies, using qualitative as well as quantitative measures, have found comparatively low correlations with intelligence (Andrews, 1930), or correlations very little higher with mental age than with chronological age (Markey, 1935). Within limits, it is likely that age differences are more important than intelligence differences, at least in very young children (Britt and Janus, 1941).

With respect to *sex*, marked differences are manifested in the nature of play and in the kinds of toys and games. Projective-play techniques reveal differences related to personality (Bach, 1945; Yarrow, 1948). Boys display more aggression and less "nicety" and stereotypy than do girls (Sears, 1951), probably, to a large degree, as a function of different upbringing. Activities preferred by boys in comparison with girls no doubt reflect these conditions (Britt and Janus, 1941; T. D. Jones, 1939; Lehman and Witty, 1927). In general, sex differences in play become greater with increasing chronological age, up to about eight to ten years, after which they seem to decrease (Lehman and Witty, 1927; Marshall, 1931). The stories children tell spontaneously clearly reflect sex differences (Ames, 1966). Although violent accidents are a major theme, girls employ more "protective" devices, such as attributing bad things to others or emphasizing that the episodes were not really happening. Girls mention people more than boys do, are more concerned with morality, and their stories are more realistic and closer to home. Boys mention vehicles more than girls do, are more fanciful, and deal more with far away places. Whereas boys portray the mother as more friendly than girls do, the reverse holds for the father. Where the quantity and the general quality of play have been assessed, apart from preferences and types of behavior, very slight differences, if any, are found between the sexes (Markey, 1935). However, there is some evidence that the kinds of differences found in play are manifestations of the basic sex roles that operate subsequently to childhood. Thus Vinacke and Gullickson (1964) compared triads at the ages seven to eight, twelve to fourteen, and college in a simple competitive game. As shown in Figure 13-1, behavior was similar at the youngest age, but diverged at the later ages. These data suggest that little boys have not yet learned the strategy typical of the older male. The play setting affords an opportunity for such learning to occur.

So far as *group organization* is concerned, constructiveness of play and amount of time spent in play are both greater in pairs of strong friends than in pairs of weak friends; this also holds for social in comparison with solitary play (Wright, 1942).

The kind of play also appears to vary with *socioeconomic status*. Children of relatively low socioeconomic backgrounds more

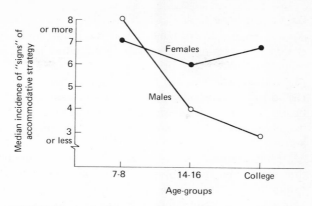

FIGURE 13–1   Incidence of accommodative strategy in triads of three age groups. (From Vinacke and Gullickson, 1964.) Explanation: *Accommodative strategy* refers to an orientation toward social relationships in a game and a concern that outcomes be as satisfactory as possible to all participants. It contrasts with *exploitative strategy*, which entails an orientation toward winning, with ruthless effort to arrive at an outcome favorable to oneself. Here accommodative strategy was assessed by the occurrence of various characteristics of the triad, including failure to form coalitions, establishing "triple alliances," equal division of the prize, low frequency of bargaining when it promotes winning, high frequency of bargaining when it is not necessary to win, and making "altruistic" offers (proposing that others ally when it is to one's disadvantage).

often engage in types of imaginative play closely connected with prosaic, everyday events; children from backgrounds of higher socioeconomic status display more fanciful imaginative activity (Markey, 1935).

Environmental conditions of many different kinds influence play, such as urban and rural conditions, climate, topography, and so on (Lehman and Witty, 1927). Jumping-rope rhymes reflect current events of the adult world (Britt and Balcom, 1941), and current wars may apparently have a strong effect on active dramatic play and in the choice of toys (Bonte and Musgrove, 1943). It is common to find the family relationships of children entering into their play activities (Despert, 1940). The effect of frustration is shown by greater constructiveness in free play than under frustrating conditions (Wright, 1942) and, by the same token, aggressive responses related to the source of frustration increase (Bach, 1945; Barker, Dombo, and Lewin, 1937; Yarrow, 1948).

Dramatic Play

An extensive study of play by Hartley, Frank, and Goldenson (1952) is rich in reporting the variety of activities typical of children. By assuming roles in group situations, the child has an "opportunity (1) to imitate adults; (2) to play out real-life roles in an intense way; (3) to reflect relationships and experiences; (4) to express pressing needs; (5) to release unacceptable impulses; (6) to reverse roles usually taken; (7) to mirror growth; and (8) to work out problems and experiment with solutions."

Anyone who has observed children can readily cite instances that exemplify these functions. In doll play and playing house, for example, the little girl adopts the role of mother and meticulously acts as she has seen her own mother act; similarly, in operating a toy car, the little boy imitates his father or some other adult. Frequently, children who have recently had emotionally important experiences reenact them in play; for example, a trip to the circus may serve as an impetus to play the parts of clowns or horse trainers, and so on. The play situation provides an opportunity to express hostility and aggression or other disapproved impulses, such as punishing the "mother doll" or attempting to force another child into a subordinate role. The reversal of usual roles may be witnessed when a passive, docile child is stimulated to become active, aggressive, and dominant. Changes in the child's situation, such as in relationships to parents, may be reflected in play. Thus a child who becomes aware of new abilities or accomplishments, such as writing, is likely to find ways to bring them directly into the play situation. The child's problems also enter into play. For instance, a child who has acquired a new sibling may focus on such relationships and employ doll play as a setting to try out different feelings toward the new baby.

Painting

The expressive function of imagination is seen in the graphic productions of children, no less than in the great works of art. Painting can vary from the extremely spontaneous, as children in effect simply "play" with paint, to quite controlled attempts to externalize themes and to convey experiences in tangible forms. It thus ranges from the primarily autistic across the continuum toward dominantly realistic activity. As we shall see in Chapter 15, creative thinking blends the autistic with the realistic, but we need not be concerned about this distinction here. For most children, certainly, painting is more like play than like serious creativity.

An intensive longitudinal study of painting was conducted by Alschuler and Hattwick (1947, 1969). The children were two-and-a-half to five-and-a-half years old, and were observed under natural conditions, 149 of them almost daily for a year, and 21 for an additional year. Besides the creative products and detailed observations made in the nursery-school environment, large masses of data were obtained on home backgrounds and behavior. The data thus assembled were analyzed both in terms of general trends for the group as a whole, and of individual case histories.

Although five media were available to the children (easel paints, crayons, clay, blocks, and dramatic play), most of the analyses were based on performance with easel paints and crayons, partly because the products could be preserved. In general, color was strongly linked with the child's emotional life, line and form with energy and its control, and space usage with the child's reactions to his environment. Some conception of the results can be gained from Table 13-1.

Striking differences appear in the personalities of those who prefer different colors in different ways. Children who preferred red were relatively free in their reactions and comparatively well adjusted. Red was also used, sometimes, to express hostile emotion by means of heavy strokes or long wide strokes. Children who preferred blue were typically controlled rather than free in their expression. In some instances, this control appeared to reflect self-restraint or repression ("blue of controlled anxiety"); in other instances, outwardly directed, adaptive behavior ("sublimation blue"). Preference for other colors was similarly associated with particular personality characteristics. Consistent choice of yellow was made by dependent, emotional children, whereas green was preferred by restrained children who showed generally good social relationships.

Of equal interest is the manner in which the colors were used. For instance, some children tended to overlay one color with another, suggesting that the child is hiding under an assumed pattern of overt behavior. The color most frequently used for overlaying was blue, which, as noted above, is associated with tendencies toward control. The children who used cold colors to overlay warm colors were more often repressed, more often played alone, initiated contacts, and displayed such signs of control as orderly work habits and an inclination to name their paintings. In contrast, children who placed colors separately on the page seemed to be directing their energies outward, to be adapting to environmental expectancies or making an effort at control. Thus they were cooperative, self-controlled and

Table 13-1
Some Personality Differences between Nursery School Children as a Group and
Those Who Use Color in Various Ways. (Adapted from Alschuler and Hattwick,
1947.)

Color Character-istics	Personality Characteristic	Group in Col. 1 %	Total Group (N=170) %	CR*	P*
Preference for red	Dependent on adults for affection	39	24	1.88	3
(N=46)	Good adult relations	74	56	2.37	1
	Good child relations	72	49	2.99	1
	Talks a great deal	65	43	2.72	1
	Good adjustment	82	64	2.65	1
Preference for blue	Plays alone	75	52	2.95	1
(N=40)	Orderly, careful work habits	60	43	1.95	3
Overlaying cold on warm colors (N=49)	Repressed	37	24	1.57	7
	Plays alone	69	52	2.07	2
	Initiates contacts	67	51	1.91	3
	Actively seeks materials	71	56	1.85	4
Overlaying in general (N=85)	Repressed	36	24	2.00	2
	Good relations with children	62	49	2.03	2
	Protects self	53	38	2.38	1
	Orderly, careful work habits	55	43	1.88	4
Kept colors separate (N=33)	Cooperative in routines	76	55	2.50	1
	Ideas for play	70	48	2.47	1
	Shows good adjustment	88	64	3.53	1
	Good relations with adults	73	56	1.98	3
	Leads through ideas	48	31	1.79	4
	Realistic orientation	48	28	2.13	2
	Purposive, planned work habits	64	41	2.47	1
	Orderly, careful work habits	64	43	2.26	1

*CR= critical ratio; P= probability, here expressing the chances in 100 that the obtained difference
between the two percentages is not a true difference.

well-adjusted, had good relations with adults, a realistic orientation, and displayed purposive, planned work habits. Intermingling characterized children who were well-adjusted, realistic, and more emotionally free than the children who overlaid or placed colors separately; indiscriminate mixing occurred primarily in very young, immature children.

The relation between characteristics of painting and personality adjustment has received further attention in a study by H. P. Smith and Appelfeld (1965). They employed judges to identify painting produced by emotionally disturbed or normal children (ages three to five), and also to match the painting with brief personality descriptions. All but one of ten judges displayed better-than-chance accuracy, with the median percent correct 63.5 and 68.5 for the two tasks, respectively.

Paintings as expressions of personality can also be studied at later ages. For example, Stewart (1955) undertook a factor analysis of variables in the self-portraits of high school students. Revealed were clusters that could be labeled as skill quality, realism, symmetry, width and variability of line, angularity, and movement. Variables of skill quality in boys were indicative of maladjustment and neurotic introversion, in girls of creativeness and adjustive introversion. Properties of lines were related in boys to dominant extraversion, in girls to sociability and adjustment. For girls, variables of movement were associated with self-assertion and striving for recognition. Realism in the paintings of boys was associated with intelligence.

Finally, DiLeo (1970) has organized a large collection of black-and-white drawings by children ranging in age from about one year to more than five years.[1] He emphasizes developmental progressions as the child moves from kinesthetic expression (scribbling) to representational and more controlled forms of expression. DiLeo is particularly adept at viewing drawings from the child's point of view. For example, he shows quite engagingly how characteristics of drawings reflect the "intellectual" realism of the child, who draws what he knows to be true, compared to the adult's "visual" realism, or portraying things as they appear to be. Thus a child will show both eyes in a profile, or draw the people in a boat as if the hull were transparent. One source of consolation to the child psychologist is DiLeo's comparison of the child of 1967 with that of 1885 drawn from a work by C. Ricci, showing that the same characteristics appear in drawings of both epochs.[2]

---

[1] See also, Kellogg and O'Dell (1967), who present the astonishing variety and beauty of children's paintings, as they progress from scribbling through forms and structures to fully developed pictures.

[2] It should also be noted that the second half of the book is devoted to mental retardation and various neurological and personality disorders.

SUMMARY

In studying imagination, we focus on processes that approach the autistic pole of cognition. As extrinsic determinants decrease (or as intrinsic ones increase) in intensity, thinking becomes more autistic. Images, which contrast with perceptions, are especially responsive to need-states, and fall into classes of afterimages, memory images, eidetic images, hypnagogic and hypnopompic images, and images of imagination. Images may be conditioned, varying with information-processing demands of the situation, and serve functions of enjoyment, interpretation of experience, guidance of action, constructive or creative thought, and expression of anxiety. Play, especially typical of childhood, displays trends of increasing control, organization toward goals, and imitation of adults. It varies as a function of anxiety, intelligence, sex, group organization, and environmental conditions. Dramatic play and painting reveal characteristics of imagination.

14

FANTASY AND DREAMS

In this chapter we shall examine those cognitive processes in which the role of external reality is sharply reduced by virtue of the special conditions under which they are produced. Projective techniques represent the psychologist's deliberate attempt to induce autistic thinking, by presenting stimuli that minimize the demands of the environment. Fantasy and dreams occur when the person's contact with reality is reduced, and exemplify most clearly in normal persons the autistic pole of the continuum. Other special conditions, such as the taking of drugs or the development of mental disorder, produce the more extreme autistic thinking that we label pathological.

PROJECTIVE TECHNIQUES

Although the many techniques employed to study the imaginative behavior of children could properly be included under the heading of *projective techniques* (especially paintings), here we shall consider the application of more standardized instruments to the investigation of autistic effects.

Rapaport (1952) formulated the basic principle behind projective techniques, as follows: "All behavior manifestations of the human being, including the least and the most significant, are revealing and expressive of his personality, by which we mean that individual principle of which he is the carrier." The aim (Frank, 1939) is to get meaningfully at the private world of the individual, "that peculiar, individual way of organizing experience and of feeling which personality implies."

The idea is to present to the subject a situation in which the subject puts himself into the situation, or externalizes himself (Bell, 1948). Much effort has been expended to find unstructured stimulus materials that, at the same time, can be systematized, easily scored, and meaningfully interpreted (Murstein and Pryer, 1959). Since it is difficult to attain all of these criteria, very few projective tests have actually achieved widespread acceptance.

The great number of projective situations proposed up to the present actually fall into a small number of categories. They may be classified by what the subject does (Frank, 1939), as: (1) *constitutive*, representing the structuring of meaningless or amorphous material, as in the Rorschach test; (2) *interpretive*, where the subject explains the meaning of material, or suggests what is going on, as in the Thematic Apperception Test (TAT); (3) *cathartic*, in which the subject expresses more or less inarticulately his emotions or impulses, as in doll play; and (4) *constructive*, in which the subject achieves some creative product, as in completing a story, or making a village in the World Test. In practice, most tests are not limited to only one of these kinds of response. The TAT, for instance, is both constitutive and interpretive. It is probable that any test may be cathartic.

Bell (1948) classified the most highly developed tests by the kind of stimulus employed, namely, verbal, visual, expressive movement, and play materials. More recently, Lindzey (1959) has differentiated eleven techniques by mode of response, stimulus attributes, manner of interpretation, purpose, method of administration, and method of construction. The fact that these techniques fall into five clusters, which are difficult to describe in any simple manner, indicates the complexity of the problem.

It is beyond the scope of this book to review the methods proposed (see Abt and Bellak, 1950; H. H. Anderson and Anderson, 1951; Murstein, 1963), but it is pertinent to suggest briefly some of the ways in which projective techniques can contribute to the study of imaginative thinking.

One fruitful line of research would be to determine interrelationships between various imaginative situations, not only to ascertain agreement between them (Munroe, Lewinson, and Waehner, 1944) but to seek a comprehensive cross section of imaginative thinking. Nor should such efforts be confined merely to projective techniques; it would be valuable to relate performance in imaginative situations to that in problem solving, in various learning situations, and in everyday life. For the most part, however, projective techniques have been used to test specific hypotheses.

Another important direction is the study of interpersonal and intergroup relations. A good example of this kind of research is afforded by Brown's (1947) extension of the Rozenweig Picture-Frustration Test to the dynamics of prejudice. There are innumerable other problems in which projective techniques may be of value—in the study of leadership, industrial relations, political behavior, and so on. For example, Sanford and Rosenstock (1952) showed that pictures can be fruitfully employed in mass surveys to assess such variables as authoritarianism and equalitarianism. A related area is the study of the relation between culture and personality, as begun in studies like those of DuBois and Oberholzer (1944) and documented by Lindzey (1961).

Still another kind of contribution lies in the application of projective techniques to investigate the influence of motives and attitudes in perception, problem solving, and other aspects of performance, for example, as in the use of TAT pictures to measure achievement motivation (McClelland et al., 1953; Atkinson, 1958). Another example appears in a series of studies, over the past 35 years, on the effects of physiological states such as hunger and thirst (R. N. Sanford, 1936; Levine, Chein, and Murphy, 1942; Gilchrist and Nesberg, 1952; Lazarus, Yousem, and Arenberg, 1953; Wispé and Drambarean, 1953; Klein, 1954; Segal, 1968). Winter (1969) has shown that nursing mothers of first babies, compared to control mothers (tested a month after the end of breast-feeding), produce TAT stories higher in oral references, positive feelings, and non-chronological treatment of time. There was no difference in the incidence of sexual themes. Not only do such experiments show that perception is influenced by autistic factors, but also that the effect depends on the relative intensity of autistic compared to realistic forces: as the former increase in strength and/or as the latter decrease in their demands, behavior is increasingly influenced by intrinsic states.

The relationship is not necessarily as direct as these studies suggest. R. A. Clark (1952), for instance, first aroused sexual motivation by presenting subjects with slides of attractive nude females, then administered TAT pictures. A control group witnessed slides of landscapes instead. Under normal conditions the experimental groups displayed *less* sexual imagery and guilt than did the controls, but under alcoholic conditions (the context of a fraternity beer party), this effect was reversed (see Figure 14-1). That repression operated under the normal conditions was demonstrated by R. A. Clark and M. R. Sensibar (1955) who found that the stories of the sexually aroused subjects under nonalcoholic conditions contained significantly more sexual symbolism than those of the controls. Further analysis disclosed a curvilinear relationship, with subjects who expressed either high-or low-manifest sex displaying a high degree of symbolism.

The projective approach can be tied to theoretical principles, nicely illustrated by the Blacky test, developed by Blum (1949). It consists of cartoons that present a dog (Blacky) in a series of familial situations, each intended to tap some psychodynamic process. For instance, cartoon VII, "Positive Identification," shows Blacky sternly shaking a finger at a little toy model of a dog.

With respect to sex differences, it is well known that psychoanalytic theory outlines a process whereby the boy comes to identify himself with his father and the girl with her mother. On questions about who Blacky is imitating, the men significantly tended to respond "Papa," whereas the women responded "Mama." It was confirmed that identification is more ambivalent in women since a greater proportion of males said that Blacky would rather pattern himself after Papa than females said that Blacky would rather pattern herself after Mama. Further, more women express hostile impulses toward the identified parent. When presented with four alternatives to the question, "What would Blacky have an impulse to do if he (she) were in the position of the toy dog?," significantly more females chose "start fighting." Psychoanalytic theory suggests that males who prefer narcissistic love objects have unresolved Oedipal conflicts and identify themselves with the mother rather than with the father. In Blum's experiment, responses to cartoon VII, indicating that males tend to identify with the father, had a significant negative correlation with expression of a narcissistic love object (cartoon XI): tetrachoric $r = -.46$, $P < .02$). A significant correlation was also obtained between positive identification in females and sibling rivalry (tetrachoric $r = .36$, $P < .05$), although psychoanalytic theory apparently does not deal directly with this relationship.

In general, results with the Blacky test gave striking confirmation of many points in psychoanalytic theory, but there continues to be

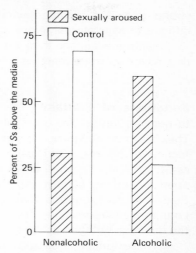

FIGURE 14–1 Manifest sexual imagery under alcoholic and nonalcoholic conditions. (Based on Clark, 1952.)

the need for experimental verification of psychoanalytic concepts. Perhaps the greatest merits of Blum's approach are the standardized procedure, the fact that apparently meaningful and objective interpretations can be made of the results, and the possibility of obtaining data from large numbers of subjects. Incidentally, it should be noted that some points of psychoanalytic theory were not confirmed (e.g., that women as well as men tend to have fatherly superegos; if, however, the possible cultural differences between American and European society are taken into account, perhaps even this result is not really counter to the theory). It is also worth mentioning that Blum's results indicate a very definite weakness in psychoanalytic theory in the realm of sex differences—a weakness not adequately remedied by psychoanalysts since Freud.

FANTASY

Fantasy signifies fairly well defined sequences of thinking in which realistic forces from the environment are secondary to autistic forces from intrinsic states. In children it is difficult to distinguish play from fantasy—if there were any reason to do so, at least in normal children; but in adults play takes the form of games, with a strong goal and reality orientation. In fact, in adults it is often difficult to separate play from problem solving.

Fantasy is autistic thinking when the person is awake, whereas dreams are autistic processes during sleep.

Functions of Fantasy

In general, fantasy for older persons is similar to play for the child. Thus we can recognize (1) *wish fulfillment,* or the vicarious satisfaction of desires, (2) *escape,* (3) *relaxation,* (4) *explanation of reality,* and (5) *preparation for realistic thinking* (as in artistic creation, reworking of past experience, and planning for the future). Singer (1966) suggests that fantasy is a cognitive skill—or even cognitive style—resulting from internalized play, varying widely in the directness of the wish and in the degree of deliberate control.

These functions suggest the conditions that promote autistic thinking. Thus the stronger the wish, together with an absence of realistic demands, the more likely it is that autistic thinking will result. Or if the environmental situation imposes constraints incompatible with intrinsic impulses, easy escape via fantasy is quite possible. In general, the more confusing, ambiguous, unreal, or unpleasant a situation, the more probable it is that autistic response will result.

Singer and Antrobus (1963) subjected data from a daydream questionnaire, various tests, and interviews, to factor analysis. Revealed were some twelve factors, including one indication of general daydreaming, and others reflecting Guilford's category of divergent thinking,[1] autistic activity involving negative affect arising from the superego, and controlled thinking. Noteworthy is the fact that daydreaming and divergent thinking were different factors, agreeing with the conception of creative thinking described in the next chapter. Further analysis also indicated a bipolar clustering, with the daydream factors opposed to controlled thinking.

Variations in Fantasy

It is easy to recognize that there is more than one degree of fantasy. It is useful to differentiate *reverie* from *daydreaming,* although there is no sharp division. Fantasy is freer and less subject to voluntary control at some times than at others. States of reverie are analogous to free association, and daydreaming to storytelling or response to

[1] See p. 364.

projective tests (without, of course, the same degree of conscious control). That is, a daydream is more likely to have a beginning, a definite structure, and a dominant theme than is the case in reverie.

Fantasy, either of the daydream or reverie variety, has certain characteristics that distinguish it from realistic thinking (H. A. Murray, 1937; Symonds, 1946). The most outstanding features are: (1) *egocentrism*, where the person himself is the hero and/or his own problems and needs occupy the central focus, although he may at times be an onlooker; (2) *anthropocentrism*, where fantasies deal with personal relationships and animals are likely to be anthropomorphized; (3) *dramatic and pictorial form*; (4) *pleasurable emotional satisfaction* (but sometimes daydreams are shocking or horrifying expressions of anxiety); (5) *exaggeration*, as in extremely aggressive, or emotionally idealized fantasy, or in imagining unlimited wealth; (6) *free manipulation of time*, where past and future may be blended, events may quickly shift from one time to another, particular moments may be greatly prolonged, and so on; (7) *privacy and secrecy*; (8) *lack of exigency*; (9) *monopolizing of attention*; (10) *reduction or even absence of contact with external stimuli*, where fantasies are hardly conscious, and the person is typically not aware that he is "fantasizing"; (11) *autonomy*, where fantasies appear and disappear without deliberate effort; and (12) *quasi-reality* where fantasy seems real.

In addition to qualitative aspects of fantasy, possible quantitative variables include "inducibility," strength of action involved or relation to action ("actional potency"), level of aspiration exhibited in the fantasy, amount of terminal satisfaction, degree of concentrated absorption, number of external incentives rejected or positive needs inhibited, endurance, frequency, accompanying emotion, and accompanying pleasure or unpleasure (Wolf and Murray, 1938).

THE STUDY OF FANTASY

Although materials about the fantasy life of individual persons are scattered extensively through clinical literature, only a few investigators have attempted to study fantasy behavior as a normal phenomenon. Except for these reports, our systematic knowledge of fantasy is closely linked with imaginative responses to projective tests. The latter have apparently diverted interest from spontaneous fantasy to the more controlled and quantifiable test situation.

Griffiths (1953) devised a technique that combined features of several procedures—observation, interview, free association, and projective testing. Five-year-old children in many successive sessions were permitted to talk and act as they pleased, with the experimenter recording everything said. At a suitable break in the conversation, one of the following test situations was introduced: free drawing, a series of irregular and asymmetrical ink blots, a request for an original story, a request for a report of the previous night's dreams, and an imagery test in which the child covered his eyes and talked about what he saw. The tests were not given in a set order, although an effort was made to obtain reactions to each one in every session. Throughout, the experimenter, in a nondirective manner, continued to question the child, endeavoring to promote spontaneity and naturalness of rapport. The experimenter adapted herself as much as possible to circumstances, and sought to draw out the subject gradually, over a long period of time. In this respect the technique borrowed from psychoanalysis. The result was that each case underwent recognizable stages of development. At first, there was a gradual lifting of inhibitions, with a consequent increase in the child's ability to reveal his fantasy and creative life. Then skill in using the "tools of expression" began to improve, and the fantasy content became clearer. Finally, the subjective content itself expanded and developed.

Griffiths concluded that fantasy has an important function in the normal emotional and intellectual development of children. The child manipulates his knowledge of the world in an effort to interpret and understand situations. Gradually, successively imagined possibilities lead to a resolution of the problem. The process of adjustment is seemingly bound up with fantasy, rather than with more objective problem-solving activities, because the child has not yet sufficient information or organized intellectual skills to deal with problems in a less subjective fashion. This study thus complements the study of play.

Jersild, Markey, and Jersild (1933) obtained data from a detailed interview that covered wishes, ambitions, best and worst happenings, likes and dislikes, daydreams, dreams, fears, and reactions to school, sex roles and so on. The subjects were four hundred children, twenty-five of each sex at each age from five to twelve years, who varied in socioeconomic status and IQ.

The daydreams included a wide range of topics (thirty different categories are listed). The younger children tended to report simpler and more direct daydreams, in contrast to the more complex and comprehensive ones of the older subjects (in this respect, daydreams resembled wishes). Emphasis in the wishes lay in a desire for specific objects or conditions, whereas daydreams more often dealt with activities and amusements. Only 8 percent of the subjects failed to report, that is, said they did not have any daydreams or gave unintelligible responses.

Adolescent Fantasy

A study by Symonds (1949) bears on the question of how closely imaginative responses to projective tests resemble spontaneous fantasy. Pictures were especially designed and drawn for use with adolescents, and stories were elicited from twenty subjects of each sex. Other data, used in interpreting the results, included associations to the completed stories, scores on other tests, and extensive case-history material.

Themes could conveniently be classified as (1) psychological, (2) environmental, or (3) stylistic. Two subcategories are listed under the stylistic heading, and a considerable number under each of the others. *Aggression* and *family relationships,* classified as psychological and environmental, respectively, occurred by far the most frequently, and were expressed by all of the forty subjects. Others that occurred in the stories of half or more of the subjects were as follows: psychological themes involving eroticism, negative emotion or depression, anxiety, altruism, success or ambition, repentance or reform, and positive emotion; and environmental themes dealing with economic matters, punishment, separation or rejection, accidents or illness or injury, school, and social relationships or gangs. The range of themes was extremely wide and included at least as many topics as, and probably more than, those displayed by the younger subjects of Jersild, Markey, and Jersild. Comparing the two sets of data as well as possible, it would appear that adolescents continue the trend previously noted—older children express more complicated themes than do younger children. In any event, the stories told by adolescents reflect to a remarkable degree problems of social adjustment and relations between the sexes, as would be expected from that stage of development.

To return now to the question raised earlier, it is well worth inquiring to what degree stories told in response to pictures accurately represent the real, everyday fantasy life of adolescents. We could follow down the list of characteristics presented above and suggest possible points of difference. For example, we would expect that stories would be more organized and coherent than spontaneous fantasy, that they would be more subject to the demands of reality, and that the highly personalized, "private" nature of fantasy would be greatly disguised in a story reported to another person (especially an adult semistranger in a rather formalized situation). Whatever the possible value of the stories in personality study, much remains to be learned about their reflection of true-life thought processes.[1] S. B. Sarason (1944) has submitted data purporting to show the similarity between dreams and TAT stories. The two kinds of reports undoubtedly supplement each other, but we require further evidence, and a more convincing analysis.

Adult Daydreams

What is the role of fantasy in adult life? It may be supposed that daydreams are fairly common, and that their characteristics and functions are essentially the same as those advanced for children's fantasy.

Singer and McCraven (1961) have developed a daydream questionnaire using categories derived from the clinical literature. They also solicited actual daydreams, night dreams, and original stories. Daydreams were reported almost universally (96 percent said that they occurred daily), and chiefly when the person was alone. They typically contain clear images of people, objects, or events, and visual forms were common. A frequent theme was planning for the future, especially events of an interpersonal character. Common themes were immediate practical concerns, including sex, altruistic feelings, and unusual good fortune. Like hypnagogic imagery—perhaps not sufficiently differentiated—daydreams were said to occur frequently before sleeping, and least often in the morning, during meals, or during sexual activity.[2]

An examination of various background factors disclosed that daydreaming has a peak frequency during the period of eighteen to twenty-nine years, and declines with age thereafter. Subjects raised in large cities daydream most, those in the suburbs least. Blacks and

---

[1] It might not be too farfetched an analogy to liken the story to the manifest content of dreams and the spontaneous fantasy to the latent content; unfortunately, it is quite possible that the latter is itself a stage removed from the true latent content. To carry the matter one step farther, it would be interesting to know whether spontaneous fantasy may not be less disguised than dreams. Perhaps the fact that fantasy occurs in a waking state, in which the contrast between autistic and realistic thinking is more readily established, permits freer thought processes. That is, the potential reversion to reality acts as a set (a controlling mechanism) as if in the ego there were a sign reading, "Go ahead, imagine anything you wish, it's only fantasy." In any case, there is a really important question here.

[2] Under these circumstances, no doubt, the vicarious satisfaction of daydreaming is not needed.

Jews reported the most daydreaming, Anglo-Saxons the least. Employing the same questionnaire, Wagman (1967) has further reported that the daydreams of males are more assertive, sexual, heroic, and self-aggrandizing; those of females are more passive, affiliative, narcissistic, oral, and concerned with physical attractiveness. The daydreams of females more often deal with practical matters and with planning for the future.

Singer and McCraven also report a significant correlation between frequency of daydreaming and creativity. Relations with parents proved to be important for both sexes. In particular, perceived similarity to the mother figure was associated with the creativeness of daydreams.

Operating on the hypothesis that daydreaming reflects a cognitive style, Singer and Schonbar (1961) administered a varied battery of tests to adult women. A distinctive cluster of relationships emerged, showing that daydreaming, achievement motivation, anxiety, relatively greater identification with the mother rather than with the father, and creativity of spontaneous daydream and story material are positively related; repression and the Minnesota Multiphasic Personality Inventory (MMPI) lie scale displayed generally negative correlations with these variables. These results suggest that "high and low daydreamers differ along a dimension which might be termed self-awareness, or acceptance of inner experience."

DREAMS

The resurgence of interest in autistic processes is strikingly apparent in the enormous body of current research on dreaming. The discovery of appropriate physiological techniques is a major reason for this outburst. Even without this development, dreams would increasingly have become a respectable psychological topic, as one facet of the turn toward cognitive processes. The study of dreaming, like other distinctively human phenomena, received impetus from humanistic psychology (Krippner and Hughes, 1970).

Freud's brilliant treatise *The Interpretation of Dreams* (1938) remains the central focus for theoretical analysis of dreaming, although research is beginning to broaden our conception of its functions. In general, systematic experimental research has not so much invalidated Freud's views as extended and somewhat revised them. The earlier evidence was surveyed by R. R. Sears (1943), and we shall look at some of the recent research below.

Freudian Theory

The major function of dreaming, according to Freud, is to protect the sleeper from awaking in response to disturbing stimuli (whether intrinsic or extrinsic): dreams are adjustive in the positive sense of providing a mechanism whereby potentially harmful or destructive impulses can be safely expressed.

A dream represents the fulfillment of a wish expressed in *disguised form,* and various *mechanisms* are utilized by the ego to bring about this disguise by censoring direct expression and adopting acceptable modes of expression.

In ordinary language, a "wish" is simply an intrinsic impulse, which Freud considered to arise from libidinal or instinctive sources. However, the concept of wish can be treated more generally to signify that a dream is motivated (R. R. Sears, 1943) rather than invariably having the kind of psychodynamic character most intriguing to the psychoanalyst: it is a cognitive process during sleep influenced primarily by autistic forces.

Freud recognized that dreams may be determined by (1) the effect of recent experiences, notably of the preceding day, which may persist into sleep and arouse dreams (e.g., an airplane may figure prominently in a dream after a trip by air); (2) memories of infantile experiences (e.g., a person may dream of a parent who died during his childhood); as Freud himself admits, this second source is very difficult to prove—even when childhood events are discovered in dreams, the specific stimulus could just as well be the trace of some recent experience; (3) somatic states, not only sexual, but also bodily needs such as thirst or hunger, or discomforts induced by an external stimulus (e.g., one may dream of food, or of traveling to the north pole, and, on awaking, find that he is hungry, or that the temperature changed during the night). The point is that something arouses the dream, which, in turn, represents a way of dealing with the stimulating conditions.

Dreams usually have two aspects, the *manifest content* and the *latent content.* Instances when there may be little difference between them are simple wish-fulfillment dreams in children and dreams that more or less directly satisfy physical needs. For the most part, however, the latent content consists of impulses, emotions, or desires that cannot be expressed or satisfied directly because they are unacceptable to the dreamer—they are dangerous, immoral, shameful, and so on. The latent wish, in short, is subject to repression by the ego, as a result of which it is permitted to achieve cognitive expression only after it has been disguised or distorted into acceptable form. Unacceptable impulses, seeking outlet from the reservoir of the unconscious id (a possibility that can never actually be proved directly) may affect dreaming, or an incidental stimulus, such as the perseveration of an experience from the preceding day or an external stimulus during sleep, may set off a series of associations involving unacceptable impulses. However aroused, impulses do not usually appear directly in the dream, but rather in the disguised form of the manifest content.

One must always infer the nature of the latent content, no matter how convincing the evidence. In attempting to uncover it, one hazard is that analysis of the manifest content may lead almost anywhere without the necessity for assuming a prior connection; that is, the elements of the manifest content can be associated with any impulse, idea, or problem of concern to the subject. Therefore the criterion of whether the latent content has really been discovered can only be, in the last analysis, whether or not it is convincing to either the analyst or the subject, or both.

Freud made his most distinctive contribution in analyzing the disguising processes since the bizarre, and often incomprehensible, nature of dreams has always been a puzzle. The explanation lies in the *dream-work,* which transforms the latent content into the manifest content.[1]

This conversion is accomplished by several mechanisms. By *condensation* the dream is "overdetermined" because elements of the latent content may be omitted or similar elements fused (e.g., to dream of one's boss, who has the face of one's brother). By *displacement* emphasis on ideas or emotion may be shifted by substituting another idea for the really significant one or an indifferent element may assume central importance (e.g., a married man dreams of a girl with a very pretty dog, which is stressed). By *symbolization* acceptable, associatively related objects are substituted for tabooed or censored objects (e.g., the male genital organ appears as a tool, sword, or faucet; a queen as a symbol for mother). By *regressive representation* ideas, feelings and modes of expression characteristic of earlier sense impressions (e.g., pictorial form, unconstrained time relationships, appearance of past events such as dreaming of being a child, and personification of animals and objects) are adopted. By *dramatization* the dream is expressed in imagery and rapid, episodic sequences rather than coherent

---

[1] Even experimental work on dreams oriented toward disproof of some aspects of Freudian theory agrees that the dream, as the individual is aware of it, transforms the condition that instigates the dream into a story of some kind, or a sequence of images, the content of which is not simply a direct statement of the stimulus.

logical form. By *secondary elaboration* the ego increasingly converts dream elements into comprehensible form, most evident when, after waking, a person reports his dream to another, tending to produce a story in which gaps are filled, relationships are made more realistic, "meaningless" components are dropped out, and so on (e.g., a fearful animal may be described as a lion, a glittering, gold, writhing object may become a snake, and so on).

Other Theoretical Views

In general, positions subsequent to Freud are not in fundamental disagreement, but rather complement and extend his theory. Some theories emphasize the role of current conflicts or problems rather than unconscious libidinal impulses, allowing for a larger role of realistic factors (Adler, 1958). Evidence provided by McReynolds, Landes, and Acker (1966) shows a tendency for the dream content to reflect material about which the dreamer is concerned, but they also report a tendency for dreams *not* to contain elements about personal matters incongruent with each other. Neither finding is incompatible with the Freudian view.

Several theories of dreaming reflect a more directly cognitive emphasis. Hall (1953a, b,1954), for example, has criticized Freud's theory as relying on too complex a conception of sleeping cognition. In particular, he sees no reason to suppose that symbolization is necessarily so disguising and subtle a matter. After examining long sequences of dreams, he concluded that pictorial representation is simply the most natural form of expression in the absence of the demands imposed by external reality. Instead of complex processes of logical ordering and conceptualizing, dreams call on simpler and freer cognitive processes. In fact, dream symbols can be regarded more as associations than as distortions of ideas; the underlying principle is not so much disguise as convenient expression. In this sense, any symbol is as good as any other—it merely happens that one rather than another occurs. Suppose the basic concept is "male sex organ." A host of potential associations are available that cluster together in memory, like those related by the idea of penetration (sword), by the idea of releasing fluids (faucet), or by the idea of instruments or tools (screwdriver). It really does not matter which object emerges as the symbol. Indeed, penis could be the expression of the idea, as well as some other exemplar. Hall and Van de Castle (1966a), in fact, present long lists of symbols that appear in dreams, and among them are the sexual or aggressive objects that supposedly are subject to disguise.

T. M. French (1954) has also proposed that dreams are simpler than Freud implied. He suggested that they have their own kind of logical organization, although considerable analysis may be required to clarify it; since a dream may have many different meanings, a sequence of dreams may be required to discover the proper interpretation. As a problem solving process, the dream originates in a conflict, and a given dream reflects efforts to solve it. Each dream may represent some way of working out of the conflict, so that the underlying organization can best be reconstructed by tracing out the whole dream sequence. More recently, a similar view invokes information-processing principles. Dreaming might be treated as the arousal of informational activity during sleep, followed by processes of assimilating and organizing "solutions" available in existing memorial systems (Breger, 1967).

Research on rapid eye-movement sleep (REMS), during which dreaming primarily occurs, compared with nonrapid eye-movement sleep (NREMS), further yields suggestions about the function of dreams. Ephron and Carrington (1966) have developed carefully the argument that REMS constitutes an important period in a homeostatic process acting to maintain cortical "tonus" by increased intrinsic stimulation (or *afferentation*), complementary to extrinsic stimulation during waking. When NREMS occurs, there is a recession (or deprivation) of cortical activity, and some mechanism is required to restore the brain to an effective functioning condition. REMS may counteract the *deafferentation* of NREMS, and reinvigorate the cortex. Dreaming is then essentially the counterpart of waking perception and thought: It is the patterned cognition of the sleeping brain that accompanies the increased sensory input of the REMS period. Dreaming is thus a normal, physiologically regulated process that fulfills essential neurological functions.

Just how mutually incompatible these views may be cannot at present be accurately assessed (Foulkes, 1964). On the whole, they do not seem to be in real conflict. Thus the theories of Hall and French do not necessarily run counter to Freudian theory since they also allow for the significance of dreaming as the expression of strong intrinsic impulses. They do discount the disguising function of symbolization, at least in many dreams if not in all, and appear to provide a more valid interpretation of cognition during sleep. However, these theories do not really oppose the view that *some* dreams—and perhaps the most significant ones psychodynamically —acquire their properties by virtue of cognitive structures corresponding to the notion of ego mechanisms (i.e., that even imagery is subject to selective and organizing systems).

Physiological interpretations also seem to broaden rather than vitiate the Freudian view. They are compatible with the principle that dreaming occurs to protect and maintain sleep. That dreaming is normal rather than "symptomatic," in the Freudian sense, of repressed impulses is not opposed to the principle that the properties of dreams are determined by intrinsic states present in the dreamer. Therefore interpretation of particular dreams (or sequences of dreams) still has the diagnostic significance that Freud attributed to it. Indeed, the activation of REMS may be just as essential to maintain the brain's control of affective states as it is to maintain its cognitive tonus.

At present then, the Freudian theory is undergoing revision and extension. Comparatively little of it has been disproven—and much has been supported—but clearly it was too narrow in its emphasis and linked dreaming too exclusively with unconscious, repressed impulses. Post-Freudian studies have shown that dreaming is a normal cognitive process, a response to autistic states relatively free from realistic determinants.

The Empirical Study of Dreams

Historically, various attempts have been made to study dreaming in a systematic fashion (R. R. Sears, 1943; White, 1944), mostly with direct or implicit derivation from Freudian theory. For example, Cubberly (1923) investigated the effects of extrinsic stimuli during sleep. He induced "tensions" by sticking small pieces of gummed paper to various parts of the body. The opposite effect was obtained by rubbing a relaxing substance, such as oil, over a small area. He found that dreams invariably resulted, of which only 5 percent could not be remembered. The dreams, although varied, showed a distinct relation to the induced "tension" or "detension." For instance, a "tensor" on the leg might result in dreams of walking, of lameness, of a threatened kick from a horse, and so on. Later studies, using the REMS technique described below, have confirmed the effect of external stimuli, although indicating that extrinsic stimulation is not usually important in dreams (Dement and Wolpert, 1958).

Analysis of Dream Reports Numerous efforts to confirm Freudian theory have used first-hand reports of naturally occurring dreams. Schonbar (1961) had forty-five graduate students submit on each of 28 days a report of their dreams during the preceding 24 hours. They were divided at the median of frequency of dreams recalled to constitute high and low groups (the latter inferred to utilize repression to a greater degree). The subjects indicated whether each dream occurred while falling asleep, just before normal wakening, or whether it awakened them during the night. Judges were used to assign each dream to pleasant or unpleasant categories, and, in turn, the latter were rated as anxious or non-anxious. Both groups recalled dreams followed by continued sleep about as well as those that awakened them, indicating that dreams are not necessarily a transition to waking. Dreams that awakened the subject were featured by greater anxiety and less pleasant effect than other dreams. In line with psychoanalytic theory, subjects high in recall more often reported dreams with emotional and unpleasant overtones, and those low in recall remembered more dreams just prior to waking.

The occurrence of strangers in dreams was examined by Hall (1963) as a test of the Oedipal theory. Supported were the hypotheses that more strangers were male than female, that male dreams contain a higher proportion of male strangers and a higher proportion of aggressive encounters involving a male stranger than a female stranger or familiar figure of either sex. Marginally supported was a greater number of associations to male strangers indicative of the father and male authority figures. In another study, the dreams of male college students were found to contain more evidence of castration anxiety than those of females, whose dreams displayed a higher incidence of castration wish and penis envy (Hall and Van de Castle, 1965).

REMS   The study of dreaming has dramatically been advanced by the discovery of techniques to ascertain when during actual sleep a subject is dreaming (Aserinsky and Kleitman, 1955; Dement, 1955; Dement and Kleitman, 1957; Foulkes, 1966; Kleitman, 1963; Murray, 1965). Two kinds of eye movements were discerned, slow and rapid, with dreams found to occur typically during the rapid eye-movement (REM) periods. Experimentally, sleep is monitored by following electroencephalograph (EEG) recordings, and eye movements are observed by recording electrical changes in the eye muscles. The incidence and character of dreaming is obtained by periodic waking of the subject and asking for reports about cognitive activity. Dreams are reported from some 60 to 90 percent of awakenings during REM periods, but from only 0 to 10 percent NREM periods.

Surveys of the entire sleeping period reveal a cylic variation in the physiological state, accompanied by cognitive changes. The cycle, defined by the characteristics of the EEG (and also by changes in bodily motility, heart rate, and respiration rate), begins with presleeping and drowsy states. During this phase, alpha waves indicative of arousal may occur, accompanied by REMs and reports of imagery.[1] This state passes into a slow eye-movement phase, followed by sleep ("descending" stage 1), with NREM and a changed EEG pattern. Stages 2, 3, and 4 ensue, each with NREM and characteristic EEG features. At least brief transitions from stage 4 to stage 3 to stage 2 occur, leading to stage 1 again. This is the typical dreaming phase, with at least some return of alpha waves and the onset of REM ("ascending" or aroused stage 1). This point in the cycle marks a period of deep sleep and, if awakened, the subject is likely to report dreaming. Although there is some variation in these phases, and also the omission of one or more stages in later cycles, the general sequence just described is repeated throughout the period of sleeping, each lasting perhaps 90 to 100 minutes. The REM periods last from a few to 50 minutes, being shorter early in sleep and longer as sleep continues.

By awakening the subject at the onset of REMs, Dement (1960) studied the effects of dream deprivation over several nights. The subjects had to be awakened increasingly often as the experiment continued, and they displayed increasing irritability, anxiety, and other indicators of emotional disturbance. When they were allowed to sleep without interruption, these subjects manifested marked increases in dreaming, compared to control subjects. On this basis there seems to be a "need for dreaming."[2]

By awakenings during REM and NREM phases, R. D. Cartwright and Monroe (1968) found that deprivation of REM states tended to increase dreaming in other sleep phases (or to increase waking fantasy, suggesting that a certain amount of autistic activity is necessary).

NREM versus REM Cognition   Evidence has accumulated—as would follow from our conception of the autistic-realistic continuum —that at least some cognition occurs in all stages of sleeping, as

[1] Perhaps corresponding to hypnagogic images or active reminiscing. There is, however, probably no exact relation between eye movements and visual imagery in dreams (Koulack, 1972). That is, eye movements do not necessarily correspond to the content, and, indeed, visual imagery is not the only component of dreams.

[2] However, there is some question whether the deprivation condition primarily pertained to dreaming itself, or to the stage of deep sleep, which may have an important physiological function apart from or in addition to dreaming (see Foulkes, 1966, pp. 206–207).

well as in waking. Subjects do, in fact, report mental activity at all stages (Foulkes, 1962), but with important differences between REM and NREM cognition. Recall of content for the former is better, with stronger affective, visual, and muscular characteristics, more elaboration, and less correspondence to the cognitions of waking stages. NREM processes are more like thoughts than dreams, are more frequent with gradual rather than abrupt awakening, decrease in frequency with the time spent in stages 2, 3, or 4, and are fewer if the subject enters the NREM period from a waking state without an intervening REM period (Goodenough et al., 1965;— see Table 14-1). Within REM periods more active eye movement is associated with a higher incidence of active dreams (Berger and Oswald, 1962).

Other Characteristics After pointing to studies that found a very low occurrence of color, Kahn, et al. (1962) suggested that spontaneous reports were not dependable. Accordingly, questions about the dream to elicit further information revealed that 70 percent of the dreams contained color, 25 percent reported spontaneously, the remainder after questioning (82 percent of the subjects reported at least one colored dream). Additional dreams were reported as vaguely colored, and only 17 percent were reported as not colored.[1] These results suggest that color is often present, although not a prominent characteristic. Probably the person who reports dreams is usually more concerned with objects and events than with sensory characteristics.

Home versus Laboratory Dreams By means of the REM technique, giant strides have been made in the systematic, controlled investigation of dreams (Tart, 1965). But it is important to inquire whether dreams produced under laboratory conditions are comparable to those reported under natural conditions. In particular, induced dreams may not adequately reflect the psychodynamic processes central to the Freudian theory.[2]

[1] That secondary elaboration was partly responsible for reporting color is indicated by a special check on the effects of the experimenter's interest in color. Color was spontaneously reported for 16 percent of the dreams. This difference, however, is not significantly different from the 25 percent mentioned above, when subjects may have been primed for color.

[2] Under either condition, interpretation depends on a report obtained *after* the dream occurred, and thus the careful use of inference is required. The role of suggestion is clearly a more serious problem in the laboratory. For example, as in the Cubberly study mentioned earlier, it is uncertain whether the extrinsic stimulus applied before dreaming is responsible for the effect, or whether the experimenter's perceived intention is the significant variable.

Table 14-1

Reported Characteristics of Cognition after REM and NREM Periods. (From Goodenough, Lewis, Shapiro, Jaret, and Sleser, 1965.)

	REM	NREM
	Stage 1	Stages 2. 3, 4
Content		
A. Total (%)	84	45
B. Dreaming (%)	76	21
C. Thinking (%)	08	24
No Content		
D. Asleep (%)	12	36
E. Awake (%)	04	19
F. Word count (mean)	115	34
G. Bizarreness (mean)	0.35	0.11
H. Activity (mean)	0.46	0.23
I. Self-representation (mean)	0.73	0.40
J. Visual imagery (mean)	0.64	0.27
K. Laboratory reference (mean)	0.16	0.26

Note: G through K are based on rating scales. All differences are significant at the 5 percent level or better, except for K.

Hall and Van de Castle (1966b) found that home dreams display more aggression, sexual interaction, misfortune, castration anxiety, and other dynamic properties. Domhoff (1967) has observed that the laboratory subject seems to employ "psychological vigilance" rather than mechanisms of selective recall. He suggests that home dreams are more valuable for an understanding of unconscious fantasies and symbolism.

Personality Variables   A number of investigators show that, however normal it may be, the incidence and character of dreams varies from one person to another (and such findings would follow from Freudian theory).

A seven-point scale to measure primary-process characteristics of dream reports has been developed by Auld, Goldenberg, and Weiss (1968) (ratings range from logical and matter-of-fact content through increasing degrees of unusual, shifting, illogical, etc. components to dreams that are "extremely bizarre, uncanny, and autistic"). The scale has a high degree of reliability (the correlation between two raters was .876). The tendency to reveal primary-process characteristics is quite stable (at least over a 3-week period). In accordance with Freudian theory, a high degree of primary process is correlated with longer dreams, supporting the principle that the censoring mechanism eliminates primary-process elements from the manifest content (and thus a short dream—or no dream at all—would result). In addition, dreams from the same night are more closely alike in primary process than dreams from different nights.

Eiduson (1959) found a significant relationship between flexibility and rigidity, as derived from Rorschach criteria and criteria considered to reflect this characteristic in dreams. This "cognitive style" was also found in ratings of overt behavior.

Another approach is represented by comparing persons who report many dreams with those who report few or no dreams. Goodenough et al. (1959) confirmed the fact that REMs occurred periodically for all their subjects, but some subjects did not recall their dreams. Significant differences in the EEG patterns appeared. Subjects low in recall more often displayed alpha bursts during the REM periods.[1] Since periodic awakenings limit our knowledge of spontaneous dreams, Antrobus, Dement, and Fisher (1964) administered a dream questionnaire after uninterrupted sleep, distinguishing "recallers" (frequent dreams reported) from those who reported fewer than one dream per month. In a laboratory study recallers reported dreams nearly as frequently as they had claimed before (although 15 percent now fell into the nonrecalling category), whereas the nonrecallers now dreamed much more than they had claimed (45 percent fell into the recalling category). There was no difference in the time spent sleeping in the laboratory, nor in the number of REM periods, although those of recallers were longer. Contrary to expectation, the REM rate was greater in the nonrecallers, leading to the view that more frequent eye movements may be "visual avoidance responses." The investigators suggest that "perhaps nonrecallers try to avoid 'seeing' what is in their dreams by rapidly shifting their gaze, much as they avoid recalling their dreams later."[2]

Other studies are suggestive, if not definitive. Lachmann, Lapkin, and Handelman (1962) found that high dream recall is associated

[1] Not confirmed in a later study (H. B. Lewis et al., 1966).
[2] This hypothesis does not imply that eye movements correspond to the content of a dream (such as the direction of an action), but only that they reflect avoidance of directly accepting the content.

with "sharpening," as measured by the "schematizing" test (Gardner et al., 1959) (but the prediction that low dream recall was not related to "leveling" was not confirmed). Thus, as intimated above, high recall is a function of low repression, but nonrecallers are not easily characterized in the opposite fashion. Pivik and Foulkes (1966) compared "repressers" and "sensitizers," identified by Byrne's (1961) special MMPI scale under deprivation and nondeprivation conditions (of REM). Dream content from a point late in the sleep period was rated for intensity of fantasylike qualities. The repressers exhibited an intensification of dreaming under the deprivation condition, whereas the sensitizers did not (see Figure 14-2).

EXTREME FORMS OF THOUGHT

The bizarre and disturbed forms of cognition that occur under unusual conditions (see Tart, 1969) shall not be described in detail although the total scope of autistic phenomena shall be indicated. In such instances thought either becomes freed from the constraints of reality or from controls imposed by properties of cognitive structure, or both. Thought then displays characteristics of exaggerated tendencies that appear only as mild and "correctable" deviations under normal conditions. Instead of fluctuating and inefficient attention to environmental objects, a person may display a strong and enduring failure to pay attention to them at all. Instead of "errors" of perception, there may be extreme distortions. Rather than expressing or symbolizing intrinsic states, images may become so strong and engrossing as to be actually mistaken for reality. Whereas thinking is usually governed by some degree of "logic" that yields organized and orderly sequences of ideas (even though often inefficient or confused), in pathological states thinking may be so disorganized as to defy a rational interpretation.

Quasi-Pathological Thinking   Here are grouped those instances when autistic factors seriously interfere with orientation to reality, without necessarily reflecting a sharp break. Anxious states illustrate this point. At times worries and fears may induce images or memories that tend to dominate cognition, with ensuing disturbances in attention, orderly control of thoughts, or realistic coping with tasks. Additional examples include states of fatigue, frustration, competition, and other conditions when special relationships to the environment render intrinsic forces temporarily dominant. In addition, altered

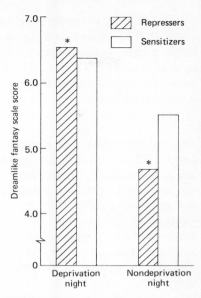

FIGURE 14-2 The effects of "dream deprivation" on the content of dreams. (Based on Pivik and Foulkes, 1966.) Deprivation produced more intense dreams in both groups, but this effect was significant only for the repressers.

physiological states induced by disease may promote cognitive disturbances. Headaches, fevers, intestinal illness, colds, and so on, may interfere with attention to the environment, augment the role of imagery in thought, or in other ways reduce the efficiency of cognition. There is an indefinable border between temporary or mild cognitive distortions and those disruptions that merit the label "pathological."

Drugs Of special current interest are the "altered states" of consciousness induced by a wide variety of drugs (Cole, 1961). Although effects vary in different individuals, some drugs (like tranquilizers) reduce levels of arousal and anxiety and attenuate attention (although sometimes having a stimulating effect), and others (like amphetamine) are stimulants that increase activity, wakefulness, and the rate of cognitive processes. Still others are "psychomimetic" (e.g., LSD) and allegedly "expand the mind." They may induce very vivid and protracted fantasy or greatly augment the intensity of sensory experiences. Alcohol may also be considered a drug, acting as a depressant to decrease the usual realistic controls over cognition, with ensuing disturbances in attention and logical thinking, often accompanied by an increase in imagery and autistic expression.

Mental Disorder   Finally, any text on abnormal psychology (e.g., Landis, 1964) may be consulted for descriptions of cognitive disturbances associated with psychotic states. These phenomena reflect on the one hand severe disorientation to reality and on the other hand the dominance of autistic forces. Among them are hallucinations (images or sequences of images, especially visual or auditory, that are treated as if they were actual perceptions induced from extrinsic sources), delusions (complex systems of ideas or beliefs that control thought regardless of available information), phobias (irrational, dominating fears), amnesia, and bizarre or distorted concepts.

SUMMARY
Projective techniques, fantasy, and dreams strongly exemplify the autistic pole of cognition. Projective devices may be used to study motivational and psychodynamic characteristics and their influence on thinking. Fantasy, varying from vaguer, freer states to more organized forms, serves functions of wish fulfillment, escape, relaxation, and coping with reality. It has qualitative and quantitative properties. Daydreaming reaches a peak in postadolescence, and varies with environmental conditions as well as circumstances in a person's life. People who daydream frequently are high in self-awareness and acceptance of inner experience. The Freudian theory of dreams is based on principles of wish fulfillment and ego defense, distinguishes between latent and manifest content, and invokes the operation of mechanisms of disguise. Other theories stress the role of current conflicts, associational processes, and maintenance of cortical tonus. Empirical approaches use dream reports and physiological indexes. Important contributions stem from the study of the sleep cycle, in which REMS is indicative of dreams. Individual differences in dreaming are associated with primary-process characteristics, cognitive style, and ego-defensive mechanisms. Extreme forms of autistic thinking occur in quasi-pathological states, drug-induced states, and mental disorder.

15

CREATIVE THINKING

Often linked with imagination is creative thought. Stirring wonder and speculation, this activity appears marvelous and mysterious— yielding products in the arts and in science wonderful in their construction, meaning, perfection, and emotional or intellectual power. The creator, as well as the observer, has been fascinated with the question of what mental processes could have led to something so remarkable. These processes appear to be quite different from everyday thought, which does not produce such results.

In company with other difficult psychological problems, creativity is becoming steadily more amenable to systematic empirical investigation. More attention has been devoted to the special characteristics of creative persons than to their cognitive processes, so that we know more about the former than the latter. We shall regard these issues as different problems: The highly creative person may differ in personality from the noncreative person without necessarily engaging in different processes of thinking, or, conversely, the secret of creativity might lie in the cognitive events that produce the final product. More likely, creativity is a function both of special personal characteristics and of certain modes of thinking. At the outset we must recognize that no simple picture will emerge.

DEFINING CREATIVITY

Efforts to define and measure creativity focus on *originality*, or the production of rare or unusual outcomes in the form of ideas or actual objects. Although in a strict sense we might insist on the uniqueness of the outcome, in practice originality signifies some point along a potential continuum of frequency of response, thus meaning rare rather than absolutely unique. The truly new or unique, which might accord better with conceptions of creative art or the greatest advances in science, is not discontinuous with the relatively new or unusual, but simply represents an extreme occurrence. If, in fact, the greatest original works *are* discontinuous, then they constitute special cases that must be treated differently from the general psychological problem of creativity. We recognize the significance of these occurrences, but they lie beyond the scope of this discussion, except by implication.

Still, originality by itself is an insufficient mark of creativity. Otherwise, any novel or even random response would be considered creative. (This possibility cannot invariably be discounted.) Instead, we must invoke the additional criterion of *appropriateness*[1]—a term I shall purposely leave ambiguous. I mean that the product must somehow satisfy the conditions of the situation and also the creator, including one or more of the following: have impact on others, realize the creator's intention, have value, or otherwise be perceived as qualitatively significant and important. Part of the ambiguity in this criterion lies in the fact that appropriateness may only be judged at a time subsequent to the outcome, when a perspective can be attained that is larger than the immediate circumstances provide. Again, in practice, the investigator would be obliged to employ some reasonable standard, such as the judgments of hopefully qualified experts.

The criterion problem is perhaps the most difficult one to solve in the study of creativity. Its importance is apparent in the work of Dreher (1968), for example, who indicates that authentic works of art produce reactions significantly different from reproductions or imitations. Such matters remain to be fully clarified. An overemphasis on originality, to the exclusion of qualitative variables, can yield a distorted view of creativity.

The Creative Situation

Within my framework, creative thinking lies between the extremes previously outlined as autistic and realistic. Creative thinking is the

[1] See also, Jackson and Messick (1965).

intimate interweaving of intrinsic activities and demands imposed by external conditions, with characteristics both of problem solving and of fantasy. It is a kind of problem solving without a predetermined or "correct" solution and with self-expression or externalization as its dominant feature. It resembles fantasy by calling on the free reorganization of past experience and by being continuously influenced by inner need-states. Yet it differs from fantasy because it is under greater voluntary control (at least during much of its course), and because it aims at externalization and eventually some tangible final product that, unlike a typical problem solution, is new or satisfying rather than "correct" in an objective sense.

These general characteristics do not have a fixed pattern but range from a stronger role of autistic forces to the salience of realistic conditions. Sometimes creative activity is less subject to voluntary control than at others. At times it may have almost a simple problem solving character, at others it may have almost the properties of a fantasy (or dream) seemingly reproduced by the creator. Fairbairn (1938) and others have viewed art as "restitutitive," comparable to the dream-work. According to my view, however, this process is only one aspect of creativity, and is too limited a conception.

Consider the creative situation more carefully. It may arise from an external stimulus. For example, an artist may be commissioned to paint a mural or a composer to write a cantata. Creative situations also frequently arise from the creator's exposure to environmental conditions that induce (or inspire) creative activity. In contrast, an internal state may touch off the process. A dream may suggest images to a poet, or an emotional state may instigate a painter to begin a painting. Regardless of its origin, however, a creative situation entails an effort to convert feelings, images, and ideas into a tangible product.

Beyond particular creative events, the creative situation may be regarded as a continuous state of the creator in a certain field (Murphy, 1947). The person whose aim in life it is to create, whether painter, composer, inventor, writer, poet, or scientist, is not striving simply to express an immediate state, but also to fulfill a lifework. Thus the instigating factor is a continuing need for self-expression, or self-realization, although a specific stimulus may be required to channel the person's efforts in some particular direction. For a full understanding of creativity therefore, we need to distinguish between that sequence of events associated with the evolution of a particular product and the successive stages in the developmental history of a creator, of which a given creative situation is but a momentary part.

PROCESSES OF CREATIVE THINKING

In the traditional view, creative thinking consists of a series of distinct phases. Impetus for this conception came from introspective reports by Helmholtz (1896) and Poincaré (1913) who described their own thought processes while pursuing the answer to an original problem. Helmholtz specified a period of initial investigation of the problem until further progress was impossible, then, following a period of rest and recovery, a possible solution would occur to him in an apparently sudden and unexpected manner. To this sequence of events Poincaré added the requirement of a second period of conscious work, consequent to inspiration or illumination. Both scientists emphasized the role of unconscious activity, especially in the second period prior to the illumination. Many later writers have also stressed this side of the total process.

Wallas (1926) labeled these aspects of creative thinking *preparation, incubation, illumination*, and *verification*, terms still used today. Some early experimental studies have employed this formulation as a point of departure. Dewey (1933) described reflective thinking as a process that originates in a disturbance of some sort—perplexity, doubt, or, simply, the occurrence of a need or problem, followed by a period of searching, from which the problem emerges more definitely. Then successive hypotheses or suggestions are used to assemble pertinent material. In the next period (reasoning) elaboration of a possible solution occurs, and finally it is tested either by overt or imaginative action. Dewey's scheme, to be sure, is more that of the disciplined thinker, or reasoner, than that of the creative thinker, as ordinarily conceived, but his stages are similar to those identified in other fields.

These stages were tested by Patrick (1935, 1937, 1938) in a laboratory situation. She successively investigated the writing of a poem, the painting of a picture, and the solution of a scientific problem. In the last experiment no attempt was made to include professional scientists, but in each of the other two the subjects consisted of groups of professional poets and artists, and control groups of nonpoets and nonartists.

Each subject was asked to create in response to a stimulus—a landscape painting for the poets, a portion of Milton's *L'Allegro* for the painters. The subject was asked to talk aloud, and worked without a definite time limit. The experimenter observed the subject and wrote down his running commentary verbatim. The time was recorded in 5-minute intervals, permitting the experimenter to trace various trends through the working session. In addition, answers were obtained to a questionnaire covering methods of work. In the scientific-thought experiment, one group of fifty subjects planned an experiment in one sitting, and another group of fifty kept diaries during the course of 2 weeks during which they thought about the problem.

In order to make possible some kind of statistical treatment, Patrick arbitrarily divided the total time spent in the experimental session into four quarters, and then sought to determine what kind of activity was most typical of each. She found that "thought changes" occurred most often during the first quarter, indicating *preparation*; the recurrence of ideas at a later stage occurred in a majority of cases, showing *incubation*—Patrick does not locate it, other than to say that it follows preparation, but the single session probably reduced incubation to a minimum; as evidence for *illumination*, writing the first lines of a poem or first drafting the general shapes of a picture predominantly appeared in the second and third quarters; finally, most of the revisions were made in the fourth quarter, supporting the *verification* process.

The first three stages were found also in the experiment on scientific thought, but the nature of the problem appeared to preclude evidence on the fourth.

Other investigators who have identified these (or similar) stages include Rossman (1931) who studied inventors; Hutchinson (1939, 1940, 1941, 1942) who drew on reports by artists; and Hadamard (1945) who examined the work of mathematicians.

Patrick's experiments have a number of serious limitations. First, it is doubtful that a single brief session (in the poem experiment the time averages 21 minutes) is really typical of a creative situation; it would appear more natural to allow as many sessions as the subject requires. Second, the task was explicitly stated and the available materials were very limited. Third, the talking aloud method may be criticized. It is even more doubtful in this situation than in problem solving or concept formation, for example, that overt verbalization corresponds closely enough to covert mental processes to be relied on. Fourth, the arbitrary definitions and statistical procedures utilized appear very much to oversimplify the results. It might be said that she depended too much on a priori conceptions of creative processes.

Eindhoven and Vinacke (1952) tried to overcome some of these limitations. The task was to paint a picture, which would serve as a "publishable illustration" for a poem. The subjects were professional artists and a control group of nonartists, the two groups equated for sex, age, and intelligence. To avoid strict dependence on verbal report, the experimenter sat where he could unobtrusively observe, time, and record the subject's actual behavior; in addition, all the work done during the experiment was available for later analysis. Several devices were used to increase freedom of expression. Time restrictions were kept at a minimum. The subjects were allowed as many visits to the laboratory as they desired, up to maximum of four. Almost all subjects, in fact, came for more than one period, although relatively few came for all four. A variety of materials were available: four monochrome media consisting of black drawing pencils ranging from hard to soft, charcoal sticks, india ink with pens ranging from fine to wide points, and black poster paint with brushes of various sizes. The stimulus poem was relatively "unstructured" and abstract, and presented a variety of fanciful and unusual images.

The subjects, as in Patrick's (1938) experiment on scientific thought, were supplied with drawing paper and a pocket notebook to use for ideas relevant to the project which might occur while they were away from the laboratory. Although few subjects actually used these diary materials, invaluable data for understanding the creative activities of at least one subject were obtained.

The results considerably amplify those obtained by Patrick.

1. *Time relationships.* Given the opportunity to choose as many sessions at the task as the creator wishes, it is apparently typical for creation to extend over more than one period, with considerable variability in this respect among individuals. Most of the time in all the laboratory periods was spent in actual sketching; more time was spent in the first period than in later sessions in reading the poem. When the first sketch in a series was compared with the final sketch,[1] it was found that artists spent very little time on the former and much more time on the latter; the nonartists tended to spend the same amount of time on both.

2. *Products of creativity.* It was typical for the subjects to produce more than one sketch; artists tended to make more sketches in early than in late stages. Sketches varied considerably in size, with artists showing a change from very small sketches in the first period to larger ones in later periods, but nonartists tended to produce very large sketches during all periods. With respect to placement of sketches, those of the smallest size were usually off-center, those of largest size were centered. Artists most often used pencil for small sketches in the first period, and brush for larger sketches made later;

[1] Not all subjects achieved what they regarded as a "publishable" sketch; those selected as "publishable" were not always final sketches; however, the results for comparing initial and "publishable" sketches are very similar to those comparing initial and final.

nonartists more often used brush for early sketches, and pen for later ones.

Various aspects of painting were traced through the sketch series. In general the motif appearing in the first sketch was repeated in later sketches, whereas subject matter, composition, the number of objects, and the size relationships of elements in the picture were often dissimilar from sketch to sketch. Artists usually employed the same style throughout the series but varied the activities portrayed, whereas nonartists reversed this pattern, that is, varied their style but repeated the activities shown in early sketches.

Thus these results go beyond those of Patrick in two principal ways. In the first place, artists are seen to differ strikingly in their manner of painting from nonartists, and important additional light is cast on the nature of the four alleged stages of creative thought in relation to the final product.

Processes, Rather than Stages

The real weakness in the view that creative thinking consists in a sequence of fairly well defined phases is not that these stages do not exist but that they are regarded as universal, clearly recognizable, successive, and distinct from each other. In actuality it would be better to conceive of creative thinking in more holistic terms, as a total pattern of behavior in which various processes overlap and interweave between the occurrence of the original stimulus and the formation of the final product (Wertheimer, 1959).

In this regard let us consider more carefully those aspects of creative thinking that have been called incubation and illumination, which I prefer to define as processes rather than successive periods. In the Eindhoven and Vinacke experiment, nearly all the subjects came to the laboratory more than once and produced more than one sketch. At what point could it be said that illumination took place? There were rather a *series of illuminations*, which began in the first sketch and continued throughout the series. In the case of one artist, a classicial illustration of illumination occurred. She had an idea, suddenly, for her publishable sketch while at home, and simply reproduced and elaborated it in later periods. Incidentally, one artist never did have an illumination of any kind pertaining to the problem, but simply sketched the experimenter. One nonartist was totally unable to sketch, even with the experimenter out of the room.

The plan for the publishable or final sketch sometimes appeared in the first sketch, sometimes later, after a series of experimental sketches; more typically, it evolved gradually so that the final sketch combined many illuminations. The fuller view of illumination is clearly exemplified in the analysis of various aspects of the picture, motif, subject matter, composition, style, and so on. Any of these, or a combination, may be involved in any single illumination. Decisions regarding none of them were reached exclusively at any stage of the painting process. Nor is it possible to consider each separate sketch as an embodiment of the four alleged stages, since they represent for each subject parts of a more inclusive whole, the evolution of the ultimate product.

Incubation, similarly, does not occur at a particular stage, rather sharply differentiated from preceding and succeeding stages, but operates to varying degrees throughout the creative process. By definition, one would suppose that incubation took place, in the Eindhoven and Vinacke experiment, predominantly between laboratory sessions; but nearly all the subjects painted more than one sketch in at least one session, so that incubation can be said to have occurred during any session when more than one sketch was made—as a matter of fact continuously during the preparation of a single sketch, for instance when the outline of an object is drawn, then attention is given to some other part of the picture, and later shifted back to the earlier activity, etc.

Other studies, incidentally, which have analyzed in considerable detail the creative thought of individual artists further confirm the belief that creative processes run parallel, interweaving courses (e.g., the studies of the poet Coleridge, by Lowes [1930] and Nethercot [1939], and Armstrong's analysis of the imagery in Shakespeare's plays [1946]). The composing of a poem may involve an extremely intricate interplay between the reservoir of memories and the deliberate formulation of phrases and lines, the whole process continuing over a long period of time during which the future poetic materials are accumulated. According to Lowes and Nethercot, "The Rime of the Ancient Mariner," "Khubla Khan," and "Christabel" did not emerge suddenly nor completely, but were gradually developed by Coleridge, with many incubations and illuminations. Many of the introspective reports gathered by Rossman (1931) from inventors similarly indicate that creative thought in invention is more often a train of inspirations and incubations than of sharply defined stages.[1]

[1]Other works that go deeply into the relations between personality dynamics end creative expression include Freud's (1947) *Leonardo da Vinci*; Heider's (1941) study of Marcel Proust; Squires's (1938a, b) examination of the composers Franck and Weber; Arnheim's (1962) analysis of Picasso's *Guernica*; Graetz's (1963) analysis of themes in Van Gogh's paintings; Brenner's (1952) look at autistic components in the work of W. S. Gilbert; and Riviere's (1952a) analysis of Ibsen's *Master Builder*, together with her discussion of unconscious influences on literature (1952b).

The other two periods, preparation, and verification, are similarly continuing processes rather than stages. In the Eindhoven and Vinacke experiment, preparation can be said to have occurred at the start of each laboratory period, and at the start of each sketch, as well as in the very first period. In the picture unfolded by Lowes and Nethercot, preparation in Coleridge's work did not cease after the poems were begun but actually seemed to continue to the end, when Coleridge was still having new ideas. Verification, by the same token, accompanies early as well as late stages in the creative process. An illumination in a preliminary sketch, for example, may be followed up, criticized, refined, and carried throughout the sketch series.

Thus it is necessary to conceive of creative thinking in terms of dynamic, interplaying activities rather than as more or less discrete stages. Preparation, regarded as the process of recognizing and formulating the problem and having ideas about its solution, may lead to some preliminary decisions, a kind of illumination, and an effort made along that line. This same action, however, may serve as preparation for a later stage of development. Incubation may follow illumination as well as precede it; that is, the individual may not think consciously about the problem following an illumination, which has actually resulted in setting down an idea, but resume thinking later. Even when the product is in the final stages of refinement, or elaboration, or polishing (verification), incubation may occur between two attacks on the problem.

There are wide individual differences in patterns of creative thinking—no fixed and invariant sequence in which the several processes occur. They vary and interweave as the product is developed. But clearly to speak about the kinds of activities typical of creative situations tells only part of the story. We must still consider the issue of creativity itself, that is, factors responsible for the more successful (original, appropriate) utilization of creative processes by some persons compared to others.

AN ASSOCIATIVE VIEW

Creative thinking has been viewed by Mednick (1962) as the recombining of "associative elements" that "either meet specified requirements or are in some way useful." Of the two criteria mentioned, originality is included but "usefulness" is not fully equivalent to appropriateness since it merely refers to successful solution of a problem, without stressing the expression or satisfaction of the creator's intrinsic state. Thus this approach rests on realistic considerations rather than the merging of both autistic and real-istic forces. Mednick proposes that creativeness depends on how many "requirements" the product meets.

Solutions, in this vein, may occur through (1) *serendipity* (accidental contiguity of stimuli leading to a new combination of elements; see also, D. T. Campbell, 1960); (2) *similarity of elements* (perhaps depending on primary stimulus generalization); or (3) *mediation* (combination via common elements). The last process is considered especially typical of the manipulation of symbols.

Individual differences arise from variations in characteristics of associative resources, such as availability of elements, hierarchical relationships, and efficiency of search.

To assess creativity, the Remote Associates Test (RAT) was devised. Consisting of sets of three words, a common associate provides the solution word (and the common link is difficult to discover). Here are two examples: (1) RAILROAD—GIRL—CLASS ————; (2) OUT—DOG—CAT ————. The test has high reliabil-ity, is negatively correlated with college grades, and displays signifi-cantly positive correlations with other tests of originality (between .30 and .40).

On a word association test, a group scoring high on RAT produced more associations and maintained a faster rate of associa-tion than medium or low scorers (Mednick, Mednick, and Jung, 1964). A priming technique was employed to study incubation, as a period when new associative elements enter and facilitate the forma-tion of new combinations (Mednick, Mednick, and Mednick, 1964). Ten items missed on RAT were selected, five were primed by analogies, five as controls (for example, BREAK—TRAIN—BATTLE [a RAT item] was primed by TV: channel as radio: s————, the letter provided as a cue). On readministration of the RAT items, the primed items were solved significantly more often than control items. High scorers benefited more than did low scorers. Another study showed that high scorers are more responsive to incidental cues (Mendelsohn and Griswold, 1964).

Remarking that Mednick's view focuses on too simple a level, Riegel, Riegel, and Levine (1966) proposed that differences in per-formance depend on skills at complex levels of organization that recognize and employ class relationships—analogously to the con-cept of "chunking" (G. A. Miller, 1956). Subjects high and low in creativeness on a test different from RAT (but reported as agreeing with it) were administered a variety of tasks, including free associa-tion, "creative responding" (writing words typical of an immature person), and restricted association (e.g., superordinates, similars, antecedents, location). Type-token ratios were computed (number of different responses per stimulus divided by total number of responses). The variability of high scorers on the creativity test was greater in free association, logical tasks (e.g., subordinates), and imitational tasks ("creative responding"), but less on tasks that called on functions, parts, or attributes. The low scorers displayed greater overlap (repetition) among the tasks, indicating conceptual confusion. Differences in performance therefore depend on the type of task, and complexity of associative functioning emerges as more important than mere remoteness of association.

The associative approach may be criticized for ignoring the intimate role of autistic (emotional, expressive) components, not to mention unconscious influences. More specifically, close scrutiny of RAT shows that it is primarily a difficult problem solving task, with a single, predetermined correct response that can be discovered by sufficient ingenuity. Test scores should reflect some aspect of intelligence more than they do creativity (Jackson and Messick, 1965). In fact, they correlate significantly with the Wechsler Adult Intelligence Scale (WAIS) vocabulary score ($r = .34$), and although intelligence was related to performance on a concept task, RAT was not (Jacobson et al., 1968). Other studies, however, indicate that RAT scores and intelligence are both related to concept attainment, but that the relation between RAT and performance is especially evident on incidental (i.e., more remote) concepts, whereas intelligence displays a stronger relation to intentional (i.e., more direct or obvious) concepts (Laughlin, 1967; Laughlin, Doherty, and Dunn, 1968). In a situation more appropriate for assessing actual creativity, Andrews (1965) found no relation between RAT and creative performance by scientists, but significant negative correlations under conditions of a restricted environment.

CREATIVE ABILITIES

The bulk of the evidence points to an independence of creativity from conventional measures of intelligence (Dellas and Gaier, 1970). More accurately, there is a marked discontinuity between lower and higher IQ, so that little or no creativity occurs at levels below high average (say, IQ 120), and above that point the correlation is negligible (Barron, 1963a; Getzels and Jackson, 1962). That is, although highly creative people are typically high in intelligence, the reverse does not necessarily hold true.

Guilford and his coworkers (Guilford, 1957; Wilson et al., 1954; Guilford, 1967) have therefore sought to isolate the special abilities conducive to creative products. In their model of intellect, these abilities fall within the domain of *divergent production*, and include originality, fluency, flexibility, sensitivity to problems, and redefinition of problems. The exercise of such abilities is conceived to lead toward new or unknown solutions (hence the term *divergent*).

Guilford has been extremely ingenious in devising tests for these hypothesized abilities. Especially familiar are unusual uses (list as many uses as possible for a common object such as a brick or a paper bag), plot titles (given a short story, suggest possible titles), consequences (list consequences of some eventuality, such as that people no longer need or want sleep), and various kinds of figure use (given several simple forms or lines, construct objects of them), and unusual or remote associations. Responses may be scored for total number of responses, for unusualness, or for quality (such as cleverness).

Although factor-analytic studies have provided a substantial basis for formulating these abilities, Dellas and Gaier (1970), after reviewing applications to various criteria of creativity (that continuing knotty problem in this area!), point out that only quite low or non-significant correlations are typical (see also, Torrance, 1962; MacKinnon, 1961; Gough, 1961). Nevertheless, some investigators find significant relationships (e.g., Drevdahl, 1956; Barron, 1963b; Elliott, 1964). As Dellas and Gaier point out, the Guilford measures "leave unilluminated the personalogical context in which the creative process functions." Indeed, it is quite likely that personality variables play a role similar to intelligence: in certain combinations or degrees they are conducive to the creative exercise of divergent abilities, but the existence of the latter does not necessarily guarantee creative performance.

These abilities may at least partly be viewed as dependent on "information searching" (Karlins, Lee, and Schroder, 1967). In their experiment, Peace Corps volunteers participated in three quite natural and relevant tasks, such as imagining that one is assigned to help build a hospital—in order to build it, one must obtain information about the locale and people. The number of questions asked and the number of categories searched displayed significant correlations with Guilford's unusual uses (ranging from .27 to .37, with one non-significant coefficient). The three tasks were significantly inter-correlated, indicating consistency for this cognitive style. In line with other findings, intelligence displayed low and mostly negative correlations with all the other measures.

Divergent thinking is affected by environmental conditions. Hinton (1968) found that performance on several of Guilford's tests was reduced during periods of general frustration. Experimentally induced stress (exposure to an emotionally disturbing film about subincision rites of Australian aborigines) has the same kind of effect (Krop, Alegre, and Williams, 1969)—but convergent thinking was not affected.

Although verbatim recall shows a decrement with working time, production of responses in inventive tasks such as unusual uses and impossibilities, where the subject is asked to list as many impossible things as he can think of, does not; originality increases but cleverness does not; and instructions to be clever decrease output but facilitate cleverness (Christensen, Guilford, and Wilson, 1957).

The work of Guilford, marked by an awareness of the contribution of nonintellective conditions, has enriched conceptions of creative performance. Divergent abilities offer a logically meaningful basis for further research. If they are too narrow in their emphasis, then we require a better balance by adding personality, motivational, and experiential variables to the context. Nor should we discount the possibility that better tests of the abilities might yield better results— they are typically low in reliability as well as validity.

PERSONALITY CHARACTERISTICS

The thesis that creatively productive persons differ in personality traits from noncreative persons has been intensively investigated in recent years. In general two strategies are recognizable: (1) identifying and assessing contrasting groups (such as established artists versus nonartists or eminent scientists versus their less-outstanding colleagues), and (2) applying some criterion, such as teacher ratings or scores on a test designed to measure creativity, to form contrasting high and low groups.[1]

Running through the quite diverse studies are several salient themes: (1) Creative persons are relatively lacking in repressive control of impulses and imagery, which allows "to the creative fuller

---

[1]Some examples of studies dealing with recognized creative individuals are Roe (1951, 1953) Munsterberg and Mussen (1953), Eiduson (1958), Hersch (1962), and Helson (1967a, b). Studies that utilized test procedures to identify high- and low-creative persons include Rust (1948), Getzels and Jackson (1962), Garwood (1964), Andrews (1965), Chambers (1964), Cashdan and Welsh (1966), Trowbridge and Charles (1966), and Parloff, et al. (1968).

access to his conscious and unconscious experiences, and therefore a greater opportunity to combine dissociated items" (Dellas and Gaier, 1970; see also, Barron, 1955). (2) Creative persons are open to external and internal stimuli, permitting the complexity and imbalance from which unusual organizations can emerge. Creative males are higher in femininity than noncreatives, and accept this side of their nature, leading to wide interests, openness to emotion, aesthetic sensitivity, and self-awareness (see Hammer, 1964). (3) Creative persons are typically marked by independence of attitudes and comparative immunity from the opinions of others, allowing them freedom of self-expression.

Barron (1963b, p. 246) has written, "In the creative process there is an incessant dialectic and an essential tension between two seemingly opposed tendencies: the tendency towards disruption of structure and diffusion of energy and attention."

In one study, industrial research chemists were administered ambiguous stimuli (Rorschach cards). A score based on quality of integrated form was highly correlated with creativity ($r_{bis} = .88$). As predicted, the most creative chemists, as rated by superiors and colleagues, offered more hypotheses, a higher proportion of which were judged high in quality, and produced many more well-integrated responses. They also gave more autistic responses, but this difference decreased as level of exposure increased (Stein and Meer, 1954).

The principle of "regression in the service of the ego" (Kris, 1952; Schafer, 1958) is derived from psychoanalytic theory. It signifies a temporary reduction in the level of cognitive functions (secondary process), permitting the intrusion and use of drive-determined material (primary process). Occurring in the illumination phase, regression of this kind, unlike psychotic regression, remains under control in relation to the creative product—and hence is adaptive. By contrast, the verification phase involves more strictly secondary-process thinking—and is therefore more directly realistic. Thus this principle agrees well with the view of creativity as an interplay between intrinsic and extrinsic forces.

Myden (1959) analyzed Rorschach responses of recognized creative persons (dramatic arts, painting, literature) compared to a matched sample of noncreators. He found clear evidence for a greater use of primary process by the creative subjects and for its effective integration with secondary-process thinking. (Incidentally, the creators liked and enjoyed the inkblots, whereas none of the non-creators liked them and many found them unpleasant.)

Pine and Holt (1960) point out also that it is not merely the expression of primary-process material that is distinctive but the effective control over it. Accordingly, in addition to using the Rorschach to assess the expression and control of primary process,[1] a variety of tests, including the TAT, a humor test, animal drawing, and consequences, were administered to measure creative responses. The male subjects displayed the predicted relationships, but results were not consistent for the females.

Wild (1965) has further suggested that if adaptive regression is more typical of creative persons, then they should more readily shift appropriately from a regulated to an unregulated condition; furthermore, they should find the unregulated condition easy and enjoyable. To vary creativity, she used groups of art students, teachers, and schizophrenics. The shift measure was obtained in word association and object-sorting tests, first administered under spontaneous conditions by presenting character sketches. The regulated sketch described "a conventional, cautious, reliable person, who prefers an orderly, structured universe and values good common sense . . ."; the unregulated one, a person who has "novel thoughts and whimsical yet acute perceptions that may startle other people (and) points to the contradictions in experience and enjoys fanciful speculations." The subject was instructed to take the test as the person described would.

Shift scores consisted of the difference between the regulated and unregulated conditions.[2] As predicted, the hypothesis was confirmed that the art students shifted most adaptively, the schizophrenics least (see Figure 15-1). In addition, the art students were significantly more original under the spontaneous condition. Gamble and Kellner (1968) also found that more-creative subjects (with RAT as a criterion) performed better on the Stroop test, which requires a shift in response when interference is introduced. Experiments with hypnosis also bear out the principle (P. G. Bowers, 1967; K. S. Bowers and S. J. van der Meulen, 1970) since individuals more responsive to regressive states in hypnosis perform better on creativity tests.

Barron and Welsh (1952) developed a test to assess artistic

[1] This characteristic is determined on the basis of "defense demand" (social acceptability) and "defense effectiveness" (success in controlling primary-process materials). For example, "two people holding hands" exemplifies low demand, compared to "two people having intercourse"; "this part looks like a horse but the rest makes me think it's a man" is less effectively controlled than "it's a centaur."

[2] Responses were scored as original or unconventional. The scores reflect degree of increased originality.

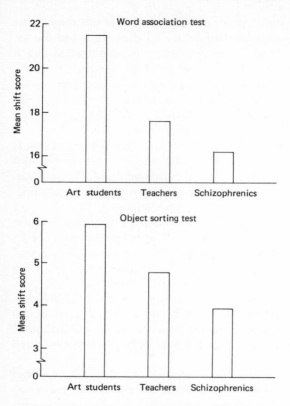

FIGURE 15-1   Tendency to shift toward originality
from regulated to unregulated conditions as evidence
for "regression in the service of the ego" in creative
persons. (Based on Wild, 1965.)

preferences, with items consisting of drawings. As indicated above,
artists liked the complex asymmetrical figures, whereas nonartists
preferred the simple, symmetrical ones. In a study by Pyron (1966),
preferences were elicited for examples of avant-garde, popular, and
classical art from the media of painting, literature, and music.
Personality measures administered to the college-student subjects
showed that preference for avant-garde art, which has characteristics of ambiguity, novelty, and unexpected arrangement, was related
to flexibility and complexity of attitudes. Still another study, with
high school subjects, has shown that creativity is associated with
preference for complex shapes (Eisenman and Robinson, 1967).

Creative Architects

An example of more elaborate studies is research by MacKinnon (1963) on the self-concepts of architects. Of the 124 subjects, 40 were chosen nationwide by 5 professors of architecture at the University of California on the basis of their outstanding creativeness. A second group of forty-three were matched with the first group in age and geographic location and also had worked with them. The third group of forty-one were similarly matched, but had not worked with the others. The expectation that this procedure would yield a fairly good sampling was borne out by creativity ratings from a variety of experts. On a seven-point scale, the means for the three groups were 5.46 (group 1), 4.25 (group 2), and 3.45 (group 3) (differences significant at better than the .001 level).

To assess self-concepts and ideal self-concepts, the architects were administered the adjective check list (Gough, 1961). Each subject checked those of the 300 adjectives he thought most descriptive of himself, and, on a subsequent presentation, those that described how he would like to be.

Although all three groups judged themselves in favorable and generally similar terms, there was a distinctly different pattern of emphasis between the more- and less-creative architects (see Table 15-1). The most creative subjects regarded themselves as inventive, independent, individualistic, determined, enthusiastic, and industrious. Their less-creative peers stressed to a greater degree such qualities as responsibility, integrity, logical and practical thinking, and understanding of others.

More detailed analysis also disclosed that the less-creative architects tended to be more defensive in their self-descriptions, and that the more-creative subjects were more willing to admit flaws in themselves. Other derived scores showed the more-creative architects to be lower in self-control and adjustment and higher in ability.

With respect to the ideal self, the most creative group displayed the greatest discrepancies from the real self. In general they expressed wishes for greater personal attractiveness, self-confidence, maturity, more favorable interpersonal relations, energy, and sensitivity.

MacKinnon interprets these results as showing that the more-creative architects display greater self-actualization, deriving from freedom to express themselves according to their own standards, accompanied by effective and confident ego control. The less-creative architects, on the other hand, follow more conventional standards, with more concern for the opinions of others. The former

Table 15-1
Adjectives Checked as Self-descriptive by 80 Percent of One Sample but Less than 80 Percent of the Other. (From MacKinnon, 1963.)

Checked by 80% or More of Group 1 But Less than 80% of Group 3	Checked by 80% or More of Group 3 But Less than 80% of Group 1
INVENTIVE*	RESPONSIBLE†
DETERMINED*	SINCERE†
INDEPENDENT*	RELIABLE†
INDIVIDUALISTIC*	DEPENDABLE†
ENTHUSIASTIC*	CLEAR-THINKING†
INDUSTRIOUS*	TOLERANT†
ARTISTIC	UNDERSTANDING†
PROGRESSIVE	PEACEABLE
APPRECIATIVE	GOOD-NATURED
	MODERATE
	STEADY
	PRACTICAL
	LOGICAL

*Checked by 80% or more of group 1, but less than 80% of groups 2 and 3.
†Checked by 80% or more of groups 2 and 3, but less than 80% of group 1.

are marked by integration between ego and id, whereas the latter show a stronger integration between ego and superego.[1]

Motivation

Since creative persons seem especially receptive to and capable of utilizing directly their emotional and motivational impulses, Pine (1959) looked in TAT stories for evidence of "drive content" and "drive material" (derivatives of instinctual aggressive and libidinal drives). Data pertinent to the formation of hypotheses came from a science test (e.g., a question posing the possibility of coal in Antarctica, despite the absence of trees). The stories rated highest in literary quality and the scientific productions highest in theoretical quality were both characterized by high drive content. In addition, quality was related to controlled expression of drive and its integra-

[1]Space does not permit a detailed survey of distinctive patterns of personality in various fields of creativity. However, the general picture presented so far is oversimplified since various investigators in addition to MacKinnon have identified subtypes of creative persons. Helson (1968), for instance, has outlined sex differences between highly creative men and women. Furthermore, Helson and Crutchfield (1970) have distinguished five types of creative mathematicians, each displaying a distinctive pattern of personality characteristics and family background.

tion into the product. These findings agree with the principle of regression in the service of the ego.

Self-actualizing tendencies (Rogers, 1961; Maslow, 1970) have been linked with creativity. Support for this proposition is shown by the fact that in comparison with noncreative persons, creative individuals prefer ambiguous and "evocative" stimuli and express greater liking for situations and activities calling for independence, self-expression, and application of creativity (Golann, 1962). Needs for quality and novelty, which operate independently of achievement, affiliation, and so on, are important components of self-actualizing tendencies (Maddi, 1965). The aspirations of creative high school seniors reflect these needs (Torrance and Dauw, 1965). Csikszentmihalyi and Getzels (1970) relate "concern for discovery" (assessed by an interview) to the quality of drawings produced by high school fine arts students. By distinguishing styles of formulating the problem, attempting the solution, and completing the solution, they show that concern for discovery is significantly correlated with originality, regardless of stage, and with aesthetic value at the first two stages. However, analysis by partial correlation showed that the relation for originality primarily occurred at the first stage (see Figure 15-2).

Conceived as a self-actualizing process, creativity therefore arises from needs for novelty and quality, accompanied by a concern for discovery.

THE CREATIVE PERSON

Thus we find a number of well-defined properties of creative persons. Not only does a pattern emerge of originality, preference for complex and expressive situations, and independence from conventional environmental constraints, but also of sensitivity and responsiveness to intrinsic needs and feelings. Apparently these characteristics mark creative persons in a wide variety of fields, scientific as well as artistic. Rogers (1961) has suggested as common denominators: *openness to experience, an internal locus of evaluation, and the ability to toy with elements and concepts.* These conditions point to the peculiar effectiveness of creative individuals in moving toward self-actualization.

However, studies (e.g., Eindhoven and Vinacke, 1949) of the differences between creators and noncreators, together with evidence for controlled or disciplined utilization of intrinsic resources, further indicate that special kinds of experience or training are required.

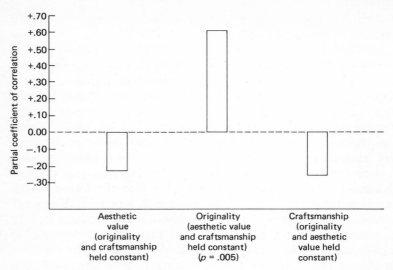

FIGURE 15-2   Relation between concern for discovery and qualitative aspects of drawing at the stage of formulating the problem. (Based on Csikszentmihalyi and Getzels, 1970.)

The artist, whatever his perceptual-emotional sensitivity, must nevertheless possess the basic skills that serve as an agent for expression—that is, drawing, knowledge of color, grasp of composition, and so on. The scientist must acquire knowledge and understanding of his subject matter as part of the raw material for his ideas, as well as the technical proficiencies that enable him to put his ideas into practice. In short, the creator must develop the skills that serve as media for the product that fulfills his ultimate aim. He must be able to translate his experience, feelings, and ideas into the form that he desires. Therefore the difference between creator and noncreator depends on training as much as on special personal resources.

Training, however, is a complex matter. Dellas and Gaier (1970) observe that personality characteristics may be either determinants or consequences of creativity. Probably they are both. That is, the releasing of creative potential depends initially on favorable conditions, which experience and training reinforce and facilitate. But experience and training also help to establish the trends that lead to greater creativity. For example, as the person becomes better acquainted with his chosen mode of expression, he learns better how to discriminate between the conventional and the original, and inaugurates his own quest for his distinctive métier. In this way, perhaps, the ego strength and controlled expression of the creator stem partly from training.

The point is especially pertinent to differences between artists and scientists. The development of the artist involves the cultivation of perceptual-emotional expression, whereas that of the scientist is more nearly an actualization of cognitive-emotional states.

One area of difference clearly lies in patterns of interest, associated, at least partly, with family, school, and other developmental conditions (Roe, 1958).

Significant differences between art and physics majors were found by Dickinson (1967). Each group of subjects performed more creatively on tasks especially appropriate to its discipline—contour drawing and inkblots in the case of the artists, consequences and verbal concept formation in the case of the scientists. Although neither repressive tendencies nor need for cognition was related to performance on concept formation, both of these variables interfered with creativity on the inkblot test, with evidence again that this relationship depends on the task. The more-creative scientists who were high in repression were more creative on verbal-concept formation, whereas this difference did not appear for the artists. In both groups the more-creative subjects, who were also low in repression, produced more creative responses to the inkblots.

Feeling is central to the artist's resources, whereas ideas are inherent in the scientist's expression. The artist is oriented more to autistic forces, the scientist to realistic ones. (Some commentaries suggest that the artist seeks to express himself, the scientist to express the natural world.) This distinction is, of course, difficult to draw. In a groping fashion, however, I wish to suggest that the blending of autistic and realistic forces is the key factor in creative activity, that the interplay differs in various fields, and that training has much to do with the form it assumes.

As yet there is no simple answer concerning the possible prerequisites of creativity, once certain basic requirements are present (such as sufficiently high intelligence). But there are at least two ways in which creativity is not the mysterious prerogative of a special group of people. First, creative situations are common to everyone. When a problem arises for which there is no predetermined "correct" answer, or when a need is aroused that leads the person to externalize himself, a potential creative situation is present. Under these circumstances any individual may engage in that kind of activity that combines imagination and realistic thinking. Thus wider and more explicit recognition of such instances can augment creative thinking.

They need not be "artistic" or "scientific" in any self-conscious sense but simply instances when creative processes are appropriate. Second, creative potentials can be released and improved by introducing suitable training conditions. Here we must consider both general-developmental conditions and the possibility that special instructional procedures can promote creativity.

Developmental Factors

Evidence suggests that the characteristics of creative persons typically develop early (Meier, 1933; Reid, King, and Wickwire, 1959; Torrance, 1964). A family or school environment that provides rich opportunities for emotional expression, an orientation toward individual standards of meaning, and an emphasis on varied experience is conducive to the release of creativity. Rogers (1961) adds attitudes of acceptance, a climate that emphasizes internal standards of evaluation, and empathic understanding, thus promoting an atmosphere of "psychological safety" and "psychological freedom."

More specifically, Torrance (1964) has advanced the notion of *inhibitors* and *facilitators* of creative thinking. The former are such conditions as the discouraging of fantasy, demands for conformity and conventional modes of accomplishment, insistence on narrow and specified methods of work, drawing too sharp a distinction between play and work, and derogation of emotional response. Facilitators include recognizing and rewarding special talents or individualistic responses, encouraging participation in learning, valuing personal perceptions and experiences, and providing varied and diverse media for expression.

Important also is promoting the disciplined gearing of expression to desired outcomes—that is, the mastery of appropriate skills and their direction toward creative products. Spontaneity is not solely opposed to conformity, but may also be inchoate without guidance toward significant goals. Thus we face two problems, not solely the release of spontaneity, but also its effective utilization. Development entails both release and direction of creative potential.

Training

Stemming from behavioral theory, originality has been seen by Maltzman (1960) as a problem of increasing the frequency of uncommon responses. Practice in emitting them might induce a general tendency to be original. In one procedure (Maltzman, Bogartz, and

Breger, 1958), a list of words was administered five times, with instructions to give a different response each time. One subgroup was reinforced occasionally for uncommon associations. Then a new list was presented, with half the subjects instructed to be as original as possible. The originality instructions increased uncommon responses, with some benefit from reinforcement. Transfer to Guilford's unusual uses was equivocal. Introducing lists of uncommon uses for pertinent objects significantly facilitated performance of females, but not of males, on Maier's two-string problem. Although the word-association technique and instructions to be original are both effective, "heuristics" training is superior (Ridley and Birney, 1967). The latter involves describing and illustrating various strategies.

Word-association training can be criticized for overemphasis on sheer frequency of response, without sufficient attention to appropriateness. Caron, Unger, and Parloff (1963) pointed out that it could just as well increase the response strength of irrelevant rather than relevant responses. No effect of originality training appeared on the RAT. Arguing that RAT actually depends more on *common* than on uncommon associates, so that quickness and variety of association may be crucial, Freedman (1965a) developed a facilitation technique. A stimulus was presented with instructions to say whatever words came to mind for 30 seconds; under nonfacilitation, subjects merely defined each word. The facilitation procedure yielded significantly better performance on RAT, evidently by promoting quickness of association. (See also, Miller et al., 1970.) In another study, subjects allowed to continue working on RAT problems previously failed did better than those interrupted to work on another task ("incubation" condition); association training during the interruption period, however, facilitated the solutions of females (Gall and Mendelsohn, 1967).

Still another technique has sought to facilitate the combining of previously correlated ideas, as implied in the associative conception of originality (Davis and Manske, 1966). Subjects imagined themselves in a situation such as a picnic, party, or classroom, then listed uses for a hanger, a tire, or a screwdriver. Other groups listed uses under neutral instructions or under instructions to be both original and practical. The "situations" condition yielded significantly more uses, and a higher proportion of original responses. They were, however, judged lower in practicality.

A more traditional training method was used by Renner (1970). Art slides were presented, accompanied by taped talks that dealt with the "novel and significant attributes of the complexities in each painting." One control group simply viewed the slides and wrote down comments, feelings, or associations, another was administered the test measures without any experimental treatment. These measures included the Revised Art Scale (Welsh, 1959), a music attitude scale (Mueller et al., 1934), and tests of divergent thinking such as consequences (Christensen, Merrifield, and Guilford, 1958), and Torrance's (1962) circles test.

Figure 15-3 shows that the explanatory talks produced increased scores on all the measures. Note that there is not only a gain on the most obviously relevant test (the Revised Art Scale), but also generalization to the music attitude scale, and transfer to originality tests. This approach appears to have greater potential than the more mechanical and specific training procedures adopted by other investigators.

A particularly good illustration of the efficacy of seeking to capitalize on a deep understanding of creativity is provided by the research of Dellas (1970) on seventh graders. In line with the conception of interplaying autistic and realistic forces, she proposed that a special feature of creativity is the "ability to associate elements from two distinct and diverse sensory modalities—the affective and the visual." Therefore training to stimulate or enhance this ability should facilitate creative performance. However, the visual experiences themselves should be treated, not in their "conventional, geometric-technical-pragmatic aspects," but rather as "representatives or analogues of affective experience" with emphasis on "sensitivity to the unconventional, dynamic-affective-expressive aspects."

Experimental classes were given a series of training sessions with increasingly abstract materials, accompanied by a psychologically free atmosphere to elicit emotional expression. Compared to control classes, which did not have this training, there was increased flexibility on an alternate uses task, and greater originality on consequences and plot titles tasks.

The predicted negative correlation between defensiveness and creativity was found (greater for boys) ; and the relationship was increased by the pretest. As predicted also, a low positive correlation was found between intelligence and creativity.

This study has special merit because it is based on a more penetrating understanding of creativity than has characterized many attempts to introduce special training. The training was not only sensitively conceived and conducted, but had many features particularly natural and relevant to the classroom situation—characteristics of openness, freedom, unconventionality, and emotional

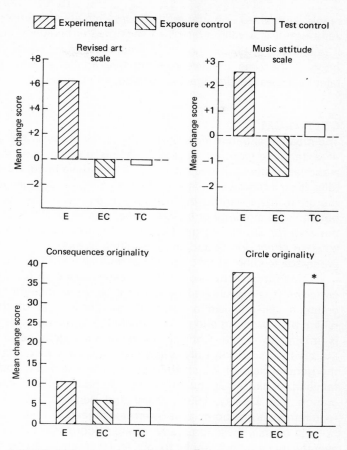

FIGURE 15-3 Increased creativity as a function of special training in the understanding of paintings. (Based on Renner, 1970.) (The test control for the circles test was not significantly different from the experimental group.)

expression stressed by Rogers, Torrance, Barron, and others. It is true that individual differences in susceptibility to training (save for defensiveness) are not elucidated. We might also criticize the ignoring of the criterion of appropriateness (did the children improve in the *quality* of their productions?). But these weaknesses merely point toward additional research. The study suggests that certain aspects of creative performance can be significantly enhanced—a quite important finding—but it leaves open the relative effects and long-range outcomes on more and less creatively gifted children. Although it is a valid strategy to seek greater creativity in everyone, it is still worth examining the question of *which* children can best hope to become creatively productive adults, and of how such talent can best be discovered, fostered, and trained.

CRITICISM

The creative situation does not really terminate with the attainment of a tangible product because, having permanence, it evokes a response in the audience for whom it was developed. Here, incidentally, is an important variable of the realistic pole of creative activity— the artist, the inventor, the mathematician, even the amateur radio builder is, to a greater or lesser degree, creating not for himself alone but also for others. He must expect therefore that his product will have an effect on the audience, resulting in emotional and cognitive processes leading to favorable or unfavorable judgments.

This further extension of the creative situation has been called *criticism.* It is exemplified by the process of verification, where the creator's self-criticism arises from his knowledge of the field in which he is working and in his knowledge of the particular object he is striving to create. Criticism by others is a genuine extension of the creative situation only when the critic knows something about the general field of which the object is an exemplar, and when he familiarizes himself adequately with the specific object under consideration (see Dewey, 1934; Maier and Reninger, 1933). A further requirement is an appreciative interest in objects of the kind criticized.

Of course, these requirements are seldom adequately met in the average person, but apply to his representative, so to speak, the professional critic, who plays an important part in the creative situation by analyzing, interpreting, and evaluating the creative product. These functions are fulfilled to the degree that the requirements set forth above are met. Deficient criticism may result from insufficient acquaintance with the particular work in question. The history of the arts is filled with too hasty adverse or favorable judgments, on the first appearance of new works. And science is replete with similar instances. The second requirement may be lacking also, as when there has been insufficient time for a new movement in art or knowledge to be understood, to say nothing of occasions when persons have acted as critics with little knowledge of the field in which they are acting.

But the average person is not a professional critic, and therefore, participates in a creative situation somewhat differently from the critic. His role is that of *appreciation*. It may range from a sheerly emotional reaction, induced without delay, to an elaborate pattern of analysis and interpretation similar to that of the professional critic.

SUMMARY

A creative situation presents a problem without a fixed or "correct" solution. Creative activity calls on self-expression and blends realistic and autistic forces. To originality as a criterion of creativity must be added appropriateness. Creative thinking involves processes of preparation, incubation, illumination, and verification. Views have been advanced based on associative processes and on the structure of intellect. Personality studies of creative persons have brought out characteristics of lack of repressive control, openness to external and internal stimuli, independence, regression in the service of the ego, preference for complexity, and the salience of self-actualizing tendencies and concern for discovery. Special training promotes creativity, with differences between artists and scientists. Favorable developmental conditions include the fostering of emotional expressiveness and emphasis on individual meaning, varied experience, personal worth, and freedom. Criticism and appreciation are extensions of the creative situation to everyday life.

16

THE INTERNALIZATION OF EXPERIENCE

The character of thinking depends on the *mental context*—the organized ongoing system composed of past experience and of current intrinsic processes, in the midst of which any momentary thought occurs. As repeatedly emphasized, this system consists of interrelated components: affective and motivational, memorial, and the input of information from extrinsic sources. The outcome of the system, in the form of cognitive, verbal, or motor acts depends on the properties of cognitive structure, or concepts and attitudes.

In outlining some of the conditions that produce the experiential background of the mental context, inevitably there will be some imbalance since systematic knowledge is much greater on some conditions than on others. For example, psychologists have displayed considerably more ingenuity in studying the influence of imitation than of more subtle individual modes of acquiring experience. Similarly, the acquisition of knowledge, verbal habits, and motor responses has been investigated more intensively than the development of emotional characteristics.

During the course of development, the person incorporates into his own system characteristics originally external to himself, such as symbolic representations of environmental objects, the norms of his culture, and the real or ideal traits of persons with whom he has close emotional ties. More broadly, this process is a matter both of progressive absorption of external influences and of the continuous shaping and modification of those characteristics and tendencies already present, whether stemming from inherent biological properties or from prior learning. We shall call this aspect of development the *internalization of experience.*

Internalization involves not only the specific, recognizable learning processes studied extensively in the laboratory, but also more gradual, subtle experiential continuities, not yet adequately investigated. Contributing to our understanding of this latter dimension of experience are studies of cultural differences, of selective and organizing influences on perception, learning, memory, conceptualization, and interpersonal relations, and of clinical investigations of personality dynamics. Psychoanalytic theory has powerfully influenced much of this work.

Forces from the organism and from the environment continuously interplay—in combinations so complex that the possibilities for their interaction are unlimited. This principle shall be treated as an axiom, without examining in detail the evidence that justifies it. And, as a corollary, the principle that the combination of conditions is always different for each individual shall also be accepted. Beyond that, as learning progresses, there is a "self-organizing" property of the developing mental context, which tends to preserve and increase individualized aspects of it.

A cross section of experience would reveal general components or themes arising from the conditions under which development proceeds, namely, biological, physical-environmental, societal, and cultural. Certain ones confront every individual (i.e., are universal) in all cultures; other conditions are present only in a particular culture, or in a particular group within a culture, or in the immediate circumstances of a particular individual (i.e., are idiosyncratic) (Kluckhohn and Mowrer, 1944). In consequence, an infinite variety of combinations is possible, so that a unique pattern characterizes each person. Even where the same general condition can be postulated for a set of people, such as a system of family relationships, or a mode of infant care, great variation occurs within the framework in responding to and imposing the condition.

As development proceeds, all these factors interplay : *biological* properties providing general bases for social experience, *cultural* influences determining how biological characteristics will be expressed, *social* forces emphasizing certain features of the *physical environment,* and so on in an intricate fashion.

BEGINNINGS OF EXPERIENCE

Since the human infant is born in a relatively unformed and helpless state, development has barely started at birth, rather than being nearly completed as is generally the case in lower organisms. Knowledge about the biological nature of man tells us comparatively little about the process and results of internalization; instead, we must look to the learning and development of the person in relation to relevant external conditions. A vast change in viewpoint in the social sciences has come about during the past fifty years as a consequence of studies of cultural differences, of the increasingly systematic investigation of child development, and of intensive research on the nature and functions of learning. Building on these bases, social psychologists and sociologists have contributed ever more sophisticated insights into the effects of roles and interpersonal influences.

It is not necessary to belabor the point. We may accept as an axiom that the starting points of behavior in the infant owe their direction and outcomes to the internalization process. But the developing organism is not passive either, is not simply the recipient of environmental pressures. It acts on the environment, is stimulated by and reacts to stimuli; and, as time goes on, along with increasing organization of behavior, participation becomes greater as intrinsic selective and regulative systems become established and strengthened. Thus later experience depends on previous experience. As development proceeds, behavior tends to become more and more organized, with the effects of later experience owing their character in greater or lesser degree to the effects of earlier experience.

The starting points of behavior reside in the need system of the infant (food, affection, fairly constant temperature, sleep, etc.). However, the conditions that will satisfy those needs, and the circumstances attendant on their satisfaction, are not at all fixed but vary according to the general schema given above: the pattern characteristic of the infant's role, the groups of which he will become a member, his culture, together with the idiosyncratic events that apply to him alone (including his relationships with particular people). Within this framework the general directions of the individual's behavior and the bases for further modification are established. One aspect of development then is the elaboration of the motive system. The original needs and impulses of the infant form starting points on which learning acts to shape the complex pattern of striving and impulse satisfaction of later stages in development.

In addition to the elaboration of the motive system, other trends also originate in biological properties of the organism; namely, the distinctive ways in which activity is carried out. These trends may be called *traits*. They represent in later behavior characteristics of the organism that determine *how* a response is made—quickly or slowly, forcefully or weakly, positively or negatively, vocally or silently, emotionally toned in one way or another way, and so on. As learning proceeds, such trends not only become more definite but also more complex as they acquire organized relations to particular classes of stimuli, particular symbolic systems, particular patterns of emotional control and expression, and so on. Hence the simple trends suggested by words like "quickly," "forcefully," or "positively" come to demand more precise and distinctive definition, so that the characteristics of responses now require names like "persistently," "extrovertedly," "dominantly," "optimistically," "absent-mindedly," and so on.

In addition to motives and traits, fundamental directions in the organization of experience are represented by the inauguration of *attitudes* and *concepts.* These terms (or others like them) refer to the systems in the mental context, established by learning, that link motives and traits with specific stimuli and responses. It is particularly to these cognitive properties that we refer when speaking about mediation.

HOW EXPERIENCE IS INTERNALIZED

Let us now consider more explicitly the processes of learning responsible for the internalization of experience, and hence for intrinsic organization.

A first point concerns the fact that two kinds of learning intertwine during the course of development: (1) learning that depends on an individual relation to the physical environment, and (2) learning that depends on a relationship to one or more other persons. Learning of the first kind may be called *individual acquisition.* Under this heading may be included learning that results from the child's explorations and manipulations and from the mere repetition of stimuli. Later on the process of individual acquisition becomes increasingly *deliberate*—that is, under the voluntary control of the individual—although some habit systems derived from individual acquisition, as well as from other learning, may be quite nonvoluntary, or automatic. Learning of the second kind, involving other persons, may be called *social learning.* Its basis lies in the prolonged state of plasticity of the human infant, during which time, perforce, at least one other person is present in the environment. Through the agency of this person (usually the mother), and of other persons, the child learns about society and the ways of behaving that are rewarded or punished by others. At one level, situations in which social learning takes place depend on the cultural setting where they occur; at a more immediate level, however, they are always specific interpersonal situations. The person never experiences cultural settings directly, but only through the agency of its exemplars. And here again, the learning process becomes increasingly subject to voluntary control, increasingly dependent on the organization of past experience.

Neither kind of learning is independent of the other—they are contrasting aspects of the total interaction between organism and environment. Neither is one-way, for the child influences and acts on his or her environment, as well as receiving impressions from it.

The second general problem of internalization concerns *immediate versus long-term* effects. Although we shall presently discuss conditioning as the specific mechanism by which learning occurs, at least in the beginning, how to account for the permanent effects of learning has been a more difficult question to answer. Since conditioning is specific and subject to extinction, psychologists have suggested various additional principles to explain more lasting and generalized effects of learning, for example, canalization (Murphy, 1947); trauma (Allport, 1951); fixation (Freud, 1938); sentiment (McDougall, 1933); habit strength (Hull, 1943); response strength (Skinner, 1938); incentive (Spence, 1956); and expectancy (Tolman, 1932).

The Conditioned Response Character of Learning

The basic modification and elaboration of the organism result from *conditioning*—the establishment of new relationships between stimuli and responses. The principle of classical conditioning is that when two stimuli occur in close temporal proximity, one of which naturally evokes a response, the other may also come to evoke that response. In addition to contiguity, it is usually necessary for the two stimuli to occur together repeatedly until the association is strong enough for the new (conditioned) stimulus to evoke the response without the natural (unconditioned) stimulus. At later stages, further contiguous presentations may be necessary to reestablish and further strengthen the connection. Controversy continues about whether these conditions are sufficient to account for the basic learning itself, or whether some other factor or factors are essential. This issue is clarified by distinguishing between *learning* and *performance*, in which the former refers to an intrinsic effect (cognitive or emotional), the latter to observable response. Changes in performance as a function of experience depend on such conditions as attention, incentive, and immediate intrinsic states such as properties of the mental context and motivational arousal. We can label, for convenience, all such relations between prior learning and performance as the *significance* or *relevance* of experience to the situation. Since for all practical purposes we are concerned here with the behavioral effects of basic learning, we shall add relevance as a third requirement.

Complementary to classical conditioning is the principle of *operant* (or *instrumental*) conditioning, developed by Skinner (1938). Here reinforcement is contingent on the individual's making a specified response, which becomes conditioned following reinforcement. Thus the conditioned response serves to produce a reward. The same basic requirements apply to operant as to classical conditioning, but rather than contiguity of stimuli, contiguity of conditioned response (operant) and reinforcement is necessary.

All three requirements (contiguity of stimuli or responses, repetition, and relevance) are preeminently present in the life of the infant. Simple sequences of events recur over and over involving very much the same patterns of stimuli and responses and bearing a relation to the infant's motivational and emotional states. In this way the first modifications of behavior can meaningfully be understood in rather mechanistic terms, allowing sufficiently for variations in extrinsic conditions, individual differences in sensitivity and responsiveness, and gradients of stimulus and response equivalence.

Mowrer (1960a, b) has developed a theory that incorporates both classical conditioning and instrumental (or trial-and-error) learning into a unified conception. The former he calls *sign* learning, the latter *solution* learning. Most situations, he indicates, involve both kinds of learning. For example, in avoidance learning, sign learning comes first (fear is conditioned to a previously neutral stimulus or signal), then this acquired motive instigates trial-and-error behavior leading to a behavioral solution. Contrasted with the behavioristic one-step S-R formula, Mowrer postulates a two-stage formula—S-r: s-R, with S the danger signal, r the conditioned fear response, s the fear motive, and R the learned response.

Mowrer proposes that only intrinsic *emotional* responses are conditioned, and that such states serve as the fundamental mediators in learned behavior. Therefore all learning has a single common denominator in Mowrer's theory—the establishment of emotional relationships between stimuli and responses. However, he recognizes that there may be two kinds of reinforcement—punishment, which has an incremental effect (i.e., increases response tendencies), and reward (decremental), which decreases response tendencies (terminates a specific sequence of acts). Either type of reinforcement may be primary—that is, reward or punishment appropriate for an unlearned drive, such as hunger or pain; or secondary—that is, reward or punishment appropriate for a learned motive, such as social approval or conditioned fear. On this basis Mowrer arrives at four basic effects of conditioning: (1) fear: learning that a signal threatens punishment; (2) disappointment: learning that response does not produce a reward; (3) relief: learning that response does not lead to punishment or to absence of reward; and (4) hope: learning that response may produce reward.

In general then, Mowrer sees all learning as yielding the fundamentals of mediating processes. He does, however, allow for other kinds of mediators, although without clearly indicating whether they are derived from conditioned emotions, or develop in some other fashion. He suggests, in fact, that there may be three types of mediators: (1) emotions, mediators of the first order; (2) pure stimulus acts (the $r_g s_g$ mechanism), to which emotions are conditioned, mediators of the second order; and (3) expectancies, or cognitive representations, mediators of the third order. Despite ambiguities, Mowrer's theory is the most advanced conception of conditioning yet to be formulated. Clearly, the concept of conditioned emotions, with their ready extension to expectancy and mediation, is powerful.

Enduring Effects of Conditioning   To extend the conditioning principle into later stages of development, we must suppose that early conditioning has enduring effects.

1. *Early conditioning.* Because of the combination of extreme plasticity and continual reinforcement, the earliest conditioned responses may be so deeply established that they become permanent. This early, deep, permanent conditioning may continue up to some period when other learning mechanisms (notably mediation) can take over. In this case the further elaboration of behavior may represent the conditioning of prior conditioned responses; that is, conditioned stimuli and responses may function in the way that the original stimuli and responses functioned (i.e., as reinforcers in their own right).

2. *Sensitization.* The earliest conditioning may sensitize the organism, making it easier for certain kinds of connections, rather than others, to be established later on. Directions are laid down such

that stimuli are more and more likely to have particular consequences —as perhaps especially implied by Mowrer's contention that it is really emotions that are conditioned rather than overt responses. Basic conditioning may lead to states of emotional responsiveness that generalize widely, so that new stimuli or situations elicit intrinsic responses that link them with previous experience. Reinforcement need not always be explicit and direct, but may come about via already-acquired emotional systems. To the extent that conditioning has generalized, rather than only specific effects, any stimulus that lies along a gradient of similarity to the original conditioned stimulus has already been somewhat incorporated into the individual's repertory of response elicitation; similarly, any response along a gradient of association with the original conditioned response is to some degree ready to be strengthened under suitable conditions of reinforcement. Subsequent to early conditioning, already-present tendencies may indirectly be strengthened. For example, conditioned responses to the mother may be strengthened by any mother-related reinforcement; or any reinforcement by the mother may simultaneously strengthen a ramifying system of responses.

3. *Intermittent reinforcement*. The persistence of instrumental behavior is very greatly increased by interspersing reward among the events of a sequence rather than supplying it for every event. This condition creates a state in which the person must continue to produce the response (so far as he knows) *every* time in order to receive *any* reward—he cannot afford to cease responding since at some unpredictable time in the future his response will actually yield the hoped-for reward. Once symbolic mediating processes enter into behavior, the instrumental act is represented by an *expectancy* of reward. Thus operant responses provide an important basis for intentional or choice strategies. Having grown out of experience in which intermittent reinforcement was present, such intentions are highly resistant to extinction.

Intermittent reinforcement is also remarkably typical of the infant's experience. Other persons—or even elements in the physical environment—rarely, if ever, provide wholly regular or predictable reinforcement. A child who babbles or laughs often elicits a social response from the parent, but not always, and may therefore babble even when the parent does not respond. Similarly, an infant may discover that a certain toy is available at some location in a room. But although the toy is not always there, it is there often enough to make crawling in that direction a highly desirable activity.

Furthermore, the reward situation itself is not a single, homogeneous event, but involves various components. In addition to a physical gain, such as food, the situation also contains varied acts of another person, such as verbalization, smiling, caressing, and so on. From the principle of generalization, any of these components may be reinforcing, and any of them may be intermittent. Thus an act may become instrumental for a number of reward elements, which may have differential rewarding properties, as well as acquiring different degrees of resistance to extinction. In this fashion, nonmaterial, symbolic, or "self-rewarding" expectancies can develop. A child who acquires certain response patterns in relation to a parent may persist in making them in the absence of material reward, merely to elicit verbal approval or, beyond that, to receive his own intrinsic approval.

4. *Conditioning of emotions.* If, indeed, it is emotions rather than overt (or sensorimotor) responses that are conditioned, there is a further basis for long-enduring influences on subsequent learning. If extinction occurs primarily for bodily or overt behavioral responses, with the underlying emotional (or autonomic) state persisting, then earlier effects can certainly have an important bearing on subsequent experience, as demonstrated especially by research on negative reinforcement (conditioned fear).

5. *Generalization.* Generalization gradients on both the stimulus and response side show that a particular event is not initially a highly specific one-to-one relation between a particular stimulus and a particular response, but rather between a *kind* of stimulus and a *kind* of response. Although special procedures can be introduced to narrow the relation, so that it is specifically discriminated, probably most learning events have the complexities signified by generalization: conditioned responses are not distinctly separate so much as potentially general experiences. And because a learning event has a general effect, it no doubt overlaps many other events. Conditioned events are not so much additive as interrelated.

For example, the mother is the focal point for numerous perceptions and the source of many rewards (or punishments). She acquires generalized properties, any of which can elicit many responses, not just one. An object has many properties and is experienced in varied contexts. A stimulus event overlaps many previously encountered stimuli and a reward has overlapping reinforcement value. An apple is not only a taste but also round, as are bottles, balls, and oranges— and any of these objects not only produces its particular kind of reward but also perhaps verbal reward and other types of social reinforcement. Thus many stimuli may elicit similar response elements and any stimulus may elicit various responses (compare with reintegration as discussed by Hollingworth, 1927). In this fashion conditioning may be viewed as the basis for concepts and attitudes.

The Trial-and-Error Character of Learning

We have already mentioned instrumental learning, which leads the individual to act on the environment to secure reinforcement. As such acquisitions achieve representation through expectancies (or, more broadly, concepts and attitudes, for which expectancies are immediate foci), the infant begins to participate actively in his contacts with the environment. By the term *trial-and-error*, I therefore mean to stress the importance of exploration, manipulation, and intentional effort to carry out a series of responses that bring the child by his own actions into commerce with the environment in a variable fashion. Of course, this variable behavior is not purely accidental, but is influenced by existing properties of intrinsic organization (motives, traits, concepts, attitudes), and also partly by such objects as are available in the environment (i.e., perceptual and feedback processes help to shape behavior). The seemingly paradoxical fact that the person is both molded by the particular properties of his environment (and hence made like others of his group and culture), and yet becomes increasingly individualized is partly a matter of the trial-and-error character of learning.

The consequences of exploring and manipulating depend on what there is to explore and manipulate, on the codes that govern the child's activities, and the rewards (or punishments) that accrue from them. At the same time the child's own tissue system determines to a large degree how active he is in exploring, how rapidly he develops, how he reacts emotionally, and so on. Beyond this, as organization progresses farther, the child behaves to an ever-increasing degree as his own intrinsic organization determines. Thus at one and the same time learning makes the individual more and more like what is permitted and required by his environment and yet more and more like himself.

The Permanent and Self-organizing Character of Experience

The enduring effects of early learning form the substratum for later learning, as seen in the reinforcement of earlier trends, emotional responses, and symbolic representations. Gradually, selective and regulative systems (motives, traits, concepts, attitudes) are established, and behavior displays increasing organization. Since the formation of these systems depends so much on the internalization of experience, it is through their agency that previous experience influences present behavior. The strength and character of previous experience determine the properties of intrinsic organization. Stimuli impinge on already partially organized systems, and responses emerge out of those systems.[1]

The self-organizing property of learning also implies that intrinsic systems are not independent of each other. They are really subsystems, making up the person as a whole. Within this more inclusive system they have active relationships to each other—close or remote, tight or loose, as the case may be. A useful analogy here is a field of forces, in which each component bears a direct or indirect relation to each other component. A change or disturbance at one point produces an effect that depends on all these relationships. It may institute a shifting about, a realignment of forces, so that a different organization ensues. (Gestalt principles of cognitive organization are historically important along these lines.)

The field of forces is so complex, and disturbance so continuous, that a stable organization never exists. Subsystems are interrelated, communicate with each other, and activate each other. A disturbance at onepoint depends for its effect on many interrelationships. By "disturbance" we mean some activity within a subsystem, however aroused—a nervous impulse triggered by an external stimulus, the eroding of barriers between subsystems, the input of emotion, or whatever. Applying this principle on a psychological level, we might say that motives are not single and separate instigations. Hunger may be accompanied by needs for reassurance and social interaction; the desire to meet a pretty girl may be accompanied by the desire to avoid humiliation by making a socially acceptable approach, and so on. The arousal of one motive also arouses others, as a rule. Concepts are not discrete, separate packages, either. A dog is not merely a specific object but a member of numerous sets, such as animals, pets, sources of danger, and so on. It may even be a member of a class such as "things I own" or "things I wish I had," and thus belong with a new catcher's mitt and a baby brother. Similar

[1]This point of view does *not* maintain that intrinsic systems are rigid and unchangeable—although all degrees of susceptibility to change no doubt can be found both within the same person and from one person to another. On the contrary, this discussion points to the *continuity* of experience. Intrinsic systems can and do change, depending on their properties and on the character of subsequent experience. But such changes are not simple accretions or extraneously induced, but are modifications of and incorporations into antecedently acquired systems.

considerations apply to traits and attitudes. Experience does not consist of separate, isolated events, but of ramifying systems of intrinsic processes with focal and receding components.

The Symbolic Character of Learning

The development of language vastly complicates the internalization process. As time goes on, objects and acts come to have internal, or symbolic, counterparts that can serve in lieu of the external object or act. The possibilities thus offered for additional learning are un-limited because experience can be communicated efficiently from one person to another, short-cutted by employing symbols rather than physical objects and overt acts, and utilized in elaborate and rapid ways by manipulating symbols instead of the original percep-tions and acts.

At least in its earliest stages, the acquisition of symbolic re-sponses can be explained as simple conditioning, from the repeated linkage of words (or other symbolic representations, such as images) and objects.[1] In due course the word (or cognitive event) substitutes for the object. Eventually, also, words can themselves act as rein-forcements, and further learning be built on them. As Murphy (1947) pointed out, once language develops, the conditioning process need no longer involve laborious sequences of stimuli and physical re-sponses, but can be cut across or abbreviated by verbal responses. Furthermore, symbolic responses make it possible to bring large segments of past experience into a present situation, as shown, for instance, in connotational dimensions of concepts, and in mediation processes generally.

CULTURAL DETERMINANTS

Social learning molds the child in two ways: (1) by training him in the general pattern of norms, codes, beliefs, practices, and systems of behavior typical of the group, and (2) by providing direct contact with other individuals who interpret the cultural norms and who enforce them in their own ways.

Central Affectional Relationships

The central consideration is *emotional relationships*, through the medium of which specific acquisitions occur.

[1] It remains controversial whether the process of symbolizing itself is inherent in the functioning of the brain, so that some kind of symbolizing occurs even without conditioning. However, we mean here to emphasize the systematic relation between experience and its expression—that is, the organization of cognitive processes, or the introduction of order into experience.

Case studies particularly well illustrate the decisive role of central affectional relationships. One instance is the case of Harry, sensitively described by Bettelheim (1949). A seven-year-old delinquent, Harry came from a home of severe marital discord. His mother was punitive and rejecting; his father was violent when intoxicated, then submissive and remorseful; and both treated Harry with extreme inconsistency. After referral to a special school, an effort was made to establish a stable, secure, and comprehensible environment, to aid Harry in building a new self-concept, and to provide more dependable and supportive parental figures. Progress in these directions led not only to improved social learning, but also to more satisfactory performance in school. Once Harry had begun to achieve satisfying affectional relationships with acceptable parental substitutes, the internalization process also began to proceed more efficiently.

Another illustration comes from Keniston's (1963) report on the case of Inburn. From a conventional middle-class background, he displayed characteristics of "alienation," shown by distrust, pessimism, resentment, egocentricity, feeling himself to be an outsider, rejection of conventional values, and disavowal of happiness as a goal. These characteristics grew out of a special set of affectional relationships. Thus Inburn had deep-lying ambivalent attitudes toward his mother. As a small child he enjoyed an especially intimate relation with her, enhanced by the absence of his father for 4 years on military duty. He failed to achieve a truly close and rewarding relation with his father when the family was reunited. Indeed, some incipient signs of his later alienation appeared at that time (such as moodiness and estrangement). Basic considerations include his earliest intimacy with his mother, followed by "expulsion from early oral paradise," only partial resolution of Oedipal conflicts with continuing ambivalence toward his mother and resistance to identifying with his father. Affectional aspects of his early development had far-reaching effects, both quite explicit (e.g., anger directed at older males) and more generalized (such as his "existential pessimism" and distrust). Unlike in the case of Harry, no further information is available because Inburn disappeared from view. Thus we do not know what processes of later affectional relationships might alter his personality.

Other kinds of research also reveal the effects of sociocultural variables. Studying three generations of a southern Italian peasant family, Campisi (1948) illustrates the effects of changes in the family. Moving from one country to another brought about many important modifications in central family relationships. For instance, the family in America has tended to become more democratic, the mother coming to share status and authority with the father, and the children coming to be treated equally. Other important changes have occurred in the enforcement of basic disciplines, such as those related to weaning. Such changes are not, however, sudden, but transpire over a period of time accompanied by conflict and readjustment.

Davis (1948) has summarized differences between socio-economic groups, found some years ago in studies by him and his coworkers.[1] For example, babies in lower-class families were more likely to be breast-fed only and to be fed at will, the infants were weaned later, sphincter training was begun later, and greater freedom was permitted in staying up late, going to the movies, and so on. Patterns of anxiety also differ at different socioeconomic levels. In the lower class there are many worries about physical dangers such as cold, insufficient food, darkness, and eviction from home. Classes differ in socially defined pressures (represented, for instance, by the police) that impinge on them. Davis suggests that the special social dangers of slum life originate in the context of family, peer group, and other institutions. Compared to the middle-class child, the lower-class youngster is conditioned to fear exploitation by teachers, and learns that serious study is almost a disgrace, that street fighting, cursing, and other acts disapproved of in middle-class society are signs of virility. In a slum community, such behavior is realistic and adaptive.

Thus the internalization process not only operates at the level of central affectional relationships but also in a wider sense depends on the subcultural environment.

One focus for understanding this principle appears in studies of changing attitudes and other personality characteristics in black Americans. Brazziel (1964) administered the Edwards Personal Preference Schedule to groups of black college students in the upper South. Compared to white norms, the black subjects were significantly higher in deference, and lower in autonomy and dominance (there were also sex differences). However, the upper-South students were typically closer to the white norms than were the lower-South students. Social class differences were also apparent. Middle-income subjects from the upper-South displayed higher mean scores for achievement, order, and dominance, and a lower mean for nurturance; but middle-income lower-South subjects were higher on order and endurance, lower on autonomy and nurturance.

That migration and sociocultural forces induce changes in attitudes, motives, and self-concepts is shown clearly in analyses of

[1]See also, Bronfenbrenner (1965) and Zigler and Child (1969), who indicate that these differences are decreasing. Hess (1970) has also reviewed this topic.

young black militants. A study by Forward and Williams (1970) was based on interviews just after a riot in Detroit in 1967. Tests indicated that *personal control* ("feeling of control over [one's] own future") was associated with positive evaluation of the riot, whereas no such association appeared with *control ideology* ("general beliefs about the relationships among ability, effort, and success in the society at large"). Persons who were uncertain about whether the riot was good or bad displayed significantly higher self-blame scores. Over time these differences polarized, so that the riot greatly increased the tendency by young black militants to blame external sources, with an opposite effect for nonmilitants. Findings like these led the investigators to conclude that the self-concept of young black militants differs from that of their peers. Rejecting the fatalistic stereotype that ghetto existence stems from weakness or inability to improve their lot, they believe strongly in their potential to control their lives and to affect their futures. At the same time they have a realistic view of external barriers like discrimination, prejudice, and exploitation.

The heightened sense of personal effectiveness combined with the change from self-blame to blaming the system helps to explain why young ghetto militants resort to violence. An augmentation of personal efficacy leads to increased frustration with the conditions responsible and also to strong impulses to employ violent action to fight these conditions. Blaming the system rather than themselves serves to justify the use of violence.

Cultural Patterns

Kardiner's (1939, 1945) investigations demonstrate the significance of cultural differences. A special technique ("psychodynamic analysis") was followed to identify the primary and secondary institutions of a culture and to trace their effects in personality development. The consequences of exposure to the same institutions are represented in the basic personality structure.

Kardiner's analyses of various cultures strikingly reveals fundamental differences in internalization and, as a result, in behavior among cultures. Fundamentally important is the role of central affectional relationships. Thus in traditional Marquesan culture, the mother was a frustrating object to the child. Her relation to the child was characterized by neglect and lack of tenderness and care. Therefore the infant's longing for protection and love was not satisfied, and many adult anxieties stemmed from this condition (most directly evinced in direct or disguised hostility toward women). The real protectors of the child were the secondary husbands (polyandry was practiced among the Marquesans) and the father. An outcome of this relationship was strong and friendly ties to and among men. The child, however, was not subjected to restricting or unreasonable demands or disciplines, with a resulting independence and self-confidence, and freedom and spontaneity in relations between children and adults.

In Alor, relationships with both parents were inconsistent and confused, or actually featured by neglect or rejection. This condition was at least partly responsible for the mutual hostility, distrust, and suspicion typical of the Alorese basic personality. At the same time, the many tensions in childhood appeared to stifle the development of organized, consistent modes of acting, so that, despite considerable aggression, there was no effective means to release it.

Still another pattern appeared among the Comanche. Here maternal care was consistent and helpful, and the relationship to the father was also warm and dependable. These conditions contributed to a fairly simple, self-confident personality and to strong, cooperative relations with other persons.

Our illustrations could be multiplied, but one more must suffice. Bacon, Child, and Barry (1963) have shown that cultural variations in criminal behavior can be linked with characteristics of the family. Ratings of ethnographic data revealed that the general incidence of crime varies with the structure of the family, increasing from monogamous nuclear forms through monogamous extended forms to polygynous types. By inference, crime is partly a defense against strong feminine identification. Variations in the absence of the father, reflected in the form of the family, can be generally treated as determining the strength of feminine identification. Child-training practices inferred to induce feelings of deprivation of love (e.g., indulgence, emphasis on responsibility, self-reliance, and achievement) proved to be significantly correlated with theft,[1] whereas factors conducive to a suspicious or distrustful attitude toward the environment (dependence, socialization anxiety, and prolonged mother-child sleeping arrangements) were associated with personal crime (such as intent to injure or kill, assault, rape, false accusations).

Such accounts, of necessity, extract features from the total social environment. But fundamental institutions are interdependent,

[1] In addition, a number of socioeconomic factors were found to be significantly correlated with theft, including degree of social stratification, level of political integration, and elaboration of social control. These properties of the social system may also be interpreted as inducing feelings of insecurity and resentment but, as the investigators note, may also partly result from a high incidence of crime.

and their effects are complex. The culture sets the general framework within which internalization occurs and specifies the general character of the central affectional relationships. From this background the person's social experience is selected, so to speak, and explicitly presented to him via immediate interpersonal encounters with others.

PARENT-CHILD RELATIONSHIPS

The role of child-rearing practices is especially well-revealed in cross-cultural studies. Research by Whiting and Child (1953), for example, showed how adult belief systems are associated with such practices. Thus explanations of illness that emphasize oral, dependency, or aggressive causes occur significantly more often in societies featured by severity of socialization in those spheres.

It is becoming clearer that the general relation between parent and child is more significant than the specific techniques employed. Such relations vary along dimensions of *love-hostility* and *control-autonomy* (Schaefer, 1959). A love orientation is marked by rewarding, directing, and encouraging tactics, with the use of reasoning; negative policies include isolation, scolding, and withholding of love. Such techniques induce security, confidence, and internalized reactions to transgression (conscience), but may also be associated with overcontrol of impulses and undue concern about the reactions of others. Hostility-based patterns typically involve physical punishment, verbal disparagement, or cold, aloof, and disapproving attitudes. These tactics often induce demanding attention, hostility, and aggression; or they may produce fearfulness, dependency, and withdrawal. However, this kind of relationship can engender striving, independence, and early maturity. The control dimension is seen in continuous surveillance and attempted direction, ranging from overprotectiveness to dictatorial exercise of power. Consequences include fear of punishment and responsiveness to external authority, or hostility to authority and uncooperativeness. In autonomous patterns the child is permitted relatively great freedom, typically conducing to warm and friendly interpersonal behavior, self-assurance, and assertiveness. However, a resulting concern for maintaining social relationships may be accompanied by a lack of persistence and independence.

Longitudinal studies also demonstrate continuities between the early experience of the child and adult characteristics (Sontag and Baker, 1958; Kagan and Moss, 1962). Such continuities are by no means uniform since relationships between parental behavior and personal tendencies decline as development continues, others become stronger, and still others apparently have delayed effects (see Figure 16-1). I do not mean to overstate the role of early experience, because later experience can greatly modify or alter its effects, but rather to stress the continuity of experience, in which successive events grow out of those that have preceded them.

Further evidence on the significance of parent-child relations comes from experimental studies. It has been systematically observed, for example, that highly authoritarian mothers are restricting in play situations, hostile and rejecting mothers are inattentive and display little interaction with their children, and democratic mothers are compliant and participative (Brody, 1965). In another study, a high level of punitiveness in the mother was found to be positively related in boys to dependency behavior in preschool settings, but a negative relation appeared for girls (Sears et al., 1953). Highly-punished children of both sexes displayed more aggression in doll play (a fantasy situation) than medium- or lightly-punished children. In another study, the father and mother served as reinforcing agents in an operant conditioning procedure (Patterson, 1965). Parents of either sex were quite effective in influencing the child, but highly anxious fathers were especially so. Furthermore, boys from punitive and restrictive homes and girls from nonpunitive homes were especially responsive. Following Schaefer's (1959) formulation, Heilbrun, Orr, and Harrell (1966) examined relations between such parental attitudes and the performance by college men on a concept-formation task. The rejected subjects displayed a significantly impaired performance. In a further experiment on level of aspiration, with induced failure, the rejected men were least stable and least positive in setting goals (Heilbrun and Orr, 1966).

Teachers, Peers, and Others
Affectional ties with persons outside the home and beyond infancy are continuing determinants of the internalization process. The role of teacher-pupil relationships is increasingly recognized as significant for learning (Rogers, 1968). Again, influences stem not so much from specific techniques as from the general character of the relationship, described by Rogers as reflecting qualities of realness (or genuineness), trust, acceptance, and "prizing," and empathic understanding (sensitive awareness). Similarly, the effects of peer interaction depend on affectional bonds (Lott and Lott, 1969). Positive, rewarding, and understanding attitudes—or simply liking—have

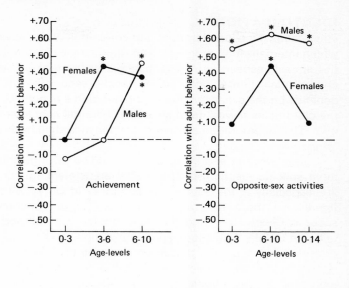

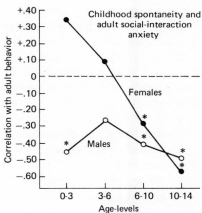

FIGURE 16-1   Examples of correlations between childhood behavior at several age levels and adult behavior. (Based on Kagan and Moss, 1962). (Significant correlations are starred.)

facilitative consequences, compared to opposing attitudes. But this is not to say that punitive and negative relationships may not have important consequences. Marshall (1965), for example, points out that punishment can at least be informative, and therefore provide an impetus to learning.

IDENTIFICATION

The relationships just described are conditions of the environment in which internalization proceeds. The significance of central affectional ties appears especially in identification, or the process whereby the child models himself after other people, especially the parents. It depends on the existence of a strong emotional attachment, whereby the child gains reward from accepting parental characteristics as his own. The incorporation of such characteristics shall be designated as *introjection*.

Identification and introjection should be distinguished from the more specific mechanisms that fulfill adjustment functions in later life, especially in the adult. A person may "identify" with a political figure or a sports hero as a means to acquire vicarious power or success. Clearly, the principle is the same as in childhood identification, but usually with short-range implications and with an indication of underlying dynamics that depend on the consequences of childhood identification, which the adult mechanism expresses. Second, identification may involve more than introjection, such as projection, displacement, hostility, and so on. Furthermore, although identification signifies a positive modeling, a negative relation may develop, in which the child opposes rather than accepts the available model.

I mean by identification, as Sanford (1955) proposes, a mainly unconscious process. It is a continuous feature of parent-child relationships, in which neither party is fully aware of its pervasive influence. The child absorbs not simply what the parent conceives himself to be instilling or instructing, but *what the parent is* as a person, *how* he acts and feels, and other acquisitions that defy a clear description. In this respect identification is distinguished from *imitation*, or the overt and directly intentional influence of a model on another person.

The Freudian theory of identification (Fenichel, 1945; Bronfenbrenner, 1960) encompasses a sequence of events involving the child's changing relationship with the parents. In early stages of development this attachment is narcissistic, and associated with the Oedipus complex. The mother first serves as a sexual love object, accompanied by dependency on her and demands for emotional satisfaction. In the case of the boy, the father is perceived as a rival, with a greater or lesser degree of hostility toward him. But a complex set of conditions soon begins to act. The mother is compelled to reject the boy's demanding advances, not only because they constitute inappropriate behavior (as determined by the social norms), but also because in fact the father is her preferred sexual love object. At the same time the father also asserts direct and continuing authority over the child, for similar reasons. Therefore the boy must alter his relationship to the mother, by repressing its sexual character and "sublimating" his love for her; accompanying this process is an acceptance of the father as a source of authority and an exemplar of acceptable masculine behavior. Thus the Oedipus complex approaches a resolution and sets the stage for identification with the father. This relationship becomes established during the latency period of later childhood.

In the case of the girl, however, the sequence is more complex. The mother also serves for her as an initial love object since she is the primary source of comfort, gratification of needs, and security. But soon a narcissistic attachment to the father begins, with a strong sexual character. However, a further shift is required, namely, a desexualization of feelings toward the father, and the development of an identification with the mother. Forces are imposed on her to recognize that her parents are the actual sexual love objects for each other, and that they have authority over her. Again, these conditions depend on social norms that guide the parents in enforcing appropriate behavior. In general, these changes are likely to be less sharply defined and less completely accomplished for girls than for boys. One reason is that our society, at least, tolerates a closer continuing and dependent emotional relationship between daughter and father than between son and mother. Another reason is that the greater complexities of the girl's Oedipal relationships may make it more difficult to resolve them.

The superego is one of the principal consequences of the identification relationship, but in addition to facilitating the acquisition of moral standards and ideals, identification also provides a basis for learning sex roles and the way of life represented by the family (the traditions and cultural perspectives characteristic of the parents).

IMITATION

The influence of other people in social learning becomes explicit in those processes that have historically been called *imitation, suggestion,* and *sympathy* (Allport, 1968). Each of these processes has been the focus of particular areas of investigation, imitation in the learning of the child (with extensions to adults), suggestion in response to persuasive communications and attitude changes, and sympathy in the investigation of emotional and helping behavior.

In imitation, a person manifests behavior that has been "modeled" by another person. Chiefly to be distinguished are "echo" or conditioned response imitation (Allport, 1937; Murphy, Murphy, and Newcomb, 1937), and "copying." In the echo form, similar behavior recurs merely because sequences of stimuli and responses are repeated. The conditioned stimulus is simply the same as the response that it evokes, either an individual's own act or the act of another. Such situations may be accidental or deliberately reinforced (e.g., by the parents). Copying occurs when an individual makes his behavior "approximate that of a model and (knows) when he has done so, that his is an acceptable reproduction of the model act" (N.E. Miller and Dollard, 1941). Some preliminary learning is necessary to equip the person with an ability to perform the required act; essential also is a reward (material, or intangible, like approval).

N. E. Miller and Dollard (1941) conducted a series of experiments on animals and children intended to specify the conditions under which learning by imitation may occur and to test principles derived from learning theory. In one experiment with first-grade children, the situation presented the subject with a choice of two boxes, in one of which a reward (candy) could be found. The subject watched a child "leader," trained in advance, proceed to one of the boxes and obtain the reward. The subject tried to find the candy until he achieved success on two successive trials. In a parallel condition, subjects were rewarded for nonimitating behavior (i.e., going to the box not chosen by the leader). The training proved very effective and generalized strongly to a four-box situation. Using an adult leader, and a more complex task, McDavid (1959) replicated the results of Miller and Dollard, and also showed that parental variables such as strictness and disapproval of dependency are related to imitation. Schein (1954) extended the experiment to a group situation with adults, demonstrating both imitation and generalization.

In recent years this general situation has been exploited in many experiments. Not only have various conditions been manipulated, but increasing effort has been devoted to exploring implications of the experimental results for a broader conception of internalization (Flanders, 1968).

Imitation depends on the characteristics of the model and of the subject. In one study (Bandura and Mischel, 1965), children, who had by previous assessment been identified as preferring immediate *or* delayed reward, were exposed to either a live or symbolic model. In a choice situation, the child actually observed the model and verbalized a "philosophy of reward" or was presented with this information in written form; control children had no model. The model's choices were opposite to the subject's preference.

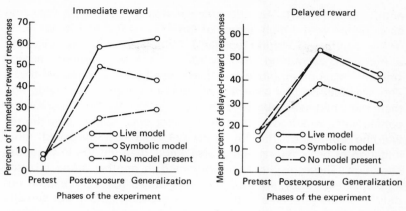

FIGURE 16-2 Mean percentage of response on each of three test periods for three model conditions. (From Bandura and Mischel, 1965.)

The live model was considerably more effective in inducing change in the immediate-reward children, with little difference for the delayed-reward group (see Figure 16-2); a generalization test after 4 to 5 weeks showed that the modeling effect persisted in both groups. Live models are also more effective with adults (Bandura, Blanchard, and Ritter, 1969; this study dealt with modification of phobic behavior, the fear of snakes). In another study, five-year-old children were exposed to films in which peer *or* adult models displayed *aggressive* behavior (Hicks, 1965). After a period of frustration, play with toys was observed. The peer model produced a greater effect on aggressive behavior immediately after the film but, after 6 months, the effect of the adult model was greater. A *nurturant* model induced more imitation of incidental behavior (e.g., manner and verbal acts) than a *nonnurturant* model, but there was little effect on a discrimination task (Bandura and Huston, 1961); similar results have been found for nurturant versus nonnurturant mothers (Mussen and Parker, 1965). But nurturance may facilitate tasks that do not involve imitation (DiBartolo and Vinacke, 1969). Observed in their own homes, children were found to imitate the *dominant* parent (Hetherington, 1965). Dominance of the parent seems to be especially significant for girls, while warmth is significant for boys (Hetherington and Frankie, 1967). In general, the child's emotional state, as elicited by the reinforcing agent's expressive behavior is the important factor (Leventhal and Fisher, 1970).

The behavior of the model has been manipulated by Mischel

and Grusec (1966). An adult female was introduced to the child as someone with a high degree of *future control* ("a new teacher") or *low control* ("a visiting teacher"). She played with the subject in a nurturant, *rewarding* fashion, or in a *nonrewarding* manner (minimal responding while the child played with unattractive toys). This was followed by a display of neutral or aversive behavior, and then the child was observed in interaction with an experimental confederate. Imitation of neutral behavior was greater after the rewarding condition; the future-control condition produced more imitation of both neutral and aversive acts than did the low-control condition. These results were confirmed in another study (Grusec and Mischel, 1966), with additional evidence that the children not only performed the acts of the highly rewarding model, but actually learned them.

McDavid (1964) investigated the consistency of the model in the learning of a color-discrimination task when a preschool child had the opportunity to observe an adult model. Although all groups displayed learning, 100 percent consistent correct response by the model and also random response were both superior to 67 percent consistency. A model who was consistently rewarded for displays of highly aggressive behavior induced more imitation than did an inconsistently treated or consistently punished model, and the inconsistent condition produced more imitation than consistent punishment did (Rosekrans and Hartup, 1967, see Figure 16-3).

Imitation is more likely when the person perceives the model as *similar* to himself. In one experiment, boy scouts were more influenced by a peer dressed as a scout and with other attributed characteristics intended to strengthen judged similarity than by the same peer dressed in street clothes and also low in similarity in other ways (Rosekrans, 1967). More imitation was displayed by girls similar to their mothers than by those who were dissimilar—but this did not hold for boys (Hetherington, 1965).

Vicarious Reinforcement

Clearly implied is the principle that children are influenced by reward and punishment administered to a model. Here the critical conditions are that one individual observe another when that person is systematically reinforced for responses that can readily be discriminated, and, further, that the observer be tested for imitation without himself being directly reinforced. It is difficult to separate vicarious reinforcement from certain instances of conditioning, when the subject learns

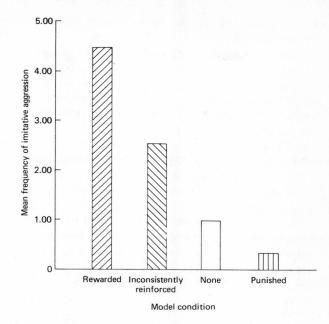

FIGURE 16-3   Imitation as a function of vicarious reinforcement. (Based on Rosekrans and Hartup, 1967.)

merely to respond to the same stimulus as does the model. However, as Flanders (1968) points out, we need only be reasonably sure that the subject makes the following assumption: "If I do that, I'll get rewarded (or punished) too." Thus children who observed a punished model manifested less imitation than did those who observed a rewarded model or one for whom there was no consequence—however, when attractive incentives were introduced, this difference was eliminated (Bandura, 1965).

Bandura, Grusec, and Menlove (1967) administered four treatments to nursery school children with a history of fear of dogs. (1) In a series of four *modeling-positive* sessions, the children first had a "jovial party," followed by observing a fearless peer who interacted with a dog, with contact progressively increasing in directness and intimacy. (2) Similar *modeling-neutral* sessions were held, but with no parties. (3) In *exposure-positive* sessions there were parties with the dog present, but no model. (4) Finally, *positive-context* sessions included just the parties, without dog or model. A test of graduated interactions with the dog, after these sessions, revealed that the two modeling conditions yielded similar extinction tendencies, in comparison with the two control conditions, which did not differ. In a further study, multiple models proved considerably more effective than a single model (Bandura and Menlove, 1968).

With adults, vicarious reinforcement has yielded conflicting results. In some studies, verbal reinforcement of a model facilitated verbal conditioning (Kanfer and Marston, 1963). In others, the introduction of control groups to permit a better comparison of vicarious and direct reinforcement failed to produce significant effects for the former, although the latter was very effective (Phillips, 1968a,b). Since typical experimental conditions are artificial and contrived, clarification will require further research. If the crucial factor is the subject's perception that he might profit from acting like the model, attention should be directed to how such expectations are established. Although direct reinforcement as a rule is probably more effective, it would be surprising if vicarious reinforcement were not also significant. How many graduate students, for example, have been influenced by rewards (or punishments) administered to their mentors?

The Role of Imitation
In general, exposure to a model is an important condition in shaping early experience (and also affects adult behavior). Models serve to identify response sequences, to demonstrate the outcomes to which they lead, and to make a situation meaningful—that is, significant in an interpersonal fashion. The presence and behavior of the model elicit affectional relationships that mediate the child's orientation to the task.

SUGGESTION
Other persons may also influence the child in indirect ways when no explicit reinforcement is involved. Verbal and gestural acts convey some response desired by the source person, but without actual indication of what reward or punishment will ensue if the response is carried out. Origins of suggestion can be traced to conditioning, by which words and gestures become conditioned stimuli to evoke appropriate responses, and the essential affectional relationships are established. With the acquisition of language, suggestion may become quite efficient in guiding the behavior of the child. To be sure, the absence of direct reinforcement does not signify that *no* reinforcing conditions are present. Rather, intrinsic rewards may be

gained (via expectancies of approval, for example, or of punishment—and such expectancies may either lead to self-reward or self-punishment or to future reward or punishment from the source of influence).

Much of the discipline exerted in love-oriented patterns is conducted through the use of suggestion. Remaining to be clarified are the conditions antecedent to its efficacy and under which it works. For example, does consistent contingent reward (or punishment) lead to situations where suggestion can be dependably utilized? Or is an intermittent schedule better? Evidence on such antecedent conditions could be obtained from parents, and experiments devised to test the effectiveness of suggestion in relation to parental differences. It would be interesting to learn more about differences between positive and negative suggestion (i.e., implied reward versus punishment). Then the role of suggestion in the basic internalization process might be more fully brought into the kind of perspective offered by Bandura and Walters (1963) for imitation.

SYMPATHY

A third process in social learning is based on feeling or emotion that one person induces in another. Here, again, conditioning equips the child to respond emotionally to others. The emotional acts of another must acquire cue-value—that is, become conditioned stimuli for evoking response, and the child must learn in a more general way to be aware of and to respond to other persons. The social environment of the child typically provides continuous opportunity for these prerequisites to develop. "Sympathy," however, is only one aspect of emotional learning. Since it signifies a "sharing" of emotion—that is, a congruence between the feeling of two persons—we must also recognize other outcomes, such as when one person's emotion induces a different emotion. Thus the crying of another may evoke joy (as in sadism) or anger. Kindliness may elicit annoyance, rather than a fellow feeling, as when the befriending of a new child in the neighborhood induces jealousy in a third child. Such reactions are more complex than the concept of sympathy implies.[1]

L. B. Murphy (1937) studied sympathy experimentally, and by observations in the natural environment of the nursery school.

---

[1] A variety of meanings have been attached to the terms *sympathy* and *empathy*. I would differentiate the former from the latter by proposing that empathy involves cognitive understanding of another person's emotion, but that sympathy is primarily a state of feeling like another does, or participating in his emotion. Thus a therapist may understand and appreciate a patient's distress, experiencing empathy, compared to the witness of an accident who feels the same fear of pain as the victim. Complex emotions such as compassion appear to blend the two states.

Emphasizing the role of learning, she showed that despite individual patterns of sympathetic response, the following general forms can be identified:(1) *cooperative*, or practical sympathy, where children respond spontaneously to the needs of their playmates; (2) *masked aggression*, or behavior a child may adopt to avoid disapproval; (3) *projected anxiety*, where a child attributes his own anxieties to others; (4) *emotional identification*, occurring primarily in well-adjusted children as a response to the distress of persons they love; and (5) *conventional morality*, or responses often employed as an overt bid for approval.

Altruism

More recently the study of sympathy has become focused on manifestations of *altruism* (helping behavior). This phenomenon involves considerations of superego development (see Chapter 18) and the learning of social norms. In a recent review, Bryan and London (1970) suggest that affective experience is crucial in altruistic tendencies, pointing to a number of significant findings, including the fact that generosity increases with age (Wright, 1942; Fischer, 1963; Handlon and Gross, 1959), that altruistic behavior depends on the role of the model, and that family background is related to expressions of altruism.

In a study by Staub (1970), children, either alone or in same-sex pairs, overheard a tape-recorded episode in which a child, apparently in the next room, was experiencing distress. When given an opportunity to help, a curvilinear relation to grade level appeared (see Figure 16-4). The reversal at older ages may be a function of social norms such as fear of disapproval for inappropriate behavior and concern over evaluation by peers.

After surveying research on adults, Krebs (1970) noted that altruism may be elicited by positive states (such as success) or by negative states (such as harm to another). Other facilitative conditions include observation of altruistic models and dependency or attractiveness of the recipient. Sex differences appear, since adult males act less altruistically toward highly dependent others (especially if they seem threatening), with the reverse for females. Coming from a large family is also conducive to altruism. In general, altruism tends to be greater toward others who are similar, prestigious, or potential benefactors.

In adult social life, emotional response to others becomes complicated by many factors, including perception of the consequen-

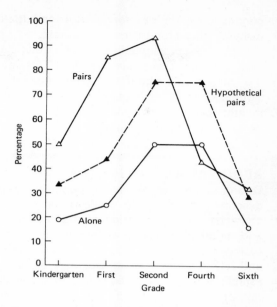

FIGURE 16-4   Percentage of help at each grade level (active help and volunteering information combined) by individuals, pairs, and hypothetical pairs. (Percentages of hypothetical pairs were derived on the basis of individuals' helping behavior.) (From Staub, 1970.)

ces of one's actions (rewards and costs), the characteristics of the other person, and norms that govern appropriate behavior (e.g., the *social responsibility norm* [Berkowitz and Daniels, 1964]). For example, feelings of gratitude vary with perception of the benefactor's intentions, the cost of the generous behavior to the benefactor, and the value of the benefit received (Tesser, Gatewood, and Driver, 1968); the attractiveness of another person decreases when the other is seen to be responsible both for his own suffering and for a desirable outcome to oneself (Lerner and Matthews, 1967). In a field study, Hornstein, Fisch, and Holmes (1968) found that helping behavior was enhanced by an expression of positive feelings on the part of a symbolic social model, if an individual did not perceive himself as dissimilar to the model. However, expression of positive or negative feelings made no difference when the model was perceived as dissimilar.

Thus the role of emotional response in adult behavior depends on attitudes that govern its expression. Especially significant in this connection is the development of the superego, and we can better discuss other studies in that context.

Processes originating in sympathetic response constitute an essential aspect of social learning. Through emotional experience, the child learns about the experience of others—and about the significance of that experience. Such learning becomes elaborated in later years into patterns of interpersonal judgment and systems of response to emotional cues.

REDIRECTING ACTIVITIES

During the course of development, the relationships and processes described in preceding sections have basic consequences in the character and organization of the person. Initial trends are shaped and modified and new experience is continuously integrated into that which has been internalized earlier. Directions (such as goals and relationships with others) may be changed, or new directions established. These consequences of social learning entail the formation of ego structure and its effects on behavior and the acquisition of values and ideals (the superego).

SUMMARY

Processes in the internalization of experience determine the mental context, associated with variations in biological, physical-environmental, social, and cultural conditions. Trends of individual and social learning are evident in the development of traits, motives, attitudes, and concepts. General characteristics of internalization processes include (1) conditioning, (2) trial-and-error learning, (3) the permanence and self-organization of learning, and (4) symbolic representation. Central affectional relationships serve as the medium for socialization in the family, varying from one society to another. Parent-child relationships have basic love-hostility and control-autonomy dimensions—and such factors are important in the extension of socialization to peer groups and other settings. Identification processes are crucial. Social learning also depends on imitation, suggestion, and sympathy; experimental research has been especially concerned with the first of these, revealing effects associated with the characteristics and behavior of models, similarity to the model, and conditions of reinforcement. Studies show that altruistic behavior increases with age, and is influenced by models, family background, social responsibility norms, and other factors.

17

EGO AND SELF

In the last chapter the groundwork was laid for examining more closely the properties of the mental context, which depend on the *organization* of experience. More specifically, we turn now to a discussion of cognitive systems.

Freudian theory contributes, in this respect, the ego and the superego; biosocial and Rogerian theory, the self. I find it necessary to retain all three of these organizational principles,[1] as I shall hope to make clear. Attitudes that fall under these headings serve to "personalize" thinking—to render it relevant to the experience and needs of a particular person. Although, as we have seen, individuals during the internalization process are subject to the influence of similar conditions (associated with general social and cultural contexts, and with their contingent prescriptions), nevertheless, even the strictest of culturally specified disciplines depends on the actions of particular agents interacting with a specific person; beyond that, the continuously self-organizing character of learning conduces to an increasing individualization of experience.

Therefore when we consider the operation of attitudes that

[1]Jung also recognizes both ego and self.

stem from the organization of the ego, self, and superego, we are seeking to understand the personal expression and direction of cognition. That is, we are concerned with the *regulation* of thinking.[1]

EGO MECHANISMS

In the Freudian view the ego begins to develop from the earliest sensations and perceptions of the infant (Fenichel, 1945). Opposed to the biological needs of the organism are the conditions of the external environment, which require the matching of impulses to stimuli. Gradually the infant begins to discriminate objects and to orient his actions toward them. He begins to learn what is possible and necessary. This process entails a distinction between the *pleasure principle* and the *reality principle*. The pleasure principle signifies that biological impulses (arising from the id) seek direct expression in behavior with consideration of consequences other than their immediate gratification. The reality principle—the keynote of the ego—refers to the control of impulses in relation to the immediate environmental situation, and therefore is apparent in delay of gratification (or a change in behavior from that which would otherwise occur). As experience continues, the ego increasingly acquires resources for controlling impulses and bringing them into relation with the external environment, thus acting as a mediating or regulating system between motives and situational conditions.[2]

Accompanying the development of the ego then, is an increasing tendency for perceptual and cognitive activities to determine behavior, in contrast to the primitive impulses arising from the id. The id utilizes *primary process* to express its impulses—that is, direct, affectively toned images (hallucinations). But the ego employs *secondary process*, or realistic thinking, to accomplish its aims. Manifestations of the primary process are wish fulfillments; of the secondary process, planning and rational cognitions. With the acquisition of secondary-process resources, the ego converts the fluid energies of the id into organized cognitive processes. In this fashion conscious activities become differentiated from unconscious forces. More accurately, the free expression of impulses comes under the control of the organized ego, so that special relationships develop between unconscious and conscious forces. These relationships

---

[1] As earlier pointed out, regulatory processes depend not only on the operation of enduring attitudes but also on the immediate situation and on feedback from behavior therein. In these last chapters this point is always implied, if not explicitly stated.

[2] Acting also, in the Freudian view, to accommodate both these forces with the structure of the superego.

are vested, on the one hand, in repression and mechanisms for the altered direction and expression of unconscious impulses, and, on the other hand, in the integration of biological resources and realistic thinking resulting from sublimation.

REPRESSION AND SUBLIMATION

It is a historical curiosity that until recently psychoanalytic theorists have been unable to convincingly reconcile instinctual forces with the "higher" forms of human activity that we link with society and culture, save by the doctrine of repression. So long, in fact, as attention is preoccupied with neurosis, no other resolution is easily seen. But when one turns to healthy personality (or focuses on culture itself), another alternative appears. A full understanding of the ego therefore requires clarification of this issue.[1]

Repression

The reality principle stems from the frustration of free gratification of impulses. The ego utilizes energy to prevent them from entering consciousness—and thus interposes barriers between unconscious and conscious realms of the mind. Following repression, various mechanisms may be employed to permit an impulse to achieve expression in disguised or indirect forms. Thus the threat or danger from primitive wishes is reduced or alleviated or made to serve the interests of acceptable goals. This general process has already been described in relation to dreams. More broadly, whenever the ego must use repression we would expect to see distortions of cognition (whether of memory, perception, judgment, conceptualizing, logic, etc.).

Repression is a function of conflict between the ego and the id, serving to maintain balance between them. The degree and intensity of repression depends on the amount of conflict. In the classical psychoanalytic conception, conflict is regarded as nearly perpetual, the ego constantly needing to monitor unconscious impulses, exert repression, and redirect wishes into acceptable or safe modes of expression. This relation between unconscious and conscious processes is, *par excellence,* typical of the neurotic, who is more or less continuously besieged by threatening instinctual impulses, and must devote great quantities of ego energy to their restraint and

[1] My view derives partly from necessary inferences drawn over the years, and from the critical extensions of Freudian theory by Marcuse (1955), N. O. Brown (1959), and Madison (1961). See also the revisions of psychoanalytic theory advanced by ego psychology (e.g., Hartmann, 1964).

control. As a consequence, comparatively little energy is left over for activity oriented toward coping constructively with environmental demands. The ego of the neurotic is disproportionately occupied with the reduction of anxiety and with the maintenance of defenses.

How then does the "normal" person manage? The psycho-analytic view really treats the normal person as being basically the same as the neurotic, except that he is less subject to conflict. Repression is more successful in reducing anxiety, and the ego is left with sufficient resources to pursue its own end. Instead of perpetual defensive tactics, the normal ego much of the time can engage in realistic commerce with the environment. However, such activity still rests on a balance between unconscious and conscious processes, albeit a relatively harmonious one. This means that if we were to probe deeply enough we would find underlying the normal person's behavior essentially the same repressions that harass the neurotic. Conscious behavior is simply a superstructure, or facade, built on repressed impulses. The neurotic has a difficult—if not impossible—task in preventing unconscious wishes from exploding into consciousness and thus destroying the ego's management of behavior. The normal person has a much easier time—and may, indeed, hardly need to worry that his defenses will break down.

This conception makes the id and the ego (and the superego) into separate functions opposed to each other. Personality organization involves the allocation of energy among these systems.

Sublimation

The negative pessimistic conception of man as fundamentally dominated by original instincts that can only be restrained or distorted, has elicited much criticism (e.g., currently by humanistic psychologists). Freud himself recognized that man can acquire more than defensive systems, and presented, in this connection, the principle of sublimation. This term refers to the desexualization of instinctive impulses,[1] followed by the directing of energy toward "higher" goals, such as in aesthetic, religious, humanitarian, or other spheres. We must, however, distinguish between two meanings of sublimation. As just described, sublimation is essentially a "successful defense" of the ego—that is, a process whereby the threat of unconscious impulses is effectively removed, and their energies acquired by the ego—the distinction between id and ego remains,

---

[1]Or to the deenergizing of instincts, if we include aggressive and destructive impulses.

but with an altered relation between them. It is clear, however, that in this case there is *no repression* (in effect, none is necessary since the original instinctive property is eliminated). Thus sublimation is an alternative to repression.

In contrast, sublimation may refer to an integration of impulse and cognition, a blending, so to speak, of unconscious and conscious, so that they compose wholly compatible new intrinsic systems. The impulse is not necessarily "desexualized" or deprived of its original character, but contributes directly and without repression to the ego's activity.[1] There is no longer any distinction between id and ego, nor any break between unconscious and conscious. (However, there is an unconscious *level*, or simply an unverbalized or latent or nonconscious component.)

Conformity and Creativity

But to cite sublimation raises still another issue. Close consideration of the principle shows that society not only imposes repressions on its members, but also apparently sublimations. What is the aim of socialization? Is it to promote the repression of libidinal impulses and thereby to facilitate the establishment of defenses? In general, this view has probably characterized the psychoanalytic orientation. Or is the aim to promote the establishment of sublimations, and thereby to adopt the "higher" goals prescribed by the culture? In either case, the difficulty arises that *someone* decides what repressions and/or sublimations are most desirable or necessary. Since the conventional view regards the parents as the primary socializing agents and treats them as exemplars of society, it is easy to conclude that the aim of socialization is to perpetuate the existing culture in its new members. But if this be the case, then where do individual choice and social change lie? This age-old dilemma is not readily, if at all, recognized in either the principle of repression or in the principle of sublimation (especially if the latter is itself formulated as a defense built on repression).

What does the sublimation of impulses accomplish that is fundamentally any better than repression? In both instances the outcome seems to be a person who has been made to adapt to the prescriptions of society, in the one case by suffering continuous anxiety, in the other by a happier acceptance and conformity to the

---

[1]When carried to its conclusion, this principle of sublimation converges on the principle of the functional autonomy of motives, and on other formulations of self-sustaining acquired motivational systems.

social system. The ego built on repression, it is true, is less productive because disproportionate energy must be devoted to defense, whereas the ego founded on sublimation can pursue with minimal distraction such goals as work and play. In addition, the notion that sublimation involves the desexualization of impulses, if carried to an extreme, is clearly quite unsatisfactory to the extent that it rules out sexual gratification. In pyschoanalytic theory, presumably, this problem could be handled by the notion that there always remains some surplus of libidinal instinct that occasionally overcomes or bypasses repressive or sublimational systems.

Thus it is necessary to recognize that sublimation, like repression, leads to *two* possible outcomes. Sublimation may produce *conformity* or *creativity*. The key point, in sublimation as in repression, is the bringing of impulses under the control of the ego. But rather than defending against them, in sublimation the ego *uses* them and *incorporates* them into inclusive systems, in which the division between ego and id disappears. In this way an individual is not merely a reflection of society but is also free to choose goals and courses of action that deviate from it.

This issue points to the necessity for research to examine more broadly the implications for cognitive behavior of various kinds of development in the ego. Investigation from psychoanalytic theory especially needs to get away from an exclusive preoccupation with repression and defense. As we have seen, the study of creativity—particularly in emphasizing regression in the service of the ego—has taken a considerable step in this direction.

Humanistic Psychology

Criticisms of the foregoing kinds have been advanced by humanistic psychologists. Among their theses is the insistence that psychology should concern itself with the distinctive features of the human condition. They see growth, creativity, the pursuit of higher goals (signified by sublimation), and the enduring influence of values as essential properties of human behavior. In contrast to psychoanalytic theory, they emphasize the positive, healthy release of potentials. This tendency is attributed to an inherent need for *self-actualization*. Neurosis and other personality disorders stem from conditions that interfere with the process of self-actualization. However, rather than a precarious, almost accidental arrival at culturally valued goals, as implied in psychoanalytic theory, every human being is considered to strive for the realization of the potentials represented by the transcendent goals of experience: aesthetic, religious, humanitarian, truth, and so on. Cogent advocates of this view include Rogers (1961), Frankl (1966), and Maslow (1967) [the work of Jung (1956) also contributes to it].

The study of cognition must pay serious attention to those aspects of human experience to which humanistic principles point. The role of the ego is otherwise severely misunderstood. We shall not here argue whether an extension of the principle of sublimation or the principle of an inherent self-actualizing motive will in the long run prove to account better for the higher forms of human behavior. In either case the ego must be treated as potentially a constructive, active, creative force than can transcend the primitive, unconsciously based, defensively managed conflicts mainly envisaged in psychoanalytic theory.

EGO-DEFENSIVE FUNCTIONS
Psychoanalysts have described a host of ego defenses (Fenichel, 1945; A. Freud, 1937). We have already discussed displacement, condensation, and other mechanisms in dreams, and in earlier contexts cited evidence for defensive processes.

Repression
Derived from psychoanalysis is the hypothesis that threatening stimuli will be forgotten. Early studies were equivocal on the differential recall of pleasant and unpleasant material (Rapaport, 1942) and their adequacy with respect to Freudian theory is questionable.

Rosenstock (1951) sought to increase the relevance of stimuli by using sentences expressing aggressive and sexual attitudes toward parents. Compared to neutral sentences, the recognition threshold of such material was significantly higher, and was interpreted as evidence for primal repression.

Another approach induces actual conflict that might lead to repression. Zeller (1950) had subjects learn nonsense syllables, then experience failure in a different task (to induce repression), followed by success (to remove repression). Retention was impaired after failure, and a later experiment demonstrated that when failure was *specific* to the interpolated task, it had little effect on the critical retention task.

This procedure has been criticized because it does not actually reveal whether or not the unreported material was available so that response suppression or competition, rather than repression, might be responsible (D'Zurilla, 1965; Eriksen and Pierce, 1968). D'Zurilla obtained results like Zeller's using allegedly homosexual words following a relevant threat. From interviews he found, however, that significantly more of the threatened subjects reported consciously thinking about the task, along with greater preoccupation with ideas irrelevant to the specific words. Contrary to the repression theory then, this study supports the principle of response competition. Furthermore, distraction during the interpolated task impairs recall similarly to threat (Holmes and Schallow, 1969).

Unfortunately, these later experiments are no more definitive than Zeller's. Although recall was significantly impaired in all three, the principle of repression was treated superficially and over a very brief period. We do not know whether *some* experimental subjects, but not others, may have repressed the threatening words. In the D'Zurilla experiment, it is not reported whether those who did not report thinking about the threat differed in recall from those who did; in the Holmes and Schallow study, it is unknown whether both experimental groups actually had the nonrecalled material available. The repression principle does not maintain that all individuals utilize repression under the same conditions—quite the contrary.

Repression and Sensitization

Holzman and Gardner (1959) assessed repressive tendencies by Rorschach indicators (few responses, few movement responses, emphasis on color, stereotypy, etc.). A task of judging the size of successively larger squares was used to identify levelers and sharpeners, the former marked by errors and lagging behind in adapting to increased size, the latter by accuracy and adaptation. High repressive tendencies were associated with leveling, low repressive tendencies with sharpening. Using other criteria, Gordon (1957) assigned repressers and sensitizers to homogeneous or mixed pairs. Repressers were more accurate in predicting similarities between themselves and others, sensitizers more accurate in predicting differences. Furthermore, sensitizers better discriminated similarities and differences when paired with repressers, and less often attributed similarities to the other. Both groups were better at predicting repressers, probably because they produced readily identified socially desirable responses. Repressers apparently have smaller self-ideal discrepancies, while sensitizers assign more negative traits to themselves (Altrocchi, Parsons, and Dickoff, 1960; but see Lomont, 1966).

A scale derived from the MMPI has been developed to measure repression and sensitization (Byrne, 1961; Byrne, Barry, and Nelson, 1963). Reliability is high and several studies provide evidence for its validity.

Under the stress of pregnancy, repressers attribute less hostility to themselves than do sensitizers (or "expressers") (McDonald, 1967). Threatening instructions (allegation that the task measured intelligence) were employed by Markowitz (1969) in a learning situation, with trigrams as intentional stimuli, and English words, which varied in affective connotation, as incidental stimuli. Threat impaired the incidental learning of positive words for the repressers, but facilitated learning for the sensitizers. Contrary to prediction, there was little effect for the negative words.

Weinstein and his coworkers (1968) have pointed out that self-report indicators of stress tend to disagree with physiological measures. By examining several studies, they show that defensive style is responsible. Discrepancies were larger for repressers, signifying that they display greater autonomic than self-report reactions; the opposite holds for sensitizers. This finding underlines the defensive function of repressive mechanisms.

Reaction Formation

The conversion of an impulse into its opposite is called reaction formation. Clinical examples can readily be cited, such as when hostility toward a younger sibling may be repressed and protective or loving attitudes expressed instead, or when generosity stems from repressed stinginess.

Sarnoff (1960b) has presented a hypothesis in the opposite direction, to the effect that cynicism may be a reaction formation against unconscious affection for others. Cynicism and manifestation of reaction formation were measured by tests. High arousal of affection was induced 2 weeks later by a performance of an excerpt from Saroyan's *Hello Out There,* low arousal by a tape with the actors expressing less emotion. The tests were then readministered; data from a control group who were not exposed to the play were collected a year later. The control subjects who were high and low in reaction-formation tendencies displayed little difference, but under low arousal both experimental groups markedly decreased in

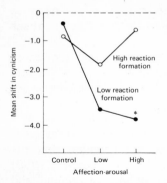

FIGURE 17–1   Shifts in cynicism as a function of arousal of affection for persons low and high in reaction-formation tendencies. (Based on Sarnoff, 1960.) *Different from high reaction formation at 3 percent level (one tail).

cynicism. However, in support of the hypothesis, the change was not only much less for subjects high in reaction formation but especially so under high arousal (see Figure 17-1).

Denial

Lazarus and his associates have induced stress by requiring subjects to watch a highly disturbing film depicting the subincision rites of aboriginal tribes, with special sound tracks (Speisman et al., 1964). The "trauma" commentary emphasized threatening aspects (painfulness, cruelty, etc.); the "denial and reaction formation" commentary stated that the operations were not painful and mentioned their social benefits in initiating youths to adulthood; and the "intellectualizing" commentary was cast in an objective, scientific fashion. Physiological measures showed that the trauma condition induced considerably greater stress, whereas the defense-inducing conditions reduced responsiveness. Introductory orientations, without the commentary, produced supporting results (Lazarus and Alfert, 1964). In addition, defensive attitudes were pretested, with the discrepancy noted above: deniers did not report as much disturbance as others, despite high levels of physiological responding. It would appear that such persons employ denial to reduce the conscious threat.

Houston and Hodges (1970) have employed discrepancies between verbal reports of affective state and heart rate to define denial, neutral, and accentuator groups. As anticipated, the denial subjects displayed less impairment of performance under stress (failure or electric shock) than the accentuator subjects, with the neutral group intermediate. Thus denial proved an effective adaptation to the stress.

Displacement

In this mechanism, affect is diverted from one object and expressed toward a different object. This process has especially been viewed as one possible consequence of frustration (Dollard et al., 1939), and is one factor in manifestations of prejudice, to be discussed in Chapter 19. In classic experiments with rats , N. E. Miller (1948) has demonstrated that displacement may be explained on the basis of principles of stimulus generalization, and that the strength of displacement varies with the similarity of alternative objects to the original stimulus. Furthermore, he has suggested that displacement stemming from unconscious forces should be greater than that at a conscious level since repression removes the verbal responses that facilitate discriminations between objects, and hence there should be greater generalization.

Experimental approaches typically induce aggressive feelings by frustrating subjects, and then provide opportunities for subjects to express aggression toward some target. For example, N. E. Miller and Bugelski (1948) imposed very severe frustration on a group of youths, and found that prejudice toward minority groups significantly increased. (But milder and less natural experimental inductions may not produce this effect, as shown by Stagner and Congdon [1955]. Or they *may,* as later shown by Cowen, Landes, and Schaet [1959].)

Berkowitz and Holmes (1959) suggested that displacement depends on conditions such as prior dislike for the available target and attitude (degree of hostility) toward the frustrating agent. Their subjects were unjustifiably punished (electric shock) by a partner, thus presumably inducing dislike, compared to a control condition without the shock. The experimenter imposed frustration on half the subjects by accusing them of cheating in a new task on which they worked alone. Then they were brought together for a third task. As predicted, negative attitudes toward the partners increased for the group who initially disliked them, who had been frustrated, and who had expressed high hostility toward the agent of frustration (the experimenter).

Displacement is not necessarily confined to aggression. Darlington and Macker (1966), for example, have shown that altruism may sometimes be a function of guilt. They arranged a situation in which female subjects were apparently responsible for the failure of another person, who, in turn, enabled them to succeed. When they were subsequently given the chance to volunteer as blood donors, the "guilty" subjects were more responsive to the appeal.

Projection

Ample evidence for the generalized role of attributing one's own tendencies to other persons can be found in the results of projective tests. Many experiments on social perception also reveal this process (Shrauger and Altrocchi, 1964).

A widely cited study was derived from the psychoanalytic conception of the "anal syndrome" (Sears, 1936). Fraternity men rated both themselves and their fellows for the traits of stinginess, obstinacy, disorderliness, and bashfulness. Subjects were considered to possess the trait themselves if others gave them an above-average rating, and not to possess it if they received a below-average rating. Those who thus had the trait were classified as "insightful" if they rated themselves higher than they rated others, and conversely for the "noninsightful" subjects. Sears found that the noninsightful individuals rated as having a trait tended to attribute the trait to others to a higher degree than did the insightful individuals, apparently reflecting a projection mechanism, with an opposite effect for those who did not have the trait.

Subsequent studies failed to confirm these findings (Lemann and Solomon, 1952; Rokeach, 1945). Replicating the Sears experiment as precisely as possible, Wells and Goldstein (1964) found similar results, when analyzed in the same way. However, peculiarities of Sears's technique in classifying subjects make his results questionable (for instance, his use of average, rather than more extreme, ratings would place some individuals in the stingy category who were actually rated close to average). Reclassification by a more stringent criterion left very few subjects who were judged to possess the trait, and a sizable number who did not. For these individuals the results were opposite to Sears's: the noninsightful subjects (judged *not* to possess the trait) attributed more of the trait to others than did the insightful subjects. Actually, the same point appears here as in previous contexts—the concept of projection does not signify that every person will display it under the same conditions. It is doubtful that these studies actually identify significant "anal characteristics," and certainly they do not permit any assessment either of the repression on which it presumably rests, or of the individual's tendency to employ projection rather than other defenses.

Other studies reveal projection in general interpersonal relationships. Pepitone (1950) showed that perception of important stimulus figures may be significantly distorted in a way that positively facilitates goal attainment. Vroom (1959) obtained measures of attitudes of industrial supervisors toward themselves and two subordinates, and similar data for the subordinates. Thus he could derive indicators of perceived similarity (of subordinate to supervisor), of real similarity (correspondence between the supervisor's self-judgments and the subordinate's self-judgments), and accuracy (agreement between supervisor's judgments about the subordinate and the latter's actual judgments about himself). Projection was assessed by examining attitudes toward the subordinate (evaluation of job performance) in relation to perceived similarity, holding constant real similarity. Subordinates toward whom the supervisors had positive attitudes were perceived as more similar to themselves than those toward whom they held negative attitudes, especially for central traits. In general, when attitudes were positive, perceived similarity was greater than it actually was, with an opposite (negating) effect when attitudes were negative.

Situational stress appears in a study by Murray (1933). He had eleven-year-old girls judge photographs of men on a scale of goodness-badness before and after pleasurable (an automobile ride) and fear-arousing (the game of "murder") conditions. The latter induced increased judgment of badness, compared to the former.

Bellak (1944) presented pictures of the Thematic Apperception Test, under neutral conditions or severe and derogatory criticism. Aggressive words in the stories increased when the criticism was introduced, thus confirming the hypothesis that resentment would be projected as increased aggression.

Feshbach and Singer (1957a) administered electric shock to

subjects while they watched a film, with either instructions calculated to arouse and express fear or to suppress fear; the shock and instructions were omitted for control subjects. Both experimental groups saw the stimulus figure as more fearful and aggressive than did the controls, with some evidence that projection was greater in the "fear-suppressed" group.

Projection, like other defenses, is selective. Markowitz and Ford (1967) compared the effects of low and high stress for subjects who were low or high in defensive denial tendencies (measured by the Ford Social Desirability Scale), and also provided targets who were either allegedly similar or dissimilar to them. Under conditions of low stress only, the subjects high in defensiveness projected less positive affect onto the dissimilar target, those low in defensiveness onto the similar target.

Bramel (1962) has argued that projection is, at least partly, a mode of reducing cognitive dissonance. Subjects were first given information, allegedly based on personality tests, either favorable or unfavorable, and led to believe that they had homosexual tendencies, presumed to be more dissonant for the favorably assessed group. Projection was greater under the dissonant condition, as predicted, since these subjects attributed greater homosexual arousal to another person, when viewing photographs of males, than did those in the unfavorable (low dissonant) condition. This effect, however, occurred only when the other person had previously been favorably evaluated.

Defenses in Everyday Life

In the foregoing sampling of research, we have focused on attempts to bring defensive processes under objective scrutiny.

Frenkel-Brunswik (1939), on the other hand, studied the everyday manifestation of defenses. She devised a procedure for comparing the actual conduct of her subjects with their statements about themselves. Reports about their behavior (scientific work, relations to fellow students, etc.), ideals and "guiding principles," and their "demands on the environment" (regarding changes in rules, for instance) were compared with descriptions by four judges of personality traits and conduct in several concretely defined situations. She found evidence of many kinds of defensive processes, such as *distortion into the opposite* (considering that one has a certain trait in which others regard him as deficient), *omission* of significant characteristics of one's conduct, *justification* of action, *belittling* traits by shifting emphasis. The analysis of guiding principles also revealed defensive thinking. Ideals pertaining to attitudes and social conduct were lived up to far less than those dealing with achievement. Guiding principles of the former kinds may serve to compensate for the lack of the traits and attitudes involved. The manner of expressing guiding principles constituted a clue to their function since the subject who spontaneously added further explanation may well have been striving to justify his statement or to convince the experimenter of its truth. With respect to demands on the environment, a third were simply matter-of-fact statements, whereas the other two-thirds seemed to be rationalizations, for example, the environment should satisfy one's personal shortcomings and help to overcome them.

EGO-CONSTRUCTIVE FUNCTIONS

Conceptions of the role of the ego have obviously drawn very heavily on the Freudian model of repression, with nearly all research dominated by the search for evidence of defense. And yet the ego also possesses coping and constructive resources. We would expect to find them operating especially in systems built on sublimation. Although infrequently discussed from this standpoint, constructive processes appear by implication in various contexts. Distinctive labels, like those for defensive processes, are mostly lacking, but nevertheless their importance can scarcely be overestimated.

Creative Functions

As we saw in Chapter 15, research on creativity has begun to clarify properties of the ego that facilitate the production of original and expressive work. Although we might refer to freedom of expression, flexibility, openness to experience, and other characteristics as ego-constructive functions, especially explicit is regression in the service of the ego.

Fitzgerald (1966) administered several tests to college students, including MMPI scales, a self-description adjective checklist, and the experience inventory. The latter, derived from several sources (see, especially, Ås, O'Hara, and Munger, 1962), assessed characteristics like tolerance and capacity for regressive experiences and logical inconsistencies, constructive use of repression, and experience with altered states of consciousness and peak experiences. This inventory displayed little relation to the ego-strength scale, a significant negative relation to the repression scale (as expected), and a significant tendency for high-scoring males (not females) to be high in anxiety. The self-descriptions of high-scoring males often contained words like artistic, complicated, individualistic, moody (an "alienated artist" pattern); those of females words like adventurous, aggressive, assertive, imaginative, impulsive, original, quick, spontaneous, and versatile. Thus the high males appeared to be open to *inner* experience, the high females to *outer* experience. In word-association and object-sorting tasks, the highs of both sexes produced many more original responses under spontaneous conditions and greater ability to shift from more to less regulated thinking (see Wild, 1965). These results support Schachtel's (1959) point that regression in the service of the ego depends on *openness to experience* rather than regression to primitive levels—and accord better with the principle of sublimation than repression.

Sensitization
By implication, although repressers are adversely affected by stress, sensitizers cope effectively with it. The latter, apparently, muster responses to counteract the threat by recognizing it and engaging in positive action that takes it into account.

Realistic Cognitive Styles
Our earlier discussion of strategy in concept formation and other problem solving tasks implied ego-constructive functions, for example, ability to adopt an appropriate mode of attack or to shift from one mode to another as task requirements change. Other important characteristics are cognitive complexity versus simplicity and field independence (Witkin et al., 1954). The role of understanding and recentering approaches are other possible directions to look for constructive problem solving styles.

Ego Strength
Perhaps the chief way in which ego-constructive functions have entered directly into research efforts arises from the concept of ego strength—the degree that the ego's energies are bound up with the maintenance of repression. A person low in ego strength has little energy available to cope effectively with environmental demands,

especially under stress (Barron, 1963b), whereas a person high in ego strength, having relatively less inner conflict, possesses more energy to cope competently with the environment. Ego strength clearly overlaps with other ways of describing ego functions—but the same holds for most of the variables under consideration, whether defensive or constructive.

One experiment (Ringuette, 1965) employed a conflict situation. Subjects first learned to draw a line toward the corner of a drawing board at which a light appeared, and to the opposite corner at a different signal. Conflict was induced by presenting incompatible signals. Persons high in ego strength, based on the Barron scale, more often produced an effective compromise response by drawing a line midway between two conflicting corners, whereas those low in ego strength more often made a double response, such as drawing a line to both corners.

Under sensory deprivation, subjects low in ego strength (based on Rorschach indicators) displayed disturbances like negative affect, anxiety, and desire to quit, whereas those high in ego strength were flexible, adaptive, and resourceful (Goldberger and Holt, 1961).

From such studies, and others, it is becoming evident that a realistic orientation and the availability of competent coping attitudes represent significant ego-constructive functions. There has long been a pronounced tradition of referring to the "well-adjusted person" simply as a rather pale abstraction, with less defensive or neurotic or anxious traits than his more interesting pathologically marked peer.

THE SELF

The ego contains conceptual and attitudinal subsystems organized with reference to particular objects, such as a wife, mother, son, daughter, God, one's country, and so on. Especially important in our society at least, as many theorists have recognized, is that system that refers to one's own person, or the *self*. Such subsystems may be pervasive throughout the ego, or narrowly circumscribed, may be interrelated or tightly held in separate compartments, or vary in other ways (Vinacke, 1968). The functions of the ego depend on the properties of its substructures, which determine the salience and significance of environmental objects, the intensity and direction of motive regulation, the instrumental character of behavior in relation to goals, and other trends that reflect the organization of experience.

Although it is not necessarily true that the self is the central and dominant system in the ego, it is clearly the one most universally emphasized.

Development

Theorists agree that the self originates in the infant's perceptions of his body (Allport, 1961; Sarbin, 1952), leading to a gradual differentiation of this part of the environment from other parts. With continued growth the child begins to recognize and practice functions such as perception, manipulation, and locomotion, which serve as processes by which he acts on and relates himself to other objects. As time goes on, other persons become significant objects also, and the child begins to acquire a repertory of relationships with them that forms the nucleus for social roles and ultimately for adult systems of behavior. Sarbin (1952) regards these successive stages as providing progressive components, or layers, of the total self, representing the accumulation of experience—or the ingredients for the complex *concept* of the self. Furthermore, the individual acquires expectations and enduring modes of regulating behavior—or well-defined *attitudes* toward the self—as he expresses and fulfills his own needs. In this fashion, the self-system operates as a point of reference for behavior, as that part of the ego concerned with one's own person as an object in the experiential field.[1]

Just as we can solicit evidence for cognitive processes that involve other objects, so can we assess the self. An "I" or a "me" has conceptual dimensions just as does a "red square" or an "apple." The self has denotative and connotative properties, although the latter no doubt generally assume much greater importance in the self than in other representations of objects—and, in fact, constitute the primary interest in studies of the self-concept (for example, the use of the Semantic Differential [S. D.] as in studies by Osgood, Suci, and Tannenbaum [1961] and P. A. Smith [1962]).

Similarly, attitudes toward the self may be determined in ways familiar in research on the formation and change of attitudes. Just as one can obtain judgments about the degree of approval or disapproval of an "object" such as the leader of a group, so may one ask subjects to judge themselves. Although other attitudinal

---

[1]As noted above, the self-system extends in the ego as widely as the person-object dominates it. Our own society makes the self so important that it is easy to assume that it corresponds wholly with the ego.

dimensions have been studied, including complexity, salience, and stability, investigators have concentrated on affective attitudes.

Aspects of the Self

Perhaps no term throughout psychology has been employed in so many different ways as the "self" (Chein, 1944; Wylie, 1968; Hall and Lindzey, 1970).

In general, it may signify a person's attitudes and feelings about himself (*self as object*) or the intrinsic processes that govern behavior (*self as process*). The latter conception makes the self correspond with the ego (except with explicit reference to the person himself).

Distinguished from the "real self"—representations of what the person perceives himself to be—is the "ideal self"—what he would like to be. Both kinds of characteristics may vary widely in clarity or accuracy of judgment, as revealed in appraisal against other criteria based on ratings by others or by psychometric assessment. At the verbal level, an individual can be asked to describe himself as he *actually* is and as he *would like* to be. For this purpose, investigators employ devices like adjective checklists (Gough, 1960) and the S. D.

Furthermore, the *ego ideal* may be distinguished from the *ideal self*. The latter is an aspect of the self-system, whereas the former is part of the superego system (Chapter 18), referring to generalized values or internalized goals. The ego ideal represents standards the person already has and that can be lived up to, but the ideal self represents wished-for (and perhaps unattainable) modes of behavior.

I do not intend to force artificial distinctions but rather to emphasize that these terms refer to different problems in understanding the role of cognitive variables. At the same time, theory must also allow for relations and integrations among self, ideal self, and ego ideal. The Freudian conception, for example, appears to separate ego and superego too sharply to apply adequately to a mature, integrated personality.

Self-evaluation

One body of research focuses on affective attitudes toward the self (see Diggory, 1966). A central interest is the effect of situational variables, such as success and failure or the character of interpersonal relationships. Another concern is conditions that enhance or degrade self-esteem. Although this problem is important, we shall here consider the effects on behavior of already-present properties of the self-system. Studies of self-evaluation tend to examine transient, situationally bound changes in perception or judgment, without much attention to their further consequences. Self-evaluation is thus treated mainly as a dependent variable, but in this chapter emphasis will be on properties of the self as independent variables.

Self-acceptance and Attitudes toward Others

Prominent in Rogerian principles is the thesis that positive self-regard is accompanied by positive feelings about other persons. This relationship has been confirmed in several studies, together with the fact that changes in self-acceptance produce corresponding changes in acceptance of others (Sheerer, 1949; Stock, 1949; Berger, 1952; Omwake, 1954). A positive correlation has been found between self-rating and ratings of others both before the introduction of stress (.74) and also afterward (.77), and both ratings are more positive after stress (Levanway, 1955). However, such relationships depend on characteristics of the other person since Suinn (1961) found that self-acceptance and acceptance of another is greater the more similar the other is to the person.

Self-ideal Discrepancy

The difference between self-concept and ideal self-concept has been investigated by the Q-sort technique (W. Stephenson, 1953), in which the subject allocates descriptive items into categories of a scale from "like me" to "unlike me," and then, similarly, into categories that refer to one's ideal person (as one would like to be). Arguing that nondirective counseling should reduce the discrepancy, Butler and Haigh (1954) obtained ratings before and after treatment and at a later period. Counseling typically produces a change from a negative to a positive self-concept (Raimy, 1948), but the ideal self-concept, as a representation of societal values, should be less likely to change. Therefore correlations between self- and ideal self-concepts should increase. This effect did, in fact, occur, contrasted with no change in matched control subjects (see Figure 17-2).

Congruence between self-concept and ideal self-concept serves as an index to adjustment. One study found a correlation of .70 between congruence and self-adjustment, and of .59 with social adjustment (Hanlon, Hofstaetter, and O'Connor, 1954). Zimmer

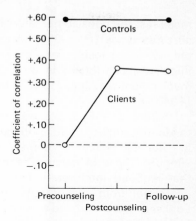

FIGURE 17-2 Self-ideal correlations in client and control groups. (Based on Butler and Haigh, 1954.)

(1954), however, found a nonsignificant relation between self-ideal discrepancy and indicators of complexes (word-association data), suggesting that discrepancy reflects general personality organization rather than specific conflicts.

Chodorkoff (1954) obtained self-descriptions by the Q-sort procedure, together with clinical evaluations by independent judges. The difference between recognition thresholds for neutral and threatening words was employed to measure perceptual defense. As hypothesized, the following significant relations appeared : the greater the agreement between self- and objective descriptions, the better the personal adjustment and the less the perceptual defense, and the better the adjustment, the less the degree of perceptual defense.

Self-esteem

A dominant theme in discussions of the self is that a person acts to enhance his self-concept and defend himself against threats to it. One example of confirmatory research is an experiment by Cartwright (1956). Procedures were adopted to render material consistent or inconsistent with self-concepts. In one task subjects first copied a list of nonsense syllables, then made up their own list; in another they sorted object names into piles representing how likely they were to possess them; and in a third task they sorted descriptive statements into categories from "most unlike me" to "most like me." In a recall test the consistent material was recalled significantly better for all three types ($P < .005$). Adjusted and maladjusted groups displayed similar results, except that the latter showed relatively more impaired recall for the inconsistent items. (See also, studies of ego involvement by Alper [1946]; Lewis and Franklin [1944]; Prentice [1943].)

Dittes (1959) employed both tests and situational manipulations to identify subjects high, moderate, and low in self-esteem; variations in "general desire for clarity" were also assessed. To determine "impulsiveness of closure," these groups were compared in tasks that required interpretation of an incoherent parable, forming an impression from a list of traits, and recognizing a "jammed" message. Low self-esteem proved to be associated with impulsiveness (so was high desire for clarity).

Silverman (1964b) investigated the interaction of success and failure and self-esteem. Contrived information about performance on a quiz was provided to manipulate perceived success and failure. When the quiz was readministered, subjects high in self-esteem showed greater improvement after success, with the opposite effect for those low in self-esteem. Dabbs (1964) in a related study showed that subjects high in self-esteem were more influenced by a source of communication characterized by "coping" behavior (confident and active), than one who manifested "noncoping" behavior (passive, ineffectual).

Internal-External Control

This variable, proposed by Rotter (1966), is somewhat ambiguous since it might be regarded as a generalized ego function rather than a process in which the self is salient. However, the central theme pertains to the individual's feelings of self-reliance and conceptions of his own competence. *External control* refers to perceptions that a person's actions depend on luck, chance, fate, others are powerful, or unpredictable external forces. *Internal control* refers to perceptions that events depend on one's own behavior or characteristics.

Studies of internal-external control have generally found, despite some conflicting results (e.g., Watson and Baumal, 1967), that differences between "internals" and "externals" depend on the kind of task. Internals take longer to reach decisions in tasks determined by skill (Rotter and Mulry, 1965) and take longer as difficulty increases (Julian and Katz, 1968), with an opposite effect in tasks that involve chance. Differences also appear in situational conditions such as success and failure, since externals tend to display greater confidence after success, internals after failure (Ryckman and Rodda, 1971).

Less crucial than task conditions themselves, however, are the perceptions of the subject. Lefcourt, Lewis, and Silverman (1968) employed the level of aspiration board, a task that calls for the subject to shoot a ball along a graduated groove so that it reaches a target area. Overshooting or undershooting yields scores progressively lower in both directions. On each trial the subject states the score he expects to make, which can be compared to his actual performance. Instructions were manipulated to emphasize that performance depends on skill *or* on chance. The difference between previous performance and subsequent expectancy (D scores) was significantly greater for the internals, reflecting a self-confident, assertive attitude. Otherwise there was little difference, but when the actual perceptions of subjects were determined, the expected differences appeared. That is, internals who saw the task as calling on skill took longer to make decisions, recalled their expectancy statements better, paid more attention to the task, and reported more task-relevant thoughts.

Variables Based on the Self-concept

These studies thus indicate that differences in properties of the self-system play a considerable role in accounting for variations in performance. At the same time, it is essential to recognize that the effect of these variables depends on the kind of task presented to the subject, and the degree to which the situation enlists the self as a factor. As a cautionary note, I feel that merely classifying subjects as high or low on some variable involving the self may be quite insufficient to identify differences in performance. The effect depends on the *relevance* of conditions to the self and to the person's perceptions thereof.

SUMMARY

Ego mechanisms are determined by the reality principle (opposed to the pleasure principle of the id). The secondary process (corresponding to thinking) characterizes the ego, with activities arising from the id described as primary process. In considering the ego, we can distinguish processes built on repression from those founded on sublimation. Four general models result: neurotic and "normal neurotic" (repression), and conformity and creativity (sublimation). Humanistic psychology stresses the importance of growth, creativity, values, and self-actualization. Ego-defensive processes studied experimentally include repression (and sensitization), reaction formation, denial, displacement, and projection. In contrast, we can also recognize ego-constructive functions such as those displayed in creative activity, sensitization to environmental stimuli, realistic cognitive styles, ego strength, and emotional understanding (empathy). The self is conceptualized as a subsystem within the ego, with the person as an object. The self develops through successive phases of differentiation from the environment, the incorporation of social relationships, and the acquisition of social roles. The self-system has both conceptual and attitudinal components, and both real and ideal aspects. Research has dealt with self-evaluation, relations between self-acceptance and attitudes toward others, self-ideal discrepancy, and self-esteem. Internal-external control has been proposed as a variable in the functioning of the self.

18

THE SUPEREGO
AND VALUES

We turn now to attitudinal processes that govern behavior in relation
to standards of conduct. One of Freud's most significant contributions was the explicit recognition that behavior is governed by
internalized standards, apart from external agencies of control. His
work *Civilization and Its Discontents* (1961) is a monumental explication of this development as the fundamental basis for man's existence in society.

My concern is primarily with the behavioral consequences of
individual differences in properties of the superego. I shall present a
brief perspective on theoretical conceptions, including some distinctions not clearly apparent in the monolithic Freudian conception.
Unlike in the case of ego defense, investigation remains for the most
part on a preliminary level, with interest chiefly in the moral development of children, in certain aspects of interpersonal relations (such
as compliance and helping), and in attempts to study values.

ORIGINS AND CHARACTER OF THE SUPEREGO
The superego is the "heir to the Oedipus complex."[1] With the resolution of his attachment to the parent of the opposite sex, the child

[1]See Bronfenbrenner (1960) for the important distinction between anaclitic identification and
identification with the aggressor, with its implications, especially, for sex differences in the development of the superego.

begins to develop an identification with the parent of the same sex that serves as a basis for accepting and internalizing the precepts, aims, and characteristics represented (and enforced) by that model. The resolution of the Oedipus complex is accompanied by a recession in the direct expression of instinctive impulses, so that the post-Oedipal phase may be called the *latency period*. As a consequence, the formative influences of parents, teachers, and individual learning processes gain ascendency over primitive impulses, and the establishment of standards and ideals begins in earnest. The Freudian conception allows for three kinds of determinant of behavior: biological energies from the id, regulating and expressing attitudes of the ego and supervising attitudes of the superego that demand accommodation to moral and ideal principles. Thus the ego is not free to act as it pleases, solely in accordance with environmental situations, but must interpret and make decisions in the light of internal standards that determine what is permissible and acceptable.

The superego contains four components, arising from the complex demands made on the child. Agents of socialization not only endeavor to induce the child to obey desired standards but also to avoid acting in unacceptable ways; furthermore, they seek to instill both moral principles and intentions to attain goals higher and more remote than those in the immediate present (see Table 18-1). Since combinations of these four aims vary widely, the superego is far from a unitary, uniform system.

Conscience refers to moral precepts, with two components— avoiding of transgressions (negative) and abiding by moral principles. *Ego ideal* refers to the goals that transcend immediate situations, with two aspects—relationships to higher aspirations (positive) and the revulsion from failures to act in good taste or in ways appropriate to higher goals. To each component I have attached, tentatively, a central, conscious emotional-cognitive state. Of these, guilt has been especially stressed by theorists. In a more general fashion, we could say that conscience concerns judgments of right and wrong, whereas the ego ideal pertains to judgments of good and bad. The superego imposes on the ego pressures to act both rightly and well, and to avoid acting wrongly and badly.

In this connection we may invoke Mowrer's (1960a, b) conception of the fundamental conditioning of emotions. The negative component of conscience may be linked with conditioned fear, the positive component with relief; the positive component of the ego ideal may arise from conditioned hope, the negative component from conditioned disappointment. It is, however, apparent that if these

Table 18-1
Components of the Superego

Conscience	Ego Ideal
1. Moral prohibitions (negative aspect), transgressions subject to punishment, characterized by *guilt* or shame.	1. Aspirations or symbolic goals (positive aspect), higher or remote states of attainment subject to reward, characterized by *pride* or success.
2. Moral principles (positive aspect), standards of good conduct, adherence to which is rewarded, characterized by *worth* or virtue.	2. Canons of conduct (negative aspect), transgressions against taste or misbehavior subject to punishment, characterized by *disgust,* embarrassment, or degradation.

primitive processes constitute a source for aspects of the superego, they lie much earlier in childhood than the latency period and lead to more complex systems than the simple conditioning view allows.[1]

Despite our differentiation of these four components, we must recognize that they do not remain separate from each other but become interrelated. Conscience and ego ideal may merge so that, for example, moral excellence becomes integral to one's aspirations; similarly, good conduct may acquire a significant place in one's moral principles: to behave well is, so to speak, both good and right. On the negative side as well, attitudes of avoiding transgression and of sustaining good conduct may synthesize into inclusive systems.

Integration also takes place in the achievement of intimate relationships between ego and superego, which do not necessarily remain separate. The notion of a strict, distinct monitor, implied in psychoanalytic theory, generally applies more to the neurotic than to the healthy person, in whose case morals and aspirations become interwoven with the attitudes of the ego. Action is carried out without any issue of right or wrong (they are simply right, as it were), in the absence of guilt, and with no necessity to consider whether it is a transgression. Much behavior is automatically governed morally, with no implication whatever of temptation to transgress. Of course, situations *may* occur that tempt transgression, with accompanying guilt, but such events, frequent for the neurotic, are rather rare for the well-integrated, healthy person. The processes in which superego and ego blend shall be called *values*.

Finally, any component of the superego may become part of the

[1]For example, cognitive (conceptual) dimensions complicate the structure.

self-system. Principles or aspirations, in such instances, have a personal character: they are *in* me, *belong* to me, are *inseparable* from me (and the way I wish to be). If this integration proceeds very far, the difference between self and superego breaks down. Behavior acquires a personally relevant and expressive moral (and/or ideal) dimension, inseparable from its other aspects.

Child-Rearing and Culture
The development of superego characteristics depends on the internalization process previously described. High parental standards of neatness and obedience are related to temptation in boys; strong pressures associated with oral, anal, and sex training display this relation in girls (Sears, Maccoby, and Levin, 1957; Grinder, 1961, 1962). Such patterns vary with culture. For example, in Hawaii, Samoan schoolchildren were found to have lower resistance to temptation, and showed less remorse and restitution after transgression (Grinder and McMichael, 1963).

Whiting (1959) has significantly broadened the Freudian conception by differentiating among mechanisms of social control. One type, the superego, resides in internalized moral strictures; another, sorcery, represents a belief in magical powers by which others may induce punishment or retribution; and a third, sin, rests on the fear of ghosts, who can punish transgression. Data from the Human Relations Area Files were employed to classify societies on appropriate indexes. Depending on fear of retaliation from others, sorcery arises from socialization conditions that promote defense against sexual anxiety, and occurs more frequently in societies with a long postpartum sex taboo (indicative of at least symbolic seduction in infancy), and those that punish sex behavior in childhood. Sin depends on early parental indulgence, with subsequent punishment for aggression, which produces a projected dread. Finally, the superego is most likely to occur in societies with monogamous families and those that emphasize early weaning.

There is no reason to suppose that these mechanisms are either unitary or confined within particular cultures. Even though the superego may be dominant in our own society, the other mechanisms are not necessarily absent.

Social Learning
In contrast to the psychoanalytic theory of the development of the superego, Bandura (1969a) invokes principles of imitation (see

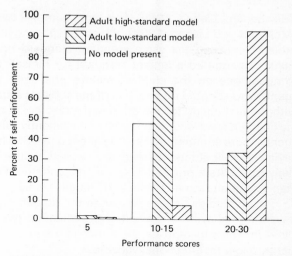

FIGURE 18-1   The distribution of self-reinforcement as a function of performance level by control children and those exposed to adult models adopting high and low criteria for self-reinforcement. (From Bandura and Kupers, 1964.)

Chapter 16), treating identification as essentially the same process. As a function of reinforcement, the child acquires characteristics of a model, including moral acts. Rate and efficiency of such learning depend on the behavior and characteristics of the model and on conditions of reinforcement—just as for any behavior.

Children can learn, through imitation, to reinforce themselves (Bandura and Kupers, 1964). The experimenters prearranged the scores attained in a bowling game; candies were available with which the seven- to nine-year-old subjects could reward themselves. First they observed while either an adult or peer model played under conditions of either stringent self-reward or lenient self-reward, accompanied by verbal statements of approval or self-criticism when the standard was successfully reached or failed. When the child played the game, after departure of the model, a marked tendency to imitate appeared (see Figure 18-1). The child more often rewarded himself in accordance with the stringency or leniency of the adult model, with similar but less pronounced results for the peer model. Subsequent self-reward was most stringent when both adult model and child were initially held to high standards, least when the child was allowed to reward himself for a low level of performance

(Mischel and Liebert, 1966). In a more complex two-phase situation (McMains and Liebert, 1968), the agent (playing alternately with the subject) imposed the same stringent standard on himself and the child, or permitted a lenient standard for himself while imposing a stringent one on the child; thereafter the child observed another agent, who adopted for one-half of the subjects a standard consistent with the first agent, for the other half a discrepant one. When tested, the children rewarded themselves more leniently following discrepant agents, more stringently after consistent ones. Similarly, when models deviate from a stringent standard imposed on the child, the child is likely to violate a previously specified standard—more so with a live than a symbolic model (Allen and Liebert, 1969).

Such studies thus demonstrate the influence of models on self-rewarding behavior, but whether the imitation theory is sufficient to allow for the superego remains uncertain because it does not sufficiently allow for affectional variables.

MORAL DEVELOPMENT

Another body of research has grown out of Piaget's (1965b) description of moral development. He postulated a series of stages progressing from an absolutistic, prelogical ("realistic") phase (age seven to eight) in which right and wrong are judged on the basis of external consequences, through a stage (age seven to eleven) in which equality of treatment for everyone regardless of conditions becomes paramount, to a final stage (age eleven on) of balancing equality and equity so that transgression and punishment become relative to the situation.

To test Piaget's view, Uğerel-Semin (1952) asked pairs of children of ages four to sixteen how they planned to divide odd numbers of nuts and to give their reasons. "Selfish" behavior declined and responses indicative of "equality" increased with age. At the later ages, generosity and equality tended to alternate from year to year. Age six appeared to be critical for "selfish" responses. The results were interpreted to reflect a shift from egocentrism through sociocentrism toward justice.

Piaget used stories that presented two actions, like the following: a boy plays with his father's inkwell and makes a blot, versus a boy who tries to help his father by filling his inkwell but accidentally makes a big blot. Children are queried regarding which action is worse. MacRae (1954) found that responses do not display a general factor but subclusters that represent separate aspects of moral development, such as intentions and consequences, punishment, perspective, and violation of norms. Parental authority was not related to these clusters, although two authority measures were significantly correlated with a moral-judgment index based on violation of lying and stealing norms. MacRae suggested that Piaget's questions pertain to cognitive components, whereas violation of norms is related to emotional components (parental authority).

Immanent justice (the inevitability of punishment) was described by Piaget as a characteristic of the young child, decreasing with age, and attributed to the authority of the parents. Consistent decrease, however, was not found by MacRae (1954) or Medinnus (1959) who found that it depends on meaningfulness or relevance of the stories, experience, and availability of rational explanations. In a study of lying, Medinnus (1962) also failed to confirm the supposed stages (most subjects, at all ages, fell into stage 2). Reclassification of answers yielded a distinction between objective and subjective responsibility. Jahoda (1958b) found the concept of immanent justice in West African children, but ambiguities of definition made classification difficult.

R. C. Johnson (1962b) identified as kinds of response immanent justice, moral realism, retribution versus restitution, efficacy of severe punishment, and communicable responsibility. Maturity of judgment displayed significant, but low, intercorrelations among the areas of moral realism and retribution versus restitution and efficacy of severe punishment, but the other two areas were slightly, if at all, related to each other or the other areas. Such results lend some support to Piaget.

Grinder (1964) points out that the Piagetian conception deals primarily with cognitive aspects of conscience, but that it is a social-learning theory with behavioral aspects. Measures of moral judgment and resistance to temptation, respectively, showed little relation, indicating that a cognitive definition cannot be assumed to agree with a behavioral definition.

Whiteman and Kosier (1964) found that maturity of judgment increases both with age and IQ, with females displaying a non-significantly greater maturity than males. The effects of experience were shown by greater maturity of children in combined-grade classrooms than in conventional graded classrooms, attributable to greater diversity of experience in the former setting.

Taking issue with the principle of stages, Bandura and McDonald (1963), in line with social-learning theory, proposed that reinforcement schedules are more important than time schedules.

They derived from Piaget a distinction between early objective responsibility (to age seven), in which wrongdoing is viewed as the amount of damage (rather than the intention), and subjective responsibility, followed by increasing personal autonomy. The child's dominant response ("subjective" or "objective") was determined. Then one of the following conditions was instituted: (1) a model made a judgment opposed to the child's moral orientation, and the experimenter reinforced the model's response and also the child when he imitated; (2) only the model was reinforced; (3) the model was absent, and the child reinforced whenever his response ran counter to his dominant orientation. Modeling and reinforcement readily modified the child's responses but, although subjective responsibility increased with age, both conceptions were concurrently present at all ages (five to eleven years). After replicating these results, Cowan and his associates (1969) argue that they reveal the complexity of moral development rather than directly supporting or refuting Piaget. In reply, Bandura (1969a) states that social learning does not deny the importance of developmental status, but merely emphasizes that responsiveness, regardless of its character, is partly under the control of external stimuli.

A REVISED CONCEPTION

The general trends described by Piaget have been identified in a variety of cultural groups (Kohlberg, 1969), but, in line with other research, the stages do not appear as sharply or consistently as he specified. Therefore Kohlberg has proposed a more systematic and detailed formulation.

Kohlberg recognizes three levels of development, each with two stages (see Table 18-2) resting on an orientation to the external event itself: behaving properly in response to social expectations and approval, and meeting the requirements of internal standards (corresponding to the role of conscience). To test for the stages in development, Kohlberg uses story situations that pose dilemmas. One describes a woman dying from cancer (Kohlberg, 1969, from Rest, 1968). A druggist in the same town has discovered a drug that might save her, but charges an exorbitant price. Her husband, unable to borrow enough money, appeals to the druggist, who refuses to help him. The man therefore breaks into the store to steal the drug. The issue is, Should the husband have done this, and why? There follow pro and con arguments corresponding to each of the six stages. They include considerations of how unfair the druggist was versus the

Table 18-2
Classification of Moral Judgment into Levels and Stages of Development. (From Haan, Smith, and Block, 1968, as adapted from Kohlberg, 1967.)

Levels	Basis of Moral Judgment	Stages of Development
I	Premoral Moral value resides in external, quasi-physical happenings, in bad acts, or in quasi-physical needs rather than in persons and standards	Stage 1. Obedience and punishment orientation; egocentric deference to superior power or prestige, or a trouble-avoiding set; objective responsibility. Stage 2. Instrumental relativists: Naively egoistic orientation. Right action is that instrumentally satisfying the self's needs and occasionally others; awareness of relativism of value to each actor's needs and perspective; naive egalitarianism and orientation to exchange and reciprocity.
II	Conventional Moral value resides in performing good or right roles, in maintaining the conventional order and the expectancies of others	Stage 3. Personal concordance: Good-boy orientation. Orientation to approval and to pleasing and helping others; conformity to stereotypical images of majority or natural role behavior, and judgment by intentions. Stage 4. Law and order: Authority and social-order maintaining orientation. Orientation to "doing duty" and to showing respect for authority and maintaining the given social order for its own sake; regard for earned expectations of others.
III	Principled Moral value resides in conformity by the self to shared or sharable standards, rights or duties	Stage 5. Social contract: Contractual legalistic orientation. Recognition of an arbitrary element or starting point in rules or expectations for the sake of agreement; duty defined in terms of contract, general avoidance of violations of the will or rights of others, and majority will and welfare. Stage 6. Individual principles: Conscience or principle orientation. Orientation not only to actually ordained social rules but to principles of choice involving appeal to logical universality and consistency; orientation to conscience as a directing agent and to mutual respect and trust.

damage done (stage 1) ; the wife's need versus the purely business-like attitude of the druggist (stage 2) ; the man's love for his wife versus his having done all he legally could, so that blame lies on the druggist (stage 3) ; the man's responsibility not to let his wife die and his intention to pay later versus his knowledge that stealing is always wrong, no matter how much he wants to save his wife (stage 4) ; although stealing is wrong, in such cases it is justified since the law doesn't cover them versus even though he could not be blamed, extreme conditions do not justify taking the law into your own hands (stage 5), and, forced to choose between stealing and letting his wife die, the former was morally right versus the fact that decision also involves other people, who equally need the drug, so that the man should not act simply on the basis of his own feelings (stage 6).

The test is intended not just to measure the decision itself so much as the kind of argument employed (leading to ratings of maturity of judgment). In addition to the intentions and consequences represented by the arguments, Kohlberg identifies numerous other aspects of moral judgment, including relation of the respondent to the hypothetical actor, attitudes toward punishment, conceptions of norms, rules, and rights, reciprocity, and so on. Although the task of scoring free responses to the dilemmas is difficult in the light of so many possible elements, it may prove to be very useful in investigating relations between superego characteristics and behavior.

Turiel (1966) suggested that Bandura and McDonald mis-interpreted Piaget's view, and actually may have measured only one component. Adopting Kohlberg's six stages, he argued that learning should be more effective when the child is exposed to the stage directly above his conceptual level rather than to stages farther removed. After initial assessment of the stage attained, seventh-grade boys were exposed to moral-reasoning situations, in which an adult played roles corresponding to a stage just below the subject's, one step above, or two steps above. One week later the subjects were retested for moral orientation, confirming the hypothesis (further supported by Rest, Turiel, and Kohlberg, 1969). Training also substantially influences children at immature levels. Crowley (1968) helped first-grade children to identify who was "naughtier" (in stories about moral situations) or "better" (more competent in non-moral situations), and, in addition, engaged the child in a discussion that led to verbalizing the intention of the story figure. These techniques produced significant increases in maturity of judgment on a posttest 18 to 19 days later—the moral stories were much superior, but the discussion added nothing to simple labeling.

Glassco, Milgram, and Youniss (1970) confirmed the long-lasting effect of such training, and see it as facilitating decentering and thus leading to an ability to shift the focus of interpretation (as Piaget proposed). Also invoking the principle of decentration as essential in shifting from immature to mature concepts, Stuart (1967) suggested that it should predict better than either chronological or mental age. Basing decentration on ability to recognize differences in opinion, relativity of judgment, and integration of information, he found that moral judgment is in fact significantly related to decentration, and that both these variables are related to age and intelligence.

The effect of social influence appears in a study of thirteen-year-old adolescents by LeFurgy and Woloshin (1969). Groups classified as realistic (less mature) and relativistic (more mature) listened to stories with tape-recorded answers attributed to peers, with the answers arranged to be contrary to the subject's own scale position. Posttests immediately afterward, after 1 week, and after 100 days, showed that compared to controls both groups displayed immediate shifts. Although this effect had practically disappeared for the relativistic group by 100 days, it remained largely unchanged for the realistic children. Thus the more-mature subjects were quite responsive to social influence but quickly recovered, whereas the less-mature children showed progressive change.

Adult behavior was investigated by Haan, Smith, and Block (1968). From populations of college students and Peace Corps volunteers, 54 percent could be assigned to one of the moral types (see Figure 18-2). The low incidence in types 1 and 2 indicates that such persons have mostly advanced beyond premoral levels. Conventional types are most frequent, with the most mature noticeably less frequent. Data on behavior, self-descriptions, and reported child-rearing practices revealed that subjects of "principled moral reasoning" (stages 5 and 6) were more active in political and social affairs, expressed views more discrepant from their parents, and their self- and ideal-concepts more strongly emphasized interpersonal responsibility, self-expression, and willingness to oppose others. The "conventionally moral" displayed less family conflict.

This study also points to sex differences that warrant further investigation. The "individual principle" type of female felt greater conflict and emotional discomfort compared to males in this category. The male "instrumental relativist" had an expressive, impulsive, irresponsible, and nonconforming orientation; the female "instrumental relativist," on the other hand, emphasized qualities like aloof, practical, and idealistic.

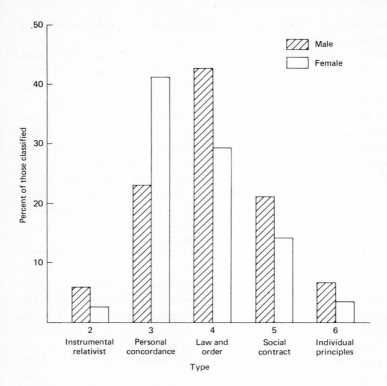

FIGURE 18-2   Representative moral types among college students and Peace Corps volunteers. (Based on Haan, Smith, and Block, 1968.) Note: Percents of the two sexes are computed separately (*N*=253 males, 257 females).

Another interesting direction lies in exploring other kinds of behavior. Do the relationships found necessarily reflect *effectiveness*? Or would the logical progression from less to more mature forms of moral thinking be associated in the same progression in other realms of activity—for example, artistic and scientific creativity? The "instrumental relativist" males superficially, at least, seem to have characteristics resembling the creative personality described in Chapter 15.

TRANSGRESSION, COMPLIANCE, AND EQUITY

In 1928 Hartshorne and May devised a variety of ingenious situations to ascertain the tendency of children to cheat, if the opportunity was given. For example, the children could change or falsify scores on tests, or "peep" when told to keep their eyes closed. They sought to determine whether honesty is a general trait or depends more specifically on the situation, and their findings have historically been interpreted as supporting the specificity view. Burton (1963), however, has pointed out that their data actually contained some evidence for a general characteristic. When he applied factor analysis to their correlations, a general factor common to all the tests was extracted, but there was considerable variance attributable to the different tests. Burton suggests that a learning model may account for this result. The common factor of honesty may extend across the situations as a function of a generalization gradient; as the tests become less similar to each other, more specific conditions affect behavior, leading to greater divergence of response. Invoking a cognitive-mediation gradient of generalization, he suggests that situations may contain cues by which subjects define situations similarly. The more the situation elicits such cues, the more probable it is that honesty will be consistently manifested.

Grim, Kohlberg, and White (1968) have reported significant correlations between measures of attention (from performance in a reaction-time test) and resistance to temptation in tasks like those of Hartshorne and May. They suggest that cheating is at least partly a function of ego strength. That is, moral distractors may operate aimilarly to other environmental distractors.

In a partial replication of Hartshorne and May, Medinnus (1966a) found some support for a positive relation between age and resistance to temptation. He also obtained some evidence that the two sexes display less resistance on tasks particularly approved socially for the opposite sex (this held in one task for sixth graders, but not for third graders). S. H. Schwartz and coworkers (1969) used Kohlberg's test to identify college students low and high in moral development, and also classified the students on measures of achievement and affiliation motivation. Situations provided opportunity to cheat and to be helpful to an accomplice of the experimenters. Level of moral thought proved to be positively related both to not cheating and to helpfulness (the latter relationship only equivocally). Achievement was related to not cheating, whereas affiliation was not. In contrast, achievement was negatively related to helpfulness, but affiliation was positively related. Thus both general and specific tendencies appeared.[1]

[1] Pittel and Mendelsohn (1966) have pointed to several weaknesses in tests of moral values, including inadequacies in the conceptualization of values. However, they do not refer to Kohlberg's approach, which appears to be potentially useful.

Guilt and Compliance

Studies suggest that after guilt is induced, subjects are more likely to comply with requests (but Silverman [1967] failed to support this proposition with sixth graders). Freedman, Wallington, and Bless (1967) induced high school subjects to tell a lie, then asked them to volunteer for another study. Significantly more complied compared to control subjects. This effect was subsequently found to occur primarily when the request pertained to a situation irrelevant to the guilt-arousing one, as if there were a desire to expiate guilt, but also a defense against confronting the source. College students display similar behavior (Carlsmith and Gross, 1969). "Self-blame" may be a factor since the higher the level of this variable, the greater the degree of conformity (Costanzo, 1970).

Brock (1969) pointed out that experiments have not adequately defined "guilt," and usually have failed to determine that inductions actually arouse "guilt." He suggests that experiments reveal a tendency to maintain "social consistency." A person given an opportunity to "transgress" may perceive himself as affecting the fate of another person (such as the experimenter) and thus will wish to do so again if the chance comes. Brock has some difficulty in accounting for experiments in which compliance is greater for requests that do not require encounters with an injured party, but he suggests that there is a common role factor (i.e., the experimenter's needs), so that by complying a kind of redress, or reciprocity, results. However, the consistency principle is hardly sufficient either, and must await evaluation in the light of better manipulation (and confirmation) of guilt.

Situational Antecedents of Transgression

Much ingenuity has been exercised in devising situations in which subjects—usually children—are given an opportunity to violate a norm or rule. Most of these studies reveal the effects of general situational conditions on the acquisition of *self-criticism*. Principles of social learning are prominent in this approach, and attention is directed more to the consequences of an act than to its intrinsic determinants. Despite this limitation, this research illustrates the role of extrinsic variables.

Aronfreed (1964, 1968) has argued that self-criticism is a response instrumental for reducing anxiety, rather than a mechanism of conscience, with contiguity of evaluative labels to punishment as a basis. In this way transgression responses may produce cues that serve as signals for anxiety (i.e., self-criticism "replicates" this verbal medium of punishment).

Self-criticism is thus seen to depend on situational conditions. In one experiment Aronfreed (1963) had fifth graders perform an aggressive act that entailed punishment. A condition of high cognitive structure and high control provided explicitly verbalized standards of performance with the subject assigned responsibility for the amount of punishment; under low structure and low control, the statements about standards were omitted and the experimenter assumed responsibility for punishment. On a final critical trial, it was made to appear that the subject had broken a key component of the apparatus. In response to inquiries, the high-cognitive-structure, high-control children significantly more often expressed self-criticism and offered reparation. In a second experiment, self-criticism occurred primarily under high cognitive structure, independently of control, supporting the principle that it depends on contiguity of punishment and verbalized labels. Reparation was associated mainly with high control (significant only under high structure), indicating that it is a different response to transgression.

Another situational factor is social recognition of transgression. Wallace and Sedalla (1966) contrived to make it appear that the subject, in the presence of a confederate of the experimenter, had broken a crucial piece of apparatus, and he was either "caught" or "not caught." Compared to controls (the apparatus was simply found by the experimenter to be defective), the transgressors significantly more often volunteered for an additional experiment—especially when "caught."

It is clear, however, that emotional relationships are also important. Grusec (1966) employed a situation in which the termination of punishment was either contingent on verbalizing self-criticism or not contingent. In one condition, withdrawal of love was instituted on punishment trials by having a model remark that she was unhappy with the way the child played, followed by an appearance of distress. In contrast, withdrawal of material reward was imposed by announcing that the supply of chips to be exchanged for toys was shut off. Self-criticism was facilitated by high rewardingness and contingent reinforcement, but only under the withdrawal of love. Generalization of self-criticism to a new situation appeared only under contingent reinforcement and withdrawal of love.

Personality variables are also related to cheating (Aronson and Mettee, 1968). Transgression is more frequent in subjects low in self-esteem, especially when negative feedback intended to reduce self-esteem is provided. In another study (Jacobson, Berger, and Millham 1970), most cheating was by subjects high on both need for approval and self-satisfaction. Females high in self-satisfaction cheated most.

Aronfreed's principle of contiguity implies that the effect of situational conditions should vary with their timing. For example, punishment at the inception of an act leads to greater resistance to temptation (Aronfreed and Reber, 1965; Hoffman, 1970), despite some inconclusive results (Walters and Demkow, 1963). However, interpretations by reference to reinforcement conditions is inadequate without more attention to mediational variables (Hoffman, 1970).

Evidence for internalized resistance to temptation comes from studies on delay of gratification. The latter variable has been assessed by preferences for an immediate small reward or a deferred larger one (e.g., a small magnifying glass now versus a larger one next week, or 15 cents now versus 30 cents in 3 weeks). Mischel and Gilligan (1964) found, for sixth-grade boys, significant correlations between preference for immediate reward and cheating ($r = .31$, $P < .05$) and latency of cheating and preference for immediate reward ($r = .38$, $P < .02$). In addition, achievement motivation (based on the TAT measure) was significantly related to cheating, showing the importance of motive strength. Furthermore, subjects who prefer larger delayed rewards are more realistic and concern themselves more with future events (Klineberg, 1968), suggesting that delay of gratification is as much a function of ego as of superego properties.

Risk, Reward, and Cost

Some studies deal with the relation between ethical behavior and risk. Rettig and Rawson (1963) employed items calling for a judgment of whether or not a student should steal money. The test varied reinforcement value of gain, expectancy of gain, reinforcement value of censure, expectancy of censure, severity of offense, and reference group—each in high and low versions. All conditions except the reference group proved significant, but *reinforcement value of censure* was most important (further confirmed when an actual opportunity to cheat was provided by Rettig and Pasamanick [1964]). Using attitudes toward evaluation by parents and teachers as measures of cost, Piliavin, Hardyck, and Vadum (1968) found that low-cost high school boys cheat more than their high-cost peers.

A simple reward-cost model, however, is inadequate. For example, in a study by Bandura and Perloff (1967), schoolchildren imposed on themselves very unfavorable schedules of reinforcement, exerting high effort (a cost) for minimum self-reward. Furthermore, when given an opportunity to reward themselves in a different task, children who had supposedly been successful in a previous task gave themselves higher rewards than those who believed they had failed (Mischel, Coates, and Raskoff, 1968).

Equity
In an experiment with four-year-old children, Masters (1968) created equitable and inequitable conditions of reward. When playing a game with a younger partner, the children received equal, higher, or lower rewards. Both sexes in a subsequent situation rewarded themselves more generously after experiencing the lower-reward condition, as also did girls who had previously received high reward. With *equal* antecedent reward, more stringent standards were adopted.

In a study by Stephenson and White (1968), ten-year-old boys played a game with model racing cars. *Privileged* boys raced the cars while *absolutely deprived* boys had to retrieve the cars for them; under *relative deprivation*, boys retrieved cars for adults; and under *equity*, boys raced and retrieved half the time. When given an opportunity to cheat on a motor-racing quiz, most cheating occurred in the absolutely deprived group, least in the equity and privileged groups. In a later experiment, privilege and deprivation were made to appear either *just* or *unjust* (Stephenson and White, 1970), and now cheating was greatest in the justly privileged and the unjustly deprived boys, suggesting the principle of *distributive justice* (Homans, 1961). Whereas the former may go to great lengths (even cheating) to justify their status, the latter endeavor to restore equity.

Alternative responses occur under inequity (Leventhal and Bergman, 1969). The person for whom inequity is profitable tends to decrease his share, if an opportunity to modify the allocation is available. The person for whom inequity is unprofitable, however, may either restore equity by increasing or decreasing his share. This second response may result from loss of interest, defensiveness, or the influence of goals that supersede the task. It was found that the magnitude of inequity partly determines self-depriving behavior. If unprofitable inequity is moderate, the subject tended to *increase* his share, but to *decrease* it with extreme inequity. Questionnaire data indicated that self-deprivation serves to defend feelings of prestige by such behaviors as displaying contempt or arousing the other's shame.

ALTRUISM AND HELPING BEHAVIOR
Although consideration for others depends, at least partly, on super-ego functions, research has been dominated by situational condi-

tions. Terms like "responsibility," for example, lack adequate conceptualization. Of course, interpersonal perceptions influence altruism, as well as the person's other values. Thus Midlarsky and Bryan (1967) have shown that the learning of altruism in children is facilitated by positive interpersonal relationships and explicit verbal reinforcement.

With college students, *dependency* as a perceived trait of another is a factor. Horowitz (1968) found that more help was given to a dependent person when the subject had no obligation to do so (high choice) than when helping was required (no choice). Furthermore, under high choice, an internally dependent person (one whose predicament was attributed to personal failings) was helped more than an externally dependent person (one who was caught by circumstances beyond his control). In contrast, R. A. Jones (1970), on the basis of reactance theory (Brehm, 1966) argued that restrictions on freedom of action induce a defensive process ("reactance") that aims to restore or protect the threatened behavior. The hypothesis was confirmed that, when one is not free to refuse a request, the more dependent the other is on one's aid, the greater the help given ; but when one is free to refuse, increased dependency leads to less willingness to help. Rejection also increased when it was implied that a future solicitation might be made. These results apparently disagree with Horowitz, but differences in procedure may be responsible. In the Horowitz study, dependency was a perceived personal characteristic of the other person, but Jones treated dependency as a situational variable.

The complexities suggested by the preceding experiments is further revealed by Y. M. Epstein and Hornstein (1969). They manipulated liking in a situation in which the subject either expected or did not expect to be punished. Liking was associated with helping more when punishment was anticipated than when it was not, with the reverse when the other was disliked (see Figure 18-3). This relationship seems to be supported by Landy and Aronson (1969) who found that simulated jurors sentenced an attractive (or neutral) defendant less severely than an unattractive one. In a field study, Feldman (1968) found that perceptions may operate differently in various cultural contexts. Several situations were contrived that enabled people in Boston, Paris, and Athens to respond to a solicitation from an experimenter who was either a compatriot or a foreigner. In both Paris and Boston, compatriots were generally provided more assistance than foreigners, but less in Athens. Feldman cites the probability that Greek norms include foreigners as temporary members of the ingroup.

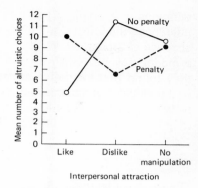

FIGURE 18-3 The effect of interpersonal attraction on altruistic choices.
(Based on Epstein and Hornstein, 1969.)

Lerner (1965a, b) and Lerner and Simmons (1966) have suggested that altruism depends on a "search for justice." Subjects were
led to believe that a partner, whom they were apparently supervising,
either rewarded or betrayed them (Simmons and Lerner, 1968).
When they were assigned the role of working for one of these types
of partners, more work was performed for a previously betrayed
supervisor by those who had themselves been ostensibly betrayed.
A previously betrayed supervisor elicited a higher level of performance than one who had been rewarded or had worked alone. These
results were interpreted as a function of belief in a "just world," in
which social norms lead one to help those who deserve it and to
withhold help from those who do not. Probably, perceived injustice
and guilt are somewhat different determinants of altruism. Regan
(1971), for instance, found that the former is especially important in
witnesses of misfortune, whereas the latter factor influences the
person who does the harm.

The influence of norms of appropriate behavior is shown in
experiments by Staub (1971), in which a child heard someone in
distress in an adjoining room. When the seventh-grade subjects had
information that they were permitted to enter that room, they more
often tried to help than when no information was supplied or when
the children were prohibited from entering. Adult female subjects
helped more often under both permission and no information conditions, compared to prohibition.

The characteristics of a model may influence altruistic behavior.
Rosenhan and White (1967) had an adult model donate half his

winnings in a bowling game to charity. This behavior significantly influenced the fourth- and fifth-grade subjects to act similarly, in the absence of the model. Wagner and Wheeler (1969) pointed out that a model may be selfish as well as generous. Using adult subjects, they found that charitable donations increased with the generosity of the model, but decreased with his selfishness. The effect of generosity was greater under low cost (it was easy to make the donation) than under high cost, but cost had little effect with the selfish model.

Response to Victims

The apparent failure of observers to take any action when someone is in serious trouble prompted Darley and Latané (1968) to hypothesize that the presence of multiple bystanders leads to a "diffusion of responsibility." A subject believed that he was participating in a discussion group via an intercom system, and heard another participant apparently having an epileptic attack. As hypothesized, there was a significant relation between the number of observers and the extent to which the subject helped by reporting the seizure to the experimenter. In a further experiment, a simulated crisis was least likely to be reported when passive bystanders were present, and most likely when the subject was alone (Latané and Darley, 1968). Still another study (Latané and Rodin, 1969) also showed that one of two friends was more likely to help than one of two strangers.

These studies are limited by the artificiality of the laboratory situation. Piliavin, Rodin, and Piliavin (1969) staged episodes on the New York subway, in which a victim, seemingly either drunk or ill, suffered collapse.[1] The apparently ill person was more likely to receive aid than the apparently drunk person. It was also observed that people tended more often to leave the critical area as the length of the emergency increased, especially with the drunken victim. Finally, counter to the diffusion of responsibility principle, speed of helping did not increase with the size of the bystander group—but rather the reverse.

In these studies, intrinsic variables have received little attention. Darley and Latané found no relation between helping and several

---

[1] The race of the victim was also varied but had little effect, except that the helper was somewhat more likely to be of the same race, especially for the drunken victim. Race and sex were also varied by Wispé and Freshley (1971) in a carefully controlled field setting. Here there were no general racial differences, but an interaction appeared between race and sex. In the black sample, males helped more, regardless of the race of the victim, whereas the black females helped less; there was no difference for the white helpers. A slight tendency was also found for the white females to help the white more than the black victim, but the black females helped neither.

personality tests, including a social responsibility scale (Daniels and Berkowitz, 1963). However, Sulzer and Burglass (1968) reported that, compared to others, more-empathic and less-punitive subjects treat others as less personally responsible for negative outcomes produced carelessly or under coercion by external agencies.

A different approach is exemplified by studies in which one person is actually the agent for the suffering of a victim. Milgram (1963) devised a situation in which the subject acted as the "teacher" of another person (a confederate of the experimenter). On the pretext of studying the effects of punishment on learning, the naive subject was induced to administer electric shock to the "learner." The latter simulated severe distress as the intensity of the shock supposedly increased (actually no shock was administered). Sixty-five percent of the subjects continued to punish the victim even at the highest level of intensity (designated as well beyond the point of "Danger: Severe Shock"). This result may partly, at least, be explained by obedience to the authority of the experimenter, who had not only required that the punishment be administered but had also stated that the shock, although extremely painful, would not produce permanent injury.[1]

Situational effects are shown by a reduction in obedience with increased proximity of either the victim or the authority figure (experimenter), although some subjects complied with the instructions even when the victim was in the same room and the subject had physically to force him to touch the "shock plate" (Milgram, 1965). Personality variables are revealed by differences between obedient and defiant subjects. The former were higher in authoritarianism (California F scale), reported more distance from and negative attitudes toward their fathers as children, and rated the "learner" more negatively (Elms and Milgram, 1966).

Tilker (1970) has investigated the effect of responsibility of an observer in the Milgram situation. The observer was assigned the function of recording the "learner's" response and the shock level received, but he had either (1) *no responsibility* for the well-being or punishment of the "learner" (all such decisions were vested in the "teacher"), or (2) *ambiguous responsibility* (decisions had to be resolved between observer and "teacher"), or (3) *total responsibility*. Victim feedback varied among *none, auditory* (the "victim's" vocal

---

[1] This study has engendered controversy over the question of how ethical it is to treat subjects in these ways, since the experiment may be harmful to them. Another issue concerns the appropriateness of the laboratory with its special relationships between experimenter and subject, along with other constraints, for investigating such problems. (See Baumrind [1964] for a critique of Milgram's study, and Milgram's [1964] reply.)

reactions could be heard), and *auditory and visual* (the "victim's" reactions could be seen as well as heard). The verbal protests of the observer were most frequent under the condition of total responsibility, as was physical interference with continuing the experiment. Furthermore, protests increased with greater feedback. Thus socially responsible behavior increases the more a person is forced to become involved or to feel responsible for the other.

Another point concerns the degree to which a person will compensate his victim. Although the perpetrator tends to utilize an opportunity to compensate, Berscheid and Walster (1967) found that compensation is more likely if an available bonus is sufficient to repay the harm than if it is either insufficient or excessive. Reactions of defensive justification are more likely when a person is strongly committed to his action, whereas overcompensating responses are more likely when he is not committed (Walster and Prestholdt, 1966). An expectation of retaliation significantly reduces the perpetrator's derogation of his victim (Berscheid et al., 1968).

Rawlings (1968) has pointed out that altruistic behavior need not merely be an expiation of guilt about harming another but may also arise from sensitivity to the plight of the victim. She found that subjects who merely observed another receive punishment behaved as altruistically as those who were responsible for it.

Comment

Thus a variety of ingenious experiments have begun to investigate superego processes. Much of the research looks for interpersonal and situational conditions that influence manifestations of honesty, altruism, responsibility, and so on, rather than searching out the role of the intrinsic, antecedent properties that may be attributed to moral and ideal attitudes. However, studies of moral development offer important clues that will surely be exploited in future research, although, like other efforts, research seems to be more concerned with conscience than with ego ideal. Whether these two components can be fruitfully separated, with a resulting orientation to different dependent variables, remains to be determined.

VALUES

It will be recalled that superego and ego processes may become fused into more inclusive systems of attitudes. The humanistic conception of self-actualizing values, mentioned in the last chapter, is significant in providing a basis for viewing such systems.

It is not easy to reach a generally acceptable definition of "value." In line with the general views outlined in this chapter and the last, we shall simply regard a value as an attitude that directs behavior into acceptable or preferred directions. A value represents an integration between the ego and the superego, in which abstract moral or ideal standards attain explicit status as points of reference for judgments and decisions. A value system, however, must be viewed more broadly, by considering relationships among its components, by appraising behavior in complex choice situations, and by looking at different levels of organization, as shown by direct preferences between alternatives, or by general, multidimensioned outlooks on life. Although both affective and cognitive elements are apparent at all levels, it is clearly different to treat a liking for opera as a value and to speak about dedication to social responsibility as a value.

Values as Determining Tendencies

In an earlier section we discussed the effects on cognitive responses of variations in attitudes. In this sense values may operate like other intrinsic properties. A test, the Study of Values (Allport, Vernon, and Lindzey, 1960), has been devised to measure values as attitudes. It is based on Spranger's (1928) classification of values into six categories: theoretical, economic, aesthetic, social, political, and religious. Each category is conceived to entail patterns of preferred interests, such as being a sculptor versus being a social worker, or helping a political candidate in his campaign for election versus doing volunteer work for a religious organization. In the second part of the test, the subject ranks four alternatives in order of preference, such as whether a university should strive mainly to improve the morals of students, involve students in public affairs, instill in students scientific knowledge, or promote in students an appreciation of great literature and art. Profiles reveal the relative importance of the six value areas. Such patterns are especially typical of occupational groups. For example, a sample of male teachers was highest on religious and theoretical values, ministers on religious and social values, and graduate students in business on economic and political values; female nurses were highest on religious and social values.

This test has proved useful in clinical settings, such as vocational counseling. But it can also be employed to demonstrate the effects of individual differences on behavior. For example, Postman, Bruner, and McGinnies (1948) found a significant relation between value score and recognition threshold for relevant words—the higher the value, the lower the threshold.

Stability and Change in Values

Rokeach (1968, p. 124) treats values as "abstract ideals, positive or negative, not tied to any specific attitude object or situation, representing a person's beliefs about ideal modes of conduct and ideal terminal goals." He distinguishes between *instrumental* and *terminal* values, or desirable behavior and desirable ends. Values cut across other attitudes, thus transcending specific situations and serving to direct or control other attitudes. Rokeach lists eighteen values of each kind. Among instrumental values are independence, imagination, logic, love, ambition, cleanliness, honesty, and self-control; and among terminal values are a comfortable life, a sense of accomplishment, a world of beauty, freedom, pleasure, self-respect, true friendship, and wisdom.

Basic is the thesis that change in values depends on recognition by a person that his values are discrepant. To this end Rokeach asked subjects to rank both sets of values, so that he could point out apparent contradictions. For example, individuals were found to rank "equality" first, but "freedom" eleventh (on the average). Next, attitudes toward civil rights were measured. The results of a survey were then presented, showing a close association between this attitude and the ranking of the equality value but, despite the relation, showing that many people who profess equality as an important value do not support or participate in civil rights activities. This discrepancy served as a point of departure for challenging the subject's own inconsistencies in values: For example, did "equality" mean his own personal freedom rather than freedom for all?

Next, a test for self-dissatisfaction was administered. Value and attitude ratings were also obtained from a control group, which had no opportunity to examine inconsistencies. Changes in behavior were related to degree of self-dissatisfaction. Some 3 to 5 months after the induction, experimental subjects solicited by mail to join the National Association for the Advancement of Colored People (NAACP) responded significantly more often than control subjects (see Figure 18-4); a second solicitation after 15 to 17 months produced similar, although nonsignificant, results.

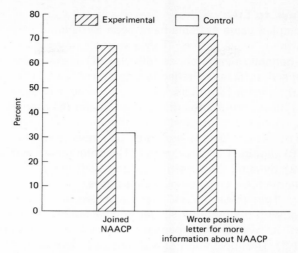

FIGURE 18-4 Difference between subjects in whom self-dissatisfaction over value inconsistencies was induced and control subjects. (Based on Rokeach, 1971.) Note: Total $N=366$ with 197 and 169 in experimental and control groups, respectively. The percents in the figure refer to those who joined (40) and those who wrote (13), and are corrected for difference in N.

Rokeach's approach offers impressive evidence for the importance of values in behavior, and his results should especially be compared with the transient changes usually reported in other studies of attitude change. We might, however, criticize the linking of values with simple verbal labels. An especially valuable step would be to examine individual differences in value rankings, rather than employing averages. Clearly there must be many individuals among those who did not reply to the solicitation whose major values were quite irrelevant to civil rights or the NAACP. In addition, an unknown number of subjects among those who did reply may simply have responded on the basis of consistent values rather than as a function of reordering and validating their values. Finally, the technique itself requires that a subject rank all eighteen values, producing a purely ordinal scale. In this way, no account can be taken of the internal properties of the value system—that is, relative salience, importance, or other variations. The method does not allow one to determine, for example, whether the lowest-ranked values are rejected or merely indifferent.

Ways to Live

Complex value systems have been formulated by Morris (1956), as thirteen "ways to live." These systems present detailed descriptions of general orientation, as follows: (1) preserve the best in society; (2) self-sufficiency, reflection, and meditation; (3) altruistic affection and concern for others; (4) abandonment to sensuous enjoyment; (5) group action toward common goals; (6) progress through realistic solution of problems; (7) integration of diversity; (8) wholesome enjoyment of simple comforts; (9) quiet receptivity to experience; (10) dignified self-control; (11) contemplation of a rich inner life; (12) dynamic physical interaction with the environment; and (13) humble obedience to cosmic purposes.

That these "ways" can be scaled has been ascertained, together with the fact that similar general factors emerge cross-culturally, but, as would be expected, with variations in salience (see Table 18-3). The application of S.D. scales has revealed not only distinctive patterns of liking and disliking, but more general factors of meaning. "Dynamism" is represented by ways 9, 11, and 13 at the passive pole, ways, 5, 6, 7, and 12 at the active pole; "socialization" by ways 1, 3, and 8 as highly socialized, and ways 2 and 4 as highly egocentric; "control" by ways 1, 2, and 10 as highly controlled, and ways 4, 8, and 12 as uncontrolled or "abandoned"; and "venturousness" by ways 4, 5, 7, and 12 as adventuresome, and ways 2, 8, and 10 as cautious and colorless.

The S.D. ratings revealed connotational factors of "successfulness," "predictability," and "kindness." The first was highly correlated with preference ratings, indicating its similarity to the evaluative dimension. When the thirteen ways were located in the semantic space defined by the three major factors, an incomplete representation of possible value systems was revealed. Thus dynamism divides the ways fairly equally, but socialization and control do not—there are few ways on the egocentric and uncontrolled sides of the space. Thus ample room exists to provide for additional value systems that may characterize other persons (or cultures). Some of these inadequately represented orientations may be quite rare or idiosyncratic, or special groups, such as "alienated" or radical subjects, may supply additional ways.

Internal Controls

The various approaches examined here are making considerable progress in bringing under systematic treatment those properties of

Table 18-3
Ways to Live Factors Especially Distinctive of Five Cultural Groups. (Based on Morris and Jones, 1955.)

Factors*	Highest	Lowest
A. Social restraint and self-control Ways 10, 1, 3, 4 (negative)	India	U. S.
B. Enjoyment in action Ways 5, 12, 8, 10 (negative), 2 (negative), 11	China	Japan
C. Withdrawal and self-sufficiency Ways 9, 2, 11, 6 (negative)	U.S. (negative)	Japan (negative)
D. Receptivity and sympathetic concern Ways 13, 3, 10, 5, 2 (negative), 4 (negative)	China	U.S. (negative)
E. Self-indulgence Ways 4, 12, 3 (negative)	Norway (negative)	India (negative)

*Derived from factor analysis of U. S. ratings.

Note: Based on factor analysis of Indian ratings, rather than American, similar results were obtained, especially for factors A, B, D, and E.

the mental context that represent internalized standards of conduct. This development is one of the most significant features of the past 10 years in psychology, and it shows every sign of vigorous growth in the future. Ego, self, superego, and value aspects of the mental context represent general regulatory processes. In addition, however, there are controlling systems linked more obviously to particular kinds or classes of eliciting stimuli—that is, those processes typically called "social attitudes." They will be the concern in the next two chapters.

SUMMARY
Originating in the resolution of the Oedipus complex, the superego governs behavior in relation to standards of conduct. The sub-divisions of conscience and ego ideal have both positive and nega-tive aspects. Superego attitudes may become integrated with those of the ego and self. Development depends centrally on parent-child relations, varying with cultural differences. Social-learning theory

treats imitation as the basic process. Piagetian theory sees moral development as proceeding through a series of stages, revised to encompass premoral, conventional, and principled levels, each with two stages. Research has focused on cheating, guilt, and compliance, resistance to temptation, delay of gratification, conditions of reward and cost, and perceived inequality. Studies of altruism and helping reveal the effects of characteristics of the other person and of situational variables. Although several principles have been advanced, a definitive theory has not yet emerged. Values are seen to be attitudes that integrate ego and superego processes, directing behavior in preferred directions.

19

SOCIAL ATTITUDES AND PREJUDICE

Throughout this book the term *attitude* has referred to components of mediating processes that regulate motives. As arousal varies quantitatively or changes qualitatively, attitudes control and direct responses. This view is compatible with the classical definition formulated by Allport (1935), as follows: *An attitude is a mental and neural state of readiness, organized through experience, exerting a directive or dynamic influence upon the individual's response to all objects and situations with which it is related.* The "readiness" feature of the definition may be an enduring predisposition, which broadly determines response in relevant situations, or an immediately induced state, which influences response in a given situation. In this fashion we can distinguish between general and specific attitudes. I prefer to reserve "attitude" for the general regulator and "set" for the specific determinant (or "adjustor").

Problems arise concerning the *formation* of attitudes, their *influence* on response, and the *changes* induced by extrinsic influences. Although it is difficult and perhaps artificial to differentiate sharply among these problems, it is evident that we have so far dealt primarily with the formation and effects of attitudes as properties of the person antecedent to behavior in given situations.

Within social psychology, attention has been directed mainly to the third problem. The issue may be phrased in this fashion: Social life is featured by transactions between and among persons, in which one individual (or agent) serves as a stimulus for eliciting responses from another. Each individual comes into the transaction equipped with already-established cognitive systems; such systems, however, do not operate autonomously to determine response but are subject to inducing and adapting forces released in the situation. Therefore the important mark of social interaction is not so much the establishment of attitudes as *change* in them, inferred from the behavior observed. But the social transaction is not merely a simple, passive relationship—each agent is an active force, exerting influence on the other. That is, the pervasive condition of society is the active attempt by one person to change in a desired direction the attitudes of the other. Social transactions are not only the expression of attitudes, but the influencing of attitudes.

Since Allport, many other definitions have been proposed (see McGuire, 1969), but none really improves on Allport's, although more specific and limited views have focused on particular components or properties of cognitive structure.

We infer an attitude from responses (notably verbal), whether overtly stated, written, or symbolized by a check mark on a scale. A response that expresses a social attitude may be called an *opinion*. But since opinions are observed responses, the drawing of inferences from them about enduring regulators requires care. An experimental induction may produce changes in opinions but only superficial or transient changes in cognitive structure—that is, sets may vary but attitudes are relatively unaffected.

Theories differ in their emphasis on the role of intrinsic and extrinsic determinants of opinions (and hence of attitudes). In general, interest has been directed toward situational influences. Comparison of pre- and posttests is usually intended to ascertain changes in response rather than to assess changes in the cognitive system itself, and thus reveals the effects of sets rather than of attitudes. This point is important in considering the broad implications of much experimental work. One cannot determine from opinions stated at a particular time whether they represent responses primarily reflecting immediate stimulus conditions, or whether they express enduring characteristics of a person. Only by examining the consistency and transsituational properties of opinions can inferences be drawn about attitudes. Otherwise the intrinsic determinant can only be designated safely as a set—or as a specific, situationally induced regulator. In the latter instance, our description and prediction are highly limited, but in the former, they are more general and less dependent on designated stimuli. In this chapter we shall examine approaches to general attitudes, and in Chapter 20, studies oriented more toward the effect of specific attitudes or sets.

Newcomb (1943) showed the importance of considering long-range effects. Women at Bennington College, which provided a liberal atmosphere, were given a test of attitudes toward political and economic issues in the mid-1930s and again in 1939. Liberalism generally increased over the college years. However, although those girls who remained at the college for 3 or 4 years maintained the change several years later, those who left the college after 1 or 2 years had reverted to their original level by the time of the follow-up study. The role of the reference group was apparent since girls who became more liberal identified with the college and participated in its affairs, whereas the girls who did not change much clung more closely to their familial identification and to special cliques of friends. (See also, Siegel and Siegel (1957) for another demonstration of the effect of reference groups in promoting change or nonchange in attitudes, in this instance authoritarianism.) Study of these women 20 years or more later (Newcomb et al., 1967) revealed that these effects persisted. Women who were conservative at the end of their college careers continued to be conservative, and those who were liberal remained liberal. Thus the subjects who were changed by their college experience have generally been permanently affected.

Investigation of students in the 1960s showed that the current population, like the earlier one, was quite liberal. The apparently more general norm of liberalism (or anticonservatism) has become differentiated into emphasis on individualism and unconventionality and on intellectuality. Definite sanctions for enforcing these norms were identified, with evidence that the college environment induces changes in these directions.

PROPERTIES OF ATTITUDES

Although the *behavioral* effects of attitudes have received most attention, some theorists have also allowed for other aspects. Thus Katz and Stotland (1959; Katz, 1960) point to *affective* and *cognitive* components, in addition to conative (behavioral) properties, suggesting that measurement of one aspect may not do justice to another. Although some studies (see McGuire, 1969) indicate that these three aspects tend to be highly correlated, at least for some categories of attitudes, nevertheless a comprehensive understanding of the functioning of attitudes requires that all these components be adequately assessed.

Ostrom (1969) has employed scales to measure each of the three aspects of attitudes toward the church. The affective component was defined as favorable or unfavorable feelings, the behavioral component as statements of positive or negative actions, and the cognitive component as conceptual views or beliefs. In addition, nonverbal indicators were obtained from information about church attendance and activities. Measures of the same component displayed higher correlations than measures of different components, although the difference was not very great (on the order of .70 versus .60). Although the nonverbal measures were similar, this relationship was also not much greater than the correlations between components. For example, church attendance correlated .66 with the verbal behavioral items, and .56 and .59 with the affective and cognitive items. Triandis (1964) has pointed to the inadequate attention paid to behavioral indexes, and suggested that a more systematic approach to their classification would be helpful.

After examining a variety of studies relating attitude measures to behavior, Tittle and Hill (1967) concluded that lack of correspondence partly results from deficiencies of the measures, using behavioral criteria lying outside the normal experience of the subject, and reliance on too limited (even single) acts.

TECHNIQUES OF MEASUREMENT

A wide variety of techniques have been developed for measuring attitudes. D. T. Campbell (1950) classified them into the following categories: (1) *nondisguised, structured methods* require direct expression in standardized fashion, with no attempt to conceal the purpose of the test, for example, typical questionnaires and rating scales, like those devised by Thurstone and Chave (1929), Likert (1932), and Guttman (1944); (2) *nondisguised, nonstructured methods* also do not hide the aim of the test, but the subject is free to respond as he pleases, for example, interviews with open-ended questions, biographical materials, essay materials (Hill and Ackiss, 1945), and preference rankings and judgments of stimulus materials like those used by Horowitz (1936) to investigate the racial attitudes of children; (3) *disguised, nonstructured methods* such as projective techniques elicit responses to ambiguous or incomplete material, for example, the thematic apperception pictures used by Proshansky (1943) to assess attitudes toward organized labor, versions of the Rosenzweig picture-frustration study used to investigate intergroup hostility (Brown, 1947; Vinacke, 1959a); and play-therapy situations (Axline, 1948); and (4) *disguised structured methods* present organized tasks with the concealed purpose of revealing attitudes, for example, experiments on selective factors in perception and memory (Cook and Selltiz, 1964), tests of critical thinking constructed to reveal biases (Morgan, 1945), and tests of information (Newcomb, 1946), the error-choice technique of Hammond (1948) containing items with two "wrong" answers, and judgments of the plausibility of arguments (Waly and Cook, 1965).

Attitude Scales

Although many kinds of techniques have been tried, most studies of attitudes rely on nondisguised, structured procedures. Sophisticated, highly developed scales of general attitudes are used for assessment purposes, with more limited single items or a few items for the specific purposes of measuring change resulting from experimental inductions. Methodological difficulties, recognized from the beginning (McNemar, 1946), are still evident (Scott, 1968).

Equal-appearing Intervals Designated by Scott (1968) as *consensual location scaling,* the method proposed by Thurstone (1928) and Thurstone and Chave (1929) sought to standardize variations in attitude independently of the subject's own position. The problem is twofold—to order views from one extreme to the other, and to provide for a sampling of opinion at successive degrees along the scale. These requirements were met by using a large sample of judges to sort statements referring to the attitude into categories corresponding to an eleven-point scale.

These judgments, it should be noted, are not based on the judge's own views but on his perception of where the statement belongs on the scale. This works very well, but there is always the risk that inescapable orientations may distort the location of statements. For example, Hovland and Sherif (1952) found that judges extremely favorable toward blacks tended to displace presumably moderate statements about blacks toward the unfavorable side (see also, Eiser, 1971b). Studies by Ward (1965, 1966) support the effect of attitude on judging statements, but not that this especially characterizes the neutral items.[1] Ostrom and Upshaw (1970) have shown how interpretation of items may shift over time. During the current period, statements are judged as more anti-black than they were in 1929. This shift is greater for whites than for blacks.

Statements on which there is very high agreement (ideally nearly perfect) are chosen and the median location then becomes the scale value. Other criteria may also be invoked to determine such points as suitability for assessing present rather than past attitudes, applicability to a wide range of respondents, and freedom from confusing or awkward language.

In administering the scale, subjects check items with which they agree, and the attitude score is the median scale value of these items.

Summated Ratings   The technique developed by Likert (1932; Likert, Roslow, and Murphy, 1934) is based on the principle that every person should display *some* degree of approval for every statement about the attitude object. Accordingly, items are provided with five steps (e.g., strongly approve, approve, undecided, disapprove, and strongly disapprove). Ideally, all statements are related in the same way to the object (monotonically), and are chosen on such criteria as whether all five points are represented, the degree of skewness, and whether bimodality exists. In addition, since the items are to be treated as components of a general attitude, they are correlated with the total score,[2] and those that produce the highest correlations are retained. The sum of the responses expresses the general attitude.

In Likert's original proposal, scale values were based on the standard deviations of the distributions. Subsequently, however, it has been determined that this laborious procedure is not necessary since simply scoring the five steps from 1 to 5 agrees closely with standard-score weightings.

In general, Thurstone and Likert scales are equivalent in reliability as well as correlating highly with each other. Although both techniques involve a tedious amount of work, especially the Thurstone approach, standardized forms are available that are readily adaptable to virtually any attitude object (see Ferguson, 1952).

[1]Eiser (1971a), however, questions this lack of confirmation, pointing to the exclusion of subjects as a possible reason.

[2]A correction may be applied to eliminate the inflation of the correlation by the inclusion of the item in the total score (see Scott, 1968, p. 219).

Cumulative Scales   Guttman (1944, 1950) attempted to arrive at simple unidimensional scales. His assumption is that several statements can be found that fall into an exact order of acceptance, so that each point represents the maximum degree of the attitude that a subject is willing to endorse. Constructing this kind of scale involves the identification of patterns of response to select those statements on which subjects are ordered as desired. Failures to produce the proper order (e.g., a subject who agrees with 1, 2, and 4, but not with 3) are treated as "errors." The aim is to reduce these errors to an absolute minimum as shown by the coefficient of reproducibility. The criterion of .90 is taken as sufficient to indicate unidimensionality.

This approach clearly has considerable merit for measurement purposes, but it is difficult to achieve in practice. Usually it yields a very simple, highly specific set of statements. The cumbersomeness of the procedures and the susceptibility of items to "random" errors and response sets renders this technique generally unsatisfactory.

Reliability and Validity   The scales just described can be constructed to produce high coefficients of consistency, as determined by the split-half technique. Stability offers a greater problem since the test ought to reflect changes. In the case of general attitudes (like those toward religion, peace, marriage), one would expect that change would usually be slow, so that test-retest reliability over reasonable periods of time is also generally high. When specific attitudes, more properly called *opinions,* are measured, as in experiments on attitude change, the items must obviously be more sensitive to the particular conditions under investigation, so that stability is not really desired. Instead, one would commonly employ a control group to show that little change occurs in the absence of the experimental induction. Thus transient and situation-specific change can be detected.

Studies of validity vary widely, some producing good relationships between attitude scores and behavioral criteria, for example, A. Campbell and his associates (1960) on political behavior, and others displaying little or no relation. The assessment of validity continues to be inadequate (Shaw and Wright, 1967), and is more often taken for granted than actually ascertained, or relies on construct validity.

Dimensions of Attitudes   Scales have mostly been designed to assess the *direction* and *intensity* of attitudes. The former refers to favorability versus unfavorability (e.g., approval or disapproval) and the latter to the degree of this orientation. These dimensions, of course, also dominate most measures of personality variables.

Although the evaluative, or affective, aspect of attitudes appears to be very important—and, in fact, it may be the major basis on which every individual can be measured on the same scale—nevertheless, other dimensions deserve attention (Krech, Crutchfield, and Ballachey, 1962). *Salience* refers to the degree to which an attitude is actually involved in the individual's behavior at the time (corresponding to its arousal rather than its latent existence). In one study Charters and Newcomb (1958) made groups of students aware of their religious affiliations by assembling them in groups of the same religion and then notifying them of this condition. Compared to control groups, for whom this salience was not induced, Catholic subjects displayed greater orthodoxy of view, but Protestant and Jewish subjects did not. Salience of group membership may still have operated, according to the investigators, since there was evidence both that religious norms were less important for the latter subjects and that at least some of them reacted negatively as a function of emphasis on their religious identification. *Importance* concerns the significance to the individual of the attitude, relative to other attitudes. Thus two persons may have similar positions on a scale of attitude toward the United Nations, but whereas this view plays a strong, continuing, and compelling role in the thinking of one, it is of some indifference to the other. *Complexity* pertains to organizational features of attitude systems, that is, how differentiated their components are, how diverse the content, how harmonious or conflicting the elements. *Consciousness* or verbalizability signifies the degree to which the individual can state and explain his views. Two people may be similarly opposed to "campus radicals," yet one may be hardly aware of his views (except that he is opposed)— that is, much of his attitude system is composed of unconscious elements, while the other person may have a well-elaborated position that he can verbalize extensively.

GENERAL ATTITUDES

If social attitudes are general regulators of response, then the specific items employed to measure them, that is, opinion statements, are potential indicators of them. A general attitude represents an inferred common denominator of a set of items. We see such consistencies in the ego-defensive and ego-constructive processes previously discussed, in measures of parental behavior, and in values. In the present context our interest lies in consistencies of response toward objects of significance in society, whether actual "objects," symbols, or abstract ideas. Thus we may attempt to identify general tendencies with respect to religion, marriage, economic or political policies, peace, or population control. In each such instance the reference for opinion has complex features, no one of which by itself is necessarily indicative of the total object. Thus a person may typically support the Democratic party, but may oppose one or more of the policies it endorses.

From a commonsense standpoint quite general orientations cut across a wide assortment of judgments. We readily classify economic and political views as "liberal" or "conservative," speak assuredly about "humanitarian" positions, and so on. The implication is that opinions are specific expressions of an enduring, underlying general attitude, such as a conservative-liberal continuum (Lentz, 1939; Kerr, 1944; Vetter, 1947), or a democratic-authoritarian variable (Adorno et al., 1950), or dogmatism (Rokeach, 1960).

Factor analysis is a basic approach to this problem (Ferguson, 1939, Eysenck, 1947). In one such study three primary social attitudes were identified: religionism, humanitarianism, and nationalism (Ferguson, 1940, 1942). In another, a conservative-aggressive factor appeared (Stagner, 1944). Radicalism and tender-minded factors were defined in a third study (Eysenck, 1947). A fourth brought out two religious factors, nearness to God and fundamentalism-humanitarianism (Broen, 1957). By utilizing a wide variety of items, Digman (1962) found the following eight factors: authoritarianism-humanitarianism, equalitarianism, social liberalism–conservatism, religionism, political liberalism–conservatism, nationalism, tender-mindedness–tough-mindedness, and sexual permissiveness.

Although these studies support the principle of general social attitudes, they cannot readily be reduced to a simple classification since somewhat different factors appear, or similar factors emerge with different degrees of importance. Like Kerr (1946), Digman indicates, for example, that liberalism-conservatism actually covers several distinct orientations. All may represent positions that range from preserving the status quo to altering the social order (or some such underlying continuum—see Mannheim, 1936). Nevertheless, a given individual who is "conservative" in one realm of social policies may evidently be "liberal" in another. This point has recently been documented by Hicks and Wright (1970). Five tests intended to measure liberalism–conservatism were administered along with several measures of possible contaminants (social desirability, acquiescence, authoritarianism, intelligence). Seven factors were identified, four of them well specified by Kerr's subscales: economic, political, aesthetic, and religious. Three other tests (Centers, 1949; Adorno et al., 1950[1]; and Wright and Hicks, 1966) all proved to measure only economic liberalism–conservatism. The fifth test (D. P. Campbell, 1965) did not appear on any of these factors, but instead belonged in a separate ethnocentrism factor, defined also by the F scale (see discussion on authoritarianism) and low intelligence. All the scales, except for those measuring the economic orientation, were to some degree contaminated by the discriminant correlates. Clearly, then, distinctions can be drawn among degrees of liberalism–conservatism, but only by reference to appropriate objects.

Kerlinger (1967) suggested that the bipolarity assumption is misleading, if not incorrect. Instead he proposed that orientations tend to be dualistic. Thus liberalism is not necessarily the opposite of conservatism, but instead may simply entail a different set of opinions. A liberal, that is, endorses one group of policies, a conservative another group, but the former does not necessarily disagree with the latter. The difference lies in what is critical for a given individual. For example, with respect to higher education, criterial referents may include student participation in college governance, independent study, and no required courses, or they may include faculty control, traditional courses, and planned curricula. If the former is labeled a "liberal" orientation, the latter "conservative," then not all elements of each position are necessarily opposed to those of the other (although they may be)—that is, the liberal may be indifferent to, or even support, aspects of the conservative cluster. It is thus conceivable that these attitudes should be treated as dualistic and orthogonal rather than bipolar. Kerlinger suggests that items be made more "natural," that is, correspond with what people actually think and say. More attention should also be paid to the attitudinal object itself, distinguishing among its different aspects and their significance to different persons.

To provide some perspective on issues that arise in the study of general attitudes, we shall discuss some of those with special interest for interpersonal relationships, namely, authoritarianism, dogmatism, and prejudice.

---

[1] The political-economic conservatism scale, not the F scale.

AUTHORITARIANISM

During the 1950s an intensive effort was made to establish the proposition that a certain complex of attitudes can be labeled as "authoritarianism," contrasting with a more democratic or equalitarian syndrome. This thesis was stimulated primarily by the work of Adorno and his associates (1950).

A variety of techniques provided information about the characteristics and development of attitudes toward minorities, political issues, and religious practices. The E scale deals with attitudes toward Jews, blacks, and other minorities ("ethnocentrism"). The F scale ("fascism") includes items on conventional values, submission, aggression, superstition, stereotypy, power, and "toughness", and other presumed manifestations of authoritarianism. Since these two scales display high correlations (about .70), they have both been used as measures of authoritarianism.

Although several patterns were actually identified within high and low scoring categories, most attention was devoted to groups described as strongly prejudiced and markedly tolerant (equalitarian). In the realm of socialization, the high scorers came from homes featured by harsh and threatening parental discipline, conventional goals, and sharply defined familial and sex roles. Stemming from these conditions were tendencies toward superficial and externalized relations with others, ambivalence in which submission to parents accompanied by repressed hostility extended also to social institutions generally, and an orientation toward power and status with contempt for those judged weak or inferior. These persons were found to be moralistic and insecure, dependent on external support, and low in ego strength. Their cognitive functioning was marked by rigidity and intolerance of ambiguity.

The great importance of these principles prompted a detailed critical appraisal (Christie and Jahoda, 1954). Methodological shortcomings, for example, pointed out by Hyman and Sheatsley (1954), included the tendency to overgeneralize, sampling biases, focusing on extremes without adequate attention to intermediate levels, various weaknesses in the scales and the coding of data, and the lack of rigor in interpreting statistical evidence.

On a conceptual basis, Shils (1954) pointed out that Adorno and his associates were really concerned with authoritarianism of the "right." Further examination suggests that, in fact, individuals with an extreme "leftist" orientation bear many important resemblances to the pattern described in the California studies. The fact that implicit values guided Adorno and his associates has been emphasized by Masling (1954), since research fails to support the notion that authoritarians are necessarily neurotic. In his view the term "authoritarian" may often be loosely employed as a derogatory label.

A review by Titus and Hollander (1957) indicated the general lines of research to which the F scale has been applied. One line searched for the personality correlates that would appear if authoritarianism is a general variable. Thus D. T. Campbell and McCandless (1951) found high intercorrelations among a variety of tests of attitudes toward minority groups, indicating a general factor of xenophobia, as the California study proposed. Radke-Yarrow and Lande (1953) showed that the F scale correlates with reaction to minority-group membership, as well as the other way around. In this study Jewish students with high scores were more anti-Semitic than those with low scores. The personality differences cited by Adorno and his associates appeared as well.

Several personality variables were found by Siegel (1954) to be significantly correlated with a version of the F scale, including manifest anxiety, intolerance of ambiguity, and compulsiveness. Jones (1957) constructed an instrument to assess personality components presumably linked with authoritarianism, including items on dependency, rigidity, anxiety, and hostility. The resulting Pensacola Z survey correlated .43 with the F scale, again providing some evidence for a general personality syndrome. Other studies also show that high scorers tend to be sensitive, schizoid, withdrawing, depressive, and antisocial (Davids, 1955; Spilka and Struening, 1956), and that prejudiced subjects are characterized by nationalistic attitudes, intolerance of ambiguity, superstition, suspicious competitiveness, higher F-scale scores, religiosity, and endorsement of strict, authoritarian parental child-rearing practices, and, in addition, are lower on educational and occupational status (J. G. Martin and Westie, 1959).

However, the correlations are low enough to indicate that authoritarianism is far from a unitary or simple variable. Its manifestation depends on social, educational, and cultural factors. General subcultural variations were reported by Christie and Garcia (1951), with Southwestern subjects displaying higher scores. Prothro (1952) found that prejudice against blacks in the South is not necessarily associated with prejudice against other minority groups, indicating that a context of unfavorable norms contributes to ethnocentrism, apart from personality dynamics. In a cross-cultural study, Melikian (1956) compared a Middle Eastern with an American sample, finding that the former were considerably higher on the measure of authoritarianism, but that the two cultures differed markedly in the variables related to it. Pettigrew (1959) further identified sociocultural variables associated with prejudice. In the South, political independents were found to be more tolerant of blacks than were party identifiers, veterans were more tolerant than nonveterans, and persons who attended church frequently were less tolerant than nonattenders. Such variables were much less related to prejudice in the North, indicating that personality characteristics are the major determinant of racial attitudes in that region. In the South, however, sociocultural factors add a significant contribution.

The California study postulated that highly authoritarian persons are "intolerant of ambiguity," tending to think in absolute "black and white" terms and to engage in premature closure in situations that call for evaluative decisions. This proposition has been confirmed by more stable "norms" reached in the autokinetic situation by individuals high in ethnocentrism (Block and Block, 1951; Taft, 1956; Millon, 1957). In addition, intolerance of ambiguity correlates significantly ($r = .43$) with difficulty in seeing certain illusions (Martin, 1954). Jones (1956) found a low negative correlation between the F scale and the rate of fluctuation of the plane cube illusion (Necker cube). However, no evidence for these relationships was apparent in studies by Davids (1955), Kenny and Ginsberg (1958), and McCandless and Holloway (1955).

Finally, Budner (1962) has constructed a scale to measure intolerance of ambiguity as a personality variable. This instrument correlated significantly with the F scale, religious dogmatism, conventionality, belief in a divine power, and other measures, providing evidence that authoritarianism and intolerance of ambiguity are related.

Persons who score high on the F scale were also described as relatively insensitive in interpersonal situations. In one study, nonauthoritarians proved more accurate in judging the F-scale scores of authoritarian partners than the reverse (Scodel and Mussen, 1953). However, when pairs were alike in F-scale scores, authoritarians were more accurate (Scodel and Freedman, 1956). Rabinowitz (1956) pointed out that these apparently contradictory results may simply reflect a tendency for the judge's own score to determine his estimates. When college students were asked for judgments of the scores that a typical student would make, they tended to give estimates higher than their own scores. Since the nonauthoritarians gave significantly higher estimates relative to their own scores, they only appeared to be accurate (i.e., closer to the mean score for the total group). Crockett and Meidinger (1956) replicated these studies, but incorporated all three types of pairs in the same design. Clearly in line with Rabinowitz, both high and low F scorers made similar estimates, regardless of their partners' characteristics; the high scorers generally produced markedly higher scores. In all these studies, however, the high scorers were less variable, which, in addition to the lack of difference between their own scores and their estimates of their partners, indicates something like rigidity. But evidently the low scorers are not better able to discriminate actual differences in authoritarianism between their partners.

Certain special factors complicate the distinction between high and low F-scale scores. Several investigators have noted a negative correlation with intelligence (Cohn, 1952; Davids, 1955). But to some extent this reflects the greater ability of persons with high intelligence to "fake good," that is, to conceal their actual opinions or to create a favorable impression (Cohn, 1952). This factor may partly account for the apparently greater concreteness and simplified thinking attributed to high scorers. In addition, the original scale was susceptible to the response set known as *acquiescence,* or the tendency for a subject to agree with positively worded statements. Evidence that high F scorers are more acquiescent appears in several studies (Cohn, 1953; Leavitt, Hax, and Roche, 1955; Bass, 1955; Chapman and Campbell, 1957; P. W. Jackson and Messick, 1957; Beloff, 1958), suggesting that it is the authoritativeness of the statements rather than their meaning that influences the high scorer. This factor is more a weakness of the scale than of the theory, since scales revised to provide better reversed statements, or to allow for acquiescence (Christie, Havel, and Seidenberg, 1958; Budner, 1962) have still confirmed some of the characteristics of authoritarianism. Furthermore, Mogar (1960) showed that reversed versions are not equivalent and that their correlations with the F scale itself, although significant, are both very low and in opposite directions. The reversed scales were not related to extreme judgments on the S. D. judgment of controversial and noncontroversial concepts, but the F scale did display this relation. Samelson and Yates (1967) have concluded that the supposed evidence for acquiescence is an artifact of the procedure used in reversing items.

In general, then, the conception of a general system of authoritarian attitudes has received some support, albeit in a variable manner. The F scale, as a measure, has serious weaknesses, but even so appears to have some relation to hypothesized behavioral effects.

DOGMATISM

Another general property of social attitudes has been labeled *dogmatism,* or narrow-mindedness. Rokeach (1951b) analyzed responses to political and religious names (Buddhism, Catholicism, Christianity, Judaism, Protestantism, Capitalism, Communism, Democracy, Fascism, and Socialism). The highest and lowest quartiles of the ethnocentrism scale (Levinson, 1949) differed markedly in cognitive organization, with the former characterized by narrowness and concreteness, the latter by comprehensiveness and abstractness. Rokeach (1954, 1956) suggested that the conception of an authoritarian personality in the Adorno and associates study rests on a narrow orientation to prejudice and political-economic conservatism when in fact these characteristics are not the only manifestations. Accordingly, he pointed to distinctions between "open" and "closed" cognitive systems, as follows: low versus high rejection of disbelief, free versus constrained communication within and between belief and disbelief, little versus considerable discrepancy in differentiating belief from disbelief, high versus little differentiation within disbelief systems, benign versus threatening outlook on the world, nonabsolutist versus absolutist view of authority, well-integrated attitudes toward authority versus subsystems of isolated attitudes, and broad versus narrow time perspective.

Acting on this formulation, he devised a dogmatism scale with items based on the postulated differences between open and closed systems, including political beliefs, notions about knowledge and "isms," the basic human condition, feelings about the future, power and status, authority, intolerance, and so on. Rokeach distinguished between *rigidity* (which pertains to limited, specific sets) and *dogmatism* (which represents a closed system of beliefs and attitudes). Therefore the person high in dogmatism should have difficulty in synthesizing information, but the rigid person should find it difficult to analyze information.

This distinction was investigated with the "doodelbug problem." It presents the subject with this problem: Joe Doodelbug can jump in only four directions—north, south, east, and west (not diagonally). He can only move by jumping (any distance, large or small); he cannot turn around. He must jump four times before he can change direction. His master places food 3 feet directly west of him. Joe stops where he is, facing north, and concludes that he must jump four times to get the food. He is correct, and the problem is to explain why. Rokeach points out that one must first overcome three beliefs, replace them with new ones, and then combine them to reach the solution (analytic phase, followed by synthetic phase).

The three old and new beliefs are : (1) we must face the food to eat it (Joe need not face the food, but can land on top of it) ; (2) we can change directions at will (Joe is fixed, facing north, but he can jump sideways or backwards) ; (3) we are free to change direction immediately but Joe must move four times in a given direction (Joe may be at any point in the sequence).[1]

As predicted, subjects high in rigidity showed greater difficulty in overcoming the three beliefs, but there was no difference between the open and closed groups on synthesis (Rokeach, McGovney, and Denny, 1960). But the expected difference in synthesis did appear in other tasks, such as the reconstruction of block designs (involving synthesis), on which the open subjects were superior.

Plant, Telford, and Thomas (1965) reported that persons high in dogmatism are relatively immature, impulsive, defensive, conventional, and stereotyped in their thinking. Anderson (1962) has shown that dogmatism declines significantly during adolescence, that more intelligent females are more dogmatic than intelligent males, and that dogmatism is associated with manifest anxiety and low socioeconomic status.

Support for Rokeach's principles was obtained in a study of problem solving by Restle, Andrews, and Rokeach (1964). Open-minded subjects were superior in oddities problems (which may be considered as requiring the synthesis of information), the closed-minded subjects on reversal shift, which involves accepting the arbitrary decision of the experimenter about the correct answer. Subjects high in both dogmatism and ethnocentrism are less able to achieve binocular fusion of discrepant stimuli (Iverson and Schwab, 1967), a judgment that calls on the synthesis posited by Rokeach.

Despite some negative evidence (Fillenbaum, 1964a ; Feather, 1969), dogmatism is associated with difficulty in handling inconsistent information (Foulkes and Foulkes, 1965 ; Kleck and Wheaton, 1967 ; M. F. Hunt and Miller, 1968), and with preference for information supporting the individual's own position, under private (by mail) conditions, but less so under public (discussion and debate) conditions (P. Clarke and James, 1967).

After reviewing research on dogmatism, Ehrlich and Lee (1969) conclude that, in general, the difference between closed- and open-minded persons has been supported, namely, that the former have difficulty in acquiring new attitudes and in changing old ones.

[1] The solution is that Joe has just completed a jump to the east. He must jump sideways three times to the east, then once sideways back to the food landing on top of it.

These effects depend on such conditions as authoritativeness of the source, congruence between new and old opinions, novelty of new opinions, and importance of the issue to the person.

PREJUDICE AND STEREOTYPING

Racial and religious prejudice has long been recognized as a widespread phenomenon in our society (Allport, 1954; Harding et al., 1969). Although authoritarian personality, as we have seen, and prejudice are associated, one cannot be equated with the other. If we were to follow the California conception, prejudice would be confined to a small segment of the population—that is, those who fit the syndrome—but prejudice, in various degrees, is far more evident than could be predicted on the presumption of a well-defined, distinctive personality type. For this reason, a great deal of research has focused on prejudice as a special kind of attitude.

Prejudice can best be understood as a complex attitude system, containing the two essential ingredients of a favorable or an unfavorable orientation toward the object that elicits it, and overgeneralization (thus erroneous judgment) about the characteristics of the object (Allport, 1954).

All that we have said about the internalization process applies also to prejudices, which are relatively permanent intrinsic regulating systems acquired during socialization, which determine responses in a variety of situations. Their distinctive character resides in activation by special classes of stimuli (cues or symbols of membership in some social category), and the important role of strong emotional responses leading to aversive behavior—condemnation, rejection, withdrawal, and the like. The inclusion of favorable or preferential approach to objects is logical but does not really accord with the social significance of prejudice. It is, of course, meaningful to recognize positive attitudes toward groups, but the central problem of prejudice is clearly its negative aspects, and therefore we can best employ them as defining chracteristics, treating positive attitudes as a contrasting category.

As in the case of other attitudes, prejudice is partly an ethnocentric phenomenon, arising from learning the norms of the society. To the extent that such norms include particular ways of judging social groups and of acting toward them, individuals will acquire similar prejudices. But prejudices, like other attitudes, also fulfill ego-defensive functions. Depending on the individual personality organization, they vary in the degree to which they enter into the expression of anxiety and hostility, the enhancement of self-esteem, and so on.

Stereotypes

The attribution of unfavorable characteristics to a class of people is an important concomitant of prejudice. Actually, as we shall see, stereotyping is not necessarily unfavorable but rather represents a well-defined concept of a group. However, because of the association between prejudice and unfavorable conceptions, it is appropriate to discuss this aspect of intergroup relations at this point.

Stereotyping may be defined as "the tendency to attribute generalized and simplified characteristics to groups of people in the form of verbal labels" (Vinacke, 1949). The stereotype is a conceptual structure with verbal labels as expressions of it.[1]

Pioneering studies of the content of stereotypes were conducted by Katz and Braly (1933, 1935). A checklist of eighty-four commonly used terms was derived from spontaneous characterizations of ten national-racial groups. One hundred white male college students then indicated the five terms they considered most typical of each group. In a second study, ratings were obtained of the desirability of the traits, together with preferential ratings of the groups. High agreement on traits attributed to each group revealed stereotyping. Many subsequent investigations have demonstrated comparable phenomena in other kinds of subjects (Brigham, 1971).

In all these studies one or more terms are used with a high degree of consistency to characterize the target groups, and diverse groups of subjects display considerable agreement (Prothro, 1954). Nevertheless, as might be expected, important differences exist between the stereotypes of various groups. A marked discrepancy, for instance, appears in the stereotype of blacks held by blacks and other groups. Bayton (1941) and Meenes (1943) showed that black subjects do not employ some of the less favorable terms, use various terms more or less frequently, and include terms not emphasized by others. In addition to stereotyping, however, other factors such as the sex of the group being characterized and the sex of the judge influence attribution of traits (Bayton, Austin, and Burke, 1965).

This point is well illustrated by a study in Hawaii (Vinacke, 1949). Following the procedures of Katz and Braly, a checklist was

---

[1] Prothro and Keehn (1957) showed that trait names, treated as S. D. scales, yield general factors similar to those derived by Osgood.

developed on the basis of spontaneous characterizations of eight groups: Japanese, Chinese, Haole (Caucasian), Korean, Filipino, Hawaiian, Negro and Samoan. Judgments were obtained from 14 groups, each sex of Japanese, Chinese, Haole, Korean, Filipino, Chinese-Hawaiian, and Caucasian-Hawaiian. Although there were many resemblances among the stereotypes, numerous differences also appeared, not only between national-racial groups, but also between the two sexes.[1]

Change in Stereotypes   The general characterization remains quite stable (Sinha and Upadhyay, 1960; Diab, 1962) but nevertheless may reflect events involving the groups characterized (Meenes, 1943; Stagner and Osgood, 1946). For example the black stereotype of Italians in 1935 was strongly influenced by the invasion of Ethiopia (Meenes, 1943), concepts of Germans have reflected the events of recent years [Katz and Braly (1933) versus Schoenfeld (1942)], and conceptions that Americans and Russians had of each other in 1950 differed from those of 1945 (Klineberg, 1950).

There may also be a gradual change in the tendency to think in stereotyped terms. Gilbert (1951) replicated the Katz and Braly study on a comparable sample (Princeton students) and found a general attenuation of the stereotypes, although the content remained similar (except for Germans and Japanese). A still later replication by Karlins, Coffman, and Walters (1969) did not confirm the weakening of stereotypes, but instead revealed changes in content—for example, 45 percent checked "intelligent" for the Japanese in 1933, compared to 11 and 20 percent in 1951 and 1957; in 1933 the most frequent term for the Chinese was "superstitious" (35 percent), while in 1967 it was "loyal to family ties" (50 percent). The stereotypes generally appeared to reflect a "liberalized" view. In addition, the methods of direct rating frequently used tended to enhance the operation of response sets, such as social desirability. Thus an atmosphere of overt liberalism may induce subjects to provide a more favorable stereotype of blacks than would appear in their private concepts (Sigall and Page, 1971). It is thus not so much a question of whether or not the typical person possesses stereotypes of significant social groups, as of the *content and properties* of such concepts.

---

[1] Even this study failed to allow for different stereotypes of males and females of the same ancestry, not, perhaps, uncommon in heterogeneous societies. For example, black men may hold quite different conceptions of white men and white women, and vice versa.

A group typically displays considerable agreement between self-stereotypes and stereotypes held of them by other groups (see, especially, Vinacke, 1949). Exceptions occur in the case, at least, of unfamiliar groups: for example, Koreans in Hawaii displayed a well-defined self-stereotype, not only higher in uniformity than the stereotype other groups had of them, but also quite different in quality.

A basic difference between self-stereotypes and stereotypes held by others lies in the "value" of the terms assigned. Terms often used either by a group for itself, or frequently attributed by others, are more favorably rated, with good traits overvalued and bad traits deprecated (see Table 19-1 ; see also, D. T. Campbell, 1967).

Such findings demonstrate that stereotyping works in both directions. Bettelheim (1947) reported these phenomena in his analysis of relations between Jews and the Gestapo in a Nazi concentration camp. Each had a stereotyped conception of the other, which influenced their interpretations of each other and their behavior toward each other.

The "Kernel of Truth" Hypothesis

To the extent that there is contact between groups, we would suppose that they should correspond at least to some degree with the actual traits manifested (Klineberg, 1950). At the same time, like all concepts, they are clearly abstractions for which individual instances are only approximations, if not outright exceptions. Although the person learns about other groups partly from established modes of thinking, which do not necessarily correspond with reality, nevertheless, stereotypes may contain valid components. Prothro and Melikian (1955), for instance, showed how they change as a function of contact with other groups. During the interval between two studies of Near Eastern subjects, increased contact with Americans produced an amplification of stereotypes of that group, whereas the stereotypes of four other groups changed little. Schuman (1966) found that stereotypes in Pakistan corresponded with actually determined typical characteristics, especially in rural areas where little cultural change had occurred.

An intensive study by Triandis and Vassiliou (1967) revealed that increased contact between Greeks and Americans sharpened both the self-stereotype and the stereotype of the other group (heterostereotype) for the Americans, but not for the Greeks. The

Table 19-1
Examples of "Overvaluing" Traits by the Group to which They Are Attributed.
(Modified from Vinacke, 1956.)

Terms Attributed by self	Terms Attributed by Other Groups	Group (Male)	Self-value	Values of Other Groups*
Traditional		Japanese	0	−43
	Neat	Japanese	93	86, 86
Money-conscious		Chinese	5	−48, −27, −14
	Thrifty	Chinese	70	65, 65, 64
Talkative		Haole	22	−37, 3, −21
	Cultured	Haole	91	86, 86, 50, 71
Hot-tempered		Filipino	−64	−90, −68, −83
	Industrious	Filipino	100	91
Stubborn		Korean	−27	−49, −52, −43
	Quiet	Korean	23	24, 13, 14

*Figures for groups that did not also attribute the trait to themselves.

Greek stereotype of Americans was more favorable with maximum than with minimum contact, with an opposite effect for the American stereotype. Other analyses also supported the "kernel of truth" hypothesis.

Stereotyping and Prejudice

Some writers have treated stereotyping and prejudice as virtually synonymous (LaViolette and Silvert, 1951), or as the cognitive component of prejudice (Saenger and Flowerman, 1954). But this view is clearly very misleading, and would only hold if stereotypes are defined as unfavorable concepts. Studies amply demonstrate that generalized conceptions of others (as well as of one's own group) are widespread, or even universal.

The fact that self-stereotypes may correspond closely to the attributed conception also raises severe problems for equating of stereotyping with prejudice. Quality, uniformity, and direction may all be closely similar. Intensity, as we have seen, may be the major difference, as if the same characteristic is acceptable if it belongs to oneself.

In addition, a stereotype of another group may be held with high uniformity and yet be accompanied by different degrees of prejudice.

Whether valid or not, the stereotype is simply a concept, it does not by itself indicate the attitude one has toward the group or its members.

Finally, it must be recognized that prejudice may operate even in the absence of a well-defined stereotype. Thus a person may simply dislike all foreigners or all Orientals, without having subordinate categories.

The Process of Stereotyping

These considerations reinforce the potential dangers of relying purely on verbal expressions of a concept as indicators of the total cognitive system. Although prejudiced people employ stereotyping in an unfavorable way, unprejudiced people also have stereotypes, which are not necessarily favorable. Prejudice is associated with the derogatory or ego-defensive *use* of stereotyping, and the special intent is difficult to deduce from the terms themselves. There is thus much room to differentiate within the stereotyping process those aspects or properties that may properly be linked with prejudice.

It appears most useful to treat stereotypes as a special class of concepts—that is, concepts of social groups—and to differentiate them from prejudices as a special class of social attitudes (Vinacke, 1957). In this respect both stereotypes and prejudices can be understood in the light of social-learning processes and ego functioning. It should be possible to illuminate more fully the properties of the larger cognitive system in which stereotype and prejudice are components, on the one hand representing the organization of "knowledge" about groups and on the other hand the regulative determinants of behavior toward those groups or symbols that refer to them.

SUMMARY

Basic problems in the study of attitudes concern their formation, influence on response, and change as a function of extrinsic forces. Immediate responses (opinions) must be distinguished from attitudes. Techniques of measurement fall into categories defined by whether the method is disguised or nondisguised and structured or nonstructured. The chief standardized scales are based on equal-appearing intervals, summated ratings, and cumulative items, and primarily assess direction and intensity. Other dimensions include salience, importance, complexity, and verbalizability. Factor-analytic studies bring out primary religious, political, and other social attitudes. Authoritarianism and dogmatism are extensively investigated general attitude systems. Prejudice cannot be explained solely on the basis of authoritarian personality, but arises from sociocultural conditions and the dynamics of individual personality. Stereotypes, as conceptual systems, must be distinguished from prejudice.

20

OPINION CHANGE

In the preceding chapters we discussed attitudes as inferred general regulators of response—that is, as relatively enduring components of the mental context. In this sense judgments in response to specific statements are potential indicators of an attitude. Such a response— an *opinion*—expresses or reflects the intrinsic system as it becomes focused in a particular situation. An opinion may be quite unstable since a momentary change in the relation between intrinsic state and environmental situation may affect it. This point is particularly well demonstrated in the long history of experiments on set. The conception of interplaying autistic and realistic forces has the same implication. By altering the relative strength of either component, we can change the character of response, either qualitatively or quantitatively or both. It is only by examining recurrent situations or classes of events that the properties of attitudes and concepts can dependably be identified.

Since it is the responses themselves that can be observed, social psychologists naturally enough look for principles to explain their properties. This interest is closely tied to an abiding concern with social influence. In the social environment persons respond to each other, influencing each other and shaping each other according to their separate needs. In these processes, verbal interchanges are highly conspicuous, and thus their consequences in the change of opinion have intensively been studied.

Apart from legitimate interest in opinions themselves, research in this area also rests on the implicit assumption that by understanding social influence and its effects on the expression and change in opinion, we move farther toward a knowledge of attitudes, as well. As learned cognitive systems, attitudes are established through the interactions of socialization and subsequent interpersonal experience (education, discussion, mass persuasion). Any single event may potentially be a miniature opinion-change situation. By sufficient incrementing of the principles that account for particular events, we may come to understand better the total lengthy process itself. This argument is an implicit application of the notion of conditioning to the formation and change of attitudes. Thus, if one can demonstrate that a certain condition elicits (or fails to elicit) a significant change in a specific opinion, it may be justified to believe that repetitive instances of the same condition would consolidate and strengthen the behavioral tendency.

Some investigators may object that this assumption is supererogatory. Attitudes cannot be observed, only their expression. The study of attitudes, in this view, is the investigation of opinions and nothing more. This position, in the behaviorist tradition, focuses quite contentedly on specific situations and their parameters with little or no intention of drawing inferences about general cognitive properties. The aim of research is merely to construct systematic principles about situational (stimulus) and response (opinion) variables. Compared to other psychological enterprises, opinion statement and change has special interest because the situation is interpersonal and the response is verbal or judgmental.

This antinomy underlies much of the controversy in attitude research, with no final resolution in sight.[1] Some perspective, however, comes from recognizing that theorists display different orientations in the kinds of variables emphasized, on the one hand linking opinions with personality, and on the other hand with immediate situational conditions. One strategy relies on specific experimental inductions and response measures, thus explicitly emphasizing opinions and the conditions that influence their expression. The other strategy utilizes antecedent measures and broader sequences or classes of response, thus looking for the

---

[1] Some general sources include Abelson et al. (1968), and Insko (1967).

deeper structure and more enduring dynamics of cognitive functioning. Most of the work mentioned in this chapter is prompted by the first of these strategies, with the second primarily apparent in previous chapters.

VARIABLES IN OPINION CHANGE

Research on maintenance of and change in opinion generally rests on the conception of a communication process of information input (influence attempts), reception by a person, followed by response output. For experimental purposes this process is divided into several categories of variables. *Source* conditions consist of properties of the individual (or an impersonal entity) who issues the communication, that is, such as credibility or reference-group character. *Message* variables pertain to the direction (pro or con) of the communication, its intensity, clarity, and so on. The *medium* or *channel* may vary in mode (visual, auditory), or form (written, physical demonstration, etc.). Variables of the *context* or *situation* include passive reception versus active participation, presence or absence of others, private or public response, and such direct inductions as instructions, incentives, or arousal techniques. Associated with the *target* or *recipient* are specific states (sets) and relevant personality variables (motives, general attitudes, amount of information, concepts). In addition, McGuire (1968) points to *destination* variables that transcend the situation and that concern long-range effects, including the intent of the message [e.g., behavioral change versus verbal expression (Cartwright, 1949)], and issue-relevant considerations (such as changes in general voting patterns).

BALANCE THEORY

The point of departure for much of the theorizing about opinion change comes from the work of Heider (1958), who, in turn, was greatly influenced by Lewin. Interpersonal perception occupies a central position in Heider's analysis. If we think of a person p and another person o, then when they interact, their characteristics or actions induce in each other responses that Heider designates as *sentiments* (such as liking, disliking, enjoying, discomfort, etc.) and *unit* relations (connections between the two). These two effects are not readily separated (see Jordan, 1968), but they can be identified as different aspects of p's relations to o. The mere presence of o may be sufficient to establish a unit relation—that is, that p and o belong together in some fashion, are acting together, are oriented to the same task, are teacher and pupil, and so on. Unit relations depend on such factors as similarity, proximity, causality, familiarity, and ownership, which tend to make elements of the perceptual field cohere. Sentiment refers to the affective dimension of p's relation to o, and a unit relation between p and o (e. g., they are brothers) does not necessarily determine the sentiment relation. However, the two kinds of relations influence each other. For example, proximity may produce a unit relation, which in turn tends to induce a positive sentiment (liking) but, at the same time, liking leads to a unit relation. In a way, neither can really exist without the other—sentiments can scarcely occur without the perception that p and o somehow belong together, nor is a unit relation likely without some accompanying sentiment. It is nevertheless important to recognize that both relationships characterize interpersonal behavior, and that the properties of one cannot automatically be predicted by specifying the other.

The relationships just mentioned are *dyadic*, but the special power of balance theory enters when we realize that two persons are not isolated from the environment but are oriented to some object x, which yields a *triadic* system of components, a p-o-x system. Viewed from p's standpoint, the perceptual-cognitive state involves p's relation to o, p's relation to x, and o's relation to x (as perceived by p). If we express these three components simply as having positive or negative signs, we arrive at the conception of *balanced* and *imbalanced* states (see Figure 20-1). A balanced state is present if the net product of the signs is positive, an imbalanced state if the net product is negative.

The core of Heider's theory is that cognitive processes tend toward balanced states. When imbalance exists, the system will change in the direction of harmony, or balance. For example, if the sentiment between p and o is positive (liking), and the relation between p and x negative (hostile), but p perceives a positive relation between o and x, then p might reevaluate x so that x is perceived as less hostile. A simple logic can be applied to other situations to demonstrate other routes to balance, in which actual or attributed change in one of the relations may lead to greater balance (or imbalance).

Complications arise when the implied stability of cognitive systems is examined more closely, since it is not always obvious. For example, Figure 20-1d is presumably unstable since it is apparently imbalanced, and one of the signs should change. How-

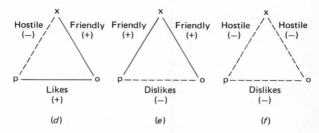

BALANCED STATES

(a) (b) (c)

IMBALANCED STATES

(d) (e) (f)

FIGURE 20-1 Instances of balanced and imbalanced cognitive states.

ever, p's liking for o, accompanied by perception of o's friendliness with x may induce jealousy, which might constitute a stable system, resistant to change. The all-negative triad may also be ambiguous, when negative relations imply avoidance and thus a lack of genuine relations. Heider discusses a variety of such considerations, including the likelihood that the character of the relation (sentiment or unit) between p and o is an important factor in the system.

Cartwright and Harary (1956) have developed a mathematical treatment of balance theory through the use of signed digraphs, thus seeking to objectify the variables, in contrast to Heider's more phenomenological approach. A *digraph* (or "directed graph") is a set of points in which lines indicate relationships. By using arrows to depict direction and separate designations (e.g., solid and broken lines) for positive and negative relationships, one can specify in detail the structure and subcomponents of a system of points. Furthermore the model can be extended to cover any system of relations and any number of components (see Figure 20-2).

Further modifications of balance theory are evident in the work

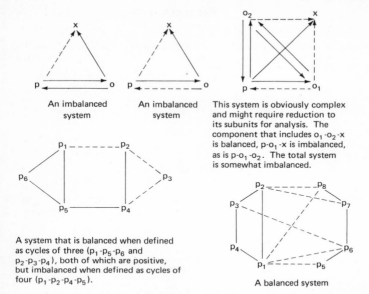

An imbalanced system

An imbalanced system

This system is obviously complex and might require reduction to its subunits for analysis. The component that includes o_1-o_2-x is balanced, p-o_1-x is imbalanced, as is p-o_1-o_2. The total system is somewhat imbalanced.

A system that is balanced when defined as cycles of three (p_1-p_5-p_6 and p_2-p_3-p_4), both of which are positive, but imbalanced when defined as cycles of four (p_1-p_2-p_4-p_5).

A balanced system

FIGURE 20-2   Examples of systems described by signed graphs. (Based on Cartwright and Harary, 1956.) (Solid lines represent positive relations, broken lines negative relations.) Note: A general definition of balanced is based on the principle that all cycles of a stated size must be positive. The degree of imbalance may be determined by the ratio of positive cycles to the total number of cycles.

of Rosenberg and Abelson (Rosenberg, 1956, 1968; Abelson, 1968; Abelson and Rosenberg, 1958; Rosenberg and Abelson, 1960). They distinguish between affective and cognitive components of the system, with the principle that a change in one induces changes in the other. (For instance, change in opinion—that is, position on an issue—is more likely when the direction of change has significant value for the person, as when influence is exerted by a strongly admired figure compared to a more neutral one.) Relations are also further refined to allow for ambivalent and neutral (null) orientations. This approach also deals with alternative modes of resolving imbalance (Abelson, 1959). By *denial,* a person alters one or more of the relations (as partly illustrated above). *Bolstering* represents a process of strengthening one of the elements so that the other is, so to speak, submerged. *Differentiation* involves the separation of elements in one of the relations, described, for instance, by Heider (1958) as recognizing that x may have both good and bad features, thus at least splitting the imbalanced from the balanced portions, although not removing the imbalance completely. Finally, *transcendence* is the process of incorporating conflicting elements into a larger and more acceptable structure.

BALANCED AND IMBALANCED SITUATIONS

A central issue in balance theory concerns the proposition that imbalanced structures are unpleasant and therefore more likely to change.

In an early study, Jordan (1953) generated sixty-four instances that incorporate possible combinations of liking and unit relations, with positive and negative signs, half of them balanced, half imbalanced. On the average, balanced structures were rated as pleasant, imbalanced ones as unpleasant, but there were marked exceptions, indicating that the relation between p and o is critical. If p disliked o, the situation was judged unpleasant whether or not it was "balanced."

Morrissette (1958) investigated triads in which p's relation to o and o's relation to q (a person rather than an object) were given (like or dislike). Subjects judged p's probable relation to q. In the two cases of similar sign (p-o and o-q both positive or negative), as predicted, the p-q relation was positive (liking). In the other two cases, the situation was unstable, with p-q judged as either positive or negative.

Rodrigues (1967) found good agreement with balance theory for impersonal (p-o-x) situations. Balanced triads were judged more pleasant and the all-positive triad more than the others. A positive p-o relation was judged more pleasant than a negative one, and agreement between p and o about x was also judged more pleasant. Imbalance was most important for willingness to change p-x and for differentiating p-o; a negative p-o relation induced change in p-o; and disagreement favored change in o-x. By manipulating the reciprocity of liking between p and o, Burnstein (1967) found that either balanced or reciprocated liking situations were changed less frequently. In imbalanced situations, changes were toward balance, typically involved the fewest possible changes, and occurred mostly in interpersonal rather than orientation components.

Further studies document the importance of affectively positive relations between p and o. When p-x and o-x are equivalent, attraction between p and o determines judged pleasantness, but discrepancy becomes most influential when attraction is held constant (Price, Harburg, and McLeod, 1965). Carrying the specifications farther, Price, Harburg, and Newcomb (1966) devised p-o-q triads in which subjects inserted actual initials of best friends or disliked persons. With a positive p-o relation, balanced types were generally judged pleasant, imbalanced types judged uneasy. But with a negative p-o relation, only one imbalanced type was typically rated unpleasant, the others were neutral or pleasant, and neither balanced situation was clearly judged pleasant or uneasy.

Other studies also demonstrate that relationships are more important than envisaged by formal definitions of balance. Zajonc and Burnstein (1965a, b) reported that positive structures were easiest to learn, but Gerard and Fleischer (1967) found that balanced positive structures were less readily recalled. Attempting to reconcile these results, Gerard and Fleischer postulate that in the Zajonc and Burnstein studies the subjects *assumed* balance and positivity, thus making errors on unbalanced and negative items, but that in their experiment items that induced tension were better recalled (like a Zeigarnik effect, the tendency to recall incompleted tasks better than completed ones). They suggested that pleasantness corresponded to difficulty: the most pleasant (but worst recalled) were balanced positive and imbalanced negative items. It is, however, possible that balanced structures were merely more overlearned than the imbalanced ones in the Zajonc and Burnstein study. The strong influence of positivity and agreement between p and o is further shown in a cross-cultural study (Whitney, 1971) and inferences from sets of statements (Wyer and Lyon, 1970).

Heider (1958, pp. 180–181) understood that the definition of imbalance and the prediction of change are not simple—for example, that imbalance may be interesting rather than simply noxious. Research is contributing to better specification of components and relations.

FURTHER DERIVATIVES: CONSISTENCY THEORIES

The basic features of balance theory—the principle of conflicting cognitive elements, the attempt to specify properties of the cognitive system and their determinants, and the assumption that there is a tendency to resolve states of imbalance in the direction of harmonizing the system[1]—have spurred numerous efforts to improve on balance theory. Gradually the term *cognitive consistency* has come into use to refer to these approaches.

[1]Whether simply cast in the form of an unstable field of forces (essentially Heider's heritage from Lewin), or treated as an actual intrinsic motivational force, as in Rosenberg's (1960, 1968) conception of thresholds of intolerance of inconsistency and Festinger's (1957) drive to reduce dissonance.

Congruity

Osgood and his associates (especially, Osgood and Tannenbaum, 1955; Tannenbaum, 1967, 1968) have concentrated on the evaluative dimensions. When a communication is presented to a person, each element is treated as having an evaluative aspect— p feels positively or negatively about the source o, about the object of the communication x, and the communication itself is perceived positively (pro) or negatively (con). Incongruity exists when these evaluations are incompatible either qualitatively (as in balance theory) or quantitatively, and cognitive change will occur to produce a more consistent system. Such change will involve opinions about *both* o and x. However, elements may either be associative or dissociative, and incongruity occurs only in the former case. When there is no reason to link p and o, two discrepant elements may coexist.

The congruity model predicts that evaluations change in the direction of greater simplicity. This process is considered to be a movement toward polarization—that is, an intensification of positive or negative judgment.

Rokeach and Rothman (1965) have criticized the assumption of congruity theory that cognitive elements judged in isolation from each other will interact in an additive manner. They propose instead a *configurationist* (or congruence) model, in which effects depend on the particular system that obtains when elements occur in some stated relation to each other, and on the *importance* of the resulting assertion. Following the procedures of Rokeach, Smith, and Evans (1960) (see Chapter 19), they show that congruence of beliefs yields a considerably better prediction of evaluative judgments in which elements are linked than does the addition of ratings of the elements obtained separately.[1]

Logical Coherence

McGuire (1960a, b, 1968) has emphasized the internal connectedness of cognitive elements and the tendency for their organization to be as coherent as possible. He suggests that cognitive elements can be stated as propositions, a series of which may be interrelated in various ways. When his cognitions are externalized in this fashion, the individual is induced to resolve inconsistencies that would perhaps otherwise remain latent. In that way the total system tends to become more coherent. Although formal logic provides the most readily apparent framework for cognitive coherence (see Chapter 12),

[1]It should be noted that congruity and congruence theories both invoke mediational principles (see Tannenbaum, 1966; Tannenbaum and Gengel, 1966).

it is not the only one. Nonrational components may be reconciled within the system, even if they would not withstand systematic, objective scrutiny. The essential point is, then, coherence, rather than accuracy per se. However, the imposition of rules of thought and procedures that facilitate discipline in treating propositions are very likely to promote change toward objectively definable coherence, rather than a further elaboration of subjective acceptance of propositions.

COGNITIVE DISSONANCE

The theory of *cognitive dissonance*, formulated by Festinger (1957), can properly be called a *consistency* theory. He did not differentiate among cognitive components, but stated his theory merely by reference to "cognitive elements," or bits of knowledge. Any two elements may be related in a consonant, dissonant, or irrelevant way. In a consonant relation, one element follows from another consistently, for example, the fact that Professor Adams always gives tough examinations and the belief that one had better study hard in preparation. In a dissonant relation, considering only the two elements, "the obverse of one element would follow from the other" (p. 13). Festinger gives, as an example, the situation in which a person feels afraid even though he knows that there are only friends around him. An irrelevant relation occurs when there is no likelihood that two elements would be associated. For example, the belief that a new stadium will be built has no relation to the knowledge that drugs are harmful.

The magnitude of dissonance depends partly on the importance of the elements, partly on the number of dissonant elements. Suppose that a course examination is pending. If the professor has the reputation of giving tough tests, but the rumor of an easy exam is bruited about, a student is likely to experience dissonance. But dissonance would be greater if the test is announced as a midterm, rather than just one in a series of weekly quizzes. This illustrates the factor of importance. The other contribution to dissonance would be exemplified if the professor is not only tough, but also cold and aloof, as well as having recently announced that he intends to give more thorough exams in the future. Each of these elements is discrepant with the rumor of an easy test, and therefore dissonance should be greater than if only one of the reasons to expect a tough exam were operating.

Festinger postulates that dissonance is uncomfortable, so that a person will seek to reduce the dissonance. In addition he will actively avoid conditions and information that might increase dissonance.

Criticisms

One difficulty arises from the vagueness of the phrase cognitive element, which subsequent theories have endeavored to render more precise. Furthermore, there is no clear specification of conditions when dissonance actually exists, or how it will be reduced. To rectify this deficiency, Brehm and Cohen (1962) invoked a principle of *commitment*, signifying that dissonance is more likely when a person has actually made a decision to act (evident, perhaps, by carrying out the act) than if he merely verbalizes an intention or responds indifferently. Dissonance-reducing behavior, then, should be stronger for those elements for which commitment is greatest. Even so, the theory does not specify *how* dissonance will be reduced, so much as *which* element is likely to change. In the example about exams, suppose the student decides to accept the rumor and not to waste time studying. Has he reduced dissonance by altering his opinion of the professor (judging him to be an easier mark than he had thought), or by concluding that the exam cannot be significant after all, or in some other way?

Dissonance theory has not allowed sufficiently for individual differences. Persons not only perceive the same conditions differently, but also evaluate them differently. The importance variable, for example, appears to require the assessment of individual variations. The assumption that dissonance is a noxious state is open to question. Some persons probably find dissonance stimulating, provocative, or a stage on the way to further dissonance—and might actually seek to become cognitively dissonant! Something like Rosenberg's (1968) principle of variation in the tolerance of inconsistency is required.

Silverman (1971) assessed consistency principles under naturally occurring conditions. Questionnaires were administered about an episode in which a nationally famous political figure displayed difficult-to-understand behavior that reflected adversely on his character. Some of the findings agreed with consistency principles —for example, respondents favorable to the politician reduced their approval of him or displayed changed views in accordance with the information available. However, considerably more tolerance of inconsistency appeared than laboratory studies predicted. For example, of the subjects who maintained their initially positive opinion, 29 percent believed that the man had been treated too leniently, and 61 percent believed that more severe treatment would have been meted out to a private citizen. One reason lies in the greater significance and personal relevance of the natural event compared to a contrived situation, rendering it more difficult to achieve consistency. Such studies indicate the necessity to test experimental principles in nonlaboratory settings.

Selective Exposure to Information

The theory of cognitive dissonance argues that, under voluntary exposure, a person tends to seek dissonance-reducing information and to avoid dissonance-increasing information. Therefore material supporting one's view should be preferred, and contrary material rejected.

Some studies confirm both points (Festinger, 1957; Mills, Aronson, and Robinson, 1959; Mills, 1965), others find a preference for dissonant information (Freedman, 1965b), and still others report avoidance of dissonant information but not seeking of consonant information (Rhine, 1967a). Although Sears and Freedman (1965), after surveying the evidence, concluded that neither part of the proposition is tenable, subsequent research indicates a tendency for people to seek supportive information. Mills (1968) invokes a principle of certainty, suggesting that the more uncertain one is about his own position, the more likely he is to seek for support, but that this does not apply to discrepant information. Brock and Balloun (1967) propose that it depends on how much supportive information has already been assimilated—as experience increases, one is more willing to expose himself to dissonant information. Furthermore, when arguments are difficult to refute, supportive information is preferred, with the reverse for arguments easy to destroy (Lowin, 1967). Contrary to the Mills principle, confidence in the correctness of decisions had little effect in Lowin's (1969) studies.

Methodological difficulties have interfered with a definite verdict (Rhine, 1967b). "Seeking" has not adequately been distinguished from "avoiding," since a measure like low interest in information does not necessarily indicate avoidance. Beyond that, studies have so far failed to consider the role of curiosity, which influences information seeking, apart from a desire to reduce dissonance.

Forced Compliance

Festinger (1957) cited the commonsense observation that dissonance arises in situations when a person has publicly stated an opinion contrary to his own actual view. Such a situation may occur accidentally or as an interpersonal strategy. For example, in discussion with others an individual may inadvertently and hastily say something discrepant with his general position, or may utter challenging remarks to make an impression or to advance an argument, and so on. Although such instances probably induce or increase dissonance, the case of special interest to the theory is when a person has been forced to comply with a position with which he privately disagrees.

According to Festinger, two principal conditions of forced compliance create cognitive dissonance: (1) the threat of punishment for noncompliance which presents alternatives of complying or of enduring the punishment; and (2) the offer of a reward for complying, with complementary alternatives. In general, the more important the opinion is, the greater the magnitude of reward or punishment required to induce compliance and the greater the resulting dissonance. But once the point of actual compliance has been reached, dissonance is assumed to be at a maximum, and increased punishment or reward produces decreasing degrees of dissonance. And the greater the dissonance, the greater the tendency to reduce it. That is, when reward (or punishment) is just barely sufficient to elicit the discrepant public statement, there is maximum conflict between preserving the consonance of private opinion and public statement and the temptation (or threat). As the magnitude of the incentive increases, however, it becomes easier to comply without jeopardizing one's private opinion. One may, so to speak, simply shrug his shoulders feeling that "if you're willing to go that far, then why shouldn't I say whatever you want me to?"

This apparently contradicts our usual notions of incentive effects, which state that the greater the reward or punishment, the greater its effect in changing opinion. To test this notion, Festinger and Carlsmith (1959) set up the following sequence of events: (1) The subject was set to work at a pointless and boring task, filling, emptying, and refilling a tray with spools. (2) After a half-hour, he was engaged in another tedious task, turning pegs in a board, for another half-hour. (3) At this point, the experimenter indicated that the experiment was finished, but in reality the crucial stages remained. Explanation was provided about two ostensible conditions for the experiment—in one the task was to be performed without prior expectations, while in the other the task was described beforehand as enjoyable. It was explained that in this latter condition another student usually talked first to the prospective subject, but owing to his inability to assist on this day, the subject would be asked to replace him. For this service, either 1 or 20 dollars was offered. (4) The subject then met an alleged new subject (actually a confederate of the experimenter) and presented statements about how enjoyable the task would be. (5) Finally, an interview was conducted during which opinions about the experiment were measured. Control subjects proceeded directly from stage 3 to stage 5, except that no reward was offered.

Supporting the theoretical predictions, the 1-dollar reward elicited a more favorable judgment of the experiment than did the 20-dollar condition.[1] Although some later studies also report positive evidence (Brehm and Crocker, 1962; Brehm, 1962), it appears that these results occur under quite special conditions. Both an increase in the perceived value of a boring task and the amount of reward were found by Leventhal (1964) to increase liking for the task. In another experiment, the amount of the reward had no effect under dissonant conditions, although under consonant conditions, a lower reward produced a more favorable reaction, interpreted as a function of embarrassment (Nuttin, 1966).

Among other criticisms of dissonance theory, Chapanis and Chapanis (1964) remarked on the use of implausibly large rewards; Silverman (1964a) countered by pointing out that no actual evidence was cited concerning credibility, and that some experiments (Cohen, 1962) show that differences even between small rewards accord with dissonance predictions. The role of "evaluation apprehension" has been emphasized by Rosenberg (1965), since offering an unduly large reward may confirm the subject's suspicions that he is being evaluated. He replicated the experiment by Cohen (1962), but separated counterattitudinal behavior from assessment of opinion. As hypothesized, the amount of change varied with the magnitude of reward. Rosenberg advances a consistency, rather than dissonance, theory to explain these results. Both cognitive and affective inconsistency were aroused, the former by counterattitudinal arguments, the latter by the reward (actually paid in this case). Linder, Cooper, and Jones (1967), however, pointed out that Rosenberg "inadver-

[1] This experiment has been criticized for the elimination of eleven subjects (26 percent in the 1-dollar condition, 17 percent in the 20-dollar condition) on various grounds. To a large degree these cases represented alternative ways to avoid dissonance. Eliminating them may have been justified, if one argues that actual compliance under stated conditions is the only requisite for testing the theory.

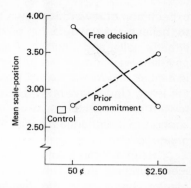

FIGURE 20-3 Attitude scores under three conditions of commitment and two incentives. (Based on Linder, Cooper, and Jones, 1967.)

tently" made it difficult for subjects not to comply with the task of writing counterattitudinal essays, since they had already committed themselves to obey the experimenter. When subjects were free not to comply, dissonance theory was supported, with the reinforcement principle sustained when this freedom did not exist (see Figure 20-3; see also, Holmes and Strickland, 1970). The context of the experiment may have unintended effects. Janis and Gilmore (1965) established conditions more natural than the laboratory, by having subjects in their residences write essays on the proposition that physics and mathematics be added as college requirements. Sponsorship was attributed either to a research agency or a commercial publishing company. Writing the essays constituted *overt role playing*, whereas control subjects were assessed immediately after the explanation. Either a 1- or 20-dollar reward was offered and paid in advance. None of the main effects was significant, but role playing under plausible sponsorship (the research agency) yielded more change in opinion. Subjects under high incentive tended to produce better arguments, despite their perceiving it as grossly inappropriate.

Carlsmith, Collins, and Helmreich (1966) suggested that these conditions are impersonal and intellectual, in contrast to the face-to-face situation of Festinger and Carlsmith, and therefore do not induce dissonance. In a replication, they found in fact that the dissonance prediction was supported in face-to-face encounters, with an opposite effect under essay-writing conditions. The importance of expectation of reward is shown by Gerard (1967). Subjects were led to believe they would be paid 2 dollars, but then were offered either a dollar and a half or 7 dollars; in a contrasting condition, no payment was announced and the reward was simply given. In both instances, moderate reward yielded greatest change, lowest reward the least. Under low reward, greater change occurred when a large reward was expected than without such expectation, lending some support to dissonance theory but, in general, the incentive effect was greater than the dissonance effect.

Helmreich and Collins (1968) invoked the principle of commitment, finding that with greater commitment, low reward elicits greater change, with the reverse for low commitment. In the same vein, Rossomando and Weiss (1970) obtained a direct relation between size of reward and change in opinion (incentive effect) when the reward was paid during the session, but when the payment was promised after completing the session, an inverse relation appeared (dissonance effect).

Cook (1969) suggested that lapsed time is an important variable, with dissonance effects likely over brief periods, but dissipating as performance continues. Thus the subject initially likes a tedious task he is required to perform briefly (as in the Festinger and Carlsmith experiment), but begins to dislike it if it continues (as in Rosenberg's and other studies).

In general, then, this issue remains controversial, with evidence that dissonance effects occur under certain conditions, but that the incentive principle probably has a more general explanatory power (Elms, 1967).

OTHER THEORIES

Although numerous commentators have supplied sparks that will probably be fanned eventually into flame, I shall mention only three other approaches to the problem of attitude change.

Behaviorist Views

Very productive experimental paradigms have emerged from applying principles of general learning theory in the neobehaviorist tradition. Hovland, Janis, and Kelley (1953), especially, have dealt systematically with the effects of stimulus conditions (e.g., the characteristics of messages and of sources of communication), reinforcement, generalization, and conditioning. To some extent the theoretical basis is implied in the general theory, rather than explicitly developed with reference to opinions, and, further, much of this work has been directed to the testing of challenges posed by other theories (such as cognitive dissonance). For the most part this treatment is compatible with mediation principles.

A "radical" behaviorist conception has also been applied to opinion change (Bem, 1967). Based on Skinnerian principles, this approach concerns itself solely with relations between current stimuli and observable responses, without recourse to inferred internal processes. Attitudes are simply treated as "statements" a person makes in response to the stimulus variables at the time, or merely a person's self-description of his own behavior, with his statements (or acts) as information. Change in "attitudes" depends on the controlling or shaping of his responses by the situations in which he finds himself. Bem sees no need to infer a motivational principle, such as a drive to reduce dissonance.

Principles of Judgment

Some investigators view change in opinion as a function of perceptual processes, with successive events influenced by preceding ones (Sherif and Hovland, 1961 ; Hovland, Harvey, and Sherif, 1957). A series of events provides a point of internal reference (or an "anchor"). When a new stimulus is discrepant with it, there is a tendency to bring it into line. *Assimilation* occurs if the new stimulus (a persuasive message) agrees fairly closely with the anchor—and the recipient will judge the communication as less extreme than it is. With marked discrepancy from the anchor, *contrast* is predicted— and the communication will be judged more extreme than it is. Other predicted effects are favorable judgment of a communication where it is not too discrepant, but unfavorable judgment when it is highly discrepant. The *latitude of acceptance* defines the boundaries of assimilation and contrast, with assimilation predicted for stimuli within this latitude, contrast for those outside it. Peterson and Koulack (1969) report supporting evidence. It is not easy to specify the latitude of acceptance since it depends on the net effect of personal involvement, perception of the source of influence (e.g., credibility or likability), etc. Direct attention to such intrinsic variables might yield better predictions than those based on latitude of acceptance.

Helson (1964) invokes similar principles from the theory of adaptation level, to suggest that change in opinion arises when

influence attempts depart from the reference point established in a
series of judgments. Thus statements that oppose preceding arguments would be judged as negative, followed by a shift in the
adaptation level in that direction.

Functional Views

We come, finally, to several related positions that correspond in many
ways to the general orientation of this book. These theories treat
attitudes as fulfilling several different functions, see opinions as
expressions of broader cognitive systems (although influenced by
situational conditions), and allow for personality variables in determining individual variations in the statement and change in opinions.

One version is represented by the work of M.B. Smith, Bruner,
and White (1956) who employed a wide variety of measures in an
intensive case study treatment of political opinions. They revealed
how attitudes toward Russia fulfill different functions—similar
attitudes may have different functions, or different attitudes may have
similar functions. Thus a given orientation may satisfy *social adjustment* needs (e.g., by gaining approval from members of a reference
group), or operate to facilitate *object appraisal*[1] (the means to act
appropriately toward an object, as when one identifies a political
candidate as a Democrat), or serve ego defensive functions in the form
of *externalization* (e.g., by acting in a hostile fashion to "war hawks,"
thus protecting oneself from threats posed by their arguments).

Somewhat more influential has been the approach advanced by
Katz, mentioned in Chapter 19 (Katz, 1960; Katz and Stotland,
1959), which distinguishes among affective, cognitive, and behavioral components of attitudes. He describes their functions as
instrumental (by which objects are treated in learned and utilitarian
ways in accordance with needs), *ego defensive*, and *knowledge*
(treating objects in accordance with personal values and conceptions of the self)[2].

Functional theories have been criticized for their apparent
failure to define or measure variables adequately. This objection

---

[1] I would prefer to treat this function primarily as a conceptual component of the total cognitive
system.

[2] Falling in the same category are the more limited views of Sarnoff (1960a), who applies psychoanalytic concepts to attitude change, and Kelman (1961), who distinguishes among compliance,
identification, and internalization as processes of social influence. See also, Insko and Schopler
(1967) for an analysis of affective, cognitive, and behavioral relationships in consistency terms,
with the conclusion that change toward consistency is greater when behavior changes than when
the attitude-belief components change.

might be overcome if investigators were more willing to employ the demanding and time-consuming techniques required to assess the properties of cognitive systems. These theories imply that single, simple, situationally bound experiments have limited merit in understanding attitude formation and change.

Generality and complexity of conceptualization are also sources of criticism. Difficulties arise in deriving testable hypotheses since it is hard to decide which variables to choose or which effects to predict. At present, functional views balance the narrow focus on situational variables by emphasizing person variables.

SUMMARY

Balance and consistency principles have been advanced to explain opinion change. Behavioristic views focus on stimulus factors, and functional theories emphasize the role of attitudes in expressing or satisfying individual motives. The influential theory of cognitive dissonance has generated research on such issues as the effects of exposure to information, forced compliance, and evaluation apprehension. The effects of reward and role playing represent major areas of controversy. Research has confirmed some of the general hypotheses of balance theory, but positivity of the relation between persons and agreement between them prove more important than balance, as formally defined. Situational variables include characteristics of the source of communication, the message, the medium, the target or recipient, and the destination.

21

SOME CENTRAL THEMES

We have surveyed in this book a great body of material on cognitive psychology. Although the proliferation of theory and research generates excitement, it may also at times be overwhelming. While the hopes of the past that we can resolve the mysteries of the human mind have not as yet been realized, nevertheless progress is clearly evident. There is so much activity in so many directions that we cannot expect at this point to foretell which ones will ultimately prove most fruitful. Sometimes a new avenue becomes a main road, at other times it proves long and winding before it gradually disappears in the desert, converges on another course, which has unexpectedly become a main artery, or rounds a corner to a dead end.

The "rat psychology" of the first half of this century seems to have reached one of these outcomes—I hesitate to say which, since different problems have met different fates. It is likely that the computer model of cognition will also fail to be the grand boulevard to an understanding of cognition. In the meantime, however, this fascinating enterprise will undoubtedly be pursued with great vigor, and will have considerable impact on psychology. But as advocates of this approach come increasingly to grips with the difficulties of simulating thinking, and find the means to incorporate the characteristics of human cognition, perhaps they will eventually conclude that one might as well study human subjects directly. These comments in no sense deny the technological advantages of computer simulation, but rather emphasize that the origins of the propositions to be tested lie in their appropriate location, namely, the human thinker. Fortunately, the more formal treatments of simulation and information processing are balanced by a healthy—even lusty—interest in probing the functions of intrinsic states. There is every reason to suppose that these avenues will sooner or later converge to produce a truly systematic cognitive psychology.

Theoretical Derivation

One impressive advance has been the increasing sophistication and discipline with which investigators have wedded theory and experiment. Theoretical propositions may be premature, if not mistaken, but at least they are likely to be quickly and systematically tested. This strategy has certainly supplanted mere speculation or the quest for new phenomena, and has powerfully brought the study of cognition under the mantle of science. It has disadvantages, to be sure, to the extent that the demands of elegant experimental techniques may impose constraints on sheer discovery and on the flexible interpretation of findings. Luckily, theorists find ways to free themselves from these boundaries, and to add new propositions to be tested. Theories themselves are developing structures that grow and change and thus lead to new propositions. (And psychology is blessed with some good theorists.) In any case, the task of the cognitive psychologist is no longer mainly to describe the characteristics of thinking, but to relate as best he can the evidence to the principle.

Methodological Advances

Equally striking is the ingenuity with which investigators have developed procedures to bring variables under control. It is not so much that really new methods have been invented as that a wealth of specific techniques now provide increasingly efficient tools for research. Fundamental to this progress is the use of inferences drawn from measures. Examples include the implicit chaining paradigm to investigate mediation, various devices to influence mediating processes, measures that reflect differences in imagery and its effects, the quantification of meaning, and so on. Just as important is the hard-headed translation of intuitively based notions into objective measures that permit experimental manipulation. Examples include the systematic study of functional fixedness in problem solving; the careful specification of dimensions, rules, and classifications; strategies in concept attainment; the standardization of conditions pertaining to conservation and transitivity in Piagetian theory; the assessment of connotative meaning; and the definition of variables relative to principles of cognitive balance and consistency. We also now have a wealth of tests for personality variables, which are increasingly employed in determining the effects on performance of the variables of ego, self, motivation, and cognitive style. Finally, we can see the development of important physiological indexes, accompanied by their increasing adaptation for investigating cognitive processes. Examples here include measures of arousal and of phases of the sleep cycle.

Rational and Counterrational Controversy

The history of psychology has always been marked by the interplay of formal and functional conceptions—the external fitting of logical formulations versus examination of processes themselves. It is difficult to separate them in any simple fashion since they differ more in strategy than in the essence of the problems to which they are directed.

One example is the continuing opposition between an orientation strictly to response processes versus a concern for inferences about cognitive processes. These preferences in subtle ways determine how propositions are stated, what measures will be chosen, and what conclusions will be drawn. Thus a preoccupation with response processes leads investigators to ignore individual differences and to avoid the incorporation into their experimental designs of personality tests. Similarly, we noted that many studies of mediation rely on paradigmatic definition and fail to seek for evidence that mediation actually occurred or to ascertain the degree to which some subjects (perhaps the faster learners) mediated, but not others (perhaps the slower learners). On the opposite side, however, advocates of inferring cognitive processes often blithely stake their faith in appealing measures without sufficient account of situational conditions or of the relevance of their measures to the performance observed.

Both parties have insufficiently examined the role of situational factors. The response-oriented psychologist focuses on specific immediate events and respects transient effects. He justifies this strategy by pointing to the objective testing of specific hypotheses, a sound enough argument. But we do not very often receive convincing evidence for the generality of the findings to other situations or tasks. In short, perspective is lacking on the purely situational determinants of response, entirely aside from intrinsic determinants or from the broader experiential context. The cognitively oriented psychologist has apparently felt that any task is suitable for investigating the variable he is interested in. He therefore encounters disappointment when nonsignificant differences are found between the groups he has specified. He thus fails to take into account the powerful and overriding role that immediate situational factors may play. No matter how people may differ in their motivational characteristics, for example, they may nearly all find a paired-associate task equally boring, or a financial reward equally appealing. In order to clarify relationships between cognitive and response processes, there must be more-penetrating scrutiny of how each is a function of, or interacts with, the immediate situation to which the person is exposed.

We could cite many other ways in which rational and counter-rational conceptions oppose each other. We saw that formal logic encounters attitudinal and "psycho-logical" influences on reasoning, that the specification of classes of intellectual abilities faces affective and intrinsic organizing determinants of thought, that extrinsically defined properties of meaning compete with intrinsically identified properties, that frequency of response as an index of creativity conflicts with an emphasis on expressiveness and appropriateness, that the formal statement of balance theory finds difficulties with the role of interpersonal perceptions, and so on.

The Autistic-Realistic Continuum

Throughout this treatment of thinking, I have employed as a general framework the principle that cognitive processes range between the poles of dominance by intrinsic, affective, impulsive, expressive, need-fulfilling forces and of dominance by extrinsic, goal-orienting, ego-controlled, directed, and problem-solving forces. In this respect, I have regarded conceptual behavior, verbal learning, and problem solving as primarily realistic, and imagination, fantasy, dreaming, and pathological forms of thinking as primarily autistic. Creative thinking has been viewed as a process in which neither autistic nor realistic forces dominate, but are rather intimately bound up together. But I have also attempted to show that no cognitive process is free from either autistic or realistic determinants (except possibly for extreme instances, on the autistic side exemplified by hallucinations, and on the realistic side by very simple, direct choice situations).

In many places I have pointed to conditions when even though a process can be understood by reference to either autistic or realistic forces, it can also be influenced by conditions of the other kind. Thus the induction of anxiety or ego-defensive mechanisms may alter performance in a conceptual or problem-solving task; special instructions or environmental factors may modify the dreaming process. Creative thinking, too, is not an equal and continuing blend of autistic and realistic forces but varies in its character, depending on the relative potency of these forces.

This formulation may require modification as our understanding increases. In particular, it may be artificial to treat autistic and realistic forces as opposite poles of a continuum since I believe that both forces nearly always exert some influence. (The person always is active intrinsically and always exists in an environment.) The critical point may concern not so much relative input as control of the effects of input. In short, some feedback process may be involved that determines successive cognitive outputs. For example, it is not necessarily true that autistic forces decrease in strength as realistic forces dominate behavior; rather, their influence may be controlled or attenuated. Or their effect may change in character—for example, rather than shaping the content or direction of response, intrinsic forces may be reflected in increased or decreased attention, greater or lesser arousal, or in some other general change. By the same token, the role of realistic forces is not necessarily less important when autistic forces determine cognition; rather, a feedback process may determine their effects on response, dissipating their influence, rerouting them (as into memory), or otherwise determining their fate. To some extent our discussion of ego- and self-regulative systems concerns feedback processes.

This argument places greater weight on cognitive systems and their properties than does a simpler view of opposed sources of the determinants of thinking. We must allow for the possibility that behavior is not so much a function of autistic and realistic forces, as of the mechanisms that control their effects. Thinking thus appears neither as the expression of needs nor as the coping with stimulus situations, but as treatment of these inputs (and in this way the information-processing model has much to offer, if it can adequately incorporate autistic input). Clearly, at least four feedback mechanisms must be involved: (1) the handling of autistic input, (2) the management of realistic input, (3) the relaying of information to and from memory, and (4) the monitoring of the immediate and continuing integration of information from the first three sources (i.e., keeping up with the cognitive activity itself). I do not pretend to have the answers to these questions, but merely raise them as issues for future attention.

Mediation Theory

The foregoing discussion really concerns the character of mediation. A pervasive theme of this book is that mediation processes, in one fashion or another, have become a dominant interest in experimental psychology. It appears in all contexts. Beginning with attempts to demonstrate the fact of mediation itself—that is, that linkages between stimuli and responses are not direct and one to one—research has moved rapidly into problems concerned with principles that govern mediation (such as the properties of associative structure).

In the preceding paragraphs and elsewhere, we have searched for implications that point to a more adequate model of mediation than is presently apparent. It is likely that something on the order of what I have called "intrinsic organization" will ultimately be worked out. I have emphasized that mediation theory requires principles of cognitive structure, memory, affective-motivational input, expectancy, and feedback. At present, however, theorists concentrate on only some combination of these variables, especially cognitive structure and memory, with some attention to expectancy and feedback, although both these important factors have received uneven or tangential treatment. (I need not repeat that mediation is often a vague and ill-defined concept, utilized by default when interest is really directed toward stimulus and/or response variables.)

Whatever theoretical developments there may be, it is safe to remark that mediation theory is moving to the center of the stage.

New Problems of Investigation

One rather concrete theme emerges in this book, namely, the vigorous activity in opening new avenues of research. The problems themselves are really not new, but it is startling to observe the ways in which gifted investigators have brought them under systematic experimental study. Some of these problems are: connotative meaning, altruism and helping behavior, imitation, values, ego attitudes and self-attitudes, imagery, dreams, creative processes, cognitive style, guilt and resistance to temptation, conservation and transitivity, and arousal and social motives. If these developments are exciting, then the future is even more promising.

BIBLIOGRAPHY

ABELSON, R., 1959. Modes of resolution of belief dilemmas. *J. Conflict Resolution,* **3**, 343–353.

ABELSON, R., 1968. Psychological implication. In R. Abelson et al. (Eds.), *Theories of cognitive consistency: A sourcebook.* Chicago: Rand McNally.

ABELSON, R. et al., (Eds.), 1968. *Theories of cognitive consistency: A sourcebook.* Chicago: Rand McNally.

ABELSON, R., & ROSENBERG, M., 1958. Symbolic psychologic: A model of attitudinal cognition. *Behavioral Sci.,* **3**, 1–13.

ABRAMSON, Y., TASTO, D. L., & RYCHLAK, J. F., 1969. Nomothetic vs. idiographic influences of association value and reinforcement value on learning. *J. Exptl. Res. Personality,* **4**, 65–71.

ABT, L. E., & BELLAK, L. (Eds.), 1950. *Projective psychology.* New York: Knopf.

ADAMS, D. K., 1929. Experimental studies of adaptive behavior in cats. *Psychol. Monographs,* No. 27.

ADAMS, J., 1953. Concepts as operators. *Psychol. Rev.,* **60**, 241–251.

ADAMS, J. A., 1954. Multiple vs. single problem training in human problem solving. *J. Exptl. Psychol.,* **48**, 15–18.

ADAMS, J. A., 1956. Vigilance in the detection of low-intensity visual stimuli. *J. Exptl. Psychol.,* **52**, 204–208.

ADAMS, J. A., 1968. Response feedback and learning. *Psychol. Bull.,* **70**, 486–504.

ADAMSON, R., 1959. Inhibitory set in problem solving as related to reinforcement learning. *J. Exptl. Psychol.,* **58**, 280–282.

ADAMSON, R. E., 1952. Functional fixedness as related to problem solving: A repetition of three experiments. *J. Exptl. Psychol.,* **44**, 288–291.

ADLER, A., 1958. *What life should mean to you*. New York: Capricorn.

ADLER, A., 1964. On the origin of the striving for superiority and of social interest. In H. L. Ansbacher & R. R. Ansbacher (Eds.), *Superiority and social interest: A collection of later writings*. Evanston, III.: Northwestern University Press.

ADORNO, T. W., FRENKEL-BRUNSWIK, E., LEVINSON, D. J., & SANFORD, R. N., 1950. *The authoritarian personality*. New York: Harper.

ALLEN, M. K., & LIEBERT, R. M., 1969. Effects of live and symbolic deviant-modeling cues on adoption of a previously learned standard. *J. Personality & Social Psychol.*, **11**, 253–260.

ALLPORT, G. W., 1935. Attitudes. In C. M. Murchison (Ed.), *Handbook of social psychology*. Worcester, Mass.: Clark University Press.

ALLPORT, G. W., 1937. *Personality*. New York: Holt.

ALLPORT, G. W., 1954. *The nature of prejudice*. Reading, Mass.: Addison-Wesley.

ALLPORT, G. W., 1961. *Pattern and growth in personality*. New York: Holt.

ALLPORT, G. W., 1968. The historical background of modern social psychology. In G. Lindzey & E. Aronson (Eds.), *Handbook of social psychology*. Vol. 1. (2nd. ed.) Reading, Mass.: Addison-Wesley.

ALLPORT, G. W., VERNON, P. E., & LINDZEY, G., 1960. *Manual for Study of Values: A scale for measuring the dominant interests in personality*. Boston: Houghton Mifflin.

ALMY, M., 1966. *Young children's thinking: Studies of some aspects of Piaget's theory*. New York: Teachers College Press.

ALPER, T. G., 1946. Task-orientation vs. ego-orientation in learning and retention. *Am. J. Psychol.*, **59**, 236–248.

ALPERT, A., 1928. The solving of problem-situations by preschool children. *Teachers Coll. Contrib. Educ.*, No. 323.

ALSCHULER, R. H., & HATTWICK, L. W., 1947. *Painting and personality*. Chicago: The University of Chicago Press.

ALTROCCHI, J., PARSONS, O. A., & DICKOFF, H., 1960. Changes in self-ideal discrepancy in repressors and sensitizers. *J. Abnormal & Social Psychol.*, **61**, 67–72.

AMEN, E. W., 1941. Individual differences in apperceptive reaction: A study of the response of pre-school children to pictures. *Genet. Psychol. Monographs*, **23**, 319–385.

AMEN, E. W., & RENISON, N., 1954. A study of the relationship between play patterns and anxiety in young children. *Genet. Psychol. Monographs*, **50**, 3–41.

AMES, L. B., 1966. Children's stories. *Genet. Psychol. Monographs*, **73**, 337–396.

AMSTER, H., 1964. Semantic satiation and generation: Learning? Adaptation? *Psychol. Bull.*, **62**, 273–286.

AMSTER, H., 1965. The relation between intentional and incidental concept learning as a function of type of multiple stimulation and cognitive style. *J. Personality & Social Psychol.*, **1**, 217–223.

AMSTER, H., & GLASMAN, L. D., 1966. Verbal repetition and connotative change. *J. Exptl. Psychol.*, **71**, 389–395.

ANDERSON, B., & JOHNSON, W., 1966. Two methods of presenting information and their effects on problem solving. *Perceptual & Motor Skills*, **23**, 851–856.

ANDERSON, C. C., 1962. A developmental study of dogmatism during adolescence with reference to sex differences. *J. Abnormal & Social Psychol.*, **65**, 132–135.

ANDERSON, H. H., & ANDERSON, G. L., 1951. *An introduction to projective techniques.* New York: Prentice-Hall.

ANDERSON, N. H., 1961. Group performance in an anagram task. *J. Social Psychol.*, **55**, 67–75.

ANDERSON, R. C., 1966. Sequence constraints and concept identification. *Psychol. Repts.*, **19**, 1295–1302.

ANDREWS, E. G., 1930. The development of imagination in the preschool child. *Univ. Iowa Studies in Character*, **3**, No. 4.

ANDREWS, F. M., 1965. Factors affecting the manifestation of creative ability by scientists. *J. Personality*, **33**, 140–152.

ANTHONY, W. S., 1966. Working backward and working forward in problem solving. *Brit. J. Psychol.*, **57**, 53–59.

ANTROBUS, J. S., DEMENT, W., & FISHER, C., 1964. Patterns of dreaming and dream recall: An EEG study. *J. Abnormal & Social Psychol.*, **69**, 341–344.

ANTROBUS, J. S., SINGER, J. L., GOLDSTEIN, S., & FORTGANG., M., 1970. Mindwandering and cognitive structure. *Trans. N.Y. Acad. Sci.*, **32**, (2) 242–252.

ARBUCKLE, T. Y., & CUDDY, L. L., 1969. Discrimination of item strength at time of presentation. *J. Exptl. Psychol.*, **81**, 126–131.

ARCHER, E. J., 1960. A re-evaluation of the meaningfulness of all possible CVC trigrams. *Psychol. Monographs*, **74**, (Whole No. 497).

ARCHER, E. J., BOURNE, L. E., Jr., & BROWN, F. G. 1955. Concept identification as a function of irrelevant information and instructions. *J. Exptl, Psychol.*, **49**, 153–164.

ARMSTRONG, E. A., 1946. *Shakespeare's imagination.* London: Lindsay Drummond.

ARNHEIM, R., 1962. *Picasso's Guernica: the genesis of a painting.* Berkeley: University of California Press.

ARONFREED, J., 1963. The effects of experimental socialization paradigms upon two moral responses to transgression. *J. Abnormal & Social Psychol.*, **66**, 437–448.

ARONFREED, J., 1964. The origins of self-criticism. *Psychol. Rev.*, **71**, 193–218.

ARONFREED, J., 1968. *Conduct and conscience: The socialization of internalized control over behavior.* New York: Academic.

ARONFREED, J., & REBER, A., 1965. Internalized behavioral suppression and the timing of social punishment. *J. Personality & Social Psychol.*, **1**, 3–16.

ARONSON, E., & METTEE, D. R., 1968. Dishonest behavior as a function of differential levels of self-esteem. *J. Personality & Social Psychol.*, **9**, 121–127.

ÅS, A., O'HARA, J. W. & MUNGER, M. P. 1962. The measurement of subjective experiences presumably related to hypnotic susceptibility. *Scand. J. Psychol.*, **3**, 47–64.

ASCH, S. E., 1956. Studies of independence and conformity: I. A minority of one against a unanimous majority. *Psychol. Monographs*, **70**, (9, Whole No. 416).

ASCH, S. E., 1969. A reformation of the problem of associations. *Am. Psychologist*, **24** 92–102.

ASERINSKY, E., & KLEITMAN, N., 1955. Two types of ocular motility during sleep. *J. Appl. Physiol.,* **8**, 1–10.

ATKINSON, J. W. (Ed.), 1958. *Motives in fantasy, action, and society.* Princeton, N. J.: Van Nostrand.

ATKINSON, J. W., 1964. *An introduction to motivation.* New York: Van Nostrand.

ATKINSON, J. W., & REITMAN, W. R., 1956. Performance as a function of motive-strength and expectancy of goal-attainment. *J. Abnormal & Social Psychol.,* **53**, 361–366.

AULD, F., GOLDENBERG, G. M., & WEISS, J. V., 1968. Measurement of primary-process thinking in dream reports. *J. Personality & Social Psychol.,* **8**, 418–426.

AXLINE, V., 1948. Play therapy and race conflict in young children. *J. Abnormal & Social Psychol.* **43**, 300–310.

BACH G. R. 1945. Young children's play fantasies. *Psychol. Monographs,* No. 272.

BACON, M. K., CHILD, I. L., & BARRY, H., III, 1963. A cross-cultural study of correlates of crime. *J. Abnormal & Social Psychol.,* **66**, 291–300.

BAGGALEY, A. R., 1955. Concept formation and its relation to cognitive variables. *J. Gen. Psychol.,* **52**, 297–306.

BAHRICK, H. P., FITTS, P. M., & RANKIN, R. E., 1952. Effect of incentives upon reactions to peripheral stimuli. *J. Exptl. Psychol.,* **44**, 400–406.

BAKAN, P., 1959. Extroversion-introversion and improvement in an auditory vigilance task. *Brit. J. Psychol.,* **50**, 325–332.

BAKER, C. H., 1959. Towards a theory of vigilance. *Can. J. Psychol.,* **13**, 35–42.

BAKER, J. A., WARE, J. R., & SIPOWICZ, R. R., 1962. Vigilance: A comparison in auditory, visual, and combined audio-visual tasks. *Can. J. Psychol.,* **16**, 192–198.

BANDURA A., 1965. Influence of models' reinforcement contingencies on the acquisition of imitative responses. *J. Personality & Social Psychol.,* **1**, 589–595.

BANDURA, A., 1969a. Social learning of moral judgments. *J. Personality & Social Psychol.,* **11**, 275–279.

BANDURA, A., 1969b. Social-learning theory of identification processes. In D.A. Goslin (Ed.), *Handbook of socialization theory and research.* Chicago: Rand McNally.

BANDURA, A., BLANCHARD, E. B., & RITTER, B., 1969. Relative efficacy of desensitization and modeling approaches for inducing behavioral, affective, and attitudinal changes. *J. Personality & Social Psychol.,* **13**, 173–199.

BANDURA, A., GRUSEC, J. E., & MENLOVE, F. L., 1967. Vicarious extinction of avoidance behavior. *J. Personality & Social Psychol.,* **5**, 16–23.

BANDURA, A., & HUSTON, A. C., 1961. Identification as a process of incidental learning. *J. Abnormal & Social Psychol.,* **63**, 311–318.

BANDURA, A., & KUPERS, C. J., 1964. Transmission of patterns of self-reinforcement through modeling. *J. Abnormal & Social Psychol.,* **69**, 1–9.

BANDURA, A., & McDONALD, F. J. 1963. Influence of social reinforcement and the behavior of models in shaping children's moral judgment. *J. Abnormal & Social Psychol.,* **67**, 274–281.

BANDURA, A., & MENLOVE, F. L., 1968. Factors determining vicarious extinction of avoidance behavior through symbolic modeling. *J. Personality & Social Psychol.,* **8**, 99–108.

BANDURA, A., & MISCHEL, W., 1965. Modification of self-imposed delay of reward through exposure to live and symbolic models. *J. Personality & Social Psychol.,* **2**, 698–705.

BANDURA, A., & PERLOFF, B., 1967. Relative efficacy of self-monitored and externally imposed reinforcement systems. *J. Personality & Social Psychol.,* **7**, 111–116.

BANDURA, A., & WALTERS, R. H., 1963. *Social learning and personality development.* New York: Holt.

BARBER, T. X., 1959. The "eidetic image" and "hallucinatory" behavior: A suggestion for further research. *Psychol. Bull.,* **56**, 236–239.

BARKER, R., DEMBO, T., & LEWIN, K., 1937. Experiments on frustration and regression in children. *Psychol. Bull.,* **34**, 754–755.

BARNLUND, D. C., 1959. A comparative study of individual, majority, and group judgment. *J. Abnormal & Social Psychol.,* **58**, 55–60.

BARRON, F., 1955. The disposition toward originality. *J. Abnormal & Social Psychol.,* **51**, 478–485.

BARRON, F., 1963a. *Creativity and psychological health: Origins of personality and creative freedom.* Princeton, N. J.: Van Nostrand.

BARRON, F., 1963b. Diffusion, integration, and enduring attention in the creative process. In R. W. White (Ed.), *The study of lives: Essays in honor of Henry A. Murray.* New York: Atherton.

BARRON, F., & WELSH, G. S., 1952. Artistic perception as a possible factor in personality style: Its measurement by a figure preference test. *J. Psychol.,* **33**, 199–203.

BARTLETT, F., 1958. *Thinking: An experimental and social study.* New York: Basic Books.

BARTLETT, F. C., 1967. *Remembering: A study in experimental and social psychology.* New York: Cambridge University Press. (Originally published: 1932).

BARTLETT, F. C., & SMITH E. M., 1921. Is thinking merely the action of language mechanisms? *Brit. J. Psychol.,* **11**, 55–62.

BASETTE, M. F., & WARNE, C. J., 1919. On the lapse of verbal meaning with repetition. *Am. J. Psychol.,* **30**, 415–418.

BASS, B. M., 1955. Authoritarianism or acquiescence? *J. Abnormal & Social Psychol.,* **51**, 616–623.

BATESON, N., 1966. Familiarization, group discussion, and risk taking. *J. Exptl. Social Psychol.,* **2**, 119–129.

BATTIG, W. F., & BOURNE, L. E., Jr., 1961. Concept identification as a function of intra- and inter-dimensional variability. *J. Exptl. Psychol.,* **61**, 329–333.

BAUMRIND, D., 1964. Some thoughts on ethics of research: After reading Milgram's "Behavioral study of obedience." *Am. Psychologist,* **19**, 421–423.

BAYTON, J. A., 1941. The racial stereotypes of Negro college students. *J. Abnormal & Social Psychol.,* **36**, 97–102.

BAYTON, J. A., AUSTIN, L. J., & BURKE, K. R. 1965. Negro perception of Negro and white personality traits. *J. Personality & Social Psychol.,* **1**, 250–253.

BEAM, J. C., 1955. Serial learning and conditioning under real-life stress. *J. Abnormal & Social Psychol.,* **51**, 543–551.

BECKMAN, F. H., & STEIN, M. I., 1961. A note on the relationship between per cent alpha time and efficiency in problem solving. *J. Psychol.,* **51**, 169–172.

BEGG, I., & DENNY, J. P., 1969. Empirical reconciliation of atmosphere and conversion interpretations of syllogistic reasoning errors. *J. Exptl. Psychol.,* **81**, 351–354.

BEILIN, H., 1965. Learning and operational convergence in logical thought development. *J. Exptl. Child Psychol.,* **2**, 317–339.

BEILIN, H., 1968. Cognitive capacities of young children and a replication. *Science,* **162**, 920–921, 924–925.

BEILIN, H., & FRANKLIN, I. C., 1962. Logical operations in area and length measurement: Age and training effects. *Child Develop.,* **33**, 607–618.

BEILIN, H., & HORN, R., 1962. Transition probability effects in anagram problem solving. *J. Exptl. Psychol.,* **63**, 514–518.

BELL, J. E., 1948. *Projective techniques.* New York: Longmans.

BELLAK, L., 1944. The concept of projection. *Psychiatry,* **7**, 353–370.

BELOFF, H., 1958. Two forms of social conformity: Acquiescence and conventionality. *J. Abnormal & Social Psychol.,* **56**, 99–104.

BEM, D. J., 1967. Self-perception: an alternative interpretation of cognitive dissonance phenomena. *Psychol. Rev.,* **74**, 183–200.

BENDIG, A. W., 1953. Twenty questions: An information analysis. *J. Exptl. Psychol.,* **46**, 345–348.

BENJAFIELD, J., 1969. Logical and empirical thinking in a problem solving task. *Psychonomic Sci.,* **14**, 285–286.

BERGER, E. M., 1952. The relation between expressed acceptance of self and expressed acceptance of others. *J. Abnormal & Social Psychol.,* **47**, 778–782.

BERGER, R. J., & OSWALD, I., 1962. Eye movements during active and passive dreams. *Science,* **137**, 601.

BERGUM, B. O., & LEHR, D. J., 1962. Vigilance performance as a function of interpolated rest. *J. appl. Psychol.,* **46**, 425–427.

BERKOWITZ, L., & DANIELS, L. R., 1964. Affecting the salience of the social responsibility norm: Effects of past help on the response to dependency relationships. *J. Abnormal & Social Psychol.,* **68**, 275–281.

BERKOWITZ, L., & HOLMES, D. S. 1959. The generalization of hostility to disliked objects. *J. Personality,* **27**, 565–577.

BERLYNE, D. E., 1954. Knowledge and stimulus-response psychology. *Psychol. Rev.,* **61**, 245–254.

BERSCHEID, E., BOYE, D., & WALSTER, E., 1968. Retaliation as a means of restoring equity. *J. Personality & Social Psychol.,* **10**, 370–376.

BERSCHEID, E., & WALSTER, E., 1967. When does a harm-doer compensate a victim? *J. Personality & Social Psychol.,* **6**, 435–441.

BETTELHEIM, B., 1947. The dynamism of anti-Semitism in Gentile and Jew. *J. Abnormal & Social Psychol.,* **42**, 153–168.

BETTELHEIM, B., 1949. A study in rehabilitation. *J. Abnormal & Social Psychol.,* **44**, 231–265.

BETTS, G. H., 1909. The distribution and functions of mental imagery. *Teachers Coll. Contrib. Educ.,* No. 26.

BEVAN, W. 1964. Subliminal stimulation: A pervasive problem for psychology *Psychol., Bull.,* **61**, 81–99.

BEVAN, W., 1967. Behavior in unusual environments. In H. Helson & W. Bevan (Eds.), *Contemporary approaches to psychology.* Princeton, N.J.: Van Nostrand.

BEVER, T. G., MEHLER, J., & EPSTEIN, J., 1968. What children do in spite of what they know. *Science,* **162**, 921–924.

BIEDERMAN, I., & CHECKOSKY, S. F., 1970. Processing redundant information. *J. Exptl. Psychol.,* **83**, 486–490.

BILLS, A. G., & STAUFFACHER, J. C., 1937. The influence of voluntarily induced tension on rational problem solving. *J. Psychol.,* **4**, 261–272.

BINDRA, D., 1959. *Motivation: A systematic reinterpretation.* New York: Ronald Press.

BIRCH, H. E., 1945. The role of motivational factors in insightful problem solving. *J. Comp. Psychol.,* **38**, 295–317.

BIRCH, H. G., & RABINOWITZ, H. S. 1951. The negative effect of previous experience on productive thinking. *J. Exptl. Psychol.,* **41**, 121–125.

BIRNBAUM, I. M., 1966. Context stimuli in verbal learning and the persistence of associative factors. *J. Exptl. Psychol.,* **71**, 483–487.

BLATT, S. J., ALLISON, J., & FEIRSTEIN, A., 1969. The capacity to cope with cognitive complexity. *J. Personality,* **37**, 269–288.

BLOCK, J., & BLOCK, J., 1951. An investigation of the relationship between intolerance of ambiguity and ethnocentrism. *J. Personality,* **19**, 303–311.

BLODGETT, H. C., 1929. The effect of the introduction of reward upon the maze performance of rats. *Univ. Calif. Publ. Psychol.,* **4**, 113–134.

BLOOMBERG, M., 1965. Anagram solutions of field-independent and field-dependent persons. *Perceptual & Motor Skills,* **21**, 766.

BLUM, G. S., 1954. An experimental reunion of psychoanalytic theory with perceptual vigilance and defense. *J. Abnormal & Social Psychol.,* **49**, 94–98.

BLUM, G. S., 1955. Perceptual defense revisited. *J. Abnormal & Social Psychol.,* **51**, 24–29.

BLUM, G. S., 1961. *A model of the mind.* New York: Wiley.

BOBROW, S. A., & BOWER, G. H., 1969. Comprehension and recall of sentences. *J. Exptl. Psychol.,* **80**, 455–461.

BOLLES, M. M., 1937. The basis of pertinence: A study of the test performance of aments, dements, and normal children of the same mental age. *Arch. Psychol.,* No. 212.

BOND, J. R., & VINACKE, W. E., 1961. Coalitions in mixed-sex triads. *Sociometry,* **24**, 61–75.

BONTE, E. P., & MUSGROVE, M., 1943. Influence of war as evidenced in children's play. *Child Develop.,* **14**, 179–200.

BOOTZIN R. R., & NATSOULAS, T., 1965. Evidence for perceptual defense uncontaminated by response bias. *J. Personality & Social Psychol.,* **1** 461–468.

BORING, E. G., 1950. *A history of experimental psychology.* (2nd ed.) New York: Appleton Century Crofts.

BORNSTEIN, R., & GRIER, J. B., 1968. Pretask information in concept identification. *J. Exptl. Psychol.,* **78**, 306–309.

BOURNE, L. E., Jr., 1957. Effects of delay of information feedback and task complexity on the identification of concepts. *J. Exptl. Psychol.,* **54**, 201–207.

BOURNE, L. E., Jr., 1963. Long-term effects of misinformative feedback upon concept identification. *J. Exptl. Psychol.,* **65**, 139–147.

BOURNE, L. E., Jr., 1965. Hypotheses and hypothesis shifts in classification learning. *J. Gen. Psychol.,* **72**, 251–262.

BOURNE, L. E., Jr., GOLDSTEIN, S., & LINK, W. E., 1964. Concept learning as a function of availability of previously presented information. *J. Exptl. Psychol.,* **67**, 439–448.

BOURNE, L. E., Jr., & GUY, D. E., 1968a. Learning conceptual rules: I. Some interrule transfer effects. *J. Exptl. Psychol.,* **76**, 423–429.

BOURNE, L. E., Jr., & GUY, D. E., 1968b. Learning conceptual rules: II. The role of positive and negative instances. *J. Exptl. Psychol.,* **77**, 488–494.

BOURNE, L. E., Jr., GUY, D. E., DODD, D. H., & JUSTESEN, D. R., 1965. Concept identification: The effects of varying length and informational components of the intertrial interval. *J. Exptl. Psychol.,* **69**, 624–629.

BOURNE, L. E., Jr., & HAYGOOD, R. C., 1959. The role of stimulus redundancy in concept identification. *J. Exptl. Psychol.,* **58**, 232–238.

BOURNE, L. E., Jr., & HAYGOOD, R. C., 1961. Supplementary report: Effect of redundant relevant information upon the identification of concepts. *J. Exptl. Psychol.,* **61**, 259–260.

BOURNE, L. E., Jr., & PENDLETON, R. B., 1958. Concept identification as a function of completeness and probability of information feedback. *J. Exptl. Psychol.,* **56**, 413–420.

BOURNE, L. E., Jr., & RESTLE, F., 1959. Mathematical theory of concept identification. *Psychol. Rev.,* **77**, 278–296.

BOUSFIELD, W. A., 1953. The occurrence of clustering in the recall of randomly arranged associates, *J. Gen. Psychol.,* **49**, 229–240.

BOUSFIELD, W. A., & PUFF, C. R., 1965. Determinants of the clustering of taxonomically and associatively related word pairs. *J. Gen. Psychol.,* **73**, 211–221.

BOWER, A. C., & KING, W. L., 1967. The effect of number of irrelevant stimulus dimensions, verbalization, and sex in learning biconditional classification rules. *Psychonomic Sci.,* **8**, 453–454.

BOWER, G., & TRABASSO, T., 1963. Reversals prior to solution in concept identification. *J. Exptl. Psychol.,* **66**, 409–418.

BOWERS, K. S., & van der MEULEN, S. J., 1970. Effect of hypnotic suscepti-bility on creativity test performance. *J. Personality & Social Psychol.,* **14**, 247–256.

BOWERS, P. G., 1967. Effect of hypnosis and suggestions of reduced defensive-ness on creativity test performance. *J. Personality,* **35**, 311–322.

BOYNTON, P. L., & FORD, F. A., 1933. The relationship between play and intelligence. *J. Appl. Psychol.,* **17**, 294–301.

BRAINE, M. D. S., 1959. The ontogeny of certain logical operations: Piaget's formulation examined by nonverbal methods. *Psychol. Monographs,* **73**, (5, Whole No. 475).

BRAINERD, C. J., & ALLEN, T. W., 1971. Experimental inductions of the con-servation of "first-order" quantitative invariants. *Psychol. Bull.,* **75**, 128–144.

BRALEY, L. S., 1962. Some conditions influencing the acquisition and utilization of cues. *J. Exptl. Psychol.,* **64**, 62–66.

BRAMEL, D., 1962. A dissonance theory approach to defensive projection. *J. Abnormal & Social Psychol.,* **64**, 121–129.

BRAZZIEL, W. F., 1964. Correlates of Southern Negro personality. *J. Social Issues,* **20**, 46–53.

BREGER, L., 1967. Functions of dreams. *J. Abnormal Psychol. Monographs,* **72**, (5, Pt. 2, Whole No. 641).

BREHM, J. W., 1962. Motivational effects of cognitive dissonance. In M. R. Jones (Ed.), *Nebraska symposium on motivation.* Lincoln, Neb.: University of Nebraska Press.

BREHM, J. W., 1966. *A theory of psychological reactance.* New York: Academic.

BREHM, J. W., & COHEN, A. R., 1962. *Explorations in cognitive dissonance.* New York : Wiley.

BREHM, J. W., & CROCKER, J. C., 1962. An experiment on hunger. In J. W. Brehm & A. R. Cohen, *Explorations in cognitive dissonance.* New York : Wiley.

BRENNER, A. B., 1952. The fantasies of W. S. Gilbert. *Psychoanal. Quart.,* **21,** 373–401.

BRETT, G. S., 1928. *Psychology, ancient and modern.* New York : Longmans.

BRIGHAM, J. C., 1971. Ethnic stereotypes. *Psychol. Bull.,* **76,** 15–38.

BRISON, D. W., 1966. Acceleration of conservation of substance. *J. Genet. Psychol.,* **109,** 311–322.

BRITT, S. H., & BALCOM, M. M., 1941. Jumping rope rhymes and the social psychology of play. *J. Genet. Psychol.,* **58,** 289–306.

BRITT, S. H., & JANUS, S. Q., 1941. Toward a social psychology of human play. *J. Social Psychol.,* **13,** 351–384.

BROADBENT, D. E., 1953. Classical conditioning and human watch-keeping. *Psychol. Rev.,* **60,** 331–339.

BROADBENT, D. E., 1957. A mechanical model for human attention and immediate memory. *Psychol. Rev.,* **64,** 205–215.

BROCK, T. C., 1969. On interpreting the effects of transgression upon compliance. *Psychol. Bull.,* **72,** 138–145.

BROCK, T. C., & BALLOUN, J. L., 1967. Behavioral receptivity to dissonant information. *J. Personality & Social Psychol.,* **6,** 413–428.

BRODY, G. F., 1965. Relationship between maternal attitudes and behavior. *J. Personality & Social Psychol.,* **2,** 317–323.

BROEN, W. E., Jr., 1957. A factor-analytic study of religious attitudes. *J. Abnormal & Social Psychol.,* **54,** 176–179.

BRONFENBRENNER, U., 1960. Freudian theories of identification and their derivatives. *Child Develop.,* **31,** 15–40.

BRONFENBRENNER, U., 1965. Socialization and social class through time and space. In H. Proshansky & B. Seidenberg (Eds.), *Basic studies in social psychology.* New York : Holt.

BRONOWSKI, J., & BELLUGI, U., 1970. Language, name, and concept. *Science,* **168,** 669–673.

BROTSKY, S. J., 1968. Classical conditioning of the galvanic skin response to verbal concepts. *J. Exptl. Psychol.,* **76,** 244–253.

BROVERMAN, D. M., 1960. Dimensions of cognitive style. *J. Personality,* **28,** 167–185.

BROWER, D., 1947. The experimental study of imagery. II. The relative predominance of various imagery modalities. *J. Gen. Psychol.,* **37,** 199–200.

BROWN, J. F., 1947. A modification of the Rosenzweig Picture-Frustration Test to study hostile interracial attitudes *J. Psychol.,* **24,** 247–272.

BROWN, J. S., 1948. Gradients of approach and avoidance responses and their relation to level of motivation. *J. Comp. & Physiol. Psychol.,* **41,** 450–465.

BROWN, J. S., 1961. *The motivation of behavior.* New York : McGraw-Hill.

BROWN, N. O., 1959. *Life against death. The philosophical meaning of history.* New York : Random House.

BROWN, R., 1965. *Social psychology.* New York : Free Press.

BROWN, S. C., & READ, J. D., 1968. Addition of context cues to response terms of paired-associate lists. *J. Exptl. Psychol.,* **78,** 692–693.

BRUCE, M., 1941. Animism vs. evolution of the concept "alive." *J. Psychol.,* **12,** 81–90.

BRUNER, J. S., 1964. The course of cognitive growth. *Am. Psychologist,* **19,** 1–15.

BRUNER, J. S., 1966. On the conservation of liquids. In J. S. Bruner, R. R. Olver, & P. M. Greenfield et al., *Studies in cognitive growth.* New York: Wiley.

BRUNER, J. S., & GOODMAN, C. C., 1947. Value and need as organizing factors in perception. *J. Abnormal & Social Psychol.,* **42,** 33–44.

BRUNER, J. S., GOODNOW, J. J. & AUSTIN, G. A., 1956. *A study of thinking.* New York: Wiley.

BRUNER, J. S., OLVER, R. R., GREENFIELD, P. M., et al., 1966. *Studies in cognitive growth.* New York: Wiley.

BRUNER, J. S., & POSTMAN, L., 1947. Emotional selectivity in perception and reaction. *J. Personality,* **16,** 69–77.

BRUSH, F. R., 1956. Stimulus uncertainty, response uncertainty, and problem solving. *Can. J. Psychol.,* **10,** 239–247.

BRYAN, J. H., & LONDON, P., 1970. Altruistic behavior by children. *Psychol. Bull,* **73,** 200–211.

BUDNER, S., 1962. Intolerance of ambiguity as a personality variable. *J. Personality,* **30,** 29–50.

BUGELSKI, B. R., 1962. Presentation time, total time, and mediation in paired-associate learning. *J. Exptl. Psychol.,* **63,** 409–412.

BUGELSKI, B. R., 1968. Images as mediators in one-trial paired-associate learning. II. Self-timing in successive lists. *J. Exptl. Psychol.,* **77,** 328–334.

BUGELSKI, B. R., 1970. Presentation time and the total-time hypothesis. *J. Exptl. Psychol.,* **84,** 529–530.

BUGELSKI, B. R., KIDD, E., & SEGMEN, J., 1968. Image as a mediator in one-trial paired-associate learning. *J. Exptl. Psychol.,* **76,** 69–73.

BUGELSKI, B. R., & McMAHON, M. L., 1971. The total time hypothesis: A reply to Stubin, Heurer, and Tatz. *J. Exptl. Psychol.,* **90,** 165–166.

BUGELSKI, B. R., & RICKWOOD, J., 1963. Presentation time, total time, and mediation in paired-associate learning: Self-pacing. *J. Exptl. Psychol.,* **65,** 616–617.

BUGELSKI, B. R., & SCHARLOCK, D. P., 1952. An experimental demonstration of unconscious mediated generalization. *J. Exptl. Psychol.,* **44,** 334–338.

BULGARELLA, R. G., & ARCHER, E. J., 1962. Concept identification of auditory stimuli as a function of amount of relevant and irrelevant information. *J. Exptl. Psychol.,* **63,** 254–257.

BURGESS, M., & HOKANSON, J. E., 1964. Effects of increased heart rate on intellectual performance. *J. Abnormal & Social Psychol.,* **68,** 85–91.

BURKE, R. J., 1965. Sex differences in recognizing the correct answer to a problem. *Psychol. Repts.,* **17,** 532–534.

BURKE, R. J., & MAIER, N. R., 1965. Attempts to predict success on an insight problem. *Psychol. Repts.,* **17,** 303–310.

BURKE, R. J., MAIER, N. R. F., & HOFFMAN, R., 1966. Functions of hints in individual problem solving. *Am. J. Psychol.,* **79,** 389–399.

BURNSTEIN, E., 1967. Sources of cognitive bias in the representation of simple social structures: Balance, minimal change, positivity, reciprocity, and the respondent's own attitude. *J. Personality & Social Psychol.,* **7,** 36–48.

BURTON, R. V., 1963. Generality of honesty reconsidered. *Psychol. Rev.*, **70**, 481–499.

BUSS, A. H., 1950. A study of concept formation as a function of reinforcement and stimulus generalization. *J. Exptl. Psychol.*, **40**, 494–503.

BUSS, A. H., 1953. Rigidity as a function of reversal and nonreversal shifts in the learning of successive discriminations. *J. Exptl. Psychol.*, **45**, 75–81.

BUSS, A. H., 1956. Reversal and nonreversal shifts in concept formation with partial reinforcement eliminated. *J. Exptl. Psychol.*, **52**, 162–166.

BUTLER, J. M., & HAIGH, G. V., 1954. Changes in the relation between self-concepts and ideal concepts consequent upon client-centered counseling. In C. R. Rogers & R. F. Dymond (Eds.), *Psychotherapy and personality change*. Chicago : The University of Chicago Press.

BYERS, J. L., & DAVIDSON, R. E., 1967. The role of hypothesizing in the facilitation of concept attainment. *J. Verbal Learning & Verbal Behavior*, **6**, 595–600.

BYERS, J. L., DAVIDSON, R. E., & ROHWER, W. D., Jr., 1968. The effects of strategy instructions and memory on concept attainment. *J. Verbal Learning & Verbal Behavior*, **7**, 831–837.

BYRNE, D., 1961. The repression-sensitization scale : Rationale, reliability, and validity. *J. Personality*, **29**, 334–349.

BYRNE, D., BARRY, J., & NELSON, D., 1963. Relation of the revised repression-sensitization scale to measures of self-description. *Psychol. Repts.*, **13**, 323–334.

BYRNE, D., & WONG, T. J., 1962. Racial prejudice, interpersonal attraction, and assumed dissimilarity of attitudes. *J. Abnormal & Social Psychol.*, **65**, 246-253.

CALLENTINE, M. F., & WARREN, J. M., 1955. Learning sets in human concept formation. *Psychol. Repts.*, **1**, 363–367.

CAMPBELL, A., CONVERSE, P. E., MILLER, W. E., & STOKES, D. E., 1960. *The American voter*. New York : Wiley.

CAMPBELL, A. C., 1968. Selectivity in problem solving. *Am. J. Psychol.*, **81**, 543–550.

CAMPBELL, D. P., 1965. *A study of college freshmen—twenty-five years later*. Minneapolis : University of Minnesota. (Coop. Res. Proj. No. 2160. Office Educ., U.S. Dept. Health, Education, and Welfare.)

CAMPBELL, D. T., 1950. The indirect assessment of social attitudes. *Psychol. Bull.*, **47**, 15–38.

CAMPBELL, D. T., 1960. Blind variation and selective retention in creative thought as in other knowledge processes. *Psychol. Rev.*, **67**, 380–400.

CAMPBELL, D. T., 1967. Stereotypes and the perception of group differences. *Am. Psychologist*, **22**, 817–829.

CAMPBELL, D. T., & McCANDLESS, B. R., 1951. Ethnocentrism, xenophobia, and personality. *Human Relations*, **4**, 185–192.

CAMPISI, P. J., 1948. Ethnic family patterns : The Italian family in the United States. *Am. J. Sociol.*, **53**, 443–449.

CAREY, G. L., 1958. Sex differences in problem-solving performance as a function of attitude differences. *J. Abnormal & Social Psychol.*, **56**, 256-260.

CARLSMITH, J. M., COLLINS, B. E., & HELMREICH, R. L., 1966. Studies in forced compliance : I. The effects of pressure for compliance on attitude change produced by face-to-face role playing and anonymous essay writing. *J. Personality & Social Psychol.*, **4**, 1–13.

CARLSMITH, J. M., & GROSS, A. E., 1969. Some effects of guilt on compliance. *J. Personality & Social Psychol.*, **11**, 232–239.

CARON, A. J., UNGER, S. M., & PARLOFF, M. B., 1963. A test of Maltzman's theory of originality training. *J. Verbal Learning & Verbal Behavior,* **1**, 436–442.

CARPENTER, B., WIENER, M., & CARPENTER, J. T., 1956. Predictability of perceptual defense behavior. *J. Abnormal & Social Psychol.*, **52**, 380–383.

CARROLL, J. B., & BURKE, M. L., 1965. Parameters of paired-associate verbal learning : Length of list, meaningfulness, rate of presentation, and ability. *J. Exptl. Psychol.*, **69**, 543–553.

CARTWRIGHT, D., 1949. Some principles of mass persuasion. *Human Relations,* **2,** 253–267.

CARTWRIGHT, D., & HARARY, F., 1956. Structural balance : A generalization of Heider's theory. *Psychol. Rev.*, **63**, 277–293.

CARTWRIGHT, D. S., 1956. Self-consistency as a factor affecting immediate recall. *J. Abnormal & Social Psychol.*, **52**, 212–218.

CARTWRIGHT, R. D., & MONROE, L. J., 1968. Relation of dreaming and REM sleep : The effects of REM deprivation under two conditions. *J. Personality & Social Psychol.*, **10**, 69–74.

CASHDAN, S., & WELSH, G. S., 1966. Personality correlates of creative potential in talented high school students, *J. Personality*, **34**, 445–455.

CENTERS, R., 1949. *The psychology of social classes: A study of class consciousness*. Princeton, N.J. : Princeton.

CERASO, J., & PROVITERA, A., 1971. Sources of error in syllogistic reasoning. *Cognitive Psychol.*, **2**, 400–410.

CHAMBERS, J. A., 1964. Relating personality and biographical factors to scientific creativity. *Psychol. Monographs*, **78**, (7, Whole No. 584).

CHAPANIS, N. P., & CHAPANIS, A., 1964. Cognitive dissonance : Five years later. *Psychol. Bull.*, **61**, 1–22.

CHAPMAN, L. J., & CAMPBELL, D. T., 1957. Response set in the F scale. *J. Abnormal & Social Psychol.*, **54**, 129–132.

CHAPMAN, L. J., & CHAPMAN, J. P., 1959. Atmosphere effect re-examined. *J. Exptl. Psychol.,* **58**, 220–226.

CHARTERS, W. W., & NEWCOMB, T. M., 1958. Some attitudinal effects of experimentally increased salience of a membership group. In E. E. Maccoby T. M. Newcomb, & E. L. Hartley (Eds.), *Readings in social psychology* (3rd. ed.), New York : Holt.

CHEIN, I., 1944. The awareness of self and the structure of the ego. *Psychol. Rev.*, **51**, 304–314.

CHILD, I. L., & DOOB, L. W., 1943. Factors determining national stereotypes. *J. Social Psychol.,* **17**, 203–219.

CHLEBEK, J., & DOMINOWSKI, R. L., 1970. The effect of practice on utilization of information from positive and negative instances in identifying disjunctive concepts. *Can. J. Psychol.,* **24**, 64–69.

CHODORKOFF, B., 1954. Self-perception, perceptual defense and adjustment. *J. Abnormal & Social Psychol.,* **49**, 508–512.

CHOMSKY, N., 1965. *Aspects of the theory of syntax.* Cambridge, Mass. : MIT Press.

CHOWN, S. M., 1959. Rigidity—a flexible concept. *Psychol. Bull.,* **56**, 195–223.

CHRISTENSEN, P. R., GUILFORD, J. P. & WILSON, R. C., 1957. Relations of creative responses to working time and instructions. *J. Exptl. Psychol.,* **53**, 82–88.

CHRISTENSEN, P. R., MERRIFIELD, P. R., & GUILFORD, J. P., 1958. *Consequences: Manual for administration, scoring, and interpretation.* (2nd. ed.) Beverly Hills, Calif.: Sheridan Supply.

CHRISTIE, R., & GARCIA, J., 1951. Subcultural variation in authoritarian personality. *J. Abnormal & Social Psychol.,* **46**, 457–469.

CHRISTIE, R., HAVEL, J., & SEIDENBERG, B., 1958. Is the F scale irreversible? *J. Abnormal & Social Psychol.,* **56**, 143–159.

CHRISTIE, R., & JAHODA, M., (Eds.), 1954. *Studies in the scope and method of the "Authoritarian personality."* New York: Free Press.

CLAPARÈDE, E., 1934. Genése de l'hypothése. *Arch. de Psychol.,* **24**, 1–154.

CLARK, H. H., 1969a. Influence of language in solving three-term series problems. *J. Exptl. Psychol.,* **82**, 205–215.

CLARK, H. H., 1969b. Linguistic processes in deductive reasoning. *Psychol. Rev.,* **76**, 387–404.

CLARK, R. A., 1952. The projective measurement of experimentally induced levels of sexual motivation. *J. Exptl. Psychol.,* **44**, 391–399.

CLARK, R. A., & SENSIBAR, M. R., 1955. The relationship between symbolic and manifest projections of sexuality with some incidental correlates. *J. Abnormal & Social Psychol.,* **50**, 327–334.

CLARK, R. D., III, & WILLEMS, E. P., 1969. Where is the risky shift? Dependence on instructions. *J. Personality & Social Psychol.,* **13**, 215–221.

CLARKE, H. M., 1911. Conscious attitudes. *Am. J. Psychol.,* **22**, 214–249.

CLARKE, P., & JAMES, J., 1967. The effects of situation, attitude intensity, and personality on information-seeking. *Sociometry,* **30**, 235–245.

CLARKE, R., 1922. An experimental study of silent thinking. *Arch. Psychol.,* No. 48.

CLITES, M. S., 1935. Certain somatic activities in relation to successful and unsuccessful problem-solving. *J. Exptl. Psychol.,* **18**, 708–724.

COFER, C. N., 1957. Reasoning as an associative process: III. The role of verbal responses in problem solving. *J. Gen. Psychol.,* **57**, 55–68.

COFER, C. N., 1967. Some data on controlled association. *J. Verbal Learning & Verbal Behavior,* **6**, 601–608.

COFER, C. N., & APPLEY, M. H., 1965. *Motivation: Theory and research.* New York: Wiley.

COFER, C. N., & FOLEY, J. P., Jr., 1942. Mediated generalization and the interpretation of verbal behavior. I. Prolegomena. *Psychol. Rev.,* **49**, 513–540.

COFER, C. N., JANIS, M. G., & ROWELL, M. M., 1943. Mediated generalization and the interpretation of verbal behavior. III. Experimental study of antonym gradients. *J. Exptl. Psychol.,* **32**, 266–269.

COHEN, A. R., 1962. An experiment on small rewards for discrepant compliance and attitude change. In J. W. Brehm & A. R.Cohen, *Explorations in cognitive dissonance.* New York: Wiley.

COHEN, A. R., STOTLAND, E., & WOLFE, D. M., 1955. An experimental investigation of need for cognition. *J. Abnormal & Social Psychol.,* **51**, 291–294.

COHEN, D., WHITMYRE, J. W., & FUNK, W. H., 1960. Effect of group cohesiveness and training upon creative thinking. *J. Appl. Psychol.,* **44**, 319–322.

COHEN, J. L., 1968. The effect of letter frequency on anagram solution times. *Psychonomic Sci.,* **11**, 79–80.

COHEN, M. R., & NAGEL, E., 1934. *An introduction to logic and scientific method.* New York: Harcourt, Brace.

COHN, T. S., 1952. Is the F scale indirect? *J. Abnormal & Social Psychol.,* **47**, 732.

COHN, T. S., 1953. The relation of the F scale to a response set to answer positively. *Am. Psychologist,* **8**, 335. (Abstract)

COLE, M., GUY, J., & GLICK, J.. 1968. Reversal and nonreversal shifts among Liberian tribal people. *J. Exptl. Psychol.,* **76**, 323–324.

COLEMAN, E. B., 1964. Verbal concept learning as a function of instructions and dominance level. *J. Exptl. Psychol.,* **68**, 213–214.

COMBS, A. W., & TAYLOR, L., 1952. The effect of the perception of mild degrees of threat on performance. *J. Abnormal & Social Psychol.,* **47**, 420–424.

CONANT, M. B., & TRABASSO, T., 1964. Conjunctive and disjunctive concept formation under equal-information conditions. *J. Exptl. Psychol.,* **67**, 250–255.

COOK, S. W., & SELLTIZ, C., 1964. A multiple-indicator approach to attitude measurement. *Psychol. Bull.,* **62**, 36–55.

COOK, T. D., 1969. Temporal mechanisms mediating attitude change after under-payment and overpayment. *J. Personality,* **37**, 618–635.

COOPER, E. H., & PANTLE, A. J., 1967. The total-time hypothesis in verbal learning. *Psychol. Bull.,* **68**, 221–234.

COOPER, J. B., & SINGER, D. N., 1956. The role of emotion in prejudice. *J. Social Psychol.,* **44**, 241–247.

CORSO, J. F., 1963. A theoretico-historical review of the threshold concept. *Psychol. Bull.,* **60**, 356–370.

COSTANZO, P. R., 1970. Conformity development as a function of self-blame. *J. Personality & Social Psychol.,* **14**, 366–374.

COWAN, P. A., LANGER, J., HEAVENRICH, J., & NATHANSON, M., 1969. Social learning and Piaget's cognitive theory of moral development. *J. Abnormal & Social Psychol.,* **11**, 261–274.

COWEN, E. L., 1952. The influence of varying degrees of psychological stress on problem-solving rigidity. *J. Abnormal & Social Psychol.,* **47**. 512–519.

COWEN, E. L., LANDES, J., & SCHAET, D. E., 1959. The effects of mild frustra-tion on the expression of prejudiced attitudes. *J. Abnormal & Social Psychol.,* **58**, 33–38.

COWEN, E. L., & THOMPSON, G. G., 1951. Problem-solving rigidity and person-ality structure. *J. Abnormal & Social Psychol.,* **46**, 165–176.

COWEN, E. L., WIENER, M., & HESS, J., 1953. Generalization of problem-solving rigidity. *J. Consulting Psychol.,* **17**, 100–103.

CRAMER, P., 1965. Mediated clustering and importation with implicit verbal chains. *Psychonomic Sci.,* **2**, 165.

CRAMER, P., 1966. Mediated priming of associative responses: The effect of time lapse and interpolated activity. *J. Verbal Learning & Verbal Behavior,* **5**, 163–166.

CREELMAN, M. B., 1966. *The experimental investigation of meaning: A review of the literature.* New York: Springer.

CROCKETT, W. H., & MEIDINGER, T., 1956. Authoritarianism and interpersonal perception. *J. Abnormal & Social Psychol.,* **53**, 378–380.

CROWDER, R. G., 1968. Evidence for the chaining hypothesis of serial verbal learning. *J. Exptl. Psychol.,* **76**, 497–500.

CROWELL, D. H., & DOLE, A. A., 1957. Animism and college students. *J. Educ. Res.,* **50**, 391–395.

CROWLEY, P. M., 1968. Effect of training upon objectivity of moral judgment in grade-school children. *J. Personality & Social Psychol.,* **8**, 228–232.

CSIKSZENTMIHALYI, M., & GETZELS, J. W., 1970. Concern for discovery: An attitudinal component of creative production. *J. Personality,* **38**, 91–105.

CUBBERLY, A. J., 1923. The effects of tensions of the body surface upon the normal dream. *Brit. J. Psychol.,* **13**, 245–265.

DABBS, J. M., Jr., 1964. Self-esteem, communicator characteristics, and attitude change, *J. Abnormal & Social Psychol.,* **69**, 173–181.

D'AMATO, M. F., & RYAN, R., 1967. Intradimensional and extradimensional shifts in compound concept learning. *Psychonomic Sci.,* **7**, 207–208.

DANIELS, L., & BERKOWITZ, L., 1963. Liking and response to dependency relationships. *Human Relations,* **16**, 141–148.

DANZIGER, K., 1957. The child's understanding of kinship terms: A study in the development of relational concepts. *J. Genet. Psychol.,* **91**, 213–232.

DARLEY, J. M., & LATANÉ, B., 1968. Bystander intervention in emergencies: Diffusion of responsibility. *J. Personality & Social Psychol.,* **8**, 377–383.

DARLINGTON, R. B., & MACKER, C. E., 1966. Displacement of guilt-produced altruistic behavior. *J. Personality & Social Psychol.,* **4**, 442–443.

DASHIELL, J. F., 1935. Experimental studies of the influence of social situations on the behavior of individual human adults. In C. Murchison (Ed.), *Handbook of social psychology.* Worcester, Mass: Clark University Press.

DAVIDON, R. S., 1952. The effects of symbols, shift, and manipulation upon the number of concepts attained. *J. Exptl. Psychol.,* **44**, 70–79.

DAVIDS, A., 1955. Some personality and intellectual correlates of intolarrance of ambiguity. *J. Abnormal & Social Psychol.,* **51**, 415–420.

DAVIDSON, M., 1969. Positive versus negative instances in concept identification problems matched for logical complexity of solution procedures. *J. Exptl. Psychol.,* **80**, 369–373.

DAVIS, A., 1948. *Social-class influences upon learning.* Cambridge, Mass.: Harvard.

DAVIS, G. A., 1966. Current status of research and theory in human problem solving. *Psychol. Bull.,* **66**, 36–54.

DAVIS, G. A., 1967. Detrimental effects of distraction, additional response alternatives, and longer response chains in solving switch-light problems. *J. Exptl. Psychol.,* **73**, 45–55.

DAVIS, G. A., & MANSKE, M. E., 1966. An instructional method for increasing originality. *Psychonomic Sci.,* **6**, 73–74.

DAVIS, J. H., 1969. Individual-group problem solving, subject preference, and problem type. *J. Personality & Social Psychol.,* **13**, 362–374.

DAVIS, J. H., & RESTLE, F., 1963. The analysis of problems and prediction of group problem solving. *J. Abnormal & Social Psychol.,* **66**, 103–116.

DAVIS, R. C., 1938. The relation of muscle action potentials to difficulty and frustration. *J. Exptl. Psychol.,* **23**, 141–158.

DEESE, J., 1955. Some problems in the theory of vigilance. *Psychol. Rev.,* **62**, 359–368.

DEESE, J., 1962. On the structure of associative meaning. *Psychol. Rev.,* **69**, 161–175.

DEESE, J., 1965. *The structure of associations in language and thought.* Baltimore: Johns Hopkins.

DELLAS, M., 1970. Effects of creativity training, defensiveness, and intelligence on divergent thinking. Unpublished doctoral dissertation, State University of New York at Buffalo.

DELLAS, M., & GAIER, E. L., 1970. Identification of creativity: The individual. *Psychol. Bull.,* **73**, 55–73.

DEMENT, W., 1955. Dream recall and eye movements during sleep in schizophrenics and normals. *J. Nervous & Mental Disease,* **122**, 263–269.

DEMENT, W., 1960. The effect of dream deprivation. *Science,* **131**, 1705–1707.

DEMENT, W., & KLEITMAN, N., 1957. The relation of eye movements during sleep to dream activity. An objective method for the study of dreaming. *J. Exptl. Psychol.,* **53**, 339–346.

DEMENT, W., & WOLPERT, E. A., 1958. The relation of eye movements, body motility, and external stimuli to dream content. *J. Exptl. Psychol.,* **55**, 543–553.

DENNIS, W., 1940. Piaget's questions applied to Zuni and Navaho children. *Psychol. Bull.,* **37**, 520.

DENNY, J. P., 1966. Effects of anxiety and intelligence on concept formation. *J. Exptl. Psychol.,* **72**, 596–602.

DENNY, N. R., 1969. Memory and transformations in concept learning. *J. Exptl. Psychol.,* **79**, 63–68.

DESOTO, C. B., LONDON, M., & HANDEL, S., 1965. Social reasoning and spatial paralogic. *J. Personality & Social Psychol.,* **2**, 513–521.

DESPERT, J. L., 1940. A method for the study of personality reactions in preschool-age children by means of analysis of their play. *J. Psychol.,* **9**, 17–29.

DEUTSCHE, J. M., 1937. *The development of children's concepts of causal relations.* Minneapolis: University of Minnesota Press.

DEWEY, J., 1933. *How we think.* New York: Heath.

DEWEY, J., 1934. *Art as experience.* New York: Minton.

DEWEY, J., 1938. *Logic: The theory of inquiry.* New York: Holt.

DIAB, L. N., 1962. National stereotypes and the "reference group" concept. *J. Social Psychol.,* **57**, 339–351.

DIBARTOLO, R., & VINACKE, W. E., 1969. Relationship between adult nurturance and dependency and performance of the preschool child. *Develop. Psychol.,* **1**, 247–251.

DICK, R. D., & COMBS, R. H., 1965. Generalization of paired associates and concepts. *J. Gen. Psychol.,* **73**, 249–256.

DICKEN, C. F., 1961. Connotative meaning as a determinant of stimulus generalization. *Psychol. Monographs,* **75**, (1, Whole No. 505).

DICKINSON, T. C., Jr., 1967. The effects of profession, creativity level, and relevant personality variables upon creative performance in concept formation tasks. Unpublished doctoral dissertation, State University of New York at Buffalo.

DIGGORY, J. C., 1966. *Self-evaluation: Concept and studies.* New York: Wiley.

DIGMAN, J. M., 1962. The dimensionality of social attitudes. *J. Social Psychol.,* **57**, 433–444.

DILEO, J. H., 1970. *Young children and their drawings.* New York: Brunner-Mazel.

DION, K. L., BARON, R. S., & MILLER, N., 1970. Why do groups make riskier decisions than individuals? In L. Berkowitz (Ed.), *Advances in experimental social psychology.* New York: Academic.

DITTES, J. E., 1959. Effect of changes in self-esteem upon impulsiveness and deliberation in making judgments. *J. Abnormal & Social Psychol.,* **58,** 348–356.

DIVESTA, F. J., 1965. The developmental patterns in the use of modifiers as modes of conceptualization, *Child Develop.,* **36,** 185–213.

DIVESTA, F. J., 1966. A normative study of 220 concepts rated on the semantic differential by children in grades 2 through 7. *J. Genet. Psychol.,* **109,** 205–229.

DIVESTA, F. J., & INGERSOLL, G. M., 1969. Influence of pronounceability, articulation, and test mode on paired-associate learning by the study-recall procedure. *J. Exptl. Psychol.,* **79,** 104–108.

DIVESTA, F. J., & STOVER, D., 1962. Semantic mediation of evaluative meaning. *J. Exptl. Psychol.,* **64,** 467–475.

DODD, D. H., & BOURNE, L. E., Jr., 1969. Test of some assumptions of a hypothesis-testing model of concept identification. *J. Exptl. Psychol.,* **80,** 69–72.

DODWELL, P. C., 1962. Relations between the understanding of the logic of classes and of cardinal number in children. *Can. J. Psychol.,* **16,** 152–160.

DODWELL, P. C., 1963. Children's understanding of spatial concepts. *Can. J. Psychol.,* **17,** 141–161.

DOLLARD, J., DOOB, L. W., MILLER, N. E., MOWRER, O. H. & SEARS, R. R., et al., 1939. *Frustration and aggression.* New Haven, Conn.: Yale.

DOMHOFF, B., 1967. Home dreams versus laboratory dreams: Home dreams are better. In M. Kramer, *Dream psychology and the new biology of dreaming.* Springfield, Ill.: Charles C. Thomas.

DOMINOWSKI, R. L., 1965. Role of memory in concept learning. *Psychol. Bull.,* **63,** 271–280.

DOMINOWSKI, R. L., 1967. Anagram solving as a function of bigram rank and word frequency. *J. Exptl. Psychol.,* **75,** 299–306.

DOMINOWSKI, R. L., 1968. Anagram solving as a function of letter-sequence information. *J. Exptl. Psychol.,* **76,** 78–83.

DOMINOWSKI, R. L., & EKSTRAND, B. R., 1967. Direct and associative priming in anagram solving. *J. Exptl. Psychol.,* **74,** 84–86.

DONAHOE, J. W., 1961. Change in meaning as a function of size. *J. Genet. Psychol.,* **99,** 23–28.

DONALDSON, M., 1959. Positive and negative information in matching problems. *Brit. J. Psychol.,* **50,** 253–262.

DOOB, L. W., 1966. Eidetic imagery: A cross-cultural will-o'-the-wisp? *J. Psychol.,* **63,** 13–34.

DREHER, R. E., 1968. Esthetic responses to paintings: As originals, Kodachrome prints, and black-and-white photographs. *Proc. APA Conv.,* **3,** 451–452.

DREVDAHL, J. E., 1956. Factors of importance for creativity. *J. Clin. Psychol.,* **12,** 21–26.

DuBOIS, C., 1944. *The people of Alor.* Minneapolis: University of Minnesota Press.

DUNCAN, C. P., 1959. Recent research on human problem solving. *Psychol. Bull.,* **56,** 397–429.

DUNCAN, C. P., 1961. Attempts to influence performance in an insight problem. *Psychol. Repts.,* **9,** 35–42.

DUNCKER, K., 1926. A qualitative (experimental and theoretical) study of productive thinking (solving of comprehensible problems). *J. Genet. Psychol.,* **33,** 642–708.

DUNCKER, K., 1945. On problem-solving. *Psychol. Monographs,* No. 270.

DUNN, R. F., 1968. Anxiety and verbal concept learning. *J. Exptl. Psychol.,* **76,** 286–290.

DUNNETTE, M. D., CAMPBELL, J., & JAASTAD, K., 1963. The effect of group participation on brainstorming effectiveness for two industrial samples. *J. Appl. Psychol.,* **47,** 30–37.

DURAN, P., Jr., 1969. Imagery and blindness: A personal report. *J. Humanistic Psychol.,* **9,** 155–166.

DURKIN, H. E., 1937. Trial-and-error, gradual analysis, and sudden reorganization: An experimental study of problem-solving. *Arch. Psychol.,* No. 210.

D'ZURILLA, T. J., 1965. Recall efficiency and mediating cognitive events in "experimental repression." *J. Personality & Social Psychol.,* **1,** 253–257.

EAGLE, M., 1959. The effects of subliminal stimuli of aggressive content upon conscious cognition. *J. Personality,* **27,** 578–600.

EARHARD, B. & EARHARD, M., 1967. Role of interference factors in three-stage mediation paradigms. *J. Exptl. Psychol.,* **73,** 526–531.

EARHARD, B., & EARHARD, M., 1968. Interference, strategies, and the mechanism of mediation. *J. Exptl. Psychol.,* **78,** 216–227.

EASTERBROOK, J. A., 1959. The effect of emotion on cue utilization and the organization of behavior. *Psychol. Rev.,* **66,** 183–201.

EDDY, E. M., 1964. Attitudes towards desegregation among Southern students on a Northern campus. *J. Social Psychol.,* **62,** 285–301.

EHRENFREUND, D., 1948. An experimental test of the continuity theory of discrimination learning with pattern vision. *J. Comp. & Physiol. Psychol.,* **41,** 408–422.

EHRLICH, H. J., & LEE, D., 1969. Dogmatism, learning, and resistance to change: A review and a new paradigm. *Psychol. Bull.,* **71,** 249–260.

EIDUSON, B. T., 1958. Artist and nonartist: A comparative study. *J. Personality,* **26,** 13–28.

EIDUSON, B. T., 1959. Structural analysis of dreams: Clues to perceptual style. *J. Abnormal & Social Psychol.,* **58,** 335–339.

EIMAS, P. D., 1966. Effects of overtraining and age on intradimensional and extradimensional shifts in children. *J. Exptl. Child Psychol.,* **3,** 348–355.

EINDHOVEN, J., & VINACKE, W. E., 1952. Creative processes in painting. *J. Gen. Psychol.,* **47,** 139–164.

EISENMAN, R., & ROBINSON, N., 1967. Complexity-simplicity, creativity, intelligence, and other correlates. *J. Psychol.,* **67,** 331–334.

EISER, J. R., 1971a. Comment on Ward's "Attitude and involvement in the absolute judgment of attitude statements." *J. Personality & Social Psychol.,* **17,** 81–83.

EISER, J. R., 1971b. Enhancement of contrast in the absolute judgment of attitude statements. *J. Personality & Social Psychol.,* **17,** 1–10.

EKSTRAND, B. R., & DOMINOWSKI, R. L., 1968. Solving words as anagrams: II. A clarification. *J. Exptl. Psychol.,* **77,** 552–558.

ELKIND, D., 1961a. Children's discovery of the conservation of mass, weight, and volume: Piaget replication study II. *J. Genet. Psychol.,* **98,** 219–227.

ELKIND, D., 1961b. The child's conception of his religious denomination: I. The Jewish child. *J. Genet. Psychol.,* **99,** 209–225.

ELKIND, D., 1961c. The development of the additive composition of classes in the child: Piaget replication study III. *J. Genet. Psychol.,* **99,** 51–57.

ELKIND, D., 1961d. The development of quantitative thinking: A systematic replication of Piaget's studies. *J. Genet. Psychol.,* **98,** 37–46.

ELKIND, D., 1962a. Children's conceptions of brother and sister: Piaget replication study V. *J. Genet. Psychol.,* **100,** 129–136.

ELKIND, D., 1962b. The child's conception of his religious denomination: II. The Catholic child. *J. Genet. Psychol.,* **101,** 185–193.

ELKIND, D., 1962c. Quantity conceptions in college students. *J. Social Psychol.,* **57,** 459–465.

ELKIND, D., 1963. The child's conception of his religious denomination: III. The Protestant child. *J. Genet. Psychol.,* **103,** 291–304.

ELKIND, D., KOEGLER, R. R., & GO, E., 1963. Field independence and concept formation. *Perceptual & Motor Skills,* **17,** 383–386.

ELLIOTT, J. M., 1964. Measuring creative abilities in public relations and in advertising work. In C. W. Taylor (Ed.), *Widening horizons in creativity.* New York: Wiley.

ELLSON, D., 1941. Hallucinations produced by sensory conditioning. *J. Exptl. Psychol.,* **28,** 1–20.

ELMS, A. C., 1967. Role playing, incentive, and dissonance. *Psychol. Bull.,* **68,** 132–148.

ELMS, A. C., & MILGRAM, S., 1966. Personality characteristics associated with obedience and defiance toward authoritative command. *J. Exptl. Res. Personality,* **1,** 282–289.

ENGLISH, H. B., 1922. An experimental study of certain initial phases of the process of abstraction. *Am. J. Psychol.,* **33,** 305–350.

EPHRON, H. S., & CARRINGTON, P., 1966. Rapid eye movement sleep and cortical homeostasis. *Psychol. Rev.,* **73,** 500–526.

EPSTEIN, W., ROCK, I., & ZUCKERMAN, C. B., 1960. Meaning and familiarity in associative learning. *Psychol. Monographs,* **74** (4, Whole No. 491).

EPSTEIN, Y. M., & HORNSTEIN, H. A., 1969. Penalty and interpersonal attraction as factors influencing the decision to help another person. *J. Exptl. Social Psychol.,* **5,** 272–282.

ERICKSON, J. R., & ZAJKOWSKI, M. M., 1967. Learning several concept-identification problems concurrently: A test of the sampling with replacement hypothesis. *J. Exptl. Psychol.,* **74,** 212–218.

ERICKSON, J. R., ZAJKOWSKI, M. M., & EHMANN, E. P., 1966. All-or-none assumptions in concept identification: Analysis of latency data. *J. Exptl. Psychol.,* **72,** 690–697.

ERIKSEN, C. W., 1958. Unconscious processes. In M. R. Jones (Ed.), *Nebraska symposium on motivation.* Lincoln, Neb.: University of Nebraska Press.

ERIKSEN, C. W., & BROWNE, C. T., 1956. An experimental and theoretical analysis of perceptual defense. *J. Abnormal & Social Psychol.,* **52,** 224–230.

ERIKSEN, C. W., & PIERCE, J., 1968. Defense mechanisms. In E. F. Borgatta & W. W. Lambert (Eds.), *Handbook of personality research and theory.* Chicago: Rand McNally.

ERIKSON, J. R., 1968. Hypothesis sampling in concept identification. *J. Exptl. Psychol.,* **76,** 12–18.

ERNST, R. L., 1967. Effect of the number of alternative response choices on transfer and retention of verbal maze learning. *J. Exptl. Psychol.,* **75,** 472–478.

ERVIN, S. M., & FOSTER, G., 1960. The development of meaning in children's descriptive terms. *J. Abnormal & Social Psychol.*, **61**, 271–275.

ESPOSITO, N. J., & PELTON, L. H., 1971. Review of the measurement of semantic satiation. *Psychol. Bull.*, **75**, 330–346.

ESTES, B. W., 1956. Some mathematical and logical concepts in children. *J. Genet. Psychol.*, **88**, 219–222.

ESTES, W. K., 1960. Learning theory and the new mental chemistry. *Psychol. Rev.*, **67**, 207–223.

ESTES, W. K., 1964. All-or-none processes in learning and retention. *Am. Psychologist*, **19**, 16–25.

EWART, P. H., & LAMBERT, J. F., 1932. The effect of verbal instructions upon the formation of a concept. *J. Gen. Psychol.*, **6**, 400–413.

EYSENCK, H. J.. 1947. Primary social attitudes: I. The organization and measurement of social attitudes. *Intern. J. Opinion Attitude Res.*, **1**, 49–84.

FAIRBAIRN, W. R. D., 1938. Prolegomena to a psychology of art. *Brit. J. Psychol.*, **28**, 288–303.

FALLON, D., & BATTIG, W. F., 1964. Role of difficulty in rote and concept learning. *J. Exptl. Psychol.*, **68**, 85–88.

FALMAGNE, R., 1968. A direct investigation of hypothesis-making behavior in concept identification. *Psychonomic Sci.*, **13**, 335–336.

FAUCHEUX, C., & MOSCOVICI, S., 1958. Études sur la créativité des groupes: I. Tache, situation individuelle et groupe. *Bull. Psychol.*, **11**, 863–874.

FAUST, W. L., 1959. Group versus individual problem-solving. *J. Abnormal & Social Psychol.*, **59** 68–72.

FEATHER, N. T., 1969. Cognitive differentiation, attitude strength, and dogmatism. *J. Personality*, **37**, 111–126.

FEIFEL, H., & LORGE, I., 1950. Qualitative differences in the vocabulary responses of children. *J. Educ. Psychol.*, **41**, 1–18.

FEIGL, H. 1959. Philosophical embarrassments of psychology. *Am. Psychologist*, **14**, 115–128.

FELDMAN, R. E., 1968. Response to compatriot and foreigner who seek assistance. *J. Personality & Social Psychol.*, **10**, 202–214.

FENDRICH, J. M., 1967. Perceived reference group support: Racial attitudes and overt behavior. *Am. Sociological Rev.*, **32**, 960–970.

FENICHEL, O.. 1945. *The psychoanalytic theory of neurosis.* New York: Norton.

FERGUSON. L. W., 1939. Primary social attitudes. *J. Psychol.*, **8**, 217–223.

FERGUSON, L. W., 1940. The measurement of primary social attitudes. *J. Psychol.*, **10**, 199–205.

FERGUSON, L. W., 1942. The isolation and measurement of nationalism. *J. Social Psychol.*, **16**, 215–228.

FERGUSON, L. W., 1952. *Personality measurement.* New York: McGraw-Hill.

FESHBACH, S., & SINGER, R. D., 1957a. The effects of fear arousal and suppression of fear upon social perception. *J. Abnormal & Social Psychol.*, **55**, 283-288.

FESHBACH, S., & SINGER, R. D., 1957b. The effects of personal and shared threats upon social prejudice. *J. Abnormal & Social Psychol.*, **54**, 411–416.

FESTINGER, L., 1957. *A theory* of *cognitive dissonance.* Stanford, Calif.: Stanford.

FESTINGER, L., & CARLSMITH, J. M., 1959. Cognitive consequences of forced compliance. *J. Abnormal & Social Psychol.*, **58**, 203–210.

FILLENBAUM, S., 1963. Verbal satiation and changes in meaning of related items. *J. Verbal Learning & Verbal Behavior,* **2**, 263–271.

FILLENBAUM, S., 1964a. Dogmatism and individual differences in reduction of dissonance. *Psychol. Repts.,* **14**, 47–50.

FILLENBAUM. S., 1964b. Semantic satiation and decision latency. *J. Exptl., Psychol.,* **68**, 240–244.

FINDLAY, D. C., & McGUIRE, C., 1957. Social status and abstract behavior *J. Abnormal & Social Psychol.,* **54**, 135–137.

FISCHER, W. F., 1963. Sharing in preschool children as a function of amount and type of reinforcement. *Genet. Psychol. Monographs,* **68**, 215–245.

FISHER, S. C., 1916. The process of generalizing abstraction, and its products: The general concept. *Psychol. Monographs,* No. 90.

FITTS, P. M., & BIEDERMAN, I., 1965. S-R compatibility and information reduction. *J. Exptl. Psychol.,* **69**, 408–412.

FITZGERALD, E. T., 1966. Measurement of openness to experience: A study of regression in the service of the ego. *J. Personality & Social Psychol.,* **4**, 655–663.

FLANDERS, J. P., 1968. A review of research on imitative behavior. *Psychol. Bull.,* **69**, 316–337.

FLANDERS, J. P., & THISTLETHWAITE, D. L., 1967. Effects of familiarization and group discussion upon risk-taking. *J. Personality & Social Psychol.,* **5**, 91–97.

FLAVELL, J. H., 1963. *The developmental psychology of Jean Piaget.* Princeton, N.J.: Van Nostrand.

FLAVELL, J. H., & WOHLWILL, J. F., 1969. Formal and functional aspects of cognitive development. In D. Elkind & J. H. Flavell (Eds.), *Studies in cognitive development: Essays in honor of Jean Piaget.* New York: Oxford.

FOLEY, J. P., Jr., & COFER, C. N., 1943. Mediated generalization and the interpretation of verbal behavior: II. Experimental study of certain homophone and synonym gradients. *J. Exptl. Psychol.,* **32**, 168–175.

FOLEY, J. P., Jr. & MacMILLAN, Z. L., 1943. Mediated generalization and the interpretation of verbal behavior: V. "Free association" as related to differences in professional training. *J. Exptl. Psychology,* **33**, 299–310.

FOLEY, J. P., Jr., & MATHEWS, M., 1943. Mediated generalization and the interpretation of verbal behavior: IV. Experimental study of the development of interlinguistic synonym gradients. *J. Exptl. Psychol.,* **33**, 188–200.

FORD, L. H., Jr., 1970. Predictive versus perceptual responses to Piaget's waterline task and their relation to distance conservation. *Child Develop.,* **41**, 193–204.

FORGUS, R. H., & SCHWARTZ, R. J., 1957. Efficient retention and transfer as affected by learning method. *J. Psychol.,* **43**, 135–139.

FORSTER, N. C., VINACKE, W. E., & DIGMAN, J. A., 1955. Flexibility and rigidity in a variety of problem situations. *J. Abnormal & Social Psychol.,* **50**, 211–216.

FORWARD, J. R. & WILLIAMS, J. R., 1970. Internal-external control and Black militancy. *J. Social Issues,* **26**, 75–92.

FOULKES, D., 1964. Theories of dream formation and recent studies of sleep consciousness. *Psychol. Bull.,* **62**, 236–247.

FOULKES. D., 1966. *The psychology of sleep.* New York: Scribners.

FOULKES, D., & FOULKES, S. H., 1965. Self-concept, dogmatism, and tolerance of trait inconsistency. *J. Personality & Social Psychol.,* **2**, 104–111.

FOULKES, W. D., 1962. Dream reports from different stages of sleep. *J. Abnormal & Social Psychol.,* **65**, 14–25.

FOWLER, W., 1962. Cognitive learning in infancy and early childhood. *Psychol. Bull.,* **59**, 116–152.

FRANK, L. K., 1939. Projective methods for the study of personality. *J. Psychol.,* **8**, 389–413.

FRANKL, V., 1966. Self-transcendence as a human phenomenon. *J. Humanistic Psychol.,* **6**, 97–106.

FRANKMANN, J. P., & ADAMS, J. A., 1962. Theories of vigilance. *Psychol. Bull.,* **59**, 257–272.

FRASE, L. T., 1968a. Associative factors in syllogistic reasoning. *J. Exptl. Psychol.,* **76**, 407–412.

FRASE, L. T., 1968b. Effects of semantic incompatibility upon deductive reasoning. *Psychonomic Sci.,* **12**, 64.

FREEDMAN, J. L., 1965a. Increasing creativity by free-association training. *J. Exptl. Psychol.,* **69**, 89–91.

FREEDMAN, J. L., 1965b. Preference for dissonant information. *J. Personality & Social Psychol.,* **2**, 287–289.

FREEDMAN, J. L., WALLINGTON, S. A., & BLESS, E., 1967. Compliance without pressure: The effect of guilt. *J. Personality & Social Psychol.,* **7**, 117–124.

FREIBERGS, V., & TULVING, E., 1961. The effect of practice on utilization of information from positive and negative instances in concept identification. *Can. J. Psychol.,* **15**, 101–106.

FRENCH, E., 1958. Effects of the interaction of motivation and feedback on task performance. In J. W. Atkinson (Ed.), *Motives in fantasy, action, and society.* Princeton, N. J.: Van Nostrand.

FRENCH, E. G., & LESSER, G. S., 1964. Some characteristics of the achievement motive in women. *J. Abnormal & Social Psychol.,* **68**, 119–128.

FRENCH, E. G., & THOMAS, F. H., 1958. The relation of achievement motivation to problem-solving effectiveness. *J. Abnormal & Social Psychol.,* **56**, 45–48.

FRENCH, T. M., 1954. *Integration of behavior.* Vol. 2. *The integrative process in dreams.* Chicago: The University of Chicago Press.

FRENKEL-BRUNSWIK, E., 1939. Mechanisms of self-deception. *J. Social Psychol.,* **10**, 409–420.

FREUD, A., 1937. *The ego and the mechanisms of defense.* London: Hogarth.

FREUD, S., 1938. *The interpretation of dreams.* New York: Modern Library. (First German edition, 1900).

FREUD, S., 1947. *Leonardo da Vinci.* New York: Random House. (First German edition, 1910).

FREUD, S. 1961. *Civilization and its discontents.* New York: Norton. (First German edition, 1930).

FRYATT, M. J., & TULVING, E., 1963. Interproblem transfer in identification of concepts involving positive and negative instances. *Can. J. Psychol.,* **17**, 106–117.

FURTH, H. G., 1961. The influence of language on the development of concept formation in deaf children. *J. Abnormal & Social Psychol.,* **63**, 386–389.

GAGNÉ, R. M., 1965. *The conditions of learning.* New York: Holt.

GAGNÉ, R. M., 1968. Contributions of learning to human development. *Psychol. Rev.,* **75**, 177–191.

GAGNÉ, R. M., & BROWN, L. T., 1961. Some factors in the programming of conceptual learning. *J. Exptl. Psychol.,* **62**, 313–321.

GAGNÉ, R. M., & SMITH, E. C., Jr., 1962. A study of the effects of verbalization on problem solving. *J. Exptl. Psychol.*, **63**, 12–18.

GALANTER, E., 1962. Contemporary psychophysics. In R. Brown, E. Galanter, E. H. Hess, & G. Mandler (Eds.), *New directions in psychology*. New York: Holt.

GALL, M., & MENDELSOHN, G. A., 1967. Effects of facilitating techniques and subject-experimenter interaction on creative problem solving. *J. Personality & Social Psychol.*, **5**, 211–216.

GAMBLE, K. R., & KELLNER, H., 1968. Creative functioning and cognitive regression. *J. Personality & Social Psychol.*, **9,** 266–271.

GAMPEL, D. H., 1966. Temporal factors in verbal satiation. *J. Exptl. Psychol.*, **72**, 201–206.

GARDNER, R., HOLZMAN, P. S., KLEIN, G. S., LINTON, H., & SPENCE, D. P., 1959. *Cognitive control: A study of individual consistencies in cognitive behavior. Psychological Issues.* **1**, No. 4. New York: International Universities Press, Inc.

GARDNER, R. A., & RUNQUIST, W. N., 1958. Acquisition and extinction of problem-solving set. *J. Exptl. Psychol.*, **55,** 274–277.

GARDNER, R. W., & SCHOEN, R. A.,1962. Differentiation and abstraction in concept formation. *Psychol. Monographs,* **76**, (41, Whole No. 560).

GARDNER, W. R., 1962. *Uncertainty and structure as psychological concepts.* New York: Wiley.

GARTLEY, W., & BERNASCINI, M., 1969. The concept of death in children. *J. Genet. Psychol.,* **110**, 71–86.

GARWOOD, D. S., 1964. Personality factors related to creativity in young scientists. *J. Abnormal & Social Psychol.*, **68**, 413–419.

GAVURIN, E. I., 1967. Anagram solving under conditions of letter order randomization. *J. Psychol.*, **65**, 179–182.

GELLERMAN, L. W., 1931. The double alternation problem. I. The behavior of monkeys in a double alternation temporal maze. II. The behavior of children and adults in a double alternation temporal maze. III. The behavior of monkeys in a double alternation box-apparatus. *J. Genet. Psychol.*, **39**, 50–72, 197–226, 359–392.

GELLERT, E., 1962. Children's conceptions of the content and functioning of the human body, *Genet. Psychol. Monographs*, **65**, 293–405.

GERARD, H. B., 1967. Compliance, expectation of reward, and opinion change. *J. Personality & Social Psychol.*, **6**, 360–364.

GERARD, H. B., & FLEISCHER, L., 1967. Recall and pleasantness of balanced and unbalanced cognitive structures. *J. Personality & Social Psychol.*, **7**, 332–337.

GETTYS, V. S. & GETTYS, C. F., 1968. Hypothesis sampling in successive solutions of a concept-ID task. *Psychonomic Sci.*, **10**, 121–122.

GETZELS, J. W., & JACKSON, P. W., 1962. *Creativity and intelligence: Explorations with gifted students.* New York: Wiley.

GIBSON, D., & HALL, M. K., 1966. Cardiovascular change and mental task gradient. *Psychonomic Sci.*, **6**, 245–246.

GIDDAN, N. S., 1967. Recovery through images of briefly flashed stimuli. *J. Personality*, **35**, 1–19.

GILBERT, G. M., 1947. *Nuremberg diary.* New York: Farrar, Straus.

GILBERT, G. M., 1951. Stereotype persistence and change among college students. *J. Abnormal & Social Psychol.*, **46**, 245–254.

GILCHRIST, J. C., and NESBERG, L. S., 1952. Need and perceptual change in need-related objects. *J. Exptl. Psychol.*, **44**, 369–376.

GILSON, C., & ABELSON, R. P., **1965**. The subjective use of inductive evidence. *J. Personality & Social Psychol.*, **2**, 301–310.

GLASSCO, J. A., MILGRAM, N. A., & YOUNISS, J., 1970. Stability of training effects on intentionality in moral judgment in children. *J. Personality & Social Psychol.*, **14**, 360–365.

GLAZE, J. A., 1928. The association value of nonsense syllables. *J. Genet. Psychol.*, **35**, 255–269.

GLICK, J., & WAPNER, S., 1968. Development of transitivity: Some findings and problems of analysis. *Child Develop.*, **39**, 621–637.

GLIXMAN, A. F., 1965. Categorizing behavior as a function of meaning domain. *J. Personality & Social Psychol.*, **2**, 370–377.

GLIXMAN, A. F., & WOLFE, J. C., 1967. Category membership and interitem semantic-space distances. *J. Personality,* **35**, 134–144.

GLUCKSBERG, S., 1964. Problem solving: Response competition and the influence of drive. *Psychol. Repts.,* **15**, 939–942.

GLUCKSBERG, S., & DANKS, J. H., 1968. Effects of discriminative labels and of nonsense labels upon availability of novel function. *J. Verbal Learning & Verbal Behavior,* **7**, 72–76.

GLUCKSBERG, S., & KING, L. J., 1967. Motivated forgetting mediated by implicit verbal chaining: A laboratory analog of repression. *Science,* **158**, 517–519.

GLUCKSBERG, S., & WEISBERG, R. W., 1966. Verbal behavior and problem solving: Some effects of labeling in a functional fixedness problem. *J. Exptl. Psychol.,* **71**, 659–664.

GOLANN, S. E., 1962. The creativity motive. *J. Personality,* **30**, 588–600.

GOLDBERGER, L., & HOLT, R. R., 1961. Experimental interference with reality contact: Individual differences. In P. Solomon et al., *Sensory deprivation.* Cambridge, Mass.: Harvard.

GOLDIAMOND. I., 1958. Indicators of perception: I. Subliminal perception, subception, unconscious perception: An analysis in terms of psychological indicator methodology. *Psychol. Bull.,* **55**, 373–411.

GOLDSTEIN, K., & SCHEERER, M., 1941. Abstract and concrete behavior: An experimental study with special tests. *Psychol. Monographs,* **53** (2, Whole No. 239).

GOODENOUGH, D. R., LEWIS, H. B., SHAPIRO, A., JARET, L., & SLESER, I., 1965. Dream reporting following abrupt and gradual awakenings from different types of sleep. *J. Personality & Social Psychol.,* **2**, 170–179.

GOODENOUGH, D. R., SHAPIRO, A., HOLDEN, M., & STEINSCHRIBER, L., 1959. A comparison of "dreamers" and "nondreamers": Eye movements, electroencephalograms, and the recall of dreams. *J. Abnormal & Social Psychol.,* **59**, 295–307.

GOODNOW, J. J., 1962. A test of milieu effects with some of Piaget's tasks. *Psychol. Monographs,* **76** (36, Whole No. 555).

GOODNOW, J. J., & PETTIGREW, T. F., 1956. Some sources of difficulty in solving simple problems. *J. Exptl. Psychol.,* **51**, 385–392.

GOODNOW, J. J., & POSTMAN, L., 1955. Probability learning in a problem-solving situation. *J. Exptl. Psychol.,* **49**, 16–22.

GOODSTEIN, L. D., 1953. Intellectual rigidity and social attitudes. *J. Abnormal & Social Psychol.,* **48**, 345–353.

GORDON, J. E., 1957. Interpersonal predictions of repressors and sensitizers. *J. Personality,* **25**, 686–698.

GORMAN, A. M., 1961. Recognition memory for nouns as a function of abstractness and frequency. *J. Exptl. Psychol.,* **61**, 23–29.

GOSS. A. E., 1961. Verbal mediating responses and concept formation. *Psychol. Rev.,* **68**, 248–274.

GOSS, A. E., & NODINE, C. F., 1965. *Paired-associates learning: The role of meaningfulness, similarity, and familiarization.* New York: Academic.

GOUGH, H. G., 1960. The adjective check list as a personality research technique. *Psychol. Repts. Monograph Suppl.,* **2**, (6), 107–122.

GOUGH, H. G., 1961. Techniques for identifying the creative research scientist. In *Conference on the creative person.* Berkeley: University of California Institute of Personality Assessment and Research.

GRAETZ. H. R., 1963. *The symbolic language of Vincent van Gogh.* New York: McGraw-Hill.

GRANT, D. A., 1951. Perceptual vs. analytical responses to the number concept of a Weigl-type card sorting test. *J. Exptl. Psychol.,* **41**, 23–29.

GRANT, D. A., & BERG, E. A., 1948. A behavioral analysis of degree of reinforcement and ease of shifting to new responses in a Weigl-type card sorting problem. *J. Exptl. Psychol.,* **38**, 404–411.

GRANT, D. A., & COST, J. R., 1954. Continuities and discontinuities in conceptual behavior in a card-sorting problem. *J. Gen. Psychol.,* **50**, 237–244.

GRANT, D. A., JONES, O. E., & TALLANTIS, B., 1949. The relative difficulty of the number, form, and color concepts of a Weigl-type problem. *J. Exptl. Psychol.,* **39**, 552–557.

GREEN, R. F., & GOLDFRIED, M. R., 1965. On the bipolarity of semantic space. *Psychol. Monographs,* **79** (6, Whole No. 599).

GREENACRE, P., 1959. Play in relation to creative imagination. *Psychoanal. Study Child,* **14**, 61–80.

GREENFIELD, P. M., 1966. On culture and conservation. In J. S. Bruner, R. R. Olver, P. M. Greenfield et al., *Studies in cognitive growth.* New York: Wiley.

GREENFIELD, P. M., REICH, L. C., & OLVER, R. R., 1966. On culture and equivalence: II. In J. S. Bruner, R. R. Olver, P. M. Greenfield et al., *Studies in cognitive growth.* New York: Wiley.

GREGG, L. W., 1967. Internal representations of sequential concepts. In B. Kleinmuntz (Ed.), *Concepts and the structure of memory.* New York, Wiley.:

GRIFFITHS, R., 1935. *A study of imagination in early childhood.* London: Kegan Paul, Trench, Trubner & Co., Ltd.

GRIGSBY, O. J., 1932. An experimental study of the development of concepts of relationship in preschool children as evidenced by their expressive ability. *J. Exptl. Educ.,* **1**, 144–162.

GRIM, P. F., KOHLBERG L., & WHITE, S. H., 1968. Some relationships between conscience and attentional processes. *J. Personality & Social Psychol.,* **8**, 239–252.

GRINDER, R. E., 1961. New techniques for research in children's temptation behavior. *Child Develop.,* **32**, 679–688.

GRINDER, R. E., 1962. Parental childrearing practices, conscience, and resistance to temptation of sixth-grade children. *Child Develop.,* **33**, 803–820.

GRINDER, R. E. 1964. Relations between behavioral and cognitive dimensions of conscience in middle childhood. *Child Develop.,* **35**, 881–891.

GRINDER, R. E., & McMICHAEL, R. E., 1963. Cultural influence on conscience development: Resistance to temptation and guilt among Samoans and American Caucasians. *J. Abnormal & Social Psychol.,* **66**, 503–507.

GRUEN, G. E., 1965. Experiences affecting the development of number conservation in children. *Child Develop.,* **36**, 963–979.

GRUSEC, J., 1966. Some antecedents of self-criticism. *J. Personality & Social Psychol.,* **4**, 244–252.

GRUSEC, J., & MISCHEL, W., 1966. Model's characteristics as determinants of social learning. *J. Personality & Social Psychol.,* **4**, 211–215.

GUANELLA, F. M., 1934. Block building activities of young children. *Arch. Psychol.,* No. 174.

GUETZKOW, H., 1951. An analysis of the operation of set in problem solving behavior. *J. Gen. Psychol.,* **45**, 219–244.

GUILFORD, J. P., 1957. Creative abilities in the arts. *Psychol. Rev.,* **64**, 110–118.

GUILFORD, J. P., 1960. Basic conceptual problems in the psychology of thinking. In E. Harms (Ed.), *Fundamentals of psychology: The psychology of thinking.* Vol. 91. New York: New York Academy of Science Annals.

GUILFORD, J. P., 1967. *The nature of human intelligence.* New York: McGraw-Hill.

GUILFORD, J. P., KETTNER, N. W., & CHRISTENSEN, P. R., 1956. The nature of the general reasoning factor. *Psychol. Rev.,* **63**, 169–172.

GUMENIK, W. E., & PERLMUTTER, E. S., 1966. Verbal repetition, set, and decision latency. *J. Exptl. Psychol.,* **72**, 213–215.

GUTHRIE, E. R., & HORTON, G. P., 1946. *Cats in a puzzle box.* New York: Rinehart.

GUTHRIE, G., & WIENER, M., 1966. Subliminal perception or perception of partial cue with pictorial stimuli. *J. Personality & Social Psychol.,* **3**, 619–628.

GUTTMAN, L., 1944. A basis for scaling qualitative data. *Am. Sociological Rev.,* **9**, 139–150.

GUTTMAN, L., 1950. The problem of attitude and opinion measurement. In S. A. Stouffer (Ed.), *Measurement and prediction.* Princeton, N.J.: Princeton.

GUY, D. E., 1969. Developmental study of performance on conceptual problems involving a rule shift. *J. Exptl. Psychol.,* **82**, 242–249.

GUY D. E., VAN FLEET, F. M., & BOURNE, L. E., Jr., 1966. Effects of adding a stimulus dimension prior to a nonreversal shift. *J. Exptl. Psychol.,* **72**, 161–168.

HAAN, N., SMITH, M. B., & BLOCK, J., 1968. Moral reasoning of young adults: Political-social behavior, family background, and personality correlates. *J. Personality & Social Psychol.,* **10**, 183–201.

HABER, R. N., 1969. Perception and thought: An information-processing analysis. In J. F. Voss (Ed.), *Approaches to thought.* Columbus, Ohio: Merrill.

HABER, R. N., & HABER, R. B., 1964. Eidetic imagery: I. Frequency. *Perceptual & Motor Skills,* **19**, 131–138.

HABER, W. B., 1956. Observation on phantom-limb phenomena. *AMA. Arch. Neurol. & Psychiat.,* **75**, 624–636.

HADAMARD, J., 1945. *The psychology of invention in the mathematical field.* Princeton, N.J.: Princeton.

HALL, C. S., 1953a. A cognitive theory of dream symbols. *J. Gen. Psychol.*, **48**, 169–186.

HALL, C. S., 1953b. *The meaning of dreams.* New York: Harper.

HALL, C. S., 1954. A cognitive theory of dreams. *J. Gen. Psychol.*, **49**, 273–282.

HALL, C. S., 1963. Strangers in dreams: An empirical confirmation of the Oedipus complex. *J. Personality, 31*, 336–345.

HALL, C. S., & LINDZEY, G., 1970. *Theories of personality.* (2nd ed.) New York: Wiley.

HALL, C. S., & VAN De CASTLE, R. L., 1965. An empirical investigation of the castration complex in dreams. *J. Personality, 33*, 20–29.

HALL, C. S., & VAN De CASTLE, R. L., 1966a. *The content analysis of dreams.* New York: Appleton Century Crofts.

HALL, C. S., & VAN De CASTLE, R. L., 1966b. Studies of dreams reported in the laboratory and at home. Santa Cruz, Calif.: *Inst. Dream Res. Monograph Series*, No. 1.

HALL, E. J., MOUTON, J. S., & BLAKE, R. R., 1963. Group problem solving effectiveness under conditions of pooling vs. interaction. *J. Social Psychol.*, **59**, 147–157.

HAMMER, E. F., 1964. Creativity and feminine ingredients in young male artists. *Perceptual & Motor Skills,* **19**, 414.

HAMMOND, K. R., 1948. Measuring attitudes by error-choice: An indirect method. *J. Abnormal & Social Psychol., 43*, 38–48.

HANAWALT, N. G., 1954. Recurrent images: New instances and a summary of the older ones. *Am. J. Psychol., 67*, 170–174.

HANDLON, B. J., & GROSS, P., 1959. The development of sharing behavior. *J. Abnormal & Social Psychol., 49*, 425–428.

HANFMANN, E., 1941. A study of personal patterns in an intellectual performance. *Character & Personality, 9*, 315–325.

HANFMANN, E., & KASANIN, J., 1937. A method for the study of concept formation. *J. Psychol., 3*, 521–540.

HANFMANN, E., & KASANIN, J., 1942. Conceptual thinking in schizophrenia. *Nervous-Mental Disease Monographs,* No. 67.

HANLON, T. E., HOFSTAETTER, P. R., & O'CONNOR, J. P., 1954. Congruence of self and ideal self in relation to personality adjustment. *J. Consulting Psychol., 18*, 215–218.

HARBIN, S. P., & WRIGHT, J. H., 1967. Connotative meaning in verbal learning. *J. Exptl. Psychol., 74*, 106–113.

HARDESTY, D., TRUMBO, D., & BEVAN, W., 1963. Influence of knowledge of results on performance in a monitoring task. *Perceptual & Motor Skills,* **16**, 629–634.

HARDING, J., PROSHANSKY, H., KUTNER, B., & CHEIN, I., 1969. Prejudice and ethnic relations. In G. Lindzey & E. Aronson (Eds.), *Handbook of social psychology.* Vol. 5. (2nd ed.) Reading, Mass.: Addison-Wesley.

HARLESTON, B. W., SMITH, M. G., & AREY, D., 1965. Test-anxiety level, heart rate, and anagram problem solving. *J. Personality & Social Psychol.,* **1**, 551–557.

HARLOW, H. F., 1949. The formation of learning sets. *Psychol. Rev.,* **56**, 51–65.

HARRINGTON, A. L., 1969. Effects of component emphasis on stimulus selection in paired-associate learning. *J. Exptl. Psychol., 79*, 412–418.

HARRIS, R., & LOESS, H., 1968. Anagram solution times as a function of individual differences in stored diagram frequencies. *J. Exptl. Psychol.,* **77**, 508–511.

HARROW, M., 1964. Stimulus aspects responsible for the rapid acquisition of reversal shifts in concept formation. *J. Exptl. Psychol.,* **67**, 330–334.

HARROW, M., & BUCHWALD, A. M., 1962. Reversal and nonreversal shifts in concept formation using consistent and inconsistent responses. *J. Exptl. Psychol.* **64**, 476–481.

HARROW, M., & FRIEDMAN, G. B., 1958. Comparing reversal and nonreversal shifts in concept formation with partial reinforcement controlled. *J. Exptl. Psychol.,* **55**, 592–598.

HARTLEY, R. E., FRANK, L. K., & GOLDENSON, R. M., 1952. *Understanding children's play.* New York : Columbia.

HARTLEY, R. E., & GOLDENSON, R. M., 1957. *The complete book of children's play.* New York : Crowell.

HARTMANN, H., 1964. *Essays on ego psychology: Selected problems in psycho-analytic theory.* New York : International Universities Press, Inc.

HARTSHORNE, H., & MAY, M. A., 1928. *Studies in deceit.* Vol. 1. *Studies in the nature of character.* New York : Macmillan.

HARVEY, O. J., HUNT, D. E., & SCHRODER, H. M., 1961. *Conceptual systems and personality organization.* New York : Wiley.

HAYAKAWA, S. I., 1964. *Language in thought and action* (2nd ed.). New York : Harcourt Jovanovich, Inc.

HAYES, J. R., 1965. Problem typology and the solution process. *J. Verbal Learning & Verbal Behavior,* **4**, 371–379.

HAYGOOD, R. C., 1966. The use of semantic differential dimensions in concept learning. *Psychonomic Sci.,* **5**, 305–306.

HAYGOOD, R. C., & BOURNE, L. E., Jr., 1965. Attribute- and rule-learning aspects of conceptual behavior. *Psychol. Rev.,* **72**, 175–195.

HAYGOOD, R. C., & DEVINE, J. V., 1967. Effects of composition of the positive category on concept learning. *J. Exptl. Psychol.,* **74**, 230–235.

HAYGOOD, R. C., SANDLIN, J., YODER, D. J., & DODD, D. H., 1969. Instance contiguity in disjunctive concept learning. *J. Exptl. Psychol.,* **81**, 605–607.

HAYGOOD, R. C., & STEVENSON, M., 1967. Effects of number of irrelevant dimensions in nonconjunctive concept learning. *J. Exptl. Psychol.,* **74**, 302–304.

HEBB, D. O., 1949. *The organization of behavior.* New York : Wiley.

HEBB, D. O., 1968. Concerning imagery. *Psychol. Rev.,* **75**, 466–477.

HEIDBREDER, E., 1924. An experimental study of thinking. *Arch. Psychol.,* No. 73.

HEIDBREDER, E., 1928. Problem solving in children and adults. *J. Genet. Psychol.,* **35**, 522–545.

HEIDBREDER, E., 1946. The attainment of concepts : I. Terminology and method-ology. *J. Gen Psychol.,* **35**, 173–189.

HEIDBREDER, E., 1947. III. The process. *J. Psychol.,* **24**, 93–138.

HEIDBREDER, E., 1949. VII. Conceptual achievement during card-sorting. *J. Psychol.,* **27**, 3–39.

HEIDER F., 1941. The description of the psychological environment in the work of Marcel Proust. *Character & Personality,* **9**, 295–314.

HEIDER, F., 1958. *The psychology of interpersonal relations.* New York : Wiley.

HEILBRUN, A. B., Jr., & ORR, H. K., 1966. Perceived maternal child-rearing history and subsequent motivational effects of failure. *J. Genet. Psychol.,* **109**, 75–90.

HEILBRUN, A. B., ORR, H. K., & HARRELL, S. N., 1966. Patterns of parental child bearing and subsequent vulnerability to cognitive disturbance. *J. Consulting Psychol.,* **30**, 51–59.

HEISE, D. R., 1965. Semantic differential profiles for 1000 most frequent English words. *Psychol. Monographs,* **78** (Whole No. 601).

HEISE, D. R., 1969. Some methodological issues in semantic differential research. *Psychol. Bull.,* **72**, 406–422.

HELMHOLTZ, H. VON, 1896. *Vorträge und Reden.* Vol. 1. (5th ed.) Brunswick, Germany: Friedrich Vieweg und Sohn.

HELMREICH, R., & COLLINS, B. E., 1968. Studies in forced compliance: Commitment and magnitude of inducement to comply as determinants of opinion change. *J. Personality & Social Psychol.,* **10**, 75–81.

HELSON, H., 1964. *Adaptation-level theory: An experimental and systematic approach to behavior.* New York: Harper & Row.

HELSON, R., 1967a. Personality characteristics and developmental history of creative college women. *Genet. Psychol. Monographs,* **76**, 205–256.

HELSON, R., 1967b. Sex differences in creative style. *J. Personality,* **35**, 214–233.

HELSON, R., 1968. Generality of sex differences in creative style. *J. Personality,* **36**, 33–48.

HELSON, R., & CRUTCHFIELD, R. S., 1970. Creative types in mathematics. *J. Personality,* **38**, 177–197.

HENDRICK, C., BIXENSTINE, V. E., & HAWKINS, G., 1971. Race versus belief similarity as determinants of attraction: A search for a fair test. *J. Personality & Social Psychol.,* **17**, 250–258.

HENLE, M., 1962. On the relation between logic and thinking. *Psychol. Rev.,* **69**, 366–378.

HENLE, M., & MICHAEL, M., 1956. The influence of attitudes on syllogistic reasoning. *J. Social Psychol.,* **44**, 115–127.

HENRY, N., & VOSS, J. F., 1970. Associative strength growth produced via category membership. *J. Exptl. Psychol.,* **83**, 136–140.

HERSCH, C., 1962. The cognitive functioning of the creative person: A developmental analysis. *J. Projective Tech.,* **26**, 193–200.

HESS, R. D., 1970. Social class and ethnic influences upon socialization. In P. M. Mussen (Ed.) *Carmichael's manual of child psychology.* Vol. 2. (3rd ed.). New York: Wiley.

HETHERINGTON, E. M., 1965. A developmental study of the effects of sex of the dominant parent on sex-role preference, identification, and imitation in children. *J. Personality & Social Psychol.,* **2**, 188–194.

HETHERINGTON, E. M., & FRANKIE, G., 1967. Effects of parental dominance, warmth, and conflict on imitation in children. *J. Personality & Socal Psychol.,* **6**, 119–125.

HICKS, D. J., 1965. Imitation and retention of film-mediated aggressive peer and adult models. *J. Personality & Social Psychol.,* **2**, 97–100.

HICKS, J. M., & WRIGHT, J. H., 1970. Convergent-discriminant validation and factor analysis of five scales of liberalism-conservatism. *J. Personality & Social Psychol.,* **14**, 114–120.

HILGARD, E. R., 1962a. Impulsive versus realistic thinking: An examination of the distinction between primary and secondary processes in thought. *Psychol. Bull.*, **59**, 477–488.

HILGARD, E. R., 1962b. What becomes of the input from the stimulus? In C. W. Eriksen (Ed.), *Behavior and awareness: A symposium of research and interpretation.* Durham, N.C.: Duke.

HILGARD, E. R., EDGREN, R. D., & IRVINE, R. P., 1954. Errors in transfer following learning with understanding: Further studies with Katona's card-trick experiments. *J. Exptl. Psychol.,* **47**, 457–464.

HILGARD, E. R., IRVINE, R. P., & WHIPPLE, J. E., 1953. Rote memorization, understanding, and transfer: An extension of Katona's card-trick experiments. *J. Exptl. Psychol.,* **46**, 288–292.

HILL, M. C., & ACKISS, T. D., 1945. The "insight interview" approach to race relations. *J. Social Psychol.,* **21**, 197–208.

HILLIX, W. A., LAWSON, R., & MARX, M. H., 1956. Reinforcement of components of similar patterns as factors in determining hypothesis selection in problem solving. *J. Gen. Psychol.,* **54**, 39–43.

HINTON, B. L., 1968. Environmental frustration and creative problem solving. *J. Appl. Psychol.,* **52**, 211–217.

HIRSCHENFANG, S., & BENTON, J. G., 1966. Assessment of phantom limb sensation among patients with lower extremity amputations. *J. Psychol.,* **63**, 197–199.

HOFFMAN, L. R., 1961. Conditions for creative problem solving. *J. Psychol.,* **52**, 429–444.

HOFFMAN, L. R., & MAIER, N. R. F., 1966. Social factors influencing problem solving in women. *J. Personality & Social Psychol.,* **4**, 382–390.

HOFFMAN, M. L., 1970. Moral development. In P. H. Mussen (Ed.), *Carmichael's manual of child psychology.* Vol. 2. New York: Wiley.

HOFSTAETTER, P. R., 1952. A factorial study of prejudice. *J. Personality,* **21**, 228–239.

HOLLAND, J. G., 1967. Discussion of papers. In B. Kleinmuntz (Ed.), *Concepts and the structure of memory.* New York: Wiley.

HOLLINGWORTH, H. L., 1927. *The psychology of thought.* New York: Appleton Century Crofts.

HOLMES, D. S., & SCHALLOW, J. R., 1969. Reduced recall after ego threat: Repression or response competition? *J. Personality & Social Psychol.,* **13**, 145–152.

HOLMES, J. G., & STRICKLAND, L. H., 1970. Choice, freedom, and confirmation of incentive expectancy as determinants of attitude change. *J. Personality & Social Psychol.,* **14**, 39–45.

HOLZMAN, P. S., & GARDNER, R. W., 1959. Leveling and repression. *J. Abnormal & Social Psychol.,* **59**, 151–155.

HOMANS, G. C., 1961. *Social behavior.* London: Routledge.

HORNSTEIN, H. A., FISCH, E., & HOLMES, M., 1968. Influence of a model's feeling about his behavior and his relevance as comparison other on observers' helping behavior. *J. Personality & Social Psychol.,* **10**, 222–226.

HOROWITZ, E. L., 1936. The development of attitudes toward the Negro. *Arch. Psychol.,* No. 194.

HOROWITZ, I. A., 1968. Effect of choice and locus of dependence on helping behavior. *J. Personality & Social Psychol.,* **8**, 373–376.

HORTON, D. L., & KJELDERGAARD, P. M., 1961. An experimental analysis of associative factors in mediated generalizations. *Psychol. Monographs,* **75** (11, Whole No. 515).

HOUSTON, B. K., & HODGES, W. F., 1970. Situational denial and performance under stress. *J. Personality & Social Psychol.,* **16,** 726–730.

HOVLAND, C. I., 1938. Experimental studies in rote-learning theory. III. Distribution of practice with varying speeds of syllable presentation. *J. Exptl. Psychol.,* **23,** 172–190.

HOVLAND, C. I., 1952. A "communication analysis" of concept learning. *Psychol. Rev.,* **59,** 461–472.

HOVLAND, C. I., 1960. Computer simulation of thinking. *Am. Psychologist,* **15,** 687–693.

HOVLAND, C. I., HARVEY, O. J., & SHERIF, M., 1957. Assimilation and contrast effects in communication and attitude change. *J. Abnormal & Social Psychol.,* **55,** 242–252.

HOVLAND, C. I., JANIS, I. L., & KELLEY, H. H., 1953. *Communication and persuasion.* New Haven, Conn.: Yale.

HOVLAND, C. I., & KURTZ, K. H., 1952. Experimental studies in rote-learning theory: X. Pre-learning syllable familiarization and the length-difficulty relationship. *J. Exptl. Psychol.,* **44,** 31–39.

HOVLAND, C. I., & SHERIF, M., 1952. Judgmental phenomena and scales of attitude measurement: Item displacement in Thurstone scales. *J. Abnormal & Social Psychol.,* **47,** 822–832.

HOVLAND, C. I., & WEISS, W., 1953. Transmission of information concerning concepts through positive and negative instances. *J. Exptl. Psychol.,* **45,** 175–182.

HOWES, D., 1954. A statistical theory of the phenomenon of subception *Psychol. Rev.,* **61,** 98–110.

HOWES, D., & OSGOOD, C. E., 1954. On the combination of associative probabilities in linguistic contexts. *Am. J. Psychol.,* **67,** 241–258.

HOYT, G. C., & STONER, J. A. F., 1968. Leadership and group decisions involving risk. *J. Exptl. Social Psychol.,* **4,** 275–284.

HUANG, I., 1943. Children's conception of physical causality: A critical summary. *J. Genet. Psychol.,* **63,** 71–121.

HUANG, I., & LEE, H. W., 1945. Experimental analysis of child animism. *J. Genet. Psychol.,* **66,** 69–74.

HUANG, I., YANG, H. C., & YAO, F. Y., 1945. Principle of selection in children's "phenomenistic" explanations. *J. Genet. Psychol.,* **66,** 63–68.

HULL, C. L., 1920. Quantitative aspects of the evolution of concepts. *Psychol. Monographs,* No. 123.

HULL, C. L., 1930. Knowledge and purpose as habit mechanisms. *Psychol. Rev.,* **37,** 241–256.

HULL, C. L., 1933. The meaningfulness of 320 selected nonsense syllables. *Am. J. Psychol.,* **45,** 730–734.

HULL, C. L., 1952. *A behavior system: An introduction to behavior theory concerning the individual organism.* New Haven, Conn.: Yale.

HUMPHREY, G., 1951. *Thinking: An introduction to its experimental psychology.* New York: Wiley.

HUNT, E. B., 1961. Memory effects in concept learning. *J. Exptl. Psychol.,* **62,** 598–604.

HUNT, E. B., 1962. *Concept learning: An information processing problem.* New York: Wiley.

HUNT, E. B., 1967. Utilization of memory in concept-learning systems. In B. Kleinmuntz (Ed.), *Concepts and the structure of memory.* New York: Wiley.

HUNT, E. B., & HOVLAND, C. I., 1960. Order of consideration of different types of concepts. *J. Exptl. Psychol., 59,* 220–225.

HUNT, E. B., MARIN, J., & STONE, P. J., 1966. *Experiments in induction.* New York: Academic.

HUNT, J. McV., 1961. *Intelligence and experience.* New York: Ronald Press.

HUNT, J. McV., 1969. The impact and limitations of the giant of developmental psychology. In D. Elkind & J. H. Flavell (Eds.), *Studies in cognitive development: Essays in honor of Jean Piaget.* New York: Oxford.

HUNT, M. F., Jr., & MILLER, G. R.. 1968. Open- and closed-mindedness, belief-discrepant communication behavior, and tolerance for cognitive inconsistency. *J. Personality & Social Psychol., 8,* 35–37.

HUNTER, I. M. L., 1957a. Note on an atmosphere effect in adult reasoning. *Quart. J. Exptl. Psychol., 9,* 175–176.

HUNTER, I. M. L., 1957b. The solving of three-term series problems. *Brit. J. Psychol., 48,* 286–298.

HUNTER, I. M. L., 1961. Further studies on anagram solving. *Brit. J. Psychol., 52,* 161–165.

HUNTER, W. S., & BARTLETT, S. C., 1948. Double alternation behavior in children. *J. Exptl. Psychol., 38,* 558–567.

HUPKA, R. B., & GOSS, A. E., 1969. Initial polarity, semantic differential scale, meaningfulness, and subjects' associative fluency in semantic satiation and generation. *J. Exptl. Psychol., 79,* 308–311.

HURLOCK, E. B., 1934. Experimental investigations of childhood play. *Psychol. Bull., 31,* 47–66.

HUSBAND, R. W., 1931. Analysis of methods in human maze learning. *J. Genet. Psychol., 39,* 258–278.

HUTCHINSON, E. D., 1939. Varieties of insight in humans. *Psychiatry. 2,* 323–332.

HUTCHINSON, E. D., 1940. The period of frustration. *Psychiatry, 3,* 351–359.

HUTCHINSON, E. D., 1941. The nature of insight. *Psychiatry, 4,* 31–43.

HUTCHINSON, E. D., 1942. The period of elaboration. *Psychiatry, 5,* 165–176.

HUTTENLOCHER, J., 1962. Some effects of negative instances in the formation of simple concepts. *Psychol. Repts., 11,* 35–42.

HUTTENLOCHER, J., 1968. Constructing spatial images: A strategy in reasoning. *Psychol. Rev., 75,* 550–560.

HYMAN, H. H., & SHEATSLEY, P. B., 1954. The authoritarian personality—a methodological critique. In R. Christie & M. Jahoda (Eds.), *Studies in the scope and method of "The authoritarian personality."* Glencoe, Ill.: Free Press.

INSKO, C. A., 1967. *Theories of attitude change.* New York: Appleton Century Crofts.

INSKO, C. A., & SCHOPLER, J., 1967. Triadic consistency: A statement of affective-cognitive-conative consistency. *Psychol. Rev., 74,* 361–376.

ISAACS, I. D., & DUNCAN, C. P., 1962. Reversal and nonreversal shifts within and between dimensions in concept formation. *J. Exptl. Psychol., 64,* 580–585.

IVERSON, M. A., & SCHWAB, H. G., 1967. Ethnocentric dogmatism and binocular fusion of sexually and racially discrepant stimuli. *J. Personality & Social Psychol.,* **7**, 73–81.

JACKSON, D. N., & MESSICK, S. J., 1957. A note on "ethnocentrism" and acquiescent response sets. *J. Abnormal & Social Psychol.,* **54**, 132–134.

JACKSON, P. W., & MESSICK, S., 1965. The person, the product, and the response : Conceptual problems in the assessment of creativity. *J. Personality* **33**, 309–329.

JACOBSON, E., 1931. VI. A note on mental activities concerning an amputated limb. *Am. J. Physiol.,* **96**, 122–125.

JACOBSON, E., 1932. The electrophysiology of mental activities. *Am. J. Psychol.,* **44**, 677–694.

JACOBSON, L. I., BERGER, S. E., & MILLHAM, J., 1970. Individual differences in cheating during a temptation period when confronting failure. *J. Personality & Social Psychol.,* **15**, 48–56.

JACOBSON, L. I., ELENEWSKI, J. J., LORDAHL, D. S., & LIROFF, J. H., 1968. Role of creativity and intelligence in conceptualization. *J. Personality & Social Psychol.,* **10**, 431–436.

JACOBY, L. L., & RADTKE, R. C., 1969. Effects of contiguity and meaningfulness of relevant and irrelevant attributes on concept formation. *J. Exptl. Psychol.,* **81**, 454–459.

JAENSCH, E. R. 1930. *Eidetic imagery* New York : Harcourt, Brace.

JAHODA, G., 1958a. Child animism : II. A study in West Africa. *J. Social Psychol.,* **47**, 213–222.

JAHODA, G., 1958b. Imminent justice among West African children. *J. Social Psychol.,* **47**, 241–248.

JAKOBOVITS, L. A. 1965. Semantic satiation in concept formation. *Psychol. Repts.,* **17**, 113–114.

JAKOBOVITS, L. A., 1966. Mediation theory and the "single-stage" S-R model : Different ? *Psychol. Rev.,* **73**, 376–381.

JAMES, W., 1890. *The principles of psychology.* New York : Holt.

JANIS, I. L., & FRICK, F., 1943. The relationship between attitudes toward conclusions and errors in judging logical validity of syllogisms. *J. Exptl. Psychol.,* **33**, 73–77.

JANIS, I. L. & GILMORE, J. B., 1965. The influence of incentive conditions on the success of role playing in modifying attitudes. *J. Personality & Social Psychol.,* **1**, 17–27.

JENKIN, N., 1957. Affective processes in perception. *Psychol. Bull.,* **54**, 100–127.

JENKINS, J. J., FOSS, D. J., & GREENBERG, J. H., 1968. Phonological distinctive features as cues in learning. *J. Exptl. Psychol.,* **77**, 200–205.

JENKINS, J. J., RUSSELL, W. A., & SUCI, G. J., 1958. An atlas of semantic profiles for 360 words. *Am. J. Psychol.,* **71**, 688-699.

JERSILD, A. T., MARKEY, F. V., & JERSILD, C. L., 1933. *Children's fears, dreams, wishes, daydreams, likes, dislikes, pleasant and unpleasant memories.* New York : Columbia.

JOHNSON, D. M., 1960. Serial analysis of thinking. In E. Harms (Ed.), *Fundamentals of psychology : The psychology of thinking.* Vol. 91. New York : The New York Academy of Sciences Annals.

JOHNSON, D. M., 1966. Solution of anagrams. *Psychol. Bull.,* **66**, 371–384.

JOHNSON, D. M., LINCOLN, R. E., & HALL, E. R., 1961. Amount of material and time of preparation for solving problems. *J. Psychol.,* **51**, 457–472.

JOHNSON, P. J., 1966. Factors affecting transfer in concept-identification problems. *J. Exptl. Psychol.,* **72**, 655–660.

JOHNSON, P. J., 1967. Nature of mediational responses in concept-identification problems. *J. Exptl. Psychol.,* **73**, 391–393.

JOHNSON, P. J., & WHITE, R. H., Jr., 1969. Effects of pretaining and stimulus composition on rule learning. *J. Exptl. Psychol.,* **80**, 450–454.

JOHNSON, R. C., 1962a. Reanalysis of "Meaningfulness and verbal learning". *Psychol. Rev.,* **69**, 233–238.

JOHNSON, R. C., 1962b. A study of children's moral judgments. *Child Develop.,* **33**, 327–354.

JOHNSON, R. C., THOMSON, C. W., & FRINCKE, G., 1960. Word values, word frequency, and visual duration thresholds. *Psychol. Rev.,* **67** 332–342.

JOHNSTON, R. A., 1955. The effects of achievement imagery on maze-learning performance. *J. Personality,* **24**, 145–152.

JONES, M. B., 1956. Authoritarianism and intolerance of fluctuation. *J. Abnormal & Social Psychol.,* **50**, 125–126.

JONES, M. B., 1957. The Pensacola Z Survey: A study in the measurement of authoritarian tendency. *Psychol. Monographs,* **71** (23, Whole No. 452).

JONES, R. A., 1970. Volunteering to help: The effects of choice, dependence, and anticipated dependence. *J. Personality & Social Psychol.,* **14**, 121–129.

JONES, T. D. 1939. The development of certain motor skills and play activities in young children. *Child Develop. Monographs,* No. 26.

JORDAN, N., 1953. Behavioral forces that are a function of attitudes and of cognitive organization. *Human Relations,* **6**, 273–287.

JORDAN, N., 1968. Cognitive balance as an aspect of Heider's cognitive psychology. In R. P. Abelson et al. (Eds.), *Theories of cognitive consistency: A sourcebook.* Chicago: Rand McNally.

JULIAN, J. W., & KATZ, S. B., 1968. Internal versus external control and the value of reinforcement. *J. Personality & Social Psychol.,* **8**, 89–94.

JUNG, C. G., 1956. *Two essays on analytical psychology.* New York: Meridian Books, Inc.

JUNG, J., 1968. *Verbal learning.* New York: Holt.

JUZAK, T., 1955. The effects of praise and reproof on the generalization of learned concepts. *J. Psychol.,* **39**, 329–340.

KAGAN, J., & MOSS, H.A., 1962. *Birth to Maturity   A study in psychological development.* New York: Wiley.

KAGAN, J., ROSMAN, B. L., DAY, D., ALBERT, L., & PHILLIPS, W., 1964. Information processing in the child: Significance of analytic and reflective attitudes. *Psychol. Monographs,* **78** (1, Whole No. 578).

KAHN, E., DEMENT, W., FISHER, C., & BARMACK, J. E., 1962. Incidence of color in immediately recalled dreams. *Science,* **137**, 1054–1055.

KAHN, L. A., 1951. The organization of attitudes toward the Negro as a function of education. *Psychol. Monographs,* No. 330.

KAHNEMAN, D., & PEAVLER, W. S., 1969. Incentive effects and pupillary changes in association learning. *J. Exptl. Psychol.,* **79**, 312–318.

KAHNEMAN, D., TURSKY, B., SHAPIRO, D., & CRIDER, A., 1969. Pupillary, heart rate, and skin resistance changes during a mental task. *J. Exptl. Psychol.,* **79**, 164–167.

KAMMANN, R., 1968. Associability: A study of the properties of associative ratings and the role of association in word-word learning. *J. Exptl. Psychol. Monographs,* **78** (4, Pt. 2).

KANFER, F. H., & MARSTON, A. R., 1963. Human reinforcement: Vicarious and direct. *J. Exptl. Psychol.,* **65**, 292–296.

KANUNGO, R. N., LAMBERT, W. E., & MAURER, S. M., 1962. Semantic satiation and paired-associate learning. *J. Exptl. Psychol.,* **64**, 600–607.

KAPLAN, I. T., & CARVELLAS, T., 1968. Effect of word length on anagram solution time. *J. Verbal Learning & Verbal Behavior,* **7**, 201–206.

KAPLAN, I. T., & SCHOENFELD, W. N., 1966. Oculomotor patterns during the solution of visually displayed anagrams. *J. Exptl. Psychol.,* **72**, 447–451.

KARDINER, A., 1939. *The individual and his society.* New York: Columbia.

KARDINER, A., 1945. *The psychological frontiers of society.* New York: Columbia.

KARLINS, M., 1967. Conceptual complexity and remote-associative proficiency as creativity variables in a complex problem solving task. *J. Personality & Social Psychol.,* **6**, 264–278.

KARLINS, M., COFFMAN, T., LAMM, H., & SCHRODER, H., 1967. The effect of conceptual complexity on information search in a complex problem solving task. *Psychonomic Sci.,* **7**, 137–138.

KARLINS, M., COFFMAN, T. L., & WALTERS, G., 1969. On the fading of social stereotypes: Studies in three generations of college students. *J. Personality & Social Psychol.,* **13**, 1–16.

KARLINS, M., LEE, R. E., & SCHRODER, H. M., 1967. Creativity and information search in a problem solving context. *Psychonomic Sci.,* **8**, 165–166.

KATONA, G., 1940. *Organizing and memorizing.* New York: Columbia.

KATZ, D., 1960. The functional approach to the study of attitudes. *Public Opinion Quart.,* **24**, 163–204.

KATZ, D., & BRALY, K. W., 1933. Racial stereotypes of one hundred college students. *J. Abnormal & Social Psychol.,* **28**, 280–290.

KATZ, D., & BRALY, K. W., 1935. Racial prejudice and racial streotypes. *J. Abnormal & Social Psychol.,* **30**, 175–193.

KATZ, D., & STOTLAND, E., 1959. A Preliminary statement of a theory of attitude structure and change. In S. Koch *Psychology: The study of a science.* Vol. 3, New York: McGraw-Hill.

KAUFMANN, H., & GOLDSTEIN, S., 1967. The effects of emotional value of conclusions upon distortion in syllogistic reasoning. *Psychonomic Sci.,* **7**, 367–368.

KEELE, S. W., & ARCHER, E. J., 1967. A comparison of two types of information in concept identification. *J. Verbal Learning & Verbal Behavior,* **6**, 185–192.

KELLEHER, R. T., 1965. Discrimination learning as a function of reversal and nonreversal shifts. *J. Exptl. Psychol.,* **51**, 379–384.

KELLEY, H. H., & THIBAUT, J. W., 1969. Group problem solving. In G. Lindzey & E. Aronson (Eds.), *Handbook of social psychology.* Vol. 4. (2nd ed.) Reading Mass: Addison-Wesley.

KELLOGG, R., & O'DELL, S., 1967. *The psychology of children's art.* New York: Random House.

KELLOGG, W. N., 1968. Communication and language in the home-raised chimpanzee. *Science,* **162**, 423–427.

KELLY, G. A., 1955. *The psychology of personal constructs*. Vol. 1. *A theory of personality*. New York: Norton.

KELMAN, H. C., 1961. Processes of opinion change. *Public Opinion Quart.*, **25**, 57–78.

KENDLER, H. H., & D'AMATO, M. F., 1955. A comparison of reversal shifts and nonreversal shifts in human concept formation behavior. *J. Exptl. Psychol.*, **49**, 165–174.

KENDLER, H. H., GLUCKSBERG, S., & KESTON, R., 1961. Perception and mediation in concept learning. *J. Exptl. Psychol.*, **61**, 186–191.

KENDLER, H. H., & KARASIK, A. D., 1958. Concept formation as a function of competition between response produced cues. *J. Exptl. Psychol.*, **55**, 278–283.

KENDLER, H. H., & KENDLER, T. S., 1956. Inferential behavior in preschool children. *J. Exptl. Psychol.*, **51**, 311–314.

KENDLER, H. H., & KENDLER, T. S., 1961. Effect of verbalization in reversal shifts in children. *Science,* **134**, 1619–1620.

KENDLER, H. H., & KENDLER, T. S., 1962. Vertical and horizontal processes in problem solving. *Psychol. Rev.,* **69**, 1–17.

KENDLER, H. H., KENDLER, T. S., & MARKEN, R. S., 1970. Stimulus control and memory loss in reversal shift behavior of college students. *J. Exptl. Psychol.*, **83**, 84–88.

KENDLER, H. H., KENDLER, T. S., & SANDERS, J., 1967. Reversal and partial reversal shifts with verbal materials. *J. Verbal Learning & Verbal Behavior*, **6**, 117–127.

KENDLER, H. H., & MAYZNER, M. S., Jr., 1956. Reversal and nonreversal shifts in card-sorting tests with two or four sorting categories. *J. Exptl. Psychol.*, **51**, 244–248.

KENDLER, H. H., & VINEBERG, R., 1954. The acquisition of compound concepts as a function of previous training. *J. Exptl. Psychol.,* **48,** 252–258.

KENDLER, H. H., & WATSON, G. W., 1968. Conceptual behavior as a function of associative strength between representational responses. *J. Verbal Learning & Verbal Behavior,* **7**, 321–325.

KENDLER, H. H. & WOERNER, M., 1964. Nonreinforcements of perceptual and mediating responses in concept learning. *J. Exptl. Psychol.*, **67**, 591–592.

KENDLER, T. S., 1963. Development of mediating responses in children. In J. C. Wright & J. Kagan (Eds.), Basic cognitive processes in children. *Monograph, Soc. Res. Child Develop.*, **28** (86, No. 2).

KENDLER T. S., & KENDLER, H. H., 1961. Inferential behavior in children: II. The influence of order of presentation . *J. Exptl. Psychol.*, **61**, 442–448.

KENDLER, T. S., & KENDLER, H. H., 1962. Inferential behavior in children as a function of age and subgoal constancy. *J. Exptl. Psychol.*, **64**, 460–466.

KENDLER, T. S., KENDLER H. H., & WELLS, D., 1960. Reversal and nonreversal shifts in nursery school children. *J. Comp. & Physiol. Psychol.,* **53**, 83–88.

KENISTON, K., 1963. Inburn: An American Ishmael. In R. W. White (Ed.), *The study of lives: Essays in honor of Henry A. Murray*. New York: Atherton.

KENNY, D. T., & GINSBERG, R., 1958. The specificity of intolerance of ambiguity measures. *J. Abnormal & Social Psychol.*, **56**, 300–304.

KENOYER, C. E., & PHILLIPS, J. L., 1968. Some direct tests of concept identification models. *Psychonom. Sci.,* **13**, 237–238.

KEPPEL, G., 1963. Word value and verbal learning. *J. Verbal Learning & Verbal Behavior,* **1**, 353–356.

KEPPEL, G., & MALLORY, W. A., 1969. Presentation rate and instructions to guess in free recall. *J. Exptl.. Psychol.,* **79,** 269–275.

KEPPEL, G., & REHULA, R. J., 1965. Rate of presentation in serial learning. *J. Exptl. Psychol.,* **69,** 121–125.

KERLINGER, F. N., 1967. Social attitudes and their internal referents: A structural theory. *Psychol. Rev.* **74,** 110–122.

KERR, W.A., 1944. Correlates of politico-economic liberalism-conservatism. *J. Social Psychol.,* **20,** 61–77.

KERR, W. A., 1946. *Tulane factors of liberalism-conservatism.* Chicago: Psychometric Affiliates.

KETTNER, N. W., GUILFORD, J. P., & CHRISTENSEN, P. R., 1959. A factor-analytic study across the domains of reasoning, creativity, and evaluation. *Psychol. Monographs,* **73** (9, Whole No. 479).

KILLIAN, L. M., & HAER, J. L., 1958. Variables related to attitudes regarding school desegregation among white Southerners. *Sociometry,* **21,** 159–164.

KING, D. J., 1971. Influence of interitem interval in the learning of connected discourse. *J. Exptl. Psychol.,* **87,** 132–134.

KLECK, R. E., & WHEATON, J., 1967. Dogmatism and responses to opinion-consistent and opinion-inconsistent information. *J. Personality & Social Psychol.,* **5,** 249–252.

KLEIN, G. S., 1954. Need and regulation. In M. R. Jones (Ed.), *Nebraska symposium on motivation.* Lincoln, Neb.: University of Nebraska Press.

KLEIN, G. S., 1958. Cognitive control and motivation. In G. Lindzey (Ed.), *Assessment of human motives.* New York: Rinehart.

KLEIN, G. S., SPENCE, D. P., HOLT, R. R., & GOUREVITCH, S. 1958. Cognition without awareness: Subliminal influences upon conscious thought. *J. Abnormal & Social Psychol.,* **57,** 255–266.

KLEITMAN, N., 1963. *Sleep and wakefulness.* (Rev. ed.) Chicago, Ill.: The University of Chicago Press.

KLINEBERG, O., 1950. Tensions affecting international understanding: A survey of research, *Social Sci. Res. Council Bull.,* No. 62.

KLINEBERG, S. L., 1968. Future time perspective and the preference for delayed reward. *J. Personality & Social Psychol.,* **8,** 253–257.

KLINGENSMITH, S. W., 1953. Child animism: What the child means by "alive." *Child Develop.,* **24,** 51-61.

KLINGER, E., 1969. Development of imaginative behavior: Implications of play for a theory of fantasy. *Psychol. Bull.,* **72,** 277–298.

KLUCKHOHN, C., & MOWRER, O. H., 1944. Culture and personality. *Am. Anthropologist,* **46,** 1–29.

KNIGHT, K. E., 1963. Effect of effort on behavioral rigidity in a Luchins water jar task. *J. Abnormal & Social Psychol.,* **66,** 190–192.

KOFFKA, K., 1935. *Principles of gestalt psychology.* New York: Harcourt, Brace.

KOGAN, N., & WALLACH, M., 1964. *Risk-taking: A study in cognition and personality.* New York: Holt.

KOHLBERG, L., 1967. Moral and religious education and the public schools: A developmental view. In T. R. Sizer (Ed.), *Religion and public education.* Boston: Houghton Mifflin.

KOHLBERG, L., 1969. *Stages in development of moral thought and action.* New York: Holt,

KOHLER, W., 1927. *The Mentality of apes.* New York: Harcourt, Brace.

KOMACHIYA, M., 1957. A note on concept attainment. *J. Psychol.,* **43**, 261–263.

KOULACK, D., 1972. Rapid eye movements and visual imagery during sleep. *Psychol. Bull.,* **78**, 155–158.

KREBS, D. L., 1970. Altruism—an examination of the concept and a review of the literature. *Psychol. Bull.,* **73**, 258–302.

KRECH, D., CRUTCHFIELD, R. S., & BALLACHEY, E. L., 1962. *Individual in society: A textbook of social psychology.* New York: McGraw-Hill.

KRECHEVSKY, I., 1932. "Hypotheses" in rats. *Psychol. Rev.* **39**, 516–532.

KRIPPNER, S., & HUGHES, W., 1970. Dreams and human potential. *J. Humanistic Psychol.,* **10**, 1–20.

KRIS, E., 1952. *Psychoanalytic explorations in art.* New York: International Universities Press, Inc.

KROP, H. D., ALEGRE, C. E., & WILLIAMS, C. D., 1969. Effect of induced stress on convergent and divergent thinking. *Psychol. Repts.,* **24**, 895–898.

KUO, Z. Y., 1923. A behavioristic experiment on inductive inference. *J. Exptl. Psychol.,* **6**, 247–293.

KURTZ, K. H., & HOVLAND, C. I., 1956. Concept learning with differing sequences of instances. *J. Exptl. Psychol.,* **51**, 239–243.

LACEY, H. M., 1961. Mediating verbal responses and stimulus similarity as factors in conceptual naming by school age children. *J. Exptl. Psychol.,* **62**, 113–121.

LACEY, H. M., & GOSS, A. E., 1959. Conceptual block sorting as a function of type of assignment of verbal labels and strength of labeling responses. *J. Genet. Psychol.,* **94**, 221–232.

LACEY, J. I., 1967. Somatic response patterning and stress: Some revisions of activation theory. In M. H. Appley & R. Trumbull (Eds.), *Psychological stress.* New York: Appleton Century Crofts.

LACHMAN, R., & SANDERS, J. A., 1963. Concept shifts and verbal behavior. *J. Exptl. Psychol.,* **65**, 22–29.

LACHMANN, F. M., LAPKIN, B., & HANDELMAN, N. S., 1962. The recall of dreams: Its relation to repression and cognitive control. *J. Abnormal & Social Psychol.,* **64**, 160–162.

LADD, F. E., 1967. Concept learning in relation to open- and closed-mindedness and academic aptitude. *Psychol. Repts.,* **20**, 135–142.

LAMBERT, W. E., & JAKOBOVITS, L. A., 1960. Verbal satiation and changes in intensity of meaning. *J. Exptl. Psychol.,* **60**, 376–383.

LANDIS, C., 1964. *Varieties of psychopathological experience* (F. A. Mettler, Ed.), New York: Holt.

LANDY, D., & ARONSON, E., 1969. The influence of the character of the criminal and his victim on the decisions of simulated jurors. *J. Exptl. Social Psychol.,* **5**, 141–152.

LAPPIN, J. S., 1967. Attention in the identification of stimuli in complex visual displays. *J. Exptl., Psychol.,* **75**, 321–328.

LARRABEE, H. A., 1964. *Reliable knowledge.* (Rev. ed.) Boston: Houghton Mifflin.

LASHLEY, K. S., 1917. The accuracy of movement in the absence of excitation from the moving organ. *Am. J. Physiol.,* **43**, 169–194.

LASHLEY, K. S., 1923. The behavioristic conception of consciousness. *Psychol. Rev.,* **30**, 237–272; 329–353.

LASHLEY, K. S., 1967. The problem of serial order in behavior. In L. A. Jeffress (Ed.), *Cerebral mechanisms in behavior: The Hixon symposium.* New York: Hafner.

LATANÉ, B., & DARLEY, J. M., 1968. Group inhibition of bystander intervention in emergencies. *J. Personality & Social Psychol.,* **10**, 215–221.

LATANÉ, B., & RODIN, J., 1969. A lady in distress: Inhibiting effects of friends and strangers on bystander intervention. *J. Exptl. Social Psychol.,* **5**, 189–202.

LAUGHLIN, P. R., 1964. Speed versus minimum-choice instructions in concept attainment. *J. Exptl. Psychol.,* **67**, 596.

LAUGHLIN, P. R., 1965. Selection strategies on concept attainment as a function of number of persons and stimulus display. *J. Exptl. Psychol.,* **70**, 323–327.

LAUGHLIN, P. R. 1966. Selection strategies in concept attainment as a function of number of relevant problem attributes. *J. Exptl. Psychol.,* **71**, 773–776.

LAUGHLIN, P. R., 1967. Incidental concept formation as a function of creativity and intelligence. *J. Personality & Social Psychol.,* **5**, 115–119.

LAUGHLIN, P. R., 1968a. Conditional concept attainment as a function of if factor complexity and then factor complexity. *J. Exptl. Psychol.,* **77**, 212–222.

LAUGHLIN, P. R., 1968b. Focusing strategy for eight concept rules. *J. Exptl. Psychol.,* **77**, 661–669.

LAUGHLIN, P. R., 1969. Information specification in the attainment of conditional concepts. *J. Exptl. Psychol.,* **79**, 370–372.

LAUGHLIN, P. R., DOHERTY, M. A., & DUNN, R. F., 1968. Intentional and incidental concept formation as a function of motivation, creativity, intelligence, and sex. *J. Personality & Social Psychol.,* **8**, 401–409.

LAUGHLIN, P. R., McGLYNN, R. P., ANDERSON, J. A., & JACOBSON, E. S., 1968. Concept attainment by individuals versus cooperative pairs as a function of memory, sex, and concept rule. *J. Personality & Social Psychol.,* **8**, 410–417.

LAURENDEAU, M. & PINARD, A., 1962. *Causal thinking in the child.* New York: International Universities Press, Inc.

LAVIOLETTE, F., & SILVERT, K. H., 1951. A theory of stereotypes. *Social Forces,* **29**, 257–262.

LAWRENCE, D. H., 1949. Acquired distinctiveness of cues. *J. Exptl. Psychol.,* **39**, 770–784.

LAWRENCE, D. H., 1950. Acquired distinctiveness of cues. *J. Exptl. Psychol.,* **40**, 175–188.

LAWRENCE, D. H., & COLES, G. R., 1954. Accuracy of recognition with alternatives before and after the stimulus. *J. Exptl. Psychol.,* **47**, 208–214.

LAWRENCE, D. H., & LABERGE, D. L., 1956. Relationship between recognition accuracy and order of reporting stimulus dimensions. *J. Exptl. Psychol.,* **51**, 12–18.

LAZARUS, R. S., & ALFERT, E., 1964. Short-circuiting of threat by experimentally altering cognitive appraisal. *J. Abnormal & Social Psychol.,* **69**, 195–205.

LAZARUS, R. S., & McCLEARY, R. A., 1951. Autonomic discrimination without awareness: A study of subception. *Psychol., Rev.,* **58**, 113–122.

LAZARUS, R. S., YOUSEM, H., & ARENBERG, D., 1953. Hunger and perception. *J. Personality,* **21**, 312–328.

LEAVITT, H. J., HAX, H., & ROCHE, J. H., 1955. "Authoritarianism" and agreement with things authoritative. *J. Psychol.*, **40**, 215–221.

LEE, S. S., & GAGNÉ, R. M., 1969. Effects of chaining cues on the acquisition of a complex conceptual rule. *J. Exptl. Psychol.*, **80**, 468–474.

LEFCOURT, H. M., LEWIS, L., & SILVERMAN, I. W., 1968. Internal vs. external control of reinforcement and attention in a decision-making task. *J. Personality*, **36**, 663–682.

LEFFORD, A., 1946. The influence of emotional subject matter on logical reasoning. *J. Gen. Psychol.*, **34**, 127–151.

LEFURGY, W. G., & WOLOSHIN, G. W., 1969. Immediate and long-term effects of experimentally induced social influence in the modification of adolescents' moral judgments. *J. Personality & Social Psychol.*, **12**, 104–110.

LEHMAN, H. C., & WITTY, P. A., 1927. *The psychology of play activities*, New York: Barnes.

LEMANN, T. B., & SOLOMON, R. L., 1952. Group characteristics as revealed in sociometric patterns and personality ratings. *Sociometry*, **15**, 7–90.

LENTZ, T. F., 1939. Personage admiration and other correlates of conservatism-radicalism. *J. Social Psychol.*, **10**, 81–93.

LERNER, M. J., 1965a. The effect of responsibility and choice on a partner's attractiveness following failure. *J. Personality*, **33**, 178–187.

LERNER, M. J., 1965b. Evaluation of performance as a function of performer's reward and attractiveness. *J. Personality & Social Psychol.*, **1**, 355–360.

LERNER, M. J., & MATTHEWS, G., 1967. Reactions to suffering of others under conditions of indirect responsibility. *J. Personality & Social Psychol.*, **5**, 319–325.

LERNER, M. J., & SIMMONS, C. H., 1966. Observer's reaction to the innocent victim: Compassion or rejection? *J. Personality & Social Psychol.*, **4**, 203–210.

LESSER, G. S., 1958. Extrapunitiveness and ethnic attitude. *J. Abnormal & Social Psychol.*, **56**, 281–282.

LEUBA, C., 1940. Images as conditioned sensations. *J. Exptl. Psychol.*, **26**, 345–351.

LEUBA, C., BIRCH, L., & APPLETON, J., 1968. Human problem solving during complete paralysis of the voluntary musculature. *Psychol. Repts.*, **22**, 849–855.

LEUBA, C., & DUNLAP, R., 1951. Conditioning imagery. *J. Exptl., Psychol.*, **41**, 352–355.

LEVANWAY, R. W., 1955. The effect of stress on expressed attitudes toward self and others. *J. Abnormal & Social Psychol.*, **50**, 225–226.

LEVENTHAL, G. S., 1964. Reward magnitude, task attractiveness, and liking for instrumental activity. *J. Abnormal & Social Psychol.*, **68**, 460–463.

LEVENTHAL, G. S., & BERGMAN, J. T., 1969. Self-depriving behavior as a response to unprofitable inequity. *J. Exptl. Social Psychol.*, **5**, 153–171.

LEVENTHAL, H., & FISCHER, K., 1970. What reinforces in a social reinforcement situation—words or expressions? *J. Personality & Social Psychol.*, **14**, 83–94.

LEVINE, M., 1962. Cue neutralization: The effects of random reinforcements upon discrimination learning. *J. Exptl. Psychol.*, **63**, 438–443.

LEVINE, M., 1963. Mediating processes in humans at the outset of discrimination learning. *Psychol. Rev.*, **70**, 254–276.

LEVINE, M., 1966. Hypothesis behavior by humans during discrimination learning. *J. Exptl. Psychol.,* **71**, 331–338.

LEVINE, M., 1970. Human discrimination learning: The subset-sampling hypothesis. *Psychol. Bull.,* **74**, 397–404.

LEVINE, R., CHEIN, I., & MURPHY, G., 1942. The relation of the intensity of a need to the amount of perceptual distortion: A preliminary report. *J. Psychol.,* **13**, 283–293.

LEVINGER, G., & SCHNEIDER, D. J., 1969. Test of the "risk is a value" hypothesis. *J. Personality & Social Psychol.,* **11**, 165–169.

LEVINSON, D. J., 1949. An approach to the theory and measurement of ethnocentric ideology. *J. Psychol.,* **28**, 19–39.

LEVITT, E. E., 1956. The water jar Einstellung test as a measure of rigidity. *Psychol. Bull.,* **53**, 347–370.

LEWIN, K., 1936. *Principles of topological psychology.* New York: McGraw-Hill.

LEWIS, H. B., & FRANKLIN, M., 1944. An experimental study of the role of the ego in work: II. The significance of task-orientation in work. *J. Exptl. Psychol.,* **34**, 195–215.

LEWIS, H. B., GOODENOUGH, D. R., SHAPIRO, A., & SLESER, I., 1966. Individual differences in dream recall. *J. Abnormal Psychol.,* **71**, 52–59.

LEWIS, M., RANSCH, M., GOLDBERG, S., & DODD, C., 1968. Error, response time, and IQ: Sex differences in cognitive style of preschool children. *Perceptual & Motor Skills,* **26**, 563–568.

LEY, R., 1968. Associative reaction time, meaningfulness, and presentation rate in paired-associate learning. *J. Exptl. Psychol.,* **78**, 285–291.

LIKERT, R., 1932. A technique for the measurement of attitudes. *Arch. Psychol.,* No. 140.

LIKERT, R., ROSLOW, S., & MURPHY, G., 1934. A simple and reliable method of scoring the Thurstone attitude scales. *J. Social Psychol.,* **5**, 228–238.

LINDER, D. E., COOPER, J., & JONES, E. E., 1967. Decision freedom as a determinant of the role of incentive magnitude in attitude change. *J. Personality & Social Psychol.,* **6**, 245–254.

LINDLEY, R. H., 1960. Association value and familiarity in serial verbal learning. *J. Exptl. Psychol.,* **59**, 366–370.

LINDLEY, R. H., 1963. Association value, familiarity, and pronounceability ratings as predictors of serial verbal learning. *J. Exptl. Psychol.,* **65**, 347–351.

LINDZEY, G., 1959. On the classification of projective techniques. *Psychol. Bull.,* **56**, 158–168.

LINDZEY, G., 1961. *Projective techniques and cross-cultural research.* New York: Appleton Century Crofts.

LOCKE, E. A., CARTLEDGE, N., & KOEPPEL, J., 1968. Motivational effects of knowledge of results: A goal-setting phenomenon? *Psychol. Bull.,* **70**, 474–485.

LOEB, M., & HAWKES, G. R., 1962. Detection of differences in duration of acoustic and electrical cutaneous stimuli in a vigilance task. *J. Psychol.,* **54**, 101–111.

LOMONT, J. F., 1966. Repressors and sensitizers as described by themselves and their peers. *J. Personality,* **34**, 224–240.

LOOFT, W., & BARTZ, W. H., 1969. Animism revived. *Psychol. Bull.,* **71**, 1–19.

LOTT, A. J., & LOTT, B. E., 1969. Liked and disliked persons as reinforcing stimuli. *J. Personality & Social Psychol.,* **11**, 129–137.

LOWELL, E. L., 1952. The effect of need for achievement on learning and speed of performance, *J. Personality*, **33**, 31–40.

LOWES, J. L., 1930. *The road to Xanadu.* Boston : Houghton Mifflin.

LOWIN, A., 1967. Approach and avoidance : Alternate modes of selective exposure to information. *J. Personality & Social Psychol.,* **6**, 1–9.

LOWIN. A., 1969. Further evidence for approach-avoidance interpretation of selective exposure. *J. Exptl. Social Psychol.,* **5**, 265–271.

LUBORSKY, L., RICE, R., PHOENIX, D., & FISHER, C., 1968. Eye fixation behavior as a function of awareness. *J. Personality,* **36**, 1–20.

LUCHINS, A. S., 1942. Mechanization in problem solving : The effect of Einstellung. *Psychol. Monographs,* No. 248.

LUCHINS, A. S., & LUCHINS, E. H., 1959. *Rigidity of behavior: A variational approach to the effect of Einstellung.* Eugene, Ore. : University of Oregon Press.

LUDVIGSON, H. W., & CAUL, W. F., 1964. Relative effect of overlearning on reversal and nonreversal shifts with two and four sorting categories. *J. Exptl. Psychol.,* **68**, 301–306.

LUND, F. H., & BERG, W. C., 1946. Identifiability of nationality characteristics. *J. Social Psychol.,* **24**, 77–83.

MACCOBY, M., & MODIANO, N., 1966. On culture and equivalence : I. In J. S. Bruner, R. R. Olver & P. M. Greenfield et al. *Studies in cognitive growth.* New York : Wiley.

MacKINNON, D. W., 1961. The study of creativity and creativity in architects. In *Conference on the creative person.* Berkeley : University of California Institute of Personality Assessment Research.

MacKINNON, D. W., 1963. Creativity and images of the self. In R. W. White (Ed.), *The study of lives: Essays in honor of Henry A. Murray.* New York : Atherton.

MACKWORTH, J. F., 1968. Vigilance, arousal, and habituation. *Psychol. Rev.,* **75**, 308–322.

MACKWORTH, N. H., 1948. The breakdown of vigilance during prolonged visual search. *Quart. J. Exptl. Psychol.,* **1**, 6–21.

MacRAE, D., Jr., 1954. A test of Piaget's theories of moral development. *J. Abnormal & Social Psychol.,* **49**, 14–18.

MADDI, S. R., 1965. Motivational aspects of creativity. *J. Personality,* **33**, 330–347.

MADISON, P., 1961. *Freud's concept of repression and defense: Its theoretical and observational language.* Minneapolis : University of Minnesota Press.

MAIER, N. R. F., 1930. Reasoning in humans. *J. Comp. Psychol.,* **10**, 115–143.

MAIER, N. R. F., 1931. Reasoning and learning. *Psychol. Rev.,* **38**, 332–346.

MAIER, N. R. F., 1933. An aspect of human reasoning. *Brit. J. Psychol.,* **24**, 144–155.

MAIER, N. R. F., & BURKE, R. J., 1966. Test of the concept of "availability of function" in problem solving. *Psychol. Repts.,* **19**, 119–125.

MAIER, N. R. F., & BURKE, R. J., 1967. Response availability as a factor in the problem solving performance of males and females. *J. Personality & Social Psychol.,* **5**, 304–310.

MAIER, N. R. F., & JANZEN, J. C., 1968. Functional values as aids and distractors in problem solving. *Psychol. Repts.,* **22**, 1021–1034.

MAIER, N. R. F., & RENINGER, H. W., 1933. *A psychological approach to literary criticism.* New York : Appleton Century Crofts.

MALMO, R. B., 1959. Activation : A neurophysiological dimension. *Psychol. Rev.,* **66**, 367–386.

MALTZMAN, I., 1955. Thinking : From a behavioristic point of view. *Psychol. Rev.,* **62**, 275–286.

MALTZMAN, I., 1960. On the training of originality. *Psychol. Rev.,* **67**, 229–242.

MALTZMAN, I., BOGARTZ, W., & BREGER, L., 1958. A procedure for increasing word association originality and its transfer effects. *J. Exptl. Psychol.,* **56**, 392–398.

MALTZMAN, I., BROOKS, L. W., BOGARTZ, W., & SUMMERS, S. S., 1958. The facilitation of problem solving by prior exposure to uncommon responses. *J. Exptl. Psychol.,* **56**, 399–406.

MALTZMAN, I., & MORRISETT, L., Jr., 1953a. The effects of single and compound classes of anagrams on set solutions. *J. Exptl. Psychol.,* **45**, 345–350.

MALTZMAN, I., & MORRISETT, L., Jr., 1953b. Effects of task instructions on solution of different classes of anagrams. *J. Exptl. Psychol.,* **45**, 351–354.

MANDLER, G., & EARHARD, B., 1964. Pseudomediation : Is chaining an artifact ? *Psychonomic Sci.,* **1**, 247–248.

MANDLER, G., & PEARLSTONE, Z., 1966. Free and constrained concept learning and subsequent recall. *J. Verbal Learning & Verbal Behavior,* **5**, 126–131.

MANNHEIM, K., 1936. *Ideology and utopia: An introduction to the sociology of knowledge.* New York : Harcourt, Brace.

MARCUSE, H., 1955. *Eros and civilization: A philosophical inquiry into Freud.* New York : Vintage Books, Inc.

MARKEY, F. V., 1935. Imaginative behavior of preschool children. *Child Develop. Monographs,* No. 18.

MARKOVA, I., 1969. Hypothesis formation and problem complexity. *Quart. J. Exptl. Psychol.,* **21**, 29–38.

MARKOWITZ, A., 1969. Influence of the repression-sensitization dimension, affect value, and ego threat on incidental learning. *J. Personality & Social Psychol.,* **11**, 374–380.

MARKOWITZ, A., & FORD, L. H., Jr., 1967. Defensive denial and selection of a target for projection. *J. Exptl. Res. Personality,* **2**, 272–277.

MARQUART, D. I., 1955. Group problem solving. *J. Social Psychol.,* **41**, 103–113.

MARQUIS, D. G., 1962. Individual responsibility and group decisions involving risk. *Ind. Management Rev.,* **3**, 8–23.

MARSHALL, H., 1931. Children's plays, games, and amusements. In C. Murchison (Ed.), *A handbook of child psychology.* Worcester Mass. : Clark University Press.

MARSHALL, H. H., 1965. The effect of punishment on children : A review of the literature and a suggested hypothesis. *J. Genet. Psychol.,* **106**, 23–34.

MARTIN, B., 1954. Intolerance of ambiguity in interpersonal and perceptual behavior. *J. Personality,* **22**, 494–503.

MARTIN, E., 1967. Formation of concepts. In B. Kleinmuntz (Ed.), *Concepts and the structure of memory.* New York : Wiley.

MARTIN, E., 1968. Short-term memory, individual differences, and shift performance in concept formation. *J. Exptl. Psychol.,* **76**, 514–520.

MARTIN, J. G., OLIVER, M., HOM, G., & HEASLET, G., 1963. Repetition and task in verbal mediating-response acquisition. *J. Exptl. Psychol.,* **66**, 12–16.

MARTIN, J. G., & PARROTT, G. L., 1966. Mediation and interference in verbal chaining. *J. Exptl. Psychol.,* **72**, 439–442.

MARTIN, J. G., & WESTIE, F. R., 1959. The tolerant personality. *Am. Sociological Rev.,* **24**, 521–528.

MARTIN, R. M., 1968. The stimulus barrier and the autonomy of the ego. *Psychol. Rev.,* **75**, 478–493.

MARTIN, W. E., 1951. Quantitative expression in young children. *Genet. Psychol. Monographs,* **44**, 147–219.

MASLING, J. M., 1954. How neurotic is the authoritarian ? *J. Abnormal & Social Psychol.,* **49**, 316–318.

MASLOW, A. H., 1967. A theory of metamotivation : The biological rooting of the value-life. *J. Humanistic Psychol.,* **7**, 93–127.

MASLOW, A. H., 1970. *Motivation and personality.* (2nd ed.) New York : Harper & Row.

MASTERS, J. C., 1968. Effects of social comparison upon subsequent self-reinforcement behavior in children. *J. Personality & Social Psychol.,* **10**, 391–401.

MAX, L. W., 1934. An experimental study of the motor theory of consciousness. I. Critique of earlier studies. *J. Gen. Psychol.,* **11**, 112-125.

MAX, L. W., 1935a. II. Method and apparatus. *J. Gen. Psychol.,* **13**, 159–175.

MAX, L. W., 1935b. III. Action-current responses in deaf-mutes during sleep, sensory stimulation, and dreams. *J. Comp. Psychol.,* **19**, 469–486.

MAX, L. W., 1937. IV. Action-current responses in the deaf during awakening, kinesthetic imagery, and abstract thinking. *J. Comp. Psychol.,* **24**, 301–344.

MAYZNER, M. S., 1962. Verbal concept attainment : A function of the number of positive and negative instances presented. *J. Exptl. Psychol.,* **63**, 314–319.

MAYZNER, M. S., & TRESSELT, M. E., 1958. Anagram solution times : A function of letter order and word frequency. *J. Exptl. Psychol.,* **56**, 376–379.

MAYZNER, M. S., & TRESSELT, M. E., 1959. Anagram solution times : A function of transition probabilities. *J. Psychol.,* **47**, 117–125.

MAYZNER, M. S., & TRESSELT, M. E., 1963. Anagram solution times : A function of word length and letter position variables. *J. Psychol.,* **55**, 469–476.

MAYZNER, M. S., & TRESSELT, M. E., 1966. Anagram solution times : A function of multiple-solution anagrams. *J. Exptl. Psychol.,* **71**, 66–73.

MAYZNER, M. S., TRESSELT, M. E., & HELBOCK, H., 1964. An exploratory study of mediational responses in anagram problem solving. *J. Psychol.,* **57**, 263–274.

McCANDLESS, B. R., & HOLLOWAY, H. D., 1955. Race prejudice and intolerance of ambiguity in children. *J. Abnormal & Social Psychol.,* **51**, 692–693.

McCLELLAND, D. C., ATKINSON, J. W., CLARK, R. A., & LOWELL, E. L., 1953. *The achievement motive.* New York : Appleton Century Crofts.

McCORMACK, P. D., & HANNAH, T. E., 1967. Monitoring eye movements during the learning of high and low meaningfulness paired-associate lists. *Psychonomic Sci.,* **8**, 443–444.

McCORMACK, P. D., & MOORE, T. E., 1969. Monitoring eye movements during the learning of low-high and high-low meaningfulness paired-associate lists. *J. Exptl. Psychol.,* **79**, 18–21.

McDAVID, J. W. 1959. Imitative behavior in preschool children. *Psychol. Monographs,* **73** (16, Whole No. 486).

McDAVID, J. W., 1964. Effects of ambiguity of imitative cues upon learning by observation. *J. Social Psychol.,* **62**, 165–174.

McDONALD, R. L., 1967. The effects of stress on self-attribution of hostility among ego control patterns. *J. Personality,* **35**, 234–245.

McDOUGALL, W., 1933. *The energies of men.* New York : Scribner's.

McGAUGHRAN, L. S., 1954. Predicting language behavior from object sorting *J. Abnormal & Social Psychol.,* **49**, 183–195.

McGEHEE, N. E., & SCHULZ, R. W., 1961. Mediation in paired-associate learning. *J. Exptl. Psychol.,* **62**, 565–570.

McGUIRE, W., 1960a. Cognitive consistency and attitude change. *J. Abnormal & Social Psychol.,* **60**, 345–353.

McGUIRE, W., 1960b. A syllogistic analysis of cognitive relationships. In C. Hovland & M. Rosenberg (Eds.), *Attitude organization and change.* New Haven, Conn. : Yale.

McGUIRE, W. J., 1968. Theory of the structure of human thought. In R. P. Abelson et al. (Eds.), *Theories of cognitive consistency: A sourcebook.* Chicago : Rand McNally.

McGUIRE, W. J., 1969. The nature of attitudes and attitude change. In G. Lindzey & E. Aronson (Eds.), *The handbook of social psychology.* Vol. 3. (2nd ed.) Reading, Mass. : Addison-Wesley.

McKELLAR, P., 1957. *Imagination and thinking: A psychological analysis.* New York : Basic Books.

McKELLAR, P., & SIMPSON, L., 1954. Between wakefulness and sleep : Hypnagogic imagery. *Brit. J. Psychol.,* **45**, 266–276.

McMAINS, M. J., & LIEBERT, R. M., 1968. Influence of discrepancies between successively modeled self-reward criteria on the adoption of a self-imposed standard. *J. Personality & Social Psychol.,* **8**, 166–171.

McMURRAY, G. A., 1958. A study of "fittingness" of signs to words by means of the semantic differential. *J. Exptl. Psychol.,* **56**, 310–312.

McNEMAR, Q., 1946. Opinion-attitude methodology. *Psychol. Bull.,* **43**, 289–374.

McREYNOLDS, P., LANDES, J., & ACKER, M., 1966. Dream content as a function of personality incongruency and unsettledness. *J. Gen. Psychol.,* **74**, 313–318.

MEADOW, A., PARNES, S. J., & REESE, H., 1959. Influence of brain-storming instructions and problem sequence on a creative problem solving test. *J. Appl. Psychol.,* **43**, 413–416.

MEDINNUS, G. R., 1959. Immanent justice in children : A review of the literature and additional data. *J. Genet. Psychol.,* **94**, 253–262.

MEDINNUS, G. R., 1962. Objective responsibility in children : A comparison with the Piaget data. *J. Genet. Psychol.,* **101**, 127–133.

MEDINNUS, G. R., 1966a. Age and sex differences in conscience development. *J. Genet. Psychol.,* **109**, 117–118.

MEDINNUS, G. R., 1966b. Behavioral and cognitive measures of conscience development. *J. Genet. Psychol.,* **109**, 174–150.

MEDNICK, M. T., MEDNICK, S. A., & JUNG, C. C., 1964. Continual association as a function of level of creativity and type of verbal stimulus. *J. Abnormal & Social Psychol.,* **69**, 511–515.

MEDNICK, M. T., MEDNICK, S. A., & MEDNICK, E. V., 1964. Incubation of creative performance and specific associative priming. *J. Abnormal & Social Psychol.,* **69**, 84–88.

MEDNICK, S. A., 1962. The associative basis of the creative process. *Psychol. Rev.,* **69**, 220–232.

MEENES, M., 1943. A comparison of racial stereotypes of 1935 and 1942. *J. Social Psychol.,* **17**, 327–336.

MEHLER, J., & BEVER, T. G., 1967. Cognitive capacity of very young children. *Science,* **158**, 141–142.

MEHLER, J., & BEVER, T. G., 1968. Reply. *Science,* **162**, 979–981.

MEIER, N. C. (Ed.), 1933. Studies in the psychology of art. *Psychol. Monographs,* **18** (No. 200).

MELIKIAN, L. H., 1956. Some correlates of authoritarianism in two cultural groups. *J. Psychol.,* **42**, 237–248.

MELTZER, H., 1925. Children's social concepts: A study of their nature and development. *Teachers Coll. Contrib. Educ.,* No. 192.

MENDELSOHN, G. A., & GRISWOLD, B. B., 1964. Differential use of incidental stimuli in problem solving as a function of creativity. *J. Abnormal & Social Psychol.,* **68**, 431–436.

MERRIFIELD, P. R., GUILFORD, J. P., CHRISTENSEN, P. R., & FRICK, J. W., 1962. The role of intellectual factors in problem solving. *Psychol. Monographs,* **76** (10, Whole No. 529).

METZGER, R., 1958. A comparison between rote learning and concept formation. *J. Exptl. Psychol.,* **56**, 226–231.

MIDLARSKY, E., & BRYAN, J. H., 1967. Training charity in children. *J. Personality & Social Psychol.,* **5**, 408–415.

MILGRAM, S., 1963. Behavioral study of obedience. *J. Abnormal & Social Psychol.,* **67**, 371–378.

MILGRAM, S., 1964. Issues in the study of obedience: A reply to Baumrind. *Am. Psychologist,* **19**, 848–852.

MILGRAM, S., 1965. Some conditions of obedience and disobedience to authority. *Human Relations,* **18**, 57–76.

MILLER, A. W., Jr., 1966. Conditioning connotative meaning. *J. Gen. Psychol.,* **75**, 319–328.

MILLER, B. J., RUSS, D., GIBSON, C., & HALL, A. E., 1970. Effects of free association training, retraining, and information on creativity. *J. Exptl. Psychol.,* **84**, 226–229.

MILLER, G. A., 1953. What is information measurement? *Am. Psychologist,* **8**, 3–11.

MILLER, G. A., 1956. The magical number seven, plus or minus two: Some limits on our capacity for processing information. *Psychol. Rev.,* **63**, 81–97.

MILLER, G. A., GALANTER, E., & PRIBRAM, K. H., 1960. *Plans and the structure of behavior.* New York: Holt.

MILLER, G. A., & SELFRIDGE, J. A., 1950. Verbal context and the recall of meaningful material. *Am. J. Psychol.,* **63**, 176–185.

MILLER, N. E., 1948. Theory and experiment relating psychoanalytic displacement to stimulus-response generalization. *J. Abnormal & Social Psychol.,* **43**, 155–178.

MILLER, N. E., 1959. Liberalization of basic S-R concepts: Extensions to conflict behavior, motivation, and social learning. In S. Koch (Ed.), *Psychology: A study of a science.* Vol. 2. New York: McGraw-Hill.

MILLER. N. E., & BUGELSKI, R., 1948. Minor studies of aggression: II. The influence of frustration imposed by the in-group on attitudes expressed toward out-groups. *J. Psychol.,* **25**, 437–442.

MILLER, N. E., & DOLLARD, J., 1941. *Social learning and imitation.* New Haven, Conn.: Yale.

MILLON, T., 1957. Authoritarianism, intolerance of ambiguity, and rigidity under ego- and task-involving conditions. *J. Abnormal & Social Psychol.,* **55**, 29–33.

MILLS, J., 1965. Avoidance of dissonant information. *J. Personality & Social Psychol.*, **2**, 589–593.

MILLS, J., 1968. Interest in supporting and discrepant information. In R. P. Abelson et al. (Eds.), *Theories of cognitive consistency: A sourcebook.* Chicago : Rand McNally.

MILLS, J., ARONSON, E., & ROBINSON, H., 1959. Selectivity in exposure to information. *J. Abnormal & Social Psychol.*, **59**, 250–253.

MILNER, P. M., 1957. The cell assembly : Mark II. *Psychol. Rev.*, **64**, 242–252.

MILTON, G. A., 1957. The effects of sex-role identification upon problem solving skill. *J. Abnormal & Social Psychol.*, **55**, 208–212.

MISCHEL, W., COATES, B., & RASKOFF, A., 1968. Effects of success and failure on self-gratification. *J. Personality & Social Psychol.*, **10**, 381–390.

MISCHEL, W., & GILLIGAN, C., 1964. Delay of gratification, motivation for the prohibited gratification, and responses to temptation. *J. Abnormal & Social Psychol.*, **69**, 411–417.

MISCHEL, W., & GRUSEC, J., 1966. Determinants of the rehearsal and transmission of neutral and aversive behaviors. *J. Personality & Social Psychol.*, **3**, 197–205.

MISCHEL, W., & LIEBERT, R. M., 1966. Effects of discrepancies between observed and imposed reward criteria on their acquisition and transmission. *J. Personality & Social Psychol.*, **3**, 45–53.

MISHIMA, J., & TANAKA, M., 1966. The role of age and intelligence in concept formation of children. *Japan. Psychol. Res.*, **8**, 30–37.

MITNICK, L. L., & McGINNIES, E., 1958. Influencing ethnocentrism in small discussion groups through a film communication. *J. Abnormal & Social Psychol.*, **56**, 82–90.

MOGAR, R. E., 1960. Three versions of the F scale and performance on the semantic differential. *J. Abnormal & Social Psychol.*, **60**, 262–265.

MONTAGUE, W. E., ADAMS, J. A., & KIESS, H. O., 1966. Forgetting and natural language mediation. *J. Exptl. Psychol.*, **72**, 829–833.

MONTAGUE, W. E., & KIESS, H. O., 1968. The associability of CVC pairs. *J. Exptl. Psychol. Monographs* **78** (2, Pt. 2).

MONTAGUE, W. E., & WEARING, A. J., 1967. The complexity of natural language mediators and its relation to paired-associate learning. *Psychonomic Sci.*, **7**, 135–136.

MOORE, T. V., 1910. The process of abstraction. *Univ. Calif. Publ. Psychol.*, **1**, 73–197.

MORGAN, J. J. B., 1945. Attitudes of students toward the Japanese. *J. Social Psychol.*, **21**, 219–227.

MORGAN, J. J. B., & MORTON, J. T., 1944. The distortion of syllogistic reasoning produced by personal convictions. *J. Social Psychol.*, **20**, 39–59.

MORRIS, C., 1956. *Varieties of human value.* Chicago : The Universitiy of Chicago Press.

MORRIS, C., & JONES, L. V., 1955. Value scales and dimensions. *J. Abnormal & Social Psychol.*, **51**, 523–535.

MORRISETT, L., Jr., & HOVLAND, C. I., 1959. A comparison of three varieties of training in human problem solving. *J. Exptl. Psychol.*, **58**, 52–55.

MORRISSETTE, J., 1958. An experimental study of the theory of structural balance. *Human Relations*, **11**, 239–254.

MOSCOVICI, S., & ZAVALLONI, M., 1969. The group as a polarizer of attitudes. *J. Personality & Social Psychol.,* **12**, 125–135.

MOWRER, O. H., 1960a. *Learning theory and behavior.* New York: Wiley.

MOWRER, O. H., 1960b. *Learning theory and the symbolic processes.* New York: Wiley.

MUELLER, J. H., MILL, E. G., ZANE, N. B., & HEVNER, K., 1934. Studies in appreciation and art. *Univ. Ore. Publ.,* **4** (6), 1–151.

MUELLER, J. H., & SLAYMAKER, F. L., 1970. Total time and stimulus-response imagery in paired-associate learning. *J. Exptl. Psychol.,* **85**, 288–292.

MUMBAUER, C. C., & ODOM, R. D., 1967. Variables affecting the performance of preschool children in intradimensional, reversal, and extradimensional shifts. *J. Exptl. Psychol.,* **75**, 180–187.

MUNN, N. L., & STIENING, B. R., 1931. The relative efficacy of form and background in a child's discrimination of visual patterns. *J. Genet. Psychol.,* **39**, 73–90.

MUNROE, R., LEWINSON, T. S., & WAEHNER, T. S., 1944. A comparison of three projective methods. *Character & Personality,* **13**, 1–21.

MUNSTERBERG, E., & MUSSEN, P. H., 1953. The personality structure of art students. *J. Personality,* **21**, 457–466.

MURDOCK, B. B., Jr., 1960. The immediate retention of unrelated words. *J. Exptl. Psychol.,* **60**, 222–234.

MURDOCK, B. B., Jr., 1965. A test of the "limited capacity" hypothesis. *J. Exptl. Psychol.,* **69**, 237–240.

MURPHY, G., 1947. *Personality: A biosocial approach to origins and structures.* New York: Harper.

MURPHY, G., MURPHY, L. B., & NEWCOMB, T. M., 1937. *Experimental social psychology.* (Rev. ed.) New York: Harper.

MURPHY, L. B., 1937. *Social behavior and child personality: An exploratory study of some roots of sympathy.* New York: Columbia.

MURRAY, E. J., 1965. *Sleep, dreams, and arousal.* New York: Appleton Century Crofts.

MURRAY, H. A., 1933. The effect of fear upon estimates of the maliciousness of other personalities. *J. Social Psychol.,* **4**, 310–329.

MURRAY, H. A., 1937. Techniques for a systematic investigation of fantasy. *J. Psychol.* **3**, 115–143.

MURSTEIN, B. I., 1963. *Theory and research in projective techniques (emphasizing the TAT).* New York: Wiley.

MURSTEIN, B. I., & PRYER, R. S., 1959. The concept of projection: A review. *Psychol. Bull.,* **56**, 353–374.

MUSSEN, P. H., & PARKER, A. L., 1965. Mother nurturance and girls' incidental imitative learning. *J. Personality & Social Psychol.,* **2**, 94–97.

MYDEN, W., 1959. Interpretation and evaluation of certain personality characteristics involved in creative production. *Perceptual & Motor Skills,* **9**, 139–158.

NAGY, M. H., 1948. The child's theories concerning death. *J. Genet. Psychol.,* **73**, 3–27.

NAGY, M. H., 1953. Children's conceptions of some bodily functions. *J. Genet. Psychol.,* **83**, 199–216.

NAHINSKY, I. D., 1968. A test of axioms of all-or-none concept identification models. *J. Verbal Learning & Verbal Behavior,* **7**, 593–601.

NAHINSKY, I. D., & McGLYNN, F. D., 1968. Hypothesis sampling in conjunctive concept identification. *Psychonomic Sci.,* **17**, 77–78.

NAHINSKY, I. D., & SLAYMAKER, F. L., 1969. Sampling without replacement and information processing following correct responses in concept identification. *J. Exptl. Psychol.,* **80**, 475–482.

NAHINSKY, I. D., & SLAYMAKER, F. L., 1970. Use of negative instances in conjunctive concept identification. *J. Exptl. Psychol.,* **84**, 64–68.

NASS, M. L., 1956. The effects of three variables on children's concepts of physical causality. *J. Abnormal & Social Psychol.,* **53**, 191–196.

NASS, M. L., 1964. The deaf child's conception of physical causality. *J. Abnormal & Social Psychol.,* **69**, 669–673.

NATSOULAS, T., 1970. Concerning introspective "knowledge." *Psychol. Bull.,* **73**, 89–111.

NEIMARK, E. D., 1967. Effect of differential reinforcement upon information-gathering strategies in diagnostic problem solving. *J. Exptl. Psychol.,* **74**, 406–413.

NEISSER, U., 1963a. The imitation of man by machine. *Science,* **139**, 193–197.

NEISSER, U., 1963b. The multiplicity of thought. *Brit. J. Psychol.,* **54**, 1–14.

NEISSER, U., 1967. *Cognitive psychology.* New York: Appleton Century Crofts.

NEISSER, U., & WEENE, P., 1962. Hierarchies in concept attainment. *J. Exptl. Psychol.,* **64**, 640–645.

NETHERCOT, A. H., 1939. *The road to Tryermaine.* Chicago: The University of Chicago Press.

NEWCOMB, T. M., 1943. *Personality and social change: Attitude formation in a student community.* New York: Holt.

NEWCOMB, T. M., 1946. The influence of attitude climate upon some determinants of information. *J. Abnormal & Social Psychol.,* **41**, 291–302.

NEWCOMB, T. M., KOENIG, K. E., FLACKS, R., & WARWICK, D. P., 1967. *Persistence and change: Bennington College and its students after twenty-five years.* New York: Wiley.

NEWELL, A., SHAW, J. C., & SIMON, H. A., 1958. Elements of a theory of human problem solving. *Psychol. Rev.,* **65**, 151–166.

NICKERSON, R. S., 1967. Categorization time with categories defined by disjunctions and conjunctions of stimulus attributes. *J. Exptl. Psychol.,* **73**, 211–219.

NOBLE, C. E., 1952a. An analysis of meaning. *Psychol. Rev.,* **59**, 421–430.

NOBLE, C. E., 1952b. The role of stimulus meaning (m) in serial verbal learning. *J. Exptl. Psychol.,* **43**, 437–446; **44**, 465.

NOBLE, C. E., 1954. The familiarity-frequency relationship. *J. Exptl. Psychol.,* **47**, 13–16.

NOBLE, C. E., 1963. Meaningfulness and familiarity. In C. N. Cofer & B. S. Musgrave (Eds.), *Verbal behavior and learning: Problems and processes.* New York: McGraw-Hill.

NOBLE, C. E., & McNEELY, D. A., 1957. The role of meaningfulness (m) in paired-associate verbal learning. *J. Exptl. Psychol.,* **53**, 16–22.

NORCROSS, K. J., & SPIKER, C. C., 1958. Effects of mediated associations on transfer in paired-associate learning. *J. Exptl. Psychol.,* **55**, 129–134.

NORDHϕY, F., 1962. Group interaction in decision-making under risk. Unpublished masters, thesis, Massachusetts Institute of Technology.

NUTTIN, J. M., Jr., 1966. Attitude change after rewarded dissonant and consonant "forced compliance." *International J. Psychol.,* **1**, 39–57.

OAKDEN, E. C., & STURT, M., 1922. Development of the knowledge of time in children. *Brit. J. Psychol.,* **16**, 309–336.

OAKES, M. E., 1947. Children's explanations of natural phenomena. *Teachers Coll. Contrib. Educ.,* No. 926.

O'CONNELL, D. C., 1965. Concept learning and verbal control under partial reinforcement and subsequent reversal or nonreversal shift. *J. Exptl. Psychol.,* **69**, 144–151.

O'CONNOR, P., 1952. Ethnocentrism, "intolerance of ambiguity," and abstract reasoning ability. *J. Abnormal & Social Psychol.,* **47**, 526–530.

OGDEN, R. M., 1911. Imageless thought: Résumé and critique. *Psychol. Bull.,* **8**, 183–197.

OHNMACHT, F. W., 1966. Effects of field independence and dogmatism on reversal and nonreversal shifts in concept formation. *Perceptual & Motor Skills,* **22**, 491–497.

OMWAKE, K. T., 1954. The relation between acceptance of self and acceptance of others shown by three personality inventories. *J. Consulting Psychol.,* **18**, 443–446.

ORDAN, H., 1945. *Social concepts and the child mind.* New York: King's Crown.

ORNE, M. T., 1962. On the social psychology of the psychological experiment: With particular reference to demand characteristics and their implications. *Am. Psychologist,* **17**, 776–783.

OSBORN, A. F., 1957. *Applied imagination.* New York: Scribner.

OSGOOD, C. E., 1952. The nature and measurement of meaning. *Psychol. Bull.,* **49**, 197–237.

OSGOOD, C. E., 1953. *Method and theory in experimental psychology.* New York: Oxford.

OSGOOD, C. E., 1961. Comments on Professor Bousfield's paper. In C. N. Cofer (Ed., with B. S. Musgrave), *Verbal learning and verbal behavior.* New York: McGraw-Hill.

OSGOOD, C. E., SUCI, G. J., & TANNENBAUM, P. H., 1957. *The measurement of meaning.* Urbana: The University of Illinois Press.

OSGOOD, C. E., & TANNENBAUM, P. H., 1955. The principle of congruity in the prediction of attitude change. *Psychol. Rev.,* **62**, 42–55.

OSGOOD, C. E., WARE, E. E., & MORRIS, C., 1961. Analysis of the connotative meanings of a variety of human values as expressed by American college students. *J. Abnormal & Social Psychol.,* **62**, 62–73.

OSLER, S. F., & FIVEL, M. W., 1961. Concept attainment: I. The role of age and intelligence in concept attainment by induction. *J. Exptl. Psychol.,* **62**, 1–8.

OSLER, S. F., & TRAUTMAN, G. E., 1961. Concept attainment: II. Effect of stimulus complexity upon concept attainment at two levels of intelligence. *J. Exptl. Psychol.,* **62**, 9–13.

OSTROM, T. M., 1969. The relationship between the affective, behavioral, and cognitive components of attitude. *J. Exptl. Social Psychol.,* **5**, 12–30.

OSTROM, T. M., & UPSHAW, H. S., 1970. Race differences in the judgment of attitude statements over a thirty-five year period. *J. Personality,* **38**, 235–248.

OVERSTREET, J. D., & DUNHAM, J. C., 1969. Effect of number of values and irrelevant dimensions on dimension selection and associative learning in a multiple-concept problem. *J. Exptl. Psychol.,* **79**, 265–268.

PAGE, M. M., 1969. Social psychology of a classical conditioning of attitudes experiment. *J. Personality & Social Psychol.,* **11**, 177–186.

PAIVIO, A., 1963. Learning of adjective-noun paired-associates as a function of adjective-noun word order and noun abstractness. *Can. J. Psychol.,* **17,** 370–379.

PAIVIO, A., 1965. Abstractness, imagery, and meaningfulness in paired-associate learning. *J. Verbal Learning & Verbal Behavior,* **4,** 32–38.

PAIVIO, A., 1969. Mental imagery in associative learning and memory. *Psychol. Rev.,* **76,** 241–263.

PAIVIO, A., 1970. On the functional significance of imagery. *Psychol. Bull.,* **73,** 385–392.

PAIVIO, A., & CSAPO, K., 1969. Concrete image and verbal memory codes. *J. Exptl. Psychol.,* **80,** 279–285.

PAIVIO, A., & MADIGAN, S. A., 1968. Imagery and association value in paired-associate learning. *J. Exptl. Psychol.,* **76,** 35–39.

PAIVIO, A., & YUILLE, J. C., 1969. Changes in associative strategies and paired-associate learning over trials as a function of word imagery and type of learning set. *J. Exptl. Psychol.,* **79,** 458–463.

PALERMO, D. S., 1963. Word associations and children's verbal behavior. In L. P. Lipsitt & C. C. Spiker (Eds.), *Advances in child development and behavior.* Vol. 1. New York : Academic.

PARLOFF, M. B., DATTA, L. E., KLEMAN, M., & HANDLON, J. H., 1968. Personality characteristics which differentiate creative male adolescents and adults. *J. Personality,* **36,** 528–552.

PATRICK, C., 1935. Creative thought in poets. *Arch. Psychol.,* No. 178.

PATRICK, C., 1937. Creative thought in artists. *J. Psychol.,* **4,** 35–73.

PATRICK, C., 1938. Scientific thought. *J. Psychol.,* **5,** 55–83.

PATTERSON, G. R., 1965. Parents as dispensers of aversive stimuli. *J. Personality & Social Psychol.,* **2,** 844–851.

PEAK, H., & MORRISON, H. W., 1958. The acceptance of information into attitude structure. *J. Abnormal & Social Psychol.,* **57,** 127–135.

PECHSTEIN, L. A., & BROWN, F. D., 1939. An experimental analysis of the alleged criteria of insight learning. *J. Educ. Psychol.,* **30,** 38–52.

PEPITONE, A., 1950. Motivational effects in social perception. *Human Relations,* **3,** 57–76.

PERLMUTTER, H. V., 1953. Group memory of meaningful material. *J. Psychol.,* **35,** 361–370.

PERVIN, C. A., 1967. Satisfaction and perceived self-environment similarity : A semantic differential study of student-college interaction. *J. Personality,* **35,** 623–634.

PETERS, H. N., 1935. Mediate association. *J. Exptl. Psychol.,* **18,** 20–48.

PETERSON, G. M., 1932. An empirical study of the ability to generalize. *J. Gen. Psychol.,* **6,** 90–114.

PETERSON, M. J., 1968. Concept identification as a function of the type of training series. *J. Exptl. Psychol.,* **78,** 128–136.

PETERSON, M. J., & COLAVITA, F. B., 1964. Strategies, type of solution, and stage of learning. *J. Exptl. Psychol.,* **68,** 578–587.

PETERSON, P. D., & KOULACK, D., 1969. Attitude change as a function of latitudes of acceptance and rejection. *J. Personality & Social Psychol.,* **1,** 309–311.

PETRE, R. D., 1964. Concept acquisition as a function of stimulus-equivalence pretraining with identical and dissimilar stimuli. *J. Exptl. Psychol.,* **67,** 360–364.

PETTIGREW, T. F., 1958. The measurement and correlates of category width as a cognitive variable. *J. Personality,* **26,** 532–544.

PETTIGREW, T. F., 1959. Regional differences in anti-Negro prejudice. *J. Abnormal & Social Psychol.,* **59,** 28–36.

PEZZOLI, J. A., & FRASE, L. T., 1968. Mediated facilitation of syllogistic reasoning. *J. Exptl. Psychol.,* **78,** 228–232.

PHARES, E. J., & DAVIS, W. L., 1966. Breadth of categorization and the generalization of expectancies. *J. Personality & Social Psychol.,* **4,** 461–464.

PHILLIPS, R. E., 1968a. Comparison of direct and vicarious reinforcement and an investigation of methodological variables. *J. Exptl. Psychol.,* **78,** 666–669.

PHILLIPS, R. E., 1968b. Vicarious reinforcement and imitation in a verbal learning situation. *J. Exptl. Psychol.,* **76,** 669–670.

PIAGET, J., 1929. *The child's conception of the world.* New York: Harcourt, Brace.

PIAGET, J., 1930. *The child's conception of physical causality.* New York: Harcourt, Brace.

PIAGET, J., 1952. *The origins of intelligence in children.* New York: Norton. (Originally published: 1937.)

PIAGET, J., 1962. *Play, dreams, and imitation in childhood.* New York: Norton.

PIAGET, J., 1965a. *The child's conception of number.* New York: Norton. (Originally published: 1941.)

PIAGET, J., 1965b. *The moral judgment of the child.* New York: Free Press. (Originally published: 1932.)

PIAGET, J., 1966. Response to Brian Sutton-Smith. *Psychol. Rev.,* **73,** 111–112.

PIAGET, J. 1968. Quantification, conservation, and nativism. *Science,* **162,** 976–979.

PIAGET, J., & INHELDER, B., 1940. *Le développment des quantités chez l'enfant.* Paris: Delachaux and Niestle.

PIAGET, J., & INHELDER, B., 1956. *The child's conception of space.* New York: Norton.

PILIAVIN, I. M., HARDYCK, J. A., & VADUM, A. C., 1968. Constraining effects of personal costs on the transgressions of juveniles. J. *Personality & Social Psychol.,* **10,** 227–231.

PILIAVIN, I. M., RODIN, J., & PILIAVIN, J. A., 1969. Good Samaritanism: An underground phenomenon? J. *Personality & Social Psychol.,* **13,** 289–299.

PINARD, A., & LAURENDEAU, M., 1969. "Stage" in Piaget's cognitive-developmental theory: Exegesis of a concept. In D. Elkind & J. H. Flavell (Eds.), *Studies in cognitive development: Essays in honor of Jean Piaget.* New York: Oxford.

PINE, F., 1959. Thematic drive content and creativity. *J. Personality,* **27,** 136–151.

PINE, F., & HOLT, R. R., 1960. Creativity and primary process. *J. Abnormal & Social Psychol.,* **61,** 370–379.

PISHKIN, V., 1960. Effects of probability of misinformation and number of irrelevant dimensions upon concept identification. *J. Exptl. Psychol.,* **59,** 371–378.

PISHKIN, V., 1967. Availability of feedback-corrected error instances in concept learning. *J. Exptl. Psychol.,* **73,** 318–319.

PISHKIN, V., & SHURLEY, J. T., 1965. Auditory dimensions and irrelevant information in concept identification of males and females. *Perceptual & Motor Skills,* **20,** 673–683.

PISHKIN, V., & WOLFGANG, A., 1965. Number and type of available instances in concept learning. *J. Exptl. Psychol.,* **69,** 5–8.

PITTEL, S. M., & MENDELSOHN, G. A, 1966. Measurement of moral values: A review and critique. *Psychol. Bull.,* **66**, 22–35.

PIVIK, T., & FOULKES, D., 1966. "Dream deprivation": Effects on dream content. *Science,* **153**, 1282–1284.

PLANT, W. T., TELFORD, C. W., & THOMAS, J. A., 1965. Some personality differences between dogmatic and nondogmatic groups. *J. Social Psychol.,* **67**, 67–76.

PODELL, H. A., 1958. Two processes of concept formation. *Psychol. Monographs,* **72** (15, Whole No. 468).

PODELL, H. A., 1963. A quantitative study of convergent association. *J. Verbal Learning & Verbal Behavior,* **2,** 234–241.

POINCARÉ, H., 1913. Mathematical creation. In *The foundations of science.* New York: Science Press.

POLLIO, H. R. 1963. Word association as a function of conditioned meaning. *J. Exptl. Psychol.,* **66**, 454–460.

POLLIO, H. R., DEITCHMAN, R., & RICHARDS, S., 1969. Law of contrast and oppositional word pairs. *J. Exptl. Psychol.,* **79**, 203–212.

POLLIO, H. R., KASSCHAU, R. A., & DeNISE, H. E., 1968. Associative structure and the temporal characteristics of free recall. *J. Exptl. Psychol.,* **76**, 190–197.

POSNER, M. I., 1964. Information reduction in the analysis of sequential tasks. *Psychol. Rev.,* **71**, 491–504.

POSNER, M. I., 1965. Memory and thought in human intellectual performance. *Brit. J. Psychol.,* **56,** 197–215.

POSTMAN, L., 1953. On the problem of perceptual defense. *Psychol. Rev.,* **60**, 298–306.

POSTMAN, L., 1962. The effects of language habits on the acquisition and retention of verbal associations. *J. Exptl. Psychol.,* **64**, 7–19.

POSTMAN, L., BRUNER, J. S., & McGINNIES, E., 1948. Personal values as selective factors in perception. *J. Abnormal & Social Psychol.,* **43**, 142–154.

PRATT, K. C., HARTMAN, W E., & MEAD, J. L., 1954. Indeterminate number concepts : III. Representation by children through selection of appropriate aggregation. *J. Genet. Psychol.,* **84**, 39–64.

PRENTICE, W. C. H., 1943. Retroactive inhibition and the motivation of learning. *Am. J. Psychol.,* **56**, 283–292.

PRIBRAM, K. H., 1962. Interrelations of psychology and the neurological disciplines. In S. Koch (Ed.), *Psychology: A study of a science,* Vol. 4. New York: McGraw-Hill.

PRICE, K. O., HARBURG, E., & McLEOD, J., 1965. Positive and negative affect as a function of perceived discrepancy in ABX situations. *Human Relations,* **18**, 87–100.

PRICE, K. O., HARBURG, E., & NEWCOMB, T. M., 1966. Psychological balance in situations of negative interpersonal attitudes. *J. Personality & Social Psychol.,* **3**, 265–270.

PRIEST, R. F., & HUNSAKER, P. L., 1969. Compensating for a female disadvantage in problem solving. *J. Exptl. Res. Personality,* **4**, 57–64.

PROSHANSKY, H. M., 1943. A projective method for the study of attitudes. *J. Abnormal & Social Psychol.,* **38**, 393–395.

PROTHRO, E. T., 1952. Ethnocentrism and anti-Negro attitudes in the Deep South. *J. Abnormal & Social Psychol.*, **47**, 105–108.

PROTHRO, E. T., 1954. Cross-cultural patterns of national stereotypes. *J. Social Psychol.*, **40**, 53–59.

PROTHRO, E. T., & KEEHN, J. D., 1957. Streotypes and semantic space. *J. Social Psychol.*, **45**, 197–209.

PROTHRO, E. T., & MELIKIAN, L. H., 1955. Studies in stereotypes : V. Familiarity and the kernel of truth hypothesis. *J. Social Psychol.*, **41**, 3–10.

PRUITT, D. G., 1969. The "Walter Mitty" effect in individual and group risk-taking. Paper presented at the A.P.A. Convention, Washington, D.C.

PRUITT, D. G., & TEGER, A. I., 1967. Is there a shift toward risk in group discussion? If so, is it a group phenomenon? If so, what causes it? Paper presented at the A.P.A. Convention, Washington, D.C.

PRUITT, D. G., & TEGER, A. I., 1969. The risky shift in group betting. *J. Exptl. Social Psychol.*, **5**, 115–126.

PYRON, B., 1966. Rejection of avant-grade art and the need for simple order. *J. Psychol.*, **63**, 159–178.

RAAHEIM, K., 1963. Sex differences in problem solving tasks. *Scand. J. Psychol.*, **4**, 161–164.

RABINOWITZ, W., 1956. A note on the social perceptions of authoritarians and nonauthoritarians. *J. Abnormal & Social Psychol.*, **53**, 384–386.

RADKE-YARROW, M., & LANDE, B., 1953. Personality correlates of differential reactions to minority group-belonging. *J. Social Psychol.*, **38**, 253–272.

RAIMY, V. C., 1948. Self-reference in counseling interviews. *J. Consulting Psychol.*, **12**, 153–163.

RAO, S. N. C., 1971. *Strategy in concept attainment as a function of certain personality and cognitive variables.* Allahabad, India : Indian International Publications.

RAPAPORT, D., 1942. *Emotions and memory.* New York : International Universities Press, Inc.

RAPAPORT, D., 1951. Toward a theory of thinking. In D. Rapaport (Ed.), *Organization and pathology of thought.* New York : Columbia.

RAPAPORT, D., 1952. Projective techniques and the theory of thinking. *J. Projective Tech.*, **16**, 269–275.

RAPAPORT, D., 1960. On the psychoanalytic theory of motivation. In M. R. Jones (Ed.), *Nebraska symposium on motivation.* Lincoln, Neb. : University of Nebraska Press.

RASMUSSEN, E. A., & ARCHER, E. J., 1961. Concept identification as a function of language pretraining and task complexity. *J. Exptl. Psychol.*, **61**, 437–441.

RAWLINGS, E. I., 1968. Witnessing harm to other : A reassessment of the role of guilt in altruistic behavior. *J. Personality & Social Psychol.*, **10**, 377–380.

RAY, W. S., 1966. Originality in problem solving as affected by single versus multiple-solution training problems. *J. Psychol.*, **64**, 107–112.

RAZRAN, G., 1949. Semantic and phonetographic generalization of salivary conditioning to verbal stimuli. *J. Exptl. Psychol.*, **39**, 642–652.

RAZRAN, G. H. S., 1935–1936. Salivating, and thinking in different languages. *J. Psychol.*, **1**, 145–151.

REED H. B., 1946a. Factors influencing the learning and retention of concepts. I. The influence of set. *J. Exptl. Psychol.*, **36**, 71–87.

REED, H. B., 1946b. Factors influencing the learning and retention of concepts. II. The influence of length of series. III. The origin of concepts. *J. Exptl. Psychol.,* **36**, 166–179.

REED, H. B., 1946c. Factors influencing the learning and retention of concepts. IV. The influence of the complexity of the stimuli. *J. Exptl. Psychol.,* **36**, 252–261.

REED, H. B., 1950. Factors influencing the learning and retention of concepts. V. The influence of form of presentation. *J. Exptl. Psychol.,* **40**, 504–511.

REED, H. B., & DICK, R. D., 1968. The learning and generalization of abstract and concrete concepts. *J. Verbal Learning & Verbal Behavior,* **7**, 486–490.

REES, H. J., & ISRAEL, H. E., 1935. An investigation of the establishment and operation of mental sets. *Psychol. Monographs,* **46** (6, Whole No. 210).

REESE, H. W., 1963. Discrimination learning set in children. In L. P. Lipset, & C. C. Spiker (Eds.), *Advances in child development and behavior.* Vol. 1. New York : Academic.

REEVES, J. W., 1965. *Thinking about thinking.* New York : George Braziller, Inc.

REGAN, J. W., 1971. Guilt, perceived injustice, and altruistic behavior. *J. Personality & Social Psychol.,* **18**, 124–132.

REID, J. B., KING, F. J., & WICKWIRE, P., 1959. Cognitive and other personality characteristics of creative children. *Psychol. Repts.,* **5**, 729–737.

REID, J. W., 1951. An experimental study on "analysis of the goal" in problem solving. *J. Gen. Psychol.,* **44**, 51–69.

REITMAN, W. R., 1965. *Cognition and thought: An information processing approach.* New York : Wiley.

RENNER, V., 1970. Effects of modification of cognitive style on creative behavior. *J. Personality & Social Psychol.,* **14**, 257–262.

REST, J., 1968. Development hierarchy in preference and comprehension of moral judgment. Unpublished doctoral dissertation. The University of Chicago.

REST, J., TURIEL, E., & KOHLBERG, L., 1969. Level of moral development as a determinant of preference and comprehension of moral judgments made by others. *J. Personality,* **37**, 225–252.

RESTLE, F., ANDREWS, M. & ROKEACH, M., 1964. Differences between open- and closed-minded subjects on learning-set and oddity problems. *J. Abnormal & Social Psychol.,* **68**, 649–654.

RESTLE, F., & EMMERICH, D., 1966. Memory in concept attainment : Effects of giving several problems concurrently. *J. Exptl. Psychol.,* 1966, **71**, 794–799.

RETTIG, S., 1966. Group discussion and predicted ethical risk taking. *J. Personality & Social Psychol.,* **3**, 629–633.

RETTIG, S., & PASAMANICK, B., 1964. Differential judgment of ethical risk by cheaters and noncheaters. *J. Abnormal & Social Psychol.,* **69**, 109–113.

RETTIG, S., & RAWSON, H. E., 1963. The risk hypothesis in predictive judgments of unethical behavior. *J. Abnormal & Social Psychol.,* **66**, 243–248.

RETTIG S., & TUROFF, S. J., 1967. Exposure to group discussion and predicted ethical risk taking. *J. Personality & Social Psychol.,* **7**, 177–180.

REUDER, M. E., 1956. The effect of ego orientation and problem difficulty on muscle action potentials. *J. Exptl. Psychol.,* **51**, 142–148.

RHINE, R. J., 1959. The relation of achievement in problem solving to rate and kind of hypotheses produced. *J. Exptl. Psychol.,* **57**, 253–256.

RHINE, R. J., 1965. Preference for a positive evaluative response in concept learning. *J. Exptl. Psychol.*, **70**, 632–635.

RHINE, R. J., 1967a. The 1964 presidential election and curves of information seeking and avoiding. *J. Personality & Social Psychol.*, **5**, 416–423.

RHINE, R. J., 1967b. Some problems in dissonance theory research on information selectivity. *Psychol. Bull.*, **68**, 21–28.

RHINE, R., COLE. D. F., & OGILVIE, L. P., 1968. Acquisition and change of an evaluative concept as a function of word frequency and type. *J. Verbal Learning & Verbal Behavior*, **7**, 55–57.

RICHARDSON, A., 1969. *Mental imagery*. New York: Springer.

RICHARDSON, J., 1960. Association among stimuli and the learning of verbal concept lists. *J. Exptl. Psychol.*, **60**, 290–298.

RICHARDSON, J., 1967. Latencies of implict responses and the effect of the anticipation interval on mediated transfer. *J. Verbal Learning & Verbal Behavior*, **6**, 819–826.

RICHARDSON, J., 1968. Implicit verbal chaining as the basis of transfer in paired associate learning. *J. Exptl. Psychol.*, **76**, 109–115.

RICHARDSON, J., & BERGUM, B. O., 1954. Distributed practice and rote learning in concept formation. *J. Exptl. Psychol.*, **47**, 442–446.

RICHARDSON, J., & BROWN, B. L., 1966. Mediated transfer in paired-associate learning as a function of presentation rate and stimulus meaningfulness. *J. Exptl. Psychol.*, **72**, 820–828.

RIDDOCH, G., 1941. Phantom limbs and body shape. *Brain*, **64**, 197–222.

RIDLEY, D. R., & BIRNEY, R. C., 1967. Effects of training procedures on creativity test scores. *J. Educ. Psychol.*, **58**, 158–164.

RIEBER, M., & LOCKWOOD, D., 1969. Effects of correction on double-alternation learning in children. *J. Exptl. Psychol.*, **79**, 191–192.

RIEGEL, K. F., RIEGEL, R. M., & LEVINE, R. S., 1966. An analysis of associative behavior and creativity. *J. Personality & Social Psychol.*, **4**, 50–56.

RIM, Y., 1963. Risk-taking and need for achievement. *Acta Psychol.*, **21**, 108–115.

RIM, Y., 1964. Personality and group decisions involving risk. *Psychol. Record*, **14**, 37–45.

RINGUETTE, E. L., 1965. Selected personality correlates of mode of conflict resolution. *J. Personality & Social Psychol.*, **2**, 506–512.

RIVIERE, J., 1952a. The inner world in Ibsen's *The Master Builder*. *International J. Psychoanal.*, **33**, 173–180.

RIVIERE, J. 1952b. The unconscious phantasy of an inner world reflected in examples from English literature. *Intern. J. Psychoanal.*, **33**, 160–172.

ROBINSON, E. S., 1932. *Association theory today*. New York: Appleton Century Crofts.

ROBINSON, J. A., & RABIN, B. J., 1969. Effects of solution-word categorizability and intralist rule order on learning codeable trigrams. *J. Exptl. Psychol.*, **79**, 586–588.

ROCK, I., 1957. The role of repetition in associative learning. *Am. J. Psychol.*, **70**, 186–193.

RODRIGUES, A., 1967. Effects of balance, positivity, and agreement in triadic social relations. *J. Personality & Social Psychol.*, **5**, 472–476.

ROE, A., 1951. Psychological tests of research scientists. *J. Consulting Psychol.*, **15**, 492–495.

ROE, A. 1953. A psychological study of eminent psychologists and anthropologists, and a comparison with biological and physical scientists. *Psychol. Monographs,* No. 352.

ROE, A., 1958. Early differentiation of interests. In *The second (1957) University of Utah research conference on the identification of creative scientific talent.* Salt Lake City: University of Utah Press.

ROGERS, C. R., 1961. *On becoming a person: A therapist's view of psychotherapy.* Boston: Houghton Mifflin.

ROGERS, C. R., 1968. *The interpersonal relationship in the facilitation of learning,* Columbus, Ohio: Merrill.

ROGERS, S. P., & HAYGOOD, R. C., 1968, Hypothesis behavior in a concept learning task with probabilistic feedback. *J. Exptl. Psychol.,* **76,** 160–165.

ROGERS, V. R., & LAYTON, D. E., 1966. An exploratory study of primary grade children's ability to conceptualize based upon context drawn from selected social studies topics. *J. Educ. Res.,* **59,** 195–197.

ROKEACH, M., 1945. Studies in beauty: II. Some determiners of the perception of beauty in women. *J. Social Psychol.,* **22,** 155–169.

ROKEACH, M., 1951a. A method for studying individual differences in "narrow-mindedness." *J. Personality,* **20,** 219–233.

ROKEACH, M., 1951b. "Narrow-mindedness" and personality. *J. Personality,* **20,** 234–251.

ROKEACH, M., 1954. The nature and meaning of dogmatism. *Psychol. Rev.,* **61,** 194–204.

ROKEACH, M., 1956. Political and religious dogmatism: An alternative to the authoritarian personality. *Psychol. Monographs,* **70** (18, Whole No. 425).

ROKEACH, M., 1960. *The open and closed mind: Investigations into the nature of belief systems and personality systems.* New York: Basic Books.

ROKEACH, M., 1968. *Beliefs, attitudes, and values.* San Francisco: Jossey-Bass.

ROKEACH, M., 1971. Long-range experimental modification of values, attitudes, and behavior. *Am. Psychologist,* **26,** 453–459.

ROKEACH, M., McGOVNEY, W. C., & DENNY, M. R., 1960. Dogmatic thinking versus rigid thinking: An experimental distinction. In M. Rokeach, *The Open and closed mind.* New York: Basic Books.

ROKEACH, M., & ROTHMAN, G., 1965. The principle of belief congruence and the congruity principle as models of cognitive interaction. *Psychol. Rev.,* **72,** 128–142.

ROKEACH, M., SMITH, P. W., & EVANS, R. I., 1960. Two kinds of prejudice or one. In M. Rokeach, *The open and closed mind.* New York: Basic Books.

RONNING, R. R. 1965. Anagram solution times: A function of the "rule out" factor. *J. Exptl. Psychol.,* **69,** 35–39.

ROSEKRANS, M. A., 1967. Imitation in children as a function of perceived similarity to a social model and vicarious reinforcement. *J. Personality & Social Psychol.,* **7,** 307–315.

ROSEKRANS, M. A., & HARTUP, W. W., 1967. Imitative influences of consistent and inconsistent response consequences to a model on aggressive behavior in children. *J. Personality & Social Psychol.,* **7,** 429–434.

ROSENBERG, M. J., 1956. Cognitive structure and attitudinal affect. *J. Abnormal & Social Psychol.,* **53,** 367–372.

ROSENBERG, M. J., 1960. An analysis of affective-cognitive consistency. In
C. Hovland & M. Rosenberg (Eds.), *Attitude organization and change*. New
Haven, Conn.: Yale.

ROSENBERG, M. J., 1965. When dissonance fails: On eliminating evaluation
apprehension from attitude measurement. *J. Personality & Social Psychol.*,
1, 28–42.

ROSENBERG, M. J., 1968. Hedonism, inauthenticity. and other goads toward
expansion of a consistency theory. In R. P. Abelson et al. (Eds.), *Theories
of cognitive consistency: A sourcebook*. Chicago: Rand McNally.

ROSENBERG, M. J., & ABELSON, R., 1960. An analysis of cognitive balancing.
In C. Hovland & M. Rosenberg (Eds.), *Attitude organization and change*.
New Haven, Conn.: Yale.

ROSENBERG, S., 1966. Associative clustering and repeated trials. *J. Gen.
Psychol.*, **74**, 89–96.

ROSENHAN, D., DeWILDE, D., & McDOUGAL, S., 1963. Pressure to conform
and logical problem solving. *Psychol. Repts.*, **13**, 227–230.

ROSENHAN, D., & WHITE, G. M., 1967. Observation and rehearsal as determinants of prosocial behavior. *J. Personality & Social Psychol.*, **5**, 424–431.

ROSENSTOCK, I. M., 1951. Perceptual aspects of repression. *J. Abnormal &
Social Psychol.*, **46**, 304–315.

ROSENTHAL, R., 1966. *Experimenter effects in behavioral research*. New York:
Appleton Century Crofts.

ROSS, B. M., & LEVY, N., 1960. A comparison of adjectival antonyms by simple
card-pattern formation. *J. Psychol.*, **49**, 133–137.

ROSS, B. M., RUPEL, J. W., & GRANT, D. A., 1952. Effects of personal,
impersonal, and physical stress upon cognitive behavior in a card-sorting
problem. *J. Abnormal & Social Psychol.*, **47**, 546–551.

ROSSMAN, J., 1931. *The psychology of the inventor*. Washington, D. C.:
Inventors Publishing Company.

ROSSOMANDO, N. P., & WEISS, W., 1970. Attitude change effects of timing
and amount of payment for counter attitudinal behavior. *J. Personality &
Social Psychol.*, **14**, 32–38.

ROTTER, J. B., 1966. Generalized expectancies for internal versus external
control of reinforcement. *Psychol. Monographs*, **80** (Whole No. 609).

ROTTER, J. B., & MULRY, R. C., 1965. Internal versus external control of reinforcement and decision time. *J. Personality & Social Psychol.*, **2**, 598–604.

ROWETON, W. E., & DAVIS, G. A., 1968. Effects of preresponse interval,
postinformative feedback interval, and problem difficulty in the identification
of concepts. *J. Exptl. Psychol.*, **78**, 642–645.

RUNQUIST, W. N., & FREEMAN, M., 1960. Roles of association value and syllable familiarization in verbal discrimination learning. *J. Exptl. Psychol.*, **59**,
396–401.

RUSSELL, D. C., 1956. *Children's thinking*. Boston: Ginn.

RUSSELL, R. W., 1940. II. The development of animism. *J. Genet. Psychol.*, **56**,
353–366.

RUSSELL, R. W., & DENNIS, W., 1939. Studies in animism. I. A standardized
procedure for the investigation of animism. *J. Genet. Psychol.*, **55**, 389–400.

RUSSELL, W. A., & STORMS, L. H., 1955. Implicit verbal chaining in paired-
associate learning. *J. Exptl. Psychol.*, **49**, 287–293.

RUST, R. M., 1948. Some correlates of the movement response. *J. Personality*, **16**,
369–401.

RYCHLAK, J. F., 1966. Reinforcement value: A suggested idiographic intensity dimension of meaningfulness for the personality theorist. *J. Personality,* **34**, 311–335.

RYCKMAN, R. M., & RODDA, W. C., 1971. Locus of control and initial task experience as determinants of confidence changes in a chance situation. *J. Personality & Social Psychol.,* **18**, 116–119.

SAENGER, G., & FLOWERMAN, S., 1954. Stereotypes and prejudicial attitudes. *Human Relations,* **7**, 217–238.

SAFREN, M. A., 1962. Associations, sets, and the solution of word problems. *J. Exptl. Psychol.,* **64**, 40–45.

SALTZ, E., 1961. Response pretraining: Differentiation or availability. *J. Exptl. Psychol.,* **62**, 583–587.

SALTZ, E., 1963. Compound stimuli in verbal learning: Cognitive and sensory differentiation versus stimulus selection. *J. Exptl. Psychol.,* **66**, 1–5.

SALTZ, E., 1967. Thorndike-Lorge frequency and *m* of stimuli as separate factors in paired–associates learning. *J. Exptl. Psychol.,* **73**. 473–478.

SALTZ, E., & FELTON, M., 1968. Response pretraining and subsequent paired-associate learning. *J. Exptl. Psychol.,* **77**, 258–262.

SALTZ, E., & SIEGEL, I. E., 1967. Concept overdiscrimination in children. *J. Exptl. Psychol.,* **73**, 1–8.

SALZINGER, S., SALZINGER, K., & HOBSON, S., 1967. The effect of syntactical structure in immediate memory for word sequences in middle- and lower-class children. *J. Psychol.,* **67**, 147–160.

SAMELSON, F., & YATES, J. F., 1967. Acquiescence and the F scale: Old assumptions and new data: *Psychol. Bull.,* **68**, 91–103.

SANDERS, B., ROSS, L. E., & HEAL, L. W., 1965. Reversal and nonreversal shift learning in normal children and retardates of comparable mental age. *J. Exptl. Psychol.,* **69**, 84–88.

SANFORD, F. H., & ROSENSTOCK. I. M., 1952. Projective techniques on the doorstep. *J. Abnormal & Social Psychol.,* **47**. 3–16.

SANFORD, N., 1955. The dynamics of identification. *Psychol. Rev.,* **62**. 106–118.

SANFORD, R. N., 1936. The effect of abstinence from food upon imaginal processes. *J. Psychol.,* **2**, 129–136.

SANFORD, R. N., 1937. The effect of abstinence from food upon imaginal processes. *J. Psychol.,* **3**, 145–159.

SARASON, I. G., 1956. Effect of anxiety, motivational instructions, and failure on serial learning. *J. Exptl. Psychol.,* **51**, 253–260.

SARASON, I. G., 1958. Effects on verbal learning of anxiety, reassurance, and meaningfulness of material. *J. Exptl. Psychol.,* **56**, 472–477.

SARASON, I. G., 1960. Empirical findings and theoretical problems in the use of anxiety scales. *Psychol. Bull.,* **57**, 403–415.

SARASON, I. G., & PALOLA, E. G., 1960. The relationship of test and general anxiety, difficulty of task, and experimental instructions to performance. *J. Exptl. Psychol.,* **59**, 185–191.

SARASON, S. B., 1944. Dreams and Thematic Apperception Test stories. *J. Abnormal & Social Psychol.,* **39**, 486–492.

SARBIN, T. R., 1952. A preface to a psychological analysis of the self. *Psychol. Rev.,* **59**, 11–22.

SARGENT, S. S., 1940. Thinking processes at various levels of difficulty: A quantitative and qualitative study of individual differences. *Arch. Psychol.,* No. 249.

SARNOFF, I., 1960a. Psychoanalytic theory and social attitudes. *Public Opinion Quart.*, **24**, 251–279.

SARNOFF, I., 1960b. Reaction formation and cynicism. *J. Personality*, **28**, 129–143.

SASSENRATH, J. M., 1967. Denotative meaningfulness, connotative directionality, and verbal learning. *J. Verbal Learning & Verbal Behavior.*, **6**, 817–818.

SAUGSTAD, P., 1955. Problem solving as dependent on availability of functions. *Brit. J. Psychol.*, **46**, 191–198.

SAUGSTAD, P., 1957. An analysis of Maier's pendulum problem. *J. Exptl. Psychol.*, **54**, 168–179.

SAUGSTAD, P., & RAAHEIM, K., 1960. Problem solving, past experience, and availability of functions. *Brit. J. Psychol.*, **51**, 97–104.

SCHACHTEL, E., 1959. *Metamorphosis.* New York: Basic Books.

SCHACHTER, S., GOLDMAN, R., & GORDAN, A., 1968. Effects of fear, food, deprivation, and obesity on eating. *J. Personality & Social Psychol.*, **10**, 91–97.

SCHAEFER, E. S., 1959. A circumplex model for maternal behavior. *J. Abnormal & Social Psychol.*, **59**, 226–235.

SCHAFER, R., 1958. Regression in the service of the ego: The relevance of a psychoanalytic concept for personality assessment. In G. Lindzey (Ed.), *Assessment of human motives.* New York: Rinehart.

SCHEIN, E. H., 1954. The effect of reward on adult imitative behavior. *J. Abnormal & Social Psychol.*, **49**, 389–395.

SCHLAG-REY, M., & SUPPES, P., 1968. Higher-order dimensions in concept identification. *Psychonomic Sci.*, **11**, 141–142.

SCHOENFELD, N., 1942. An experimental study of some problems relating to stereotypes. *Arch. Psychol.*, No. 270.

SCHOLNICK, E. K., OSLER, S. F., & KATZENELLENBOGAN, R., 1968. Discrimination learning and concept identification in disadvantaged and middle-class children. *Child Develop.*, **39**, 15–26.

SCHONBAR, R. R., 1961. Temporal and emotional factors in the selective recall of dreams. *J. Consulting Psychol.*, **25**, 67–73.

SCHRODER, H. M., & ROTTER, J. B., 1952. Rigidity as learned behavior. *J. Exptl. Psychol.*, **43**, 141–150.

SCHUESSLER, K., & STRAUSS, A., 1950. A study of concept learning by scale analysis. *Am. Sociological Rev.*, **15**, 752–762.

SCHULZ, R. W., & LOVELACE, E. A., 1964. Mediation in verbal paired-associate learning: The role of temporal factors. *Psychonomic Sci.*, **1**, 95–96.

SCHULZ, R. W., & WEAVER, G. E., 1968. The A-B, B-C, A-C mediation paradigm: The effects of variation in A-C study- and test-interval lengths and strength of A-B or B-C. *J. Exptl. Psychol.*, **76**, 303–311.

SCHULZ, R. W., WEAVER, G. E., & RADTKE, R C., 1965. Verbal satiation? *Psychonomic Sci.*, **2**, 43–44.

SCHUMAN, H., 1966. Social change and the validity of regional stereotypes in Pakistan. *Sociometry*, **29**, 428–440.

SCHVANEVELDT, R. W., 1966. Concept identification as a function of probability of positive instances and number of relevant dimensions. *J. Exptl. Psychol.*, **72**, 649–654.

SCHWARTZ, M., 1969a. Instructions to mediate, recall time, and type of paired-associate list. *J. Exptl. Psychol.*, **81**, 398–400.

SCHWARTZ, M., 1969b. Instructions to use verbal mediators in paired-associate learning. *J. Exptl. Psychol.*, **79**, 1–5.

SCHWARTZ, M., 1971. Subject-generated versus experimenter-supplied mediators in paired-associate learning. *J. Exptl. Psychol.*, **87**, 389–395.

SCHWARTZ, M., BUNDE, D. C., KNITTER, R. W., & KOTTLER, P. D., 1970. Instructions to use verbal mediators in learning a mixed paired-associate list. *J. Exptl. Psychol.*, **85**, 245–248.

SCHWARTZ, S. H., 1966. Trial-by-trial analyses of processes in simple and disjunctive concept-attainment tasks. *J. Exptl. Psychol.*, **72**, 456–465.

SCHWARTZ, S. H., FELDMAN, K. A., BROWN, M. E., & HEINGARTNER, A., 1969. Some personality correlates of conduct in two situations of moral conflict. *J. Personality*, **37**, 41–57.

SCODEL A., & FREEDMAN, M. L., 1956. Additional observations on the social perceptions of authoritarians and nonauthoritarians. *J. Abnormal & Social Psychol.*, **52**, 92–95.

SCODEL, A., & MUSSEN, P., 1953. Social perceptions of authoritarians and nonauthoritarians. *J. Abnormal & Social Psychol.*, **48**, 181–184.

SCOTT, W. A., 1968. Attitude measurement. In G. Lindzey & E. Aronson (Eds.), *Handbook of social psychology.* (2nd ed.) Reading, Mass.: Addison-Wesley.

SEARS, D. O., & FREEDMAN, J. L., 1965. Selective exposure to information. *Public Opinion Quart.*, **31**, 194–213.

SEARS, P. S., 1951. Doll play aggression in normal young children: Influence of sex, age, sibling status, father's absence. *Psychol. Monographs,* No. 323.

SEARS, R. R., 1936. Experimental studies of projection: I. Attribution of traits. *J. Social Psychol.*, **7**, 151–163.

SEARS, R R., 1943. Survey of objective studies of psychoanalytic concepts. *Social Sci. Res. Council Bull.,* No. 51.

SEARS, R. R., MACCOBY, E. E., & LEVIN, H., 1957. *Patterns of child rearing.* Evanston, III.: Row, Peterson.

SEARS, R. R., WHITING, J. W. M., NOWLIS, V., & SEARS, P. S., 1953. Some child-rearing antecedents of aggression and dependency in young children. *Genet. Psychol. Monographs,* **47**, 135–234.

SECORD, P. F., & SAUMER, E., 1960. Identifying Jewish names: Does prejudice increase accuracy? *J. Abnormal & Social Psychol.*, **61**, 144–145.

SEGAL, E. M., 1969. Hierarchical structure in free recall. *J. Exptl. Psychol.*, **80**, 59–63.

SEGAL, S. J., 1968. Patterns of response to thirst in an imagery task (Perky technique) as a function of cognitive style. *J. Personality*, **36**, 544–588.

SEGAL, S. J., & FUSELLA, V., 1970. Influence of imaged pictures and sounds on detection of visual and auditory signals. *J. Exptl. Psychol.*, **83**, 458–464.

SELLS, S. B., 1936. The atmosphere effect : An experimental study of reasoning. *Arch. Psychol.*, No. 200.

SHANNON C. E., 1948. A mathematical theory of communication. *Bell System Tech. J.*, **27**, 379–423; 623–656.

SHANTZ, C. U., & SMOCK, C. D., 1966. Development of distance conservation and the spatial coordinate system. *Child Develop.*, **37**, 943–948.

SHAPIRO, S. I., & PALERMO, D. S., 1967. Mediated clustering in free recall. *J. Exptl. Psychol.*, **75**, 365–371.

SHAW, M. E., 1932. A comparison of individuals and small groups in the rational solution of complex problems. *Am. J. Psychol.*, **44**, 491–504.

SHAW, M. E., & WRIGHT, J. M., 1967. *Scales for the measurement of attitudes.* New York: McGraw-Hill.

SHAW, W. A., & KLINE, L. H., 1947. A study of muscle action potentials during the attempted solution by children of problems of increasing difficulty. *J. Exptl. Psychol.,* **37,** 146–158.

SHEEHAN, P. W., 1967. Visual imagery and the organizational properties of perceived stimuli. *Brit. J. Psychol.,* **58,** 247–252.

SHEERER, E. T., 1949. The relationship between acceptance of self and acceptance of others. *J. Consulting Psychol.,* **13,** 169–175.

SHEFFIELD, F. D., 1946. The role of meaningfulness of stimulus and response in verbal learning. Unpublished doctoral dissertation, Yale.

SHEPARD, R. N., HOVLAND, C. I., & JENKINS, H. M., 1961. Learning and memorization of classifications. *Psychol. Monographs,* **75** (13, Whole No. 517).

SHERIF, M., & HOVLAND, C. I., 1961. *Social judgment.* New Haven, Conn: Yale.

SHILS, E. A. 1954. Authoritarianism: "Right" and "left." In R. Christie & M. Jahoda (Eds.), *Studies in the scope and method of the "Authoritarian personality."* New York: Free Press.

SHIMA, F., 1966. Sex, stimulus, association strength, duration and rate of repetition in semantic satiation. *Psychonomic Sci.,* **4,** 429–430.

SHRAUGER, S., & ALTROCCHI, J., 1964. The personality of the perceiver as a factor in person perception. *Psychol. Bull.,* **62,** 289–308.

SHUELL, T. J., 1969. Clustering and organization in free recall. *Psychol. Bull.,* **72,** 353–374.

SIEBER, J. E., & LANZETTA, J. T., 1964. Conflict and conceptual structure as determinants of decision-making behavior. *J. Personality,* **32,** 622–641.

SIEGEL, A. E., & SIEGEL, S., 1957. Reference groups, membership groups, and attitude change. *J. Abnormal & Social Psychol.,* **55,** 360–364.

SIEGEL, S., 1954. Certain determinants and correlates of authoritarianism. *Genet. Psychol. Monographs,* **49,** 187–229.

SIEGEL, S., & ANDREWS, J. McM., 1962. Magnitude of reinforcement and choice behavior in children. *J. Exptl. Psychol.,* **63,** 337–341.

SIGALL, H., & PAGE, R., 1971. Current stereotypes: A little fading, a little faking. *J. Personality & Social Psychol.,* **18,** 247–255.

SIGEL, I. E., 1953. Developmental trends in the abstraction ability of children. *Child Develop.,* **24,** 131–144.

SIGEL, I. E., 1954. The dominance of meaning. *J. Genet. Psychol.,* **85,** 201–207.

SIGEL, I. E., SALTZ, E., & ROSKIND, W., 1967. Variables determining concept conservation in children. *J. Exptl. Psychol.,* **74,** 471–475.

SILLER, J., 1957. Socioeconomic status and conceptual thinking. *J. Abnormal & Social Psychol.,* **55,** 365–371.

SILVERMAN, I., 1964a. In defense of dissonance theory: Reply to Chapanis and Chapanis. *Psychol. Bull.,* **62,** 205–209.

SILVERMAN, I. 1964b. Self-esteem and differential responsiveness to success and failure. *J. Abnormal & Social Psychol.,* **69,** 115–119.

SILVERMAN, I., 1971. On the resolution and tolerance of cognitive consistency in a natural-occurring event: Attitudes and beliefs following the Senator Edward M. Kennedy incident. *J. Personality & Social Psychol.,* **17,** 171–178.

SILVERMAN, I. W., 1967. Incidence of guilt reactions in children. *J. Personality & Social Psychol.,* **7,** 338–340.

SILVERMAN, L. H., & SILVERMAN, D. K., 1964. A clinical-experimental approach to the study of subliminal stimulation: The effects of a drive-related stimulus upon Rorschach responses. *J. Abnormal & Social Psychol.*, **69**, 158–172.

SIMMONS, A. J., & GOSS, A. E., 1957. Animistic responses as a function of sentence contexts and instructions. *J. Genet. Psychol.*, **91**, 181–189.

SIMMONS, C. H., & LERNER, M. J., 1968. Altruism as a search for justice. *J. Personality & Social Psychol.*, **9**, 216–225.

SIMON, H. A., 1967. Motivational and emotional controls of cognition. *Psychol. Rev.*, **74**, 29–39.

SIMON, H. A., & NEWELL, A., 1971. Human problem solving: The state of the theory in 1970. *Am. Psychologist*, **26**, 145–159.

SIMON, H. A., & SIMON, P. A., 1962. Trial and error search in solving difficult problems: Evidence from the game of chess. *Behavioral Sci.*, **7**, 425–429.

SIMON, S. H., & JACKSON, B., 1968. Effect of a relevant versus irrelevant observation stimulus on concept-identification learning. *J. Exptl. Psychol.*, **76**, 125–128.

SIMPSON. M. E. & JOHNSON D. M., 1966. Atmosphere and conversion errors in syllogistic reasoning. *J. Exptl. Psychol.* **72**, 197–200.

SINGER, J. L., 1966. *Daydreaming: An introduction to the experimental study of inner experience.* New York: Random House.

SINGER, J. L., & ANTROBUS, J. S., 1963. A factor-analytic study of day dreaming and conceptually related cognitive and personality variables. *Perceptual & Motor Skills*, **17**, 187–209.

SINGER, J. L., & McCRAVEN, V. G., 1961. Some characteristics of adult day-dreaming. *J. Psychol.*, **51**, 151–164.

SINGER, J. L., & SCHONBAR, R., 1961. Correlates of daydreaming: A dimension of self-awareness. *J. Consulting Psychol.*, **25**, 1–6.

SINHA, A. K. P., & UPADHYAY, O. P., 1960. Stereotypes of male and female university students in India toward different ethnic goups. *J. Social Psychol.*, **51**, 93–102.

SKINNER, B. F., 1938. *The behavior of organisms: An experimental analysis.* New York: Appleton Century Crofts.

SLAMECKA, N. J., 1967. Transfer with mixed and unmixed lists as a function of semantic relations. *J. Exptl. Psychol.*, **73**, 405–410.

SLAMECKA, N. J., 1968. A methodological analysis of shift paradigms in human discrimination learning. *Psychol. Bull.*, **69**, 423–438.

SLIGHT, D., 1924. Hypnagogic phenomena. *J. Abnormal & Social Psychol.*, **19**, 274–282.

SMEDSLUND, J., 1961a. The acquisition of conservation of substance and weight in children: II. External reinforcement of conservation of weight and of the operations of addition and subtraction. *Scand. J. Psychol.*, **2**, 71–84.

SMEDSLUND, J., 1961b. The acquisition of conservation of substance and weight in children: III. Extinction of conservation of weight aquired "normally" and by means of empirical controls on a balance. *Scand J. Psychol.*, **2**, 85–87.

SMEDSLUND, J., 1961c. The acquisition of conservation of substance and weight in children: IV. Attempt at extinction of the visual components of the weight concept. *Scand. J. Psychol.*, **2**, 153–155.

SMEDSLUND, J., 1961d. The acquisition of conservation of substance and weight in children: V. Practice in conflict situations without external reinforcement. *Scand. J. Psychol.,* **2**, 156–160.

SMEDSLUND, J., 1961e. The acquisition of conservation of substance and weight in children: VI. Practice on continuous versus discontinuous material in conflict situations without external reinforcement. *Scand. J. Psychol.,* **2**, 203–210.

SMEDSLUND, J., 1969. Psychological diagnostics. *Psychol. Bull.,* **71**, 237–248.

SMILEY, S. S., & WEIR, M. W., 1966. The role of dimensional dominance in reversal and nonreversal shift behavior. *J. Exptl. Child Psychol.,* **4**, 296–307.

SMITH, D. B., & ROTH, R. M., 1960. Problem solving behavior of preschool children in a spontaneous setting. *J. Genet. Psychol.,* **97**, 139–143.

SMITH, D. E. P., & RAYGOR, A. L.. 1956. Verbal satiation and personality. *J. Abnormal & Social Psychol.,* **52**, 323–326.

SMITH, G. J. W., SPENCE, D. P., & KLEIN, G. S., 1959. Subliminal effects of verbal stimuli. *J. Abnormal & Social Psychol.,* **59**, 167–176.

SMITH. H. P., & APPELFELD, S. W., 1965. Children's paintings and the projective expression of personality: An experimental investigaton. *J. Genet. Psychol.,* **107**, 289–294.

SMITH, I. D., 1968. The effects of training procedures upon the acquisition of conservation and weight. *Child Develop.,* **39**, 515–526.

SMITH, M. B., BRUNER, J. S., & WHITE R. W., 1956. *Opinions and personality.* New York: Wiley.

SMITH, M. O., 1969. History of the motor theories of attention. *J. Gen. Psychol.,* **80**, 243–257.

SMITH, P. A., 1962. A comparison of three sets of rotated factor analytic solutions of self-concept data. *J. Abnormal & Social Psychol.,* **64**, 326–333.

SMITH, S. M., BROWN, H. O., TOMAN, J. E. P., & GOODMAN, L. S., 1947. The lack of cerebral effects of d-tubocurarine. *Anesthesiology,* **8**, 1–14.

SMOKE, K. L.. 1932. An objective study of concept formation. *Psychol. Monographs,* No. 191.

SMOKE, K. L., 1933. Negative instances in concept learning. *J. Exptl. Psychol.,* **16**, 583–588.

SOLLEY, C. M., & SNYDER, F. W., 1958. Information processing and problem solving. *J. Exptl. Psychol.,* **55**, 384–387.

SOLSO, R. L., 1968. Functional stimulus selection as related to color versus verbal stimuli. *J. Exptl. Psychol.,* **78**, 382–387.

SOMMER, R., & KILLIAN, L. M., 1954a. Areas of value difference: I. A method for investigation. *J. Social Psychol.,* **39**, 227–235.

SOMMER, R., & KILLIAN, L. M., 1954b. Areas of value difference: II. Negrowhite relations. *J. Social Psychol.,* **39**, 237–244.

SONSTROEM, A. McK., 1966. On the conservation of solids. In J. S. Bruner, R. R. Olver, P. M. Greenfield, et al., *Studies in cognitive growth.* New York: Wiley.

SONTAG, L. W., & BAKER, C. T., 1958. II. Personality, familial, and physical correlates of change in mental ability. In L. W. Sontag, C. T. Baker, & V. L. Nelson, *Mental growth and personality development: A longitudinal study. Soc. Res. Child Develop. Monograph,* **23** (68, No. 2).

SPEISMAN, J. C., LAZARUS. R. S., MORDKOFF, A., & DAVISON, L., 1964. Experimental reduction of stress based on ego-defense theory. *J. Abnormal & Social Psychol.,* **68**, 367–380.

SPENCE, D. P., 1967. Subliminal perception and perceptual defense : Two sides of a single problem. *Behavioral Sci., 12*, 183–193.

SPENCE, D. P., & EHRENBURG, B., 1964. Effects of oral deprivation on responses to subliminal and supraliminal verbal food stimuli. *J. Abnormal & Social Psychol., 69*, 10–18.

SPENCE, D. P., & HOLLAND, B., 1962. The restricting effects of awareness : A paradox and an explanation *J. Abnormal & Social Psychol., 64*, 163–174.

SPENCE, K. W., 1945. An experimental test of the continuity and non-continuity theories of discrimination learning. *J. Exptl. Psychol., 35*, 253–266.

SPENCE, K. W., 1956. *Behavior theory and conditioning.* New Haven, Conn. : Yale.

SPENCE, K. W., 1958. A theory of emotionally based drive (D) and its relation to performance in simple learning situations. *Am. Psychologist, 13*, 131–141.

SPENCE, K. W., BERGMANN, G., & LIPPITT, R., 1950. A study of simple learning under irrelevant motivational-reward conditions. *J. Exptl. Psychol., 40*, 539–551.

SPIELBERGER, C. D., & WEITZ, H., 1964. Improving the academic performance of anxious college freshmen : A group-counseling approach to the prevention of underachievement. *Psychol. Monographs, 78* (13, Whole No. 590).

SPIKER, C. C., 1963. Verbal factors in the discrimination learning of children. In J. C. Wright & J. Kagan (Eds.), Basic cognitive processes in children. *Social Res. Child Develop. Monograph, 28* (86, No. 2).

SPILKA, B., & STRUENING, E. L., 1956. A questionnaire study of personality and ethnocentrism. *J. Social Psychol., 44*, 65–71.

SPRANGER, E., 1928. *Types of men.* Halle East Germany : Niemeyer.

SPRINGER, D. V., 1951. Development of concepts related to the clock as shown in young children's drawings. *J. Genet. Psychol., 79*, 47–54.

SQUIRES, P. C., 1938a. The creative psychology of Carl Maria von Weber. *Character & Personality, 6*, 203–217.

SQUIRES, P. C., 1938b. The creative psychology of César Franck. *Character & Personality, 7*, 41–49.

STAATS, A. W., 1969. Experimental demand characteristics and classical conditioning of attitudes. *J. Personality & Social Psychol., 11*, 187–192.

STAATS, A. W., & STAATS, C. K., 1958. Attitudes established by classical conditioning. *J. Abnormal & Social Psychol., 57*, 37–40.

STAATS, A. W., STAATS C. K., & HEARD, W. G., 1959. Language conditioning of meaning to meaning using a semantic generalization paradigm. *J. Exptl. Psychol., 57*, 187–192.

STAATS, C. K., & STAATS, A. W., 1957. Meaning established by classical conditioning. *J. Exptl. Psychol., 54*, 74–80.

STAGNER, R., 1944. Studies of aggressive social attitudes : III. The role of personal and family score s. *J. Social Psychol., 20*, 129–140.

STAGNER, R., & CONGDON, C. S., 1955. Another failure to demonstrate displacement of aggression. *J. Abnormal & Social Psychol., 51*, 695–696.

STAGNER, R., & OSGOOD, C. E., 1946. Impact of war on a nationalistic frame of reference : I. Changes in general approval and qualitative patterning of certain stereotypes. *J. Social Psychol., 24*, 187–215.

STAUB, E., 1970. A child in distress : The influence of age and number of witnesses on children's attempts to help. *J. Personality & Social Psychol., 14*, 130–140.

STAUB, E., 1971. Helping a person in distress: The influence of implicit and explicit "rules" of conduct on children and adults. *J. Personality & Social Psychol.,* **17**, 137–144.

STEIN, D. D., HARDYCK, J. A., & SMITH, M. B., 1965. Race and belief: An open and shut case. *J. Personality & Social Psychol.,* **1**, 281–289.

STEIN, M. I., and MEER, B., 1954. Perceptual organization in a study of creativity. *J. Psychol.,* **37**, 39–43.

STEINER, T. E., & SOBEL, R., 1968. Intercomponent association formation during paired-associate training with compound stimuli. *J. Exptl. Psychol.,* **77**, 275–280.

STEPHENSON, G. M., & WHITE, J. H., 1968. An experimental study of some effects of injustice on children's moral behavior. *J. Exptl. Social Psychol.,* **4**, 460–469.

STEPHENSON, G. M., & WHITE, J. H., 1970. Privilege, deprivation, and children's moral behavior: An experimental clarification of the role of investments. *J. Exptl. Social Psychol.,* **6**, 167–176.

STEPHENSON, W., 1953. *The study of behavior: Q-technique and its methodology.* Chicago: The University of Chicago Press.

STEVENS, S. S., 1951. Mathematics, measurement, and psychophysics. In S. S. Stevens (Ed.), *Handbook of experimental psychology.* New York: Wiley.

STEWART, L. H., 1955. The expression of personality in drawings and paintings. *Genet. Psychol. Monographs,* **51**, 45–103.

STOCK, D., 1949. An investigation into the interrelations between the self-concept and feelings directed toward other persons and groups. *J. Consulting Psychol.,* **13**, 167–180.

STONER, J. A. F., 1961. A comparison of individual and group decisions involving risk. Unpublished masters thesis, MIT.

STONER, J. A. F., 1968. Risky and cautious shifts in group decisions: The influence of widely held values. *J. Exptl. Social Psychol.,* **4**, 422–459.

STORMS, L. H., 1958. Apparent backward association: A situational effect. *J. Exptl. Psychol.,* **55**, 390–395.

STOTLAND, E., KATZ, D., & PATCHEN, M., 1959. The reduction of prejudice through the arousal of self-insight. *J. Personality,* **27**, 507–531.

STRAUSS, A. L., 1951. The animism controversy: Re-examination of Huang-Lee data. *J. Genet. Psychol.,* **78**, 105–113.

STRAUSS, A. L., 1952. The development and transformation of monetary meanings in the child. *Am. Sociological Rev.,* **17**, 275–286.

STRAUSS, A. L., 1954. The development of conceptions of rules in children. *Child Develop.,* **25**, 193–208.

STREUFERT, S., SUEDFELD, P., & DRIVER, M. J., 1965. Conceptual structure, information search, and information utilization. *J. Personality & Social Psychol.,* **2**, 736–740.

STROOP, J. R., 1935. Studies in interference in serial verbal reactions. *J. Exptl. Psychol.,* **18**, 643–661.

STUART, R. B., 1967. Decentration in the development of children's concepts of moral and causal judgment. *J. Genet. Psychol.,* **111**, 59–68.

STUBIN, E. J., HEIMER, W. I. & TATZ, S. J., 1970. Total time and presentation time in paired-associate learning. *J. Exptl. Psychol.,* **84**, 308–310.

SUEDFELD, P., GLUCKSBERG, S., & VERNON, J., 1967. Sensory deprivation as a drive operation: Effects upon problem solving. *J. Exptl. Psychol.,* **75**, 166–169.

SUEDFELD, P., & HAGEN, R. L., 1966. Measurement of information complexity: I. Conceptual structure and information pattern as factors in information processing. *J. Personality & Social Psychol.,* **4**, 233–236.

SUINN, R. M., 1961. The relationship between self-acceptance and acceptance of others: A learning theory analysis. *J. Abnormal & Social Psychol.,* **63**, 37–42.

SULZER, J. L., & BURGLASS, R. K., 1968. Responsibility, attribution, empathy, and punitiveness. *J. Personality,* **36**, 272–282.

SUTTON, R. S., 1962. Behavior in the attainment of economic concepts. *J. Psychol.,* **53**, 37–46.

SUTTON-SMITH, B., 1966. Piaget on play: A critique. *Psychol. Rev.,* **73**, 104–110.

SWETS, J. A., 1961. Is there a sensory threshold? *Science,* **134**, 168–177.

SWETS, J. A. (Ed.), 1964. *Signal detection and recognition by human observers: Contemporary readings.* New York: Wiley.

SYMONDS, P. M., 1946. *The dynamics of human adjustment.* New York: Appleton Century Crofts.

SYMONDS, P. M., 1949. *Adolescent fantasy.* New York: Columbia.

SZÉKELY, L., 1950. Productive processes in learning and thinking. *Acta Psychol.,* **7**, 388–407.

TAFT, R., 1956. Intolerance of ambiguity and ethnocentrism. *J. Consulting Psychol.,* **20**, 153–154.

TAFT, R., 1959. Ethnic stereotypes, attitudes, and familiarity: Australia. *J. Social Psychol.,* **49**, 177–186.

TANAKA, Y., & OSGOOD, C. E., 1965. Cross-culture, cross-concept, and cross-subject generality of affective meaning systems. *J. Personality & Social Psychol.,* **2**, 143–153.

TANNENBAUM, P. H., 1966. Mediated generalization of attitude change via the principle of congruity. *J. Personality & Social Psychol.,* **3**, 493–499.

TANNENBAUM, P. H., 1967. The congruity principle revisited: Studies in the reduction, induction, and generalization of persuasion. In L. Berkowitz (Ed.), *Advances in experimental social psychology.* Vol. 3. New York: Academic.

TANNENBAUM, P. H., 1968. The congruity principle: Retrospective reflections and recent research. In R. P. Abelson et al. (Eds.), *Theories of cognitive consistency: A sourcebook.* Chicago: Rand McNally.

TANNENBAUM, P. H., & GENGEL, R. W., 1966. Generalization of attitude change through congruity principle relationships. *J. Personality & Social Psychol.,* **3**, 299–304.

TANNER, W. P., Jr., & SWETS, J. A., 1954. A decision-making theory of visual detection. *Psychol. Rev.,* **61**, 401–409.

TART, C. T., 1965. Toward the experimental control of dreaming: A review of the literature. *Psychol. Bull.,* **64**, 81–91.

TART, C. T. (Ed.), 1969. *Altered states of consciousness: A book of readings.* New York: Wiley.

TAYLOR, D. W., BERRY, P. C., & BLOCK, C. H., 1958. Does group participation when using brainstorming facilitate or inhibit creative thinking? *Admin. Sci. Quart.,* **3**, 23–47.

TAYLOR, D. W., & FAUST, W. L., 1952. Twenty questions: Efficiency in problem solving as a function of size of group. *J. Exptl. Psychol.,* **44**, 360–368.

TAYLOR, J. A., 1951. The relationship of anxiety to the conditioned eyelid response. *J. Exptl. Psychol.,* **41**, 81–92.

TAYLOR, J. A., 1953. A personality scale of manifest anxiety. *J. Abnormal & Social Psychol.,* **48**, 285–290.

TAYLOR, J. A., & SPENCE, K. W., 1952. The relationship of anxiety to perform-ance in serial learning. *J. Exptl. Psychol.,* **44**, 61–64.

TERWILLIGER, R. F., 1962. Free association patterns as a factor relating to semantic differential responses. *J. Abnormal & Social Psychol.,* **65**, 87–94.

TESSER, A., GATEWOOD, R., & DRIVER, M., 1968. Some determinants of gratitude. *J. Personality & Social Psychol.,* **9**, 233–236.

THOMPSON, R. F., 1958. A comparison of correction and modified correction procedures on the acquisition of a 12-unit verbal maze. *J. Exptl. Psychol.,* **56**, 443–447.

THORNDIKE E. L., 1898. Animal intelligence: An experimental study of the associative processes in animals. *Psychol. Rev. Monograph Suppl.,* No. 8.

THORNDIKE, E. L., 1922. The effect of changed data upon reasoning. *J. Exptl. Psychol.,* **5**, 33–38.

THORNDIKE, E. L., & LORGE, I., 1944. *The teacher's word book of 30,000 words.* New York: Columbia.

THORSON, A. M., 1925. The relation of muscular action potentials to imaginal weight lifting. *J. Exptl. Psychol.,* **8**, 1–32.

THURSTONE, L. L., 1928. Attitudes can be measured. *Am. J. Psychol.,* **33**, 529–554.

THURSTONE, L. L., & CHAVE, E. J., 1929. *The measurement of attitude.* Chicago: The University of Chicago Press.

TIGHE, L. S., 1965. Effect of perceptual pretraining on reversal and nonreversal shifts. *J. Exptl. Psychol.,* **70**, 379–385.

TIGHE, T. J., & TIGHE, L. S., 1967. Discrimination shift performance of children as a function of age and shift procedure. *J. Exptl. Psychol.,* **74**, 466–470.

TILKER, H. A., 1970. Socially responsible bahavior as a function of observer responsibility and victim feedback. *J. Personality & Social Psychol.,* **14**, 95–100.

TITCHENER, E. B., 1909. *Lectures in the experimental psychology of the thought-processes.* New York: Macmillan.

TITCHENER, E. B., 1910. *A textbook of psychology.* New York: Macmillan.

TITCHENER, E. B., 1914. *A primer of psychology.* (Rev. ed.) New York: Macmillan.

TITTLE, C. R., & HILL, R. J., 1967. Attitude measurement and prediction of behavior: An evaluation of conditions and measurement techniques. *Socio-metry,* **30**, 199–213.

TITUS, H. E., & HOLLANDER, E. P., 1957. The California F scale in psychological research: 1950–1955. *Psychol. Bull.,* **54**, 47–64.

TOLMAN, E. C., 1932. *Purposive behavior in animals and men.* New York: Appleton Century Crofts.

TOLMAN, E. C., 1948. Cognitive maps in rats and men. *Psychol. Rev.,* **55**, 189–208.

TORCIVIA, J. M., & LAUGHLIN, P. R., 1968. Dogmatism and concept-attain-ment strategies. *J. Personality & Social Psychol.,* **8**, 397–400.

TORRANCE, E. P., 1962. *Guiding creative talent.* Englewood Cliffs, N. J.: Prentice-Hall.

TORRANCE, E. P., 1964. Education and creativity. In C. W. Taylor (Ed.), *Creativity: Progress and potential.* New York: McGraw-Hill.

TORRANCE, E. P., & DAUW, D. C., 1965. Aspirations and dreams of three groups of creatively gifted high school seniors and comparable unselected groups. *Gifted Child Quart.*, **9**, 177–182.

TRABASSO, T., 1963. Stimulus emphasis and all-or-none learning in concept identification. *J. Exptl. Psychol.*, **65**, 398–406.

TRABASSO, T., & BOWER, G., 1964. Presolution reversal and dimensional shifts in concept identification. *J. Exptl. Psychol.*, **67**, 398–399.

TRABASSO, T., & BOWER, G., 1966. Presolution dimensional shifts in concept identification : A test of the sampling with replacement axiom in all-or-none models. *J. Math. Psychol.*, **3**, 163–173.

TRABASSO, T., & BOWER, G., 1968. *Attention in learning: Theory and research.* New York : Wiley.

TRIANDIS, H. C., 1961. A note on Rokeach's theory of prejudice. *J. Abnormal & Social Psychol.*, **62**, 184–186.

TRIANDIS, H. C., 1964. Exploratory factor analyses of the behavioral component of social attitudes. *J. Abnormal & Social Psychol.*, **68**, 420–430.

TRIANDIS, H. C., & DAVIS, E. E., 1965. Race and belief as determinants of behavioral intentions. *J. Personality & Social Psychol.*, **2**, 715–725.

TRIANDIS, H. C., & VASSILIOU, V. 1967. Frequency of contact and stereotyping. *J. Personality & Social Psychol.*, **7**, 316–328.

TROWBRIDGE, N., & CHARLES, D. C., 1966. Creativity in art students. *J. Genet. Psychol.*, **109**, 281–290.

TURIEL, E., 1966. An experimental test of the sequentiality of developmental stages in the child's moral judgments. *J. Personality & Social Psychol.*, **3**, 611–618.

TURNER, M. B., 1965. *Philosophy and the science of behavior.* New York : Appleton Century Crofts.

TURSKY, B., SCHWARTZ, G. E., & CRIDER, A., 1970. Differential patterns of heart rate and skin resistance during a digit-transformation task. *J. Exptl. Psychol.*, **83**, 451–457.

TWEDT, H. M., & UNDERWOOD, B. J., 1959. Mixed vs. unmixed lists in transfer studies. *J. Exptl. Psychol.*, **58**, 111–116.

UESUGI, T. K., & VINACKE, W. E., 1963. Strategy in a feminine game. *Sociometry*, **26**, 75–88.

UĞUREL-SEMIN, R., 1952. Moral behavior and moral judgment of children. *J. Abnormal & Social Psychol.*, **47**, 463–474.

UHL, N., 1966. The intradimensional and extradimensional shifts as a function of amount of training and similarity between training and shift stimuli. *J. Exptl. Psychol.*, **72**, 429–433.

UNDERWOOD, B. J., 1952. An orientation for research on thinking. *Psychol. Rev.*, **59**, 209–220.

UNDERWOOD, B. J., HAM, M., & EKSTRAND, B., 1962. Cue selection in paired-associate learning. *J. Exptl. Psychol.*, **64**, 405–409.

UNDERWOOD, B. J., & RICHARDSON, J., 1956. Some verbal materials for the study of concept formation. *Psychol. Bull.*, **53**, 84–95.

UNDERWOOD, B. J., RUNQUIST, W. N., & SCHULZ, R. W., 1959. Response learning in paired-associate lists as a function of intralist similarity. *J. Exptl. Psychol.*, **58**, 70–78.

UNDERWOOD, B. J., & SCHULZ, R. W., 1960. Response dominance and rate of learning paired-associates. *J. Gen. Psychol.*, **62**, 153–158.

VANNOY, J. S. 1965. Generality of cognitive complexity—simplicity as a personality construct. *J. Personality & Social Psychol.,* **2**, 385–396.

VETTER, G. B., 1947. What makes attitudes and opinions "liberal" or "conservative ?" *J. Abnormal & Social Psychol.,* **42**, 125–130.

VIDMAR, N., 1970. Group composition and the risky shift. *J. Exptl. Social Psychol.,* **6**, 153–166.

VINACKE, W. E., 1942. The discrimination of color and form at levels of illumination below conscious awareness. *Arch. Psychol.,* No. 267.

VINACKE, W. E., 1949. Stereotyping among national-racial groups in Hawaii : A study in ethnocentrism. *J. Social Psychol.,* **30**, 265–291.

VINACKE, W. E., 1954. Concept formation in children of school ages. *Education,* **74**, 527–534.

VINACKE, W. E., 1956. Explorations in the dynamic processes of stereotyping. *J. Social Psychol.,* **43**, 105–132.

VINACKE, W. E., 1957. Stereotypes as social concepts. *J. Social Psychol.,* **46**, 229–243.

VINACKE, W. E., 1959a. A comparison of the Rosenzweig P-F study and the Brown interracial version : Hawaii. *J. Social Psychol.,* **49**, 161–175.

VINACKE, W. E., 1959b. Sex roles in a three-person game. *Sociometry,* **22**, 343–360.

VINACKE, W. E., 1960a. The drive-modification theory of human motivation. *J. Genet. Psychol.,* **96**, 245–268.

VINACKE, W. E., 1960b. Relations between motivational conditions and thinking. In E. Harms (Ed.), *Fundamentals of psychology: The psychology of thinking. N. Y. Acad. Sci. Annals,* **91**, 76–93.

VINACKE, W. E., 1962. Motivation as a complex problem. In M. R. Jones (Ed.), *Nebraska symposium on motivation.* Lincoln, Neb. : University of Nebraska Press.

VINACKE, W. E., 1964. Puissance, stratégie, et formation de coalitions dans les triades dans quatre conditions expérimentales. *Bull. C.E.R.P.,* **13**, 119–144.

VINACKE, W. E., 1968. *Foundations of psychology.* New York : American Book.

VINACKE, W. E., & GULLICKSON, G. R., 1964. Age and sex differences in the formation of coalitions. *Child Develop.,* **35**, 1217–1231.

VROOM, V. H., 1959. Projection, negation, and the self concept. *Human relations,* **12**, 335–344.

WACHTEL, P. L., 1968. Anxiety, attention, and coping with threat. *J. Abnormal Psychol.,* **73**, 137–143.

WAGMAN, M., 1967. Sex differences in types of daydreaming. *J. Personality & Social Psychol.,* **7**, 329–332.

WAGNER, C., & WHEELER, L., 1969. Model, need, and cost effects in helping behavior. *J. Personality & Social Psychol.,* **12**, 111–116.

WAKIN, A. H., & BRAUN, J. R., 1966. Semantic satiation and problem solving *Psychonomic Sci.,* **5**, 469–470.

WALLACE, J., & SADALLA, E., 1966. Behavioral consequences of transgression : I. The effects of social recognition. *J. Exptl. Res. Personality,* **1**, 187–194.

WALLACH, M. A., & KOGAN, N., 1965. *Modes of thinking in young children* New York : Holt.

WALLACH, M. A., KOGAN, N., & BEM, D. J., 1962. Group influence on individual risk taking. *J. Abnormal & Social Psychol.,* **65**, 75–86.

WALLACH, M. A., KOGAN, N., & BEM, D. J., 1964. Diffusion of responsibility and level of risk taking in groups. *J. Abnormal & Social Psychol.,* **68**, 263–274.

WALLACH, M. A., & WING, C. W., Jr., 1968. Is risk a value? *J. Personality & Social Psychol.,* **9**, 101–106.

WALLAS, G., 1926. *The art of thought.* New York: Harcourt, Brace.

WALSTER, E. & PRESTHOLDT, P., 1966. The effect of misjudging another: Over-compensation or dissonance reduction? *J. Exptl. Social Psychol.,* **2**, 85–97.

WALTERS, R. H., & DEMKOW, L., 1963. Timing of punishment as a determinant of resistance to temptation. *Child Develop.,* **34**, 207–214.

WALY, P., & COOK, S. W., 1965. Effect of attitude on judgments of plausibility. *J. Personality & Social Psychol.,* **2**, 745–749.

WARD, C. D., 1965. Ego involvement and the absolute judgment of attitude statements. *J. Personality & Social Psychol.,* **2**, 202–208.

WARD, C. D., 1966. Attitude and involvement in the absolute judgment of attitude statements. *J. Personality & Social Psychol.,* **4**, 465–476.

WARDEN, C. J., 1924. The relative economy of various modes of attack in the mastery of a stylus maze. *J. Exptl. Psychol.,* **7**, 243–275.

WATSON, D., & BAUMAL, E. 1967. Effects of locus of control and expectation of future control upon present performance. *J. Personality & Social Psychol.,* **6**, 212–215.

WATSON, J. B., 1924. *Psychology from the standpoint of a behaviorist.* (2nd ed.) Philadelphia: Lippincott.

WATSON, J. B., 1930. *Behaviorism.* New York: Norton. (Originally published: 1924–1925.)

WEAVER, G. E., HOPKINS, R. H., & SCHULZ, R. W., 1968. The A-B, B-C, A-C mediation paradigm: A-C performance in the absence of study trials. *J. Exptl. Psychol.,* **77**, 670–675.

WEAVER, G. E., & SCHULZ, R. W., 1968. A-B, B-C, A-C, mediation paradigm: Recall of A-B following varying numbers of trials of A-C learning. *J. Exptl. Psychol.,* **78**, 113–119.

WEAVER, H. E., & MADDEN, E. H., 1949. "Direction" in problem solving. *J. Psychol.,* **27**, 331–345.

WEIGL, E., 1941. On the psychology of so-called processes of abstraction. *J Abnormal & Social Psychol.,* **36**, 3–33.

WEINER, B., 1966. Motivation and memory. *Psychol. Monographs,* **80** (18, Whole No. 626).

WEINSTEIN, J. A., AVERILL, J. R., OPTON, E. M., Jr., & LAZARUS, R. S., 1968. Defensive style and discrepancy between self-report and physiological indexes of stress. *J. Personality & Social. Psychol,* **10**, 406–413.

WEINSTOCK, R. B., & DALY, H. B., 1971. Response learning, association formation, and repeated testing effects in a paired-associate task. *J. Exptl. Psychol.,* **87**, 343–347.

WEIR, M. W., 1964. Developmental changes in problem solving strategies. *Psychol. Rev.,* **71**, 473–490.

WEISS, S. A., & FISHMAN, S., 1963. Extended and telescoped phantom limbs in unilateral amputees. *J. Abnormal & Social Psychol.,* **66**, 489–497.

WELCH, L., 1940. A preliminary investigation of some aspects of the hierarchical development of concepts. *J. Gen. Psychol.,* **22**, 359–378.

WELCH, L., & LONG, L., 1940a. A further investigation of the higher structural phases of concept formation. *J. Psychol.,* **10**, 211–220.

WELCH, L., & LONG, L., 1940b. The higher structural phases of concept formation of children. *J. Psychol.,* **9**, 59–95.

WELLS, H., & WATSON, D., 1965. Strategy training and practice in disjunctive concept attainment. *Psychol. Repts.,* **17,** 925–926.

WELLS, W. D., & GOLDSTEIN, R., L., 1964. Sears' study of projection : Replication and critiques. *J. Social Psychol.,* **64,** 169–179.

WELSH, G. S., 1959. *Welsh Figure Preference Test: Preliminary manual.* (Rev. ed.) Palo Alto, Calif. : Consulting Psychologists Press.

WENZEL, B. M., & FLURRY, C., 1948. The sequential order of concept attainment. *J. Exptl. Psychol.,* **38**, 547–557.

WERNER, H., 1948. *Comparative psychology of mental development.* (Rev. ed.) New York : International Universities Press.

WERNER, H., & KAPLAN, B., 1963. *Symbol formation: An organismic-developmental approach to language and expressions of thought.* New York : Wiley.

WERNER, H., & KAPLAN, E., 1952. The acquisition of word meanings : A developmental study. *Monograph Soc. Res. Child Develop.,* **15**, No. 1.

WERTHEIMER, M., 1959. *Productive thinking.* New York : Harper & Row. (Originally published : 1945.)

WESTIE, F. R., & DeFLEUR, M. L., 1959. Autonomic responses and their relationship to race attitudes. *J. Abnormal & Social Psychol.,* **58**, 340–347.

WHITE, B. J., ALTER, R. D., & RARDIN, M., 1965. Authoritarianism, dogmatism, and usage of conceptual categories. *J. Personality & Social Psychol.,* **2**, 293–295.

WHITE, B. J., & HARVEY, O. J., 1965. Effects of personality and own stand on judgment and production of statements about a central issue. *J. Exptl. Social Psychol.,* **1**. 334–347.

WHITE, R. W., 1944. Interpretation of imaginative productions. In J. McV. Hunt (Ed.), *Personality and the behavior disorders.* Vol. 1. New York : Ronald Press.

WHITEMAN, P. H., & KOSIER, K. P., 1964. Development of children's moralistic judgments : Age, sex, IQ, and certain personal-experiential variables. *Child Develop.,* **35**, 843–850.

WHITFIELD, J. W., 1951. An experiment in problem solving. *Quart. J. Exptl. Psychol.,* **3**, 184–197.

WHITING, J. W. M., 1959. Sorcery, sin, and the superego : A cross-cultural study of some mechanisms of social control. In M. R. Jones, (Ed.), *Nebraska symposium on motivation.* Lincoln, Neb. : University of Nebraska Press.

WHITING, J. W. M., & CHILD, I. L., 1953. *Child training and personality: A cross-cultural study.* New Haven, Conn. : Yale.

WHITNEY, R. E., 1971. Agreement and positivity in pleasantness ratings of balanced and unbalanced social situations : A cross-cultural study. *J. Personality & Social Psychol.,* **17**, 11–14.

WICKELGREN, W. A., 1969. Context-sensitive coding, associative memory, and serial order in (speech) behavior. *Psychol. Rev.,* **76**, 1–15.

WILD, C., 1965. Creativity and adaptive regression. *J. Personality & Social Psychol.,* **2**, 161–169.

WILEY, R. E., & HORTON, D. L., 1968. Mediated clustering. *J. Exptl. Psychol.*, **76**, 373–375.

WILKINS, M. C., 1928. The effect of changed material on ability to do formal syllogistic reasoning. *Arch. Psychol.*, No. 102.

WILLIAMS, J. E., 1955. Mode of failure, interference tendencies, and achievement imagery. *J. Abnormal & Social Psychol.*, **51**, 573–580.

WILLIAMS, J. P., 1962. A test of the all-or-none hypothesis for verbal learning. *J. Exptl. Psychol.*, **64**, 158–165.

WILSON, R. C., GUILFORD, J. P., CHRISTENSEN, P. R., & LEWIS, D. J., 1954. A factor-analytic study of creative-thinking abilities. *Psychometrika*, **19**, 297–311.

WINER, G. A., 1968. Induced set and acquisition of number conservation. *Child Develop.*, **39**, 195–205.

WINNICK, W. A., & KRESSEL, K., 1965. Tachistoscopic recognition thresholds, paired-associate learning, and free recall as a function of abstractness-concreteness and word frequency. *J. Exptl. Psychol.*, **70**, 163–168.

WINTER, S. K. 1969. Characteristics of fantasy while nursing. *J. Personality*, **37**, 58–72.

WISPÉ, L. G., & DRAMBAREAN, N. C., 1953. Physiological need, word frequency, and visual duration thresholds. *J. Exptl. Psychol.*, **46**, 25–35.

WISPÉ, L. G., & FRESHLEY, H. B., 1971. Race, sex, and sympathetic helping behavior. *J. Personality & Social Psychol.*, **17**, 59–65.

WITKIN, H. A., GOODENOUGH, D. R., & KARP, S. A., 1967. Stability of cognitive style from childhood to young adulthood. *J. Personality & Social Psychol.*, **7**, 291–300.

WITKIN, H. A., LEWIS, H. B., HERTZMAN, M., MACHOVER, K., MEISSNER, P. B., & WAPNER, S., 1954. *Personality through perception: An experimental and clinical study.* New York: Harper & Row.

WOHLWILL, J. F., 1960a. Absolute vs. relational discrimination on the dimension of number. *J. Genet. Psychol.*, **96**, 353–363.

WOHLWILL, J. F., 1960b. A study of the development of the number concept by scalogram analysis. *J. Genet. Psychol.*, **97**, 345–378.

WOHLWILL, J. F., 1963. The learning of absolute and relational number discriminations by children. *J. Genet. Psychol.*, **101**, 217–228.

WOLF, R., & MURRAY, H. A., 1938. Judgments of personality. In H. A. Murray, *Explorations in personality.* New York: Oxford.

WOLFF, J. F., 1967. Concept attainment, intelligence, and stimulus complexity: An attempt to replicate Osler & Trautman (1961). *J. Exptl. Psychol.*, **73**, 488–490.

WOLFGANG, A., 1967. Exploration of upper limits of task complexity in concept identification of males and females in individual and social conditions. *Psychonomic Sci.*, **9**, 621–622.

WOOD, G., & BOLT, M., 1968. Mediation and mediation time in paired-associate learning. *J. Exptl. Psychol.*, **78**, 15–20.

WOODMANSEE, J. J., COOK, S. W., 1967. Dimensions of verbal racial attitudes: Their identification and measurement. *J. Personality & Social Psychol.*, **7**, 240–250.

WOODWORTH, R. S., 1906. Imageless thought. *J. Phil.*, **3**, 701–708.

WOODWORTH, R. S., 1938. *Experimental psychology.* New York: Holt.

WOODWORTH, R. S., 1940. *Psychology.* (4th ed.) New York : Holt.
WOODWORTH, R. S., & SCHLOSBERG, H., 1954. *Experimental psychology.*
    (Rev. ed.) New York : Holt.
WOODWORTH, R. S., & SELLS, S. B., 1935. An atmosphere effect in formal
    syllogistic reasoning. *J. Exptl. Psychol.,* **18**, 451–460.
WRIGHT, B. A., 1942. The development of the ideology of altruism and fairness
    in children. *Psychol. Bull.,* **39**, 485–486. (Abstract)
WRIGHT, J. H., & HICKS, J. M., 1966. Construction and validation of a Thurstone
    scale of liberalism-conservatism. *J. Appl. Psychol.,* **50**, 9–12.
WRIGHT, M. E., 1942. Constructiveness of play as affected by group organization
    and frustration. *Character & Personality,* **11**, 40–49.
WUNDT, W., 1907. *Outlines of psychology.* (3rd rev. English ed.) Leipzig :
    Englemann.
WYER, R. S., Jr., & LYON, J. D., 1970. A test of cognitive balance theory
    implications for social inference processes. *J. Personality & Social Psychol.,*
    16, 598–618.
WYLIE, R. C., 1968. The present status of self theory. In E. F. Borgatta & W. W.
    Lambert (Eds.), *Handbook of personality theory and research.* Chicago :
    Rand McNally.
YARROW, L. J., 1948. The effects of antecedent frustration on projective play.
    Psychol. Monographs, No. 293.
YAVUZ, H. S., 1963. The retention of incidentally learned connotative responses.
    J. Psychol., **55**, 409–418.
YELEN, D. R., & SCHULZ, R. W., 1963. Verbal satiation ? *J. Verbal Learning
    & Verbal Behavior,* **1**, 372–377.
YERKES, R. M., 1927. The mind of a gorilla. *Genet. Psychol. Monographs,* **2**,
    1–193.
YERKES, R. M., & DODSON, J. D., 1908. The relation of strength of stimulus to
    rapidity of habit-formation. *J. Comp. & Neur. Psychol.,* **18**, 459–482.
YOUNG, R. K., BENSON, W. M., & HOLTZMAN, W. H., 1960. Change in atti-
    tudes toward the Negro in a Southern university. *J. Abnormal & Social
    Psychol.,* **60**, 131–133.
OYUNISS, J., & FURTH, H. G., 1965. Discrimination shifts as a function of
    degree of training in children. *J. Exptl. Psychol.,* **70**, 424–427.
YUILLE, J. C., & PAIVIO, A., 1967. Latency of imaginal and verbal mediators as
    a function of stimulus and response concreteness-imagery. *J. Exptl. Psychol.,*
    75, 540–544.
YUILLE, J. C., & PAIVIO, A., 1968. Imagery and verbal mediation instructions
    in paired-associate learning. *J. Exptl. Psychol.,* **78**, 436–441.
ZACKS, R. T., 1969. Invariance of total learning time under different conditions of
    practice. *J. Exptl. Psychol.,* **82**, 441–447.
ZAJONC, R., & BURNSTEIN, E., 1965a. The learning of balanced and un-
    balanced social structures. *J. Personality,* **33**, 153–163.
ZAJONC, R., & BURNSTEIN, E., 1965b. Structural balance, reciprocity, and
    positivity as sources of cognitive bias. *J. Personality,* **33**, 570–583.
ZAJONC, R. B., WOLOSIN, R. J., WOLOSIN, M. A., & LOH, W. D., 1970. Social
    facilitation and imitation in group risk-taking. *J. Exptl. Social Psychol.,* **6**,
    26–46.
ZAVORTINK, B., & KEPPEL, G., 1969. Retroactive inhibition as a function of
    List 2 study and test intervals. *J. Exptl. Psychol.,* **81**, 185–190.

ZELLER, A. F., 1950. An experimental analogue of repression. II. The effect of individual failure and success on memory measured by relearning. *J. Exptl. Psychol.,* **40**, 411–422.

ZIGLER, E., & CHILD, I. L., 1969. Socialization. In G. Lindzey & E. Aronson (Eds.), *Handbook of social psychology.* Vol. 3. Reading, Mass.: Addison-Wesley.

ZIGLER, E., & DeLABRY, J., 1962. Concept-switching in middle-class, lower-class and retarded children. *J. Abnormal & Social Psychol.,* **65**, 267–273.

ZIMMER, H., 1954. Self-acceptance and its relation to conflict. *J. Consulting Psychol.,* **18**, 447–449.

ZIMRING, F. M., 1969. Structure of construct systems and word association latencies. *J. Exptl. Psychol.,* **79**, 353–357.

NAME INDEX

SUBJECT INDEX